EXPERT GUIDE TO VISUAL BASIC 6

WAYNE S. FREEZE

944 pages; 7¹/2" x 9"
ISBN 0-7821-2349-X
$49.99 US

Here is the ultimate Visual Basic secrets book—written by a recognized authority! Learn the tricks that turn programmers into gurus, and journey far beyond documentation. Advanced Win32 and registry sections let programmers integrate VB 6's newest features with Windows; Internet sections show VB programmers how to build IIS apps, integrate Transaction Server, FTP and Winsock with their existing VB apps, and create Active Server pages. VBScript coverage shows how to use the Windows 98 Scripting Host with existing VB apps. The CD includes custom applications, source code, ready-to-run examples of advanced VB applets and applications, and a dozen third-party controls and applications for the hardcore VB programmer.

VISUAL BASIC 6 DEVELOPER'S HANDBOOK

EVANGELOS PETROUTSOS AND KEVIN HOUGH

1,504 pages; 7¹/2" x 9"
ISBN 0-7821-2283-3
$49.99 US

The *Visual Basic 6 Developer's Handbook* helps every VB programmer become a pro. The book's complete discussions clearly explain the most difficult, and most important, topics faced by Visual Basic programmers today. Coverage includes new Internet tools, new HTML tags, advanced client-server programming, and VBA/VBScript's integration of Windows 98 and other Microsoft applications. Written by two leading VB developers, who have created commercial applications for clients such as COMPAQ, Exxon, Texas Instruments, and NASA, this resource offers a variety of topics and depth you won't find in any other book.

VISUAL BASIC® 6 COMPLETE

SYBEX® SAN FRANCISCO ▸ PARIS ▸ DÜSSELDORF ▸ SOEST ▸ LONDON

Associate Publisher: Gary Masters

Contracts and Licensing Manager: Kristine O'Callaghan

Acquisitions & Developmental Editor: Denise Santoro

Compilation Editor: Jeremy Crawford

Editors: Davina Baum, Dusty Bernard, Pat Coleman, Lisa Duran, Brenda Frink, Suzanne Goraj, Julie Powell, Marilyn Smith, Grace Wong, and Shelby Zimmerman

Compilation Technical Editor: Greg Guntle

Technical Editors: Jim Bonelli, Helen Feddema, Don Hergert, Rima Regas, Tyler Regas, David Shank, Renate Strub, and Scott Thompson

Book Designer: Maureen Forys, Happenstance Type-O-Rama

Interior Art Designer: Chris Gillespie

Graphic Illustrators: Andrew Benzie, Inbar Berman, Patrick Dintino, and Tony Jonick

Electronic Publishing Specialist: Maureen Forys, Happenstance Type-O-Rama

Production Coordinator: Catherine Morris

Indexer: Nancy Guenther

Cover Designer: Design Site

SYBEX is a registered trademark of SYBEX Inc.

Mastering, Developer's Handbook, Expert Guide, and In Record Time are trademarks of SYBEX Inc.

Library of Congress Card Number: 99-61303

ISBN: 0-7821-2469-0

Manufactured in the United States of America

10 9 8 7 6 5 4

ACKNOWLEDGMENTS

This book is the product of many collaborators. Denise Santoro and Gary Masters defined its overall structure and contents. Jeremy Crawford compiled and adapted the material for publication, and Greg Guntle checked the technical accuracy and consistency throughout.

Electronic publishing specialist Maureen Forys and production coordinator Catherine Morris transformed a myriad of manuscript files and illustrations into this book.

A large group of developmental editors, editors, project editors, and technical editors edited the various books from which *Visual Basic 6 Complete* was compiled.

Without the original efforts of the chapters' various authors, this book would not exist. Steve Brown, Wayne S. Freeze, Ken Getz, Mike Gilbert, Guy Hart-Davis, Kevin Hough, Susann Novalis, and Evangelos Petroutsos all contributed chapters, and Evangelos Petroutsos wrote the "The Complete Visual Basic 6 Language Reference" especially for this book.

CONTENTS AT A GLANCE

TABLE OF CONTENTS

Chapter 4 □ Object Programming with Visual Basic   169

Part V ▶ Visual Basic Reference   **739**

INTRODUCTION

Visual Basic 6 Complete is a one-of-a-kind computer book—valuable both for the breadth of its content and for its low price. This thousand-page compilation of information from seven Sybex books provides comprehensive coverage of the popular programming language Visual Basic 6. This book, unique in the computer book world, was created with several goals in mind:

▶ Offering instructions, spanning basic to advanced Visual Basic, at an affordable price

▶ Helping you become familiar with the capabilities and uses of Visual Basic so you'll know which additional Visual Basic books will best suit your needs

▶ Acquainting you with some of our best authors—their writing styles and teaching skills and the level of expertise they bring to their books—so you can easily find a match for your interests as you delve deeper into Visual Basic programming

Visual Basic 6 Complete is designed to provide all the essential information you'll need to create user-friendly, sophisticated programs with Visual Basic, while at the same time inviting you to explore the even greater depths and wider coverage of material in the original books.

If you've read other computer how-to books, you've seen that there are many possible approaches to the task of showing how to use software and hardware effectively. The books from which *Visual Basic 6 Complete* was compiled represent a range of the approaches to teaching that Sybex and its authors have developed—from the quick, concise In Record Time style to the exhaustively thorough Mastering, Expert Guide, and high-level Developer's Handbook styles. As you read through various chapters of this book, you'll see which approach works best for you. You'll also see what these books have in common: a commitment to clarity, accuracy, and practicality.

You'll find in these pages ample evidence of the high quality of Sybex's authors. Unlike publishers who produce books by committee, Sybex authors are encouraged to write in individual voices that reflect their experiences with programming, with real-world applications, and with the evolution of today's personal computers. Every book represented here is the work of a single writer or a pair of close collaborators. The authors have written and fine-tuned the programs included in their chapters and have supplied tips and warnings born of their experience.

In adapting the various source materials for inclusion in *Visual Basic 6 Complete*, the compiler preserved these individual voices and perspectives. Chapters were edited only to minimize duplication, to add helpful explanations of topics otherwise not covered here in depth, and to update references as needed so you're sure to get the most current information available.

Who Can Benefit from This Book?

Visual Basic 6 Complete is designed to meet the needs of a wide range of computer users. Therefore, while you could read this book from beginning to end, you may not need to read every chapter. The Table of Contents and the Index will guide you to the subjects you're looking for.

Beginners   Even if you have only a little familiarity with programming methods and concepts, this book will enable you to build useful Visual Basic applications.

Intermediate users   If you already know the fundamentals of Visual Basic, this book will give you more sophisticated programming skills and a deeper understanding of the capabilities of Visual Basic.

Advanced users   You, too, will find much useful information in this book, including complete explanations of concepts, methods, and processes; useful programming shortcuts and alternatives; and a wealth of reference material.

How This Book Is Organized

Visual Basic 6 Complete has fifteen chapters and two reference appendices.

Part I: Introduction to Visual Basic   In the first five chapters, you'll be introduced to fundamental Visual Basic concepts and skills. You will create your own programs immediately, without first having to wade through chapter after chapter of concepts and terminology.

Part II: Practical Visual Basic   In Part II, you'll explore Visual Basic in greater depth. Here you will learn, among other things, how to effectively debug Visual Basic programs and expand their functionality with API functions.

Part III: Introduction to Visual Basic Scripting and the Internet   Part III addresses Visual Basic's scripting capabilities and how these can be used to enhance the user experience in your programs and Web sites.

Part IV: Introduction to Visual Basic for Applications   Part IV is devoted to VBA, a powerful, flexible programming tool that allows you to extend and automate applications.

Part V: Visual Basic Reference   The references contain descriptions of the built-in statements and functions in Visual Basic, along with the API functions Visual Basic can access. This information is useful for the novice and master alike.

Program Code on the Sybex Web Site

Some of the examples you'll work through in this book refer to program code you can download from the Sybex Web site (`www.sybex.com`). Once there, go to the Catalog page and enter **2469** into the search engine (these are the first four digits of the last five in the book's ISBN). Follow the link for this book that comes up, and then click the Downloads button, which will take you to a list of files organized by chapter.

A Few Typographical Conventions

When an operation requires a series of choices from menus or dialog boxes, the ➣ symbol is used to guide you through the instructions, like this: "Select Programs ➣ Accessories ➣ System Tools ➣ System Information." The items the ➣ symbol separates may be menu names, toolbar icons, check boxes, or other elements of the Windows interface—anyplace you can make a selection.

`This typeface` is used to identify programming code and Internet URLs, and **boldface type** is used whenever you need to type something into a text box.

You'll find these types of special notes throughout the book:

TIP

You'll get a lot of these Tips—for quicker and smarter ways to accomplish tasks—based on the authors' long experience using Visual Basic.

NOTE

You'll see these Notes, too. They usually represent alternate ways to accomplish a task or some additional information that needs to be highlighted.

WARNING

In a few places you'll see a Warning like this one. When you see a warning, pay attention to it!

YOU'LL ALSO SEE "SIDEBAR" BOXES LIKE THIS

These boxed sections provide added explanations of special topics that are noted briefly in the surrounding discussion but that you may want to explore separately. Each sidebar has a heading that announces the topic so you can quickly decide whether it's something you wish to know about.

For More Information...

See the Sybex Web site, www.sybex.com, to learn more about all the books that went into *Visual Basic 6 Complete*. On the site's Catalog page, you'll find links to any Sybex book you're interested in.

PART i
INTRODUCTION TO VISUAL BASIC

Chapter 1

MASTERING THE INTEGRATED DEVELOPMENT ENVIRONMENT (IDE)

Throughout the years the computer industry has seen some radical improvements in software development tools. In the early days of computers, when a computer took up an entire room, programmers flipped switches to make the machine perform simple addition. These complex machines were the cutting edge in technology. They could add two numbers! As technology progressed, punch cards provided more functionality by allowing programmers to punch an entire line of code on a single card. Large programs were developed using stacks of cards that were fed into a reader that would interpret the holes and create programming code on mainframes. The next generation of programming tools were text-based editors and were used to write machine language, assembly language,

Adapted from *Visual Basic 6 In Record Time* by Steve Brown

ISBN 0-7821-2310-4   688 pages $29.99

and Beginners All-Purpose Symbolic Instructional Code: BASIC. Once considered a toy, the BASIC language has evolved into one of the most easy-to-use and powerful programming languages available. Microsoft's Visual Basic 6 is the newest addition to the long line of programming languages.

When using Visual Basic, the most important skill you need is to be adept at using the development environment. Without the integrated tools in the environment, Visual Basic programming would be much more cumbersome and difficult. All design would need to be done on graph paper and flow charts, and it would need to be typed in line by line. Fortunately, Visual Basic contains many integrated tools to make the application development process simpler. This collection of tools makes up the *Integrated Development Environment* (IDE). Before you jump ahead in this book, be sure to spend some time reading this chapter. The skills you learn here will save you time developing applications in the future. Visual Basic gives you the tools, and this chapter teaches you how to use them.

INTRODUCING VISUAL BASIC

Visual Basic version 6 is the newest addition to the family of Visual Basic products. It allows you to develop Windows applications quickly and easily for your PC without being an expert in C++ or other programming languages.

Visual Basic provides a graphical environment in which you visually design the forms and controls that become the building blocks of your applications. Visual Basic supports many useful tools that will help you be more productive. These include, but are not limited to, projects, forms, class objects, templates, custom controls, add-ins, and database managers. You can use these tools together to create complete applications in months, weeks, or even days; producing an application using another language can take much longer.

Version 6 of Visual Basic is specifically designed to utilize the Internet. It comes with several controls that allow you to create Web-based applications, called *ActiveX executables*. These work just like stand-alone Visual Basic applications, but they are accessed through the Microsoft Internet Explorer 4 Web browser. Using this new style of application, you can revise your existing Visual Basic applications and distribute them through the Internet. New to Visual Basic 6 are the ISAPI Application and Dynamic HTML project templates. These templates provide you with a framework to develop server-side components as well as "smart" Web pages and applications.

Visual Basic continues to sport the Explorer-style development environment, modeled after Windows Explorer. This makes it easy for a computer user to jump right into creating applications with Visual Basic. Almost all the objects and tools on the screen can be manipulated through a right-click. You can set properties, add controls, and even view context-sensitive help with this single action.

When you start Visual Basic for the first time, the Project Wizard will open, and you will notice the New Project dialog box (see Figure 1.1).

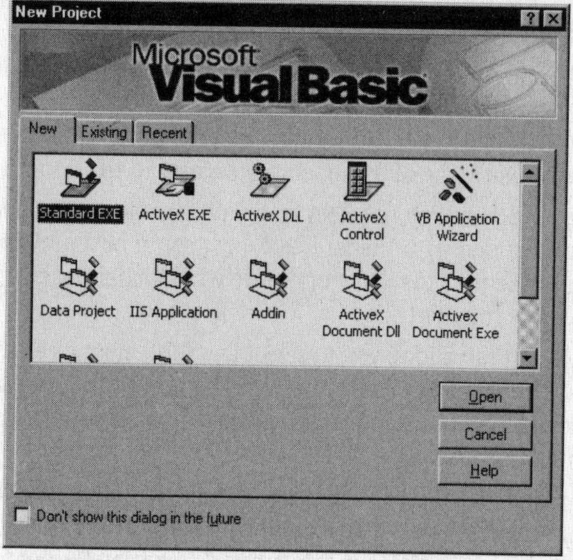

FIGURE 1.1:   The Project Wizard's New Project dialog box

From this window, you can select from several types of *projects* that will give you a head start on developing your applications. This window has three tabs: New, Existing, and Recent.

By selecting a project template from the New tab, you let Visual Basic create the foundation of your application. This can save you a lot of time designing an application, especially if you are new to Visual Basic. The New tab presents you with several project templates:

- ▶ Standard EXE

- ▶ ActiveX EXE

- ActiveX DLL
- ActiveX Control
- VB Application Wizard
- VB Wizard Manager
- Data Project
- IIS Application
- Add-In
- ActiveX Document DLL
- ActiveX Document EXE
- DHTML Application
- VB Enterprise Edition Controls

You will learn to use some of these templates later in the book.

The Existing tab allows you to select an existing project. This could be a sample project included with Visual Basic, or it could be a project you have worked on in the past. As you work more with Visual Basic, you will choose this tab more frequently.

Finally, the Recent tab allows you to select from the most recently used (MRU) projects. The tab is similar to the Existing tab, but it presents you with a list of the existing projects you have worked on recently, instead of *all* of the existing projects.

You can use any of these tabs to help get you started on a project in Visual Basic. You may also notice the small check box at the bottom of the form: "Don't show this dialog in the future." If you prefer not to be bothered with selecting a project type, you can check this box, and the window will not come up the next time you start Visual Basic.

Now let's take a closer look at the Visual Basic Integrated Development Environment (IDE).

LEARNING THE IDE FEATURES

Behind the Project Wizard window lies the Integrated Development Environment (see Figure 1.2). The IDE is an important part of Visual Basic; it's where you put together your applications and where you'll spend much of your time when you're creating applications.

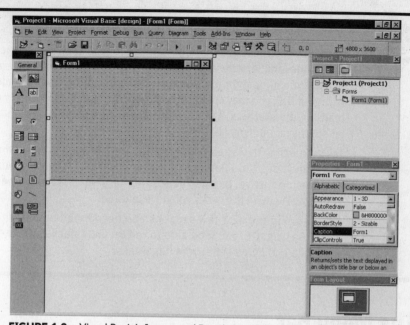

FIGURE 1.2: Visual Basic's Integrated Development Environment (IDE)

IDE is a term commonly used in the programming world to describe the interface and environment you use to create your applications. It is called *integrated* because you can access virtually all of the development tools you need from one screen, called an *interface*. The IDE is also commonly referred to as the *design environment*, the *program*, or just the *IDE*. We will use the latter term, so you can add your first programming buzz-word to your vocabulary.

The Visual Basic IDE is made up of a number of components:

▶ Menu bar

▶ Toolbar

▶ Project Explorer

▶ Properties window

▶ Form Layout window

▶ Toolbox

▶ Form Designer

▶ Object Browser

THE ALL-IMPORTANT IDE

I cannot stress enough how important it is for you as a programmer to become familiar with your Integrated Development Environment (IDE). If you jump right into coding without becoming comfortable with your IDE, you may spend a good deal of your development time learning the editor and tools, rather than writing code—which is what programming is all about.

Take some time to play around in the IDE. Tweak settings, move windows, and adjust toolbars; just get comfortable. Not only will you be more productive, but also your coworkers will sit in awe when you show them all the tricks you have learned.

After reading the next few sections and becoming familiar with Visual Basic's IDE, you'll be able to roll up your sleeves and get some bits and bytes under your fingernails!

The Menu Bar

The menu bar is the line of text that lies across the top of the Visual Basic window. It is very much like menus you may have seen in other Windows applications. The menu gives you access to many features within the development environment.

On the left is the File menu. From this menu you work with the actual files that make up your applications. You can create, open, print, and save projects. All of these menu options can also be accessed by right-clicking in the Project Explorer, explained later in this chapter.

Next to File is the Edit menu. From here you can perform the standard Clipboard options such as cut, copy, and paste. You can use the functions to store controls as well as code. In addition, you can access the Find facilities in the IDE. You can use this menu to search for text throughout a procedure, a module, or an entire project. This feature will become handy as you start developing large Visual Basic applications.

From the View menu you can view various components and tools. You can view a form and a code module, as well as other utilities that help make your development time more productive. You will learn more about these tools in detail throughout the book.

The Project menu is the heart of your project. From here you can add to and remove forms, code modules, user controls, property pages, as well as

ActiveX designers from your projects. In addition, you can add and remove custom controls and OLE references, discussed later. Many of these menu options can be accessed by right-clicking the Toolbox or Project Explorer.

The options on the Format menu deal specifically with the size and placement of controls and forms.

When you are debugging your applications, you will become very familiar with the Debug menu. From here you can start and stop your applications, set watches and breakpoints, and perform other tasks to help monitor your application's progress.

You will spend a great deal of time using the Run menu. From here you can start and stop your applications, as well as break in the middle of a program's execution and then resume. Break and Resume are handy when it comes time to debug.

The next two menus, Query and Diagram, are new to Visual Basic 6. The commands in the Query menu simplify the creation of SQL queries. The Diagram menu is used for building database applications. It especially helps when editing database diagrams.

From the Tools menu you can add procedures and set procedure properties. In addition, you can access the Menu Editor. You can also choose Options from the Tools menu to set preferences for your IDE.

The Add-Ins menu contains additional utilities called Add-Ins. By default you should have an option for Visual Data Manager and another for the Add-In Manager. Visual Data Manager is a simple but useful tool that allows you to design and populate a database in many popular formats, including Microsoft Access. The Add-In Manager allows you to select other Add-In utilities to be added to the Add-Ins menu.

The Window menu gives you options to tile and cascade windows within the IDE. You can also arrange the icons for minimized forms. However, perhaps the most important option is the window list at the bottom of the menu. This list allows you to quickly access open windows in the IDE.

The Help menu is your second stop when you get in a jam. This book, of course, should be your first.

The Toolbar

Immediately below the menu bar should be the Visual Basic toolbar (see Figure 1.3). If you can't see the toolbar, click View ➢ Toolbars ➢ Standard. You can control the whole Visual Basic environment from the menu bar, but the toolbar gives you easy access to the menu-bar commands you'll use most frequently.

FIGURE 1.3: The Visual Basic toolbar

You will notice that when you move the mouse over the buttons they appear to raise themselves up from the toolbar. If you keep the mouse pointer over a button for a moment, you will see the *tool tip* for that button.

NOTE

A tool tip is a little box that pops up and explains to you what the button's function is. You will most likely find yourself adding these helpful tips to your projects in the future.

One of the many features in the IDE is the provision of several toolbars. By selecting View ➤ Toolbars, you can also show or hide toolbars for the Edit, Debug, and Form Editor windows. If you are really finicky about your environment, you can even customize these toolbars to suit your preferences.

Moving a Toolbar Button

Let's say you want to move some buttons around on the Visual Basic toolbar to make them more accessible to you. You would follow these steps:

1. Right-click the menu bar or toolbar at the top of the screen.

2. Select Customize from the pop-up menu.

3. The Customize dialog box has three tabs: Toolbars, Commands, and Options. On the Toolbars tab, click the check box next to the toolbar you want to edit. (If the toolbar is already on the IDE like the Standard toolbar, you can go straight to it. If it is not already available, checking the toolbar option will bring up the newly selected toolbar.)

4. Click a toolbar button and hold the mouse button down. Now "drag" the button to a new position on the toolbar.

5. You will notice the I-bracket will move along the toolbar, under the button you are dragging. If the I-bracket is in the location where you want the button, let go of the mouse button and the toolbar button will "drop" into its new position.

TIP

You can move toolbar buttons to the menu as well. Just drag the button to the menu title. When the menu drops down, drag the button to a position on the menu.

If you decide you don't want to keep the changes you have just made, click the Reset button to restore the buttons to their default positions. Otherwise, click Close to save your modifications.

Removing and Adding a Menu Item

If a toolbar does not contain the shortcuts you want, or you want to add another menu item, you can customize them even further to get what you want. Try the following:

1. Right-click the menu bar or toolbar at the top of the screen.

2. Select Customize from the pop-up menu.

3. Select the Commands tab from the Customize dialog box.

4. In the Categories list, scroll down to the bottom and select Built-in Menus.

5. Now go up to the Help menu on the Visual Basic menu bar and drag it to the Commands list. Once the menu item is over the list, drop it. The Help menu has been removed from your menu.

6. Select Help from the Commands list and drag it back to the menu and drop it back in its original position.

7. Click Close to save your modifications.

Now you have a good foundation for customizing the menu bar and toolbars. Experiment and get your environment set up the way you want it.

NOTE

The previous examples showed you a common Windows task called *drag-and-drop*. You will be using this frequently within the IDE, and you may even program this functionality in your own programs.

The Project Explorer

Docked on the right side of the screen, just under the toolbar, is the Project Explorer window (see Figure 1.4). The Project Explorer is your quick reference to the various elements—forms, classes, and modules—in your project.

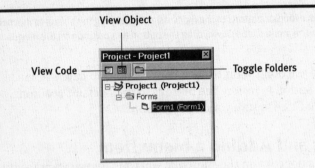

FIGURE 1.4: The Project Explorer window

The Project Explorer window is much like Windows Explorer in that it allows you to expand and collapse the subfolders.

All of the objects that make up your application are packaged in a project. If you save it for later use, testing, debugging, or improvement, Visual Basic provides the default file extension .VBP (Visual Basic Project) to the project.

A simple project will typically contain one *form*, which is the window used by your application. In addition to forms, the Project Explorer window also lists code modules and classes.

NOTE
Larger applications will often have a number of forms, modules, and classes. These too are listed in the Project Explorer window.

To view a form, select it in the Project Explorer and click the View Object button. (Any code associated with the form can be viewed in its own window by clicking the View Code button.)

If you right-click in the Project Explorer, you are presented with a pop-up menu that offers many options specific to that particular window. For instance, you can add, remove, and print forms and code modules from the pop-up menu.

If you want to remove an object from your project, right-click the name of the object in the Project Explorer window and select Remove. The name of the control will be listed after the Remove command.

TIP

Right-clicking objects in Visual Basic will expose object-specific pop-up menus. These menus will allow you to quickly access tools that you can use to operate directly on the active object. I recommend that you get used to doing this, because it will save time, as well as wear and tear on your fingers.

The Properties Window

Docked right under the Project Explorer window is the Properties window. The Properties window exposes the various characteristics (or *properties*) of selected objects. To clarify this concept, consider that each and every form in an application is an *object*. Each and every *control* (a command button, for example) that appears on a form is also an object. Now, each object in Visual Basic has characteristics such as color and size. Other characteristics affect not just the appearance of an object but the way it behaves, too. All these characteristics of an object are called its *properties*. Thus, a form has properties, and any controls placed on a form have properties, too. All of these properties are displayed in the Properties window (see Figure 1.5).

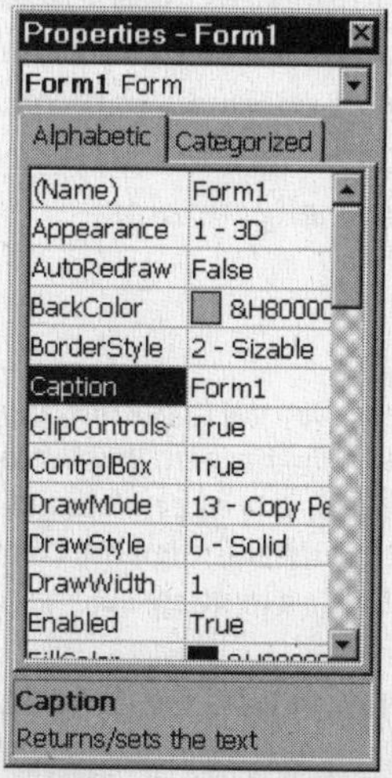

Properties - Form1	✕
Form1 Form	▼

Alphabetic	Categorized

(Name)	Form1
Appearance	1 - 3D
AutoRedraw	False
BackColor	☐ &H8000C
BorderStyle	2 - Sizable
Caption	Form1
ClipControls	True
ControlBox	True
DrawMode	13 - Copy Pe
DrawStyle	0 - Solid
DrawWidth	1
Enabled	True

Caption
Returns/sets the text

FIGURE 1.5: The Properties window

In the Properties window, you will see a list of the properties belonging to an object. There are quite a few of them, and you may have to scroll to see them all. Fortunately, many of the properties are self-explanatory (Caption, Height, Width, and so on), but some of the others are rarely used. If you are not sure what a specific property does, you can highlight it and look at the brief description at the bottom of the Properties window. Besides scrolling to view properties, you can also view properties either alphabetically or by category, by clicking the appropriate tab. Whichever method you use is a matter of preference.

TIP

If you're not sure of a property's purpose, click the property in the Properties window and press F1. This opens context-sensitive help on the highlighted property. This will give you a more in-depth description of the property and its use.

When a control (see Chapter 3, "Selecting and Using Controls") such as a command button, for example, is put on a form, the Properties window shows the properties for that control when it's selected. You can see the properties for different objects, including the underlying form, by clicking each object in turn. Alternatively, use the drop-down list at the top of the Properties window to select the control and display its properties. Most properties are set at design time, though many can be changed at run time.

Most of the time, you will set properties directly from the Properties window when you are creating an application. When you're working in the IDE, it is referred to as working in "design time" because you are still designing your program. Sometimes you will need to change properties while a program runs. You may want to disable a command button, for example. You can do this by writing code that changes the property. This is done at "run time," when your program is actually running.

NOTE

When more than one control is selected on a form, you get to see only those properties shared by all the controls. Setting a property in those circumstances affects all the selected controls. Setting, say, the Top property of a number of controls simultaneously in this manner enables you to vertically align the controls. It's not possible to include the underlying form itself in a multiple selection.

The way to change a property setting depends on the range and type of values it can hold. Since the Visual Basic IDE is a visual environment, you will set most properties at design time. This technique saves you time by not requiring you to write the code to achieve the same results. Below are some examples of the most common types of properties and their uses.

To try these examples, start a new project by selecting File ➤ New Project from the menu. When the Project Wizard appears, select Standard EXE, and click the OK button to create a standard executable project.

Boolean Value Properties

To learn how to change a Boolean value property, follow these steps:

1. Open Form1 by double-clicking it in the Project Explorer window.

    If the setting has a True or False value (called a *Boolean*), then you can change it by double-clicking the name of the property in the first column of the Properties window. Set the MaxButton property of Form1 to **False**.

2. Click Run ➤ Start. Your form will no longer have a Maximize button. This is handy if you don't want your application to cover the entire screen.

To stop the program, select Run ➤ End from the Visual Basic menu, press the End button on the toolbar, or click the [x] in the upper-right corner of Form1. This will bring you back into design mode.

Predefined Value Properties

If the setting has a number of predefined values (called an *enumerated list*), then double-clicking the property name cycles through all the permissible values. If there are a large number of options, then opening the drop-down list of values in the second column is probably quicker. To understand how an enumerated list works in the Properties window, you can experiment with the BorderStyle property of Form1.

1. Click Form1 to make it the active control.

2. In the Properties window, click the drop-down arrow to the right of the BorderStyle property. You will see a list of possible values for this property:

    ▸ Setting this value to 0-None removes all borders from the form. This is commonly seen on splash screens.

    ▸ Setting 1-Fixed Single allows you to create a thin border that cannot be resized.

▶ The default value of a form's `BorderStyle` property is `2-Sizable`. Use this setting if you want your users to be able to stretch the window to a different size.

▶ If you do not want your user to resize a dialog box for any reason, you can set the property to `3-Fixed Dialog`. Warning messages that you receive in Windows use this style of border.

▶ Finally, if you are creating a floating toolbar, also called a *tool window*, you can set the `BorderStyle` property to `4-Fixed Tool Window`, or `5-Sizable Tool Window`, depending on how you want the toolbar to behave.

3. Set the `BorderStyle` property to `3-Fixed Dialog`. This will prevent the user from resizing your form.

4. Select Run ➤ Start from the menu to test your form. You will notice now the form has no Minimize or Maximize buttons. In addition, the form cannot be resized by stretching its borders.

5. When you are done examining the form, click its Close button.

String Value Properties

Some properties require text, called *strings* in programmer jargon. Two of the properties you will encounter the most—Name and `Caption`—require strings. When the setting requires that you type an entry, then double-clicking the name is easier than clicking in the second column. The former highlights the entry (if any) in the second column so you can simply overtype instead of using the Delete or Backspace keys first. After you finish typing, it's safer to click back on the form or to press Enter—either of these removes the cursor from the settings box to prevent any accidental key presses from being added to the entry.

Let's change the name of the form and set a caption in the title bar of the form:

1. Click the form once to make it active.

2. In the Properties window, double-click the Name property. It is at the top of the properties list. The value Form1 should be completely highlighted.

3. Type **frmMain** in this field. Notice the old name was automatically deleted as you started typing.

TIP

Learning to overtype will save you time, not only in Visual Basic, but in other text applications as well. No longer do you have to continue hitting the Backspace key to edit text.

4. Hit the Enter key to set the Name property to **frmMain**.

5. Next, double-click the Caption property to highlight the text Form 1.

6. Overtype the words **I can overtype text.** in the Caption field.

As you work with Visual Basic, you will notice that you use these two properties the most. The Name property identifies the form to the application, and the Caption property visually identifies the form to the user at run time.

Hexadecimal Value Properties

Some of the entries look quite unfriendly, such as BackColor and the other color settings. Fortunately, they're not as bad as they appear. A double-click on the property name in the first column opens a dialog box that contains two tabs. The Palette tab contains a color palette where you can choose a value by selecting its color, rather than by typing a hexadecimal code. The System tab allows you to select colors based on the color scheme defined in the Windows Control Panel. You can keep a color palette permanently visible by clicking View ➤ Color Palette. In this case, a single click on the setting followed by a click in the palette is enough. BackColor is a good one to try out for frmMain—the ForeColor and FillColor will have no effect at this stage.

1. Double-click the BackColor property in the Properties window to bring up the Color dialog box.

2. Select the Palette tab to show the color palette.

3. Click the red color to change the background of the form to red.

This looks pretty ugly, so change the color back to the default window color:

4. Double-click the BackColor property again and select the System tab.

5. Select Button Face as the color. If you select Window Back-
    ground, the form will turn white. Because most controls in
    Windows are now 3-D controls, you can set the form's color
    to the same as the command button's color. This way it will
    be 3-D gray.

TIP

While this is an easy way to set colors on your forms, you will almost always
want to stick with the system colors defined on the System tab. This will allow
your application to inherit the colors your users prefer. Keep them happy.

Filename Properties

A couple of properties have the setting (None). These are the ones that
require a file reference. To pick a file, double-click the property name. For
example, the Icon property for a form determines the icon that is displayed if you minimize the form at run time. Under Windows 95/98 and
Windows NT it also sets the icon that appears on the Taskbar and as the
Control menu on the form. There are plenty of icons to evaluate in the
\Graphics\Icons sub-directory of the Visual Basic directory. To reset
one of these properties to (None), click once in the settings column and
press Delete. To add an icon to the form

1. Double-click the Icon property of frmMain. This will bring
    up the Load Icon dialog box.

2. Select Face02.ico from the \Graphics\Icons\Misc
    sub-directory. Click the Open button.

The icon for your application is now a little yellow smiley face.

Size Properties

Four properties—Left, Top, Width, and Height—appear on the toolbar
as well as in the Properties window. You can, if you want, type the values
directly into the second column of the Properties window. However, there's
another, easier way: If you drag the form in the Form Layout window and
release the mouse button, the Left and Top property coordinates are
updated on the toolbar—they're also updated in the Properties window.
When you drag one of the form's borders and release the mouse button,

then the Width and Height property coordinates are updated. You can move and resize controls on the form as well, only this time the coordinates are updated as you drag.

The Form Layout Window

The Form Layout window is a simple but useful tool (see Figure 1.6). Its purpose is to simply give you a thumbnail view of the current form, showing you what it looks like and how it is positioned on the screen at run time.

FIGURE 1.6: The Form Layout window

The Form Layout window is useful for determining what screen real estate your form will use when your application is running. To use the Form Layout window, do the following:

1. Click the form in the Form Layout window and move it to the center of the monitor graphic in the middle of the window.

2. Run your program by selecting Run ➣ Start.

The Toolbox

As the name implies, the Toolbox contains the bits and pieces you need to build your application interface. All the tools shown in Figure 1.7, with the exception of the pointer at the top left, correspond to the objects, or items, you might want to place on a form in your application. These tools or objects are referred to as *controls*. Most of them are an intrinsic part of Visual Basic and are called *built-in* or *standard* controls. Some examples include the command button control and the text box control. Chapter 3 covers these controls in more detail. Depending on your Visual Basic setup, there may be a few more controls in the Toolbox.

FIGURE 1.7:   The Visual Basic Toolbox with the custom controls

Organizing the Toolbox

The Toolbox in version 6 is similar to the Toolbox in previous version of Visual Basic. It allows you to define tabs, which you can then use to organize your controls. You may want to organize your custom controls by category. For example, I like to keep all of my Internet custom controls on a separate tab.

To add a new Internet tab to your Toolbox, follow these steps:

1. Right-click a blank area of the Toolbox.

2. Select Add Tab from the pop-up menu.

3. When Visual Basic prompts you to enter a new tab name, type **Internet**.

4. Click the OK button.

5. Now that you can create a new Toolbox tab, you can drag whatever controls you'd like to the tab; for example, drag the image control to the Internet tab you just created. (You will not have any Internet-related controls on your toolbar at this time.)

6. To add custom controls—like those created by Microsoft and other third-party companies—right-click the Toolbox and select Components from the pop-up menu, or select Project ➤ Components.

7. Check the box next to the control you want to add from the list of available controls, in this case, Microsoft Internet Controls.

8. Click the OK button to add the controls to the toolbox.

The names of the tabs and the categories you define are strictly a matter of your personal preference. Create tabs you are comfortable with, and organize your controls the way you like them.

Removing a Toolbox Control

To remove a control, simply turn off the appropriate check box in the Custom Controls dialog box. Be aware that you can't add or remove the built-in controls from the toolbox, so controls such as the command button will always be present. To remove the Internet controls

1. Right-click the Toolbox.

2. Select Components from the pop-up menu.

3. Just as you added the components in the previous exercise, you remove them by removing the check from the box next to the control. Remove the check next to Microsoft Internet Controls.

4. Click the OK button.

The Form Designer

In the center of the screen, you will see the Form Designer. This is the workspace where you actually design the visual layout of the form and the controls that lie on it.

In the Visual Basic IDE, you will see either one form at a time, or the Code window, in this space. (The Code window is discussed in the next section.)

Notice in Figure 1.8 that the form has little black dots in the center of each side. These boxes are called anchors. You can drag an anchor with the mouse to resize the form.

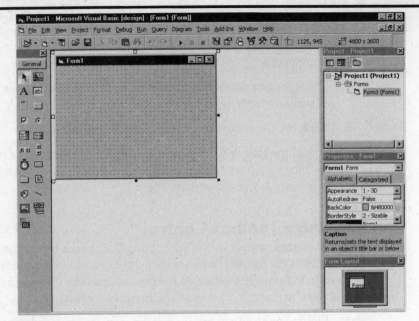

FIGURE 1.8: The Form Designer

TIP

If you want to make a form that is larger than the Form Designer window, you can stretch the border over the Project Explorer and Properties windows and Visual Basic will resize it accordingly. The form will then lie under the Project Explorer and Properties windows. You can use the scroll bars at the right and bottom of the Form Designer to uncover the hidden portions of the form.

The Object Browser

The Object Browser, shown in Figure 1.9, allows you to browse through the various properties, events, and methods that are made available, or exposed, to you. You can access it by selecting Object Browser from the View menu, or by pressing F2. We will cover the Object Browser in more detail in Chapter 4, "Object Programming with Visual Basic."

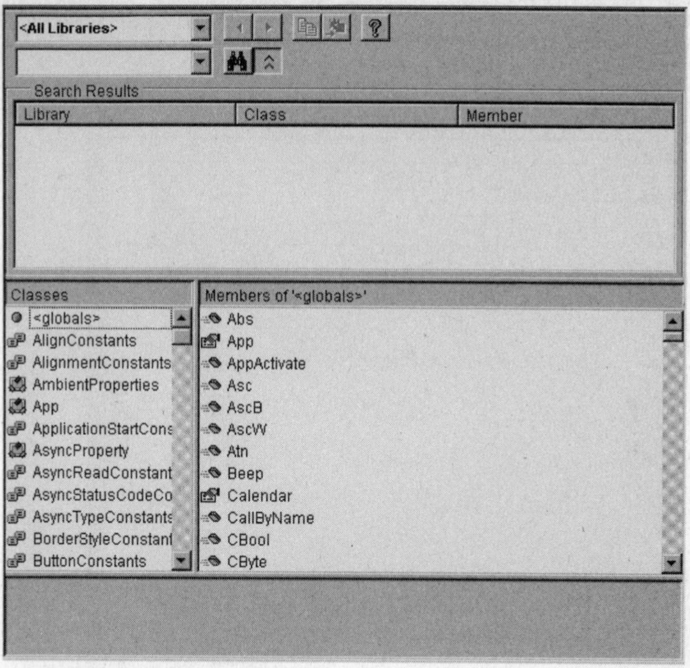

FIGURE 1.9: The Object Browser

KNOW YOUR VISUAL BASIC EDITOR, AND KNOW IT WELL

My Unix instructor's first words to the class were "Know your editor!" If you have ever had the dubious pleasure of working with the Unix's Vi Editor, you know exactly what he meant. These words have proven their meaning over and over to me during my years of programming.

In Visual Basic, the editor is called the *Code window* (see Figure 1.10). It's actually a turbo-charged text editor with many productivity tools built in. Regardless of what you want to call it, this is the window where you will do most of your work.

You can open the Code window by double-clicking a form or control in the Form Layout window. If you double-click a form, you will be taken to a *procedure* for the form. Open the form by double-clicking in the Project Explorer window, or select the View Code button in the Project Explorer. If you double-click a control, you will be taken to a procedure for that control. Once the Code window is open, you can go to any procedure for any object on the selected form.

```
Form                          ▼   Unload                      ▼
  Option Explicit                                               ▲
  Private Sub Form_Load()

  End Sub

  Private Sub Form_MouseUp(Button As Integer, Shift As Integer, X As Single, Y

  End Sub

  Private Sub Form_Unload(Cancel As Integer)
  |
  End Sub

                                                               ▼
```

FIGURE 1.10:   The Visual Basic Code window

NOTE

A procedure is a collection of lines of code that are grouped together to perform a set of related tasks.

Like I said, you should get *real* familiar with your editor. Learn as much about its features as possible. Learn all of the shortcuts and keystrokes. Set your fonts and colors exactly the way you want them. Becoming as comfortable as possible now with the Visual Basic editor will save you time later.

Depending on how you set your IDE options, you can have your Code window display multiple procedures at one time, as described in the next section. In addition, it can display object properties as you type, as well as give you visual cues as to the state of your code. We will cover these features in more detail later in this chapter.

WORKING WITH MULTIPLE PROJECTS

Visual Basic allows you to work on multiple projects simultaneously. The Project Explorer window shows you the projects and their components in a tree view. If you are a beginner, you may not have an immediate need to open multiple projects at one time. However, when you start creating ActiveX objects, you may want to open one project for the object and another to test the object.

If you have not already done so, you need to install the sample applications that come with Visual Basic. To install them, follow these steps:

1. Start the MSDN Library - Visual Basic 6 Setup program by selecting Add/Remove Programs from the Windows Control Panel.

2. Click the Add/Remove button to start the installation process.

3. When the MSDN Library - Visual Studio 6 dialog box appears, press the Add/Remove button.

4. Once the MSDN Library - Visual Studio 6 - Custom dialog box appears, check the box next to VB Product Samples. If the check box is grayed, press the Select All button.

5. Press Continue to finish the setup process.

Once you have installed the sample applications that come with Visual Basic, then you can try the following example to open multiple projects:

1. From the Visual Basic IDE select File ➤ Add Project.

2. In the Add Project dialog box, click the Existing tab.

3. Select `FirstApp.vbp` from the `\MSDN98\98vs\1033\ Samples\VB98\Firstapp` sub-directory.

4. Click the Open button. This will add the FirstApp project to the IDE.

5. Select File ➤ Add Project to add another project.

6. Again, click the Existing tab in the Add Project dialog box.

7. Select `Controls.vbp` from the `\MSDN98\98vs\1033\ Samples\VB98\Controls` sub-directory. This will add the Controls project to the IDE.

That's all there is to opening multiple projects. You can add more projects if you wish, but it will be very rare that you will need to do so. You will most likely start working with multiple projects when you start creating ActiveX servers and clients.

CUSTOMIZING THE IDE

While version 6 of Visual Basic has many productivity features in the IDE, you may still want to customize the IDE to suit your preferences. You can define the number of spaces of a tab, change the color of your Code window, dock your toolbars, and much more. If you want to change any settings within the IDE, select Tools ➢ Options. The tabs of the Options dialog box categorize many IDE options you will become familiar with.

The Editor Tab

The first tab of the Options dialog box to be examined is the Editor tab, shown in Figure 1.11. Many of these options may be unfamiliar to you if you are new to Visual Basic, but as you become more comfortable, you can use the Editor tab to customize your working environment.

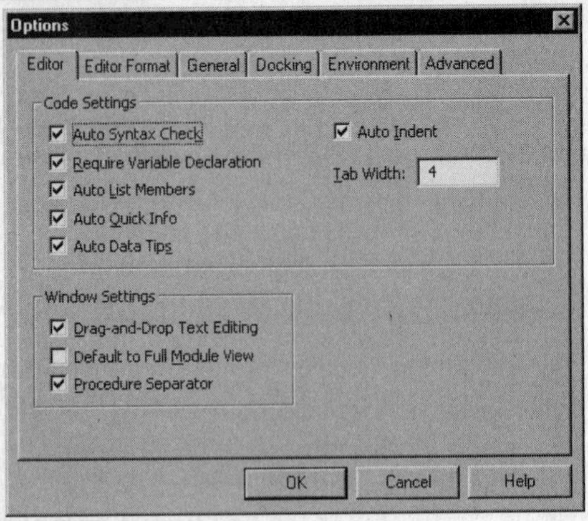

FIGURE 1.11:   The Editor tab

Within the Code Settings frame are the options that will affect your editor. After selecting Tools ➢ Options, experiment with these choices:

► Check the Auto Syntax Check box to force the editor to check your code for errors during design mode. Keep this setting enabled so you won't program errantly only to discover you have an error in your code.

▶ Check the Require Variable Declaration box to force you to declare all variables before using them in your code.

Part i

TIP

You should check Require Variable Declaration when you customize your IDE. This will make Visual Basic place one line—Option Explicit—in the General Declarations portion of every form, module, and class. This will save you many hours of frustration when you start debugging larger applications. As you gain programming experience, you will discover that most of your errors will be the result of incorrect variable types and miscalculations. Setting variables to the appropriate type will minimize these types of errors. If you have not developed the habit of using this feature, take time to do so now.

▶ Check the Auto List Members box to have the editor display a list of members belonging to the object, which you can easily reference as you type. As you type, the properties and methods are automatically listed at the cursor point. All you need to do is click the desired property or method.

▶ Check the Auto Quick Info box to show or suppress information about functions and their parameters. This is a useful setting if you are new to Visual Basic; by enabling this, Visual Basic will make recommendations to you as you type in the Code window.

▶ Check the Auto Data Tips box to toggle the display of the value of a variable under the cursor. This option is especially helpful when you are debugging your applications.

▶ Check the Auto Indent box to automatically indent your code a number of spaces. This is good for structured code. Neat code is easier to read, which is very helpful during the debugging process. As you read through the examples in the chapters to follow, you will see what structured code looks like.

▶ Use the Tab box to set the number of spaces the editor will insert when you press the Tab button. The default is four spaces. Although this is the default, you may desire to have more or less spaces. What you choose is a matter of preference.

Within the Window Settings frame you can experiment with three options:

- ▶ Check the Drag-and-Drop Text Editing option if you want to drag text within the Code window.

- ▶ Check the Default to Full Module View if you want to see all of the procedures within an object in the editor. If you prefer viewing one procedure in the editor at a time, disable this option.

- ▶ Check the Procedure Separator option if you are in Full Module View mode and want a visual separator between your procedures. If you choose to view code in Full Module View, I recommend checking this box.

The Editor Format Tab

As you can see in Figure 1.12, you use this tab to set your color and font preferences for your editor. Because this tab is self-explanatory, I will not cover it in detail.

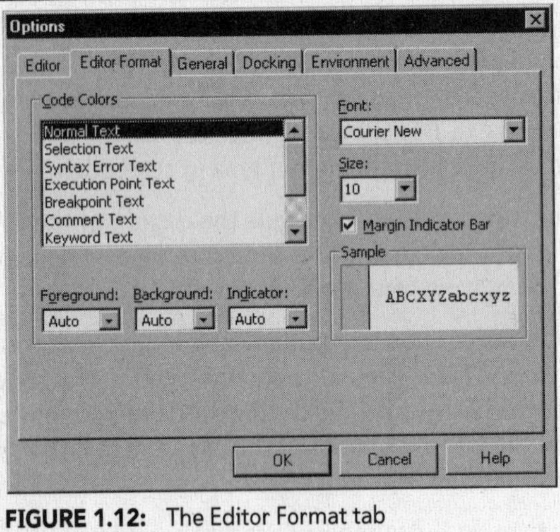

FIGURE 1.12: The Editor Format tab

The General Tab

The General tab, shown in Figure 1.13, allows you to fine-tune various aspects of the IDE, such as the gridlines on forms, error trapping, and compiling. Don't worry if some of these terms are unfamiliar to you at the moment. These terms will be explained throughout the text as you hone your Visual Basic programming skills.

▶ You can set the grid-spacing units in the Form Grid Settings section. You use these lines to align controls on the form. Usually, the default settings will be sufficient.

▶ The Error Trapping section allows you to set the sensitivity of error trapping. You can have your application break on all errors, break in class modules, or break on all unhandled errors. Unhandled errors are errors that may be encountered that you have not written an error-trapping function for. Leave this option at its default, Break in Class Module.

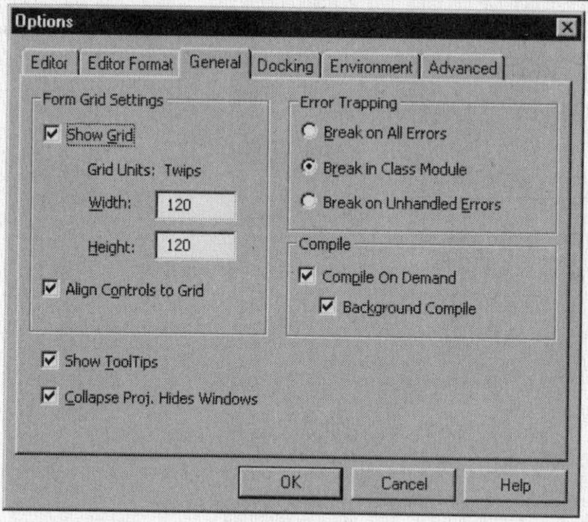

FIGURE 1.13:   The General tab

The Compile section contains the following options:

▶ Set Compile on Demand to allow Visual Basic to compile your code as you write your code. This helps your program start sooner when you select Run ➤ Start. This setting is enabled by default.

▶ Enable Background Compile to allow yourself to continue working in Visual Basic while it compiles your application. This setting is enabled by default.

Checking Show ToolTips will allow Visual Basic to show you tool tips that describe the control under the mouse pointer. This is a helpful feature, especially if you are new to Visual Basic. Finally, selecting Collapse Proj. Hides Windows will collapse the associated windows of a project when a project is collapsed in the Project Explorer window.

The Docking Tab

By selecting the Docking tab shown in Figure 1.14, you can determine which windows within the IDE are dockable. These are self-explanatory.

NOTE

Docking allows windows to physically position themselves along borders of the screen or other objects and lock themselves into place. This is another feature that allows you to keep various windows out of your way.

Options

Editor | Editor Format | General | Docking | Environment | Advanced

Dockable

- ☑ Immediate Window
- ☑ Locals Window
- ☑ Watch Window
- ☑ Project Explorer
- ☑ Properties Window
- ☐ Object Browser
- ☑ Form Layout
- ☑ Toolbox
- ☑ Color Palette

OK | Cancel | Help

FIGURE 1.14: The Docking tab

The Environment Tab

The Environment tab is perhaps the most important place to customize settings within the IDE (see Figure 1.15).

If you decide you do not want the Project Wizard window disturbing you when you create a new project, you can deselect the Create Default Project option in the When Visual Basic Starts frame. However, leave this option checked for now.

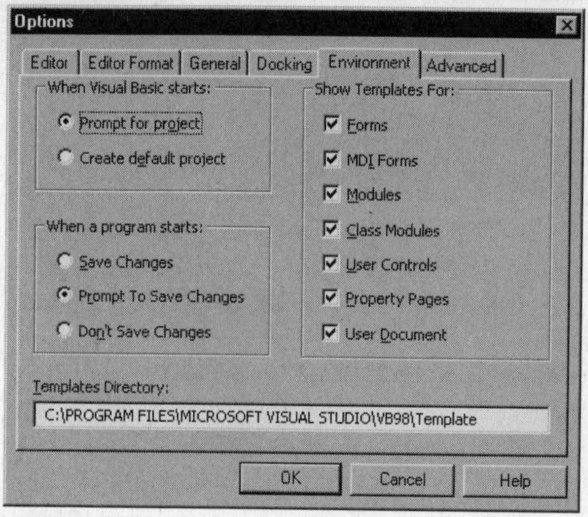

FIGURE 1.15:   The Environment tab

In addition, if you do want the Project Wizard window but you want to remove some of the templates from the window, you can select and deselect them in the Show Templates For frame.

The most important settings, perhaps in the whole IDE, are the ones listed in the When a Program Starts frame. When you are involved in serious project development, you will want to save your work often. The best way to do this is to check the Prompt to Save Changes option. This will cause Visual Basic to ask you to save your project just before your application is run from the IDE.

I find that the Don't Save Changes option is helpful when I am experimenting or demonstrating a series of programs that I do not want to keep. You can choose this option if you wish, but if you want to keep the projects you work on in this book, I recommend that you check Prompt to Save Changes.

The Advanced Tab

Finally, the Advanced tab (Figure 1.16) has a few options that you will not need to worry about at this time, but I will briefly discuss them here.

▶ Selecting the Background Project Load option will force Visual Basic to load projects while you continue working. This is useful because it allows you to continue working while a project loads. This option is set by default.

Options   ✕

Editor | Editor Format | General | Docking | Environment | Advanced

☑ Background Project Load

☑ Notify when changing shared project items

☐ SDI Development Environment

┌─ External HTML Editor: ─────────────────────┐
│ C:\WIN95\notepad.exe   │...│ │
└───┘

                        OK   Cancel   Help

FIGURE 1.16: The Advanced tab

▶ Leave the Notify When Changing Shared Project Items option checked. Some Visual Basic projects can use shared objects such as forms or modules. If you load multiple projects that use the same objects and change one of the shared objects, Visual Basic will notify you that a shared object has been changed. Although you will not use shared objects within this book, you may do so as you become more proficient with Visual Basic.

▶ The SDI Development Environment option allows you to change your IDE from a multiple document interface (MDI) to a single document interface (SDI). All of the projects and examples used in this book were created in an MDI environment, so leave this option unchecked.

▶ Finally, Visual Basic 6 adds some more Internet functionality. If you are familiar with Hypertext Markup Language, or HTML, you may find yourself designing Web pages from within VB. You can select your Web editor from the External HTML Editor field.

TIP

Because we cannot possibly cover every aspect of the IDE in this chapter, I recommend you take some time to snoop through each menu option and experiment with what it does. As I mentioned earlier, get to know the Code window—as well as the whole IDE. With practice, using the IDE will become second nature to you, and your efforts will be spent on coding rather than fumbling through the IDE.

CREATING YOUR FIRST APPLET

Now that you have had a chance to get familiar with the IDE and its new-and-improved tools, it's time to put all this knowledge to work by creating a simple application. You might not know it, but most programmers' first "real" application is the little Hello World program.

The Hello World program is historically the first application when one learns a new programming language. While very simple, it gives you tangible results with a minimal amount of coding, and it will give you a feel for working with Visual Basic and using the IDE environment. So let's continue and you can join the legions of programmers who have tackled the Hello World application.

Hello World!

To create the Hello World application, follow these steps:

1. Click File ➢ New Project. You might be asked to save changes to the current project if you've been experimenting. If so, click the No button. If you want to keep your work, click Yes.

2. If it is not already visible, open the Form Layout window by selecting View ➢ Form Layout Window.

3. Right-click the form in the Form Layout window. Select Startup Position ➢ Center Screen from the pop-up menu.

TIP

You can move the form by dragging it around in the Form Layout window. The pop-up menu also offers positioning options.

4. Resize the form by dragging its borders until it's about 3 inches wide and 2 inches high.

5. Double-click the Command Button control in the toolbox to create a command button of default size in the center of the form. Drag the button near the bottom center of the form.

6. Double-click the Label control in the toolbox to create a label on the form. Drag the label so it sits just below the top of the form. Resize the label so it is roughly the height of one line

of text and wide enough to contain the text "Hello World."
Your form should now look similar to the one shown here.

7. Now, click the form once to select it. You can tell that the
   form (as opposed to any of the controls) is selected because
   its properties are listed in the Properties window. If you can't
   see the Properties window, press F4.

8. Set the following two properties for the form by typing in the
   text under the Setting column in the appropriate property field:

Property	Setting
Caption	**My First Application!**
Name	**frmHelloWorld**

   The Caption property setting appears in the title bar of the
   form. The Name property is a very important one and is used
   to refer to the form in program code. In Chapter 3, I'll have a
   lot more to say about the Name property. For now, take it on
   faith that frmHelloWorld is a better name than the default
   one of Form1, which is the same as the default Caption
   property. The same applies to the Name property of the controls in this application. In each case, the default Name property has been changed.

9. Now, click the label and set the next two properties:

Property	Setting
Name	**lblHelloWorld**
Text	**Hello World.**

10. Click the Command button and set its properties as follows:

Property	Setting
Name	**cmdOK**
Caption	**&OK**

This time the Caption property shows as the text on the button. The ampersand character (&) before the first letter adds an underline to the letter *O*; this provides a quick keyboard alternative to a mouse-click to activate the button (here it's Alt+O). Happily, you can make many of your shortcut keys a mnemonic (*O* for *OK*, in this example).

11. Now double-click the cmdOK button. Double-clicking a control (or a form) opens the Code window at the default event for the control. The default event for a command button is the Click event. You should be looking at a procedure template or *stub* for cmdOK_Click, as in Figure 1.17. You can afford to ignore the Private Sub prefix for now; the important point is the name of the procedure: cmdOK_Click. This means that any code entered in the procedure will be executed when the user clicks the cmdOK button.

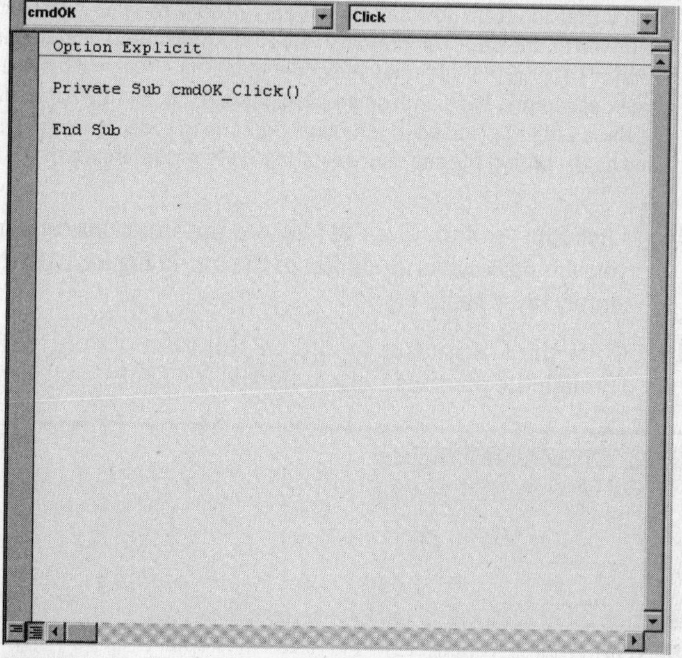

```
Option Explicit

Private Sub cmdOK_Click()

End Sub
```

FIGURE 1.17: The procedure in the Code window

12. Type the following line of code between the `Private Sub` and `End Sub` lines:

```
Unload Me
Set frmHelloWorld = Nothing
```

When the user clicks the cmdHelloWorld button, the `cmdOK_Click` event occurs. This event tells the form to unload itself. Because this is the only form in the application, it also tells the application to end.

13. Click File ➤ Save Project. Enter **frmWorld.frm** as the name of the form and **HelloWorld.vbp** as the name of the project. Before a project as a whole is saved, all the individual component files are saved. In this application there is one form and therefore one file corresponding to the form. The project file is basically a list of the component files.

NOTE

Notice that the form now has three descriptors—the `Name` property (frm-HelloWorld), the `Caption` property (My First Application), and the filename (`frmWorld.frm`). It's vital that you understand the difference between these three descriptors. The `Caption` property appears in the title bar of the form, the `Name` property is used to reference the form in code, and the filename is used by the project file and your operating system to reference the form.

14. Click Run ➤ Start. If you've followed the directions correctly, you should see a form, similar to the one in Figure 1.18, that simply says "Hello World."

15. Click the OK button to end. If things go wrong, check through the previous steps to find your mistake.

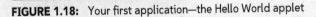

FIGURE 1.18: Your first application—the Hello World applet

You've just created your first application! Congratulations—you're well on your way to being a master Visual Basic programmer.

Creating this simple applet was an example of how you will be working in the Visual Basic IDE. Although the Hello World applet was very easy, it allowed you to get a feel for working in Visual Basic. The following chapters will present you with more information about the various tools you will be working with to build your killer app.

What's Next?

One of the tools you'll employ is the Form object, the main control for creating an interface for your application. Chapter 2 will introduce you to forms and show you how to create them and change their properties. You'll also gain familiarity with form events and methods, creating multiple document interface (MDI) forms, using the Form Wizard, and adding forms to your projects. Learning these skills will prove fundamental to your Visual Basic programming.

Chapter 2

WORKING WITH FORMS

This chapter will focus on laying the foundation for your Visual Basic programming. In Visual Basic, the Form object is the foundation of any application that presents an interface. This is the main control that will allow you to place other controls on top of it to create a window, called an *interface*, that the user can see on the screen.

You will learn about the various parts of the form that you can manipulate to get the style of form you desire for your application. In addition, you will be introduced to menus as well as more complex interfaces using Multiple Document Interfaces, or MDIs.

Adapted from *Visual Basic 6 In Record Time*
by Steve Brown

ISBN 0-7821-2310-4   688 pages $29.99

THE ANATOMY OF A FORM

The most basic object you will be working with in Visual Basic is the *form* object, which is the visual foundation of your application. It is basically a window that you can add different elements to in order to create a complete application. Every application you can see on the screen is based on some type of form. Before delving into the details of application development, let's take a look at the basic form object that you will probably use the most often in your projects: the single form.

As you learn Visual Basic, most of your applications will only have one interface, which is the single form. When you become more experienced and start writing larger, editor-styled applications like Notepad or Microsoft Word, you will want to use multiple forms, often referred to as *documents*. We will introduce these types of forms toward the end of this chapter (see "Working with Multiple Document Interface (MDI) Forms"). To create a new form, open Visual Basic and select File ➢ New Project ➢ Standard EXE; you'll then see the various parts of a single form object, as shown in Figure 2.1. In the following sections, we will go through each of the parts that make up this object so you can become familiar with what forms are and how you will use them.

All of these elements should be familiar to you if you have spent any time using the Windows operating systems. Let's take a look at how these features are referenced in Visual Basic.

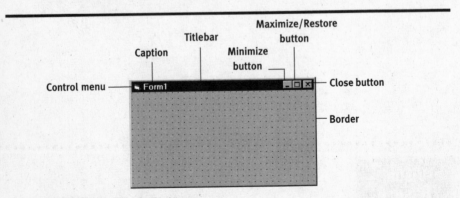

FIGURE 2.1: The form object

The Border

The form's border is what gives the form its elasticity. Depending on the type of form you want to display, you can program the border to be fixed, sizable, or even nonexistent. These features can be set with the Border-Style property.

The Title Bar

The title bar is the colored bar on the top of most forms. If your desktop color scheme is set to the Windows default scheme, this bar will be blue. You can use the title bar to drag the window around the screen. In addition, double-clicking it will alternately maximize and restore the form.

The Caption

The form's caption is the text you see in the form's title bar. It can be used to identify the name of the application, the current function of the form, or as a status bar. What you put in the caption depends on what your program is trying to achieve.

If you set a form's BorderStyle property to None, then the caption (along with the whole title bar) is hidden. You can set the caption to display the text you want by setting the form's Caption property in the Properties window.

The Control Menu

The Control menu is a simple menu that allows you to restore, move, resize, minimize, maximize, and close a form. To enable this button on your form, set the form's ControlBox property to True in the form's Properties window.

The Minimize Button

The Minimize button is used to minimize the current form, that is, move it out of the way, to the Windows Taskbar. To enable this button on your form, set the form's MinButton property to True in the form's Properties window.

NOTE

In MDI forms, minimized forms move to the lower-left corner of the MDI parent. Apps initiated from the System Tray get minimized back to the tray.

The Maximize/Restore Button

The Maximize button has two purposes. If the form is in its normal state, that is, its normal size, you can click the Maximize button to automatically expand the current form to the size of the screen or container of the form. A form's *container* is also known as a multiple document interface (MDI) form, which is described in "Working with Multiple Document Interface (MDI) Forms" later in this chapter. If the form is maximized, you can click this button again to restore the form to its original size. To enable this button on your form, set the form's `MaxButton` property to `True` in the Properties window.

The Close Button

The Close button's sole purpose is to close the current window. In Visual Basic, you can control whether the Close button is visible to the user with the `ControlBox` property. The Close button will not be visible if the Control box is not visible. If you decide not to enable the Close button or the Control box, then you must provide a way for the form to unload. This can be done automatically, or by using a menu or a button to close the form. You will learn more about this in the next section.

WORKING WITH FORM PROPERTIES

As you learned in Chapter 1, properties describe the characteristics of an object. They can be used to manipulate the identity of an object, its appearance, or even its behavior. Every Visual Basic object has at least one property, but most have many more. Certainly the form is no exception. The following shows the properties for a form object:

ActiveControl	DrawWidth	HelpContextID	NegotiateMenus
ActiveForm	Enabled	HWnd	Picture

Part i

Appearance	FillColor	**Icon**	ScaleHeight
AutoRedraw	FillStyle	Image	ScaleLeft
BackColor	Font	KeyPreview	**ScaleMode**
BorderStyle	FontBold	**Left**	ScaleTop
Caption	FontItalic	LinkMode	ScaleWidth
ClipControls	FontName	LinkTopic	**ShowInTaskbar**
ControlBox	FontSize	**MaxButton**	Tag
Controls	FontStrikethru	MDIChild	Top
Count	FontTransparent	**MinButton**	Visible
CurrentX	FontUnderline	MouseIcon	WhatsThisButton
CurrentY	**ForeColor**	MousePointer	WhatsThisHelp
DrawMode	HDC	Moveable	**Width**
DrawStyle	**Height**	**Name**	**WindowState**

If you glance at the list of properties for a form in the Properties window, you'll see there are quite a lot of them. Fortunately, only a few of the properties are used frequently—these are boldface in the above list—the rest you'll probably only use occasionally. It's important to note that these properties are specific to the Form object. As you will soon learn in Chapter 3, many objects share many of the same properties, but each property is specific to the control it belongs to. For example, a person could be described using properties. My Name property would be set to Steve and my EyeColor property would be set to Blue. However, my wife's Name would be set to Susan and her EyeColor property would be set to Brown.

TIP

You won't see all these form properties in the Properties window. If you can't see a certain property, it means it's a run-time–only property and can't be set at design time (see "Tweaking a Form's Properties" later in this chapter for more information).

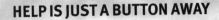

HELP IS JUST A BUTTON AWAY

You can get help with a property at any time. Just highlight it in the Properties window and press the F1 function key. For example, highlight the Caption property in the Properties window, and you will see a screen similar to the one shown below.

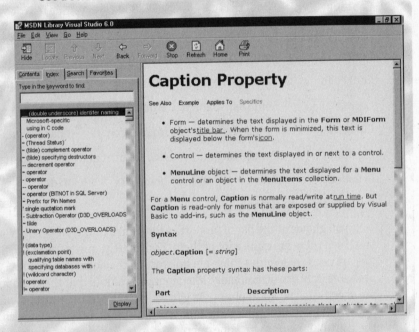

You can scroll through the information or click links (text that is underlined) to find related information. The tabs at the top of the screen—Contents, Index, Search, and Favorites—offer you more options for finding help with Visual Basic topics.

You may notice that the Help window does not look like the familiar Windows Help style that has been used in the past. With version 6, Microsoft has started using the Microsoft Developer Network, or MSDN, using the HTML Help system, to provide extensive online help facilities.

Let's take a closer look at some of the properties that are used most often (the next sections are listed alphabetically to act as a quick reference; the properties also appear in the Properties window in alphabetical order).

The BackColor Property

The BackColor property sets the background color of the form. You briefly met this property in Chapter 1. You can set a form's background color to any color on the palette. When you double-click BackColor in the Properties window or click the drop-down arrow next to the color selection, the Properties window will display a dialog box containing a color palette and a system color palette.

Usually you would not want to set a form's background color because this prevents the user from utilizing their own color scheme, which they may have defined in the Control Panel. In fact, it is required that you do not set it if you want the "Designed for Windows" logo on your software.

The BorderStyle Property

The BorderStyle property determines how the border of a form behaves. A form can have fixed borders that cannot be stretched or sizeable borders that can be stretched by dragging them with the mouse. Table 2.1 shows each option for the BorderStyle property.

TABLE 2.1: BorderStyle Settings

SETTING	DESCRIPTION
0–None	Selecting this setting means the form can't be resized or moved. The Control menu, Close button, Maximize and Minimize buttons, and the form's title bar are all suppressed. Although you will not use this setting often, it is useful for making splash screens and screen savers.
1 - Fixed Single	This setting means the form can't be resized by dragging its borders. However, you can use the Maximize and Minimize buttons.
2–Sizable	This is the default setting for Visual Basic forms and for most other Windows applications windows. The user can resize the form by dragging the form borders or by using the relevant buttons on the title bar.
3 - Fixed Dialog	As its name implies, this is usually the setting chosen for forms that act as dialog boxes. The user can't resize the form—the only options are to move or close it. If you want to force the user to interact with the form, you can set the ControlBox property to False. This prevents users from even closing the form. All they can do is to move the form by dragging its title bar. In that situation you would probably place one or more command buttons on the form—the Click events containing a line of code to close the form (for example, frmFormName.Hide).

TABLE 2.1 (continued): BorderStyle Settings

SETTING	DESCRIPTION
4 - Fixed ToolWindow	This acts the same as the Fixed Dialog setting, but with the addition of a Close button (the caption in the title bar is also shown in a smaller font). The form will not appear on the Taskbar.
5 - Sizable ToolWindow	This is just the same as the Sizable style but does not include a Maximize or Minimize button. Under Windows 95/98 it shows the Close button but doesn't appear on the Taskbar.

Try out these options—you can use the form in the Hello World application that you created in Chapter 1 to do this. Open the `frmHelloWorld` project from Chapter 1 by selecting File ➢ Open Project. Select the project you saved in Chapter 1.

1. In the Form Designer, click the form once to make it the active control.

2. Because the Hello World form acts more as a dialog box than a useful form, set its `BorderStyle` property to **3 - Fixed Dialog**.

3. Run your modified Hello World program by selecting Run ➢ Start.

Notice that the form doesn't stretch. Now you have created a true dialog box.

The Caption Property

A caption is the text that appears on the title bar of the form. If you set the `BorderStyle` property to None, then the caption (along with the entire title bar) is hidden. You can read more about changing the Caption property in "Tweaking a Form's Properties" later in this chapter.

The ControlBox Property

The `True` and `False` settings determine whether the Control menu is visible. Keep in mind that the settings for `BorderStyle`, `ControlBox`, `MaxButton`, and `MinButton` are interdependent. For example, if you turn off the Maximize button and have the Control menu visible, the latter will not contain an option for maximizing the form. Or, to look at another example, if you set the BorderStyle to FixedToolWindow, then this turns off the ControlBox even if you explicitly turn it on.

Stop your Hello World application if you have not already done so. In design mode, do the following:

1. Make the form the active control by clicking it.

2. In the Properties window, set the ControlBox property to False.

3. Run the program again (Run ➤ Start).

Notice this time there is no Control menu on the left side of the title bar or a Close button on the right side. The only way to close this form is to click the OK button.

The ForeColor Property

This doesn't affect the color of objects you place on a form, though it does affect the color of text you print to a form. For example, if you wanted to print red text directly on the form, you would set the form's ForeColor property to red. Whenever you print text directly on the form using the Print method, it would be red. Don't worry too much about printing text directly on a form. It is very rarely used. Remember the color of the form itself is set through the BackColor property.

Let's try adding a command button (described in detail in Chapter 3) to a form and changing the color of the text and the form itself:

1. Start a new project by Selecting File ➤ New Project.

2. Add a command button to Form1 by double-clicking the command button control in the Toolbox.

3. Once the button is on the form, double-click it to open the button's Click() event.

4. In the Click event procedure for the command button, enter the following line:

   ```
   Print "Hello World"
   ```

Now experiment by changing the BackColor and ForeColor properties at design time using the Properties window. You can see how these properties work together. If you want to hide the text, you can set the BackColor and ForeColor properties to be equal. For example:

```
BackColor = ForeColor
```

The Height Property

Use this property to change the height of a form. You can also set the height by dragging the form's borders in design view. The default units for measuring the Height property (as well as for the Width, Left, and Top properties) are *twips*. Don't worry too much about the units of measurement right now. These are more important when you become more skilled in Visual Basic. If you require precise measurements for a form, or any other control for that matter, you can set its size in the Height and Width properties.

Using your form from the previous example:

1. In the Properties window, set the Width property to **3600**.

2. Set the Height property to **3600**.

Notice that even without running the program, the form has been resized in the Form Designer. This is not much use to you at this time, because you can visually size the form by dragging its borders in the Form Designer. You will find that the dimensions of a form will be set in code at run time. Try this example to see what I mean:

1. Double-click the form to open the Code window. The two boxes at the top of the Code window, called drop-down list boxes, should say Form and Load respectively. This means you are currently in the Form's Load event. Don't worry too much about the details of an event.

2. Scroll down the list on the right until it says Resize. This will take you to the form's Resize event.

3. In the Resize event, type the following line of code:
    ```
    Width = Height
    ```

4. Select Run ➢ Start to run the project.

Resize the form by dragging the top or bottom border. Notice how the form automatically resizes itself to a perfect square? This is an example of setting properties at run time.

Try dragging the left or right border. The form does not resize, but it instead snaps back. This happens because the width will always equal the height, according to the code you entered. The width cannot change unless the height changes.

The Icon Property

Select an icon by double-clicking this property. The Icon property determines the icon to display on the Taskbar when the form is minimized at run time. This property has no effect if you can't minimize the form—you may have set its BorderStyle to Fixed Dialog.

If you installed all of the options for Visual Basic, then there are a large number of icons in the Common\Graphics\Icons folders—if they're not there, they'll always be found in the same directory on your Visual Basic CD-ROM. Windows 95/98 helpfully lets you preview the icons before choosing one.

The Left Property

The Left property functions much like the Height and Width properties you learned about earlier. The difference is this property determines the distance of the form from the left of the screen. This property is commonly used in conjunction with the form's Top property, which sets the vertical spacing of the form. Try this example that centers the form on the screen:

1. Stop the program if you have not already done so.

2. Double-click the form to get back to the form's Resize event.

3. Add these two lines of code to the Resize event, below the Width = Height statement:
   ```
   Left = (Screen.Width - Width) / 2
   Top = (Screen.Height - Height) / 2
   ```

4. Run the program.

This time, the form will not only resize itself, but it will center itself as well. If you want to see a cool elastic-style form, then change the last statement in the Resize event to:
```
Width = (Screen.Height - Height) / 2
```

The MaxButton Property

By setting this property to True, your form will show the standard Maximize button on the right side of the title bar. If you do not want your users to maximize the form, set this property to False.

The MinButton Property

By setting this property to True, your form will show the standard Minimize button on the right side of the title bar. If you do not want your users to minimize the form, set this property to False.

TIP

There may be instances when you do not want your users to resize the form. For example, you may have a graphic that must keep the same proportions on the form. Setting the MaxButton and MinButton properties to False will prevent this.

The Name Property

The Name property is the single most important property in Visual Basic. This is the name of a control that Visual Basic refers to when the program runs. In order to know exactly what your forms are, you should give them a descriptive name and prefix it with the letters frm. If you look back at your Hello World application in Chapter 1, you will notice you named the form "frmHelloWorld." Although it is not so important to give a descriptive name in that particular application, imagine if you had 20 or 30 forms in your program! You wouldn't want to have to remember their names as Form17 or Form20; names like frmLogon, frmLogoff, and frmChangePassword are more descriptive. Descriptive names make it easier for you to identify forms and controls in your code.

As you read Chapter 3, you will learn how to apply more three-letter prefixes called *naming conventions* to your controls.

The ScaleMode Property

Although the Height, Width, Left, and Top properties of a form are in twips, you have a choice of scales for any controls you place on a form. If you wanted to set the size and position of a command button using the more familiar system of pixels, then set the ScaleMode property for the form to 3 - Pixel.

The ShowInTaskbar Property

This property is interesting because it allows you to hide the form from the Taskbar. If you write an application that you want to reside in that little box in the right side of the Taskbar, called the *System Tray*, or you just don't want your program noticed by the user, you will need to set this property to False. You can do this at run time in the form's Load event, as shown below:

```
Private Sub Form_Load()
   ShowInTaskBar = False
End Sub
```

The Width Property

This specifies the width of the form in twips. This is similar to and is commonly used in conjunction with the Height property.

The WindowState Property

The WindowState property is responsible for how the form starts up. There are three options; the following shows you what each option does:

You type...	Option	Effect
0	Normal	The form will open in its normal state.
1	Minimized	The form will open, but it will be minimized.
2	Maximized	The form will be maximized when it opens.

TWEAKING A FORM'S PROPERTIES

Now that you are familiar with several of the form properties, let's manipulate them so you can see how they work. Many properties can be set at run time as well as design time. A few can be set only at design time (for example, BorderStyle), and one or two can be set or read only at run time. Those that are only available at run time (for instance, a property called hWnd) do not appear in the Properties window at design time.

NOTE

To set properties at design time, you use the Properties window. To set them at run time, you set the properties through code.

One property you can easily change at run time is the Caption property. Here's a hands-on example to show you how to change "Hello" to "Bye." Afterward, you'll see how to extend the code slightly, and you'll learn to change the caption of an object on a form, too.

1. Start a new project (File ➤ New Project ➤ Standard EXE) and set the Name property of Form1 to **frmForm1** in the Properties window. Also set the Caption property to **Hello**.

2. Double-click the command button in the Toolbox to add a button to the form. Set its Name property to **cmdHello** and set its Caption property to **&Hello** in the Properties window.

3. Double-click the command button on the form to display the cmdHello_Click event procedure. Add the following lines to the procedure (as shown in Figure 2.2):

```
If frmForm1.Caption = "Hello" Then
   frmForm1.Caption = "Bye"
Else
   frmForm1.Caption = "Hello"
End If
```

NOTE

If-Then-Else statements allow your program to make decisions. They operate much like they sound: *If* condition1 is true, *then* do something, or *else* do something else.

4. Run the application (Run ➤ Start) and click the command button.

All the code does is to check the current Caption property of the form. As you can see in Figure 2.3, if the caption of the form is "Hello" when you click the command button, then it gets set to "Bye." If the form's caption is set to "Bye" (that's the meaning of the Else statement), then it gets set back to "Hello."

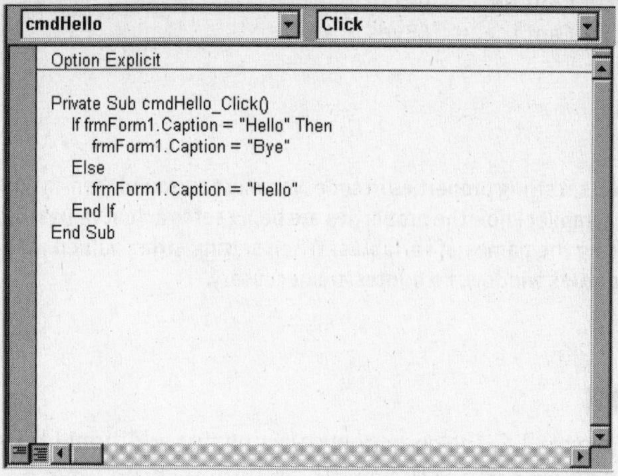

```
cmdHello            ▼    Click                ▼
  Option Explicit

  Private Sub cmdHello_Click()
     If frmForm1.Caption = "Hello" Then
        frmForm1.Caption = "Bye"
     Else
        frmForm1.Caption = "Hello"
     End If
  End Sub
```

FIGURE 2.2: Adding lines to a procedure

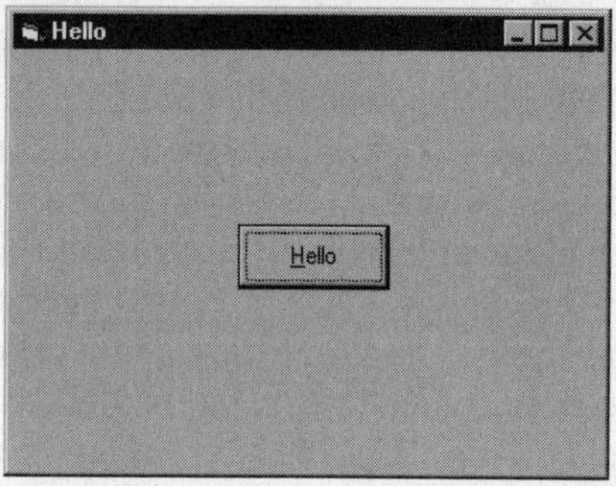

```
Hello                        _ □ ×



              ┌─────────┐
              │  Hello  │
              └─────────┘
```

FIGURE 2.3: Caption manipulation

Extending the Code

The second example takes this a step further. Double-click the command button to open the Code window for the command button's Click event. Amend the code to read the following:

```
If frmForm1.Caption = "Hello" Then
   frmForm1.Caption = "Bye"
   cmdHello.Caption = "&Hello"
Else
```

```
          frmForm1.Caption = "Hello"
          cmdHello.Caption = "&Bye"
      End If
```

NOTE

When you set string properties in code, you must surround them in quotes. This lets the compiler know the properties are being set to actual values, rather than referencing the names of variables. When setting string valued properties in the Properties window, no quotes are necessary.

Fixing a Bug

As shown in Figure 2.4, the code now contains two additional lines that set the Caption property of the cmdHello button at run time:

```
      cmdHello.Caption = "&Hello"
```

and

```
      cmdHello.Caption = "&Bye"
```

If you're using Windows 95/98, watch how the entry in the Taskbar is updated to reflect the current caption of the form. Also note there's something wrong with the application—when it first starts, the caption of the button is "Hello" and so is the caption of the form. The command button should be the opposite of the form caption. (This way they toggle each other.) You will also notice that the very first time the command button is clicked, the button's caption does not change; it stays at Hello. What should transpire is the command button should be "Bye" when the application begins. Of course, this is fixed by simply altering the Caption property of the button at design time, but there's also another way of doing it.

To fix the small bug in the code:

1. Double-click the form in the Form Designer to see the Form_Load event procedure.

2. Add the next line
   ```
   cmdHello.Caption = "&Bye"
   ```
   to that procedure (between the Private Sub and End Sub lines, as shown in Figure 2.5).

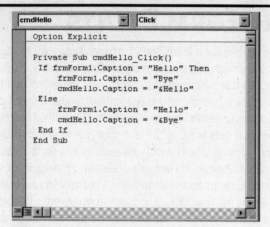

FIGURE 2.4: Setting the Caption property

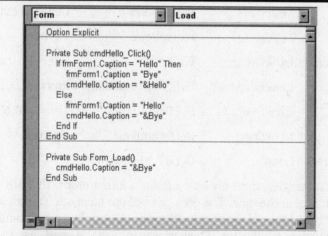

FIGURE 2.5: Adding another line of code

3. Now run the application (Run ➢ Start) and all is well.

What you did here was to use one of the events associated with a form. In the event procedure you changed one of the control properties at run time. Now let's look at some of those events.

INTRODUCING FORM EVENTS

Before looking at the events for a form, let's learn what an event actually is. Windows is an *event-driven* operating system. This means it utilizes system events to react to the environment. Events are triggered by messages. Whenever you click a button, move the mouse, resize a form, or anything else, Windows will generate a message that describes your action. This message then gets sent to the message queue. From here the message is sent to the appropriate control—for example, a form. When the control receives this message, it then generates an appropriate event. You can write your own code in an event to force a control to react precisely the way you want it to. You will learn more about events in this skill, and in the ones to follow. The more you program, the more familiar you will become with events. Now let's look at a form's events:

Activate	KeyDown	LostFocus	OLESetData
Click	KeyPress	MouseDown	OLEStartDrag
DblClick	KeyUp	MouseMove	Paint
Deactivate	LinkClose	MouseUp	QueryUnload
DragDrop	LinkError	OLECompleteDrag	**Resize**
DragOver	LinkExecute	OLEDragDrop	Terminate
GotFocus	LinkOpen	OLEDragOver	**Unload**
Initialize	**Load**	OLEGiveFeedback	

Just like properties, there are only a few of a form's events that are used a great deal of the time. The ones you will use most often are shown in boldface type. Many of the events are rarely used, unless you're building a very complex application. The best way to view the events associated with a form is to double-click the form in design view to display the Code window. The form is already given in the Object drop-down box, so all you have to do is open the Procedure drop-down list associated with it, shown in Figure 2.6.

The list of events is quite long, and some of them may appear to be fairly similar to their names—for example, the Activate event sounds similar to the Load event. You might think that a form can be displayed by activating it. The form must be loaded into memory, however, before it can do anything. Once it is loaded, it can be activated and deactivated as needed. It all depends on the exact nature of the applications you want to create, but it's a fairly safe bet that, rather than using the less popular events, you'll want to use the ones described in the following sections.

```
Form                  ▼  │ Load                    ▼
    Option Explicit           │ Load                    ▲
                              │ LostFocus
    Private Sub cmdHello_Click()  │ MouseDown
        If frmForm1.Caption = "Hello" Th │ MouseMove
            frmForm1.Caption = "Bye"   │ MouseUp
            cmdHello.Caption = "&Hello"  │ OLECompleteDrag
        Else                    │ OLEDragDrop
            frmForm1.Caption = "Hello"  │ OLEDragOver
            cmdHello.Caption = "&Bye"   │ OLEGiveFeedback
        End If                  │ OLESetData
    End Sub                     │ OLEStartDrag
                              │ Paint                   ▼
    Private Sub Form_Load()
        cmdHello.Caption = "&Bye"
    End Sub
```

FIGURE 2.6:   Form events appearing in a drop-down list

The Activate Event

You may think that activating a form and initializing a form are the same things, but they are not. A form is actually activated *after* it is initialized. The form then receives the focus after it has been activated.

These subtle differences appear between all of them. The most important difference is the order in which they occur in an application. The order is as follows:

Initialize   This event is triggered when a form is being configured before it is loaded.

Load   This event is called after the form has been initialized, and before the form is displayed on the screen. You can type code in a form's Load event to further tailor the appearance or behavior of the form.

Activate   The Activate event is triggered when the form has been loaded into memory and when it becomes the active form.

GotFocus   If it occurs at all, this event is triggered when the form gets the focus, either when it is loaded or when a user accesses the form with a mouse-click.

GETTING ONLINE HELP FOR EVENTS

To find out what different events are, click a form in design mode to remove the focus from any other objects or windows. Then press F1 to show the Help window for the form object, as shown below.

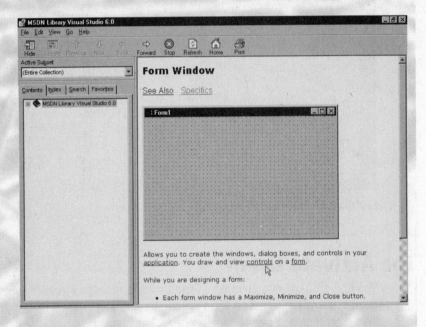

Just below the form click the controls link—the link has a solid underline and is usually blue on a color monitor. This jumps to a window that defines a Visual Basic control.

Once a particular form is open, only the Activate and possibly the GotFocus events can occur from these four events—though the Initialize event can occur in certain special circumstances.

The Initialize event happens when Visual Basic first becomes aware of the form. At run time, this happens just as you click Run ≻ Start. This is followed by the Load event, as Visual Basic reads the form from disk to memory, or from a disk cache in memory. Once the form is loaded, then the Activate event occurs as the focus shifts to the form—in other words, as the form becomes active. This happens a millisecond or so before the GotFocus event. The GotFocus event, however, can only take place if there are no visible controls on the form. If there's a visible control, then the control receives the focus rather than the form itself, and the form's GotFocus event is bypassed—though there will be a GotFocus event for the control.

In normal circumstances, then, there's always a Load event followed by an Activate event for the first form in the application when the application is started up. Of course, the application may have other windows. When the user or program switches back to the first window, it receives another Activate event, so this time there's no Load event. However, there *is* a Load event if the form has been unloaded in the meantime.

To summarize, there's a Load event followed by an Activate event when the application starts. As the focus moves to other forms and back to the first form (provided it hasn't been unloaded), then the Activate event occurs without a preceding Load event. As a beginning Visual Basic programmer, don't be too concerned with the Activate event yet. You can initialize your forms using the Load event.

The Deactivate Event

The Deactivate event is the converse of Activate. The Deactivate event occurs when the form ceases to be active. Depending on your Windows color scheme, you might see the title bar of the form turning a different color (or becoming fainter) as it deactivates and stops being the active form.

The DragDrop Event

This event takes place when a dragged control is dropped onto a form. When you run the Hello World application, you'll find if you attempt to drag a command button, nothing appears to happen. To enable the DragDrop event, you must have something to drag and drop on the form in the first place. For a quick teaser of the DragDrop event, follow these steps:

1. In the Properties window, set the DragMode property of the command button to **Automatic**.

2. Optionally, select an icon for the DragIcon property by double-clicking the DragIcon property in the Properties window.

3. Double-click the form to open the Code window.

4. Select the DragDrop event from the event drop-down list at the top of the Code window.

5. Finally, add the following statement to the DragDrop event procedure for the form:

```
Private Sub Form_DragDrop(Source As Control, _
 X As Single, Y As Single)
  Print "Dropped"
End Sub
```

NOTE

The DragDrop event can only happen if you have a "draggable" control to drag and drop. Some objects are not usually dragged around a form. For example, you would not drag a command button around. Other objects lend themselves to being dragged, such as picture boxes containing icons, or elements within list boxes. If you are unfamiliar with drag-and-drop controls, you can examine other Windows applications and see how drag-and-drop behaves in them.

The Load Event

The Load event comes after the Initialize event, but it comes before the Activate event as a form is loaded into memory from disk or from a disk cache in memory. The Load event is a particularly important one and is the one most frequently used. It's extremely handy for specifying some of the contents of the form—for example, it's often used to center a form on the screen.

WHEN TO USE *LOAD/UNLOAD* OR *ACTIVATE/DEACTIVATE*

Before a form is visible on screen, it needs to be loaded into memory. When this happens, Windows sends a message to the form and a Load event is generated by the form. If you decided you wanted to perform checks for your program or wanted to change the position of your form, you would place the code to do so in this event.

For example, if you wanted to center your form before it was displayed, you would write the following code:

```
Private Sub Form_Load()
  Move (Screen.Width - Width) / 2, (Screen.Height - _
Height) / 2
End Sub
```

CONTINUED ➡

Part i

Once the form is loaded, it gets activated because it becomes the active window. As a result, it generates an Activate event. In addition, this event is generated whenever an inactive form is acted upon. A good example of when to use the Activate event is in an e-mail program. You could write code in the Activate event that checks for new mail. As a result, every time you start working with the program, it will check for new mail for you.

The Deactivate event is generated when another form or application receives the focus. You could possibly use this event to minimize your application when you go to another program.

Finally, the Unload event is important, because this is your last chance to perform any "housekeeping" for your form. You will want to close any open databases or files in this event. This ensures that memory is not wasted when the form is removed from memory.

The Resize Event

When the user or the program code alters the size of a form, the Resize event occurs. This has two main uses:

- ▶ You can resize the controls on the form (in the event procedure) with code.

- ▶ You can set the form back to its original size.

To do these you employ the Height and Width properties of objects. You can examine the code in the example dealing with the Height and Width properties.

NOTE

You can't resize a form that has been maximized or minimized. To prevent either of these from happening, the easiest solution is to set the MaxButton and MinButton properties to False.

The Unload Event

The Unload event is, logically, the opposite of Load. The most popular choice for an Unload event procedure is one that asks the user if they're sure they want to close the form (though another event procedure, QueryUnload, is a little more flexible in this respect). If you look at the Unload event in the Code window, you can see it's a little different from some of the others you've met. It has (Cancel As Integer) after the name of the procedure. You can use this argument to cancel the unloading of the form. You can see this in action with the following example:

1. Start a new project (File ➢ New Project), and select Standard EXE.

2. Double-click Form1 in the Form Designer to open its Code window.

3. Select the Unload event from the Events drop-down list box.

4. Add the following code:

```
Private Sub Form_Unload(Cancel As Integer)
  If MsgBox("Are you sure?", vbYesNo, _
"Quit?") = vbYes Then
    Unload Me
    Set Form1 = Nothing
  Else
    Cancel = 1
  End If
End Sub
```

5. Close the Code window and run the program by selecting Run ➢ Start.

6. You should see a plain form on the screen. Click the Close button on the form. This will generate an Unload event.

NOTE

The MsgBox function is used to display a dialog box, called a *message box*, to the user.

Because you added the code to the Unload event, Visual Basic executes this code, which asks you if you really want to exit. If you click the Yes button, the form will close. However, if you click No, the program sets the Cancel parameter to 1, which notifies Visual Basic not to unload the form.

TIP

If you are creating an editor-style application—like a word processor or paint program—you should ask the user if they are sure about closing an application if they have not saved their edits and changes. You can place warning code, similar to the code in the previous example, in the form's Unload event.

INTRODUCING FORM METHODS

Before we look at a form's methods, let me take a minute to explain what a method does. A method is a command that allows you to tell an object what to do. In plain English, a method is the equivalent of a verb. For example, you can tell a form to unload itself by calling the Unload method. The following are a form's methods:

Circle	Move	Pset	TextHeight
Cls	PaintPicture	Refresh	TextWidth
Hide	Point	Scale	**Unload**
Item	Print	SetFocus	Zorder
Line	PrintForm	**Show**	

Show, Hide, and Unload are the three most popular methods to apply to a form. These are put into practice in the next section.

WORKING WITH MULTIPLE DOCUMENT INTERFACE (MDI) FORMS

Another breed of the form object is the multiple document interface (MDI) form. An MDI lets you open windows within a *parent container* window. If you look at a typical word processor—Word for Windows is a classic example—you can have many documents open simultaneously within the main window (see Figure 2.7). This main window serves as the container—it contains multiple forms. The MDI application was originally developed back when previous versions of Windows were predominant. The multiple document nature allowed users to open more than one file at a time, without having to open several copies of the program itself. This not only saves time, but it also saves memory.

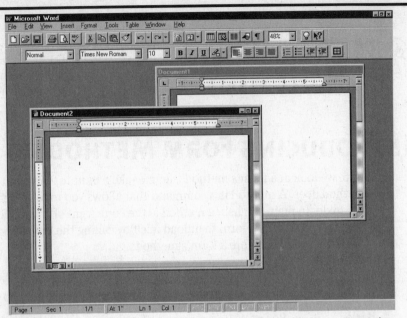

FIGURE 2.7: Multiple documents open simultaneously within a parent container window.

MDI interfaces are more commonly used for *document-centric* applications, like word processors and paint programs. A program is said to be document-centric when the main objects that you work on are documents. If you plan to allow your users to work on several similar forms at one time from within an application, you should use the MDI model. Visual Basic makes it very simple to create an MDI application.

Creating an MDI

To create an MDI application, you need at least two forms in the application. One is the *parent*, or *containing* form, and the second is the *child*, or *contained* form. To have more than one type of child form, you can add further forms to the project. But you only need one child form for the simplest of MDI projects. Here's how it's done:

1. Start a new project by selecting File ➤ New Project. Select Standard EXE as the project type if you have the Project Wizard enabled.

2. You will already have a form in the project. Set its Name property to **frmChild** and its Caption property to **MDI Child**.

3. To create the MDI parent form, right-click the Forms folder in the Project Explorer and select Add ≻ MDI Form. If the Form Wizard appears, select MDI Form.

4. Set the Name property to **frmMDI**, and the Caption property to **MDI Parent**.

5. Right-click Project1 in the Project Explorer, and select Project1 Properties from the pop-up menu. Set the Startup Object list to frmMDI. If you omit this, the application will start with the child form showing.

6. Select frmChild from the Project Explorer. Set the form's MDI Child property to True. This will cause this form, which is the child, to rest inside of the MDI Parent container.

7. Select frmMDI from the Project Explorer.

8. Start the Menu Designer by selecting Tools ≻ Menu Editor. You will see a window like the one in Figure 2.8.

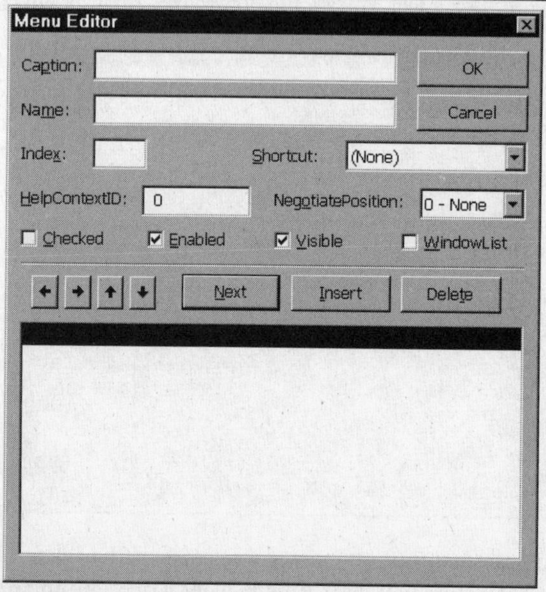

FIGURE 2.8:   The Menu Editor

Now that you have created a MDI child form to reside inside the MDI parent window, let's create a simple menu for the form.

1. Type **&File** in the Caption field.

2. In the Name field, type **mnuFile**.

3. Click the Next button.

4. Click the right arrow button. This will indent this menu item.

5. Enter **&New Form** in the Caption field.

6. Type **mnuFileNew** in the Name field.

7. Click the OK button to close the Menu Editor.

8. The frmMDI form should now have a File menu on it. Select File ➤ New from the MDI menu. This will open up the Code window.

9. In the mnuFileNew_Click() event, type the following lines of code:

    ```
    Dim frm As New frmChild
    frm.Show
    ```

10. Save and run the project. You should now see the MDI shown here.

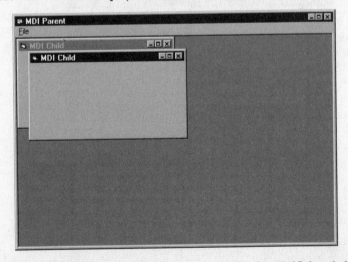

The code creates (or *instantiates*) new copies of frmChild and shows them. It does this each time you click File ➤ New. Try opening and closing a few child windows. You should have a functioning MDI application.

Improving the MDI

But there are a few additions to make before it really resembles a commercial Windows MDI application. For example, each child form has the same caption, so it's impossible to tell them apart. Let's fix that. It would also be nice to tile or cascade the children. Further, it's normal to have a menu option (called a *window list*), which lets you switch easily to children that get hidden behind other children.

1. Open the Menu Editor and add a **&Window** menu title to the MDI parent, frmMDI. Turn on the check box for WindowList in the Menu Editor as you do so.

2. Using the same methods as in steps 5 and 6 in the previous section, add a **Tile** and a **Cascade** item to this menu title. Name them **mnuWindowTile** and **mnuWindowCascade**, respectively.

3. Click OK to close the Menu Editor.

4. Enter this code for the Click event of the mnuWindowTile object:

   ```
   frmMDI.Arrange vbTileHorizontal
   ```

5. Enter this line for the mnuWindowCascade item:

   ```
   frmMDI.Arrange vbCascade
   ```

   The vbCascade and vbTileHorizontal terms are built-in Visual Basic constants. These can be obtained from Visual Basic's online help.

6. Change the code for the mnuFileNew menu item so that it looks like this:

   ```
   Private Sub mnuFileNew_Click()
     Static Counter As Integer
     Dim frm As New frmChild
     Counter = Counter + 1
     frm.Caption = "MDI Child" & Counter
     frm.Show
   End Sub
   ```

Now save and run the application, and notice the difference in Figure 2.9.

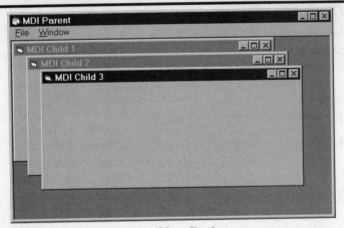

FIGURE 2.9: The improved MDI application

Deciphering the Code

The code you typed in the previous example may look like Greek to you, but don't worry. Many of the statements are explained elsewhere in this book. But let's take a quick look so you can get an idea of what's actually going on when you type in code.

The first line (Static Counter As Integer) tells Visual Basic to create a variable called Counter. The Static keyword tells Visual Basic to remember the value of Counter every time this procedure is called. This allows Counter to count the forms as they are created.

The second line (Dim frm As New frmChild) uses a Dim statement to "dimension" a variable. In this case, it is dimensioning a variable called frm and this variable will be based on, or derived from, the frmChild form. The New keyword tells Visual Basic this will be a new form, not one of the others created by this procedure.

Because Counter remembers its value, it can increment itself with the line:

```
Counter = Counter +1
```

In effect, if Counter was equal to the number 3, then it would say that Counter equals the value of Counter, three for example, plus one. The result would be that Counter equals three plus one, or four. Because Counter is a Static variable, it will remember this value, so it will be five the next time this procedure is called, six the next, and so on.

The next statement (`frm.Caption = "MDI Child" & Counter`) just changes the `Caption` property of the form to the text "MDI Child" and the number stored in `Counter`. For example, the second form would have the caption "MDI Child 2."

The last statement brings the child to life, so to speak. It tells the child form to show itself. Because you now understand how a form comes to be, you know the first event of a form is the `Load` event. Once the form is loaded, it is activated and then displayed on screen.

USING THE FORM WIZARD

As you work with Visual Basic more often, you will find yourself adding forms to your projects. You have just done this in the multiple document interface (MDI) example. Because a single document interface (SDI) form cannot perform the functions of an MDI form very well, a special MDI form was created to handle the task. When you start writing your own applications, you may find that a single form is not enough to complete the task. At this point you will need to add a new form and customize it to do the task you need. With Visual Basic 6 it is easy to include a form; you can use the Form Wizard to select the style of form you would like to add to your project. Just right-click in the Project Explorer and select Add ➤ Form and the Form Wizard will display the Add Form dialog box (see Figure 2.10).

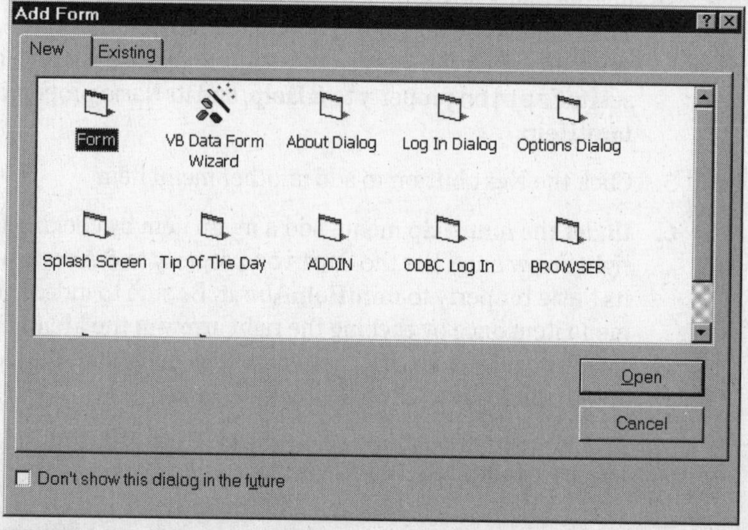

FIGURE 2.10: The Form Wizard

As you can see, you have many form choices to choose from, including About Dialog, Splash Screen, Tip of the Day, and even a Web browser! When you select a form from the Wizard, Visual Basic will create a template complete with graphics and code and add it to your project. You will find that the Form Wizard can be a real time-saver, because it writes the code for a form automatically.

TIP

If you want to have standard-looking forms and do not want to code them yourself, you can use the Form Wizard to do the work for you.

Let's use the Form Wizard to add one last form to your project to spice it up a little.

1. To bring up the Form Wizard, right-click in the Project Explorer and select Add ➤ Form from the pop-up menu.

2. Add another form to your project by selecting About Dialog in the Add Form dialog box. The form will automatically name itself frmAbout.

3. Make the multiple document interface (MDI) form active by double-clicking frmMDI in the Project Explorer.

4. Go back to the Menu Editor, and add another menu by clicking the blank space directly under the &New Form caption. There should be no ellipses (the three dots) in this space. If there are, click the left arrow button to remove them. Now set its Caption property to **&Help**, and its Name property to **mnuHelp**.

5. Click the Next button to add another menu item.

6. Under the mnuHelp menu, add a menu item by clicking the right arrow once. Set the Caption property to **&About**, and its Name property to **mnuHelpAbout**. Be sure to indent this menu item once by clicking the right arrow in the Menu Editor. This will ensure that this will be a menu item of the Help menu. Click OK to close the Menu Editor.

7. Right-click Project1 in the Project Explorer and select Project1 Properties.

8. When the Project Properties dialog box comes up, click the Make tab.

9. Change the Title field to **A Sample MDI**.

10. In the Version Information frame, click Company Name in the Type list, and type your name or your company name in the Value field.

11. Scroll down to the Product Name entry in the Type list, and enter **A Sample MDI**. Click OK when you are done.

12. Select Help ➢ About from the menu on your MDI form to open the Code window.

13. In the `mnuHelpAbout_Click()` sub, type the following line of code:

    ```
    frmAbout.Show vbModal
    ```

14. Run your application and check out the About dialog box (shown in Figure 2.11).

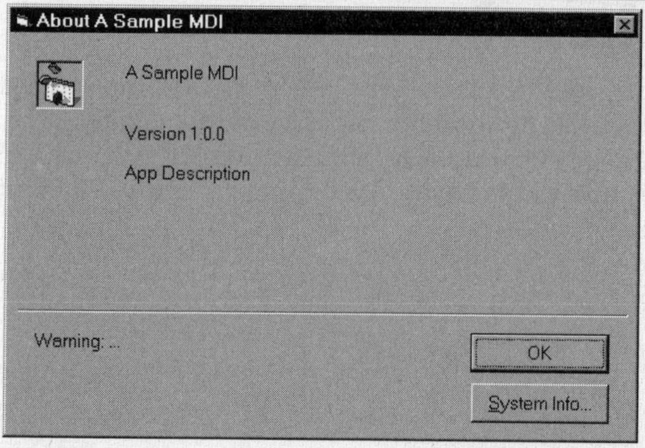

FIGURE 2.11: The About dialog box created by the Form Wizard

Now that you have tried this example, let's look at the keyword `vbModal`. In this case, the `vbModal` keyword is a parameter passed to the form's Show method. This tells Visual Basic to show the About dialog box in a modal state. A *modal* form gains the exclusive attention of the user. A user cannot access any other forms within an application until the modal dialog box has been addressed. This technique is used in many ways. You would most certainly want to make a login dialog box modal, because you do not want your users to gain access to a program without first being properly validated by the login process.

In addition to a simple modal form, you can also have *system modal* forms. These forms require the attention of the user and do not allow any other applications to be accessed until the dialog box has been addressed. A good example of a system modal dialog box is a screen saver. No applications can be accessed until the proper password is entered. This provides a small amount of security for your applications. (A full discussion of system modal dialog boxes is beyond the scope of this book; see *Mastering Visual Basic 6* by Evangelos Petroutsos [Sybex, 1998], for more information.)

TIP

If you find your Visual Basic design window becoming cluttered with lots of forms, close them. The quickest way to redisplay a form is to double-click its name in the Project Explorer.

WHAT'S NEXT?

Now that you have a handle on forms, you can move on to bigger and better things. Controls add functionality and style to your application. The next chapter will delve into this subject and covers dealing with the Toolbox, grouping controls within frames, and designing Windows 95/98–style interfaces.

Chapter 3

SELECTING AND USING CONTROLS

As you learned in the previous chapter, the form object is the foundation of your Visual Basic application. Almost every application you develop will have a form in it, and on these forms will be controls. Controls are the building blocks of your application. They give your application the enhanced functionality and personality that is required for your user to interact with your application. In this chapter, we will discuss the most common and useful controls that come with Visual Basic 6. While we cannot discuss every control in detail, those discussed in here will be the ones you will work with the most.

Adapted from *Visual Basic 6 In Record Time*
by Steve Brown
ISBN 0-7821-2310-4   688 pages $29.99

INTRODUCING CONTROLS

Custom controls are the building blocks of a Visual Basic application. Controls allow your form to do more than just sit empty on a screen. Some controls, such as labels or list boxes, give users feedback, while others, like command buttons and text boxes, elicit responses. Other controls sit quietly, invisible to the user, and perform some of the grunt work that makes your application useful. The timer control is one example of an invisible control. Controls are easy to use and, when used properly, can add significant functionality to your programs. To add a control to a form you simply double-click the control you want to add, or you can "draw" the control on a form by clicking the control and then dragging the mouse around the area on the form where you want the control to be. After you add some controls, you can set most of their properties in the Properties window. You simply click the control to make it active and change the appropriate properties in the Properties window.

The Toolbox is the containing window that holds the custom controls for your applications (see Figure 3.1). In this chapter, we are going to take a look at some of the basic controls you can use to get your applications up and running.

There are also several advanced controls that come with Visual Basic 6, many of which have been enhanced since the previous version. Some controls work with multimedia, such as the Multimedia control, and others—Winsock and Internet Transfer controls—utilize the Internet. There are also several new data-aware controls that help you work with databases. In addition, you can develop your own ActiveX custom controls and add them to your Toolbox, or you can distribute your custom controls to other developers through a variety of methods.

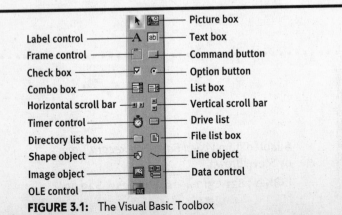

FIGURE 3.1: The Visual Basic Toolbox

USING COMMAND BUTTONS

 A command button control (shown here) is one of the most common controls found in Windows applications. Visual Basic is no exception. You can use a command button to elicit simple responses from the user or to invoke special functions on forms. You have surely encountered command buttons before: Every time you click the OK button on a dialog box you click a command button.

In the following sections we will look at some of the most important properties, methods, and events of this simple but powerful control. In "Command Button Methods" you will learn how a command button control works; follow along with the exercise to get some hands-on experience.

NOTE

Remember that properties describe the characteristics of an object. Methods are actions that you can tell the object to perform, and events are triggered when a control does something.

Command Button Properties

Below is a list of the properties of a command button. The most commonly used properties appear in boldface. If you are interested in any properties not discussed below, you can select it in the Properties window and press the F1 key to get online help.

Appearance	**Enabled**	HWnd	**Style**
BackColor	Font	Index	**TabIndex**
Cancel	FontBold	Left	**TabStop**
Caption	FontItalic	MaskColor	Tag
CausesValidation	FontName	MouseIcon	ToolTipText
Container	FontSize	MousePointer	Top
Default	FontStrikethru	**Name**	UseMaskColor
DisabledPicture	FontUnderline	OLEDropMode	Value
DownPicture	ForeColor	Parent	Visible
DragIcon	Height	**Picture**	WhatsThis-HelpID
DragMode	HelpContextID	RightToLeft	Width

The two most important properties of command buttons are Name and Caption. The Name property is used to give the control its own identity. This name is used by your code and Visual Basic to distinguish it from the rest of the controls. The Caption property determines the text that appears on the command button. Placing an ampersand character (&) in the caption gives a keyboard-access key alternative (called a *hotkey*) to a mouse-click. You access these controls by holding the Alt key down while you press the underlined letter of the control you wish to access. The user could also tab to the command button and press the spacebar to simulate a mouse-click on the button.

TIP

Access keys, also called *hotkeys*, are important to understand because not all users like to use the mouse. Users who write for a living, for example, may not like it when they have to move their hands off of the keyboard to change a font, and then resume typing. You should provide hotkeys whenever possible to make using your software easier on your users.

Two other useful properties are Cancel and Default. Setting the Default property to True means the user can simulate a click on the button by pressing Enter. Setting Cancel to True means the user can close a form by pressing Esc.

NOTE

When you add command buttons to a form, only one button can have its Default property set to True at a time. This button becomes the default button for the form. Likewise, only one command button can have its Cancel property set to True.

By setting the Style property, you can make the button contain text only, or you can add a picture to the button. If you want the button in its normal, unpressed state to have a picture, you can specify the picture's filename in the Picture property. You can also place other graphics on the button by setting them using the DisabledPicture and Down-Picture properties.

Two properties can stop the user from accessing a command button—Enabled and Visible. If either is set to False, the command button will be unusable. Disabling a command button is a handy technique if you want to force the end user to complete certain actions (such as filling in text boxes) before clicking the next button in the process.

TIP

When you want a button to be disabled, you should set the Enabled property to False rather than setting the Visible property to False. This lets the user know a control is available under certain conditions, rather than completely hiding the functionality of your program.

If the user moves around the form with the Tab key, you can determine the order in which they visit controls by specifying the TabIndex property. A control with a TabIndex of 0 (zero) is the first to receive the focus on a form, provided it's not disabled or invisible. If you alter the TabIndex of one control, the other controls' orders adjust to accommodate the new order. When you want to prevent a user from tabbing to a control, set its TabStop property to False. This does not prevent a mouse-click on a control—to stop that, use the Enabled or Visible properties described previously.

Command Button Events

Without a doubt, the most frequently coded event procedure for a command button corresponds to the Click() event; the other events for a command button are listed here:

Click	KeyPress	**MouseUp**	OLESetData
DragDrop	KeyUp	OLECompleteDrag	OLEStartDrag
DragOver	LostFocus	OLEDragDrop	
GotFocus	**MouseDown**	OLEDragOver	
KeyDown	MouseMove	OLEGiveFeedback	

In your first programs, the Click() event is probably the only event in which you'd be interested. It's the most commonly used event on a command button. You won't use many of the other events until you become more proficient in Visual Basic. However, you can also use the MouseUp() event in place of the Click() event. Many Windows 95/98 applications use this event because it gives the user a chance to back out without firing a Click() event.

Command Button Methods

Listed below are the methods for the command button. The most commonly used method is `SetFocus`.

Drag	OLEDrag	**SetFocus**	ZOrder
Move	Refresh	ShowWhatsThis	

The `SetFocus` method is sometimes used to place the focus on a particular button. This comes in handy if you want the user to return to a default button after editing a text box on a form. If that were so, the code for the focus button looks like this:

```
cmdMyButton.SetFocus
```

And it might be placed in the `Change()` event procedure for a text box.

Experimenting with a Command Button

Let's put the command button to use.

1. If you installed the sample applications from the Visual Basic CD, then open the project `\MSDN98\98vs\1033\Samples\VB98\Controls\Controls.vbp`. (This directory may be slightly different, depending on how you installed your sample applications.)

NOTE

If you haven't already installed the sample applications, take a moment to refer back to the section "Working with Multiple Projects" in Chapter 1. It covers how to install the sample applications. You will need to have these installed to do many of the exercises in this chapter.

2. Click Run ➣ Start from the Visual Basic menu to run the application. From the Control Examples dialog box, click Test Buttons. You will see a form like Figure 3.2.

3. Click the Change Signal button to watch the signal lights change. When you are done testing the buttons, click the Close button.

With the command button control, you can enhance this form by placing the signal directly on the Change Signal button.

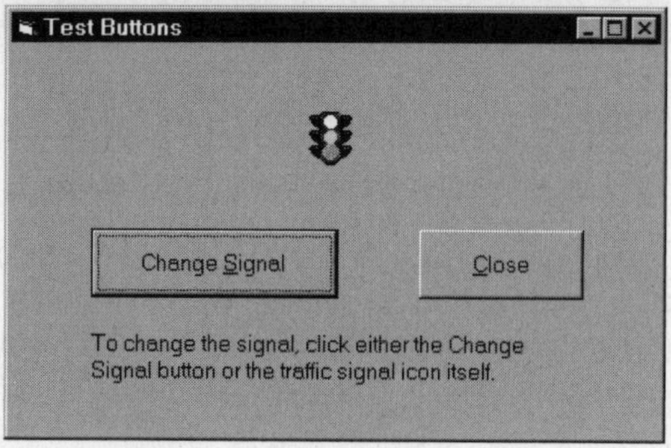

FIGURE 3.2: Testing the command button

4. Stop the application by selecting Run ➤ End from the Visual Basic menu.

5. Make the Test Buttons form active by double-clicking frmButton in the Project Explorer.

6. Stretch the Change Signal button so it can fit an icon the size of the signal on it. In the Properties window, change the button's Style property to **1 - Graphical**.

7. Set the Visible property of the controls imgGreen, imgYellow, and imgRed to False.

8. Add the following code to the form's Load() event:

```
Private Sub Form_Load()
   cmdChange.Picture = imgGreen.Picture
End Sub
```

9. Now change the ChangeSignal procedure to the following code:

```
Private Sub ChangeSignal()
  Static signal As Integer

  signal = signal + 1
  If signal > 3 Then signal = 1

  Select Case signal
    Case Is = 1
      cmdChange.Picture = imgYellow.Picture
```

```
        Case Is = 2
          cmdChange.Picture = imgRed.Picture
        Case Is = 3
          cmdChange.Picture = imgGreen.Picture
      End Select
    End Sub
```

10. Run the program again (Run ➤ Start). Click Test Buttons again to get to the Test Buttons dialog box. When you click the Change Signal button, the signal icon on the command button will change in the same manner that the signal image did previously.

Although not sophisticated, this example shows you how the command button works. You can place other commands in the Click() event so the button will perform any tasks you want it to. If you wanted the button to close your application, you could change the Click() event procedure to:

```
    Private Sub cmdChangeSignal_Click()
      End
    End Sub
```

TIP

To add a graphic to your command buttons, set the Style property to 1 - Graphical. Then add the graphic by setting the Picture property to the filename of the graphic you want to use.

USING TEXT BOXES

Nearly every Visual Basic project involves at least one text box control (shown here). Text boxes are commonly used for accepting user input or for entering data. Their properties are, of course, specifically designed for these purposes. If you only want the simplest of user responses, you might consider using an InputBox instead. The InputBox displays a dialog box and prompts the user to enter something and returns this to the application.

Text Box Properties

Here is the list of properties for the text box control. Again, the most important properties appear in boldface:

Alignment	Font	LinkItem	RightToLeft
Appearance	FontBold	LinkMode	**ScrollBars**
BackColor	FontItalic	LinkTimeout	**SelLength**
BorderStyle	FontName	LinkTopic	**SelStart**
CausesValidation	FontSize	**Locked**	**SelText**
Container	FontStrikethru	**MaxLength**	**TabIndex**
DataChanged	FontUnderline	MouseIcon	TabStop
DataField	ForeColor	MousePointer	Tag
DataFormat	Height	**MultiLine**	**Text**
DataMember	HelpContextID	**Name**	ToolTipText
DataSource	HideSelection	OLEDragMode	Top
DragIcon	HWnd	OLEDropMode	Visible
DragMode	Index	Parent	WhatsThis-HelpID
Enabled	Left	**PasswordChar**	Width

As always, the property you set first is the Name property. By convention this begins with the txt prefix. Notice that there is no Caption for a text box. Instead the text shown in the text box is determined by the Text property. You can provide a default entry in the text box by setting the Text property accordingly. It's possible you don't want any value in the text box—you want the user to enter something from scratch. In that case, delete the Text property setting and the text box appears blank. The MaxLength property is handy for limiting the user to a specified number of characters. This is often used in conjunction with the PasswordChar property. The latter is valuable for showing a default character (the asterisk character—*—is the best choice) when the user is entering a password. MaxLength and PasswordChar properties are often employed for a text box on a logon form.

The MultiLine property lets the user type more than one line of text into the text box. If MultiLine is used with the ScrollBars property, you can make a simple text editor with no coding—though you would need a couple of lines of code to save the user's typing.

The SelLength, SelStart, and SelText properties are useful for dealing with text appropriately. For example, the SelText property returns the text in the text box that the user selected with the mouse or arrow keys. From there it's easy to copy or cut the selected text to the Clipboard.

Note that the ReadOnly property from previous versions has been replaced by the Locked property. Setting the Locked property to True will cause the text box to display data, but will permit no editing. You may have noticed this type of text box on license agreement dialog boxes that appear during program installations. You can select and copy text, but you cannot type or delete text from the box.

To change the order in which the user tabs around the text boxes (and other controls) on a form, change the TabIndex setting. If you don't want the user to tab into a text box, set its TabStop property to False. To prevent a user from clicking in the text box with the mouse, set the Enabled property to False. There may be some situations where you would want to prevent the user from accessing a text box. For example, the user is not allowed to enter a message in an e-mail program until an address has been entered in the address text box. You will discover other examples of why you would want to use this feature as you become more proficient with Visual Basic.

Text Box Events

The text box control supports a few events that are listed in the table here:

Change	KeyDown	LinkOpen	OLEDragDrop
Click	KeyPress	LostFocus	OLEDragOver
DblClick	KeyUp	MouseDown	OLEGiveFeedback
DragDrop	LinkClose	MouseMove	OLESetData
DragOver	LinkError	MouseMove	OLEStartDrag
GotFocus	LinkNotify	OLECompleteDrag	Validate

The Change() event occurs every time the user inserts, replaces, or deletes a character in a text box. You can perform some elementary validation of user entry in the Change() event. You can even use it to restrict entry to certain characters only. However, you may find that the Masked Edit control or one of the Key events is more suitable for this purpose. The Microsoft Masked Edit control lets you specify entry templates or masks. It's a custom control that you need to add to the Toolbox if you want to use it. There's a full reference for all the custom controls bundled with Visual Basic in the Microsoft Developer Network, included on your Visual Basic CD.

Text Box Methods

Here is the list of methods supported by the text box control:

Drag	**LinkRequest**	OLEDrag	ShowWhatsThis
LinkExecute	**LinkSend**	Refresh	ZOrder
LinkPoke	Move	**SetFocus**	

Most of the methods here are not used very frequently, though the Link methods are necessary if your text box is involved in a DDE (Dynamic Data Exchange) conversation. DDE allows one application to communicate with another. As the user interacts with one application, it sends data automatically to the other application. Unfortunately, it is beyond the scope of this book to cover DDE in detail. If you are interested in pursuing it further, check the online help.

The SetFocus method, though, is a boon in data-entry applications. When the user clicks a command button (say, an Update button), the focus remains on that button. If the last statement in the Click() event for the command button is a SetFocus method, you can force the focus back to the data-entry text boxes. This saves the user from an extra mouse-click or excessive use of the Tab key just to get back into position. The syntax is:

```
txtMyTextBox.SetFocus
```

Experimenting with Text Box Controls

To see the SetFocus method in action, try the following example:

1. Open the project \MSDN98\98vs\1033\Samples\VB98\ Controls\Controls.vbp if it is not already open.

2. Select Run ➤ Start to run the application. From the Control Examples dialog box, click the Text Box button. You will see a form similar to the one shown in Figure 3.3.

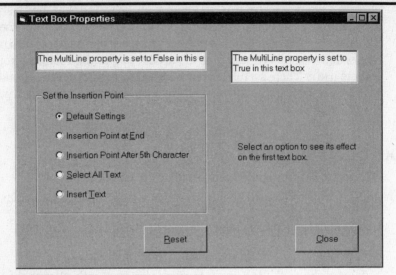

FIGURE 3.3:   Testing text box controls

The text box on the left of Figure 3.3 can be changed by selecting the options within the frame. The text box on the right has its MultiLine property set to True, as the text in the box indicates. Text editing applications often exploit the MultiLine and ScrollBars properties of a text box. Make the text box as large as the form and keep the form fixed in size (BorderStyle property). If you want the user to resize the form, or it's a multiple document interface (MDI) child form, you have to resize the text box dynamically as the user alters the size of the form. One way of doing this is to add the following code to the form's Resize event procedure:

```
txtText1.Top = frmForm1.ScaleTop
txtText1.Left = frmForm1.ScaleLeft
txtText1.Width = frmForm1.ScaleWidth
txtText1.Height = frmForm1.ScaleHeight
```

The Scale properties refer to the internal dimensions of a form. Thus a form's Height property is different from its ScaleHeight property. The latter makes allowances for title bars and borders.

3. Next, stop the application and make frmText active in the Form Designer.

4. Double-click the Insertion Point After 5th Character option to expose its procedure code, which looks like this:

```
Private Sub optInsert_Click()
  ' place the insertion point after 5th char
  txtDisplay.SelStart = 5

  ' set the focus to the text box so we can see
  ' the result of our settings
  txtDisplay.SetFocus
End Sub
```

The `SelStart` property is used to select the starting position, in characters, of a selection within a text box. Here it is set to the fifth position. The `SetFocus` method sets the focus of the application back to `txtDisplay`.

5. Open the procedure for the `Click()` event of `optSelect`:

```
Private Sub optSelect_Click()
  ' place the insertion point at the beginning
  txtDisplay.SelStart = 0
  ' find the length of the string and
  ' select that number of characters
  txtDisplay.SelLength = Len(txtDisplay.Text)

  ' set the focus to the text box so we can see
  ' the result of our settings
  txtDisplay.SetFocus
End Sub
```

This code shows how you can select all of the text within a text box. So if you had a Select All menu option, you would call a procedure similar to this example. If you want to check the text that is highlighted, you can check the `SelText` property.

6. Replace the code in the `cmdClose_Click()` event with the following:

```
Private Sub cmdClose_Click()
  If txtDisplay.SelLength > 0 Then
    MsgBox "You selected " & txtDisplay.SelText
  End If

  Unload Me    ' Unload this form.
End Sub
```

7. Run the application. In the Text Box Properties dialog box, select the word MultiLine and click the Close button. You will see something like Figure 3.4.

Text Box Properties

The MultiLine property is set to False in this e

The MultiLine property is set to True in this text box

Set the Insertion Point

- ⦿ Default Settings
- ○ Insertion Point at End
- ○ Insertion Point After 5th C
- ○ Select All Text
- ○ Insert Text

Controls

You selected MultiLine

OK

an option to see its effect
irst text box.

Reset

Close

FIGURE 3.4:   The SelText property contents

USING LABELS

A A label control (shown here) is similar to a text box control in that both display text. The main difference, however, is that a label displays read-only text as far as the user is concerned, though you can alter the caption as a run-time property.

The property of interest in a label control is the Caption property, as opposed to a text box's Text property. Labels are often used for providing information to the user. This can be in the form of a message shown on the form itself or a prompt. The prompt is usually combined with a text box, list box, or other control. It gives the user an idea of the nature of the referenced control. For example, if you had a text box that allowed the user to enter the data for a customer's name, then you might place a label to the left or above the text box with its Caption property set to Customer Name.

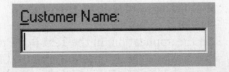

SETTING ACCESS KEYS FOR A LABEL CONTROL

Access keys, also known as *accelerators*, are actually Alt+key combinations that allow the user to access a control by holding down the Alt key while pressing the underlined letter of a text-type control. Access keys can only be set for controls that have a Caption property—for instance, command buttons and menu controls. Many controls, text box controls for example, do not have a Caption property, so it's impossible for a keyboard user to jump straight to the control—unless they press the Tab key and the control just happens to be next in the tab order.

The workaround is to place a label control before the control in question. Then you set the TabIndex property of the label to one less than the TabIndex of the control the label is describing. Include an ampersand character (&) in the Caption property for the label to define the access key.

Let's try an example to give you an idea of what's required:

1. If it's not already open, open the Controls.vbp project from the previous example.

2. Double-click frmText in the Project Explorer to make it the active form.

3. Click txtDisplay, the text box control on the upper-left side of the form, and examine its TabIndex property in the Properties window. It should be set to **o**. This makes this control the first tabstop on the form.

4. Add a label control to the form and place it above txtDisplay. Set its Name property to **lblDisplay** in the Properties window. Set its Caption property to **Dis&play**. Be sure to place the ampersand before the letter *p*.

5. The TabIndex property of lblDisplay should be 11. Change it to **o**.

6. Run the program by selecting Run ≻ Start.

7. From the Control Example form, click the Text Box button.

8. From the Text Box Properties form, click the Reset button to move the focus away from txtDisplay.

9. Now, hold down the Alt key and press the letter **P**.

CONTINUED ➥

Now pressing the Alt key with the underlined letter moves the focus to the label. But if you look at the properties, events, and methods of a label (described shortly), you see that there's no TabStop property; no GotFocus or LostFocus events; and no SetFocus method. What this means is a label can never receive the focus—so moving the focus to a label with an access key will move the focus to the next control in the TabIndex property order.

Label Properties

You have already worked with some of the properties of a label control. Here is the complete list of properties for this control:

Alignment	DataSource	Height	Parent
Appearance	DragIcon	Index	RightToLeft
AutoSize	DragMode	Left	**TabIndex**
BackColor	Enabled	LinkItem	Tag
BackStyle	**Font**	LinkMode	ToolTipText
BorderStyle	FontBold	LinkNotify	Top
Caption	FontItalic	LinkTimeout	**UseMnemonic**
Container	FontName	LinkTopic	Visible
DataChanged	FontSize	MouseIcon	WhatsThisHelpID
DataField	FontStrikethru	MousePointer	Width
DataFormat	FontUnderline	**Name**	**WordWrap**
DataMember	ForeColor	**OLEDropMode**	

As a reminder, the most important property at the outset is—once again—the Name property. For labels the prefix is normally lbl. The Caption property determines the text shown in the label. If you incorporate an ampersand (&) character in the caption, an access key is defined. This raises an interesting question: What happens if you want to show an actual ampersand in the caption? An ampersand does not display; instead, it remains hidden and causes the subsequent character to appear underlined.

Part i

> **TIP**
>
> If you do want an ampersand character to appear in a label, set the UseMnemonic property to False, because by default it's True. A mnemonic is an abbreviation or shorthand—in this context it means an access key, or accelerator.

You define the size of the label at design time. At run time you might wish to alter the Caption property, only to find it's too big to fit within the label control. You could calculate the length of the caption and adjust the label size accordingly, but this is messy and there's a danger of an enlarged label obscuring other controls. To simplify matters, use the AutoSize and WordWrap properties, either by themselves or in conjunction. That way the caption will fit and you can control whether the label expands vertically rather than horizontally.

One more interesting label control property is BorderStyle. This is not related to the form property of the same name—there are only two choices. But by setting BorderStyle to 1 - Fixed Single and the BackColor to white (or whatever), the label looks exactly like a text box, except that it's read-only. Labels were often used in this fashion in prior versions of Visual Basic to show data for browsing purposes only.

Label Events

The label control has many of the same events as any other controls:

Change	LinkClose	MouseMove	OLEGiveFeedback
Click	LinkError	MouseUp	OLESetData
DblClick	LinkNotify	OLECompleteDrag	OLEStartDrag
DragDrop	LinkOpen	OLEDragDrop	
DragOver	MouseDown	OLEDragOver	

Most of the standard events are supported. But note the absence of any Key() events. This is consistent with a label not being able to receive the focus. The Mouse() events are there, because there's nothing to stop you from clicking a label at run time. The ability to click a control does not indicate it must necessarily receive the focus. The Link() events are not shared by many other controls (with the exception of text boxes and picture controls). These events are concerned with DDE (Dynamic Data Exchange) conversations.

Label Methods

The label control also has methods, but you will probably not use them very often in your applications. The following shows the methods supported by the label control:

Drag	**LinkRequest**	OLEDrag	ZOrder
LinkExecute	LinkSend	Refresh	
LinkPoke	Move	ShowWhatsThis	

The label methods are not particularly useful, although the Link-Request method is sometimes used to update a nonautomatic DDE link.

Experimenting with a Label Control

Although there is not much that can be done to show you how a label works, we will add a label to the main form in the Controls project that you have been working with in previous examples:

1. Make frmMain the active form in the Form Designer by double-clicking frmMain in the Project Explorer.

2. Add a label on the bottom of the form. Stretch it so it is almost the width of the form.

3. Set its Name property to **lblHelp** and set the Caption property to **Click a button to see how a control works**.

4. When you run the application, the main form should look like Figure 3.5.

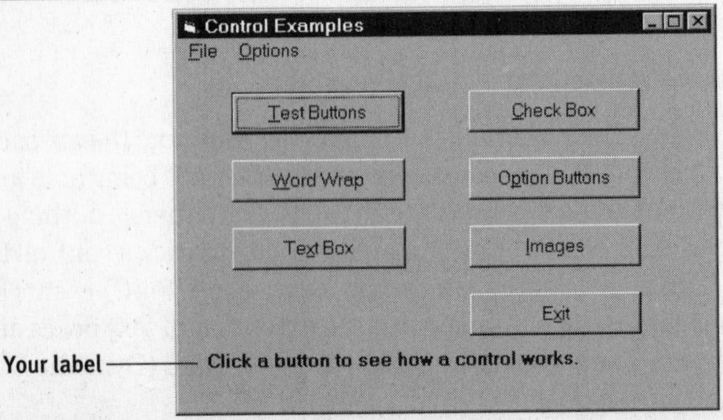

FIGURE 3.5: Your label added to the form

USING OPTION BUTTONS

Option button controls, also called radio buttons (shown here), are used to allow the user to select one, and only one, option from a group of options. Usually option buttons are grouped together within a frame control (described later in this chapter), but they can also be grouped on a plain form, if there is to be only one group of option buttons. Thus, if you had a frame specifying a delivery method, you might have one button for UPS (United Parcel Service) and another for Courier delivery. Products can only be shipped by *one* of these methods (not both—and not none). In contrast, option buttons representing, say, bold and italic settings for text would not make sense. Text can be both bold *and* italic, or neither (none).

Part I

Option Button Properties

The option button supports many properties, are shown in the table below:

Alignment	FontSize	Picture
Appearance	FontStrikethru	RightToLeft
BackColor	FontUnderline	**Style**
Caption	ForeColor	TabIndex
CausesValidation	Height	TabStop
Container	HelpContextID	Tag
DisabledPicture	HWnd	ToolTipText
DownPicture	Index	Top
DragIcon	Left	UseMaskColor
DragMode	MaskColor	**Value**
Enabled	MouseIcon	Visible
Font	MousePointer	WhatsThisHelpID
FontBold	**Name**	Width
FontItalic	OLEDropMode	
FontName	Parent	

Once again the Name property is the one to set first; option buttons have an opt prefix by convention. The Caption property helps the user determine the purpose of an option button. The other popular property is Value. This is invaluable at both design time and run time. At run time you test the Value property to see if the user has turned on (or off) the option button. The property has two settings, True and False. At design time you can set the Value property to True for one of the buttons if you wish—the default setting is False. This means that the option button (and only that option button in a group) is pre-selected when the form opens. If you try to make Value for another button in the group True, then the previous one reverts to a False setting.

A new property added in version 6 is the Style property. The default setting of 0 - Standard will draw a normal option button, as shown at the beginning of this section. However, by setting this property to 1 - Graphical, you can make the option button look just like a command button, but it allows only one selection to be made within a group. It works much like the old memory preset buttons on the old stock car radios.

TIP

If you want to present your users with multiple buttons, but only allow them to select one, then you can set the Style property of the option button control to 1 - Graphical. In addition, you can set the Picture property if you want to display a picture on the button.

Option Button Events

The option button control has a few events, but only the Click() event is really used:

Click	KeyDown	MouseMove	OLEGiveFeedback
DblClick	KeyPress	MouseUp	OLESetData
DragDrop	KeyUp	OLECompleteDrag	OLEStartDrag
DragOver	LostFocus	OLEDragDrop	Validate
GotFocus	MouseDown	OLEDragOver	

The typical way of dealing with option buttons is to test the Value property at run time to see if they're selected. Your code then initiates actions accordingly. It's common to test for the Value property in the

`Click()` event procedure for a command button that's clicked after the user has selected the option button of interest. This allows you to check for a condition before the next procedure is called. You test the `Value` property in an `If … End If` or `Select Case … End Select` construct. But there may be occasions when you want to initiate an action immediately after the user makes a choice. Then you may want to trap the option button's `Click()` event. Try this example to see what I mean:

1. Run the Controls project by selecting Run ➤ Start.

2. Click the Option Buttons button on the Control Examples form.

3. Click any of the option buttons and watch the label at the top of the form. The `Click()` event of each option button is used to change the `Caption` property of the label.

4. When you are done watching the results, click the Close button to close the dialog box.

5. End the application by clicking the Exit button on the Control Examples form.

If you want to see the code that makes this example work, follow these steps:

1. Double-click frmOptions in the Project Explorer to make it the active form.

2. Double-click the option button next to 486 to open its Code window. You will see the following code:

```
Private Sub opt486_Click()
  ' assign a value to the first string variable
  strComputer = "486"
  ' call the subroutine
  Call DisplayCaption
End Sub
```

Notice that the `Click()` event sets the value of `strComputer` to 486. Then it calls another procedure to change the caption.

3. Select (General) from the left pull-down menu, called the *object pull-down*, at the top of the Code window. Then select (DisplayCaption) from the procedure pull-down on the upper

right of the Code window. This will display the code for the `DisplayCaption` procedure:

```
Sub DisplayCaption()
   ' concatenate the caption with the two string
   ' variables.
   lblDisplay.Caption = "You selected a " & _
      strComputer & " running " & strSystem
End Sub
```

Notice how the `Caption` property of lblDisplay is set in this procedure, which is called in every `Click()` event of every option button. That's all there is to it!

Option Button Methods

The methods for the option button are of little use in the Visual Basic environment:

Drag	OLEDrag	SetFocus	ZOrder
Move	Refresh	ShowWhatsThis	

Therefore, we will not deal with their explanations here.

Open and start the Controls sample application. Click the Option Buttons button to bring up the Options dialog box (see Figure 3.6).

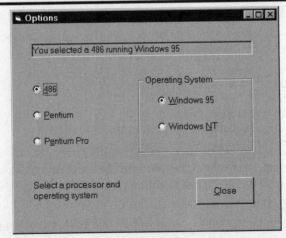

FIGURE 3.6: The Options dialog box

The five option buttons are actually in two groups. The options labeled 486, Pentium, and Pentium Pro are in their own group directly on the form. The Windows 95/98 and Windows NT options are in a separate group on the Operating System frame. This frame then rests on the form and separates the two groups of option buttons. If you click an option button, you will notice the other option buttons in the same group become deselected. Only one option can be selected in any particular group at one time.

USING CHECK BOXES

A check box control (shown here) is rather similar to an option button, which was described in the last section. Both often partake in groups, and the Value property is tested to see if a check box is on or off. But there are two fundamental differences between check boxes and option buttons: Check boxes are valid as single controls—a single option button is probably counter-intuitive. Check boxes (even when in a group) are not mutually exclusive. Finally, check boxes have three possible settings for the Value property.

An option button is either on or it's off. Therefore, Value can be either True or False. Check boxes can be in one of *three* states—on, off, or grayed. Grayed (dimmed) does *not* mean the same as disabled in this context—a grayed check box is neither on nor off, though the user can change its setting. If the check box were disabled, the user wouldn't be able to turn it on or off. A grayed check box is used to signify that some, but not all, options on another dialog box are selected. If you look at the dialog box in Figure 3.7, you will notice two of the check boxes are grayed. If you have installed Windows 95/98, then you understand what the grayed check box means. The Accessories check box is gray because I installed some, but not all, of the accessories for Windows 95/98.

Check Box Properties

The following table lists the properties for the check box control:

Alignment	DownPicture	Height	RightToLeft
Appearance	DragIcon	HelpContextID	Style
BackColor	DragMode	hWnd	**TabIndex**

Caption	**Enabled**	Index	**TabStop**
CausesValidation	**Font**	Left	Tag
Container	FontBold	MaskColor	ToolTipText
DataChanged	FontItalic	MouseIcon	Top
DataField	FontName	MousePointer	UseMaskColor
DataFormat	FontSize	**Name**	**Value**
DataMember	FontStrikethru	OLEDropMode	Visible
DataSource	FontUnderline	Parent	WhatsThis-HelpID
DisabledPicture	ForeColor	Picture	Width

Again, as with option buttons, the three most popular properties are Name, Caption, and Value. When setting the Name property it's conventional to use a chk prefix.

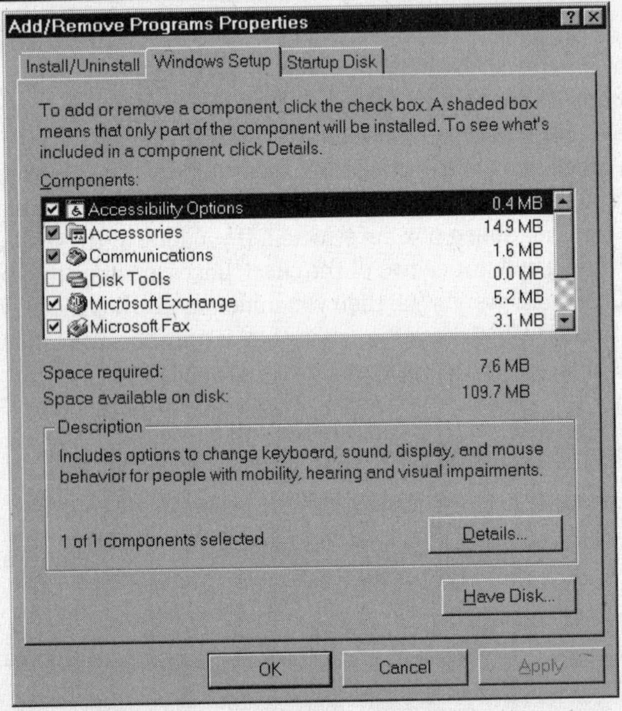

FIGURE 3.7: Grayed or "dimmed" check boxes

Check Box Events

The following table shows you that the check box has similar events to the option button control:

Click	KeyPress	MouseUp	OLESetData
DragDrop	KeyUp	OLECompleteDrag	OLEStartDrag
DragOver	LostFocus	OLEDragDrop	Validate
GotFocus	MouseDown	OLEDragOver	
KeyDown	MouseMove	OLEGiveFeedback	

To carry out further processing as soon as the user has clicked the check box, use the Click() event. Normally, though, if you do not put code directly within the Click() event, you will have another procedure that will ascertain the value of a check box by retrieving its Value property.

Check Box Methods

Like the events of the check box control, the methods are similar to those for the option button control:

Drag	OLEDrag	SetFocus	ZOrder
Move	Refresh	ShowWhatsThis	

Like option buttons, the methods for the check box control are non-vital to the operation of the control.

If you want to test the functionality of the check box control, start the Controls application and click the Check Box button. The Check Box Example dialog box has two check boxes that manipulate the text box at the top (see Figure 3.8).

Clicking the Bold check box turns the text bold, and the Italic option italicizes the text within the box. In the procedure below you can see how the FontBold property for the text box is modified in the Click() event.

```
Private Sub chkBold_Click()
    ' The Click event occurs when the check box changes state.
    ' Value property indicates the new state of the check box.
    If chkBold.Value = 1 Then    ' If checked.
        txtDisplay.FontBold = True
    Else                ' If not checked.
        txtDisplay.FontBold = False
    End If
End Sub
```

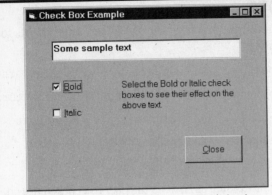

FIGURE 3.8: The Check Box Example dialog box

Experimenting with Check Box Controls

Try this example to see the check box work in all three of its states:

1. Start a new project by selecting File ➢ New Project ➢ Standard EXE.

2. In the Properties window, change the Name property of Form1 to **frmMain**.

3. Add a check box control to the form. Set its Name property to **chkOptions**, and its Caption property to **What do you want on your sandwich?**

4. Double-click chkOptions to open the Code window. Select the (General)(Declarations) section from the object and procedure drop-down lists. Add the following code:

   ```
   Public PeanutButter As Boolean
   Public Jelly As Boolean
   ```

5. Add the following code to the MouseUp event of chkOptions:

   ```
   Private Sub chkOptions_MouseUp(Button As Integer, _
   Shift As Integer, X As Single, Y As Single)

       frmOptions.Show vbModal

   If PeanutButter And Jelly Then
      chkOptions.Value = 1
      Exit Sub
   End If
   ```

```
    If PeanutButter Or Jelly Then
        chkOptions.Value = 2
        Exit Sub
    End If

    If Not PeanutButter And Not Jelly Then
        chkOptions.Value = 0
        Exit Sub
    End If
End Sub
```

6. Right-click the Project Explorer and select Add ➤ Form from the pop-up menu. Select Form from the Add Form dialog box.

7. In the Properties window, set the Name property of the new form to **frmOptions**. Set its Caption property to **Set Options**.

8. Add a check box control to frmOptions. Set its Name property to **chkPeanutButter** and its Caption to **Peanut Butter**.

9. Add another check box control. Set its Name property to **chk-Jelly** and its Caption to **Jelly**.

10. Double-click frmOptions to open the Code window. Add the following code to the Load() event of the form:

```
Private Sub Form_Load()
  If frmMain.PeanutButter Then
    chkPeanutButter.Value = 1
  Else
    chkPeanutButter.Value = 0
  End If

  If frmMain.Jelly Then
    chkJelly.Value = 1
  Else
    chkJelly.Value = 0
  End If
End Sub
```

11. Add the following code to the Click() event of chkPeanut-Butter:

```
Private Sub chkPeanutButter_Click()
  If chkPeanutButter.Value = 1 Then
    frmMain.PeanutButter = True
  Else
    frmMain.PeanutButter = False
  End If
End Sub
```

12. Add the following code to the `Click()` event of chkJelly:

```
Private Sub chkJelly_Click()
   If chkJelly.Value = 1 Then
      frmMain.Jelly = True
   Else
         frmMain.Jelly = False
   End If
End Sub
```

13. Select Run ➤ Start to start your application.

If you click the check box on frmMain, you are presented with a dialog box offering you peanut butter and jelly. Some people like both, while others may like only one or the other. If you check both and close the dialog box, you will see the check box is solid. If you only select peanut butter or jelly, but not both, then the check box will be grayed. If you don't want either, the check box will be unchecked.

USING FRAME CONTROLS

 When used by itself, the frame control (shown here) is not particularly useful. The controls normally placed in a frame are option buttons and check boxes. This has the effect of grouping them together so that when the frame is moved, the other controls move too. For this to work you can't double-click a control (say, an option button) to add it to the form and then drag it into position within the frame. Instead, you must single-click the control in the Toolbox and drag a location for it inside the frame. Then all the controls move together.

In addition, the option buttons function as a group—that is, if you select one at run time, the others become deselected. If you simply scatter option buttons randomly on a form, then they all function as one large group. To create separate groupings of option buttons, you place them in frames. The button items within each frame act as a self-contained group and have no effect on the option buttons in other frame groups.

Although a frame is often used as a container for check box groups too, each check box is completely independent. Thus the setting for one check box has no effect on the setting for the others in the same group. This is the behavior you would expect of check boxes. Check boxes are not mutually exclusive. This contrasts with option buttons, where the buttons within a single group should be mutually exclusive. The reason then for placing check boxes in a frame is to enable you to move the group as a whole, when you reposition the frame at design time. The frame also serves as a visual grouping for the check boxes. For example, the check boxes relating to a particular feature can be in one frame and those pertinent to another feature in another frame.

A frame is usually given the prefix `fra`. You place the frame on the form before you place the controls it's going to contain.

Frame Properties

The frame control has several properties, listed below:

Appearance	**Enabled**	Height	Parent
BackColor	Font	HelpContextID	RightToLeft
BorderStyle	FontBold	hWnd	TabIndex
Caption	FontItalic	Index	Tag
Container	FontName	Left	ToolTipText
ClipControls	FontSize	MouseIcon	Top
Container	FontStrikethru	MousePointer	Visible
DragIcon	FontUnderline	**Name**	WhatsThis-HelpID
DragMode	ForeColor	OLEDropMode	Width

After the Name property, perhaps the single most important property is `Caption`. You use this to give a meaningful title to the frame on the form. Then it's clear to the end user which feature the option buttons (or check boxes) in the frame refer to. To provide a clue as to how each option button affects the feature, you use the `Caption` property of the buttons. For example, in an order dispatch system you might have a frame with the caption Delivery. And within that frame you might have two option buttons, with the captions Normal and Express.

Frame Events

The frame control only supports a few events:

Click	MouseMove	OLEGiveFeedback
DblClick	MouseUp	OLESetData

DragDrop	OLECompleteDrag	OLEStartDrag
DragOver	OLEDragDrop	
MouseDown	OLEDragOver	

The frame control events are only rarely used. In an application that uses drag-and-drop, however, the DragDrop() event is sometimes used to initiate actions when the user drops an object into a frame area.

Frame Methods

A frame object supports only a few methods. None are very helpful and they're hardly ever seen in Visual Basic projects:

Drag	OLEDrag	ShowWhatsThis
Move	Refresh	Zorder

As you can see in Figure 3.9, a frame control serves as a container for other controls. You can group option buttons to separate them from other groups, or you can group other controls to provide visual organization to your form. Set the Caption property of the frame to the description of the functionality that the contained controls provide. In this example, the Caption is set to Set the Insertion Point.

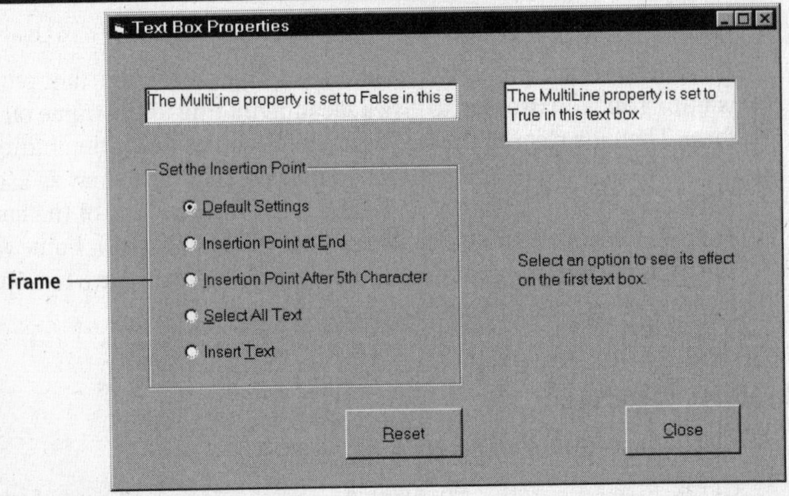

FIGURE 3.9:   A frame control

Using List Boxes

If you're a regular user of Windows, then you're familiar with list box controls (shown here). A list box is an ideal way of presenting users with a list of data. Users can browse the data in the list box or select one or more items as the basis for further processing. The user can't edit the data in a list box directly—one way around this is to use a combo box instead; combo boxes are discussed next. When the list of data is too long for the list box, Visual Basic will add a vertical scrollbar. Let's examine most of the important list box control properties, events, and methods.

List Box Properties

Many of the list box properties are shared by a combo box control, and some of them are essential for getting the best from the control:

Appearance	FontBold	**List**	**Style**
BackColor	FontItalic	**ListCount**	TabIndex
CausesValidation	FontName	**ListIndex**	TabStop
Columns	FontSize	MouseIcon	Tag
Container	FontStrikethru	MousePointer	Text
DataChanged	FontUnderline	**MultiSelect**	ToolTipText
DataField	ForeColor	**Name**	Top
DataFormat	Height	**NewIndex**	TopIndex
DataMember	HelpContextID	OLEDragMode	Visible
DataSource	hWnd	Parent	WhatsThis-HelpID
DragIcon	Index	RightToLeft	Width
DragMode	IntegralHeight	SelCount	
Enabled	ItemData	**Selected**	
Font	Left	**Sorted**	

The Columns property lets you create a multicolumn list box. Unfortunately, the columns are of the snaking, or newspaper, type. There's no direct support for the multiple columns of an Access-style list box where different data items are displayed in separate columns. Instead Visual Basic wraps the same type of data items from column to column.

TIP

You can't have a true multiple-column list box in Visual Basic. One workaround is to concatenate (join) the different data items into one string and add that string to a single-column Visual Basic list box. To line up the columns, you can embed spaces or tab characters (Chr(9)) in the concatenated string. Alternatively, use fixed-length strings to hold the items to be concatenated. However, this does not work when you're using a proportional font.

The List property sets or returns the value of an item in the list. You use the index of the item with the List property. The index positions of items in a list box start at 0 (zero) and run to 1 less than the total number of items in a list. Thus, if you had 10 items in the list box, the index positions run from 0 to 9.

NOTE

Don't confuse the index *position* in a list box with the Index *property* of a list box. The latter is displayed in the Properties window—the index position is not shown anywhere. The Index property is used when you create a control array of list boxes.

You use the List property to get the value of any item in the list. For example, to return the value of the third item in the list, use the following:

```
lstList1.List(2)
```

To get the value of the currently selected item in the list, simply use the Text property of the list box. The ListIndex property sets or returns the index position of the currently selected item—if no item is selected, the ListIndex property is -1.

NOTE

lstList1.List(lstList1.ListIndex) and lstList1.Text are the same.

You can pick up the index position of the last item added to a list (see the AddItem method shortly) with the NewIndex property. The List-Count property returns the number of items in a list box. Confusingly, this is always 1 greater than the value returned by the NewIndex property—this is because the index positions count from 0 (zero) while the ListCount property starts counting from 1 for the first item. ListCount returns 0 if the list box is empty.

The MultiSelect property determines whether the user can select one item or whether they can select more than one. List boxes support both a simple and an extended multiple selection. A simple multiple selection allows the user to select contiguous items—usually accomplished with the mouse and the Shift key. An extended multiple selection lets the user select contiguous and noncontiguous items—usually done by mouse clicks in conjunction with the Ctrl and/or Shift keys.

The Selected property is a Boolean property and is a run-time property only. A Boolean property is one that can take only a True or False setting. The following line preselects the third item in a list box:

```
lstList1.Selected(2) = True
```

Note the use of index position (2) to reference the *third* item in the list.

The final property that we're going to consider is the Sorted property. This is one of those properties that you can set only at design time. You can read it, or return it, at run time (that is, see if it's True or False) but you can't set it (that is, change an unsorted list into a sorted one or vice versa). When you set the Sorted property to True at design time, any items you add to a list box (typically, with the AddItem method) are sorted in alphabetical order. The sort can only be in ascending order and it's not case-sensitive.

List Box Events

The list box control supports a few events, shown here:

Click	KeyDown	MouseUp	OLEStartDrag
DblClick	KeyPress	OLECompleteDrag	Scroll
DragDrop	KeyUp	OLEDragDrop	Validate
DragOver	LostFocus	OLEDragOver	
GotFocus	MouseDown	OLEGiveFeedback	
ItemCheck	MouseMove	OLESetData	

Perhaps the most commonly used event for a list box is DblClick(). This coincides with the normal operation of list boxes in Windows applications. The first thing to do with a list box is usually to fill it with items for the list. The AddItem method can be used to do this (see "List Box Methods"). You can then, if you want, preselect one of the items in the list by setting the Selected property to True. The user either accepts the default selection or chooses another item with a single-click. Then clicking an OK command button carries out a process using the Text property, which returns the value of the selected item. However, a popular shortcut is to double-click the item in the list—that way, the user can both select an item and initiate a process based on that item in a single action. Many Windows applications adopt this technique to copy one item from a list box into another list box.

List Box Methods

The list box has many of its own methods, as well as some common to the other controls discussed so far:

AddItem	Move	SetFocus
Clear	Refresh	ShowWhatsThis
Drag	**RemoveItem**	Zorder

There are three methods here worthy of note—AddItem, Clear, and RemoveItem. AddItem, as already indicated, is for adding items to a list box control. The RemoveItem method, as you might expect, removes items from a list box. To remove all the items in one fell swoop, use the Clear method.

An example of the simplest syntax for the AddItem method is:

```
lstList1.AddItem "Hello"
```

This adds the word "Hello" to the list box. Often you employ a number of AddItem methods, one after the other, to populate (fill in) a list box. Many developers place the AddItem methods in a Form_Load() event procedure so the list box is filling as the form loads. You can specify the position that an item will take in a list by specifying the index position:

```
lstList1.AddItem "Hello", 3
```

This places the text "Hello" at the *fourth* position in the list. If you omit the index position, the item is added to the end of the list—or if the Sorted property is set to True, the item is placed in the correct sorted order.

WARNING

Be careful when using the AddItem method with a specified index position in a sorted list box. The Sorted property automatically calculates the index position of added items. If the position you specify does not match the one generated by the Sorted property, then the results will be unpredictable.

Experimenting with List Box Controls

Now that you have read about what makes a list box work, try this example to see it in action:

1. Start a new project by selecting File > New Project. Select Standard EXE from the Project Wizard.

2. Add two list box controls to Form1.

3. Place one list box on the upper half of the form, and the other on the lower half of the form. Size both list boxes until they are almost as wide as the form.

4. Double-click the form to open the Code window. Add the following code to the Load event:

```
Private Sub Form_Load()
    List1.AddItem "Nuts"
    List1.AddItem "Bolts"
    List1.AddItem "Nails"
    List1.AddItem "L-Brackets"
    List1.AddItem "Hammers"
    List1.AddItem "Saw"
    List1.AddItem "Drill"
    List1.AddItem "File"
    List1.AddItem "Sandpaper"
    List1.AddItem "Planer"
End Sub
```

5. Add the following code to the DblClick() event of List1:

```
Private Sub List1_DblClick()
    'Add the item to the other list
    List2.AddItem List1.Text

    'Remove the item from this list
    List1.RemoveItem List1.ListIndex
End Sub
```

Part I

6. Add the following code to the `DblClick()` event of List2:

    ```
    Private Sub List2_DblClick()
        'Add the item to the other list
        List1.AddItem List2.Text

        'Remove the item from this list
        List2.RemoveItem List2.ListIndex
    End Sub
    ```

7. Finally, run the program by selecting Run ➤ Start.

You can double-click any product to move it to the opposite list box. If you look at the code in steps 5 and 6, you will notice the item is added to the other list box before it is removed from the current one. The `AddItem` must be called *before* the `RemoveItem` method because the `AddItem` needs to know what to add to the other list. If you call `RemoveItem` first, then the wrong list item will be added to the opposite list. You will learn more about lists in the next section.

USING COMBO BOXES

The name combo box comes from "combination box"; the control is shown here. The idea is that a combo box combines the features of both a text box and a list box. A potential problem with list boxes—in some situations anyway—is that you're stuck with the entries displayed. You can't directly edit an item in the list or select an entry that's not already there. Of course, if you *want* to restrict the user, then a list box is fine in this respect. A combo box control (at least in two of its styles available in Visual Basic) allows you to select a predefined item from a list *or* to enter a new item not in the list. A combo box can also incorporate a drop-down section—that means it takes less room on a form than a normal list box. In all, there are three types of combo boxes to choose from at design time: a drop-down combo, a simple combo, and a drop-down list. You can specify the type by setting the `Style` property.

Apart from the `Style` property, the properties, events, and methods of combo boxes are very similar to those of list boxes, described shortly. However, the `Text` property is different. With a list box, the `Text` property returns the text of the currently selected item at run time. With a combo box, on the other hand, you can assign a value to the `Text` property at run time—in effect, you can set the text, even if the item is not already in the list. The results of choosing a different Style property are covered in the next section.

Note that the combo box discussed here is the built-in combo box control. There's also another combo box (DBCombo, or the data-bound combo box). This has a few more features that let you work with data from databases.

Combo Box Properties

These are the properties for the combo box control:

Appearance	FontItalic	ListCount	Style
BackColor	FontName	ListIndex	TabIndex
CausesValidation	FontSize	Locked	TabStop
Container	FontStrikethru	MouseIcon	Tag
DataChanged	FontUnderline	MousePointer	Text
DataField	ForeColor	Name	ToolTipText
DataFormat	Height	NewIndex	Top
DataMember	HelpContextID	OLEDragMode	TopIndex
DataSource	hWnd	Parent	Visible
DragIcon	Index	RightToLeft	WhatsThis-HelpID
DragMode	IntegralHeight	SelLength	Width
Enabled	ItemData	SelStart	
Font	Left	SelText	
FontBold	List	Sorted	

The List, ListCount, ListIndex, NewIndex, and Sorted properties are identical to those for a list box. The property that's different, and that consists of one of the fundamentals of designing combo boxes, is the Style property. There are three settings for Style, and the behavior and appearance of the combo box are determined by the setting you choose.

Part I

The styles are numbered from 0 to 2 and represent, in order, a drop-down combo, a simple combo, and a drop-down list:

▶ The drop-down combo looks like a standard text box with a drop-down arrow to the right. Clicking the arrow opens a list beneath the text box. The user has the choice of selecting an item from the list, which places it in the text box, or of entering their own text in the text box. In other words, this is the true combo box.

▶ The simple combo is a variation on this theme—the only difference being that the list is permanently displayed. This one's an option if your form is not too crowded.

▶ The final style, the drop-down list, is really a type of list box rather than a combo box. It looks identical to a drop-down combo but, as the name suggests, the user is confined to selecting a predefined item from the list. The advantage of this latter style is that it takes up less space than a conventional list box.

Combo Box Events

Here are the events for the combo box:

Change	**DropDown**	LostFocus	OLESetData
Click	GotFocus	OLECompleteDrag	OLEStartDrag
DblClick	KeyDown	OLEDragDrop	Scroll
DragDrop	KeyPress	OLEDragOver	Validate
DragOver	KeyUp	OLEGiveFeedback	

Most of the events for a combo box control are the standard ones. However, the DropDown() event is specific to combo boxes—though not supported by the simple combo box, which is already "dropped-down."

The Change() event is not supported by the drop-down list (style 2), because the user can't change the entry in the text box section. To see if that type of combo box has been accessed by the user, try the Click() or the DropDown() event procedures.

The DblClick() event is only relevant to the simple combo box, for it's the only one where the user can see the full list by default. Usually, the DblClick() event procedure calls the Click() event for a command button. This means the user can simply double-click an item in the list, rather than using a single-click to select followed by a click on a command button to carry out some processing based on the user selection.

Combo Box Methods

The methods you can apply to a combo box control are the same as those for a list box:

AddItem	Move	**RemoveItem**	ZOrder
Clear	OLEDrag	SetFocus	
Drag	Refresh	ShowWhatsThis	

Again, the important methods are AddItem, Clear, and RemoveItem. And, just as with a list box control, it's common practice to populate a combo box with a series of AddItem methods in the Load event of a form.

Incidentally, especially if you've worked with the database application Microsoft Access, you may be wondering about the flexibility of list and combo boxes. What do you do if the predetermined items in the list continually change? Do you continually have to re-code the AddItem methods? How can you do this anyway in a stand-alone EXE you generate from your project? Another concern of yours could be regarding the actual tedium of typing long series of AddItem methods.

All of these questions are easily resolved if you exploit the RowSource and ListField properties of a data-bound list or data-bound combo box. Even more flexibility is provided by these data-bound versions of those two controls (DBList and DBCombo). For more information on these and other data-bound controls, consult the Microsoft Developer Network online help.

Often you want the user first to select an item from a list box and then to click a command button. The button initiates an action using the selected item. An accepted alternative is for the user to simply double-click the item in the list. This both selects the item and carries out the action. To do this, you can call the button's Click() event procedure from the list box's DblClick() event procedure, as shown below:

```
Private Sub cboItems_DblClick()
    cmdAdd_Click
End Sub
```

The code listed below populates the list and combo boxes in Figure 3.10. The following example will show you the difference between a list and a combo box by simulating a grocery list. In the list I added some fruits.

The combo box lists different types of bread. Because I obviously haven't covered all of the different types of bread, you can type another kind of bread in the combo box to add it to your list.

```
Private Sub Form_Load()
    'Add items to list box
    lstItems.AddItem "Apples"
    lstItems.AddItem "Oranges"
    lstItems.AddItem "Grapes"
    lstItems.AddItem "Tangerines"
    lstItems.AddItem "Lemons"
    lstItems.AddItem "Bananas"

    'Add items to combo box
    cboCombination.AddItem "Wheat"
    cboCombination.AddItem "White"
    cboCombination.AddItem "Rye"
    cboCombination.AddItem "Sourdough"
    cboCombination.AddItem "French"
    cboCombination.AddItem "Pita"
End Sub
```

FIGURE 3.10:   The list and combo box

Experimenting with List and Combo Box Controls

Let's modify this form to function like a grocery list. You code the form to allow you to select items from the combo box and add them to your grocery list box.

1.   Start a new project and add one list box to a form and set its Name to **lstGroceries**.

2. Add a combo box below the list box and set its Name to **cbo-Products** and its Caption to **Wheat**.

3. Add two labels to a form. Place the first label above the list box and set its Caption property to **Grocery List**.

4. Place the second label between the list box and the combo box. Set its Caption to **Store Items**.

5. Add a command button to the bottom center of the form. Set its Name property to **cmdAdd** and its Caption to **&Add**.

6. Modify the Form_Load() event as follows:

```
Private Sub Form_Load()
  'Clear the list box
  lstGroceries.Clear

  'add items to combo box
  cboProducts.AddItem "Wheat"
  cboProducts.AddItem "Cereal"
  cboProducts.AddItem "Steak"
  cboProducts.AddItem "Pasta"
  cboProducts.AddItem "Candy"
  cboProducts.AddItem "Soda"
End Sub
```

7. Add the following code to the cmdAdd_Click() event:

```
Private Sub cmdAdd_Click()
  lstGroceries.AddItem cboProducts.Text
End Sub
```

8. Run the program. You can select a product from the combo box. If you want to add it to the grocery list, click the Add button.

9. Notice that this store doesn't carry any ice cream. You can type this in the combo box and click the Add button. The store will have to special order it for you.

TIP

To call the event procedure for another control, you type the name of the procedure, as in cmdListAdd_Click. But to initiate a command button's Click() event there's an alternative method. You can set the Value property of the button to True, as in cmdListAdd.Value = True.

Using Image Objects

 The image control (its prefix is often img) is a lightweight equivalent of the picture box control, which is described in a later section. But unlike the picture control, the image control can't act as a container for other objects. In some of its other properties it's not as versatile, but it's a good choice if you simply want to display a picture on a form. Image controls consume far less memory than picture controls.

The image control that comes with Visual Basic can now display bitmap (.BMP), icon (.ICO), metafile (.WMF), JPEG (.JPG), and GIF (.GIF) files. This makes it easier to display graphics from the World Wide Web, as well as graphics from other popular graphics program.

Image Properties

The image control utilizes several properties, but fewer than the picture box, discussed later.

Appearance	DragIcon	MousePointer	Tag
BorderStyle	DragMode	**Name**	Top
Container	Enabled	OLEDragMode	Visible
DataField	Height	OLEDropMode	WhatsThisHelpID
DataFormat	Index	Parent	Width
DataMember	Left	**Picture**	
DataSource	MouseIcon	**Stretch**	

As with most other graphical controls, you add the graphic by setting the Picture property. Perhaps the most interesting property here is Stretch. This is a Boolean property—meaning it takes only the values True or False. When Stretch is set to False (the default), the control resizes to the size of the picture placed inside it. If you later resize the control, then the loaded picture either is cropped or has empty space showing around it, or both, depending on the relative directions of horizontal and vertical resizing. But if you set Stretch to True, the picture resizes with the control. Thus you can make the enclosed picture larger or smaller, or fatter or thinner, by resizing the control after the picture is loaded. A picture control has no Stretch property. Its nearest equivalent is the Auto-Size property. When AutoSize is set to True for a picture box, then the control adapts to the size of the loaded picture. However, unlike an image control with Stretch turned on, if the picture box is resized the enclosed picture remains the same—the picture does not "stretch" with the picture box control.

Image Events

The image control doesn't use many events, and of those, you may only use a few, if any.

Click	MouseDown	OLEDragDrop	OLEStartDrag
DblClick	MouseMove	OLEDragOver	
DragDrop	MouseUp	OLEGiveFeedback	
DragOver	OLECompleteDrag	OLESetData	

Image controls are sometimes handy as drag-and-drop destinations. This is because you can have a picture inside that gives an indication of the results of dropping onto the control.

Image Methods

The following are properties of an image control:

Drag	OLEDrag	ShowWhatsThis
Move	Refresh	Zorder

You will most likely not use any of these methods in your applications.

TIP
There's a catalog of bundled icons included with your Visual Basic documentation. They can be found in the \Common subdirectory of Visual Basic.

Experimenting with Image Controls

Let's take a look at some image controls in action.

1. Open the Controls project from earlier in the \MSDN98\ 98vs\1033\Samples\VB98\Controls subdirectory.

2. Run the program and click the Images button.

As you can see in Figure 3.11, you can click one of the four card icons and the program will notify you that it is selected. The code listed below is fairly straightforward.

FIGURE 3.11:   The image control

```
Private Sub imgClub_Click()
  shpCard.Left = imgClub.Left
  picStatus.Cls
  picStatus.Print "Selected: Club"
End Sub

Private Sub imgDiamond_Click()
  shpCard.Left = imgDiamond.Left
  picStatus.Cls
  picStatus.Print "Selected: Diamond"
End Sub

Private Sub imgHeart_Click()
  shpCard.Left = imgHeart.Left
  picStatus.Cls
  picStatus.Print "Selected: Heart"
End Sub

Private Sub imgSpade_Click()
  shpCard.Left = imgSpade.Left
  picStatus.Cls
  picStatus.Print "Selected: Spade"
End Sub
```

The card outline is actually a shape control that is moved off the left side of the form. This is done in the Form's Load() event by setting the shape's Left property to -500. This achieves the same results as hiding a control by setting its Visible property to False.

USING PICTURE BOXES

 As you might expect, picture boxes (shown here) often display graphics (for example, bitmaps, icons, JPEGs, and GIFs). In this role, picture boxes are similar to image controls. However, picture boxes and images have slightly different properties and therefore behave differently. If you just want to show a picture, then an image control is usually a better choice than a picture box. An image control takes up less memory and is a lightweight version of the picture box control. However, if you want to move the graphic around the form, a picture box produces a smoother display. In addition, you can create text and use graphics methods in a picture box at run time. The graphics methods enable you to draw lines, circles, and rectangles at run time. But, most importantly for this application, picture boxes can act as containers for other controls. Thus, you can place a command button within a picture box. In this respect, picture boxes function as "forms within forms."

Picture Box Properties

The table below lists the properties for the picture box control. Notice that there are many more properties for this control than there are for the image control.

Align	FillStyle	MousePointer
Appearance	Font	**Name**
AutoRedraw	FontBold	OLEDragMode
AutoSize	FontItalic	OLEDropMode
BackColor	FontName	Parent
BorderStyle	FontSize	**Picture**
CausesValidation	FontStrikethru	RightToLeft
ClipControls	FontTransparent	ScaleHeight
Container	FontUnderline	ScaleLeft
CurrentX	ForeColor	ScaleMode

CurrentY	HasDC	ScaleTop
DataChanged	hDC	ScaleWidth
DataField	Height	TabIndex
DataFormat	HelpContextID	TabStop
DataMember	hWnd	Tag
DataSource	**Image**	ToolTipText
DragIcon	Index	Top
DragMode	Left	Visible
DrawMode	LinkItem	WhatsThisHelpID
DrawStyle	LinkMode	Width
DrawWidth	LinkTimeout	
Enabled	LinkTopic	
FillColor	MouseIcon	

Quite a lot of properties this time! When you put a picture into a picture box, it appears at its normal size. If it's too big for the picture box, the graphic is clipped. Setting the AutoSize property to True causes the picture box to resize to match the size of the graphic. The graphic displayed in the picture box is determined by the Picture property—you can change this property at both design time and run time. There's a similar-sounding property—the Image property. This one's only available at run time, and it's used to make a copy from one picture box to another. The syntax for doing this is:

```
Picture2.Picture = Picture1.Image
```

You can place this line of code in any event where it is relevant. For example, maybe you want to change the picture in a picture box when the user selects a different record in a database.

The line above places a copy (image) of the picture in the first picture box into the second picture box (using its Picture property). You can even change the picture directly at run time. The syntax is:

```
Picture1.Picture = LoadPicture ("filename")
```

To empty a picture box, use the Visual Basic LoadPicture function with no parameter:

```
Picture1.Picture = LoadPicture()
```

Picture Box Events

The picture box events are listed in the following table:

Change	KeyPress	MouseDown	OLESetData
Click	KeyUp	MouseMove	OLEStartDrag
DblClick	LinkClose	MouseUp	Paint
DragDrop	LinkError	OLECompleteDrag	Resize
DragOver	LinkNotify	OLEDragDrop	Validate
GotFocus	LinkOpen	OLEDragOver	
KeyDown	LostFocus	OLEGiveFeedback	

Two of the popular events for picture boxes are the Click() and DragDrop() events.

Picture Box Methods

The picture box control supports more methods than its counterpart, the image box. The most important ones are listed in boldface in the following table:

Circle	LinkRequest	**PSet**	TextHeight
Cls	LinkSend	Refresh	TextWidth
Drag	Move	ScaleX	**ZOrder**
Line	OLEDrag	ScaleY	
LinkExecute	**PaintPicture**	SetFocus	
LinkPoke	Point	ShowWhatsThis	

The Circle, Cls, Line, PaintPicture, and PSet methods are all used when drawing graphics or text in the picture box at run time—Cls (like the old DOS command for "clear screen") is actually used to erase entries. The ZOrder method is the run-time equivalent of Format ➤ Order ➤ Bring to Front or Format ➤ Order ➤ Send to Back. You can use ZOrder to determine which controls overlap other controls. However, you should be aware that there are three layers on a form—ZOrder only works within the layer that contains the control. All the nongraphical controls except labels (for example, command buttons) belong to the top layer. Picture boxes and other graphical controls (as well as labels) belong to the middle layer. The bottom layer contains the results of the graphics methods—for instance, a circle drawn with the `Circle` method is on the bottom layer. This contrasts with a circle drawn with the Shape control, which is in the middle layer. What all this means is that you can't position a picture box over a command button with `ZOrder`—the picture box is permanently relegated to the layer behind. The `ZOrder` method is for rearranging objects *within* one layer.

NOTE

`ZOrder` determines the relative positions of objects within the same layer or level of a form. In design view, use Format ➤ Order ➤ Bring to Front, or Format ➤ Order ➤ Send to Back to change relative positions. At run time you can use the `ZOrder` method.

Using Timers

The timer control (shown here) is one of the few controls always hidden at run time. This means you don't have to find room for it on a form—it can go anywhere, even on top of existing controls. The timer basically does just one thing: It checks the system clock and acts accordingly.

Timer Properties

The timer control does not have many properties, as you can see in this table:

Enabled	Left	Tag
Index	**Name**	Top
Interval	Parent	

Apart from the Name property (a `tmr` prefix is recommended), there are only two important properties for the timer control—the `Enabled` property and the `Interval` property. Indeed, you have to set these properties to get the timer to do anything at all (assuming the `Enabled` property is at its default, `True`). The `Left` and `Top` properties are virtually superfluous—it makes little difference where you put a timer on a form.

The `Interval` property is measured in milliseconds. This means if you want to count seconds, you have to multiply the number of seconds by 1,000. Once an interval has elapsed (provided the timer is enabled), the timer generates its own Timer event. It does this by checking the system clock at frequent intervals.

TIP

The Interval property is measured in milliseconds. If you want to count the number of seconds elapsed, you have to set the Interval property to the number of seconds multiplied by 1,000. Keeping this in mind, the Interval property is limited to values between 0 (the timer is disabled) and 65,535 (65.5 seconds).

The Timer Event

The timer control has only one event called, appropriately, a Timer() event. As already stated, this event takes place every time an interval elapses. The interval is determined by the Interval property. To stop the Timer() event from occurring, you can set the timer's Enabled property to False at run time.

Timer Methods

The timer control does not support any methods at all.

Experimenting with a Timer Control

To give you an idea of how the timer works, let's create a Caption Bar clock:

1. Start a new project by selecting File ➣ New project. Select Standard EXE as the project type.

2. Set the Name property of Form1 to **frmMain**. Set its Caption property to **Application Time**.

3. Add a timer to the frmMain. Set its Name property to **tmrTimer**.

4. Set the timer's Interval property to **500**. We want to have the clock check itself every half-second. We do this because the timer control is not as precise as other timer-type controls, but it will perform well for this example.

5. Add the following code to the (General)(Declarations) procedure for frmMain:

```
Option Explicit
Private OldCaption As String
```

6. Add the following code to the Form_Load() event:

```
Private Sub Form_Load()
   OldCaption = Me.Caption
End Sub
```

7. Now add the following code to the Timer() event of the timer:

```
Private Sub tmrTimer_Timer()
   Dim msg As String

   msg = OldCaption & ": " & Time$
   Caption = msg
End Sub
```

8. Save and run the application by selecting Run ➤ Start. Your Caption Bar clock should now look like Figure 3.12.

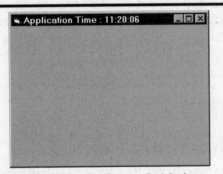

FIGURE 3.12: The Caption Bar clock

You may notice that the caption flickers a bit. You can minimize this by changing the code in the Timer() event to minimize the number of refreshes to the Caption:

```
Private Sub tmrTimer_Timer()
   Dim msg As String

   msg = OldCaption & ": " & Time$
   If msg <> Caption Then
      Caption = msg
   End If
End Sub
```

The If...Then statement checks to see if the time, returned through Time$, has changed. If the msg string is different than Caption, then you update the Caption property to reflect the time change. Otherwise you do nothing to cause a refresh on the Caption. The flicker will go away.

TIP

You can use the Format function to change the format of the display. Format accepts many named parameters as well as ones you define yourself. You can use the function to format the display of numbers and strings—it's not just confined to date and time. To see some of the possibilities, search the Microsoft Developer Network help for the Format function. Once you reach the topic entitled *Format Function*, click the See Also pop-up text at the top of the window.

Using Scroll Bars

A scroll bar control (shown here) on a form is not to be confused with a scroll bar on a large text box or list box. The scroll bar controls are completely independent objects that exist without reference to any other control (this is not the case with large text boxes or list boxes). The horizontal scroll bar and the vertical scroll bar are identical except for their orientation. Both controls share the same properties, events, and methods. When the term "scroll bar" is used in this section it means both the horizontal scroll bar and the vertical scroll bar.

A scroll bar control is typically employed to increase or decrease a value. For example, you may want to change a color setting, a number, or the volume of a digital audio device. The scroll bar acts as a sliding scale with a starting point and an ending point, including all the values in between. If you simply want to increment or decrement a number, then you should also take a look at the spin button custom control.

One problem with a scroll bar is that once it is used it retains the focus and may flicker on screen. To circumvent this you can change the focus to another control.

TIP

To avoid scroll bar flicker, add a SetFocus method on another control as the last statement in the scroll bar control's Change event procedure.

Scroll Bar Properties

The scroll bar control has a few properties worth noting:

CausesValidation	hWnd	MousePointer	Tag
Container	Index	**Name**	Top
DragIcon	**LargeChange**	Parent	**Value**
DragMode	Left	RightToLeft	Visible
Enabled	**Max**	**SmallChange**	WhatsThis-HelpID
Height	**Min**	TabIndex	Width
HelpContextID	MouseIcon	TabStop	

The most useful scroll bar properties are the Max, Min, LargeChange, and SmallChange properties. The Min and Max properties determine the limits for the Value property of the scroll bar. You can set the Min property to the lowest value allowed, for example 0. Then you would set Max to the maximum allowed value. For example, the following code could be used to define the lowest and highest volume allowed by your application:

```
Private Sub Form_Load()
    hscVolume.Min = 0      'The lowest volume
    hscVolume.Max = 255    'The maximum volume
End Sub
```

The LargeChange property determines how much the Value property changes when the user clicks in the scroll bar. The SmallChange property sets the amount the Value property changes when the user clicks one of the scroll arrows at either end of the scroll bar. You don't have to worry about the direction of the change, only the amount; Visual Basic figures out whether it's an increase or decrease, depending on where you click. There is no property setting to correspond to the user dragging the scroll box (also called *thumb* or *elevator*) within the scroll bar. This is because there's no way of predicting how far the scroll box will be dragged. However, it automatically updates the Value property. You can ascertain the new Value in the Change event procedure for the scroll bar. The Value property can also be set at design time to place the scroll box at a certain point within the scroll bar. For example, if you wanted the volume in the previous example to be set half way, you would use the following code:

```
Private Sub Form_Load()
   hscVolume.Min = 0      'The lowest volume
   hscVolume.Max = 255    'The maximum volume
   hscVolume.Value = 128  'Set the volume half way
End Sub
```

The Value, LargeChange, and SmallChange property settings must lie within the range dictated by the Min and Max properties. Value is usually set equal to Min or Max so the scroll box is at one end of the scroll bar. LargeChange is ordinarily some integral multiple of SmallChange. Max can be less than Min, which is often counter-intuitive. Max and Min, or both, can also be negative.

Scroll Bar Events

This is the list of events supported by the horizontal and vertical scroll bars:

Change	GotFocus	KeyUp	Validate
DragDrop	KeyDown	LostFocus	
DragOver	KeyPress	**Scroll**	

There are two vital events here—Change() and Scroll(). The Change() event occurs whenever the Value property of the scroll bar is altered at run time. The Value property, in turn, is changed whenever the user clicks a scroll arrow (SmallChange), clicks in the scroll bar to one side of the scroll box (LargeChange), or stops dragging the scroll box along the scroll bar. The latter induces a Value change depending on the length of the drag—though the Value change can never be greater than the difference between the Min and Max properties.

Although the Change() event is generated when the user stops dragging the scroll box, it does not occur during the drag. If you want to generate the Change() event *as the user drags,* then you must call it from the Scroll() event. The Scroll() event is continually triggered as the user drags the scroll box. By calling the Change() event from the Scroll() event, you can continually generate a Change() event. If you don't, you have to wait until the user stops dragging to ascertain the results of the action. On the other hand, any kind of click on the scroll bar produces an immediate Change() event.

Scroll Bar Methods

The following scroll bar methods are not terribly important and are rarely beneficial.

Drag	Refresh	ShowWhatsThis
Move	SetFocus	Zorder

Experimenting with Scroll Bar Controls

To see how a scroll bar works by adding a horizontal scroll bar to a project, follow these steps:

1. Start a new project by selecting File ≻ New Project ≻ Standard EXE.

2. Add a horizontal scroll bar to Form1 and set its Name property to **hscVolume** in the Properties window.

3. Set the Min property of hscVolume to **0**. Set its Max property to **100**. Set its Value property to **50**.

4. Set the SmallChange property to **1**, and the LargeChange property to **10**.

5. Add a label control to the top of the form and set its Name property to **lblVolume**. Set its Caption to **50**.

6. Click Font in the Properties window to set the Font Size property of the label to **24**.

7. Set the AutoSize property of the label to True. Center the control on the form above the scroll bar.

   Your form should now look similar to Figure 3.13.

8. Double-click the scroll bar to open the Code window.

9. Add the following code to the Change() event of the scroll bar:
   ```
   Private Sub hscVolume_Change()
      lblVolume.Caption = Trim$(Str$(hscVolume.Value))
   End Sub
   ```

10. Finally, select Run ≻ Start.

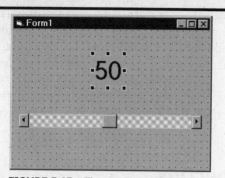

FIGURE 3.13: The scroll bar demo

The program is very simple. It just displays the volume setting, which you control by moving the slider within the scroll bar. You can move it by clicking either of the direction arrows, by dragging the slider, or by clicking between the slider and an arrow.

Perhaps the parts of the program that deserve the most attention are the Trim$ and Str$ functions. First, the Str$ function is used to convert a numeric value to a string. You need to make this conversion because the Caption of lblVolume expects either a string or a variant. However, the Value property of the scroll bar is an integer. So, the value returned by the function

```
Str$(hscVolume)
```

will be suitable for the Caption property. The Trim$ function trims the leading and trailing spaces from a string. When you convert a number to a string, the string result will contain leading spaces. So to keep the formatting neat, you can use the combination

```
Trim$(Str$(hscVolume))
```

If this were a true volume control applet, you would put code that would call the volume control application programming interface (API), and set the volume this way.

USING DRIVE LISTS

 The drive list box control (or just *drive*), which is shown here, is normally used in conjunction with the directory list and the file list controls. At its most fundamental, these three controls allow

the user to select a file in a particular directory on a particular drive. The user changes to another drive via the drive control. They switch directories with the directory control, and they select the file from the file control. You can also use the drive and directory controls to let the user choose a destination for a file they wish to save. Although a common dialog control is better suited for retrieving filenames, we will look at these three controls in the following sections. You will be able to find other uses for them as you develop your skills.

Drive List Box Properties

The following table lists the many properties for the drive list box control:

Appearance	FontItalic	List	Tag
BackColor	FontName	ListCount	ToolTipText
CausesValidation	FontSize	ListIndex	Top
Container	FontUnderline	MouseIcon	TopIndex
DragIcon	ForeColor	MousePointer	Visible
DragMode	Height	**Name**	WhatsThis-HelpID
Drive	HelpContextID	OLEDropMode	Width
Enabled	hWnd	Parent	
Font	Index	TabIndex	
FontBold	Left	TabStop	

For the Name property a drv prefix is normally adopted. Apart from the Name, the single most important property is Drive. This is a run-time property only, which is used to return the drive the user has selected in the drive control. Your application could retrieve this value and use it to synchronize the directory for file list controls explained later. The Drive property is invariably accessed in the Change event procedure for the drive control (see the next section).

Drive List Box Events

The drive list box has a few events, but few are useful to the beginning programmer.

Change	KeyDown	OLECompleteDrag	OLESetData
DragDrop	KeyPress	OLEDragDrop	OLEStartDrag
DragOver	KeyUp	OLEDragOver	Scroll
GotFocus	LostFocus	OLEGiveFeedback	Validate

The Change() event is the most popular event to trap. It is triggered whenever the user makes a selection of a drive in the drive control. The Drive property of the control is used to update the display of directories in the directory list control. Thus, the directories shown are always those on the currently selected drive. A fuller discussion of how to do this appears under the section on the file control, which follows shortly.

Drive List Box Methods

Below is the list of methods for this control.

Drag	OLEDrag	SetFocus	ZOrder
Move	Refresh	ShowWhatsThis	

These methods are rarely used.

USING DIRECTORY LIST BOXES

As already stated, the directory list box (or simply *directory*) control, which is shown here, is used in conjunction with the drive control, described earlier, and file control. The user can select a directory on the current drive from the directory list. However, it's important to update the directories displayed when the user changes drives in the drive control. It is also important to update the files shown in a file control, too. To do these, the directory's Path property and Change() event are used.

Directory List Box Properties

The following are the directory list box properties:

Appearance	FontName	List	TabIndex
BackColor	FontSize	ListCount	TabStop
CausesValidation	FontStrikethru	ListIndex	Tag
Container	FontUnderline	MouseIcon	ToolTipText
DragIcon	ForeColor	MousePointer	Top
DragMode	Height	**Name**	TopIndex
Enabled	HelpContextID	OLEDragMode	Visible
Font	hWnd	OLEDropMode	WhatsThis-HelpID
FontBold	Index	Parent	Width
FontItalic	Left	**Path**	

A directory control is often given a Name property with a dir prefix. The Path property is a run-time property that sets or returns the path to the directory in the directory list. It's usually accessed in the Change event for the *drive* control—where it updates the list of directories to match the drive selected by the user. The Path property is also used in the *directory* control's Change event procedure to update the list of files in a file control when the user changes directories or drives.

Directory List Box Events

The table below shows the events used by the directory list box.

Change	GotFocus	LostFocus	OLECompleteDrag
Click	KeyDown	MouseDown	OLEDragDrop
DragDrop	KeyUp	OLEDragOver	OLEStartDrag
DragOver	MouseMove	OLEGiveFeedback	Scroll
KeyPress	MouseUp	OLESetData	Validate

Although you may use the Click() event in your code, the Change() event procedure is where you will place code to update the files in a file list control.

Directory List Box Methods

You probably won't be working with the following directory list box methods too often:

Drag	OLEDrag	SetFocus	Zorder
Move	Refresh	ShowWhatsThis	

USING FILE LIST BOXES

 The File List Box control (shown here) comes at the end of the drive-directory-file chain. It is used to list the actual filenames that are in the directory specified by the Path property, as shown in Figure 3.14.

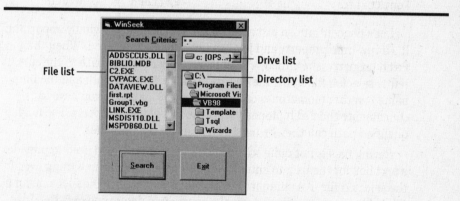

FIGURE 3.14: The drive, directory, and file list controls

To reiterate, the file control should be updated in the directory Change() event. The directory control itself is updated when the user selects a directory in the directory control—it's also updated when the user selects a new drive in the drive control. For these links to work you must code *two* Change() event procedures correctly (this is explained in the example coming up in the next section).

File List Box Properties

File list boxes have a lot of properties—and many of them quite valuable:

Appearance	FontName	ListCount	ReadOnly
Archive	FontSize	ListIndex	**Selected**
BackColor	FontStrikethru	MouseIcon	**System**
CausesValidation	FontUnderline	MousePointer	TabIndex
Container	ForeColor	MultiSelect	TabStop
DragIcon	Height	**Name**	Tag
DragMode	HelpContextID	**Normal**	ToolTipText
Enabled	**Hidden**	OLEDragMode	Top
FileName	hWnd	OLEDropMode	TopIndex
Font	Index	Parent	Visible
FontBold	Left	**Path**	WhatsThis-HelpID
FontItalic	List	**Pattern**	Width

Let's concentrate on just a few. The Path property is vitally important. It's a run-time property and is often both set and returned. When the Path property is returned, Visual Basic is aware of the path to the currently selected file in the file control. To ascertain the path and the filename together (sometimes called a *fully qualified path*), you have to concatenate the Path property with the FileName property. The fully qualified path can then be used as a basis for opening files.

Saving files is not quite so straightforward—you'll also need to provide a text box for the user to enter a new filename rather than writing over the selected file. An alternative approach is to generate the filename for a saved file automatically and use the controls to determine only the drive and directory for the file. In that case, you might want to disable the file control by setting its Enabled property to False, or make it invisible by setting its Visible property to False.

The Path is set in response to the user changing the drive (in a drive control) or the directory (in a directory control). You must code the series of possible events correctly for this to work. The following steps give you an idea of how this works:

1. In the Drive1_Change() event, you would add a line like this:

```
Dir1.Path = Drive1.Drive
```

This line updates the directory list to reflect the selected drive. The fact that the directory `Path` property changes in code generates a `Change()` event for the directory control as well. And the same event is generated if the user manually changes directories in the directory control.

2. You now code the `Change()` event for the directory as follows:

   `File1.Path = Dir1.Path`

   This ensures that the files displayed (governed by the file control's `Path` property) reflect both the currently selected drive and the directory. Changing a drive automatically selects a new directory.

The `Pattern` property can be set at design time—it can also be changed at run time. By default the `Pattern` property is `*.*`, which shows all files in the file control. You can narrow down the list of files by providing a suitable filter, for example, `*.txt` to display just your text files.

The `Archive`, `Hidden`, `Normal`, `ReadOnly`, and `System` properties can all be used to further narrow or expand the list of files. `Hidden` and `System` are `False` by default—ideally, you wouldn't want the end user even to be aware that hidden and system files exist.

TIP

If you're designing a project for a system administrator or a network manager, you may want the hidden and system files to be visible. To do this, set the `Hidden` and `System` properties to `True`.

By using the above code, you will also synchronize the controls when the application begins.

File List Box Events

This is the list of events supported by the File List Box control.

Click	KeyPress	OLECompleteDrag	**PathChange**
DblClick	KeyUp	OLEDragDrop	**PatternChange**
DragDrop	LostFocus	OLEDragOver	Scroll
DragOver	MouseDown	OLEGiveFeedback	Validate

GotFocus   MouseMove   OLESetData

KeyDown   MouseUp   OLEStartDrag

In a sense, the events for a file list control are similar to those of an ordinary list box. The standard approach is to have a command button's Click() event procedure carry out some processing based on the Path and FileName properties of the file control. However, it's often helpful to give the user a double-click alternative. The way to do this, if you recall from an earlier discussion on list boxes, is to code the file control's DblClick() event procedure to call the command button's Click() event.

Two events that are specific to a file control are PathChange() and PatternChange(). The PathChange() event occurs when the file's Path property alters. Similarly, the PatternChange() event occurs when the Pattern property is changed in code. It's common practice to let the user enter a pattern in a text box and set the Pattern property to the value of the Text property of the text box at run time. You can then use the PatternChange() event procedure to reset the Pattern if the user has entered a pattern that might be dangerous, for example, *.ini.

File List Box Methods

This control only supports a few methods, listed in the table below. None of them are particularly useful for the operation of the control.

Drag   OLEDrag   SetFocus   Zorder

Move   Refresh   ShowWhatsThis

Experimenting with File List Box Controls

To get a look at the Drive, Directory, and File List Box controls in action, let's experiment with the WinSeek.vbp sample project. This program will simply search the current drive and directory for files matching a file specification, such as an .AVI extension (see Figure 3.15).

1. Load and run the WinSeek project by double-clicking WinSeek.vbp in the \MSDN98\98vs\1033\Samples\VB98\FileCtls\ subdirectoy.

2. Set the drive list control to C: if it has not defaulted to it already.

3. Set the directory list box to the root directory of the drive. You should be in the C:\ directory.

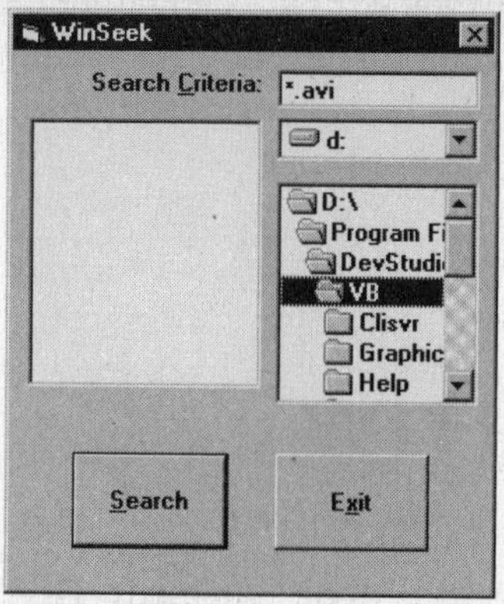

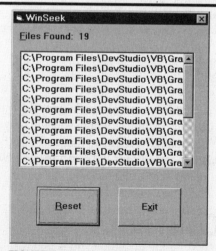

FIGURE 3.15: The WinSeek application

4. In the Search Criteria field, type a file specification (filespec) of a file type you want to search for, such as ***.AVI**. By entering an asterisk, the program will find any filename that ends with the .AVI extension.

5. Click the Search button and watch WinSeek find matching files. You will see search results similar to those in Figure 3.16.

FIGURE 3.16: The WinSeek results

When you are done experimenting with the WinSeek application, stop it by selecting Run ➤ End from the Visual Basic menu. Double-click WinSeek

to open its Code window. The procedures you want to examine are the
Change() events for drvList and dirList. Let's start by looking at the
drvList_Change() event:

```
Private Sub DrvList_Change()
  On Error GoTo DriveHandler
  dirList.Path = drvList.Drive
  Exit Sub

DriveHandler:
  drvList.Drive = dirList.Path
  Exit Sub
End Sub
```

The first thing you will notice is the On Error statement. The procedure calls an error-trapping routine because the drive list box is the most
likely of the three controls to cause an error. The reason is the user could
select a floppy drive that has no disk in it, which would cause an error. By
trapping this error, the program can resume gracefully.

Also notice that this event triggers a Change() event in the directory list
by setting the Path property. This, in turn, triggers a Change() event in the
file list box. It is sort of like the domino theory. You trigger one event and it
will trigger the next object and so on down the line. As you can see below, the
directory list Change() event modifies the path of the file list box.

```
Private Sub DirList_Change()
  ' Update the file list box to synchronize with the direc-
tory list
  ' box.
  filList.Path = dirList.Path
End Sub
```

The Drive, Directory, and File List Box controls are almost always used
together. However, there may be some instances where you will only need
the functionality of one of the controls. If you do use them all together,
you will place the relevant synchronization code in the Change() event
of each control.

ADDING OTHER CONTROLS TO THE TOOLBOX

Before we move on to the next set of controls, you will need to learn how
to add additional controls to your Toolbox. There are many more controls
included with Visual Basic than those described in this chapter.

You can add other controls by following a few simple steps:

▸ Add a tab to the Toolbox to keep it neat.

▸ Select the controls to add.

▸ Move them to the appropriate tab if necessary.

To teach you how to add controls to the Toolbox, let's add the controls used in the next sections.

1. Right-click the Toolbox to display its pop-up menu.

2. Select Add Tab from the pop-up menu.

3. When prompted for the tab name, type in **Common Controls** and click the OK button.

4. Now that the Common Controls tab has been added to the Toolbox, click it to make it the active tab.

5. Right-click the Toolbox and select Components from the pop-up menu.

6. From the Controls tab on the Components dialog box, click the check box next to Microsoft Windows Common Controls 6.0, as in Figure 3.17.

7. Click the OK button to add the controls to the tab.

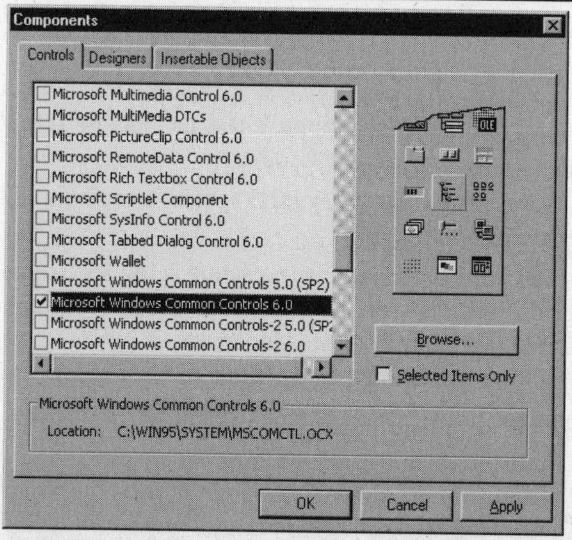

FIGURE 3.17: Adding new controls to the Toolbox

If the controls don't "land" on the appropriate tab, you can move them by dragging them to the appropriate tab on the Toolbox.

You will notice that you may not be able to see "Common Controls" on the tab you just created. You can fix this by either stretching the Toolbox to the right to make it bigger, or you can rename the tab. To rename the tab

1. Right-click in the Common Controls tab.

2. Select Rename Tab from the pop-up menu.

3. When the input box appears, rename the tab to Common.

4. Click the OK button to close the dialog box. When the dialog box closes the tab will be readable on the Toolbox.

That's all there is to adding controls to the Toolbox. Although it's not required, it is a good idea to create tabs that you can categorize your controls by. This will help make it easier for you to locate the control you need. Use the tabs to avoid Toolbox clutter.

Designing Windows 95/98–Style Interfaces

Now that you are familiar with the most common Visual Basic controls, we can learn how to design applications that look, feel, and behave just like the commercial applications written specifically for Windows 95/98 and Windows NT.

There are five controls that provide most of the functionality found in the most common Windows applications. These include the Tree View, List View, Image List, Status Bar, and Toolbar.

Figure 3.18 shows the Windows Explorer applet. It contains all of the controls that I have just described.

At the top of the window, just below the menu, is the Toolbar control. It provides buttons that allow you quick access to the most commonly used functions, such as cut, copy, paste, and delete.

The pane on the left side of the window is a Tree View control. Its name describes its function: it displays items in a tree format, or tree view.

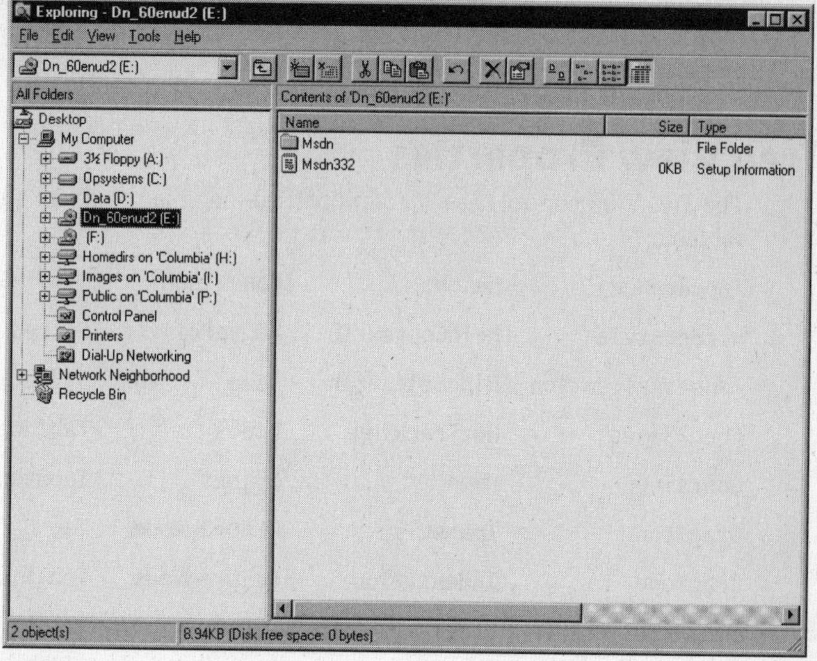

FIGURE 3.18: Windows Explorer

The pane on the right side is a List View control. Its purpose is to show a list of items. This control is most often paired with the Tree View control, and lists the contents of a selected folder in the Tree View.

At the bottom of the window is the Status Bar control. A status bar is used for many functions, including showing the number of selected objects, displaying the system date and/or time, and the amount of free disk space.

Now that you have an idea of what these controls do, and how they look, let's learn how to use them in our applications.

USING THE TREE VIEW CONTROL

 The Tree View control (shown here) provides a hierarchical view of folders or other items that can be neatly categorized in a tree-style layout. It is often used in conjunction with a List View control (explained in the next section), which is used to display the contents of the folder selected in the Tree View. Let's take a look at the Tree View's properties.

Tree View Properties

The Tree View control has a lot of properties—and many of them quite valuable:

Appearance	Height	MouseIcon	SingleSel
BorderStyle	HelpContextID	MousePointer	Sorted
CausesValidation	HideSelection	**Name**	**Style**
CheckBoxes	**HotTracking**	Nodes	TabIndex
Container	HWnd	Object	TabStop
DragIcon	**ImageList**	**OLEDragMode**	Tag
DragMode	**Indentation**	**OLEDropMode**	ToolTipText
DropHighlight	Index	Parent	Top
Enabled	**LabelEdit**	**PathSeparator**	Visible
Font	Left	**Scroll**	WhatsThis-HelpID
FullRowSelect	**LineStyle**	SelectedItem	Width

Aside from the standard properties, there are some new ones that you must get familiar with to exploit the power of this control.

The Name property is the first property you should set when working with this control. The standard naming convention prefix is tvw. For example, if you had a tree view that contained the directory structure of your hard drive, you could name the control tvwDirectories.

If you double-click the Custom field in the Properties window, you can bring up a property page like the one in Figure 3.19 that exposes the most important properties.

Of the three tabs displayed by the Tree View's property pages, the General tab is the one you will be most concerned with.

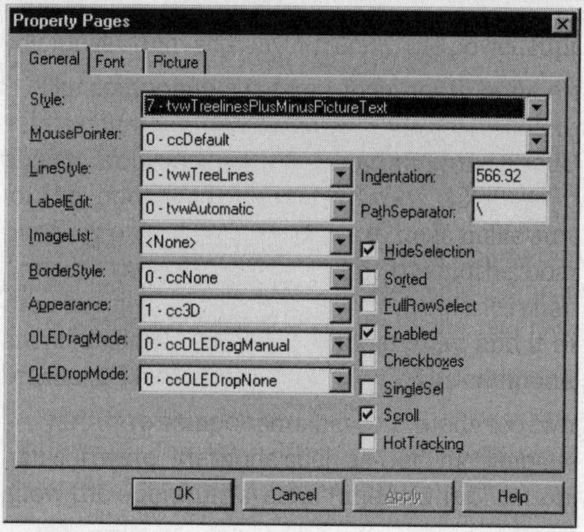

FIGURE 3.19: The Tree View's property pages

The General Tab

The Style property allows you to determine how you want the control to look and behave on the form. The possible values you can set this property to are as follows:

Setting	Description
0 – tvwTextOnly	This setting shows only the text of the node.
1 – tvwPictureText	This setting shows the nodes icon and its text.
2 – tvwPlusMinustext	Use this setting if you want the collapse/expand symbol (the plus and minus signs) and the text of the node.
3 – tvwPlusPictureText	This setting displays the collapse/expand symbol, a small icon to the left of the text, and the text itself.

Setting	Description
4 - tvwTreelinesText	If you want to have lines connect nodes that are related in the tree's hierarchy, you can use this setting to show the lines and the text for the node.
5 - tvwTreelines-PictureText	This setting displays a small icon to the left of the text, and connects related nodes.
6 - tvwTreelines-PlusMinusText	Pick this setting to show the collapse/expand symbol, connection lines, and the nodes text.
7 - tvwTreelinesPlus-MinusPictureText	If you want everything shown, choose this setting.

The LineStyle property is used to set the style of lines displayed between nodes. The possible values are

0 – TreeLines

1 – RootLines

TIP

A node is an object that can contain both images and text. You will find that nodes are the data objects used in both the Tree View or List View controls.

The LabelEdit property is a Boolean property that allows you to enable or disable the automatic label-editing feature of the control. Windows Explorer demonstrates this feature when you single-click a folder or file name. It will turn into a miniature text box that will allow you to change the name. Set this property to True to enable label editing. Set it to False to turn it off.

If you want to have pictures in your Tree View control, you should set the ImageList property to the name of an existing Image List control, explained later in this chapter.

The BorderStyle and Appearance properties are self-explanatory.

OLEDragMode configures the control for either manual or automatic dragging. You set this property to one of the following values:

0 – OLEDragManual

1 – OLEDragAutomatic

OLEDropMode configures the Tree View control to enable or disable OLE drop operations. The value of the property can be one of the following:

0 – OLEDropNone   When set to this value, the target component does not accept OLE drops and displays the No Drop cursor.

1 – OLEDropManual   The control will trigger the OLE drop events, allowing the programmer to handle the OLE drop operation in code.

The Indentation property determines the horizontal distance between nodes in the view. The lower the number, the closer the nodes are. If you prefer a tighter-looking interface, I have found that a value of 283 looks nice at run time.

The PathSeparator property allows you to set or retrieve the delimiter character used for the path returned by a node's FullPath property, as shown below:

```
Private Sub TreeView1_NodeClick(ByVal Node As Node)
    Dim rc as String
    rc = Node.FullPath
    MsgBox rc
End Sub
```

For example, you could set this property to a backslash (\) if you were showing a list of folders on your hard drive. Or, you could use a period (.) to designate an Internet-style path, as if you were mapping IP subnets on your LAN.

Set the Scroll property to True if you want the Tree View to show scroll bars; if there are more nodes than can be listed in the Tree View at one time, this may be necessary. Set it to False to disable scroll bars.

Finally, you can set the HotTracking property to True if you want the full name to be displayed in a tool tip–style box when the name does not fit horizontally within the view, as shown in Figure 3.20.

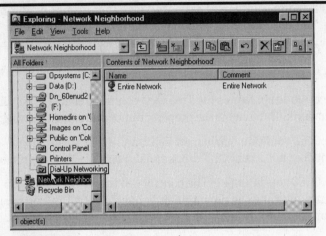

FIGURE 3.20: Hot Tracking turned on

Tree View Events

This is the list of events supported by the Tree View control.

AfterLabelEdit	Expand	MouseMove	OLEGiveFeed-back
BeforeLabelEdit	GotFocus	MouseUp	OLESetData
Click	KeyDown	NodeCheck	OLEStartDrag
Collapse	KeyPress	NodeClick	Validate
DblClick	KeyUp	OLECompleteDrag	
DragDrop	LostFocus	OLEDragDrop	
DragOver	MouseDown	OLEDragOver	

The AfterLabelEdit() event is triggered after you perform a label editing function on a node. This event is useful if you want to check the name of the node to make sure that it is valid. Its compliment, the Before-LabelEdit() event, is triggered right before the node goes into edit mode.

The Collapse() event is triggered when a user collapses a branch of the tree. This can happen by double-clicking a root of a branch, or by clicking the minus sign next to the branch's root. You could place code in this event to remove items from the Tree View if you want to conserve memory.

The Expand() event is obviously the opposite of the Collapse() event. It is triggered when a user expands a branch of the tree by either clicking the plus sign next to the root of the branch, or by double-clicking the root of the branch. You could use this event to dynamically load data into the control when the node is expanded.

The NodeClick() event is one of the most important events that the Tree View provides. You can use this event to retrieve information about the node that was clicked, or any other function that your application requires. For example, the code

```
Private Sub tvwNodes_NodeClick(ByVal Node As ComctlLib.Node)
  MsgBox Node.FullPath
End Sub
```

will display a dialog box that shows the complete path to the node you clicked. If you used the backslash character in the PathSeparator property, with a root node named C: and the node clicked named Windows, the dialog box would display C:\Windows.

OLECompleteDrag() is triggered when OLE data is dropped on the control or the OLE drag-and-drop operation is canceled.

The OLEDragDrop() event is triggered when the OLEDropMode property is set to 1 – Manual, and OLE data is dropped on the control. You would place code in the event to determine what the control should do when data is dropped. You could place code in this event to make the control move data, but not copy it. Or you could have it copy the data, but not move it. The functionality depends on the needs of your application.

The OLEDragOver() event is triggered when OLE data is dragged over the control. After this event is triggered, Visual Basic will trigger the OLEGiveFeedback() event, which will allow you to check the data and provide feedback to the user.

The OLEGiveFeedback event is triggered after every OLEDragOver() event. It allows the Tree View control to provide feedback to the user, such as changing the mouse cursor to indicate what will happen if the user drops the object, or provide visual feedback on the selection (in the source component) to indicate what can happen.

The OLESetData() event is triggered when a target control executes the GetData method on the source's DataObject object.

Finally, the OLEStartDrag() event is triggered when a user starts dragging data from the control. If the OLEDragMode property is set to 1 – Automatic, the control will automatically start. You can use this event to populate data in the control's `DataObject` object. This will allow the destination control to read the data from the `DataObject`.

Tree View Methods

These are the methods exposed by the Tree View control:

Drag	Move	SetFocus	**StartLabelEdit**
GetVisibleCount	**OLEDrag**	ShowWhatsThis	ZOrder
HitTest	Refresh		

The `GetVisibleCount` method is used to retrieve the number of nodes that can be viewed in the Tree View at one time. This is not to be confused with the total number that the control can hold, but just how many can be viewed without scrolling vertically in the control. This method is useful if you need to ensure that a given number of nodes are visible at a time.

The `HitTest` method is used to determine if a node is available as a drop target. You can use this event during an OLE drag operation to highlight a node or change the mouse pointer when the OLE data is over a target that will allow it to be dropped.

The `OLEDrag` method is called to initiate an OLE drag operation. After this operation is initiated, the control's `OLEStartDrag` event is triggered, allowing you to supply data to a target component.

The `StartLabelEdit` method is used when you want to force a node into label edit mode. You can use this method in special circumstances, for example when you have set the `LabelEdit` property to `False`, but need to change the name of this one node. A good example of this can be seen again in Windows Explorer. You can change the names of folders and files within the tree, but you cannot change the names of built-in components, such as drives, Control Panel, or Network Neighborhood.

Before we create a sample application, let's take a look at the Tree View's counterpart: the List View control.

USING THE LIST VIEW CONTROL

 As mentioned previously, the List View control is often used in conjunction with the Tree View control. There are times when it will be used separately, but for this chapter, we will use them together.

List View Properties

Below are the properties for the List View control:

AllowColumnReorder	Height	Parent
Appearance	HelpContextID	Picture
Arrange	HideColumnheaders	PictureAlignment
BackColor	HideSelection	**SelectedItem**
BorderStyle	**HotTracking**	**SmallIcons**
CausesValidation	HoverSelection	**Sorted**
Checkboxes	HWnd	**SortKey**
ColumnHeaderIcons	**Icons**	**SortOrder**
ColumnHeaders	Index	TabIndex
Container	**LabelEdit**	TabStop
DragIcon	**LabelWrap**	Tag
DragMode	Left	TextBackground
DropHighlight	**ListItems**	ToolTipText
Enabled	MouseIcon	Top
FlatScrollBar	MousePointer	Visible
Font	**MultiSelect**	WhatsThisHelpID
ForeColor	**Name**	Width
FontName	Object	**View**
FullRowSelect	OLEDragMode	
GridLines	OLEDropMode	

If you double-click the Custom field in the Property window for the List View control, Visual Basic will present you with the property pages for the control, as shown in Figure 3.21. These present the most useful, control-specific, properties that you could set to customize the look and behavior of the control.

Again, the first property you should set it the control's Name property. You can use a prefix like lvw. For example, if your control listed the files on your hard drive, you could name the control lvwFiles.

There are numerous tabs on the List View's property pages. You will be mostly concerned with the first four tabs.

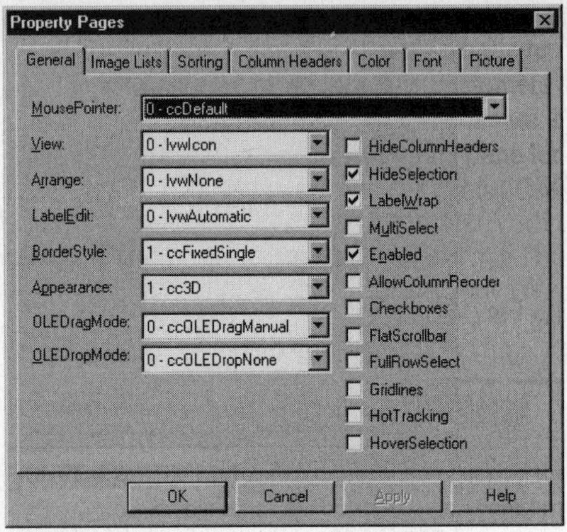

FIGURE 3.21 : List View property pages

The General Tab

The first tab on the property page, the General tab, contains many properties that control the layout of the List View control.

You can set the View property to make the List View display items in one of four different views:

0 – lvwIcon Use this value to make the List View display large icons with text for each item in the list.

1 – lvwList This value will list the items much like a List Box control.

2 – lvwReport This setting is much like lvwList, but it will also show the subitems that belong to each item in the list.

3 – lvwSmallIcon This setting is like lvwIcon, but it uses smaller icons.

The Arrange property allows you to set or retrieve the value that determines how the icons in the control's Icon or SmallIcon views are arranged. The possible values of this property are:

0 – lvwNone This setting will not control how the items are arranged.

1 – lvwAutoLeft   This setting will make the control automatically arrange the items on the left of the control.

2 – lvwAutoTop   This setting will make the control automatically arrange the items on the top of the control.

The LabelEdit property is a Boolean property that allows you to enable or disable the automatic label-editing feature of the control. Windows Explorer demonstrates this feature when you click a folder or filename. It will turn into a miniature text box that will allow you to change the name. Set this property to True to enable label editing. Set it to False to turn it off.

OLEDragMode configures the control for either manual or automatic dragging. You set this property to one of the following values:

0 – OLEDragManual

1 – OLEDragAutomatic

OLEDropMode configures the List View control to enable or disable OLE drop operations. The value of the property can be one of the following:

0 – OLEDropNone   When set to this value the target component does not accept OLE drops and displays the "No Drop" cursor.

1 – OLEDropManual   The control will trigger the OLE drop events, allowing the programmer to handle the OLE drop operation in code.

The ColumnHeaders property is set to False when you check the box next to Hide Column Headers.

The LabelWrap property allows you to set or retrieve the value that determines if labels are wrapped when the List View is in Icon view. If this box is checked, then the property is set to True.

If you want to allow the user to select more than one item at a time, you can set the MultiSelect property to True. If you want to restrict the user to one selection at a time, set this property to False.

The FullRowSelect property is interesting, because it allows the List View control to behave much like a cell in a spreadsheet that can contain graphics. You can set this property to True to make the control highlight an entire row within a column, just as a spreadsheet will highlight the entire cell, rather than just the text of the item.

Part I

If you want to make the control look and behave like a spreadsheet even further, you can set the `GridLines` property to `True`. This will make the control draw horizontal and vertical lines between each row and between each column, yielding a grid.

To make the List View control behave like a spreadsheet, you can set the `GridLines` and `FullRowSelect` properties to `True`. Then you can set the List View to display in Report view. For example, if you had a List View named lvwSheet, you would use the following code to make the spreadsheet:

```
With lvwSheet
    .View = lvwReport
    .GridLines = True
    .FullRowSelect = True
End With
```

You can set the `HotTracking` property to `True` if you want the full name to be displayed in a tool tip–style box when the name does not fit horizontally within the view.

The `HoverSelection` property allows you to set or retrieve a value that determines if an object is selected when the mouse pointer hovers over it. Set this property to `True` to enable hover selection, `False` to disable it.

The Image Lists Tab

The Image Lists tab contains the properties that enable the List View to use graphics. Normally, if you want to have pictures in your List View control, you should set the `ImageList` property to the name of an existing Image List control, explained later, in the section "Using the Image List Control".

When you set the Small field to the name of an Image List, it will set the List View's `SmallIcons` property to the Image List control. When your List View is set to display small icons, the icons will be retrieved from the Image List specified in this property.

The ColumnHeader field will set the `ColumnHeaders` property to the Image List that contains the icons to be displayed in the Column Headers of the List View.

The Sorting Tab

The Sorting tab displays fields that expose the properties related to sorting data in a List View control.

The Sorted check box sets the `Sorted` property. If it is checked, then the List View will sort the data within it. If it is unchecked, then the `Sorted` property will be set to `False`.

If you want to specify how to sort the data within the List View, you can set the `SortKey` property. If you set it to 0, then the data is sorted by the item's Text property. If you set this property to a number higher than 0, then the List View will sort based on the text within the `SubItems` properties.

The `SortOrder` property determines whether the data is sorted in an ascending or descending fashion. Set this property to 0 to sort in ascending order. Set it to 1 to sort in descending order.

The Column Headers Tab

The Index field is incremented every time you add a `ColumnHeader` object to the List View Control.

When you fill in the Text field of this tab, Visual Basic will set the `Text` property of the `ColumnHeader` object with an index specified in the Index field above.

You can set the Alignment field to one of three values:

0 – `lvwColumnLeft`

1 – `lvwColumnRight`

2 – `lvwColumnCenter`

These determine the position of the text within the `ColumnHeader` object.

The value entered in the Width field will set the Column Header's `Width` property. This will set the width of the Column Header specified in the Index field.

The `Key` property determines the Column Header's unique key within the collection of Column Headers. This value can be either numeric or text. What you enter does not matter, as long as it is unique.

The `Tag` property sets the Column Header's `Tag` property. This property can contain any miscellaneous data that you want associated with the Column Header.

You set the IconIndex field to a number that indicates the index of the desired icon within the associated Image List control. For example, if you have three icons in an Image List, and you want the third icon to be displayed on this Column Header, you would set this field to 3.

List View Events

This is the list of events supported by the List View control.

AfterLabelEdit	DragOver	KeyUp	**OLEDragDrop**
BeforeLabelEdit	GotFocus	LostFocus	**OLEDragOver**
Click	ItemCheck	MouseDown	**OLEGiveFeedback**
ColumnClick	**ItemClick**	MouseMove	**OLESetData**
DblClick	KeyDown	MouseUp	**OLEStartDrag**
DragDrop	KeyPress	**OLECompleteDrag**	Validate

As you can see, many of the events for this control are the similar to those of the Tree View control.

Again, the AfterLabelEdit() event is triggered after you perform a label editing function on an object in the List View, called a *ListItem*. This event is useful if you want to check the name of the ListItem to make sure that it is valid. Its compliment, the BeforeLabelEdit() event, is triggered right before the ListItem goes into edit mode.

NOTE

A ListItem is the object inside a List View control. It is made up of text and the index of an associated icon. If the control is in report view, then this control also contains an array of strings, called *subitems*, that further describe the ListItem.

The ColumnClick() event is triggered when a user clicks one of the column headers. A column header is the button that sits at the top of a column, and describes the contents of that column. In report view in Windows Explorer, you can see that the column headers are labeled Name, Size, Type, and Modified. By inserting code in this event, you can make your List View control re-sort the data, or even re-order the columns.

The ItemClick() event is one of the most important events in this control. You can use this event to retrieve information about the ListItem that was clicked, or any other function that your application requires. It is used in much the same way as the Tree View's NodeClick() event.

OLECompleteDrag() is triggered when OLE data is dropped on the control or the OLE drag-and-drop operation is canceled.

The OLEDragDrop() event is triggered when the OLEDropMode property is set to 1 – Manual, and OLE data is dropped on the control. You can place code in the event to determine what the control should do when data is dropped. You could place code in this event to make the control move data, but not copy it. Or you could have it copy the data, but not move it. The functionality depends on the needs of your application.

The OLEDragOver() event is triggered when OLE data is dragged over the control. After this event is triggered, Visual Basic will trigger the OLEGiveFeedback() event, which will allow you to check the data and provide feedback to the user.

The OLEGiveFeedback() event is triggered after every OLEDrag-Over() event. It allows the Tree View control to provide feedback to the user, such as changing the mouse cursor to indicate what will happen if the user drops the object, or provide visual feedback on the selection (in the source component) to indicate what can happen.

The OLESetData() event is triggered when a target control executes the GetData method on the source's DataObject object.

Finally, the OLEStartDrag() event is triggered when a user starts dragging data from the control. If the OLEDragMode property is set to 1 – Automatic, the control will automatically start. You can use this event to populate data in the control's DataObject object. This will allow the destination control to read the data from the DataObject.

List View Methods

This control only supports a few methods, listed in the table below. None of them are particularly useful for the operation of the control.

Drag	**HitTest**	Refresh	**StartLabelEdit**
FindItem	Move	SetFocus	ZOrder
GetFirstVisible	**OLEDrag**	ShowWhatsThis	

The List View has many of the same methods as the Tree View.

You can call the FindItem method to find a ListItem within the control. You can make the control find exact matches or even partial matches.

Because you can have many more ListItems in the List View control than you can see at one time, you can call the GetFirstVisible method to determine which ListItem is at the top of the list within the view when it is in List or Report View.

The HitTest method is used to determine if a ListItem is available as a drop target. You can use this event during an OLE drag operation to highlight a target ListItem or change the mouse pointer when the OLE data is over a target that will allow it to be dropped.

The OLEDrag method is called to initiate an OLE drag operation. After this operation is initiated, the control's OLEStartDrag() event is triggered, allowing you to supply data to a target component.

The StartLabelEdit method is used when you want to force a node into label edit mode. You can use this method in special circumstances, for example when you have set the LabelEdit property to False, but need to change the name of this one node. A good example of this can be seen again in Windows Explorer. You can change the names of folders and files within the tree, but you cannot change the names of built-in components, such as drives, Control Panel, or Network Neighborhood.

Let's look at the Image List control before we work on our sample. That way we can add graphics to the controls, rather than using plain old text.

USING THE IMAGE LIST CONTROL

 The Image List control does not actually appear on a form at run time. Instead, it serves as a container for icons that are accessed by other controls, such as the Tree View, List View, and Toolbar controls. You may have several Image Lists on a form at a time. One could contain the large icons, another would contain small icons, and yet another could contain icons for the Column Headers of the List View control.

Image List Properties

The Image List control has only a few properties:

BackColor	ImageWidth	MaskColor	Parent
HimageList	Index	Name	Tag
ImageHeight	ListImages	Object	UseMaskColor

The first property to set is the Name property. You can use a prefix of iml. When I link an Image List to another control, I usually set the name to be the same as the other control. For example, if I link the Image List to a Toolbar control, I would name the Toolbar `tbrToolbar`, and the Image List would be named `imlToolbar`.

The `ImageHeight` property is used to set the height of all of the images within the Image List. `ImageWidth` is set to the width of all images in the list. It is important to know that all of the images must have the same dimensions. If you require images of different sizes, you must use multiple Image Lists.

To make the backgrounds of each image transparent, you need to set the `MaskColor` property to the background color of the images within the control. Each image should use the same background color. Once the `MaskColor` property is set to the correct color, you can set the `UseMaskColor` property to `True`.

WARNING

All images within an Image List must be the same size. In addition, they should all use the same mask color.

Image List Events

The Image List control has no events, so let's look at its one and only method.

Image List Methods

The Image List has only one method: `Overlay`. You can use the `Overlay` method if you want to combine two images within an Image List. You can set the `MaskColor` property to the transparent color of the top image, so the resulting image is a nice combination of the two. For example, the code

```
'This command will overlay image 1 onto image 2
Set Picture1.Picture = imlToolbar.Overlay(1,2)
```

will overlay the first image in the control with the second image.

Putting It All Together

Now is the time you have been waiting for. This example will combine the features of the Tree View, List View, and Image List controls. Let's see how they all work together.

1. In Visual Basic, start a new project by selecting File ➢ New Project from the menu, and select Standard EXE as the project type.

2. Left-click Project1 in the Project Explorer, then set the Name property of the project to **ObjectExplorer**.

3. Select Form1 and set its Name property to **frmMain**.

4. Set the Caption property to **Object Explorer**.

5. Right-click the Toolbox and select Components from the pop-up menu.

6. When the Components dialog box appears, scroll down and select Microsoft Windows Common Controls 6.0 from the list. Click OK to add the controls to your Toolbox.

7. Add an Image List to frmMain by double-clicking the Image List control in the Toolbox. When it is added to the form, move it to the lower-right corner of the form. Set its Name property to **imlCategories**.

8. In the Property window, double-click the Custom field to open the property page for the control.

9. Select the Images tab. Click the Insert Picture button to add an image to the list.

10. When the Select picture dialog box appears, select Closed.bmp from the Common\Graphics\Bitmaps directory. Click the Open button to add the file to the control, then click OK.

11. Add another Image List to frmMain. Set its Name property to **imlItems**. Move it next to imlCategories.

12. Using the same methods as described in steps 8–10, add the image Leaf.bmp to the control and click the Open button.

13. Click the OK button to close the property page.

14. Add a Tree View control to frmMain. Set its Name property to **tvwCategories**.

15. In the Properties window, double-click the Custom property field. This will bring up the property page for the control.

16. On the General tab of the property page, set the Style property to **7 – tvwTreeLinesPlusMinusPictureText**, set the LabelEdit property to **1 – Manual**, the Indentation property to **283**, and the ImageList property to **imlCategories**.

17. Click the OK button to close the property pages.

18. Move tvwCategories to the upper-left side of the form.

19. Add a List View control to frmMain and set its Name property to **lvwItems**.

20. In the Properties window, double-click the Custom property field. This will bring up the property page for the control.

21. Set the View property to **3 – lvwReport**, the Arrange property to **2 – lvwAutoTop**, the LabelEdit property to **1 – Manual**, and the OLEDropMode property to **1 – OLEDropManual**.

22. Click the Image Lists tab to make it the active property page.

23. Set the Normal field to **imlItems**. This will link it to the Items Image List control.

24. Click the Column Headers tab to make it the active property page.

25. Click the Insert Column button. This will add the first Column Header object to the collection.

26. Set the Text field to Control Name.

27. Click the OK button to close the property pages.

28. Move imlItems to the upper-right corner of the form. The form should look like Figure 3.22.

29. Save your work by selecting File ➤ Save Project from the Visual Basic menu.

30. Double-click frmMain to open its code window.

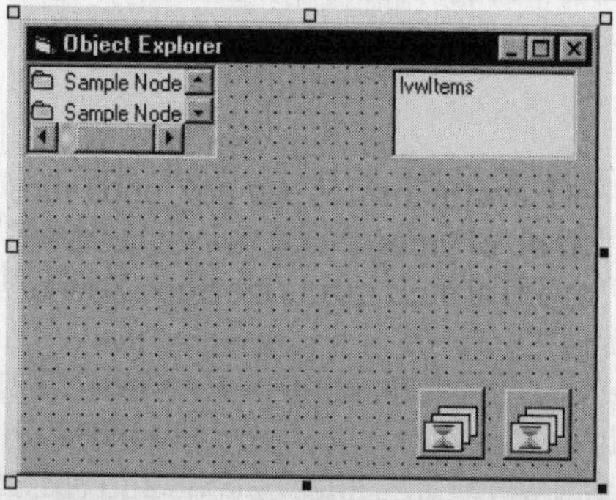

FIGURE 3.22:   The Object Explorer form under development

31. Add the following code to the Form_Resize() event:

```
Private Sub Form_Resize()

    Dim mid1 As Integer
    Dim mid2 As Integer

    mid1 = (ScaleWidth / 2) - 50
    mid2 = (ScaleWidth / 2) + 50

    If WindowState <> vbMinimized Then
        tvwCategories.Move 0, 0, mid1, ScaleHeight
        lvwItems.Move mid2, 0, ScaleWidth - mid2,
ScaleHeight
    End If
End Sub
```

The code for this example deserves some scrutiny. The first two statements dimension two variables, mid1 and mid2. The next two lines of code set these variables to values that indicate positions just to the left and right of the centerline of the form. By adding and subtracting 50 from these values, we can create a neat border between the two views.

The If...Then statement tells the program to execute the next lines of code only if the form is not minimized. If the form were minimized, then you would get an error when trying to move and size the controls.

In the Form_Load() event, add the following code:

```
Private Sub Form_Load()
    Dim cat As Node

    'Add the nodes to the tree view
    With tvwCategories.Nodes
        Set cat = .Add(, , "root", "Objects", 1)
        Set cat = .Add("root", tvwChild, , "Intrinsic", 1)
        Set cat = .Add("root", tvwChild, , "Explorer", 1)
        Set cat = .Add("root", tvwChild, , "Internet", 1)
    End With
End Sub
```

The first line creates a Node-type variable. This will allow us to work with the Nodes collection inside of the List View control. The next line (With ...) tells the Visual Basic compiler to work specifically with the Nodes collection of tvwCategories.

The first line of code under the With statement adds a node at the root level of the tree. We set its text value to "Objects" because that is what this tree contains. The following three lines of code add child nodes (tvwChild) to the root object. Each node has its own description, one for intrinsic controls, another for the Explorer-style controls, and finally some Internet controls. Remember that these nodes are actually categories. That means that they will "contain" other objects.

Add the following code to the (General)(Declarations) section of frmMain:

```
Option Explicit

Private Sub ListExplorer()
  Dim itm As ListItem

  With lvwItems.ListItems
    .Clear
    Set itm = .Add(, , "Tree View", 1)
    Set itm = .Add(, , "List View", 1)
    Set itm = .Add(, , "Image List", 1)
    Set itm = .Add(, , "Toolbar", 1)
    Set itm = .Add(, , "Status Bar", 1)
  End With
End Sub

Private Sub ListInternet()
  Dim itm As ListItem

  With lvwItems.ListItems
    .Clear
    Set itm = .Add(, , "Web Browser", 1)
    Set itm = .Add(, , "Shell Folder View", 1)
    Set itm = .Add(, , "Inet", 1)
    Set itm = .Add(, , "Winsock", 1)
  End With
End Sub

Private Sub ListIntrinsics()
  Dim itm As ListItem

  With lvwItems.ListItems
    .Clear
    Set itm = .Add(, , "Picture", 1)
    Set itm = .Add(, , "Label", 1)
    Set itm = .Add(, , "Text Box", 1)
    Set itm = .Add(, , "Frame", 1)
    Set itm = .Add(, , "Command Button", 1)
    Set itm = .Add(, , "Check Box", 1)
    Set itm = .Add(, , "Radio Button", 1)
```

```
            Set itm = .Add(, , "Combo Box", 1)
            Set itm = .Add(, , "List Box", 1)
            Set itm = .Add(, , "Horizontal Scroll Bar", 1)
            Set itm = .Add(, , "Vertical Scroll Bar", 1)
            Set itm = .Add(, , "Timer", 1)
            Set itm = .Add(, , "Drive List", 1)
            Set itm = .Add(, , "Directory List", 1)
            Set itm = .Add(, , "File List", 1)
            Set itm = .Add(, , "Shape", 1)
            Set itm = .Add(, , "Line", 1)
            Set itm = .Add(, , "Image", 1)
            Set itm = .Add(, , "Data", 1)
            Set itm = .Add(, , "OLE", 1)
        End With
    End Sub
```

The first statement, Option Explicit, forces variable declaration within the project. The three subs are very similar. Each declares a ListItem variable, named itm. This variable is used to access the ListItems collection within lvwItems.

The With... statement tells the compiler to work with the ListItems collection of the List View control. The next command, .Clear, tells the List View to clear its ListItems collection. This removes other controls if any already exist within the collection. Finally, the next commands add ListItems to the collection.

Finally, add the following code to the NodeClick() event of tvw-Categories:

```
    Private Sub tvwCategories_NodeClick(ByVal Node As _
    ComctlLib.Node)
        Select Case Node
          Case Is = "Intrinsic"
            ListIntrinsics
          Case Is = "Explorer"
            ListExplorer
          Case Is = "Internet"
            ListInternet
        End Select
    End Sub
```

Save your project by selecting File ➢ Save Project from the menu. Press the F5 key to run the project.

The form should look like Figure 3.23. The window on the left side of the form is the Tree View, and the List View is on the right. Notice that if you resize the form, the windows will automatically resize as well. Double-click the Objects folder to expand it. Then, click any of the categories to view its contents.

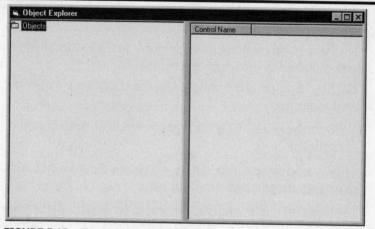

FIGURE 3.23: The Object Explorer in action

USING THE STATUS BAR CONTROL

 The Status Bar control is the next important piece of the Windows Common Controls collection. It is used to report various bits of information to the user. It resembles the System Tray, found in the right side of the Windows Taskbar. It can also be found in Windows Explorer. It can reflect the system date and time, show icons, or display statistics related to other controls, for example the number of files listed in a List View control.

Status Bar Properties

This is the list of the status bar's properties:

Align	hWnd	OLEDropMode	Tag
Container	Index	**Panels**	ToolTipText
DragIcon	Left	Parent	Top
DragMode	MouseIcon	ShowTips	Visible
Enabled	MousePointer	**SimpleText**	WhatsThisHelpID

Font	**Name**	**Style**	Width
Height	Object	TabIndex	

The Name property should be set first. You can use the prefix sts. I prefer to name the status bar stsStatus.

The Panels property returns a reference to the collection of panel objects contained in the Status Bar control.

The Style property determines how the status bar is displayed. The allowed values are:

0 – sbrNormal   This setting shows multiple panels on the status bar.

1 – sbrSimple   This setting will show only one panel, which extends the width of the status bar.

The SimpleText property allows you to set or retrieve the value of the text in the panel when the Style property is set to 1 – sbrSimple.

Status Bar Events

This is the list of events supported by the Status Bar control.

Click	MouseDown	OLEDragDrop	OLEStartDrag
DblClick	MouseMove	OLEDragOver	**PanelClick**
DragDrop	MouseUp	OLEGiveFeedback	**PanelDblClick**
DragOver	OLECompleteDrag	OLESetData	

Since the status bar is used more to give you feedback, many of these events are not that important. Let's look at the PanelClick() and PanelDblClick() events.

The PanelClick() event is triggered when the user clicks a panel. So what is a panel, you ask? A panel is a section of the status bar that contains either text or a bitmap, which may be used to reflect the status of an application. The PanelDblClick() event is triggered when a user double-clicks a panel.

Neither of these actions is likely to occur, and so these events won't be used that often. However, everything a control does depends on the design of your applications.

Status Bar Methods

This control only supports a few methods, listed below. None of them are particularly useful for the operation of the control.

Drag	OLEDrag	SetFocus	ZOrder
Move	Refresh	ShowWhatsThis	

Experimenting with the Status Bar

Let's finish the Object Explorer example from the previous section. If you have not already done so, load the ObjectBrowser project by selecting File ➤ Open Project from the Visual Basic menu.

1. Add a Status Bar control to the bottom of frmMain. It will automatically stretch to fit the width of the form. Set its Name property to **stsStatus**.

2. Open the code window for the Load() event of frmMain.

3. Add the following line of code just below the Dim cat as Node line:

   ```
   Dim pnl As Panel
   ```

4. Add the following lines of code below the With...End With block:

   ```
   'Add two panels for time and date
   With stsStatus.Panels
     Set pnl = .Add(, , , sbrTime)
     Set pnl = .Add(, , , sbrDate)
   End With
   ```

5. Go to the NodeClick() event of tvwCategories and add the following line of code above the Select Case statement:

   ```
   Dim pnl As Panel
   Dim sts As String
   ```

6. Add the following lines of code below the Select...End Select block:

   ```
   'Get the item count
   sts = lvwItems.ListItems.Count & " Objects"

   'Update the status bar
   With stsStatus.Panels(1)
   ```

```
.Text = sts
End With
```

7. In the `Form_Resize()` event, change the two lines of code with the Move statements to the following:

```
tvwCategories.Move 0,0,mid1,ScaleHeight-stsStatus.Height
lvwItems.Move mid2,0,ScaleWidth-mid2, ScaleHeight-
stsStatus.Height
```

8. Save and run the project.

Figure 3.24 shows that there are three panels in the status bar. The leftmost panel shows how many objects are listed in the List View control. The middle panel displays the system time, and the right-most panel displays the system date.

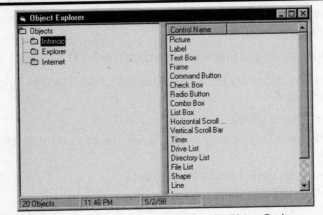

FIGURE 3.24 :   The status bar added to the Object Explorer

You can use these same techniques to customize the Status Bar control in your own applications. You are only limited by your imagination!

MOVING ON...

There are obviously too many controls to cover in this chapter. To cover all of the controls would almost require a separate book. If you have read this entire chapter, then you are more than ready to start using the controls covered here, as well as those that have not been covered yet. The nice thing about custom controls is that once you are familiar with one, it is easy to become familiar with others.

What's Next?

In the next chapter, you'll be introduced to the characteristics and benefits of object programming and how it relates to Visual Basic. You'll also discover how to create object variables, use the object browser, create controls at run time, and many other skills.

Part i

Chapter 4

OBJECT PROGRAMMING WITH VISUAL BASIC

As a term, *object-oriented programming* has been around for a quite a while now. At one time, object-oriented versions of popular programming languages, such as C and Pascal, promised to help developers solve many problems, especially with large applications or for projects on which teams of programmers worked. The catch with object-oriented languages and with the object-oriented approach to programming is that developers must learn and master new concepts and get accustomed to a new programming philosophy.

No wonder most developers worked with object-oriented versions of C in a fashion similar to the way they worked with non–object-oriented languages. The way they worked was

Adapted from *Visual Basic 6 Developer's Handbook*
by Evangelos Petroutsos and Kevin Hough

ISBN 0-7821-2283-3   1,504 pages $49.99

determined (to a large extent) by each programmer's education. Object-oriented programming didn't come naturally to those who went to school before the introduction of object-oriented programming or to those who didn't have a degree in computer science. It's a new approach to application development, and, unlike the traditional approach to programming, it's an acquired taste.

So why bother with object-oriented programming? Because you can't go very far without it. Current programming is object oriented, and you must master the object-oriented techniques necessary for developing software with development tools such as Visual Basic. Some of the benefits include the ability to:

▶ Write code that can be used in multiple applications

▶ Update objects throughout their life cycle, without breaking the applications that use them

▶ Coordinate among multiple programmers working on the same project

Much has been written about object-oriented programming, but the bottom line is this: *Object-oriented programming won't simplify your life instantly*. Actually, you'll be hard-pressed to understand topics such as inheritance, encapsulation, and polymorphism and then apply them to your projects. Down the road, however, the object-oriented approach will simplify your life. But not everyone will make the transition.

NOTE

Visual Basic is a unique environment that, over the past seven years, gradually and in subtle ways introduced programmers to the principles of object-oriented programming. Those of you who have worked with Visual Basic since version 1 (it may look arcane now, but it was an extraordinary environment for developing early Windows applications) have been using objects for many years.

The environment of Visual Basic and its approach to programming was carefully crafted so that developers wouldn't have to be aware of features such as encapsulation or polymorphism. Visual Basic literally incorporated the complexity of Windows into a simple language. The average VB developer needn't know that TextBoxes are objects derived from the TextBox class. They are boxes that can be dropped on a Form, and, once there, they carry with them the functionality of a text editor. The same programmer doesn't have to know that objects expose properties and methods and that they communicate with the operating system via events. The Properties window displays all the properties you can set to adjust the appearance of the object, and the methods are like commands that once you had to memorize. The truth is TextBoxes are objects, and they behave like objects on a Form.

So, how do you explain the principles of object-oriented programming? We'll do it gradually, starting with simple topics, such as how to manipulate objects from within your applications. We won't show you how to set properties or how to program with events or deal with other techniques you have mastered already. Instead, we'll focus on the following rather advanced topics:

▶ How to create object variables

▶ The early and late binding of variables

▶ How to create new instances of existing objects

THE CHARACTERISTICS OF OBJECTS

When you program with Visual Basic, you are actually programming objects. The ActiveX controls you place on a Form are objects, and programming in Visual Basic consists of manipulating their properties and calling their methods. All the action takes place in the events of the objects, which are raised when certain conditions are met. *Objects* are units of code and data, which can be used as black boxes. Developers don't need to know how each object is implemented. All they need to know is

▶ Which properties the object exposes

▶ Which methods the object provides

▶ Which events the object can raise

Properties and methods constitute the object's interface. This isn't a graphical interface, and it doesn't have visual elements; nevertheless, it's an interface. It stands between you and the object, as you can't access the object's code or data directly.

For example, you can add the functionality of a text editor on your application's user interface by placing a TextBox control on the Form and setting its basic properties through the Properties window (whether the TextBox can display multiple lines of text, the font to use, and so on). In your code, you can program how the TextBox reacts to user actions by providing a subroutine (handler) to the events to which it must react. The properties, methods, and events of the TextBox constitute its interface, and you can bring the functionality of this control to your application, without knowing anything about the code that implements the control. Figure 4.1 shows how this works.

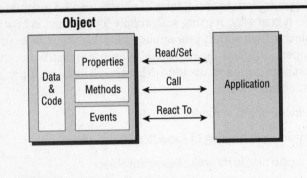

Setting a Property
Text1.ForeColor = RGB(0, 255, 255)

Reading a Property
Comments = Text1.Text

Calling a Method
Text1.SetFocus

Reacting to Events
Private Sub Text1_KeyDown(KeyCode, Shift)
If KeyCode = vbKeyF5 Then
    Text1.SelText = Date
End If
End Sub

FIGURE 4.1: Applications communicate with objects through the properties and methods they expose and the events they raise.

The Change event is raised when the user changes the contents of the control. As a developer, you don't have to monitor the mouse or the keyboard to find out when the text changes. The TextBox control itself will notify your program through an event, and all you have to do is provide the code to react to this event. If you don't provide an event handler for the Change event, the control won't react when the text is changed (it will simply accept the changes because that is its default reaction to keyboard events).

Finally, the TextBox control provides a few methods that you can call from within your code to manipulate the control. The SetFocus method lets you move the focus to a TextBox control from anywhere in your code and make it the active control. The Refresh method refreshes the control's contents. The TextBox control is in effect an object, which you can manipulate at a high level. You don't have access to its code, and you can neither enhance its operation nor break it. Actually, you can enhance its default operation by programming certain events, but still you don't have to touch its code.

For example, you can capture certain keystrokes and react differently to them. You can think of the TextBox control as an application that exposes a user interface, which consists of properties, methods, and events. Just as users of your application can control it through its user interface, you can only control the objects of your application through the members of the interface they expose.

NOTE

Restricting access to the code of a control (or any other object) isn't just a strict rule. It serves a practical purpose: It prohibits developers from breaking the control by "enhancing" it. Once users learn what they can do with a TextBox control, they can handle any TextBox, in any application. This consistency in the user interface is a fundamental characteristic of Windows, and objects are designed to enforce this consistency.

Hiding the inner workings of an object is called *encapsulation* or *abstraction*. The object encapsulates (abstracts) complicated operations, such as the breaking of multiple lines, the insertion of new characters, and so on. These are low-level details that you don't have to deal with. Instead, you can concentrate on your application, its user interface, and its operation. In this chapter, we are going to discuss the Visual Basic objects at large and the various techniques for working with them. Objects encapsulate complicated operations into a black box, which you can access through its user interface.

Encapsulation is the first buzzword in object-oriented programming; if you had to describe object-oriented programming with a single word, encapsulation would be it.

NOTE

Encapsulation is the ability to wrap code and data in a single unit that can be accessed by a well-defined interface. Developers can carry the functionality of an object to their applications and manipulate it through this interface, but they can't enhance or break the object because they can't alter the code or make it perform illegal operations.

Encapsulation is often referred to as abstraction because it abstracts complicated operations. If you have used the Data Access Objects, you understand how this abstraction works. Data in a database are stored in a file with the extension MDB. This file, however, has a complicated structure, and you never access it directly. Instead, you specify the records you're interested in and use the DAO (Data Access Objects) method to retrieve them. Information is presented in the form of rows and columns, which are easy to understand, visualize, and work with. The database file contains the data, index files, pointers, and all kinds of animals that you don't want to deal with. The DAO interface knows how to extract and/or save the desired information to the database.

COMPONENT SOFTWARE DEVELOPMENT

The concept of encapsulation leads to another important development in software design methodology: component software. What happens when you're designing applications with Visual Basic? You borrow functionality built into Windows itself and place it on your Forms by dropping controls from the Toolbox onto the Form. Your code is the glue that holds together these "pieces of functionality." And, considering what you can do with a few lines of VB code, the code you provide is really minimal. Most of the functionality of your application is concentrated in the controls.

NOTE
As operating systems and languages evolve, the code behind the applications will become less and less, but today you can't do much better than VB. It's the most compact of all major programming languages in the Windows environment.

Building applications with Visual Basic isn't unlike building a computer with components that you purchase separately. The sure way to build your dream computer is to purchase the components you need and connect them yourself. (Don't try this if you are not a computer whiz, but the best computers we've seen are custom built.) To build your own computer, you must purchase the components you need and put them together. Things may get a bit nasty when time comes to install drivers for SCSII interfaces and huge hard disks, CD-ROM units, or an inexpensive video capture card, but if you know what you're doing, you'll end up with a powerful computer. When a faster processor comes along, you can replace yours with the new processor. Power surge problem? A trip to the local computer store will take you longer than actually replacing the power supply.

The components you put together to build a custom computer encapsulate characteristics, just like the characteristics of programming objects. You don't have to know anything about power supplies, except for the input they require (110 volts, 220 volts, or switching) and the output they provide. All you have to do is make sure that the power supply provides the voltage required by the motherboard. Hard disk? Just find the one with the capacity and performance that suits your needs. They are all designed to fit in a standard bay, and if they don't, use a couple of brackets. These characteristics are the component's properties.

Hardware components have methods too, which are used by the system software. Methods such as GetThisCluster and WriteThatCluster allow the operating system (and the applications) to use the disk. The glue that makes all the components work together is the BIOS and the operating system. Fortunately, both come ready to use, and you don't have to do anything, short of setting a few parameters.

Here we are again. The operating system itself is another object, which encapsulates an incredible amount of functionality. You can adjust certain characteristics of the operating system with the applications provided in the Control Panel or even through the Registry. As a programmer, you know already that you can access the Registry's functions and use them from within your applications.

When components are designed according to a set of standards that allow them to work in tandem, they can be put together to build a larger system with minimum effort. As far as software development goes, one of the standards that allows components to interact is ActiveX (formerly OLE). Every component you build with Visual Basic supports ActiveX, and you don't have to know much about the ActiveX specifications. A software component designed according to ActiveX will work not only with Visual Basic applications, but also with any programming language, such as Visual C++. It will even work with HTML. You can actually embed ActiveX controls on a Web page by inserting a few lines of code in the page's HTML code and turn static documents into interactive applications.

To summarize, software objects have two characteristics:

1. They encapsulate certain functionality and allow developers to access their functionality through their interface.

2. They interact, which means that they can be placed together on a Form and cooperate.

What this means to you is that you can:

1. Select all the components you need for your application or develop some of them if you can't find off-the-shelf components for your application.

2. Put them together by manipulating them with VB code, using the interface components they provide (properties and methods).

This is how current software is developed, and you've been doing it with Visual Basic for many years.

Before we show you how to create your own objects, we are going to review how built-in objects are manipulated. In the rest of this chapter, we will review a few advanced topics, such as how to create new Forms and objects at run time and how to use type libraries, and then we'll introduce object-oriented programming with the built-in objects. Visual Basic provides a large number of objects, and most of you have been using them in your applications. If you plan to exploit object-oriented programming with Visual Basic, you should take a quick look at the examples in this chapter.

OBJECTS COME FROM CLASSES

The controls you see on the Toolbox are actually classes, from which the objects you use on your Forms are derived. The class is a *prototype*, and the object is an *instance* of this prototype. When you place a TextBox control on a Form, Visual Basic creates a new object based on the TextBox class. Because of the way we use ActiveX controls in building an application's user interface, this distinction between classes and objects isn't quite obvious. It will become clear when we build our own classes, and then we'll create new objects based on these classes.

The classical analogy between classes and objects is that of the cookie cutter and the cookies. All cookies cut with the same cutter are identical (at least as far as their shape and size are concerned). Each TextBox you place on your Form with the TextBox tool of the Toolbox is identical. They all come from the same class, or prototype. Once on the Form, each TextBox can be adjusted, and you can make them all look different. You can change their background and text colors, the font used for rendering the text, and so on. The basic functionality of each TextBox object, however, is the same, and it's determined by the TextBox Class.

CREATING OBJECT VARIABLES

To access the functionality of a Class, you must first create an object variable. Objects are Classes (prototypes) that can't be accessed directly. To access the functionality of an object, you must create a special variable that can store a reference to the object. In this section, we'll review the basics of creating object variables to manipulate objects.

Normally, the objects you place on a Form to create the user interface are manipulated from within code through their name (Text1, Command1, and so on). So why create variables to access them? As you will see shortly, on occasion you'll want to be able to access objects through a variable. For example, not all objects can be placed on a Form. If you have done any database programming with Visual Basic, you know that there are two approaches: the simple and limited, no-code approach (through the Data Control), and the serious approach (through the Data Access Objects). To access the objects exposed by the DAO—objects such as Recordsets, fields, and so on—you must create variables that represent these objects, just as you create variables to represent integer values or strings.

Declaring Object Variables

Object variables can be of two types:

- ▸ Generic, which can store all types of objects
- ▸ Specific, which can store objects of the same type only

Generic object variables are declared as Object type:

```
Dim myObject As Object
```

The *myObject* variable can store any type of object. The type Variant can also store objects, but this type requires more overhead than other types.

Finally, if you need an object variable to store references to controls, use the Control type:

```
Dim myControl As Control
```

The *myControl* object variable can store references to any control, but no other types of objects. If you know the type of object you want to store in an object variable, use this control's name in the declaration, as in the following statements:

```
Dim TBox As TextBox
Dim OKCancel As CommandButton
```

When an object variable is created, it contains nothing. To assign something to the object variable, you must use the Set statement to reference an existing object. The following statement allows you to use the *TBox* variable to access the Text1 TextBox:

```
Set TBox = Text1
```

Both *TBox* and *Text1* reference the same object, the Text1 TextBox (the Text1 object must already exist on the Form). You can change the bold attribute of the control with either of the following statements:

```
TBox.Bold = True
```

or

```
Text1.Bold = True
```

Both statements turn on the bold attribute of the text in the Text1 control.

The Set statement creates a reference to an existing object; it doesn't create a copy of the object. With a regular assignment operation, such as

```
amount = totalDue
```

a copy of the value of the *totalDue* variable is created, and it's accessed by the name amount. Because the two objects are distinct, changing one of the variables has no effect on the other.

NOTE

When you know the type of object you are going to store in an object variable, you should use a specific type in the Dim statement. This will make your program run faster and also simplify coding. For more details on the effect of object variable declarations, see the section "Early and Late Binding of Variables," later in this chapter.

If you don't need the object variable any longer, release it by setting it to Nothing:

```
Set myControl = Nothing
```

One common use for a Control type variable is to access variables on a different Form. If you need to access the Font property of a control on another Form frequently and if the required statement is

```
Form3!txtName.Font.Bold
```

you can simplify the code by creating an object variable that points to the control on another Form:

```
Dim TBox As Control
Set TBox = Form3!txtName
TBox.Font.Bold = True
```

You could also create an object variable that references the Font object directly:

```
Dim TBoxFont As Object
Set TBoxFont = Form3!txtName.Font
TBoxFont.Bold = True
```

The *New* Keyword

The object variables we created in the previous section refer to existing objects. To create a new instance of an existing object, you must use the *New* keyword, either in the Dim statement or in the Set statement. You can declare that an object variable create a new object with the statement

```
Dim myObject As New Object
```

and then specify the object with a Set statement:

```
Set myObject = anotherObject
```

Or, you can declare it and then assign a new instance of an object to it:

```
Dim myObject As Object
Set myObject = New anotherObject
```

NOTE
You can use the *New* keyword either when you declare the object variable (Visual Basic prepares an object for storing a new instance of the object) or when you assign an object instance to the variable with the Set statement.

With the *New* keyword, you specify that the object variable will not reference an existing instance of the control but will create a copy of the specified object. As you will see, you can create new instances of just about any object, including Forms, but you can't create new instances of controls. To create new controls at run time, you must use the Load statement, which is described in the section "Creating Controls at Run Time," later in this chapter.

Let's see now how these statements are used and what they can do for your application. In the following sections, we'll discuss a few of Visual Basic's built-in objects and see how and when object variables are used.

The Font Object

Objects represent programming entities, which can be as simple as fonts or as complicated as databases. In object-oriented programming terminology, objects encapsulate, or abstract, the entities they represent. The Font object represents the font used by a Form, by another object, or by the printer. As a programmer, you don't have to know how a font is stored in its file or how the object that uses the font reads this file. If you want the text on a Form to appear in bold, you must set the Bold property of the Font object to True:

```
Font.Bold=True
```

To print in bold on the printer, you can use this statement:

```
Printer.Font.Bold=True
```

To display text in bold on a Form, you can use this statement:

```
Form.Font.Bold=True
```

The Font object encapsulates (or abstracts) the font being used. Since both the Form and the Printer objects use a font, they provide a Font property, and you can change the attributes of the font by manipulating the Font object.

Creating a Font Object Variable

Let's create a Font object variable and make it represent the font of a specific control. You must declare an object variable that represents a font with the Font type. The variable *thisFont*, which is declared with this statement,

```
Dim thisFont As StdFont
```

is a Font object variable. You can use this variable to create a new Font property for a Form. This statement

```
Set thisFont = Form1.Font
```

makes the *thisFont* variable refer to the Font property of Form1. To change the characteristics of the font being used to render the text on the Form1 Form, you can use statements that manipulate the variable *thisFont*, such as the following:

```
thisFont.Name = "Comic Sans MS"
thisFont.Size = 12
thisFont.Bold = True
thisFont.Italic = False
```

Notice the use of the Set statement. When you want to make an object variable refer to an existing object of the same type, you must use the Set statement. The Set statement tells Visual Basic to create an object that refers to the Font property of Form1.

You can also create a new Font object, with the following declaration:

```
Dim thisFont As New StdFont
```

This object variable refers to a new Font object. You can set its properties with statements such as the following:

```
thisFont.Name = "Courier"
thisFont.Size = 10
thisFont.Bold = False
thisFont.Italic = False
```

At this point, you can assign the *thisFont* object variable to the Font property of an existing object. The statement

```
Form1.Font = thisFont
```

will cause the text on Form1 to be rendered in regular Courier typeface, at 10 points.

The FontObject Project

The FontObject project demonstrates the two distinct methods of using object variables.

NOTE

You'll find the FontObject project, along with the other projects in this chapter, at the Sybex Web site (www.sybex.com). Once there, go to the Catalog page and enter **2469** (the first four digits of the last five in the book's ISBN) into the search engine. Follow the link for this book that comes up, and then click the Downloads button, which will take you to a list of files organized by chapter.

The main Form of the project, shown in Figure 4.2, contains two Label controls. The top label's font is Verdana 14 point, and the second label has the default font (MS Serif) at 10 points. Clicking the Manipulate Font button changes the attributes of the font of the top label by manipulating its Font property.

NOTE

Load the FontObject project to see how object variables can be used to access existing fonts or represent new fonts.

FIGURE 4.2: The FontObject project, after clicking the Create Font button, which manipulates the bottom Label's Font property

The Manipulate Font button manipulates the font of the first Label control through an object variable. Code 4.1 shows the code behind the Manipulate Font button.

Code 4.1   The Manipulate Font Button

```
Private Sub Command1_Click()
Dim thisFont As StdFont

' Get original font,
' set its attributes
  thisFont.Bold = True
  thisFont.Italic = True
' and size
  thisFont.Size = 1.5 * thisFont.Size
' Clear object variable
  Set thisFont = Nothing

End Sub
```

The last statement in this subroutine releases the object variable when it's no longer needed by setting it to Nothing. The *Nothing* keyword is not equivalent to setting a string to an empty string or a numeric variable to zero. It releases the object variable *thisFont* and returns the resources allocated to the object variable when it was created.

TIP

It's solid programming practice to release any object variable when it's no longer needed.

This subroutine starts by assigning the Font property of the Label1 control to the object variable *thisFont*. It then manipulates the font of the Label control by setting the attributes of the *thisFont* variable. As each statement is executed, the appearance of the font on the Label control changes. You don't need a statement that will assign the new settings of the thisFont property to the Font object of the Label control because the variable *thisFont* and the property Label1.Font refer to the same object. If you want, you can single step through the code (by pressing F8) to see the effect of each statement on the appearance of the text on the control.

The Create Font button (see Code 4.2) modifies the font of the lower label. It starts by creating a new Font object, initializes it to the value of the Font property of the first label, changes a few attributes, and then assigns the new Font object to the Font property of the second Label control.

Code 4.2   The Create Font Button

```
Private Sub Command2_Click()
Dim thisFont As New StdFont

' Use Name and Size properties of the original font
' The Bold and Italic attributes are not inherited
  thisFont.Name = Label1.FontName
  thisFont.Size = 1.5 * Label1.FontSize
  thisFont.Underline = True
  Set Label2.Font = thisFont
  Set thisFont = Nothing

End Sub
```

The object variable *thisFont* is created with the *New* keyword, when the variable is declared, and it doesn't refer to an existing object. Therefore, it can't affect the appearance of the text on the Label control, unless you specifically assign this object variable to the Font property of the Label control. If you single-step this application and click the Create Font button, nothing will change on the Form until the second to last statement is reached. This statement assigns the characteristics of the object variable to the label's Font property.

Again, you assign the *thisFont* object variable to the Font property of the Label control with the Set statement. Every time you assign an object to another, you must use the Set statement. Simple assignment statements such as the following don't work with objects:

```
Label2.Font = thisFont
```

SIMPLE TRICKS WITH DEFAULT PROPERTIES

If you attempt to assign the *thisFont* object variable to the Font property of the Label2 control without the Set statement, the text on the label won't change, and you won't get an error message either. What's going on?

The Font object, like all other objects, has a default property, which is the Name property. The statements

```
Label2.Font.Name = "Courier"
```

and

```
Label2.Font = "Courier"
```

are equivalent. So, the statement

```
Label2.Font = thisFont
```

is the same as the following one:

```
Label2.Font.Name = thisFont
```

If *thisFont* were a string variable, Visual Basic would set the font's name to another typeface. Because *thisFont* doesn't contain a string, the last statement assigns the default font name (which is MS Sans Serif) to the Font property of the Label control.

The Screen and Printer Objects

Two useful built-in objects are the Screen and Printer objects, which represent the monitor and the current printer. You can use these objects to find out the properties of the monitor (its resolution, the fonts it can display, and so on) and of the printer. The Screen object has a Fonts property, which returns the names of the fonts that can be displayed on the screen (they are not necessarily the same as the fonts that can be used on the Printer object, which also supports the same property). If you had to display the names of the fonts in a ListBox control, you'd use a loop like this one:

```
For i = 0 To Screen.FontCount - 1
   List1.AddItem Screen.Fonts(i)
Next i
```

The Printer object is quite similar and supports many of the same properties and methods. The Screen and Printer objects demonstrate what we call encapsulation, or abstraction. As a developer, you don't have to know how the Printer and Screen objects really work. All you care about is that both objects support the Font property. The implementation details are hidden from the developer, who's free to focus on their application and not on the specifics of the various display adapters or printer models.

This is what abstraction is all about: the ability to tell an object to do something or the ability to change a characteristic of an object without having to know how each specific object carries out its operation. The ScreenPrinterObjects project, discussed later in this chapter, demonstrates how you can simplify your code by exploiting the methods that are common to these two objects.

FORMS ARE CLASSES

Forms are Classes that can be created with the Dim statement, and you can control them from within your code. Visual Basic provides four methods for manipulating Forms:

Load loads a new Form in memory but doesn't show it.

Show displays a Form that has already been loaded or loads and then displays a new Form.

Unload hides a loaded Form and unloads it from memory.

Hide hides a Form but doesn't unload it from memory.

These methods work on Forms that have already been designed and that exist in the current project. It is also possible to create new Forms at run time and display them as part of the application's user interface with the following statement:

```
Dim myForm As Form
```

Part I

This statement creates a new Form object variable, which you can use in your code to reference an existing Form or to create a new Form. For example, you can set the *myForm* variable to an existing Form,

```
Set myForm = Form1
```

or to a new instance of the Form1 object:

```
Set myForm = New Form1
```

Form1 is an existing Form, but *myForm* is a new instance of Form1 and can be loaded and displayed with the statement

```
myForm.Show
```

The Forms Project

If you need one or more special Forms in your application, you can design a prototype and then use it in your application. This prototype can have its own properties and methods and can even raise custom events.

The Forms project is a simple example of a special Form that displays a gradient on its background.

We will design a Form with a custom method, the BackGradient method, which accepts a single argument, the direction of the gradient. The gradient's direction can be horizontal or vertical.

You can call it as follows:

```
myForm.BackGradient(gradient)
```

The value of gradient can be:

- ▶ 0 (no gradient)
- ▶ 1 (horizontal gradient)
- ▶ 2 (vertical gradient)

To design a Form with the BackGradient method, start a new project and add a new Form to it. Name the new Form GradForm, and enter the code in Code 4.3 in the Form's Code window.

Code 4.3   Drawing Gradients

```
Enum Gradients
  None = 0
  Horizontal = 1
  Vertical = 2
End Enum
```

```
Public Sub BackGradient(GradientDirection As Integer)

  If GradientDirection = None Then
    Me.BackColor = RGB(128, 128, 128)
    mGradient = None
    Exit Sub
  End If
  If GradientDirection = Horizontal Then
    For i = 0 To Me.ScaleWidth - 1
      GrComponent = Int(i * 255 / Me.ScaleWidth)
      RGBColor = RGB(GrComponent, GrComponent, GrComponent)
      Me.Line (i, 0)-(i, Me.ScaleHeight - 1), RGBColor
      GrComponent = GrComponent + Me.ScaleWidth / 255
    Next
    mGradient = Horizontal
  End If

  If GradientDirection = Vertical Then
    For i = 0 To Me.ScaleHeight - 1
      GrComponent = i * 255 / Me.ScaleHeight
      RGBColor = RGB(GrComponent, GrComponent, GrComponent)
      Me.Line (0, i)-(Me.ScaleWidth - 1, i), RGBColor
      GrComponent = GrComponent + GradForm.ScaleHeight / 255
    Next
    mGradient = Vertical
  End If

End Sub
```

The Enum type at the beginning of the code allows us to refer to the gradient's direction with a descriptive name (for instance, None, Horizontal, or Vertical) instead of with a number. The BackGradient() subroutine is declared as public, which makes it a method of the Form. (In other words, other procedures outside the Form can call the BackGradient subroutine.) To create a new instance of this Form from within another Form's code, you must first create an object variable such as the following:

```
Dim myForm As GradForm
Set myForm = New GradForm
```

After you create the *myForm* instance of the GradForm Class, you can display it with the following statement:

```
myForm.Show
```

You can then access its BackGradient method as follows:

```
myForm.BackGradient 1
```

To use the GradForm, create a new Form, the MainForm, and make it the project's Startup object. The MainForm for the Forms project is shown in Figure 4.3. This Form contains a TextBox control and three buttons, which show one instance of the GradForm each. Each time you click one of these buttons, the gradient on the corresponding Form changes (from horizontal to vertical and back).

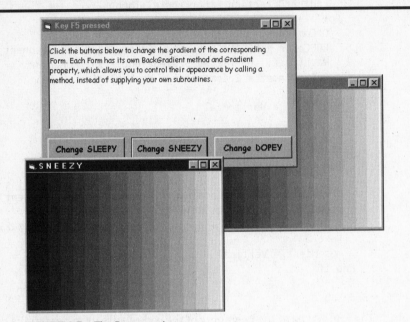

FIGURE 4.3: The Forms project

The instances of the GradForm are created with object variables, which are declared in the Main form as follows:

```
Dim Sleepy As GradForm
Dim Sneezy As GradForm
Dim Dopey As GradForm
```

Any part of the application can access these variables. When the main Form is loaded, it executes Code 4.4.

Code 4.4   Loading the Custom Forms

```
Private Sub Form_Load()

Set Sleepy = New GradForm
Load Sleepy
```

```
With Sleepy
   .Top = 2000: .Left = 4000
   .Caption = "S L E E P Y"
End With
Set Sneezy = New GradForm
Load Sneezy
With Sneezy
   .Top = 3000: .Left = 7000
   .Caption = "S N E E Z Y"
End With
Set Dopey = New GradForm
Load Dopey
With Dopey
   .Top = 3000: .Left = 2000
   .Caption = "D O P E Y"
End With
End Sub
```

Code 4.5 creates three new instances of the GradForm object and places them on the monitor at different locations. The code behind each button changes the gradient's direction on the corresponding Form and shows it, just in case it was covered by another Form.

Code 4.5   The Change Sleepy Button

```
Private Sub bttnSleepy_Click()
   Sleepy.BackGradient (Sleepy.Gradient Mod 2) + 1
   Sleepy.Show
End Sub
```

Forms with Events

In addition to custom methods, Form Classes can raise custom events. Let's say you want to capture certain keystrokes and react to each one differently. To add a new event to the Form, you declare the event's name at the beginning of the code and then use the RaiseEvent statement to raise the custom event from within the new Form:

```
Event SpecialKey(KeyCode As Integer, Shift As Integer)

Private Sub Form_KeyUp(KeyCode As Integer, Shift As Integer)
   If KeyCode >= vbKeyF1 Or KeyCode <= vbKeyF16 Then
     RaiseEvent SpecialKey(KeyCode, Shift)
   End If
End Sub
```

The SpecialKey event is raised from within the Form's KeyUp event, which examines the code of the key pressed. If it corresponds to a function key, it raises the SpecialKey event and lets the main Form of the application handle the keypress.

Custom events introduce a slight complexity to the project. To declare a Form that raises events, you use the *WithEvents* keyword in the Dim statement, as follows:

```
Dim WithEvents myForm As GradForm
```

The keyword *WithEvents* tells Visual Basic to raise the events that occur on the object so that you can handle them from within your code. If you omit this keyword, Visual Basic will create a new Form based on the GradForm Class, but it will not report the events to the object variable that represents the new Form. Now you can create a new instance of the GradForm Form with the statements:

```
Set myForm = New GradForm
myForm.Show
```

To process the special keystrokes, you provide an event handler for the SpecialKey event of the custom Form. Follow these steps:

1. Open the Objects drop-down list in the main Form's Code window and select the Sleepy object.

2. In the Events drop-down list, you will see the name of the custom event, SpecialKey. Select it and enter the following code in the event's handler:

```
Private Sub Sleepy_SpecialKey(KeyCode As Integer, _
Shift As Integer)
    Me.Caption = "Key F" & Chr(KeyCode - 63) & " pressed"
End Sub
```

3. Now run the project, display the Sleepy Form by clicking the Change Sleepy button, and press a function key.

The main Form's caption displays the key that was pressed on the Sleepy Form. This arrangement allows you to handle certain events of the GradForm's instances from within the main Form's code. The GradForm object will handle other keystrokes or mouse events and the main Form will never know.

EVENTS BELONG TO CLASSES, NOT TO OBJECTS

If you open the Code window of the GradForm Form, you will see that it doesn't have a SpecialKey event, and you can't program this event for the GradForm Form itself. The SpecialKey event can be raised by the instances of the GradForm you created in your code. This is a strange behavior, but there's a simple explanation.

The GradForm was created when you added it to the project by choosing Project ➤ Add Form. At that point, the Form didn't have the SpecialKey event, so its name didn't appear in the Events drop-down list of the Form's Code window.

CREATING CONTROLS AT RUN TIME

You have seen how to create object variables that represent existing, or new, objects, such as Forms and fonts. You might expect that it's possible to use the *New* keyword to create controls at run time, similar to the way that you create Forms. This is not the case, however. If you declare an object variable as

```
Dim myButton As CommandButton
```

you can then set it to reference an existing command button, but you can't create a new instance of the CommandButton Class. The statement

```
Set myButton = New Command1
```

will cause a run-time error. You can still use a statement like the following one:

```
Set myButton = Command1
```

This creates a reference to the Command1 button on the Form. If you change the Caption property of the myButton object, you are in effect changing the Caption of the Command1 object.

To create new instances of controls and manipulate them from within your code, you use control arrays. Declaring a Control object variable with the *New* keyword isn't going to do the trick. Creating new instances of ActiveX controls at run time is the topic of the next section.

Control Arrays to the Rescue

To create multiple instances of new controls at run time, you use a control array. Do you notice that each time you are about to paste a control you have previously copied from a Form, Visual Basic asks whether you want to create a control array? Every time you place multiple instances of the same control on a Form, you have the option of creating an array of controls. All the elements of the array share the same name, and they are distinguished from one another with the help of the Index property.

If you have three command buttons on a Form, you can create the array ThreeButtons. The first Command button is the ThreeButtons(0), the second one is the ThreeButtons(1), and the last one is the Three-Buttons(2). The Index property of the first element in the array need not be zero. You can start indexing the array at any value.

NOTE

The simplest way to create a control array at design time is to copy an existing control and paste it on the same Form. The first time, Visual Basic asks whether you want to create a control array. After that, every time you paste the same control or create a new one with the same name, it is appended to the existing control array. At run time, you must use the Load method, which is explained next.

You use control arrays when two or more controls have similar code that can be simplified with the use of the Index property. If you have the array ThreeButtons with the three elements, you need not provide three different handlers for each Command button's Click event. All the elements of the control array share common event handlers. The Click event handler for an array of controls is

```
Private Sub ThreeButtons_Click(Index As Integer)
End Sub
```

In your code, you can distinguish the various controls based on their index. When the first Command button is clicked, the *Index* argument has the value 0, and so on. For example, here is an event handler that changes the caption of the button that was clicked:

```
Private Sub ThreeButtons_Click(Index As Integer)
   ThreeButtons(Index).Caption = "I was clicked!"
End Sub
```

Let's return now to the topic of creating new controls at run time. First, you must create the control you want to repeat and assign the value zero to its Index property. It's also customary to make this control invisible. To create another instance of this control, use the Load method, with a new index value. Assuming that you have created an invisible Command button on the Form with Name = CButton and Index = 0, the following statement will create three instances of this control and display them on the Form:

```
For i = 1 to 3
    Load CButton(i)
    CButton(i).Visible = True
Next
```

When a new control is created at run time, it is initially invisible. That's why you must also set its Visible property.

The CtrlLoad Project

The CtrlLoad project demonstrates how to create new controls using index arrays by creating a Form that can accept a variable number of data points.

When you first run the application, you will see the Form shown in Figure 4.4. Click the New Data Set button, and you'll be prompted to enter the number of data points in the new set. Enter a small number, such as 10, and the Form will be stretched vertically and filled with as many TextBox controls as needed for the entry of the data values. If you specify six data values, the Form of the CtrlLoad application will look like the one in Figure 4.5.

FIGURE 4.4:   The initial state of the CtrlLoad application's main Form

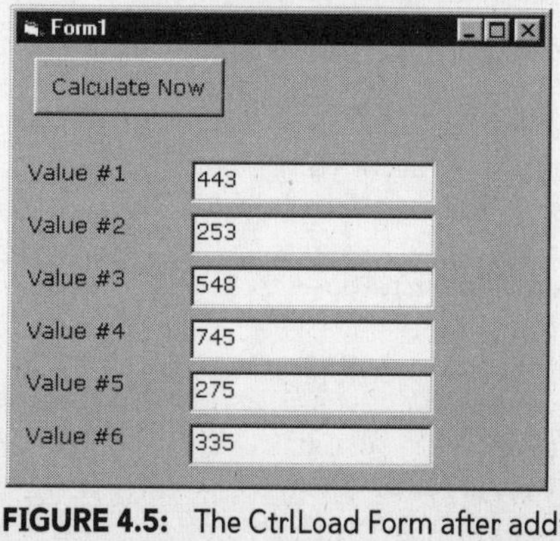

FIGURE 4.5:   The CtrlLoad Form after adding six TextBox controls at run time

To implement the Form of the CtrlLoad project, start a new project and place the following items on the Form:

- ▶ A Command button
- ▶ A Label
- ▶ A TextBox control

Because the Label and TextBox controls should be invisible when the application starts, set their Visible property to False. At run time, we want to be able to add new instances of these controls on the Form by creating new elements in the control array. The two controls placed on the Form are the first elements in the control array, and you must set their Index property to zero. At run time, you'll be able to add new elements to the array with the Load command and a new index value.

Clicking the New Data Set button executes the code in Code 4.6.

Code 4.6   Adding Controls on a Form at Run Time

```
Private Sub Command1_Click()
Dim sum As Double, avg As Double

    If Command1.Caption = "New Data Set" Then
    dataCount = InputBox("How many data values?")
    If Not IsNumeric(Count) Then
      MsgBox "please enter a valid numeric value"
      Exit Sub
    End If
    For i = 1 To dataCount
      Load Label1(i)
      Load Text1(i)
      Label1(i).Top = Label1(i - 1).Top + 1.25 * _
Label1(i).Height
      Text1(i).Top = Text1(i - 1).Top + 1.25 * _
Text1(i).Height
      Label1(i).Visible = True
      Label1(i).Caption = "Value #" & i
      Text1(i).Visible = True
    Next
    Me.Height = Text1(dataCount).Top + 2.5 * _
Text1(dataCount).Height
    Command1.Caption = "Calculate Now"
  Else
    For i = 1 To dataCount
      If IsNumeric(Text1(i).Text) Then
```

```
            sum = sum + Text1(i).Text
        End If
    Next
    avg = sum / dataCount
    MsgBox "The average is " & avg
    For i = 1 To dataCount
        Unload Text1(i)
        Unload Label1(i)
    Next
    Me.Height = 2000
    Command1.Caption = "New Data Set"
  End If

End Sub
```

This code first prompts the user for the number of data points in the data set and then creates that many instances of the Label1 and Text1 controls. It positions each new instance on the Form with respect to the previous instance (the placement of the elements Label1(0) and Text1(0) determines the appearance of the Form). In addition to creating and placing the necessary controls for entering data on the Form, the Command button changes its Caption to Calculate Now. Clicking the Calculate Now button calculates the average of the values entered and removes the controls from the Form with the Unload statement.

NOTE

When new elements are added to a control array, their Visible property is False, and you must manipulate this property from within your code to make them visible. In the CtrlLoad project, the new elements will be invisible anyway, because the initial elements of the array are invisible, but you should always set the Visible property of new control instances to True from within your code.

MANIPULATING CONTROLS AT RUN TIME

Visual Basic provides a few objects and statements for the manipulation of controls at run time. Let's start with the Control object. We mentioned that, although you can't create new controls at run time by declaring object variables, these variables are frequently used in programming controls.

The Control type represents any control on a Form, and you can create variables of Control type with statements such as

```
Dim aControl As Control
```

and then assign instances of other controls to the *aControl* variables with the Set statement

```
Set aControl = Text1
```

and perhaps later in the code

```
Set aControl = Command1
```

You can use the *aControl* object to manipulate the properties of the Command1 control. For example, you can change the Command button's Caption property with a statement such as:

```
aControl.Caption = "Click me!"
```

You may be wondering, why use object variables to manipulate controls and the control names? In some situations, you don't have direct access to a control. Instead, you can access only a variable that represents the control. For example, in programming drag-and-drop operations, you don't have access to the control being dropped. As you will see in the next section, the DragDrop event subroutine passes a reference to the control that was dropped on another control and not to the control itself. To program the DragDrop event, you must know how to handle object variables that represent controls.

Control Types

Sometimes, you need to know the type of control an object variable represents from within your code. An object variable can store references to any type of control, which is helpful should you need to determine the type of control being referenced within your code. To find out the type of the control referenced by an object variable, use the TypeOf statement, as in the following:

```
If TypeOf aControl Is TextBox Then
```

The keyword *TypeOf* is followed by the name of the object variable whose type you are seeking, followed by the keyword *Is*, which is followed by the name of a control's Class. TypeOf is not a function that returns the type of the variable; instead it compares the type of the control to a specific control type and returns a True/False value, which can be used in an If structure, like the one shown here. The TypeOf statement is used frequently in programming drag-and-drop operations to find out the type of the control that was dropped on another control. The following project provides a simple example.

The DragDrop Project

The DragDrop project demonstrates the use of the TypeOf...Is statement with drag-and-drop operations.

The Form shown in Figure 4.6 contains a TextBox, a Label, and a Picture-Box control. The contents of the first two controls can be dragged, so you must set their DragMode property to True. The PictureBox control can't be dragged, but other objects can be dropped on it. All controls can react to the drop of another control, which means you must provide a DragDrop handler for each control.

First, we must decide what happens when a control is dropped on another one. When the TextBox and Label control are dropped on each other, the source's text (Text or Caption property) is copied to the target control. When either control is dropped on the PictureBox control, it is assumed that the text is the path name of an image file, which must be displayed on the control. If the text doesn't correspond to an image file or if, for any reason, the image can't be displayed, an error message is displayed on the PictureBox control, as shown in Figure 4.7.

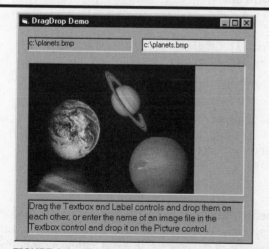

FIGURE 4.6: The DragDrop project demonstrates the use of the TypeOf...Is statement in drag-and-drop operations.

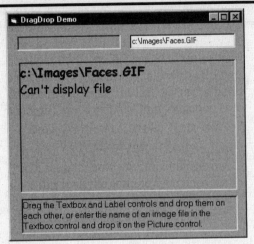

FIGURE 4.7: When the string dropped onto the PictureBox control isn't a valid image file name, an error message is displayed.

Let's start with the DragDrop events of the TextBox and Label controls (see Code 4.7), which are simpler.

Code 4.7   The DragDrop Events of the TextBox and Label Controls

```
Private Sub Text1_DragDrop(Source As Control, X As Single, _
Y As Single)
  If TypeOf Source Is Label Then
    Text1.Text = Label1.Caption
  End If
End Sub

Private Sub Label1_DragDrop(Source As Control, X As Single, _
Y As Single)
  If TypeOf Source Is TextBox Then
    Label1.Caption = Source.Text
  End If
End Sub
```

The *Source* argument represents the control being dropped, and we can use it to access any of the properties of this control. However, we must first examine the type of the control, to avoid calling a property name not supported by the Source control.

The DragDrop event handler of the PictureBox control is quite similar, but instead of copying the Text or Caption property, it attempts to display the specified file. See Code 4.8.

Code 4.8   Handling the DragDrop Event with Object Variables

```
Private Sub Picture1_DragDrop(Source As Control, X As _
Single, Y As Single)
Dim imgName
  If TypeOf Source Is TextBox Then
    imgName = Source.Text
  Else
    imgName = Source.Caption
  End If
On Error GoTo NOIMAGE
  Picture1.Picture = LoadPicture(imgName)
  Exit Sub

NOIMAGE:
  Picture1.Cls
  Picture1.Font.Bold = True
  Picture1.Print imgName
  Picture1.Font.Bold = False
  Picture1.Print "Can't display file"
End Sub
```

In addition to the event handlers shown here, the DragDrop project contains the DragOver handler for the various controls, which change the pointer's shape to indicate whether the current control can accept the control being dragged.

The Controls Collection

It is also possible to access from within your code all the controls on a Form through the Controls collection. Each element of the Controls Collection is a control. We'll discuss collections in detail in the section "Collections" later in this chapter, but we'll discuss here how you can use the Controls object to access the controls on the current Form.

The Controls object need not be initialized. It's built in to Visual Basic, and you can access it directly. The Count property of the Controls collection returns the number of controls it contains. To scan its elements, you can set up a For...Next loop such as the following one:

```
For i = 0 To Controls.Count - 1
  { process element Controls(i) }
Next
```

There is, however, a better structure for scanning the elements of a Collection, namely the For Each statement, whose syntax is

```
For Each iControl In Controls
{ process element iControl }
Next
```

The *iControl* object variable is declared as Control type. At each iteration of the loop, the *iControl* variable is automatically assigned the next control in the Collection. If this control has a `Caption` property, you can access it with the expression iControl.Caption.

Since all controls have a `Name` property, you can safely use the expression iControl.Name. Not all properties, however, apply to all controls, and you should use the TypeOf statement to find out whether the current control supports a property. For example, you can change the `Text` property of all TextBox controls or the `Caption` property of all Label controls with a loop such as the following:

```
For Each iControl In Controls
  If TypeOf iControl Is TextBox Then
    iControl.Text = "Text Changed"
  Else If TypeOf iControl Is Label Then
    iControl.Caption = "Caption Changed"
  End If
Next
```

The Controls Project

The Controls project demonstrates how to use the Controls Collection and object variables to manipulate the controls on a Form from within your code.

The main Form of the application, shown in Figure 4.8, contains two TextBox controls and a Label control, whose colors change when the Command button is clicked.

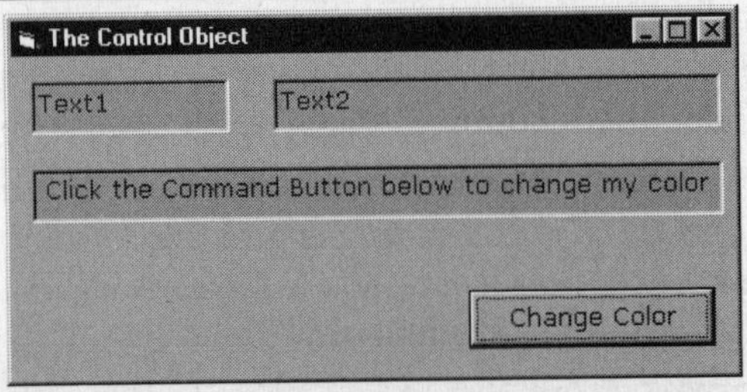

FIGURE 4.8:   The Controls application demonstrates the use of the Controls Collection.

The code behind the Command button (Change Color) scans each element of the Controls Collection and examines its type (see Code 4.9). If it's a TextBox control, it sets the control's background color to yellow. The other elements in the Controls Collection are not processed.

Code 4.9 The Change Color Button

```
Private Sub Command1_Click()
Dim iControl As Control

For Each iControl In Controls
  If (TypeOf iControl Is TextBox) Or (TypeOf iControl Is
Label) Then
     iControl.BackColor = RGB(200, 200, 0)
     iControl.ForeColor = RGB(0, 0, 200)
  End If
Next
End Sub
```

An alternative approach is to use a For...Next loop to scan all the elements of the Collection:

```
For i = 0 To Controls.Count
  Set iControl = Controls(i)
  iControl.BackColor = RGB(200, 200, 0)
  iControl.ForeColor = RGB(0, 0, 200)
Next
```

EARLY AND LATE BINDING OF VARIABLES

In this section, we are going to discuss an important topic in programming with object variables: their binding. As you do with regular variables, you should declare object variables before they are used. The more Visual Basic knows about a variable's type, the more efficiently it will handle it. If you don't declare the variable, Visual Basic automatically creates a Variant, which is good for storing all types of data values, even objects. Because of their flexibility, Variants can't be processed as quickly. Visual Basic must convert them to the proper type before using them.

The same is true for object variables. For example, if Visual Basic knows in advance that a specific object variable will be used to store a reference to a Font object, it will allocate a structure where information about a Font object can be stored and recalled efficiently. If it doesn't know the type of the object variable, it must set up a structure that can accommodate any type of object and adjust the structure according to the object assigned to the variable at run time. In addition, it must execute quite a number of lines of code at run time, which is when an object is assigned to the object variable. For example, it can't request the value of the Text property unless it makes sure that the control represented by the variable is a TextBox control (or any other control that exposes a Text property). This additional code must execute each time your code attempts to access a member of a generic object variable; this certainly can't help your code run smoothly.

So far, we have seen two ways to declare object variables:

▸ As objects

▸ As a specific object type

When the type of the variable is known at design time, Visual Basic will not only protect you from mistakes (such as using nonexistent property names), but it will also display the properties and methods that apply to the specific object variable—if you have the Auto List Members feature turned on. Most of the mistakes in your code will be caught by the editor itself as you enter the code or by the compiler before you execute the program. This is called *early binding*. The compiler knows the type of variable and will not compile lines that reference nonexistent properties or methods.

For example, if you declare an object variable as

```
Dim myBox As TextBox
```

and then attempt to set its Caption property with a statement such as

```
myBox.Caption = "This is a special box"
```

you will get an error message when you compile the application. This error simply can't go undetected. A statement that assigns a value to the *myBox* variable's Text property will compile just fine.

When you declare an object variable as Object, it can be assigned any type of object. This is called *late binding*, because the compiler can't bind members to this variable. In addition, the editor cannot validate the property names you are using. If you declare an object variable with the following statement

```
Dim thisFontObject As Object
```

it can store any object. You can even store different objects in the same object variable at run time. When you declare a variable without a specific type, it's created the first time it's referenced, which is when you assign an object instance to it. That is also when the exact type of the variable becomes known.

To create an instance of the *thisFont* object variable, you should use a statement such as:

```
Set thisFontObject = Label2.Font
```

If you go back to the FontObject project and change the declaration of the *thisFont* object variable to

```
Dim thisFont As Object
```

the rest of the code will work just as well. However, the revised application is slower. When the Visual Basic compiler runs into a statement such as

```
thisFont.Name = Label1.FontName
```

it must generate additional statements, which find out whether the object supports the Name property. These statements must be executed at run time, and if the object doesn't support the Name property, a run-time error message is generated. Had the object variable been declared with a specific type, these statements would never be introduced. Any attempt to refer to a nonexistent property name, such as `thisFont.TypeFace`, would be caught at compile time.

The main advantage of declaring variables with a specific type is that Visual Basic knows at design (or compile) time whether the object represented by the variable supports a property or a method you call in your code and generates optimal executable code. If the object's type isn't known in advance, Visual Basic generates a lot of overhead code, which is executed at run time, making the program slower. In other words, it generates code to contact the object to find out whether it supports a specific property or method. Only when Visual Basic is sure that the object supports this member does it call the member. You can avoid this overhead by declaring object variables with a specific type.

This brings us to the second advantage of declaring variables with exact types: You can write applications that run better because many potential errors can be caught at design or compile time. These two methods of declaring variables are known as early binding (object variables of exact type) and late binding (generic object variables). When an object variable's type is known at compile time, the compiler produces shorter, faster executing code. Of course, a few object variable declarations won't make your code crawl, but when you're trying to squeeze every drop of performance out of your code, it's good to know all the tricks.

To get a feel for the difference that early and late binding can make in your code, let's revise the FontObject application. Let's repeat the code of the Manipulate Font button 10,000 times with a loop and measure the elapsed time (see Code 4.10).

Code 4.10   The Revised FontObject Project

```
Private Sub Command1_Click()
Dim thisFont As StdFont

StartTime = Timer
For i = 1 To 10000
' Get original font,
  Set thisFont = Label1.Font
' set its attributes
  thisFont.Bold = True
  thisFont.Italic = True
' and size
  thisFont.Size = 1.001 * thisFont.Size
' Clear object variable
  Set thisFont = Nothing
Next
Debug.Print "10,000 repetition took : " & _
Format(Timer - StartTime, "#.00") & " seconds"
End Sub
```

On a Pentium 75, the elapsed time was 5.77 seconds. Now change the declaration of the *thisFont* object variable to

```
Dim thisFont As Object
```

and run it again. With late binding, the 10,000 iterations take 7.91 seconds. Granted, not many applications create and release object variables 10,000 times at run time, but this difference would increase with more complicated objects, such as Database objects.

Notice that we changed the line

```
thisFont.Size = 1.5 * Label1.FontSize
```

to

```
thisFont.Size = 1.0 * thisFont.Size
```

The factor 1.5 would result in an overflow after a small number of iterations.

The effect of early binding on speed can be even more dramatic if the object variable has properties that are also objects. Here's an example. An add-in is an extension to the Visual Basic integrated development environment (IDE) that manipulates the various objects of the IDE, such as the controls and code of a Form. The Collection VBProjects can have multiple components (Forms, Modules, and so on). A Form may contain multiple controls, which are accessed through the Controls Collection.

Expressions such as

```
thisForm.VBControls.Item(i).Properties("Index")
```

are common in developing add-ins. This expression represents a control on a specific Form (the variable *i* goes from 1 to the total number of controls on the Form). If Visual Basic doesn't know the exact type of the object variable *thisForm*, it generates code that will find out whether the object represented by the object variable supports the VBControls property. VBControls, in turn, is a collection. If Visual Basic doesn't know it, it will generate additional code to find out whether the *VBControls* object variable supports the Item property.

The expression up to the last dot represents a control. If Visual Basic doesn't have this information at compile time, it generates even more lines to make sure that the object represented by the expression *thisForm.VBControls.Item(i)* has a Properties property. And only if it does, will it attempt to read the value of the Index property. As you can see, expressions involving object variables can get quite messy, and the more Visual Basic knows about these variables, the better it can handle them—both at design time and at run time.

Dynamic Object Variables

Previously, we mentioned the significant advantages of early binding:

- Code is shorter.
- Code executes faster.
- There are fewer run-time errors.

The run-time errors we are talking about are actually program errors and can't be corrected at run time, as opposed to user errors or unusual conditions, which can be corrected at run time. For example, if your code detects an error with the printer or an invalid data item, it can prompt the user to check the printer connection or re-enter some data. If your code calls a property that a specific object doesn't support, there's nothing to be done about it. A statement that calls a nonexistent property, such as the following,

```
thisFont.Typeface
```

will produce a run-time error that must be caught at design (or compile) time; error trapping isn't going to help you at all. Distributing a program that contains this statement is simply going to embarrass you. Yet, you can avoid this type of error easily by declaring the *thisFont* object variable with an exact type.

This doesn't mean that generic object variables are useless. Because they can be assigned all types of objects at run time, these variables are *dynamic*. You must simply make sure that you don't attempt to access any nonexistent properties or methods.

The ScreenPrinterObjects Project

Let's look at an example of what you can do with late-bound variables. The ScreenPrinterObjects project demonstrates a common programming technique and shows the solution to a problem you may have already faced.

Most commercial applications generate output for the screen and the printer. You are already familiar with the methods that produce shapes and text on a Form or a PictureBox control. The same methods apply to the Printer object. The problem is how to redirect the program's output to the screen or the printer. Should you use statements such as

```
If PrinterOutput Then
    Printer.Line (X, Y) - (X + 100, Y + 100)
Else
    Form1.Line (X, Y) - (X + 100, Y + 100)
End If
```

or is there a more elegant method?

There is indeed a more elegant method, and it uses an object variable to draw on. If the object variable represents a Form object, the output is sent to the screen. If it represents the Printer object, the output is sent to the current printer.

The ScreenPrinterObjects project draws a few simple shapes, as you see in Figure 4.9. The project's main Form contains two option buttons (with their `Style` property set to Graphical so that they look like buttons) that you can select to specify the output. You can then click the Draw Now button to produce the output.

FIGURE 4.9: The output of the ScreenPrinterObjects project can be redirected to the screen or the printer, depending on the status of the Option buttons.

The program starts by declaring an object variable, *OutputObject*, which is set to the Form1 object or the Printer object, depending on the status of the Option buttons:

```
Dim OutputObject As Object

If Option1 Then
    Set OutputObject = Form1
Else
    Set OutputObject = Printer
End If
```

You can then call the graphics methods, which are common to both objects, to produce the desired output. The sample shapes in Figure 4.9 were produced with the following lines:

```
OutputObject.DrawWidth = 2
OutputObject.ForeColor = RGB(255, 0, 0)
OutputObject.Circle (2000, 2000), 800
OutputObject.DrawWidth = 1
OutputObject.Line (1000, 1000)-(3000, 3000), , B
OutputObject.ForeColor = RGB(0, 0, 255)
OutputObject.CurrentX = 1500
OutputObject.CurrentY = 2400
OutputObject.Print "Graphics methods"
```

Error-Trapping Considerations

The program also contains an error trap, intended for systems without a printer. If you attempt to direct the output to the printer and there's any problem with your printer, the program won't crash.

We were careful not to include any lines that call properties or methods that don't apply to both objects. What if you wanted to change the background color of the Form before printing on it? The statement

```
OutputObject.BackColor = RGB(230, 230, 0)
```

will work while the *OutputObject* variable refers to the Form1 object, but it will produce a run-time error when the object it refers to is the Printer object. To make sure that the code won't fail, regardless of the current output object, use an If structure, such as the following:

```
If TypeOf OutputObject Is Form Then
    OutputObject.BackColor = RGB(230, 230, 0)
End If
```

Late-bound object variables may have disadvantages over early-bound ones, but if you need to manipulate the object variables dynamically from within your code, you must declare them as late bound (without an exact type).

USING THE OBJECT BROWSER

Where do all these objects come from, and how do you know, at any point, which objects are available and the properties and methods they provide? Each object, whether it's built into Visual Basic or you build it, has a type library. A *type library* is a catalog of the object's properties, methods, and events, which you can consult at any time. Each object, including your custom ActiveX controls and ActiveX components (in EXE or DLL format) has a type library, which can be displayed in the Object Browser. Fortunately, you don't have to take any special action in order to display your component's members. The Object Browser will pick up their definitions from the executable file (you must provide their descriptions, however). You will find more information on this in the following two chapters.

The type libraries of the available objects are displayed in the Object Browser, which is shown in Figure 4.10. We'll demonstrate how to use the Object Browser by building a simple application that manipulates a few of the objects exposed by the Database object. As you will see, you don't have to know every object and every property of these objects in order to use them. A basic understanding of databases and their structure is all you need to program them with the help of the Object Browser.

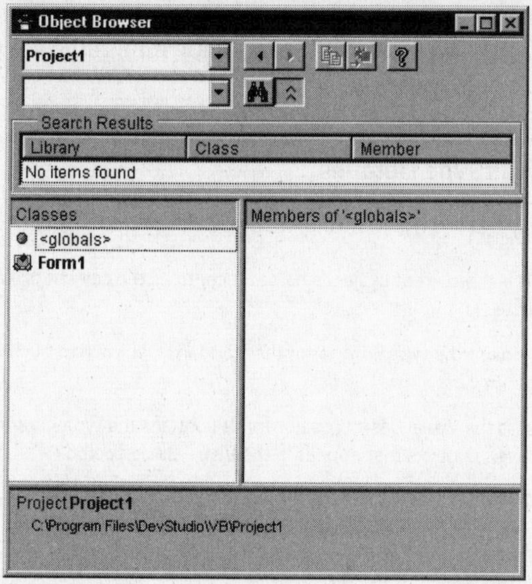

FIGURE 4.10: The Object Browser for a simple VB project

The Object Browser isn't a substitute for the help files or other reference material, but even experienced programmers can't possibly remember the structure of complicated objects such as the Database object. The Object Browser simplifies the task of programming database applications with the Database object.

The Purpose and Structure of the Object Browser

Every class available within Visual Basic or within other applications that expose objects is described in the Object Browser. The Object Browser is an application that gets these descriptions from the corresponding EXE or DLL files and displays them in an easy-to-visualize and navigate fashion. Objects can be as simple as a Form or as complex as an application such as Microsoft Excel or Microsoft Word. Let's explore the Object Browser by starting with a simple project.

Start a new project and click the Object Browser button, or choose View ➣ Object Browser (or simply press F2) to open the Object Browser.

At the top of the Object Browser window you see two drop-down boxes. The first contains the available object libraries, from which you can select one. The second contains previous search arguments, which you can activate for new searches. For a new project (a project to which no special objects have been added), the Object Libraries shown in Table 4.1 are available.

TABLE 4.1: The Default Type Libraries

LIBRARY	DESCRIPTION
Project1	This is the current project's name. It contains the current project's classes.
Stdole	These are the type libraries of the standard OLE classes, such as the StdFont class.
VB	This is the Visual Basic type library. It contains the type libraries for the ActiveX controls that appear in the Visual Basic Toolbox.
VBA	This is the VBA type library.
VBRUN	This is the Visual Basic run-time library. It contains the classes that are available at run time only.

If you select Project1 in the Type Library drop-down box, you will see the only Class in the project, which is the main Form, Form1 (you know already that, unlike controls, Forms are Classes). In the Classes pane, along with the name of the Form, you will see the entry *globals*. If the project had global variables, their names would appear in the Members pane.

Select the Class Form1, and in the Classes pane you will see all the members of the Form1 class: the properties, methods, and events that the Form1 Form recognizes, as well as any event handlers or procedures you've written. Even the code you entered in the project becomes a member of the Form1 Class, because you can access the Form1 object through the functions and event handlers it provides.

TIP

The Object Browser displays in a compact format all the functionality in a project, whether it was brought into the project by Visual Basic (through its built-in objects) or by the developer (through custom components and controls).

Add a couple of controls on the Form and a couple of event handlers. You can place a couple of Command buttons on it and enter a simple Msg-Box function in their Click event. If you open the Object Browser again, you will see that the names of the controls are displayed as properties of the Form1 Class in the Members pane. The event handlers of the Click event for the two Command buttons are also listed in this pane as methods of the Form1 Class. Something wrong here? Click is an event name for the Command1 and Command2 controls. The subroutines Command1_Click() and Command2_Click(), however, are methods, as they can be called from any other subroutine in this Form. Unless they are declared as Private, they can also be accessed by procedures contained in other Forms of the project. So, they are, in effect, members of the Form. If you click the name of the subroutine Command1_Click(), you will see in the description pane that this subroutine is a member of the Class Project1.Form1.

Using the Data Access Object

In this section, we are going to discuss an advanced topic, the Data Access Object. If you are not familiar with database programming, this section should be of particular interest.

CALLING ALL DATABASE PROGRAMMERS...

Even if you are experienced with programming the Data Access Object, don't skip this section. Our goal is not to explain the Data Access Object but to show how to use the Object Browser to find out the members of various objects and use them.

If you have any open projects in the Visual Basic editor, close them and start a new Standard EXE project. To use the Data Access Object, you must first add a reference to it, as this Class isn't added by default to every project. Follow these steps:

1. Choose Project ➤ References to open the Reference dialog box (see Figure 4.11), which displays a list of all the available objects you can add to your projects:

In this dialog box, you see the names of all available Classes on your system. Some were installed with Windows itself, others by programming languages or applications. The components referenced in the project are checked.

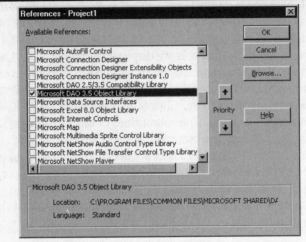

FIGURE 4.11:   The References dialog box

2. Scroll down the list, locate the entry Microsoft DAO 3.5 Object Library, and check the box in front of its name. Then click OK to close the References dialog box. You have just added a reference to the Data Access Object to your project.

3. Open the Object Browser window again and open the Type Library drop-down list. This time you will see a new object, DAO.

4. Select DAO and take a look at the Classes it exposes in the Classes pane.

In the next section, we'll show you how to use these Classes.

Using the DAO Object

The DAO object has many classes, one of them being the Database class. The Database class represents a database: a structure for storing information in Forms of tables. To work with a database, you must first select a table or a set of records, which are stored in a structure called Recordset.

NOTE

A Recordset is a collection of records, such as the invoices issued to customers in California or the best-selling products.

If you scroll down the Classes list in the Object Browser, you will see the Recordset entry. Select the Recordset entry, and you'll see the description of a Recordset at the bottom of the window: "A representation of the records in a base table or the records that result from a query" (the last few words are missing, but we had to complete the sentence anyway).

In the Members pane, you will now see the members of the Recordset class. The BOF property, for example, becomes True when the first record is reached, and the EOF property becomes True when the last record is reached. You use the methods FindFirst, FindLast, FindNext, and Find-Previous to locate records in a Recordset according to criteria you specify.

To access the members of a Database object, you must first open a database and assign it to an object variable. The function for opening a database does not appear anywhere in the Object Browser, because it's not a member of the Database object. A Database object variable doesn't exist before you actually open the database and assign it to the variable. Therefore, the method for opening the database can't be a member of the Database object. OpenDatabase is a method of the DAO object; however, you don't need to prefix it with the name of the DAO object.

To open a database and assign it to an object variable, you first declare the variable as follows:

```
Dim DB As Database
```

You then open a database and set the *DB* variable to the database:

```
Set DB = OpenDatabase("C:\PROGRAM FILES\DEVSTUDIO\VB\NWIND.MDB")
```

NOTE

We assume that the NWIND database is in the default VB folder. If you installed VB in another folder, change the path in the last statement accordingly.

The OpenDatabase() function accepts other optional arguments, and its complete syntax is as follows:

```
OpenDatabase(Name, [Options,] [Read-Only,] [Connect])
```

The arguments in square brackets are optional. The *Options* argument can be True or False, indicating whether the database will be opened exclusively or will be shared. The *Read-Only* argument is another True/False argument, indicating whether the database can be written to or is read-only. The last argument sets connection parameters, such as the user name and password.

Selecting Records in Recordsets

The next step is to create a Recordset with the records we want to work with. Let's say we want to explore the Customers table, which contains the names of all customers in the NWIND database. Locate the Recordset Class of the DAO object, and in the Members pane locate the OpenRecordset method. The description of this method is "Creates a New Recordset Object," as shown in Figure 4.12.

The syntax of the method is

```
OpenRecordset(Name As String, [Type], [Options], [LockEdit])
As Recordset
```

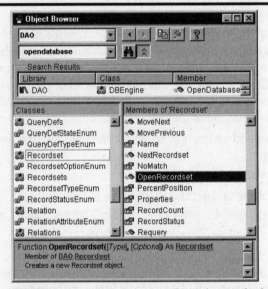

FIGURE 4.12: Locating the OpenRecordset method of the Recordset Class

The *Name* entry is the name of the table we want to open or a SQL statement that retrieves the desired records from the database. For the purposes of our example, we'll use the name of the Customers table. You could also specify a SQL statement, such as the following, to retrieve selected customers only:

```
SELECT * FROM Customers WHERE Country = 'Germany'
```

The *Type* argument specifies the type of Recordset we want to create. You should know the various types of Recordsets you can create, but if you need to be reminded of the constants that describe them, locate the

Class RecordsetTypeEnum and select it. In the Members pane, you will see all possible values for the *Type* argument:

dbOpenDynamic opens a dynamic Recordset (similar to an ODBC dynamic cursor).

dbOpenDynaset opens a Dynaset-type Recordset.

dbOpenForwardOnly opens a forward-only Recordset (it's faster than a Dynaset, but you can only issue the MoveNext and MoveLast methods against this Recordset).

dbOpenSnapshot opens a Snapshot Recordset, which you can use to read from but not write back to the database.

dbOpenTable opens a Table Recordset (an actual table in the database).

If you want to find out the constants that can be assigned to an argument, locate a Class whose name ends with *Enum* in the Classes pane (the name should resemble the name of the argument), and then look up its values in the Members pane. The last argument determines the type of locking for the Recordset, which we will not use in this example. If you want to find out the possible values of this argument, select the LockTypeEnum Class in the Class pane, and you'll see its values in the Members pane.

To create a Recordset with the names of all customers, you declare a Recordset object variable and then assign a newly created Recordset to it:

```
Dim RS As Recordset
Set RS = DB.OpenRecordset("Customers", dbOpenSnapshot)
```

The Recordset type is dbSnapShot, because this type gives the fastest possible access. We don't want to change the Customers table; we only want to read its records.

Exploring the Recordset's Structure

So far we've created a Recordset with the rows of the Customers table. What can we do with this Recordset? In this example, we want to find out the structure of each field, as well as the values of selected fields. If you select the Recordset class in the Classes pane and look at the members of the class, you will see that it has a property called `Fields`, as shown in Figure 4.12, earlier in this chapter. The icon in front of the Fields member is similar to the icon for properties with a little dot above it. This means that Fields is a Collection.

This makes sense because the Recordset contains multiple records. To access the first field, use the expression RS.Fields(i), where i goes from 0 to the number of fields (columns) in the Recordset minus one. The number of fields in the Recordset is given by the property `Fields.Count`. Don't remember the name of the property? Select the Fields Class in the Classes pane, as usual, and look it up in the Members pane.

The following loop scans all the fields in the Recordset and displays their names in a ListBox:

```
maxFields = RS.Fields.Count
For i = 0 To maxFields - 1
    List1.AddItem RS.Fields(i).Name
Next
```

Now we'll turn our attention to the rows of the Recordset. Each row is a record, with data about a different customer. The first piece of information we need is the number of rows in the Recordset. Again, select the Recordset class in the Classes pane, and search in the Members pane for a property named `RecordCount`. Its description is "Returns the number of records accessed in a Recordset." This is the property we need, but there is a detail you should be aware of here. The Object Browser won't be of much help here. The `RecordCount` property won't return the number of records in the Recordset because it hasn't seen more than the first record. You must first go to the last record in the Recordset with the MoveLast method, and then call the `RecordCount` property to find out the actual number of records in the Recordset.

The Recordset's rows can't be accessed through a Collection, similar to the Fields Collection. Instead, you must use the MoveNext method to move to the next record. The loop for scanning the rows of the RS Recordset is

```
Do
    {process fields of current row}
RS.MoveNext
Loop While Not RS.EOF
```

To process the fields of the current row, you must know the names of the fields. We're interested in the fields ContactName and Company-Name. Their values can be accessed with the `Value` property of the Fields Collection of the RS object. The following code displays the values of the fields ContactName and Company name:

```
Do
    List2.AddItem RS.Fields("ContactName").Value & ", " _
        & RS.Fields("CompanyName").Value
    RS.MoveNext
Loop While Not RS.EOF
```

Now, let's summarize what we have done so far and then build an application.

1. We opened a database and assigned it to a Database object variable (the DB variable).

2. Then, we called the DB object variable's OpenRecordset method to create a Recordset with the rows of the Customers table. This Recordset was assigned to the RS object variable.

3. Finally, with two loops we extracted the columns (field names) and rows (field values) of the Recordset.

Now we can put it all together and build a small application.

The ObjectLibrary Project

The ObjectLibrary project does the following:

▶ Opens a database and selects a table—the Customers table

▶ Displays the names of the fields in the upper ListBox control

▶ Displays all the values of two fields in the Recordset in the lower ListBox control

The application's main Form is shown in Figure 4.13.

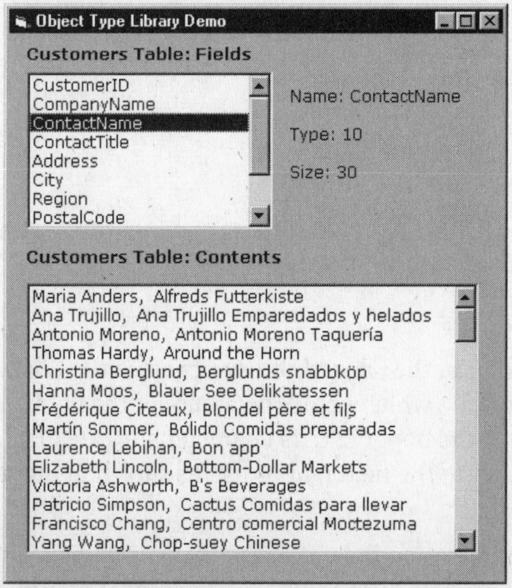

FIGURE 4.13: The ObjectLibrary project's Form

The code starts by declaring two object variables:

```
Private DB As Database
Private RS As Recordset
```

When the Form is loaded, the program opens the NWIND database and assigns it to the DB object variable. The statement that opens the NWIND database is

```
Set DB = OpenDatabase("c:\Program files\Microsoft Visual _
Studio\VB98\nwind.mdb")
```

NOTE

NWIND is a sample database that comes with Visual Basic 6, and we'll be using it a lot in this book's examples. The database's path used in the code segments is the default one. If you installed it in a different folder, you must adjust the code accordingly.

After this statement is executed, the *DB* variable refers to the NWIND database. The following line creates the Recordset with the rows of the Customers table:

```
Set RS = DB.OpenRecordset("Customers", dbOpenSnapshot)
```

After the two object variables are created, the code proceeds with the two loops we presented earlier to populate the lists:

```
List1.Clear
List2.Clear
maxFields = RS.Fields.Count
For i = 0 To maxFields - 1
List1.AddItem RS.Fields(i).Name
Next

Do
  List2.AddItem RS.Fields("ContactName").Value & ", " & _
    RS.Fields("CompanyName").Value
  RS.MoveNext
Loop While Not RS.EOF
```

Another event handler in the ObjectLibrary project is the Click event handler of the List1 control, which holds the names of the fields. When you click a field name in the upper list, its characteristics are displayed in three Label controls next to the field names list, as shown in Figure 4.13, earlier in this chapter.

COLLECTIONS

Arrays are convenient for storing related data, but accessing individual array elements can be a problem. To insert an element at a specific location in an array you may have to move down all the elements that follow it (that could mean copying a large number of elements). Likewise, if you delete an element, the elements that follow must be moved up. And because an array can't be sorted automatically, keeping its elements in some order requires a lot of work. In the past, programmers had to resort to creative programming techniques to manipulate array data to overcome its limitations.

Consider this simple example: Suppose you have a two-dimensional array in which you store city names and temperatures. You want to find out the temperature in Atlanta. Ideally, arrays would be accessed by their contents. So in this instance, you should be able to look up the temperature in Atlanta with a statement such as the following:

```
Temperatures("Atlanta")
```

However, if you haven't or couldn't use the city names to index your array, you would have to either know the index that corresponds to Atlanta or scan each element in the array until you find Atlanta. Clearly, this could be a very cumbersome and time-consuming task.

But Visual Basic provides an alternative: collections. A collection is a very common and very useful structure in working with Visual Basic objects. It is a simple structure that works like an array, storing related items. Collections are objects and, as such, have properties and methods. The advantage of a collection over an array is that the collection lets you access its items via a key. If the city name is the key in the Temperatures() array, you can recall the temperature in Atlanta instantly by providing the key

```
MsgBox "The temperature in Atlanta is " & Temperatures.Item _
("Atlanta")
```

Item is a method of the collection that returns a collection item based on its key or index. If you know the index of Atlanta's entry in the collection, you can use a statement such as the following:

```
MsgBox "The temperature in Atlanta is " & Temperatures.Item(6)
```

If you are going to access a collection's item with its index, there's no advantage in using collections over arrays.

To use a collection, you must first declare a Collection variable, as follows:

```
Dim Temperatures As New Collection
```

The *New* keyword tells Visual Basic to set up a new collection and name it Temperatures. Temperatures is not an array. You do not have to specify its size (there are no parentheses after the collection's name), and you can't assign new elements with an assignment operator. Temperatures is an object, and you must use its members to access it.

The Members of a Collection

Collection objects provide three methods and one property:

Add Method adds items to the collection.

Item Method returns an item by index or by key.

Remove Method deletes an item from the collection by index or by key.

Count Property returns the number of items in the collection.

The Add (Item, Key, Before, After) Method

To add a new item to a collection, use the Add method and assign its value to the *item* argument and its key to the *key* argument. To place the new item in a specific location in the array, specify one of the arguments *before* or *after* (but not both). To insert the new item before a specific element whose key (or index) you will specify, use the *before* argument. To place the new item after an item, specify this item's key or index with the *after* argument.

For example, to add the temperature for the city of San Francisco to the Temperatures collection, use the following statement:

```
Temperatures.Add 78, "San Francisco"
```

The number 78 is the value to be stored (temperature), and the string "San Francisco" is the new item's key. To insert this temperature immediately after the temperature of Santa Barbara, use the following statement:

```
Temperatures.Add 78, "San Francisco", , "Santa Barbara"
```

The extra comma denotes the lack of the *before* argument. The Add method supports named arguments, so the previous statement could also be written as follows:

```
Temperatures.Add 78, "San Francisco", after:= "Santa Barbara"
```

Collections aren't sorted; neither do they have a method to automatically sort their items. To maintain an ordered collection of objects, use the *before* and *after* arguments. In most practical situations, however, you don't care about sorting a collection's items. You sort arrays to simplify access of their elements; you don't have to do anything special to access the elements of collections.

The Remove (Index) Method

The Remove method removes an item from a collection based on its key or index. By passing the argument to the Remove method, the argument can be either the position of the item you want to delete or the item's key. To remove the city of Atlanta from your collection of temperatures, use the following statement:

```
Temperatures.Remove "Atlanta"
```

Or, if you know the city's order in the collection, specify the index in place of the key:

```
Temperatures.Remove 6
```

The Item (Index) Method

The Item method returns the value of an item in the collection, based on its key or index. As with the Remove method, the *Index* argument can be either the item's position in the collection or its key. To recall the temperature in Atlanta, use one of the following statements:

```
T1 = Temperatures.Item("Atlanta")
T1 = Temperatures.Item(3)
```

The Item method is the default method for a collection object, so you can omit it when you access an item in a collection. The previous example could also be written as

```
T1 = Temperatures("Atlanta")
```

TIP

Collections maintain their indices automatically as elements are added and deleted. The index of a given element, therefore, changes during the course of a program, and you shouldn't save an item's index value and expect to use it to retrieve the same element later in your program. Use keys for this purpose.

The Count Property

The Count property returns the number of items in the collection. To find out how many cities have been entered so far in the Temperatures collection, use the following statement:

```
Temperatures.Count
```

You can also use the Count property to scan all the elements of the collection with a For...Next loop such as:

```
For city = 1 To Temperatures.Count
{process elements}
Next city
```

Actually, there is a better way to scan the elements of a Collection, which is explained next.

Processing a Collection's Items

To scan all the items in a collection, Visual Basic provides the For Each...Next structure. Its syntax is

```
For Each member in Temperatures
 {process member}
Next
```

The *member* variable is the loop counter, but you don't have to initialize it or declare its type. The For...Each statement scans all the items in the collection automatically. At each iteration, the *member* variable assumes the current item's value.

You can also set up a For...Next loop to scan all the items in a collection:

```
For idx = 0 to Temperatures.Count-1
 {process current item}
Next
```

At each iteration of this loop, you can retrieve the value of the current item with the expression Temperatures(idx).

Using Collections

Let's implement a collection for storing the city names and temperatures. Start a new project, and add the following declaration in the Form:

```
Dim Temperatures As New Collection
```

This statement creates a new collection and names it Temperatures. Now enter the following code in the Form's Load event:

```
Private Sub Form_Load()
```

```
Temperatures.Add 76, "Atlanta"
Temperatures.Add 85, "Los Angeles"
Temperatures.Add 97, "Las Vegas"
Temperatures.Add 66, "Seattle"

End Sub
```

You can add as many lines as you wish, read the data from a disk file, or prompt the user to enter city names and temperatures at run time. New items can be added to the collection at any time.

Next, create a Command button, set its Caption property to Show City Temperature, and enter the following code in its Click subroutine:

```
Private Sub Command1_Click()
On Error GoTo NoItem
 city = InputBox("What City?")
 temp = Temperatures.Item(city)
 MsgBox temp
 Exit Sub

NoItem:
 MsgBox "This city was not found in our catalog"

End Sub
```

This subroutine prompts users to enter the name of the city's temperature they want to learn. The program then recalls the value of the collection's item, where the key is the city name supplied by the user. If the supplied key doesn't exist, a run-time error is generated, which is why we use the On Error statement. If the user enters a nonexistent city name, a run-time error is generated; Visual Basic intercepts it and executes the statements following the label NoItem. If the key exists in the array, then the temperature of the corresponding city is displayed in a message box.

Finally, add another command button to the Form, set its caption to Show Average Temperature, and enter the following code behind its Click event:

```
Private Sub Command2_Click()
 For Each city In Temperatures
  total = total + city
  Debug.Print city
 Next
 avgTemperature = total / Temperatures.Count
 MsgBox avgTemperature
End Sub
```

The Print statement displays each element in the Immediate window. The name of the loop variable is *city*, and its value is the temperature of the current item, not the city name. (The counter of the For Each loop in the previous example could be named *iCity*, *temp*, or *foo*.)

NOTE

The key values in a collection object are not stored as array elements in the collection. They are only used for accessing the items of the collection, just as array indices are used for accessing an array's elements.

WHAT'S NEXT?

The following chapter will help expand your Visual Basic skills further by demonstrating how to create an application that uses multiple Forms and how to distribute executable files. You'll also get to try your hand at two applications: a math and a loan application.

Chapter 5
VISUAL BASIC PROJECTS

I n this chapter, we will build some real-life applications. Among other topics, we'll look at how to write applications that have multiple windows, how to validate user input, and how to write error-trapping routines.

The bulk of the chapter demonstrates very basic programming techniques, such as building user interfaces, event programming, validating user input, and so on. The goal is to show you how to write simple applications using the most basic elements of the language. This chapter will explain the methodology for building applications. While the code of the applications will be rather simple, it will demonstrate user interface design and the basics of validating data and trapping errors.

Adapted from *Mastering Visual Basic 6*
by Evangelos Petroutsos
ISBN 0-7821-2272-8   1,312 pages $49.99

If you're a beginner, you may be thinking, "All I want now is to write a simple application that works—I'll worry about data validation later." It's never too early to start thinking about validating your code's data and error trapping. As you'll see, making sure that your application doesn't crash requires more code than the actual operations it performs! If this isn't quite what you expected, welcome to the club. A well-behaved application must catch and handle every error gracefully, including user errors. This chapter only discusses the basic concepts of error handling you'll need to build a few simple applications.

BUILDING A LOAN CALCULATOR

An easy-to-implement, practical application is one that calculates loan parameters. Visual Basic provides built-in functions for performing many types of financial calculations, and you only need a single line of code to calculate the monthly payment given the loan amount, its duration, and the interest rate. Designing the user interface, however, takes much more effort.

Regardless of the language you use, you must go through the following process to develop an application:

1. Decide what the application will do and how it will interact with the user.

2. Design the application's user interface.

3. Write the actual code.

Deciding How the Loan Application Works

Following the first step of the process outlined above, you decide that the user should be able to specify the amount of the loan, the interest rate, and the duration of the loan in months. You must, therefore, provide three textboxes where the user can enter these values.

Another parameter affecting the monthly payment is whether payments are made at the beginning or at the end of each month, so you must also provide a way for the user to specify whether the payments will be early (first day of the month) or late (last day of the month). The most appropriate type of control for entering Yes/No or True/False type of information is the CheckBox control. The CheckBox control is a toggle. If it's checked, you can clear it by clicking on it. If it's cleared, you can check it by clicking again. The user doesn't enter any data in this control and it's the simplest method for specifying values with two possible states. Figure 5.1 shows a user interface that matches our design specifications.

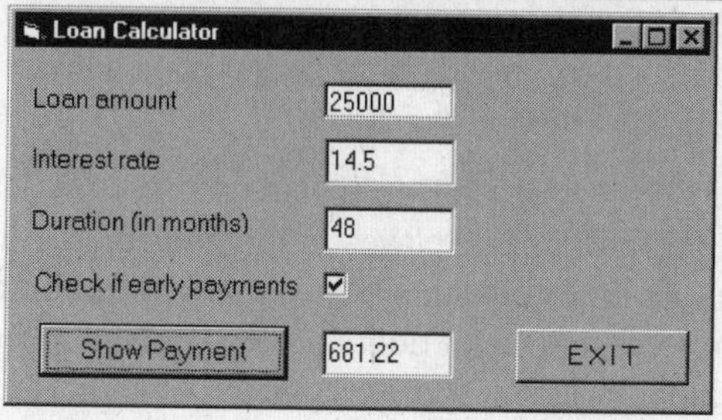

FIGURE 5.1: The loan application is a simple financial calculator.

After the user enters all the information on the Form, they can click the Show Payment Command button to calculate the monthly payment and display it in a message box. All the action takes place in the Command button's Click subroutine. The function for calculating monthly payments is called Pmt(), and it must be called as follows:

```
MonthlyPayment = Pmt(InterestRate, Periods, Amount, _
    FutureValue, Due)
```

The interest rate (variable *InterestRate*) is specified as a monthly rate. If the interest rate is 16.5%, this value should be 0.165/12. The duration of the loan *(Periods)* is specified in number of months, and *Amount* is the loan's amount. The *FutureValue* of a loan is zero (it would be a positive value for an investment), and the last parameter, *Due*, specifies when payments are due. If it's 0, payments are due at the beginning of the month; if it's 1, payments are due at the end of the month.

The present value of the loan is the amount of the loan with a negative sign. It's negative because you don't have the money now. You're borrowing it; it's money you owe to the bank. The future value of the loan is zero. The future value represents what the loan will be worth when it's paid off. This is what the bank owes you or what you owe the bank at the end of the specified period.

Pmt() is a built-in function that uses the five values in the parentheses to calculate the monthly payment. The values passed to the function are called *arguments*. Arguments are the values needed by a function (or subroutine) to carry out an action, such as a calculation. By passing different values to the function, the user can calculate the parameters of a different loan. The

Pmt() function and other financial functions of Visual Basic are described in the Language Reference at the end of this book. You don't need to know how the Pmt() function calculates the monthly payment. The Pmt() function does the calculations and returns the result. To calculate the monthly payment on a loan of $25,000 with an interest rate of 14.5%, payable over 48 months, and due the last day of the payment period (which in our case is a month), you'd call the Pmt() function as follows:

```
Debug.Print Pmt(0.145 / 12, 48, -25000, 0, 0)
```

The value 689.448821287218 will be displayed in the Immediate window (you'll see later how you can limit the digits after the decimal point to two, since this is all the accuracy you need for dollar amounts). Notice the negative sign in front of the amount. If you specify a positive amount, the result will be a negative payment. The payment and the loan's amount have different signs because they represent different cash flows. The last two arguments of the Pmt() function are optional. If you omit them, Visual Basic assumes they are zero. You could also call the Pmt() function like this:

```
Debug.Print Pmt(0.145 / 12, 48, -25000)
```

Calculating the amount of the monthly payment given the loan parameters is quite simple. What you need to know or understand are the parameters of a loan and how to pass them to the Pmt() function. You must also know how the interest rate is specified, to avoid invalid values. What you don't need to know is how the payment is calculated—Visual Basic does it for you. This is the essence of functions: they are "black boxes" that perform complicated calculations on their arguments and return the result. You don't have to know how they work, just how to supply the values required for the calculations.

Designing the User Interface

Now that you know how to calculate the monthly payment, you can design the user interface. To do so, start a new project, rename its Form to **Loan-Calc**, rename the project to **LoanProject**, and save the project as **Loan**.

NOTE

The Form and the project files, along with the files for the other projects in this chapter, can be found at the Sybex Web site (www.sybex.com). Once there, go to the Catalog page and enter **2469** (the first four digits of the last five in the book's ISBN) into the search engine. Follow the link for this book that comes up, and then click the Downloads button, which will take you to a list of files organized by chapter.

Your first task is to decide the font and size of the text you'll use for most controls on the Form. Although we aren't going to display anything on the Form directly, all the controls we place on it will have by default the same font as the Form (which is called the container of the controls). You can change the font later during the design, but it's a good idea to start with the right font. At any rate, don't try to align the controls if you're planning to change their fonts. This will, most likely, throw off your alignment efforts.

TIP

Try not to mix fonts on a Form. A Form, or a printed page for that matter, that includes type in several fonts looks like it has been created haphazardly and is difficult to read.

The Loan application, which you'll find with this chapter's files on the Sybex Web site, uses 10-point MS Sans Serif. To change it, select the Form with the mouse, double-click the name of the Font property in the Properties window to open the Font dialog box, and select the desired font and attributes.

To design the Form shown previously in Figure 5.1, follow these steps:

1. Place three labels on the Form and assign the following captions to them:

   Label1   Loan amount

   Label2   Interest rate

   Label3   Duration (in months)

   The labels should be large enough to fit their captions. You don't need to change the default names of the three Label controls on the Form because their captions are all we need. You aren't going to program them.

2. Place a TextBox control next to each label. Name the first textbox (the one next to the first label) **Amount** and set its Text property to 25,000, name the second textbox **IRate** and set its value to 14.5, and name the third textbox **Duration** and set its value to 48. These initial values correspond to a loan of $25,000 with an interest rate of 14.5% and a payoff period of 48 months.

3. Next, place a CheckBox control on the Form. By default, the control's caption is Check1, and it appears to the right of the checkbox. Because we want the titles to be to the left of the corresponding controls, we'll change this default appearance.

4. Select the checkbox with the mouse (if it's not already selected), and in the Properties window, locate the Alignment property. Its value is 0–Left Justify. If you expand the drop-down list by clicking the Arrow button, you'll see that this property has another setting, 1–Right Justify. Select the alternate value from the list.

5. With the checkbox selected, locate the Name property in the Properties window, and set it to PayEarly.

6. Change the caption by entering the string "Check if early payments" in its Caption property field.

7. Place a Command button control on the lower left corner of the Form. Name it **ShowPayment,** and set its caption to "Show Payment".

8. Finally, place a TextBox control next to the Command button and name it **txtPmt.** This is where the monthly payment will appear. Notice that the user isn't supposed to enter any data in this box, so you must set its Locked property to True. You'll be able to change its value from within your code, but users won't be able to type anything in it. (We could have used a Label control instead, but the uniform look of TextBoxes on a Form is usually preferred).

Aligning the Controls

Your next step is to align the controls on the Form. First, be sure that the captions on the labels are visible. Our labels contain lengthy captions, and if you don't make the labels long enough, the captions may wrap to a second line and become invisible like the one shown in Figure 5.2.

TIP

Be sure to make your labels long enough to hold their captions, especially if you're using a nonstandard font. A user's computer may substitute another font for a nonstandard font and the corresponding captions may increase in length.

```
Loan Calculator                    _ □ ×
  Loan amount        25000
  Interest rate      14.5
  Duration (in       48
  Check if early payments  □
     Show Payment                    EXIT
```

FIGURE 5.2: The third label's caption is too long to be displayed in a single line.

To align the controls on the Form, Visual Basic provides a number of commands, all of which can be accessed through the Format menu. To align the controls that are already on the LoanCalc Form, follow these steps:

1. Select the three labels and the checkbox, and left-align them by choosing Format ➤ Align ➤ Left.

2. Select the four textboxes, and left-align them by choosing Format ➤ Align ➤ Left. Don't include the checkbox in this selection.

TIP

When you select multiple controls to align together, use the control with blue handles as a guide for aligning the other controls.

3. With all four textboxes still selected, use the mouse to align them above and below the box of the CheckBox control.

Your Form should now look like the one in Figure 5.1. Take a good look at it and check to see if any of your controls are misaligned. In the interface design process, you tend to overlook small problems such as a slightly misaligned control. The user of the application, however, instantly spots such mistakes. It doesn't make any difference how nicely the rest of the controls are arranged on the Form; if one of them is misaligned, it will attract the user's eye.

Programming the Loan Application

Now run the application and see how it behaves. Enter a few values in the textboxes, change the state of the checkbox, and test the functionality already built into the application. Clicking the Command button won't have any effect because we have not yet added any code. If you're happy with the user interface, stop the application, open the Form, and double-click the Command button. Visual Basic opens the Code window and displays the following three lines of the ShowPayment_Click event:

```
Option Explicit

Private Sub ShowPayment_Click()

End Sub
```

Place the pointer between the lines Private... and End Sub, and enter the following lines:

```
Dim Payment As Single

Payment = Pmt(0.01 * IRate.Text / 12, Duration.Text, _
    -Amount.Text, 0, PayEarly.Value)
txtPmt.Text = Format$(Payment, "#.00")
```

The Code window should now look like the one shown in Figure 5.3. Notice the underscore character at the end of the first part of the long line. The underscore lets you break long lines so that they will fit nicely in the Code window. I'm using this convention here to fit long lines on the printed page. The same statement may appear in a single, long line in the project.

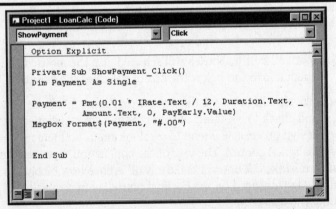

FIGURE 5.3: The Show Payment button's Click event subroutine

In Figure 5.3, the first line of code declares a variable. It lets the application know that *Payment* is a placeholder for storing a *floating-point number* (a number with a decimal part). The first really executable line in the subroutine calls the Pmt() function, passing the values of the controls as arguments:

▶ The first argument is the interest rate. The value entered by the user in the Irate textbox is multiplied by 0.01 so that the value 14.5 (which corresponds to 14.5%) is passed to the Pmt() function as 0.145. Although we humans prefer to specify interest rates as integers (8%) or floating-point numbers larger than 1 (8.24%), the Pmt() function expects to read a number less than 1. The value 1 corresponds to 100%. Therefore, the value 0.1 corresponds to 10%. This value is also divided by 12 to yield the monthly interest rate.

▶ The second argument is the duration of the loan in months (the value entered in the Duration textbox).

▶ The third argument is the loan's amount (the value entered in the Amount textbox). The fourth argument (the loan's future value) is 0 by definition.

▶ The last argument must be the value 0 or 1, which specifies when payments are due. If they are made early in the month, this value should be 0. If they are made at the end of the month, it should be 1. As you know, the CheckBox control's Value property can be either 0 (if cleared) or 1 (if checked). Therefore, you can pass the quantity PayEarly.Value directly to the Pmt() function.

The second line displays the result in the fourth TextBox control. The result is first formatted appropriately with the following statement:

```
txtPmt.Text = Format$(Payment, "#.00")
```

Because the Pmt() function returns a precise number, such as 372.2235687646345, you must round and format it nicely before displaying it. Since the bank can't charge you anything less than a penny, you don't need extreme accuracy. Two fractional digits are sufficient. That's what the Format$() function does. It accepts a number and a string and formats the number according to an argument you supply (it's called the *formatting string*).

To format a number with two fractional digits, you set the formatting string to "#.00". This tells Visual Basic to round the number to two fractional digits and throw away the rest. The integer part of the number isn't affected. Moreover, if the result is something like 349.4, Visual Basic will format it as 349.40.

TIP

You almost always use the Format$() function when you want to display the results of numeric calculations, because most of the time you don't need Visual Basic's extreme accuracy. A few fractional digits are all you need. In addition to numbers, the Format$() function can format dates and time (see the Language Reference at the end of this book for more information).

Run the application again, and when the Form opens, click the Show Payment button. The result for the loan described by the initial values of the controls on the Form is 689.45. This is the amount you'll be paying every month over the next four years to pay off a loan of $25,000 at 14.5%. Enter other values, and see how a loan's duration and interest rate affect the monthly payment.

The code of the Loan project in this book's section on the Sybex Web site is different from the one I have presented here and considerably longer. The statement discussed in the last paragraph is the bare minimum for calculating a loan payment. The user may enter any values on the Form and cause the program to crash. In the next section, we'll see how you can validate the data entered by the user, catch errors, and handle them gracefully (that is, give the user a chance to correct the data and proceed).

Validating the Data

If you were to enter a non-numeric value in one of the fields, the program would crash and display an error message. For example, if you entered "twenty" in the Duration textbox, the program would display the error message shown in Figure 5.4. A simple typing error can crash the program. This isn't the way Windows applications should work. Your applications must be able to handle most user errors, provide helpful messages, and in general, guide the user in running the application efficiently. If a user error goes unnoticed, your application will either end abruptly, or produce incorrect results without an indication.

Click the End button, and Visual Basic will take you back to the application's Code window. Obviously, we must do something about user errors. Applications must be foolproof and not crash with every mistake the user makes. One way to take care of typing errors is to examine each control's contents, and if they don't contain valid numeric values, display your own descriptive message, and give the user another chance. Here's the revised ShowPayment_Click() subroutine that examines the value of each textbox before attempting to use it in the calculations.

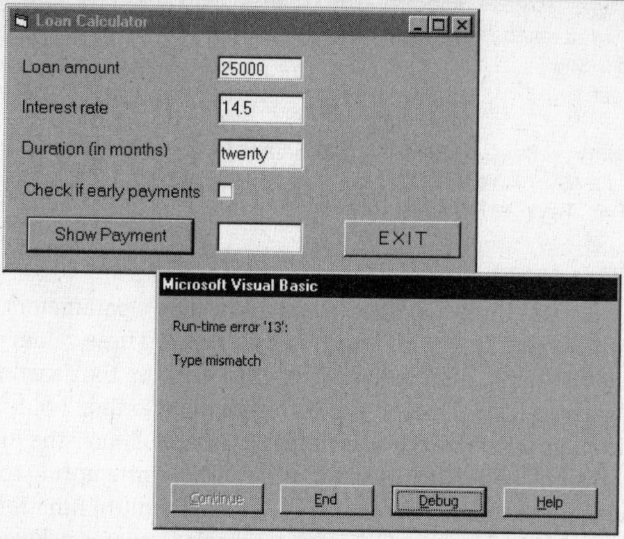

FIGURE 5.4: The "Type mismatch" error message means that you supplied a string where a numeric value was expected.

Code 5.1: The Revised ShowPayment_Click() Subroutine

```
Private Sub ShowPayment_Click()
Dim Payment As Single
Dim LoanIRate As Single
Dim LoanDuration As Integer
Dim LoanAmount As Integer

  If IsNumeric(Amount.Text) Then
   LoanAmount = Amount.Text
  Else
   MsgBox "Please enter a valid amount"
   Exit Sub
  End If
  If IsNumeric(IRate.Text) Then
   LoanIRate = 0.01 * IRate.Text / 12
  Else
   MsgBox "Invalid interest rate, please re-enter"
   Exit Sub
  End If
  If IsNumeric(Duration.Text) Then
   LoanDuration = Duration.Text
  Else
```

```
    MsgBox "Please specify the loan's duration _
        as a number of months"
    Exit Sub
End If

Payment = Pmt(LoanIRate, LoanDuration, -LoanAmount, 0, _
    PayEarly.Value)
txtPmt.Text = Format$(Payment, "#.00")

End Sub
```

First, we declare three variables in which the loan's parameters will be stored: *LoanAmount, LoanIRate,* and *LoanDuration.* These values will be passed to the Pmt() function as arguments. Each textbox's value is examined with an If structure. If the corresponding textbox holds a valid number, its value is assigned to the numeric variable. If not, the program displays a warning and exits the subroutine without attempting to calculate the monthly payment. IsNumeric() is another built-in function that accepts a variable and returns True if the variable is numeric, False otherwise.

If the Amount textbox holds a numeric value, such as 21,000 or 21.50, the function IsNumeric(Amount.Text) returns True, and the statement following it is executed. The statement following it assigns the value entered in the Amount textbox to the *LoanAmount* variable. If not, the Else clause of the statement is executed, which displays a warning in a message box and then exits the subroutine. The Exit Sub statement tells Visual Basic to stop executing the subroutine immediately, as if the End Sub line was encountered.

You can run the revised application and test it by entering invalid values in the fields. Notice that you can't specify an invalid value for the last argument; the CheckBox control won't let you enter a value. You can only check or clear it and both options are valid. The LoanCalc application you'll find in this book's section of the Sybex Web site contains this last version with the error-trapping code.

The actual calculation of the monthly payment takes a single line of Visual Basic code. Displaying it requires another line of code. Adding the code to validate the data entered by the user, however, is an entire program. And that's the way things are.

WRITING WELL-BEHAVED APPLICATIONS

A well-behaved application must contain data-validation code. This means that if the application crashes because of a typing mistake, nothing really bad will happen. The user will try again or give up on your application and look for a more professional one. However, if the user has been entering data for hours, the situation is far more serious. It's your responsibility as a programmer to make sure that only valid data are used by the application and that the application keeps working, no matter how the user misuses or abuses it.

NOTE

The applications in this book don't contain much data-validation code because it would obscure the "useful" code that applies to the topic at hand. Instead, they demonstrate specific techniques. You can use parts of the examples in your own applications, but you should provide your own data-validation code (and error-handling code, as you'll see in the following section).

Now run the application one last time and enter an enormous loan amount. Try to find out what it would take to pay off our national debt with a reasonable interest rate in, say, 72 months. The program will crash again (as if you didn't know). This time the program will go down with a different error message. Visual Basic will complain about an "overflow."

TIP

An overflow is a numeric value too large for the program to handle. This error is usually produced when you divide a number by a very small value. Dividing by zero, for example, is sure to produce an overflow.

Actually, the Loan application will crash with a small loan value. Any value greater than 32,767 will cause an overflow condition. The largest value you can assign to an integer variable is 32,767 (quite small for storing financial figures). As you'll see in the next section, Visual Basic provides other types of variables, which can store enormous values (making the national debt look really small). In the meantime, if you want to use the loan calculator, change the declaration of the *LoanAmount* variable to

```
Dim LoanAmount As Single
```

The Single data type can hold much larger values.

An overflow error can't be caught with data-validation code. There's always a chance your calculations will produce overflows or other types of math errors. Data validation isn't going to help here. We need something called error trapping. *Error trapping* tells Visual Basic to trap errors and, instead of stopping the program, inform your code that an error has occurred and give your code a chance to handle it. We'll see how to prevent these types of errors in the next example.

BUILDING A MATH CALCULATOR

Our next application is more advanced, but not as advanced as it looks. It's a math calculator with a typical visual interface that demonstrates how Visual Basic can simplify programming. If you haven't tried it, you may think that writing an application such as this one is way too complicated, but it isn't. The Math application is shown in Figure 5.5, and you'll find it in this book's section of the Sybex Web site. The Math application emulates the operation of a hand-held calculator and implements the basic arithmetic operations. It has the structure of a working math calculator, and you can easily expand it by adding more features. Adding features like cosines and logarithms is actually simpler than performing the basic arithmetic operations.

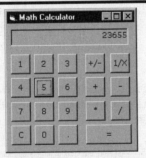

FIGURE 5.5: The Math application window

Designing the User Interface

The application's interface is straightforward, but it takes quite a bit of effort. You must align a number of buttons on the Form and make the calculator look like a hand-held calculator as much as possible. You don't have to redesign the interface or the operation of a calculator, so you can start building the application's Form. Start a new project, name its main Form **MathCalc,** and save the project as **Math** in a new folder (the project is stored on the Sybex Web site). Now, follow these steps:

1. Select a font that you like for the Form. All the Command buttons you'll place on the Form will inherit this font. The Math-Calc application on the Sybex Web site uses 10-point Verdana.

2. Add the Label control, which will become the calculator's display. Set its BorderStyle property to 1–Fixed Single so that it will have a 3-D look, as shown in Figure 5.5.

3. Draw a Command button on the Form, change its caption to "0", name it **Digits**, and set its Index to 0. We'll create an array of buttons.

4. Place the button in its final position on the Form.

Creating an array of controls may sound strange, but here's why you do it. We could create 11 buttons and give them different names, for example, Digit1, Digit2, and so on. But then we would have to provide a separate subroutine for their Click event, in other words, one subroutine per Command button. By creating an array of Command buttons, we can provide a single subroutine for the Click event of all buttons. You'll see later how this naming scheme simplifies our code.

5. Right-click the button and select Copy from the shortcut menu. The Command button is copied to the Clipboard, and now you can paste it on the Form (which is much faster than designing an identical button).

6. Right-click somewhere on the Form and from the shortcut menu select Paste to create a copy of the button you copied earlier. Visual Basic displays a dialog box with the following message:

   ```
   You already have a control named 'Digits'. Do you want
   to create a control array?
   ```

   You want to create an array of Command buttons, so click on Yes.

7. Repeat steps 5 and 6 eight more times, once for each numeric digit. Each time a new Command button is pasted on the Form, Visual Basic gives it the name Digits and sets its Index property to a value that's larger than the previous one by 1. Each button's Index property will be the same as its caption,

as long as you set the captions sequentially. If you place the Command buttons for the digits in any other order, the application won't work. As you have guessed, we'll be using the Index property to handle the buttons from within our code, and it's crucial that their captions are the same as their indices.

8. When the buttons of the numeric digits are all on the Form, place two more buttons, one for the C (Clear) operation and one for the Period button. Name them **ClearBttn** and **DotBttn**, and set their captions accordingly. Use a larger font size for the Period button to make its caption easier to read.

9. When all the Digit buttons of the first group are on the Form and in their approximate positions, align them with the commands on the Format menu.

   a. First, align the buttons in a row and make their horizontal spacing equal. Then do the same with the buttons in a column, and this time, make sure their vertical distances are equal.

   b. Now you can align the buttons in each row and each column separately. Use one of the buttons you aligned in the last step as the guide for the rest of them. The buttons can be aligned in many ways, so don't worry if somewhere in the process you ruin the alignment. You can always use the Undo command in the Edit menu.

10. Now, place the Command buttons for the operations. Table 5.1 lists their captions and names.

TABLE 5.1: Captions and Names for MathCalc Application Command Buttons

CAPTION	NAME
+	Plus
–	Minus
*	Times
/	Div
+/	PlusMinus
1/X	Over
=	Equals

11. Use the commands on the Format menu to align these buttons as shown in Figure 5.6. The control with the blue handles can be used as a reference for aligning the other controls into rows and columns.

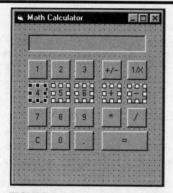

FIGURE 5.6: An alignment of Digit buttons created by using a single reference control (the one with the dark handles)

Programming the Math Application

Now you're ready to add some code to the application. Double-click one of the Digit buttons on the Form, and you'll see the following in the Code window:

```
Private Sub Digits_Click(Index As Integer)

End Sub
```

This is the Click event's handler for all Command buttons that represent digits. All buttons have the same name, and they are differentiated by their index. When the user clicks one of them, Visual Basic generates the Digits_Click event and uses the *Index* argument to report the index of the button that was clicked.

What happens on a hand-held calculator when you press a numeric button? The corresponding digit is appended to the display. To emulate this behavior, insert the following line in the Click event handler:

```
Display.Caption = Display.Caption + Digits(Index).Caption
```

This line appends the digit clicked to the calculator's display. The Caption property of the control that was clicked is the digit of the button. For example, if you have already entered the value 345, clicking the digit 0 displays the value 3450 on the Label control that acts as the calculator's display.

> **TIP**
>
> A single line of code in a single Click event takes care of all the numeric buttons. That's what an array of controls does for you. If you have multiple controls with identical behavior, create arrays of controls. All the members of the array have the same handler (subroutine) for each event, and you don't need to repeat the code over and over again.

The code behind the Digit buttons needs a few more lines. If you run the application now, you'll see what happens after an operation is performed and the result is displayed. If you click another digit, it's appended to the existing number. But this isn't the way a hand-held calculator works. The first time a Digit button is pressed after a result is displayed, the display must clear and then print the new digit. Revise the Digits_Click event handler as follows.

Code 5.2: The Digits_Click Event

```
Private Sub Digits_Click(Index As Integer)
   If ClearDisplay Then
    Display.Caption = ""
    ClearDisplay = False
   End If
   Display.Caption = Display.Caption + Digits(Index).Caption
End Sub
```

The *ClearDisplay* variable is declared as Boolean, and it can take a True or False value. Suppose the user has performed an operation and the result is on the calculator's display. The user now starts typing another number. Without the If clause, the program would continue to append digits to the number already on the display. This is not how calculators work. When a new number is entered, the display must clear. And our program uses the *ClearDisplay* variable to know when to clear the display.

The Equals button sets the *ClearDisplay* variable to True to indicate that the display contains the result of an operation. The Digits_Click() subroutine examines its value each time a new Digit button is pressed. If it's True, it clears the display and then prints the new digit on it. It also sets it to False so that when the next digit is pressed, the program won't clear the display again.

What if the user makes a mistake and wants to undo an entry? The typical hand-held calculator has no backspace key. The Clear key erases the current number on the display. Let's implement this feature. Double-click the C button and enter the following code in its Click event:

```
Display.Caption = ""
```

And now we can look at the Period button. A calculator, no matter how simple, should be able to handle fractional numbers. The Period button works just like the Digit buttons, with one exception. A digit can appear any number of times in a numeric value, but the period can appear only once. A number like 99,991 is valid, but you must make sure that the user can't enter numbers such as 23.456.55. Once a period is entered, this button mustn't insert another one. The following code accounts for this.

Code 5.3: The Period Button

```
Private Sub DotBttn_Click()
  If InStr(Display.Caption, ".") Then
    Exit Sub
  Else
    Display.Caption = Display.Caption + "."
  End If
End Sub
```

The `InStr(Display.Caption, ".")` function returns the location of the first instance of the period in the caption of the Label control. If this number is positive, the number entered contains a period already, and another can't be entered. In this case, the program exits the subroutine. If the InStr() function returns 0, the period is appended to the number entered so far, as is a regular digit.

The InStr() function accepts two string arguments and returns the location of the second string in the first one. The following function returns 12 because the string "Visual" appears in the 12th character position in the longer string:

```
InStr("Welcome to Visual Basic", "Visual")
```

However, the following function returns 0 because the string "Java" doesn't appear anywhere in the first string.

```
InStr("Welcome to Visual Basic", "Java")
```

The following expression returns a positive number if the value already on the display contains a period:

```
InStr(Display.Caption, ".")
```

If that's the case, the program exits the subroutine without taking any action. If the value returned by the InStr() function is a positive number, the value entered is an Integer, and the period is displayed.

Check out the operation of the application. We have already created a functional user interface that emulates a hand-held calculator with data entry capabilities. It doesn't perform any operations yet, but we have already created a functional user interface with only a small number of statements.

Math Operations

Now we can move to the interesting part of the application: considering how a calculator works. Let's start by defining three variables:

- *Operand1*   The first number in the operation
- *Operator*   The desired operation
- *Operand2*   The second number in the operation

When the user clicks a number, or *Operand1,* the value on the display is stored in a variable. If the user then clicks the Plus button, or *Operator,* the program must make a note to itself that the current operation is an addition, and then clear the display so that the user can enter another value. The user enters another value, or *Operand2,* and then clicks the Equals button to see the result. At this point, our program must do the following:

1. Read the *Operand2* value on the display.

2. Add that value to *Operand1.*

3. Display the result.

The Equals button must perform the following operation:

```
Operand1 Operator Operand2
```

Suppose the number on the display when the user clicks the Plus button is 3,342. The user then enters the value 23 and clicks the Equals button. The program must carry out the addition:

```
3342 + 23
```

If the user clicks the Division button, the operation is

```
3342 / 23
```

In both cases, the result is displayed (and it may become the first operand for the next operation).

The variables in the previous examples are local in the subroutines where they are declared. Other subroutines have no access to them and can't read or set their values. Sometimes, however, variables must be accessed from many places in a program. If the *Operand1*, *Operand2*, and *Operator* variables in this application must be accessed from within more than one subroutine, they must be declared outside any subroutine. The same is true for the *ClearDisplay* variable. Their declarations, therefore, must appear outside any procedure, and they usually appear at the beginning of the code Module (the first lines in the Code window are usually declarations of variables that must be accessed from within any subroutine).

Let's see how the program uses the *Operator* variable. When the user clicks the Plus button, the program must store the value "+" in the *Operator* variable. This takes place from within the Plus button's Click event. But later on, the Equals button must have access to the value of the *Operator* variable in order to carry out the operation (in other words, it must know what type of operation the user specified). Because these variables must be manipulated from within more than a single subroutine, they must be declared outside any subroutine (see Figure 5.7).

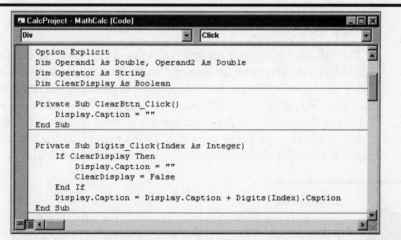

FIGURE 5.7: The first few lines in the Math application's Code window. The variables declared outside any procedure are visible from any subroutine on this Form.

To declare the variables outside a subroutine, place the pointer at the top of the Code window, right after the Option Explicit statement, and enter the following declarations:

```
Dim Operand1 As Double, Operand2 As Double
```

```
Dim Operator As String
Dim ClearDisplay As Boolean
```

The keyword *Double* is new to you. It tells Visual Basic to create a numeric variable with the greatest possible precision for storing the values of the operators. (Numeric variables and their types are discussed in detail in the next chapter.) The Boolean type takes two values, True and False. You have already seen how the *ClearDisplay* variable is used.

The variables *Operand1*, *Operand2*, and *Operator* are called *Form-wide*, or simply *Form* variables, because they are visible from within any subroutine on the Form. If our application had another Form, these variables wouldn't be visible from within the other Form(s). In other words, any subroutine on a Form on which the variables are declared can read or set the values of the variables, but no subroutine outside that Form can do so.

With the variable declarations out of the way, we can now implement the Operator buttons. Double-click the Plus button and in the Click event's handler, enter the following lines:

```
Private Sub Plus_Click()
   Operand1 = Val(Display.Caption)
   Operator = "+"
   Display.Caption = ""
End Sub
```

The variable *Operand1* is assigned the value currently on the display. The Val() function returns the numeric value of its argument. As you may recall, a Label's Caption property is a string. For example, you can assign the value "My Label" to a Label's Caption property. The actual value stored in the Caption property is not a number. It's a String such as "428", which is different from the numeric value 428. That's why we use the Val() function to convert the value of the Label's caption to a numeric value.

WARNING

If you don't use the Val() function to convert the String to a Numeric value, adding two values like "355" and "8" will produce the String "3558" and not a numeric value. The + symbol tells Visual Basic to add two strings, as well as two numbers, depending on the type of operands. If you subtract the same two values, however, you'll get the correct result. Visual Basic can't subtract a string from another, so it assumes the two operands are numeric values and subtracts them numerically. Remove the Val() function from the code to see how it will perform the various operations. The other three Operator buttons do the same. The only difference is the symbol of the operator.

Code 5.4: The Click Event Handlers for the Operator Buttons

```
Private Sub Minus_Click()
  Operand1 = Val(Display.Caption)
  Operator = "-"
  Display.Caption = ""
End Sub

Private Sub Times_Click()
  Operand1 = Val(Display.Caption)
  Operator = "*"
  Display.Caption = ""
End

Private Sub Div_Click()
  Operand1 = Val(Display.Caption)
  Operator = "/"
  Display.Caption = ""
End Sub
```

So far, we have implemented the following functionality in our application. When an Operator button is clicked, the program stores the value on the display in the *Operand1* variable and the operator in the *Operator* variable. It then clears the display so that the user can enter the second operand. After the second operand is entered, the user can click the Equals button to calculate the result. When this happens, the following code is executed.

Code 5.5: The Equals Button

```
Private Sub Equals_Click()
Dim result As Double
  Operand2 = Val(Display.Caption)
  If Operator = "+" Then result = Operand1 + Operand2
  If Operator = "-" Then result = Operand1 - Operand2
  If Operator = "*" Then result = Operand1 * Operand2
  If Operator = "/" And Operand2 <> "0" Then _
    result = Operand1 / Operand2
  Display.Caption = result
End Sub
```

The *result* variable is declared as Double so that the result of the operation will be stored with maximum precision. The code extracts the value displayed in the Label control and stores it in the variable *Operand2*. It then performs the operation with a string of If statements:

▶ If the Operator is "+", the result is the sum of the two operands.

- If the Operator is "-", the result is the difference of the first operand minus the second.

- If the Operator is "*", the result is the product of the two operands.

- If the Operator is "/", the result is the quotient of the first operand divided by the second operand, provided that the divisor is not zero.

NOTE

Division takes into consideration the value of the second operand because, if it's zero, the division can't be carried out. The last If statement carries out the division only if the divisor is not zero. If *Operand2* happens to be zero, nothing happens.

Now run the application and check it out. It works just like a hand-held calculator, and you can't crash it by specifying invalid data. We didn't have to use any data-validation code in this example because the user doesn't get a chance to type invalid data. The data entry mechanism is foolproof. The user can enter only numeric values because there are only numeric digits on the calculator. The only possible error is to divide by zero, and that's handled in the Equals button.

Adding More Features

Now that we have implemented the basic functionality of a hand-held calculator, we can add more features to our application. Let's add two more useful buttons:

- The +/- button, which inverts the sign of the number on the display

- The 1/x button, which inverts the number on the display

Open the Code window for each of the Command buttons and enter the following code in the corresponding Click event handlers. For the +/- button, enter

```
Private Sub PlusMinus_Click()
    Display.Caption = -Val(Display.Caption)
End Sub
```

For the 1/x button, enter

```
Private Sub Over_Click()
```

```
    If Val(Display.Caption) <> 0 Then Display.Caption = _
        1 / Val(Display.Caption)
    End Sub
```

As with the Division button, we don't attempt to invert a zero value. The operation 1/0 is undefined and causes a runtime error. Notice also that I use the value displayed on the Label control directly in the code. I could have stored the Display.Caption value to a variable and used the variable instead:

```
    TempValue = Val(Display.Caption)
    If TempValue <> 0 Then Display.Caption = 1 / TempValue
```

This is also better coding, but in short code segments, we all tend to minimize the number of statements.

You can easily expand the Math application by adding Function buttons to it. For example, you can add buttons to calculate common functions, such as Cos, Sin, and Log. The Cos button calculates the cosine of the number on the display. The code behind this button's Click event is a one-liner:

```
    Display.Caption = Cos(Val(Display.Caption))
```

It doesn't require a second operand and it doesn't keep track of the operation. You can implement all math functions with a single line of code. Of course, you should add some error trapping, and in some cases, you can use data-validation techniques. For example, the Sqr() function, which calculates the square root of a number, expects a positive argument. If the number on the display is negative, you can issue a warning:

```
    If Display.Caption < 0 Then
        MsgBox "Can't calculate the square root of a negative number"
    Else
        Display.Caption = Sqr(Val(Display.Caption))
    End If
```

The Log() function can calculate the logarithms of positive numbers only. Other functions, however, can easily cause overflows. For example, the Exp() function can easily produce very large numbers.

One more feature you could add to the calculator is a limit to the number of digits on the display. Most calculators can display a limited number of digits. To add this feature to the Math application (if you consider this a "feature"), use the Len() function to find out the number of digits on the display and ignore any digits entered after the number has reached the maximum number of allowed digits. But don't do anything about it yet. Let's see if we can crash this application.

Error Trapping

Crashing this application won't be as easy as crashing the Loan application, but it's not impossible either. Start multiplying very large numbers (start again with the national debt), and continue multiplying with large numbers. The result will eventually become larger than the largest number Visual Basic can represent and it will bring the program to a halt with an overflow error message.

The error's number is 6, and its description is "Overflow" (one of the worst, because it can't be remedied easily). Many errors are caused by conditions that can be remedied from within your code. If a file wasn't found, for instance, you can prompt the user for another filename. If a field's value is empty, you can ask the user to enter a different value or use a generic value. But the overflow is always the result of a series of math operations you can't undo.

How do you prevent this? Data validation isn't going to help. You just can't predict the result of an operation without actually performing the operation. And if the operation causes an overflow, you can't prevent it.

The solution is to *trap* the error. The overflow will occur no matter what, but you can trap it, and instead of letting the error message show up and embarrass you, you can handle it from within your code. To handle errors from within your code, you insert a so-called *error trap*, with the following statement:

```
On Error Goto ErrorLabel
```

The *ErrorLabel* entry is a label in your code. This statement asks Visual Basic to jump to the statement following the label ErrorLabel. (This has nothing to do with the Label control; it's a mark in the code that identifies a specific line and it can be any string.)

The structure of a subroutine with an error trap is as follows:

```
Sub MySubroutine()
On Error Goto ErrorHandler
   {statements}
   Exit Sub

ErrorHandler:
   MsgBox "Couldn't complete the operation. Aborting"
End Sub
```

The first statement isn't executable. It doesn't cause any action to be taken. It simply tells Visual Basic that if an error occurs, it must execute the lines following the label ErrorHandler. ErrorHandler is not a statement or keyword. It's a string that identifies the beginning of the error-handling code. Notice the colon at the end of the label. This is how Visual Basic knows that ErrorHandler is a label and not a procedure name.

If no error occurs during execution, the subroutine's statements are executed as if the error-trapping statements aren't there. After the subroutine's statements are executed and the Exit Sub statement is reached, the subroutine exits as usual. If an error occurs during the execution of the statements, however, the program jumps to the statement following the ErrorHandler label. The lines following the ErrorHandler label form an *error handler,* a subroutine that handles the error. The error handler shown in the example is generic; it displays a message and exits the subroutine.

Writing a Simple Error Handler

The error handler for the Math application must tell the user what kind of error occurred and then stop the operation. Let's examine its implementation. The overflow error will occur only when the Equals button is pressed, so this is the subroutine you must modify. Open the Code window, and in the button's Click event, add the underlined statements in Code 5.6.

Code 5.6:   The Revised Equals Button

```
Private Sub Equals_Click()
Dim result As Double

On Error GoTo ErrorHandler
  Operand2 = Val(Display.Caption)
  If Operator = "+" Then result = Operand1 + Operand2
  If Operator = "-" Then result = Operand1 - Operand2
  If Operator = "*" Then result = Operand1 * Operand2
  If Operator = "/" And Operand2 <> "0" Then _
        result = Operand1 / Operand2
  Display.Caption = result
  ClearDisplay = True
  Exit Sub

ErrorHandler:
  MsgBox "The operation resulted in the following error" & _
      vbCrLf & Err.Description
  Display.Caption = "ERROR"
  ClearDisplay = True
End Sub
```

Most of the time, the error handler remains inactive and doesn't interfere with the operation of the program. If an error occurs, which most likely will be an overflow error, the program's control is transferred to the error handler. It doesn't make any difference which line in the code produces the error—all errors activate the same error handler. Of course, each procedure must have its own error handler.

The error handler displays a message box with the description of the error, prints the string "ERROR" on the calculator's display and sets the *ClearDisplay* variable to True so that when another Digit button is clicked, a new number will appear on the display. The vbCrLf constant inserts a line break between the literal string and the error's description.

NOTE

Err is the name of an object that represents the error. The two most important properties of the Err object are Number and Description. In the case of the overflow error, the error's number is 6, and its description is the string "Overflow". Notice that our error handler doesn't detect the type of error that occurred. It handles all errors in the same manner (by displaying the error message and the string "ERROR" on the calculator's display).

AN APPLICATION WITH MULTIPLE FORMS

Few applications are built on a single Form. Most applications use two, three, or more Forms, which correspond to separate sections of the application. In this section, we are going to build an application that uses three Forms and lets the user switch among them at will. You'll see how to write an application that opens multiple windows on the Desktop.

VB6 at Work: The Calculators Project

The Calculators project combines the two Forms we have developed in this chapter into a single application. We'll create a new project, call it Calculators, and add the two Forms we have already designed (the project is called Calcs and is on this book's section of the Sybex Web site. We'll then design a third Form that will become our switching point. The new Form will let us load both calculators, as shown in Figure 5.8.

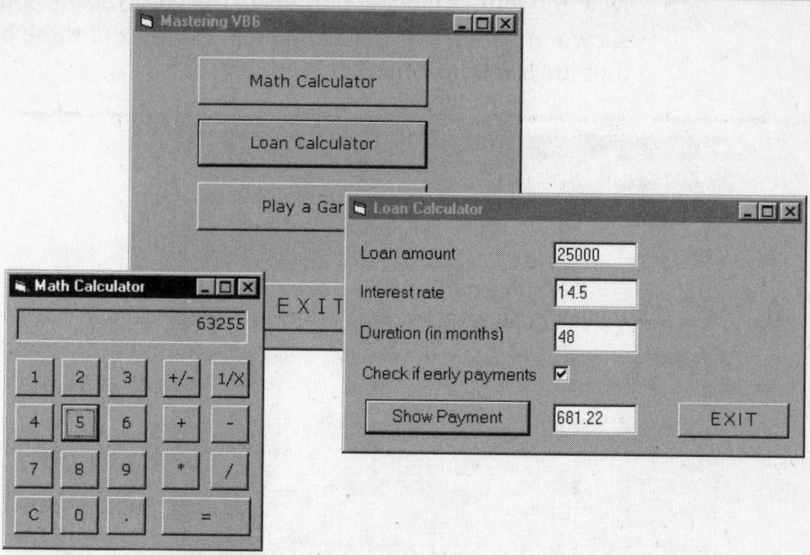

FIGURE 5.8: The window of the Calculators application loads and displays the MathCalc and Loan calculators.

To implement the new, multi-window application, follow these steps:

1. Start a new Standard EXE project.

2. Choose Project ➤ Add Form to open the Add Form dialog box (see Figure 5.9). Click on the Existing tab, and locate the Form LoanCalc on your disk (or on the Sybex Web site). The LoanCalc Form is added to the current project, and its name appears in the Forms folder under the project's name.

3. Choose Project ➤ Add Form, and locate the Form MathCalc in the Existing tab to add the Form to the project.

You now have a project with three Forms (the first one being an empty Form). If you run the application, you'll see the following error message:

```
Must have Startup Form or Sub Main()
```

To specify an application's start-up Form, do the following:

4. Open the Form1 Form in design mode, select it with the mouse, and in the Properties window, set its Name property to Calculators and its caption to Mastering VB6.

5. Now add four Command buttons to the Form, as previously shown in Figure 5.8. The names and captions of these buttons are listed in Table 5.2.

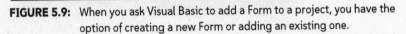

FIGURE 5.9: When you ask Visual Basic to add a Form to a project, you have the option of creating a new Form or adding an existing one.

The code behind the first two buttons should show the Math-Calc and LoanCalc Forms. To show a Form from within another, you must use the Show method, which has the following syntax where *Form* is the name of the Form you want to show:

`Form.Show`

TABLE 5.2: Names and Captions of Command Buttons

CAPTION	NAME
Math Calculator	ShowMath
Loan Calculator	ShowLoan
Play a Game	ShowGame
EXIT	bttnExit

6. Now, enter the following code in the Math Calculator button's Click event:

```
Private Sub ShowMath_Click()
    MathCalc.Show
End Sub
```

The code behind the Loan Calculator button is:

```
Private Sub ShowLoan_Click()
    LoanCalc.Show
End Sub
```

The code behind the Play a Game button should also call the Show method of another Form, but it doesn't. I regret not developing a game for your enjoyment, but I did implement a fun feature. When you click this button, it jumps to another place on the Form.

Code 5.7:   The Play a Game Button

```
Private Sub ShowGame_Click()
    ShowGame.Left = Rnd() * (Calculators.Width - _
            ShowGame.Width)
    ShowGame.Top = Rnd() * (Calculators.Height - _
            ShowGame.Height)
End Sub
```

This subroutine manipulates the Left and Top properties of the Command button to move the button to a different position.

The last button, Exit, ends the application with the End statement:

```
Private Sub ExitButton_Click()
    End
End Sub
```

This is all it takes to create a multi-window application based on some existing Forms. No changes in the existing Forms are required.

Now you can save the project. Choose File ➢ Save Project As, and in the Save dialog box, create a new folder and save the project in it.

The Startup Object

Now press F5 or choose Start ➢ Run to run the application described in the previous section. Instead of running the application, Visual Basic displays the following error message:

```
Must have a startup form or Sub Main()
```

Click OK to open the Project Properties dialog box shown in Figure 5.10. Visual Basic wants to know which Form to display when it starts. By default, Visual Basic displays the Form named Form1 or starts by executing a subroutine called Main. Our project has neither, so Visual Basic needs more information in order to start the application.

Project1 - Project Properties

General

Project Type:
Standard EXE

Startup Object:
Calculators

Project Name:
Project1

Help File Name:

Project Help
Context ID:
0

Project Description:

☐ Unattended Execution
☑ Upgrade ActiveX Controls   ○ Thread per Object
☐ Require License Key   ● Thread Pool 1 threads

OK   Cancel   Help

FIGURE 5.10:   Open the Project Properties dialog box to specify the Startup object.

Obviously, the Startup object must call the Calculators Form, as shown in Figure 5.10. This is the only Form that can call the other two. Expand the Startup Object drop-down list and select Calculators. Click OK to start the application.

NOTE

You can also open the Project Properties dialog box by choosing Project ➢ Project Properties. If you do so, the dialog box will have more tabs than those shown in Figure 5.10. I'll explain their contents later when we look at how to package an application as an EXE file.

Now, run the application and see how it works. Click the first two buttons in the main window to display the Loan and Math Forms. Switch from one window to the other, and click the main Form's buttons while the two windows are open. Visual Basic doesn't open the corresponding window again but moves the *focus* to it (brings it on top of any other window on the Desktop).

To close a window, click the Close button (the little X button at the upper right corner of the window). You can close and open the Math and Loan windows as many times as you wish. If you close the application's Main window, though, you'll have to restart the application. This action is equivalent to clicking the Exit button of the main Form.

A PROJECT'S FILES

Each Visual Basic project is made up of a number of files that are all listed in the Project Explorer window shown in Figure 5.11. This figure shows the components of the Calculators project. Notice that the files are grouped in folders, according to their types. Not only can you have more types of files in the same project, but you can also have multiple projects, or a project group. In this section, we are going to look at the structure of the files that make up a typical project: the Form and project files.

The *project file* is a list of all the files and objects associated with the project, as well as information about the environment (if you have changed some of the default settings). The contents of the project file are updated every time the project is saved. It's a text file that you can open and view with a text editor.

WARNING

Modifying the project file directly is not recommended, and you don't have good reason to do so.

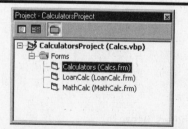

FIGURE 5.11: The components of the Calculators project

You can, however, create project files from within a special application, which is usually called a code generator. A *code generator* is an application that creates the code of an application based on user-supplied data.

The various Wizards, for instance, are code generators; they generate code for the programmer. This code is usually the skeleton of an application that you must modify according to your requirements.

The Project File

If you open the Calcs.vbp project file with a text editor, you'll find the following references in it:

```
Form=Calcs.frm
Form=..\Math\MathCalc.frm
Form=..\Loan\LoanCalc.frm
Startup="Calculators"
```

It contains a list of the Forms that make up the project and the Start-up Form (which is the Form displayed when the application starts). The project is stored in the Calcs folder, and the Forms MathCalc and LoanCalc are stored in the Math and Loan folder, respectively. The references to these files from within the Calcs project file are relative. Thus, if you move the entire parent folder with its subfolder to a new location on your disk, the project file will still be able to locate the project's components.

The Form File

The Form files (FRM) are also text files and contain the descriptions of the controls on the Form and the corresponding code. Here is the listing of the Calc.frm file:

```
VERSION 5.00
Begin VB.Form Calculators
   Caption     = "Mastering VB6"
   ClientHeight = 3675
   ClientLeft  = 60
   ClientTop   = 345
   ClientWidth = 4680
   LinkTopic   = "Form1"
   ScaleHeight = 3675
   ScaleWidth  = 4680
   StartUpPosition = 3 'Windows Default
   Begin VB.CommandButton bttnExit
      Caption  = "E X I T"
      BeginProperty Font
         Name  = "Verdana"
         Size  = 12
         Charset = 0
```

```
      Weight    = 400
      Underline = 0 'False
      Italic    = 0 'False
      Strikethrough = 0 'False
   EndProperty
   Height    = 570
   Left      = 780
   TabIndex  = 3
   Top       = 2940
   Width     = 2820
End
Begin VB.CommandButton bttnGame
   Caption   = "Play a Game"
   BeginProperty Font
      Name      = "Verdana"
      Size      = 9.75
      Charset   = 0
      Weight    = 400
      Underline = 0 'False
      Italic    = 0 'False
      Strikethrough = 0 'False
   EndProperty
   Height    = 570
   Left      = 780
   TabIndex  = 2
   Top       = 1755
   Width     = 2820
End
Begin VB.CommandButton bttnLoan
   Caption   = "Loan Calculator"
   BeginProperty Font
      Name      = "Verdana"
      Size      = 9.75
      Charset   = 0
      Weight    = 400
      Underline = 0 'False
      Italic    = 0 'False
      Strikethrough = 0 'False
   EndProperty
   Height    = 570
   Left      = 780
   TabIndex  = 1
   Top       = 1005
   Width     = 2820
End
Begin VB.CommandButton bttnMath
```

```
        Caption    =   "Math Calculator"
        BeginProperty Font
          Name      =   "Verdana"
          Size      =   9.75
          Charset   =   0
          Weight    =   400
          Underline =   0   'False
          Italic    =   0   'False
          Strikethrough =  0   'False
        EndProperty
        Height    =   570
        Left      =   780
        TabIndex  =   0
        Top       =   270
        Width     =   2820
      End
   End
   Attribute VB_Name = "Calculators"
   Attribute VB_GlobalNameSpace = False
   Attribute VB_Creatable = False
   Attribute VB_PredeclaredId = True
   Attribute VB_Exposed = False
   Private Sub bttnExit_Click()
      End
   End Sub

   Private Sub bttnGame_Click()
   bttnGame.Left = Rnd() * (Calculators.Width - bttnGame.Width)
   bttnGame.Top = Rnd() * (Calculators.Height - bttnGame.Height)
   End Sub

   Private Sub bttnLoan_Click()
      LoanCalc.Show
   End Sub

   Private Sub bttnMath_Click()
      MathCalc.Show
   End Sub
```

(No, I didn't create this listing with Visual Basic 5. The beta version I
used to prepare this book inserts the line VERSION 5.0 at the beginning
of the listing. The release version may use a different version number. It
probably won't change because the project structure has not changed
from version 5 to version 6.)

The first definition is that of the Form, which begins with the following line:

```
Begin VB.Form Calculators
```

VB.Form is a Form object, and *Calculators* is its name. Following this line is a list of Form properties. The properties whose names begin with "Client" determine the position and size of the Form on the Desktop. The ScaleWidth and ScaleHeight properties determine the coordinate system of the Form. The positions of the controls on the Form are expressed in these units.

After the properties of the Form and before the *End* keyword that closes the definition of the Form (the one that begins as Begin VB.Form), are the definitions of the controls. The following line

```
Begin VB.CommandButton bttnExit
```

marks the beginning of the first Command button control on the Form, which is the Exit button. This definition ends with the *End* keyword. In between these two keywords are all the properties of the Exit Command button. Notice that the Font property has a number of members and that they are all enclosed in a pair of *BeginProperty/EndProperty* keywords.

Following the definition of the controls is the Form's code. Code 5.8 shows the structure of a FRM file. It contains the headers of the controls only. The lines that correspond to the properties of the controls and the actual statements in the subroutines are omitted to make the structure of the file easier to see. Ellipses denote the places where properties and code lines would otherwise appear.

Code 5.8: The Object Headers of the Calculators Form

```
VERSION 5.00
Begin VB.Form Calculators
   ...
   Begin VB.CommandButton bttnExit
    BeginProperty Font
    ...
    EndProperty
   ...
   End
   Begin VB.CommandButton bttnGame
    BeginProperty Font
    ...
    EndProperty
   ...
   End
```

```
    Begin VB.CommandButton bttnLoan
     BeginProperty Font
     ...
     EndProperty
    ...
    End
    Begin VB.CommandButton bttnMath
     BeginProperty Font
     ...
     EndProperty
    ...
    End
End
Attribute VB_Name = "Calculators"
Attribute VB_GlobalNameSpace = False
Attribute VB_Creatable = False
Attribute VB_PredeclaredId = True
Attribute VB_Exposed = False

Private Sub bttnExit_Click()

End Sub

Private Sub bttnGame_Click()

End Sub

Private Sub bttnLoan_Click()

End Sub

Private Sub bttnMath_Click()

End Sub
```

As you can see, writing an application that automatically generates Visual Basic code is straightforward. You have to start with a similar project, see what information Visual Basic stores in the project and Form files, and use these files as guides.

Moving and Copying Projects

Sooner or later you'll have to move or copy a project to another folder. If you choose File ➢ Save Project As and save the project with the same (or a different) name in another folder, only the VBP file is stored in the new folder. The project's components remain in their original folders. This may not be what you expected, but that's how Visual Basic works. A project's components need not reside in the same folder, so Visual Basic doesn't copy all the files along with the project file.

TIP

Using components of existing projects is not only possible; it's desirable. You should never write code that duplicates existing code.

You shouldn't maintain multiple copies of the same file either. Suppose you create a custom Form for specifying colors. After this Form is tested and working, you can use it from within multiple projects. This Form shouldn't be replicated in each project's folder. If you decide to add a feature to it later (and believe me, you will), you'll have to update multiple files. If you save this Form in a special folder though, you can add it to any number of projects. If you update the Form in a single folder, all the projects that use it will see the new Form.

TIP

Another good way to save a Form is to place it in your vb\common\forms folder, for example, and add it to each project that needs its functionality.

This feature is why Visual Basic doesn't enforce the one-folder-per-project rule. Create a folder for each project, and store all the files that are unique to the project in it, but add existing components to a new project from their original folders.

To save a project in a different folder, you must first copy all the files of the project to a new folder and, only then, save the project file in the same folder. If you first save the project to a new folder or under a different filename, your project won't see the new files. Instead, it will refer to the original files.

As mentioned, the VBP file contains references to the project's components. Of course, if you change the name or path of even a single component in your project, Visual Basic will prompt you to save the project file before you close it. An awareness of this detail can save you a good deal of frustration.

WARNING

There's nothing more frustrating than having identically named files in several folders and not knowing which ones are the latest versions. Even worse, you may end up updating one set of files and expect to see the changes in another set. This is an accident waiting to happen, and if you decide to move a project to another folder, always delete the files in the old folder.

You can also move projects to a different folder from within the Windows Explorer. Visual Basic uses relative path names in the VBP file, so if you move all the files to a new folder, the relative references are valid. However, you shouldn't count on this. It's possible that the VBP file will end up seeing files other than those you think it does, or it might not find the referenced files at all. It's best to use File menu commands when moving projects around. Select each component of the project in the Project Explorer window and save it under a different file name with the File ➤ Save As command. After you have saved all the components to the new folder, save the project in the same folder with the File ➤ Save Project As command.

Executable Files

So far, you have been executing applications within Visual Basic's environment. However, you can't expect the users of your application to have Visual Basic installed on their systems. If you develop an interesting application, you won't feel like giving away the code of the application (the *source code*, as it's called). Applications are distributed as executable files, along with their support files. The users of the application can't see your source code, and your application can't be modified or made to look like someone else's application (that doesn't mean it can't be copied, of course).

NOTE

An *executable file* is a binary file that contains instructions only the machine can understand and execute. The commands stored in the executable file are known as *machine language*.

Applications designed for the Windows environment can't fit in a single file. It just wouldn't make sense. Along with the executable files, your application requires a number of so-called support files. If you're using any custom controls, the files in which they reside (they have the extension OCX) must be distributed with the application.

In general, Windows applications require a large number of support files, and these files may already exist on many of the machines on which your application will be installed. That's why it doesn't make sense to distribute huge files. Each user should install the main application and the support files that aren't already installed on their computer.

USING THE APPLICATION SETUP WIZARD

Distributing applications would be a complicated process if it weren't for the Application Setup Wizard. The Application Setup Wizard takes care of packaging your application for distribution.

The Wizard creates a new application whose sole purpose is to install your application on the host computer. It also breaks the installation program into pieces so that you can distribute your application on diskettes. The Application Setup Wizard comes with Visual Basic, and it's straightforward to use.

Creating an Executable File

Before preparing the setup application, you must create an executable file for your application. This file will be represented as an icon on your Desktop, and you can run the application without starting Visual Basic and loading the project. Simply double-click the application's icon on the Desktop (or a folder) to start the application.

To make an executable file for your project, follow these steps:

1. Choose File ➢ Make *project*.exe (*project* is the name of the project).

2. Enter the name and the location of the file, and Visual Basic will create the executable file.

To set options for the executable files through the Project Properties dialog box, follow these steps:

1. Choose Project ➢ Project Properties to open the Project Properties dialog box, shown in Figure 5.12.

2. Select the Compile tab.

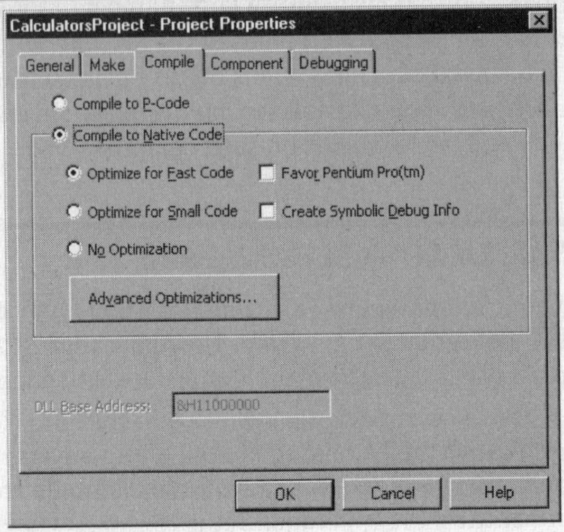

FIGURE 5.12:   In the Compile tab of the Project Properties dialog box, you specify compilation options.

Now you're ready to specify options. Visual Basic can produce two types
of executable files:

▶ P-code

▶ Native code

Compile to P-Code   When you select this option, Visual Basic compiles a project using *p-code*, which is pseudo-code that the CPU can't execute directly. BASIC has always been an interpreted language. Programs
written in an interpreted language aren't translated into machine language before they are executed. Instead, each line of code is translated as
needed and then executed.

Interpreted programs aren't as fast as compiled programs (which are
translated into optimized machine language before execution). A p-code
program is somewhere in between the two. It's highly efficient code, but
it can't be executed as is. A translation step is required. P-code, however,
is closer to machine language than it is to Visual Basic, and the process of
translating p-code to executable code is efficient.

NOTE

The main benefit of p-code is that it's compact and not much slower than pure executable code. For more information on p-code and native code-compiled applications see Chapter 12, "Optimizing VB Applications," in *Mastering Visual Basic 6*.

Part i

Compile to Native Code When you select this option, Visual Basic compiles a project using *native code*, which is the machine language that the CPU understands and executes. The generated executable is faster than the equivalent p-code executable by as much as 20 times. This is a benchmark (a best-case scenario), and you shouldn't expect such dramatic improvements with your average applications. Use this option for applications that perform involved math operations. When you compile to native code, you have the following options:

▶ **Optimize for Fast Code** Maximizes the speed of the executable file by instructing the compiler to favor speed over size. To optimize the code, the compiler can reduce many constructs to functionally similar sequences of machine code.

▶ **Optimize for Small Code** Minimizes the size of the executable file by instructing the compiler to favor size over speed

▶ **No Optimization** Compiles without optimizations

▶ **Favor Pentium Pro™** Optimizes code to favor the Pentium Pro processor. Use this option for programs meant only for the Pentium Pro. Code generated with this option runs on other Intel processors, but it doesn't perform as well as if compiled with other options.

▶ **Create Symbolic Debug Info** Generates symbolic debug information in the executable. An executable file created using this option can be debugged with Visual C++ or with debuggers that use the CodeView style of debug information. Setting this option generates a PDB file with the symbol information for your executable. This option is most likely to be used by Visual C++ programmers who also use Visual Basic.

Selecting Advanced Optimization Options

When you select Advanced Optimizations, Visual Basic opens the Advanced Optimizations dialog box, shown in Figure 5.13. You use these options to turn off certain checks that normally take place and ensure that your application works properly. To increase the speed of the executable file, you can turn off some or all of these checks by selecting the appropriate checkbox.

WARNING

Enabling these optimizations may prevent the correct execution of your program. You must understand what each option does and be sure the application doesn't require any of the options you turn off.

Advanced Optimizations

Warning: enabling the following optimizations may prevent correct execution of your program

☑ Assume No Aliasing

☑ Remove Array Bounds Checks

☐ Remove Integer Overflow Checks

☐ Remove Floating Point Error Checks

☐ Allow Unrounded Floating Point Operations

☑ Remove Safe Pentium(tm) FDIV Checks

[OK]   [Cancel]   [Help]

FIGURE 5.13: The Advanced Optimizations dialog box

Assume No Aliasing   Select this checkbox to tell the compiler that your program doesn't use aliasing. *Aliasing* is a technique that lets your code refer to a variable (memory location) by more than one name.

Remove Array Bounds Checks   By default, Visual Basic checks an array's bounds every time your code accesses the array to determine if the index is within the range of the array. If the index is not within array bounds, a runtime error is generated (which can be trapped from within the code). Select this option to turn off the array bounds checking and speed up applications that use arrays. However, the code that ensures that the array's bounds aren't exceeded may cost more in execution time. If an array bound is exceeded, the results will be unexpected.

Remove Integer Overflow Checks By default, Visual Basic checks every calculation for integer-style data types—Byte, Integer, and Long—to ensure that the value is within the range of the data type. If the magnitude of the value being put into the data type is incorrect, a runtime error is generated. Select this option to turn off error checking and speed up integer calculations. If data type capacities are overflowed, you'll get incorrect results.

Remove Floating Point Error Checks By default, Visual Basic checks every calculation of a floating-point data type—Single and Double—to be sure that the value is within range for that data type and that there are no divide-by-zero or invalid operations. If the magnitude of the value being put into the data type is incorrect, an error occurs. Select this option to turn off error checking and speed up floating-point calculations. If data type capacities are overflowed, no error occurs, and you'll get incorrect results.

Allow Unrounded Floating Point Operations When this option is selected, the compiler uses floating-point registers more efficiently, avoids storing and loading large volumes of data to and from memory, and compares floating points more efficiently.

Remove Safe Pentium™ FDIV Checks Selecting this option removes the safety checking so that the code for floating-point division is faster but may produce slightly incorrect results on Pentium processors with the FDIV bug.

WHAT'S NEXT?

After getting your hands dirty doing some actual programming in this chapter, it's time for some programming theory in the next. This won't be airy, useless theory. You'll learn how to approach programming your VB applications so that bugs will be minimized, and you'll acquire some effective debugging techniques for when those bugs do raise their ugly heads.

PART II
PRACTICAL VISUAL BASIC

Chapter 6

DEBUGGING VISUAL BASIC PROGRAMS

This chapter is a collection of debugging tips and tricks you can use with Visual Basic. Many of these tricks are those I've learned from experiences I've had writing programs in a wide variety of languages and on a number of different platforms.

I've broken this chapter into three "how-to" parts: preventing bugs, isolating bugs, and using the Visual Basic Debugger. Finally, I'll talk about some problems that you may encounter with your Visual Basic programs.

Adapted from *Expert Guide to Visual Basic 6* by Wayne S. Freeze

ISBN 0-7821-2349-X   944 pages $49.99

PREVENTING BUGS BEFORE THEY OCCUR

Perhaps the best way to fix a bug is to keep the bug from happening in the first place. For the most part, the techniques for preventing bugs are common sense things (or would be common sense if common sense were common) that most programmers would do if they took the time to think about it. But let's face it, with increasing demands on our time, we don't always have the time we need to pay such attention to detail!

THE FASCINATING STARSX PROGRAM

For the examples in this chapter, I'm using one of my favorite programs of all time: StarSX. Many years ago, I was learning how to program on a Hewlett Packard 2000 F time-share system that allowed you to program only in BASIC. One of the terminals attached to the system was an old Tektronics 4010 graphic display terminal, and one of my favorite pastimes was creating graphics programs for it.

Someone wrote a few programs for it before I started at the school (Essex Community College). One of these programs was called The Star of Essex, which was shortened to StarSX. I was so fascinated with the program that I rewrote it many times over the years. It was originally written in BASIC, but has been converted into FORTRAN, C, C++, Pascal, SPL (don't ask), and most recently, Visual Basic.

As I rewrote the program, I continued to enhance it by allowing the user to change various parameters to get different results. The version included with this book has the most parameters of any of the versions I've written. However, don't start playing with this program unless you have a lot of time on your hands—it's more addicting than it looks!

Technically, all this program does is draw a circle, by drawing a series of straight lines between two points on the circle. The closer you choose the points, the more round the circle looks. However, by choosing points fairly far apart on the circle and decreasing the radius of the circle each time you draw a point, you create a picture like the one you see below. My kids love to watch all the bright colors move and swirl across the screen.

CONTINUED ➡

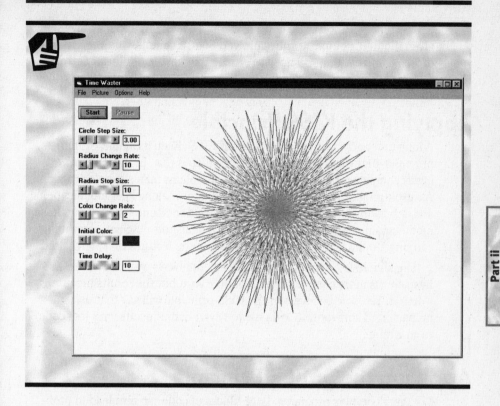

Using Option Explicit

Most programming languages in use today require that you declare a variable before you use it. In some languages, declaring variables is done to make it easier to write the compiler. With other languages, programmers declare variables just for documentation purposes; others do it simply because it was always done that way. But I've found that declaring a variable does two things: it ensures that you get the variable type you want, and it prevents you from misspelling the variable's name. Sometimes, finding a misspelled variable can be very difficult, since `Clock` and `Clock` look the same to you and me but not to the compiler.

By default, Visual Basic will create a variable automatically the first time you use it. To disable this feature, you need to include `Option Explicit` at the top of each module in your program. For new projects, you can set the Visual Basic IDE option Require Variable Declaration (in the Options dialog box). For existing projects, you can simply enter `Option Explicit` into the Global Declarations section of any module.

The big limitation of Option Explicit is that it applies only to a given module, not to the entire project. So in a complex project with a lot of forms and classes, you need to ensure that each module has Option Explicit included.

Applying the KISS Principle

A long time ago, I learned about the old KISS (Keep It Simple, Stupid) principle. In the case of Visual Basic, the idea is that, in the long run, an overly complex program will cause more problems than a simple program. A simple program is easier to understand, thus making later modifications and debugging a whole lot easier (especially if someone else is doing those modifications). A simple program may even be more efficient, since it is not carrying around a lot of baggage caused by extra features that aren't used.

The simple-is-better philosophy does not always work, however. A heap sort is more complex than a bubble sort, but the results are often worth it. Yet, true believers in the KISS principle will say that using a prepackaged sort routine will give you even better results with less code to go wrong.

Applying the SMILE Principle

Like very complex programs, large blocks of code can also lead to problems. Someone once told me years ago that if you can't see an entire subroutine or function, then it's too large. I call this the SMILE (Simple Makes It Lots Easier) principle.

I learned about applying the SMILE principle back when I used to compile large programs as a batch job. The compiler would generate a few hundred pages of paper with the program's source code and other diagnostic information. Each subroutine or function would begin on a new page, so this meant that a practical limit was about 50 lines of code per routine.

Today, I find that limit somewhat high in most cases, but a little bit restrictive in a few other cases. Now I try to use what I can fit on a typical screen—about 30 lines. This means that I can see the entire routine easily. If I can't fit the code into that much space, I'll divide the code into a few private subroutines and call them from the original.

Occasionally, I find that I want to use a large subroutine. This usually happens when I have many assignment statements or subroutine calls, or

I have a `Select Case` statement or `If...Then...ElseIf` statement with many individual conditions. In the first situation, I try to group the statements into meaningful chunks. In the second situation, I try to limit myself to less than a dozen statements in each of the individual cases.

Taking Advantage of Object-Oriented Programming

Object-oriented programming means many things to many people (especially those in the marketing department). The answer to the question "Is Visual Basic object-oriented?" doesn't really matter. What matters is that when you break your program into chunks of code with well-defined interfaces between the chunks, your programs become more reliable.

By using well-defined interfaces, you are forced to think about how the chunk will be used. Since you can't cross boundaries and change a particular value inside a chunk even though you think it's safe, you may need to include an additional interface in the future. But at least you will know all of the code that could possibly modify the chunk's data. So if the chunk's data gets corrupted, this approach simplifies the debugging process considerably.

The other advantage of chunks is that they are easy to build and easy to test by themselves. Once they have been tested, you can build other components using these chunks. Since your chunks communicate through well-defined interfaces, you can check for invalid parameters and trap more errors before they occur.

Of course, you also get the fundamental advantage of object-oriented programming. When you need to change an object's architecture, your existing program will continue to work without changes, as long as the interfaces continue to work the same way. Also, you can use the object in more than one place, which will help to reduce your overall programming effort.

Using Comments and Coding Conventions

Comments and coding conventions are also important to minimizing problems in your code. While these things may not prevent bugs per se, they will help the next person who comes along to understand what you did and why you did it. Then if something should go wrong, it will be easier for that next person to rectify the problem.

Adding Comments

There is more to writing comments than simply repeating what is obvious from reading the code. Writing good comments takes a little time and some thought, but the end result should be useful to anyone (including yourself) who may read those comments in the future.

It is important to understand that with comments, more is not always better. Take a look at the following code fragment from the StarSX program. It has one line of comments for each line of code. Note that the comments are particularly uninspired, so while the number of comments is equal to the number of lines of code, no useful information is passed.

```
' Compute new x coordinate
NewX = CenterX + Sin(Theta) * Radius
' Compute new y coordinate
NewY = CenterY + Cos(Theta) * Radius

' Draw a line from the old coordinate to the new coordinate
Form1.Line (OldX, OldY)-(NewX, NewY), RGB(Red, Green, Blue)
' Set the line mode
Form1.DrawMode = vbCopyPen

' Save the new x coordinate in place of the old x coordinate
OldX = NewX
' Save the new y coordinate in place of the old y coordinate
OldY = NewY

' Add AngleStep to Theta
Theta = Theta + AngleStep
' Subtract RadiusDecrement from Radius
Radius = Radius-RadiusDecrement
```

Now look at the next code fragment from the StarSX program. You see only one comment, but this comment spans five lines. Instead of restating each line of code, this comment tries to explain how this routine works. From reading this, you understand why DrawMode was reset after the line was drawn. Also, you can understand how the arc of the circle is drawn rather than trying to figure out what CenterX + Sin(Theta) * Radius really means.

```
' Draw the arc of a circle from the coordinates (OldX, OldY)
' to the point determined by Theta, Radius with center at
' (CenterX, CenterY). The first time, Form1.DrawMode is set to
' vbWhiteness, so the arc is not drawn. Set it to vbCopyPen so
' subsequent arcs will be visible.

NewX = CenterX + Sin(Theta) * Radius
```

```
NewY = CenterY + Cos(Theta) * Radius

Form1.Line (OldX, OldY)-(NewX, NewY), RGB(Red, Green, Blue)
Form1.DrawMode = 13

OldX = NewX
OldY = NewY

Theta = Theta + AngleStep
Radius = Radius-RadiusDecrement
```

Another tip for writing comments is to include some status information at
the head of each routine that discusses who wrote the routine, when it was
written, and a brief revision history. This information is especially useful
when you have multiple people working on the same project. Listing 6.1
shows the complete DrawArc subroutine from the StarSX program.

Listing 6.1:   DrawArc Routine in StarSX

```
Private Sub DrawArc()

' Routine:    DrawArc
' Programmer:   Wayne S. Freeze
' History:
'  1Apr98:    Initial release - WSF.
'  5Apr98:    Modified to not draw the arc the first
'         time this routine is called - WSF.
'
' Discussion:
'  Draw the arc of a circle from the coordinates (OldX, OldY)
'  to the point determined by Theta, Radius with center at
'  (CenterX, CenterY). The first time, Form1.DrawMode is set to
'  vbWhiteness, so the arc is not drawn. Set it to vbCopyPen so
'  subsequent arcs will be visible.

NewX = CenterX + Sin(Theta) * Radius
NewY = CenterY + Cos(Theta) * Radius

Form1.Line (OldX, OldY)-(NewX, NewY), RGB(Red, Green, Blue)
Form1.DrawMode = vbCopyPen

OldX = NewX
OldY = NewY

Theta = Theta + AngleStep
Radius = Radius - RadiusDecrement

End Sub
```

Following Coding Conventions

Coding conventions are another useful tool for preventing bugs. Coding conventions come in a couple of forms: they provide rules for naming variables and routines, and they identify which statements you want to avoid while programming. Both forms combine to create a style that must be comfortable for you to use.

Variable and Routine Names   Microsoft recommends a rather complex way to prefix variables. While this convention conveys a lot of information about your variables, it makes them somewhat unreadable and definitely difficult to remember. Even though Microsoft makes this suggestion, you might notice that the properties for things like the TextBox and ListBox controls refer to the Text property rather than the strText property. The same goes for the rest of the properties and methods for the other controls and objects. I suggest that you use meaningful names but leave the type information off the variable name.

TIP

Find a variable quickly: If you right-click on a variable (or subroutine or function) and select the Definition option from the pop-up menu, you will be taken to the place in your program where the variable was defined. You can return to the same line you left by right-clicking again and selecting the Last Position option from the pop-up menu.

Subroutines and functions are two places where the more descriptive you make the name, the less likely you are to use the wrong one. Properties, methods, and events in your own user controls should also be descriptive. After all, when you compile your program into machine code, it doesn't matter in the least whether you used two characters or twenty characters!

Statements to Avoid   Visual Basic includes a variety of different statements, many of which overlap other statements in terms of functionality. I strongly suggest that you choose a subset of these statements and use them, while ignoring the others. This means you'll need to remember the syntax for fewer statements, and you'll become more comfortable with the ways that you use those statements.

For instance, you can use For/Next, Do Until/Loop, Do While/Loop, and While/Wend to perform loops in your code. There is no reason to use all four. I suggest you pick one style and use it consistently. Personally, I prefer the

Do While/Loop structure, but I find myself using the For/Next anytime I'm dealing with a collection of objects (For Each), or when I need to perform a process a fixed number of times (For I= 1 to 10). I never use the Do Until/Loop or the While/Wend statements.

NOTE

There is an exception for every rule, and you'll see me use it fairly often: Being a lazy programmer, I often use short variable names. The variable name I use most often is i. I typically use this whenever I write a For/Next loop as the index variable. (Can you tell I spent too much time writing FORTRAN programs over the years?)

I also recommend avoiding the Gosub/Return statement and the GoTo statement. Both are holdovers from BASIC's early days. Gosub/ Return isn't really needed in Visual Basic, where you can declare real subroutines, and GoTo is against every structured programming rule ever written. I've debugged many programs written by professional programmers who used the GoTo statement, and I've frequently found it faster to rewrite the entire program rather than try to fix it.

WARNING

More means less: Visual Basic has the ability to include more than one statement in a single line of code. Don't do it! Breakpoints are set on the line of code, not the statement. This means that you can't stop your program on the third statement on a particular line of code.

Being a Lazy Programmer

After reading about the KISS and SMILE principles, object-oriented programming, and comments and coding conventions, you may be wondering, "What does this have to do with debugging my programs?" The answer is that following good, solid programming practices is key to creating programs that require less debugging and that can more easily be debugged. As long as I'm on my soapbox, I'm going to suggest a general philosophy that will help you to eliminate bugs before they become bugs. I call it the Lazy Programmer approach.

Here are the Ten Commandments of a Lazy Programmer:

1. Think about what you want to do before you write any code.

2. Make it work the first time—you prefer not to do it again.

3. Don't make a program more complicated than necessary because this may introduce more problems into the program in the long run.

4. Write modular programs because they are easier to test and debug.

5. Use a wide variety of tools to reduce the amount of work required to create the program and to increase the reliability of the final product.

6. Reuse code where possible, since the code has already been written and is known to work properly.

7. Write the least amount of code to solve the problem.

8. Use a lot of comments for complex code, and make sure that you provide a good overview of how the program functions.

9. Use good coding conventions so that comments aren't necessary for simple tasks.

10. Use Visual Basic to write Windows programs.

In today's world, people are paid to work. The harder they work, the more money they make (well, at least in theory). While this should be true of most professions, it is the wrong way to pay programmers.

Programmers should be paid a flat fee for creating an acceptable program. That way, it is in the programmer's best interest to make it work right the first time, so he or she can move on to the next project. It also forces a programmer to think smart. After all, the correct measure of programming is not the number of lines of code written per year but the number of acceptable programs written per year.

Isolating Bugs the Easy Way

Although you can use the techniques I've suggested so far to prevent some bugs, I don't need to tell you that you won't avoid all of them.

When you know you are getting the wrong result, or your program is not behaving properly, what do you do next? You can use the Visual Basic Debugger, but sometimes that's overkill for what may appear to be a simple problem. Here, I'll talk about some simple ways to help you find out what is going on in your program:

▶ The MsgBox statement can be used to display information about your program while it is running.

▶ By pressing Ctrl+Break, you can interrupt your program and use the Immediate window to find out what is happening with your program.

▶ The Debug object provides some facilities to your program while running in the Visual Basic development environment.

Displaying Information with MsgBox

As I mentioned earlier, I learned to program many years ago on a Hewlett Packard 2000F time-share system, and the only programming language was a version of BASIC. This version of BASIC was powerful at the time, but wasn't even close to the Visual Basic we know and love today. If your problem generated an error, it printed a cryptic error message and stopped running. There were no breakpoints and no watches. Hitting Break stopped your program without giving you an opportunity to check any of your variables.

In that situation, debugging became a matter of inserting Print statements at various places throughout the program to display critical variables. Sometimes, you would even put an Input statement after the Print statement, just to slow down the program to the point where you could see the results before they scrolled off the top of the terminal display.

Well, Visual Basic still remembers its roots. Probably the easiest way to debug a Visual Basic program is by placing statements in your program to display variable information and to interrupt execution. The MsgBox statement has the ability to both display information and interrupt your program while it is running.

Simply insert a statement like this in your program to see what value the variable x contains:

```
MsgBox Format(x)
```

Use the following type of statement to see what is in the variables x and y:

```
MsgBox Format(x) & ":" & Format(y)
```

Once you get the information you need, you can click the OK button to continue. As you can see in the example shown in Figure 6.1, the display isn't pretty, but then, you're the only one who is ever going to see it.

Part ii

STARSX

1024:10

OK

FIGURE 6.1: Displaying a message box to see the contents of multiple variables

Using Ctrl+Break and the Immediate Window

While your program is running in the development environment, you can interrupt it at any time by pressing Ctrl+Break. You can also select Run ➤ Break from the Visual Basic IDE menu. Either method invokes the Visual Basic Debugger. This will even work while you are displaying a message box. But rather than use the full power of the Visual Basic Debugger, you can use the Immediate window to check on some values and perform some basic tasks.

The Immediate window allows you to enter a single Visual Basic statement and execute it immediately. Figure 6.2 shows an example.

```
Immediate
print anglestep, radiusdecrement, colorincrement
 3              10            2
|
```

FIGURE 6.2: The Immediate window

Statements that declare variables or create subroutines can't be used in the Immediate window, but nearly any other statement can be used. For instance, you can display the contents of any of the variables that are in scope by using the Print statement. You can set the value of a variable by simply typing an assignment statement. You can even call functions, run subroutines, or invoke methods from the Immediate window.

The biggest limitation of using the Immediate window is that the variable or object must be available for you to reference. If you are waiting for input, your program may be able to access only global variables because all of the other variables may be out of scope. To ensure that the variables you want to see are in scope, you need to insert a Stop statement where you want to check them or set a breakpoint using the Visual Basic Debugger (discussed a bit later in this chapter).

WARNING

Stop means End: Use the Stop statement only when debugging your program. If you encounter a Stop statement while running a compiled program, it is treated as an End statement, and your program will be terminated.

Adding Debug.Assert

Okay, since your code is already perfect, how about making a small wager? Would you be willing to bet that everything is normal in several places throughout your program? The Debug.Assert statement let's you do just that.

For instance, you can add a statement like this one to your program:

```
Debug.Assert x > 0 and y = ""
```

This statement verifies that the variable x is greater than zero, and that y contains a null string. If x is really less than zero, the Assert method will fail and you will be transferred to the Visual Basic Debugger, with the Assert statement highlighted, as shown in Figure 6.3.

Part II

```
' Routine:        DrawArc
' Programmer:     Wayne S. Freeze
' History:
'   1Apr98:       Initial release - WSF.
'   5Apr98:       Modified to not draw the arc the first
'                 time this routine is called - WSF.

' Draw the arc of a circle from the coordinates (OldX, OldY)
' to the point on determined by Theta, Radius with center at
' (CenterX, CenterY). The first time, Form1.DrawMode is set to
' vbWhiteness, so the arc is not drawn. Set it to vbCopyPen so
' subsequent arcs will be visible.

NewX = CenterX + Sin(Theta) * Radius
NewY = CenterY + Cos(Theta) * Radius

Debug.Assert Radius > 10000

Form1.Line (OldX, OldY)-(NewX, NewY), RGB(Red, Green, Blue)
Form1.DrawMode = vbCopyPen

OldX = NewX
OldY = NewY

Theta = Theta + AngleStep
Radius = Radius - RadiusDecrement

End Sub

Private Sub Command1_Click()
```

FIGURE 6.3: The Visual Basic Debugger highlighting a failed Assert statement

Note that the Assert method works only in the development environment. When you compile your project, all references to the Assert method are dropped, so there is no need to use conditional compilation to remove these statements from your compiled program.

Adding Debug.Print

The MsgBox statement can be annoying, especially if it's inside a loop. Fortunately, the Debug object offers a viable alternative: the Debug.Print statement.

The Debug.Print statement works like a regular Print statement, except that it sends the output to the Immediate window. This can be useful when you want to check what is happening to a variable in a loop, as you can see in the example in Figure 6.4.

```
Immediate
Radius  =   1690              Theta  =  453
Radius  =   1680              Theta  =  456
Radius  =   1670              Theta  =  459
Radius  =   1660              Theta  =  462
Radius  =   1650              Theta  =  465
Radius  =   1640              Theta  =  468
Radius  =   1630              Theta  =  471
Radius  =   1630              Theta  =  471 |
```

FIGURE 6.4:   Watching variables change in a loop

USING THE VISUAL BASIC DEBUGGER

The biggest advantage of using an interpreted language is the ability to use a debugger that allows you to debug at the source-code level. The Visual Basic Debugger is a truly advanced tool that can help you identify problems with your program. Here I'll go over the basics of setting breakpoints and watching expressions.

Debugging with Breakpoints

An alternative to using Ctrl+Break or the MsgBox statement to interrupt your program is to set a breakpoint. A *breakpoint* is a marker in your program that will temporarily interrupt your program and transfer control to the Immediate window. This works in the same way as the Stop statement described earlier. However, breakpoints are never included into a compiled program, so they can never be accidentally executed.

Setting a Breakpoint

To set a breakpoint, simply click on the gray area to the right of your statement. The statement will be highlighted in brown, and a brown dot will appear beside the statement in the gray area. Figure 6.5 shows a black-and-white rendition. The breakpoint can be set while your program is in break mode or while you are in design mode.

Part ii

```
STARSX - Form1 (Code)                                    _ □ X
(General)                          ▼    DrawArc                    ▼

    Private Sub DrawArc()

    ' Routine:        DrawArc
    ' Programmer:     Wayne S. Freeze
    ' History:
    '   1Apr98:         Initial release - WSF.
    '   5Apr98:         Modified to not draw the arc the first
    '                   time this routine is called - WSF.
    '
    ' Draw the arc of a circle from the coordinates (OldX, OldY)
    ' to the point on determined by Theta, Radius with center at
    ' (CenterX, CenterY). The first time, Form1.DrawMode is set to
    ' vbWhiteness, so the arc is not drawn. Set it to vbCopyPen so
    ' subsequent arcs will be visible.

    NewX = CenterX + Sin(Theta) * Radius
    NewY = CenterY + Cos(Theta) * Radius

    Form1.Line (OldX, OldY)-(NewX, NewY), RGB(Red, Green, Blue)
    Form1.DrawMode = vbCopyPen

    OldX = NewX
    OldY = NewY

●   Theta = Theta + AngleStep
    Radius = Radius - RadiusDecrement

    End Sub

    Private Sub Command1_Click()
```

FIGURE 6.5: Setting a break point

Hitting a Breakpoint

When your program is running and encounters the breakpoint, the statement is highlighted in yellow, and the code window is displayed along with the Immediate window. You can then examine any variables local to the routine and look at any module-level variables or global variables. Figure 6.6 shows an example of what happens when you hit a breakpoint.

NOTE

Breakpoints happen at the start: A breakpoint will be triggered before the break-pointed line of code is executed. If you have multiple statements on a single line, the program will be stopped before the first statement on the line is executed.

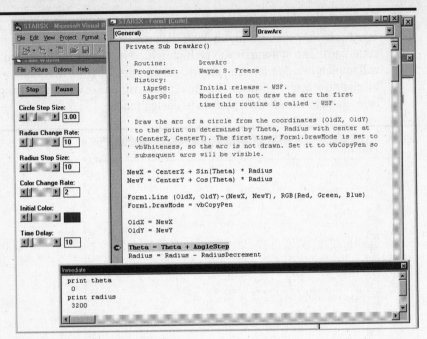

FIGURE 6.6: Hitting a breakpoint

Leaving Break Mode

Once you have finished checking your program's state while in break mode, you have two ways to resume execution: continue with regular execution or go on in step mode.

Continuing with Normal Execution   You can select Run ➤ Continue to allow your program to continue normally. It will continue to the next breakpoint or until the end of the program if no more breakpoints are encountered.

Continuing in Step Mode   Alternatively, you can resume in step mode after a breakpoint. In this mode, you can execute the current line of code and return to break mode. This is similar to setting a breakpoint on the next line of code. There are three options in step mode:

> **Step Into**   This option lets you execute the current line of code and break at the next line of code executed, even if it is in a different subroutine.

Step Over This option allows you to execute the current line of code and break at the line of code immediately following the current line, even if the current line is a call to a subroutine.

Step Out This option lets you execute all of the statements starting with the current statement until the routine completes. Then the program will reenter break mode on the statement that immediately follows the statement that called the routine.

Step mode commands work only while you are in break mode.

Watching Expressions

Setting a breakpoint is not the only way to enter break mode. You can tell Visual Basic to watch an expression and then enter break mode when the expression is true or when the value changes. If you don't specify either of these options, Visual Basic will just watch the expression and display it the next time you enter break mode. Note that unlike the Immediate window, which is updated continually as the program runs, the watch display is only updated when you enter break mode.

Setting a Watch

To set a watch, select Debug ➤ Add Watch to display the Add Watch dialog box, as shown in Figure 6.7. You fill in the Expression box with the expression you wish to watch. You can choose a simple variable as the expression, or you can choose a more complex expression involving variables, functions, properties, and methods that return a value.

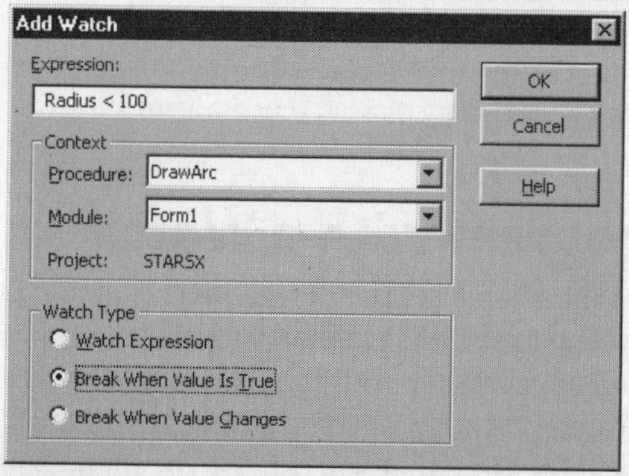

FIGURE 6.7: The Add Watch dialog box

You can also specify the watch type, which describes the action to be taken when the expression is evaluated. When you choose the Watch Expression option, the expression is tracked, but no action is taken until you enter break mode. The Break When Value is True and the Break When Value Changes options are far more useful because they enter break mode. You should think of these options as conditional breakpoints. While the expression can be as simple or as complicated as you make it, chances are you want to use something like `Radius < 100` or `ProcessingComplete = True` when you select either of the watch types that enter break mode.

NOTE

Watches are slow: Before you execute a statement, all of the watches will need to be recomputed, causing your program to slow down. In the interest of time, it is highly desirable to isolate the watch to a specific procedure or at least a specific module.

After you add a watch, the Watches window appears, listing all of the watches you set, as shown in Figure 6.8. You can highlight one of the watches and choose Debug ➣ Edit Watch or Debug ➣ Delete Watch (or right-click and select the appropriate option from the pop-up menu) to change or delete the selected watch.

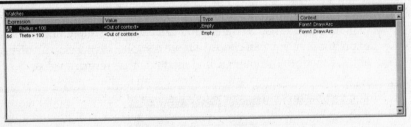

FIGURE 6.8: The Watches window before running your program

Running Your Program with a Watch

If you chose either the When Value is True or the Break When Value Changes option when you set your watch, when you run your program, the Watches window will appear when your program enters break mode. Figure 6.9 shows the Watches window and the Immediate window displayed when `Radius < 100`. Note that you can use the Immediate window to determine exact values for each watched variable.

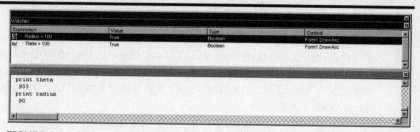

FIGURE 6.9:   The Watches and Immediate windows in break mode

TRACKING DOWN THE PROBLEM

As I said earlier in this chapter, I'm lazy. I know it. I admit it. This doesn't mean I don't work hard or that I'm not willing to devote the necessary time to a project. It's just that I want the most bang for the buck.

Under ideal circumstances, you should spend 50 (yes 50!) percent of your time in a project defining the requirements and designing the application. Another 25 percent should be spent in coding and unit testing, and the rest spent in system testing. However, in the real world, there's never enough time. Deadlines change, competitors release new products, and customers want new and different features.

In the real world, you never have enough time to define the requirements beyond "Do it now!" Project design is often done on the fly. This increases the time needed for coding and debugging the project. Because you did less design up front, you devote more time to debugging design flaws rather than simply debugging coding errors. Debugging design flaws is perhaps the most difficult debugging task of them all. Your code runs perfectly, but the program fails to perform its assigned task.

Correcting design flaws often involves making major changes to your application. You may need to add new database tables or restructure existing tables. You may need to make major changes to old forms, or even junk them and start over again from scratch. The beauty of writing Visual Basic programs is that much of the hard work is done for you automatically.

However, coding problems can still be a challenge to track down and fix. We've gone over the tools, now let's look at some problem errors. Visual Basic has a few traps of its own.

Finding Array Problems

Many controls use zero-based arrays. This means that the first element in an array has an index of zero. With Count items in the array, the last element will have an index of Count −1. However, just to keep you on your toes, some Visual Basic controls use a one-based array. Thus, valid indexes range from 1 to Count.

Remembering which type of array is used where is a challenge. When you get an error in this type of situation, you may want to pull up the documentation and review what the range of values should be.

Checking Parameter Ranges

Another area that often causes problems is ensuring that parameters are in the proper range before calling a function.

For instance, Left(mystring, len(mystring)−x) is a very useful expression. It will truncate the last x number of characters from the string mystring. This statement will work perfectly fine, until one time when x > len(mystring). Then you get that nasty runtime error saying "Invalid procedure call or argument."

Watching for Error Object Problems

The last area I want to mention involves the On Error statement and the Error object. Using an On Error statement without clearing the Error object creates a time bomb waiting to explode.

I spent an embarrassing amount of time (no, I'm not going to admit how much!) debugging a program when I first started using Visual Basic. I couldn't understand why a block of code was failing. I was doing everything right. I had an On Error Resume Next statement, followed by another statement, followed by an If statement that checked the Error object. Even though the statement succeeded, the If statement always found an error condition. It turns out that the Error object contained a minor error from another statement that I didn't care about. The statement that I thought was causing the error didn't change the Error object because no error had occurred. Therefore, the old value error condition that existed from before was caught in my If statement.

The moral of the story is that you should clear the Error object immediately before the statement you wish to check for errors. This prevents second-hand errors.

FINAL THOUGHTS

The best way to debug your program is to prevent bugs in the first place—hence, the KISS and SMILE principles and the Lazy Programmer philosophy. However, following this approach will not guarantee that your programs always will be 100 percent bug free.

When you suspect a bug, try to isolate where the problem is. The best way to do this is to look at your program and try to identify the code that could be causing the problem. Most likely, you can narrow your search considerably before you actually use any of the debugging techniques we discussed in this chapter.

Before you try to debug your program, consider making backup copies of all of your project's files. This will help you recover your original program after you've accidentally trashed it while trying to find the bug. I always try to put a project (or project group) into a single directory, so I just need to copy all the files in the directory to an empty directory to make a clean backup of the project.

One common problem in Visual Basic programs is determining when an event will occur. This is definitely a problem in a complex program where multiple events may be fired based on a single trigger. So if you are not sure of the order of the events or whether the event is even being called, simply put a message box in the event to display the name of the event.

Another common problem occurs when `If Then Else`, `Select Case`, `Do/Loop`, `While/Wend`, and `For/Next` are not coded properly. This usually happens when you have nested one of these statements inside another. The statement causing the problem is probably inside the wrong group of statements.

Use the `Debug.Assert` and `Debug.Print` methods liberally. Using `Debug.Print` inside a loop will generate a lot of output but is often helpful when debugging an infinite loop (and the output is easily recycled when you close the Immediate window).

Use breakpoints and watches to trace your program's execution. When you have an extremely complex program, these tools are invaluable in helping you find your bug.

If breakpoints and watches aren't helping you, start stripping out code from your program one piece at a time. If the program starts working, look at the hunk of code you just deleted. The best way to delete code is not to use the Delete key, but to insert an apostrophe in front of the line and turn the line of code into a comment. Eventually, you will be able to isolate where the problem occurs.

When all else fails, try to duplicate the error in a small, stand-alone program. While Visual Basic is relatively protected against bugs, it's not totally bug free. If you think you've found a Visual Basic error, having a simple program that causes the error is very helpful when you contact Microsoft.

What's Next?

Sometimes your Visual Basic application will require capabilities that are beyond the core language. These capabilities will often be within reach in dynamic-link libraries (DLLs), which your application accesses with API calls. Chapter 7 will show you how to make these calls to add to the functionality of your application.

Chapter 7

VISUAL BASIC AND THE WINDOWS API

In Visual Basic, text boxes already know how to hold and display text, list boxes and combo boxes already know how to present data, command buttons know how to process a click, and windows know how to open and close. When your application needs capabilities that go beyond the core language and these controls, you can make API calls. By calling API procedures in DLLs, or dynamic-link libraries, you can access the thousands of procedures in the WIN32 API system, as well as routines written in other languages.

As their name suggests, DLLs are libraries of procedures that applications can link to and use at run time rather than link to

Adapted from *Visual Basic 6 Developer's Handbook*
by Evangelos Petroutsos and Kevin Hough
ISBN 0-7821-2283-3   1,504 pages $49.99

statically at compile time. DLLs are not compiled into the application's executable; thus, DLLs can be updated independently of the application, and many applications can share a single DLL. Microsoft Windows itself is composed of DLLs, and other applications call the procedures within these libraries to display windows and graphics, manage system resources, manipulate the Windows Registry, and do many other tasks. These procedures are sometimes referred to as the Windows API.

Visual Basic is designed to be extended by having access to the API. VB provides a balance by hiding many of the complexities of Windows programming while still providing access to the Windows environment. More than 1,000 API calls are available and can be classified in four areas:

Application manipulation   APIs open and close applications, access menu commands, and move and resize windows.

Graphics   APIs create bitmaps and capture screen images.

System information   APIs determine the current drive, available and total memory, current user, and the computer's operating system.

Registry interaction   APIs interact with the Windows Registry beyond the built-in Visual Basic Registry functions of GetSettings and SetSettings to create and query keys and to delete keys, subkeys, and values.

The Win32 API allows Visual Basic to exploit the power of the 32-bit Windows family of operating systems. The functions, structures, messages, macros, and interfaces form a consistent and uniform API for Microsoft Windows 95, Windows 98, and Windows NT operating systems. With a simple API call, you can accomplish tasks that seem overwhelming or even impossible. This chapter introduces the fundamentals of Windows APIs, shows how to access APIs from Visual Basic, and looks at how to declare and reference function arguments. The example projects in this chapter will show you, the developer, how to unleash and harness the power of the Win32 API functions so that your VB projects are able to do the following:

▶ Find and control a window

▶ Manipulate other applications

▶ Find, access, and execute a menu option in another application

API FUNDAMENTALS

To use the Windows API functions, you need to understand the functional categories shown in Table 7.1.

TABLE 7.1: API Functional Categories

CATEGORY	DESCRIPTION
Windows Management (User32)	Creates and manages a user interface for applications
Graphics Device Interface (GDI32)	Generates graphical output for Windows devices
System Services (Kernel32)	Provides access to the operating system and computer resources
Multimedia	Accesses audio and video services
Remote Procedure Calls (RPC)	Carries out distributed computing

Part ii

Windows Management

Windows Management (User32) provides the basic functions required to build and manage the display of your program output and to capture user input. The Windows Management layer determines how your application responds to mouse and keyboard input, retrieves and processes messages sent to your application windows, and supports all the clipboard functions. The Windows Management API functions include

- ShowWindow, which sets the specified window's visibility

- IsWindowVisible, which retrieves the visibility state of the specified window

Graphics Device Interface

The Graphics Device Interface (GDI32) provides the functionality for your application to support all the devices installed on your computer, including the monitor and the printer. The GDI provides the ability to define drawing objects, such as pens, brushes, and fonts and also provides the ability to draw lines, circles, and bitmap functions. The GDI functions include:

- ▶ BitBlt, which performs a bit-block transfer of the color data corresponding to a rectangle of pixels from the specified source device context into a destination device context

- ▶ CreateCompatibleBitmap, which creates a bitmap that is compatible with the device that is associated with the specified device context

System Services

System Services (Kernel32) provide functions to access the resources of the computer provided by the operating system. These include functions for memory, the file system, and resources running on your system. System Services provide information about the hardware, including the mouse and the keyboard. System Service functions include

- ▶ GetDiskFreeSpace, which retrieves information about the specified disk, including the amount of free space on the disk

- ▶ GetVersion, which returns the current version number of Windows and information about the operating system platform

Multimedia Functions

Multimedia functions allow you to add wave audio, AVI video, joystick support, multimedia timers, and MIDI music to your applications. The MCI Command String and Command Message Interface provides support for playing various types of media files. The multimedia functions include

- ▶ mciSendCommand, which sends a command message to the specified MCI device.

- ▶ MessageBeep, which plays a waveform sound. The waveform sound for each sound type is identified by an entry in the sounds section of the Registry.

Remote Procedure Calls

Remote Procedure Calls (RPC) give applications the ability to carry out distributed computing, allowing applications to tap the resources and power of computers on a network. You use RPC to create distributed applications consisting of a client that presents information to the user and a server that stores, retrieves, and manipulates data and performs computing tasks for the client. Remote file servers, remote printer servers, and shared databases are examples of distributed applications. The RPC API functions include:

▶ RpcServerRegisterAuthInfo, which is a server side API that turns on security for the various server interfaces that are registered. It sets up the server, the principal name, the authentication service to use, and any key retrieval function in the RPC_SERVER object.

▶ RpcMgmtInqServerPrincName, which is used by the server application to inquire about the server's principal name corresponding to the supplied binding handle and the authentication service.

ACCESSING THE WIN32 API FROM VISUAL BASIC

Using a DLL procedure in Visual Basic consists of two steps: declaring it, and then calling it as many times as it is needed. You must tell Visual Basic the DLL or API function you want to use and then supply the arguments it requires.

Declaring API Functions and DLLs

To declare a DLL procedure, you add a Declare statement to the Declarations section of the Code window. If the procedure returns a value, write the Declare statement as a function:

```
Declare Function publicname Lib "libname" [Alias "alias"] _
[([[ByVal] variable [As type] [,[ByVal] variable [As _
type]]...])] As Type
```

If a procedure does not return a value, write the Declare statement as a subroutine:

```
Declare Sub publicname Lib "libname" [Alias "alias"] _
[([[ByVal] variable [As type] [,[ByVal] variable [As _
type]]...])]
```

Part ii

Later in this chapter, we will use the function FindWindow. It is declared as follows:

```
Declare Function FindWindow Lib "user32" Alias "FindWindowA" _
(ByVal lpClassName As String, ByVal lpWindowName _
As String) As Long
```

NOTE

The underscore character at the end of code lines is used to break long code into multiple lines.

The FindWindow function in this declaration finds the handle of a window. We will also demonstrate how to use this function later in this chapter.

When you declare DLL procedures in standard modules, they are public by default, and you can call them from anywhere in your application. When you declare DLL procedures in any other type of module, they are private to that module, and you must identify them as such by preceding the declaration with the Private keyword.

NOTE

Procedure names are case sensitive in 32-bit versions of Visual Basic. In versions before VB5, procedure names were not case sensitive.

Specifying the Library

The Lib clause in the Declare statement tells Visual Basic where to find the DLL file that contains the procedure. When you reference one of the core Windows libraries (User32, Kernel32, or GDI32), as we did in the FindWindow example, you don't need to include the file name extension. If you do not specify a path for *libname*, Visual Basic searches for the file in the following order:

1. In the directory containing the calling EXE file

2. In the current directory

3. In the Windows system directory (often, but not necessarily \Windows\System)

4. In the Windows directory (not necessarily \Windows)

5. In the *Path* environment variable

Table 7.2 lists the common operating environment library files.

TABLE 7.2: Common Operating Environment Library Files

DYNAMIC LINK LIBRARY	DESCRIPTION
Advapi32.dll	Advanced API services library supporting numerous APIs, including many security and Registry calls
Comdlg32.dll	Common dialog API library
Gdi32.dll	Graphics Device Interface API library
Kernel32.dll	Core Windows 32-bit base API support
Lz32.dll	32-bit compression routines
Mpr.dll	Multiple Provider Router library
Netapi32.dll	32-bit Network API library
Shell32.dll	32-bit Shell API library
User32.dll	Library for user interface routines
Version.dll	Version library
Winmm.dll	Windows multimedia library
Winspool.drv	Print spooler interface that contains the print spooler API calls

Part ii

Using the API Viewer Application

You can use the API Viewer application (shown in Figure 7.1) to browse through the declarations, constants, and types included in any text file or Microsoft Jet database. When you find the procedure you want, you can copy the code to the clipboard and paste it into your Visual Basic application.

To use the Viewer Application, follow these steps:

1. Choose Add-Ins ➤ API Viewer. If you don't see the API Viewer option, select Add-In Manager and check VB API Viewer to add the API Viewer Application to the list of available Add-Ins.

2. Choose File ➤ Load Text File or File ➤ Load Database File.

API Type:

Declares ▾

Type the first few letters of the word you are looking for:

GetW

Available Items:

| GetWindow |
| GetWindowContextHelpId |
| GetWindowDC |
| GetWindowExtEx |
| GetWindowLong |
| GetWindowOrgEx |
| GetWindowPlacement |
| GetWindowRect |

Add

Declare Scope
○ Public
○ Private

Selected Items:

Public Declare Function GetWindow Lib "user32" Alias "GetWindow"
(ByVal hwnd As Long, ByVal wCmd As Long) As Long

Remove

Clear

Insert

Copy

FIGURE 7.1: The API Viewer application

NOTE

For your convenience, Microsoft includes a Win32API file with Visual Basic 6. It
is in the WinAPI subdirectory where you installed Visual Basic.

3. Select the function you want from the Available Items list
    box. The selected function(s) are displayed in the Selected
    Items list box.

4. Click the Copy button to copy the functions to the clipboard.

5. Paste the functions from the clipboard into your application's
    Code window.

Passing Arguments

Most DLL routines, including those in the Windows API, are docu-
mented using notation from the C programming language. This is only
natural, as most DLLs are written in C or C++.

To translate the syntax of a typical API routine into a Visual Basic
Declare statement, you have to understand something about how both C
and Visual Basic pass arguments. The usual way for C to pass numeric
arguments is by *value*—a copy of the value of the argument is passed to
the routine.

Sometimes C arguments are pointers, and these arguments are said to be passed by *reference*—the called routine modifies the argument and returns it. C strings and arrays are always passed by reference.

Visual Basic usually passes all its arguments by reference (the default if not specified otherwise). To pass arguments to a C routine that expects its arguments to be passed by value, you use the ByVal keyword with the argument in the Declaration statement.

Visual Basic strings do not use the same format as C strings. In Visual Basic, the ByVal keyword is overloaded to mean "pass a C string" when it is used with a string argument in a Declare statement.

Table 7.3 shows the C argument types and their equivalent declarations in Visual Basic.

TABLE 7.3: C and Visual Basic Data Types

C DECLARATION	VISUAL BASIC DATA TYPE	ARGUMENT TYPE
Char	String	ByVal
Handle	Long	ByVal
Integer	Integer	ByVal
Integer Pointer (LPINT)	Integer	ByRef
Long	Long	ByVal
Long Integer Pointer	Long	ByRef
Void Pointer	Any	ByRef

NOTE

You will never pass a Visual Basic string or array to a DLL routine unless the DLL was written specifically for use with Visual Basic. Visual Basic strings and arrays are represented in memory by descriptors (not pointers), which are useless to DLL routines that were not written with Visual Basic in mind.

Passing Arguments by Value

When arguments are passed by value, only a copy of a variable is passed. If the procedure changes the value, the change affects only the copy and not the variable itself. Use the ByVal keyword to indicate an argument passed by value.

For example, if you create the following subroutine:

```
Public Sub customSub(ByVal addTo As Integer)
    addTo = addTo + 10
    Debug.Print addTo
End Sub
```

and call customSub() with the following code

```
x = 5
Call customSub (x)
Debug.Print x
```

the Debug.Print command displays 15 in customSub(), but the value reverts to 5 when it returns to the calling subroutine. The value changes only within the customSub() subroutine.

Passing Arguments by Reference

Passing arguments by reference gives the procedure access to the actual variable contents in its memory address location. As a result, the variable's value can be permanently changed by the procedure to which it is passed. Passing by reference is the default in Visual Basic.

For example, if you create the following subroutine

```
Public Sub customSub(addTo As Integer)
    addTo = addTo + 10
    Debug.Print addTo
End Sub
```

and call customSub() with the following code

```
x = 5
Call customSub (x)
Debug.Print x
```

the Debug.Print command displays 15 in customSub(), and the value of x is 15 when it returns to the calling subroutine. The changes to x are global since it was passed by reference.

HANDLES IN WINDOWS

One way or another, Windows API functions can access windows, program instances, bitmaps, files, icons, menus, and all types of objects in Visual Basic. Windows identifies each object with a 32-bit integer known as a *handle*. This handle is generally referred to as the *Windows hwnd*, a unique Long Integer data type.

Every window in Windows has a handle, which enables you to find a specific window among all the windows currently running in memory. Once you obtain the handle, it is easy to minimize and maximize a window, move a window, and change a window's size.

As the mouse moves over windows on the Desktop, you can use the API function WindowFromPoint to get the handle to the window currently under the mouse. To take this one step further, you can also store the window's handle and use it later in your program. To do so, you implement the same type of process that Visual Basic DragDrop uses.

Clicking the mouse button on a Visual Basic Form triggers the Mouse-Down event. This sets the Form as a starting point. Releasing the mouse button triggers the MouseUp event. You can then pass the mouse coordinates to the WindowFromPoint API function and obtain the window's handle. Now that you have the handle, you can use the API function Get-WindowRect to determine the size and position of the window. The coordinates of the window are returned from GetWindowRect in WindowRect.Left, WindowRect.Right, WindowRect.Top, and WindowRect.Bottom. Code 7.1 shows how these API functions work.

Part ii

WARNING

When you use API functions in Visual Basic, there is no built-in safety net. If you pass incorrect arguments to a function, unexpected things can happen. You can even cause a General Protection Fault that can crash the system. Therefore, it is good programming practice to use procedure-level error trapping, as we have done in Code 7.1.

Code 7.1:   Sample API Functions

```
Private Sub Form_MouseUp(Button%, Shift%, x As Single, _
y As Single)

On Error GoTo ErrorRoutineErr

Dim strCaption$
Dim ptLocation As POINT
Dim i

'Convert the current mouse position to screen coordinates
ptLocation.x = CLng(x)
```

```
    ptLocation.y = CLng(y)
    ClientToScreen Me.hwnd, ptLocation

    'Use WindowFromPoint to find out what window we are
    'pointing to
    hwndCurrentWindow = WindowFromPoint(ptLocation.x, _
      ptLocation.y)

    'Create a buffer to hold the caption, and call
    'GetWindowText to retrieve it
    strCaption = Space(1000)
    Caption = Left(strCaption, _
    GetWindowText(hwndCurrentWindow, strCaption, _
    Len(strCaption)))

    'Clear our module-level variable and restore
    'the mouse pointer hwndCurrentWindow = False
    MousePointer = vbNormal

    'Get the rectangle describing the window
    GetWindowRect hwndCurrentWindow, WindowRect

    'coordinates of the window are returned in
    '(WindowRect.Left),(WindowRect.Right)
    '(WindowRect.Top),(WindowRect.Bottom)

ErrorRoutineResume:
  Exit Sub
ErrorRoutineErr:
  MsgBox "FindWindow - frmMain, MouseMove" _
    & Err & " " & Error
  Resume Next
End Sub
```

NOTE
We'll expand on this code later in this chapter in the FindWindow project.

With WindowFromPoint, you can get the handle for any window and then use GetWindowRect to capture the style, size, and position of the window. The projects and examples that follow will give you plenty of ideas and opportunities for integrating (and controlling!) other applications from your Visual Basic application. If you combine the features from the example projects, you can build an even more robust project.

PROVIDING AN API FOUNDATION

The Windows API examples in this chapter are designed to provide a foundation from which you can build your own API libraries. Windows includes an API to perform almost any function or task, but they all work the same basic way: declare the function, pass the expected parameters, and perform the actions or manipulate the results. Keep this in mind as you work through the sample applications that follow. Then later, when you work with APIs that are not demonstrated here, you can use these samples to take some of the mystery out of programming the Windows API.

The FindWindow Project

Armed with the window's handle, manipulating the window is easy for VB. We will use the FindWindow application (shown in Figure 7.2) to find and manipulate a window.

NOTE

You will find the FindWindow project, along with the files for the other projects in this chapter, at the Sybex Web site (www.sybex.com). Once there, go to the Catalog page and enter 2469 (the first four digits of the last five in the book's ISBN) into the search engine. Follow the link for this book that comes up, and then click the Downloads button, which will take you to a list of files organized by chapter.

FIGURE 7.2:   The FindWindow application

Part ii

The FindWindow program gets the handle from a window and allows you to minimize, maximize, move, resize, and flash the title bar of the selected window with API functions. The project consists of three Forms and six Command Buttons on the main Form. These buttons are as follows:

▶ The Minimize Window button minimizes the selected window by passing SW_MINIMIZE to the ShowWindow function.

▶ The Restore Window button restores a minimized window to its original size by passing SW_SHOWNOACTIVATE to the ShowWindow function.

▶ The Set Position button displays the Set Position Form (shown in Figure 7.3). This Form allows you to pass new coordinate positions to the SetWindowPos function and move the window.

FIGURE 7.3: The SetPosition Form

▶ The Set Size button displays the Set Size Form (shown in Figure 7.4). From this Form, you can set new size values and call the SetWindowPos function to resize the window.

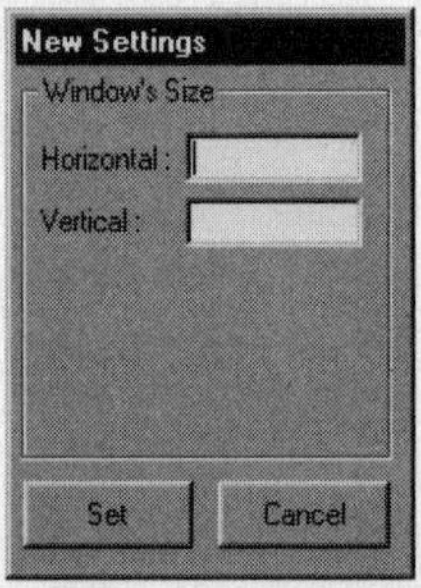

FIGURE 7.4: The SetSize Form

▶ The Identify button calls the FlashWindow API function and causes the window's title bar to change colors.

▶ The Exit button terminates the program.

The FindWindow Project API Functions

The FindWindow project calls the API functions listed in Table 7.4 to find and manipulate a window.

NOTE

You'll find a complete description of the API functions in the Function Reference located at the end of the book.

TABLE 7.4: The FindWindow API Functions

API FUNCTION	DESCRIPTION
ClientToScreen	Converts the client coordinates of a given point or rectangle on the display to screen coordinates.
DrawIcon	Draws an icon in the client area of the window.
FlashWindow	Flashes the specified window once.
GetWindowRect	Retrieves the dimensions of the rectangle of the specified window. The dimensions are given in screen coordinates that are relative to the upper-left corner of the screen.
GetWindowText	Copies the text of the specified window's title bar (if it has one) into a buffer. If the specified window is a control, the text of the control is copied.
IsIconic	Determines whether the specified window is minimized (iconic).
IsWindowEnabled	Determines whether the specified window is enabled.
IsWindowVisible	Retrieves the visibility state of the specified window.
IsZoomed	Determines whether a window is maximized.
LoadCursor	Loads the specified cursor.
SetWindowPos	Changes the size, position, and Zorder of a child, pop-up, or top-level window.
ShowWindow	Sets the specified window's visibility.
WindowFromPoint	Retrieves the handle of the window that contains the specified point.

The FindWindow Code in Action

Now that you've seen the API functions needed to convert the mouse pointer's coordinates to find a window's handle, minimize and restore a window's state, move and resize a window, and flash the title bar of a window, let's take a look at the code needed to put the functions into action.

Code 7.2 contains all the declarations, types, and constants required for the API functions in the FindWindow project.

Code 7.2:   Declarations, Types, and Constants for FindWindow

```
'API Declarations, Types, and Constants
Public Type RECT
  Left As Long
  Top As Long
  Right As Long
  Bottom As Long
End Type

Public Type POINT
  x As Long
  y As Long
End Type

'SetWindowPos() hwndInsertAfter values
Public Const HWND_TOP = 0
Public Const HWND_BOTTOM = 1
Public Const HWND_TOPMOST = -1
Public Const HWND_NOTOPMOST = -2

'SetWindowPos Flags
Public Const SWP_NOSIZE = &H1
Public Const SWP_NOMOVE = &H2
Public Const SWP_NOZORDER = &H4
Public Const SWP_NOREDRAW = &H8
Public Const SWP_NOACTIVATE = &H10
Public Const SWP_FRAMECHANGED = &H20
Public Const SWP_SHOWWINDOW = &H40
Public Const SWP_HIDEWINDOW = &H80
Public Const SWP_NOCOPYBITS = &H100
Public Const SWP_NOOWNERZORDER = &H200
Public Const SWP_DRAWFRAME = SWP_FRAMECHANGED
Public Const SWP_NOREPOSITION = SWP_NOOWNERZORDER
```

```
'ShowWindow() Commands
Public Const SW_HIDE = 0
Public Const SW_SHOWNORMAL = 1
Public Const SW_NORMAL = 1
Public Const SW_SHOWMINIMIZED = 2
Public Const SW_SHOWMAXIMIZED = 3
Public Const SW_MAXIMIZE = 3
Public Const SW_SHOWNOACTIVATE = 4
Public Const SW_SHOW = 5
Public Const SW_MINIMIZE = 6
Public Const SW_SHOWMINNOACTIVE = 7
Public Const SW_SHOWNA = 8
Public Const SW_RESTORE = 9
Public Const SW_SHOWDEFAULT = 10
Public Const SW_MAX = 10


Declare Sub ClientToScreen Lib "user32" (ByVal hwnd _
    As Long, lpPoint As POINT)
Declare Function GetWindowText& Lib "user32" Alias _
    "GetWindowTextA" (ByVal hwnd&, ByVal lpString$, ByVal cb&)
Declare Function GetWindowRect Lib "user32" (ByVal _
    hwnd As Long, lpRect As RECT) As Boolean
Declare Function WindowFromPoint Lib "user32" (ByVal _
    ptY As Long, ByVal ptX As Long) As Long
Declare Function LoadCursor Lib "user32" Alias "LoadCursorA" _
    (ByVal hInstance&, ByVal lpCursor&) As Long
Declare Function DrawIcon Lib "user32" (ByVal hdc As Long, _
    ByVal x As Long, ByVal y As Long, ByVal hIcon As _
    Long) As Long
Declare Function ShowWindow Lib "user32" (ByVal hwnd As _
    Long, ByVal nCmdShow As Long) As Long
Declare Function IsWindowVisible Lib "user32" (ByVal hwnd _
    As Long) As Long
Declare Function IsWindowEnabled Lib "user32" (ByVal hwnd _
    As Long) As Long
Declare Function IsZoomed Lib "user32" (ByVal hwnd As _
    Long) As Long
Declare Function IsIconic Lib "user32" (ByVal hwnd _
    As Long) As Long
Declare Function SetWindowPos Lib "user32" (ByVal hwnd _
    As Long, ByVal _
    hWndInsertAfter As Long, ByVal x As Long, ByVal _
    y As Long, _
    ByVal cx As Long, ByVal cy As Long, ByVal wFlags _
    As Long) As Long
```

Part ii

```
Declare Function FlashWindow Lib "user32" (ByVal hwnd _
    As Long, ByVal bInvert As Long) As Long

'Define the icon
Global Const IDC_UPARROW = 32516&

' Holds the handle to the captured window
Public hwndCurrentWindow As Long
```

Drawing the Icon   The Form_Load subroutine shown in Code 7.3 sets up the Form and draws a copy of vbUpArrow on the Form using the function DrawIcon. Table 7.5 lists the built-in cursor styles available in Visual Basic. To substitute one of these styles, change the IDC_UPARROW argument in the LoadCursor function.

Code 7.3:   The Form_Load Subroutine

```
Private Sub Form_Load()
    'Size the form and put instructions in the caption
    With frmMain
        .Caption = "Click & drag the arrow!"
    End With

    'Change the ScaleMode to pixels and turn on AutoRedraw
    ScaleMode = vbPixels
    AutoRedraw = True

    'Draw vbUpArrow into the form's persistent bitmap
    DrawIcon hdc, 170, 0, LoadCursor(0, IDC_UPARROW)

End Sub
```

TABLE 7.5: Cursor Values

VALUE	DESCRIPTION
IDC_APPSTARTING	Standard arrow and small hourglass
IDC_ARROW	Standard arrow
IDC_CROSS	Crosshair
IDC_IBEAM	Text I-beam
IDC_ICON	Obsolete for applications marked version 4 or later
IDC_NO	Slashed circle

TABLE 7.5 (continued): Cursor Values

VALUE	DESCRIPTION
IDC_SIZE	Obsolete for applications marked version 4 or later. Use IDC_SIZEALL.
IDC_SIZEALL	Four-pointed arrow.
IDC_SIZENESW	Double-pointed arrow pointing northeast and southwest.
IDC_SIZENS	Double-pointed arrow pointing north and south.
IDC_SIZENWSE	Double-pointed arrow pointing northwest and southeast.
IDC_SIZEWE	Double-pointed arrow pointing west and east.
IDC_UPARROW	Vertical arrow.
IDC_WAIT	Hourglass.

Tracking the Mouse Position   The MouseMove subroutine tracks the movement of the mouse pointer and converts the location to screen coordinates with the ClientToScreen function. With the WindowFromPoint function, we retrieve the handle to the window. Finally, we pass the handle to the GetWindowText function to set the caption of the main Form to the caption of the window under the mouse pointer.

Code 7.4:   The MouseMove Subroutine

```
Private Sub Form_MouseMove(Button As Integer, Shift As
Integer, _
  x As Single, y As Single)
  Dim strCaption$
  Dim ptLocation As POINT
  Dim i
  Dim hwndTemp As Long

  'Convert the current mouse position to screen coordinates
  ptLocation.x = CLng(x)
  ptLocation.y = CLng(y)
  ClientToScreen Me.hwnd, ptLocation

  'Use WindowFromPoint to find out what window we are
  'pointing to
  hwndTemp = WindowFromPoint(ptLocation.x, ptLocation.y)

  'If a window has been captured, then put its caption
```

```
        'in our caption
        If hwndTemp Then

            'Create a buffer to hold the caption,
            'and call GetWindowText to retrieve it
            strCaption = Space(1000)
            Caption = Left(strCaption, _
            GetWindowText(hwndTemp, strCaption, Len(strCaption)))
        End If
    End Sub
```

Getting the Handle and Filling the Main Form   The MouseUp subroutine gets the position of the mouse pointer when you release the mouse button and converts the location to screen coordinates with the ClientToScreen function. As in the MouseMove subroutine, we use the WindowFromPoint function to retrieve the handle to the window. Finally, we pass the handle to the GetWindowText function to set the caption of the Main Form to the caption of the window under the mouse pointer, and then we fill in the text boxes with the window's size, position, and state.

Code 7.5:   The MouseUp Subroutine

```
Private Sub Form_MouseUp(Button%, Shift%, x As Single, _
y As Single)

On Error GoTo ErrorRoutineErr

Dim strCaption$ ' Buffer used to hold the caption
Dim ptLocation As POINT ' The location of the window
Dim i

'Convert the current mouse position to screen coordinates
ptLocation.x = CLng(x)
ptLocation.y = CLng(y)
ClientToScreen Me.hwnd, ptLocation

'Use WindowFromPoint to find out what window we are
'pointing to
hwndCurrentWindow = WindowFromPoint(ptLocation.x, _
  ptLocation.y)

'If a window has been captured, then put its caption
'in our caption
If hwndCurrentWindow Then

    'Create a buffer to hold the caption, and call
```

```
         'GetWindowText to retrieve it
         strCaption = Space(1000)
         Caption = Left(strCaption, _
         GetWindowText(hwndCurrentWindow, strCaption, _
         Len(strCaption)))

         'If this window does not a caption,
         'it is not a main window, exit out
         If Len(Caption) = 0 Then
           Exit Sub
         End If

         'Fill the form with the current windows attributes
         Call GetWindowAttributes

         'If we found a window, enable the action buttons
         For i = 0 To 4
           cmdWindowAction(i).Enabled = True
         Next

       End If
       'Restore the mouse pointer
       MousePointer = vbNormal
   ErrorRoutineResume:
       Exit Sub
   ErrorRoutineErr:
       MsgBox "frmMain, MouseUp " & Err & " " & Error
       Resume Next
   End Sub
```

Managing the Window   The cmdWindowAction button is a control array that minimizes and restores the window with the ShowWindow function, flashing the window's title bar with the FlashWindow function and displaying the NewSize and NewPosition Forms as shown in Code 7.6. Table 7.6 lists the possible values for the ShowWindow function.

Code 7.6:   The cmdWindowAction Button

```
   Private Sub cmdWindowAction_Click(Index As Integer)
     On Error GoTo ErrorRoutineErr
     Dim rc
     Select Case Index
       Case 0 'minimize window
         rc = ShowWindow(hwndCurrentWindow, SW_MINIMIZE)
       Case 1 'show window
         rc = ShowWindow(hwndCurrentWindow, SW_SHOWNOACTIVATE)
       Case 2 'set new size
```

Part ii

```
              frmNewSize.Show 1
          Case 3 'set new position
              frmNewPosition.Show 1
          Case 4 'identify the window, make the title flash
              rc = FlashWindow(hwndCurrentWindow, -1)
          Case 5 'exit
              End
      End Select
  ErrorRoutineResume:
      Exit Sub
  ErrorRoutineErr:
      MsgBox "frmMain, cmdWindowAction " & Err & " " & Error
      Resume Next
  End Sub
```

TABLE 7.6: The ShowWindow Visibility Values

VALUE	DESCRIPTION
SW_HIDE	Hides the window and activates another window.
SW_MAXIMIZE	Maximizes the specified window.
SW_MINIMIZE	Minimizes the specified window and activates the next top-level window in the Zorder.
SW_RESTORE	Activates and displays the window. If the window is minimized or maximized, Windows restores it to its original size and position. An application should specify this flag when restoring a minimized window.
SW_SHOW	Activates the window and displays it in its current size and position.
SW_SHOWDEFAULT	Sets the show state based on the SW_ flag specified in the STARTUPINFO structure passed to the CreateProcess function by the program that started the application.
SW_SHOWMAXIMIZED	Activates the window and displays it as a maximized window.
SW_SHOWMINIMIZED	Activates the window and displays it as a minimized window.
SW_SHOWMINNOACTIVE	Displays the window as a minimized window. The active window remains active.
SW_SHOWNA	Displays the window in its current state. The active window remains active.
SW_SHOWNOACTIVATE	Displays a window in its most recent size and position. The active window remains active.
SW_SHOWNORMAL	Activates and displays a window. If the window is minimized or maximized, Windows restores it to its original size and position. An application should specify this flag when displaying the window for the first time.

Moving the Window

To move the window, enter the new Top and Left positions into the text boxes on the NewPosition Form (shown in Figure 7.5 with the Main FindWindow Form) and click the Set button.

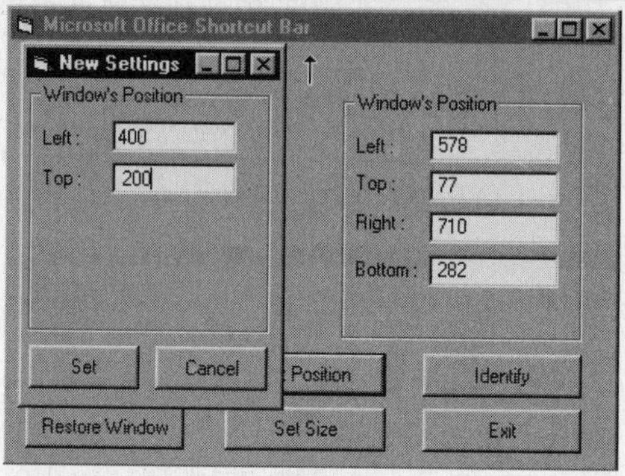

FIGURE 7.5: The NewPosition and Main FindWindow Forms

The Set button calls the SetWindowPos function and moves the window to its new location. You must identify the window to precede the positioned window in the Zorder as shown in Code 7.7. This parameter must be a window handle or one of the values in Table 7.7.

Code 7.7: Moving a Window with the SetWindowPos API

```
Private Sub cmdWindowAction_Click(Index As Integer)
  On Error GoTo ErrorRoutineErr
  Dim rc As Long
  Select Case Index
    Case 0 'OK
      rc = SetWindowPos(hwndCurrentWindow, _
        HWND_TOP, txtLeft, txtTop, _
        frmMain.lblHorizontal, frmMain.lblVertical, _
        SWP_NOSIZE)
    Case 1 'cancel
      'cancel the changes and unload the form
      Unload Me
  End Select
ErrorRoutineResume:
  Exit Sub
ErrorRoutineErr:
  MsgBox "frmNewPosition, cmdWindowAction " _
    & Err & " " & Error
  Resume Next
End Sub
```

TABLE 7.7: The SetWindowPos Values

VALUE	DESCRIPTION
HWND_BOTTOM	Places the window at the bottom of the Zorder. If the hWnd parameter identifies a topmost window, the window loses its topmost status and is placed at the bottom of all other windows.
HWND_NOTOPMOST	Places the window above all nontopmost windows (that is, behind all topmost windows). This flag has no effect if the window is already a nontopmost window.
HWND_TOP	Places the window at the top of the Zorder.
HWND_TOPMOST	Places the window above all nontopmost windows. The window maintains its topmost position even when it is deactivated.

Resizing the Window   To resize the window, enter the new Horizontal and Vertical dimensions in the text boxes on the NewSize Form (shown in Figure 7.6 with the Main FindWindow Form), and click the Set button. The Set button calls the SetWindowPos function and resizes the window.

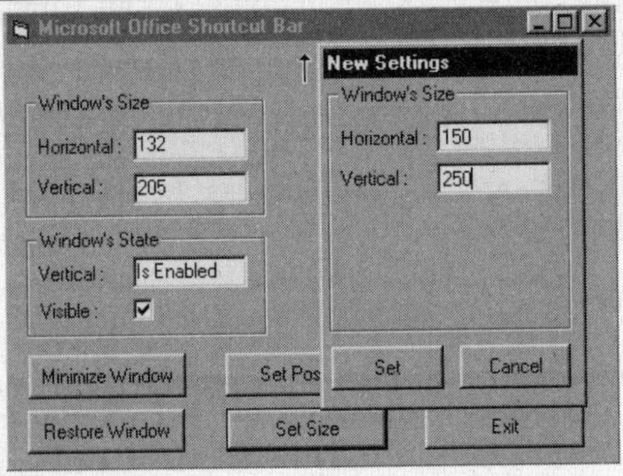

FIGURE 7.6: The NewSize and Main FindWindow Forms

Code 7.8:   Setting the Window's Size with the SetWindowPos API Function

```
Private Sub cmdWindowAction_Click(Index As Integer)
   On Error GoTo ErrorRoutineErr
   Dim rc As Long
   Select Case Index
     Case 0 'OK
```

```
                rc = SetWindowPos(hwndCurrentWindow, HWND_TOP _
                    , frmMain.lblLeft, frmMain.lblTop, _
                    txtHorizontal, txtVertical, SWP_NOMOVE)
            Case 1 'cancel
                'Cancel the changes and unload the form
                Unload Me
        End Select
    ErrorRoutineResume:
        Exit Sub
    ErrorRoutineErr:
        MsgBox "frmNewSize, cmdWindowAction " & Err & " " & Error
        Resume Next
    End Sub
```

Taking FindWindow for a Test Run

Now that everything is set up, let's test the FindWindow application and move some windows around. Press F5 to start the program and follow these steps:

1. Move the mouse pointer over the Main Form and press and hold the mouse button.

2. With the mouse button still pressed, move the pointer over a window. Notice that the caption of the Main Form changes to display the title of the window.

3. Release the mouse button, and the Form displays the window's statistics (see Figure 7.7).

4. Now you can experiment with the features of the program.

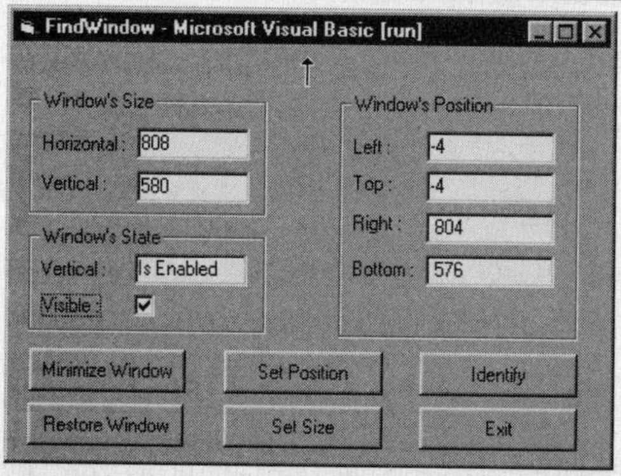

FIGURE 7.7: The FindWindow application at work

As you can see from the code samples, finding a window's handle is not difficult. Once you have the handle to a window, it is easy to manipulate it with the API functions. In the next section, we'll explore some of the API functions needed to manipulate an application.

MANIPULATING APPLICATIONS

Visual Basic is designed to give you, the developer, lots of control over your application as you are designing and running it, but VB does not give you much control over other applications that may be running concurrently. At times, you need to be able to do the following:

▶ Start another application from within your VB program.

▶ Terminate the application and know when that application has ended.

▶ Start another application and deny access to your VB program until the user closes the new application.

▶ Terminate any application from within your program.

You can take care of all these tasks with the help of Windows API calls. Here are a few API functions that you can call from within VB to launch a new application:

▶ OpenProcess opens a handle to an existing process. You can use this function after the Visual Basic Shell function, or you can incorporate the Shell function into the call.

▶ CreateProcess creates a new process.

▶ PostMessage terminates a running application after you obtain the handle.

The AppShell Project

We will use the AppShell project (shown in Figure 7.8) to demonstrate the application manipulation API functions.

NOTE

You'll find the AppShell project in this book's section of the Sybex Web site.

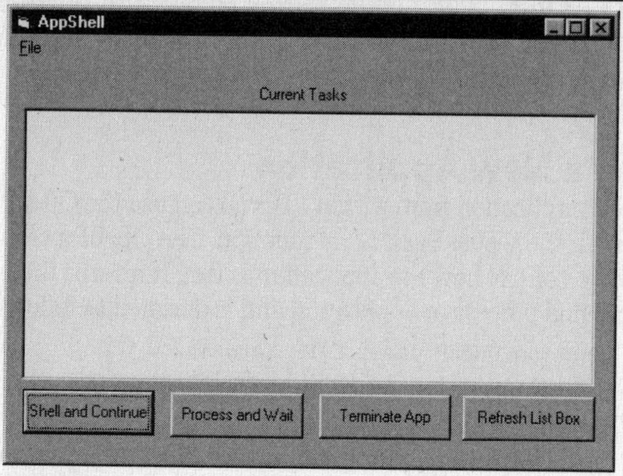

FIGURE 7.8:   The AppShell project

AppShell loads a ListBox control with the name and Windows handle of all the processes currently running in memory. These processes include Windows level processes and applications such as Notepad and Calculator. The project has four Command Buttons:

Shell and Continue   Clicking this button displays a File Open dialog box in which you can choose an application (EXE) file to launch. Your VB program monitors the new application and notifies you, through a message box, when it is closed. You remain in control of the VB program.

Process and Wait   This button differs from the Shell and Continue button in that you do not maintain control over the VB program while the new process is active. Clicking this button "freezes" the VB program. Your VB program will notify you through a message box and will again gain control when the new application is terminated.

Terminate App   Clicking this button terminates the application you selected from the ListBox.

WARNING

Terminate App is a powerful command. You can terminate any process, even Windows itself. Since this example program does not employ a lot of error trapping, use caution and only terminate applications such as Calculator or Notepad.

Refresh List Box   Clicking this button refreshes the ListBox control. You can click this button if you launch an application from the Start menu.

Launching a New Application

To launch a new application from within VB, you can use the OpenProcess API function with the Visual Basic Shell function. The OpenProcess function allows you to control how the application is run. It returns the handle to the newly opened process or application and is declared as follows:

```
Declare Function OpenProcess Lib "kernel32" _
    (ByVal dwDesiredAccess As Long, ByVal bInheritHandle _
    As Long, ByVal dwProcessID As Long) As Long
```

When you have the process handle to the new process, you can use the GetExitCodeProcess function to determine whether the process is still running in memory. Code 7.9 uses the OpenProcess function to start the Notepad application.

Code 7.9:   The OpenProcess API Function

```
Private Sub Command1_Click()
    On Error GoTo ErrorRoutineErr

    Dim hProcess As Long
    Dim RetVal As Long
    Dim slAppToRun As String

    slAppToRun = "c:\Windows\Notepad.exe"

    'The next line launches Notepad.
    hProcess = OpenProcess(PROCESS_QUERY_INFORMATION, 1, _
    Shell(slAppToRun, vbNormalFocus))

ErrorRoutineResume:
    Exit Sub
ErrorRoutineErr:
    MsgBox "AppShell.Form1.Command1_Click" & Err & Error
    Resume Next
End Sub
```

The GetExitCodeProcess function returns a value of STILL_ACTIVE if the opened process or application is still running. You can code a subroutine to check this value periodically to determine the state of the new process.

Launching a New Application and Waiting

You can use the CreateProcess API function to load and run any application or process you want. Unlike the OpenProcess function, which uses the Shell function to start the application, CreateProcess actually starts the application before it creates a Windows process. When you use this function, you have complete control over how the launched application is run. After you call the CreateProcess function, you can call the WaitForSingleObject function and force the system to wait until a specified process has finished to continue. You declare the CreateProcess function as follows:

```
Declare Function CreateProcessA Lib "kernel32" _
  (ByVal lpApplicationName As Long, ByVal lpCommandLine As _
  String, ByVal lpProcessAttributes As Long, ByVal _
  lpThreadAttributes As Long, ByVal bInheritHandles As _
  Long, ByVal dwCreationFlags As Long, ByVal _
  lpEnvironment As Long, ByVal _
  lpCurrentDirectory As Long, lpStartupInfo As STARTUPINFO, _
  lpProcessInformation As PROCESS_INFORMATION) As Long
```

For the WaitForSingleObject function, you pass the handle of the process you want to wait for and the length of time to pause, in milliseconds. You can set the time-out value to INFINITE and cause the system to wait until the user stops the process.

After the user stops the process, the final step is to close the open handle for the just-launched process. This removes all references to the new process. Code 7.10 uses the CreateProcess function to start the Notepad application.

Part ii

Code 7.10: The CreateProcess API Function

```
Private Sub Command1_Click()
  On Error GoTo ErrorRoutineErr

  Dim NameOfProc As PROCESS_INFORMATION
  Dim NameStart As STARTUPINFO
  Dim rc As Long
  Dim slAppToRun As String

  slAppToRun = "c:\Windows\Notepad.exe"

  NameStart.cb = Len(NameStart)
  rc = CreateProcessA(0&, slAppToRun, 0&, 0&, 1&, _
    NORMAL_PRIORITY_CLASS, _
    0&, 0&, NameStart, NameOfProc)
```

```
ErrorRoutineResume:
  Exit Sub
ErrorRoutineErr:
  MsgBox "AppShell.Form1.Command1_Click" & Err & Error
  Resume Next
End Sub
```

Terminating an Application

To terminate an application, you use the FindWindow function to retrieve the handle. After you have the handle, it is a good idea to check and be sure that you are not getting ready to close your Visual Basic program. To do this, use the GetWindow function, and compare the handle with your program and with the application you want to terminate. If they are the same, you're getting ready to terminate your Visual Basic program. After this check, use the PostMessage function to actually terminate the application. You declare the PostMessage function as follows:

```
Declare Function PostMessage Lib "user32" Alias _
  "PostMessageA" (ByVal hwnd As Long, ByVal wMsg _
  As Long, ByVal wParam _
  As Long, ByVal lParam As Long) As Long
```

Code 7.11 shows how you can use the PostMessage function to terminate an application whose handle is passed in as TargetHwnd. The FindWindow function ensures that you do not close the current window.

Code 7.11:   The EndTask Subroutine

```
Function EndTask(TargetHwnd As Long) As Long

  Dim rc As Integer
  Dim ReturnVal As Integer
  If TargetHwnd = Form1.hwnd Or GetWindow(TargetHwnd, _
    GW_OWNER) = Form1.hwnd Then
    End
  End If
  If IsWindow(TargetHwnd) = False Then
    GoTo EndTaskFail
  End If
  If (GetWindowLong(TargetHwnd, GWL_STYLE) _
    And WS_DISABLED) Then
    GoTo EndTaskSucceed
  End If
```

```
If IsWindow(TargetHwnd) Then
  If Not (GetWindowLong(TargetHwnd, GWL_STYLE) _
  And WS_DISABLED) Then
  rc = PostMessage(TargetHwnd, WS_CANCELMODE, 0, 0&)
  rc = PostMessage(TargetHwnd, WM_CLOSE, 0, 0&)
   DoEvents
  End If
End If
GoTo EndTaskSucceed

EndTaskFail:
  ReturnVal = False
  GoTo EndTaskEndSub
EndTaskSucceed:
  ReturnVal = True
EndTaskEndSub:
  EndTask = ReturnVal
End Function
```

The AppShell Project API Functions

The AppShell project calls the API functions listed in Table 7.8 to give Visual Basic a boost in manipulating applications.

NOTE

You'll find a complete description of these API functions in the Function Reference at the end of this book.

TABLE 7.8: The AppShell API Functions

API Function	Description
CloseHandle	Closes an open object handle.
CreateProcess	Creates a new process and its primary thread. The new process executes the specified executable file.
GetExitCodeProcess	Retrieves the termination status of the specified process.
GetParent	Retrieves the handle of the specified child window's parent window.
GetWindow	Retrieves the handle of a window that has the specified relationship (Zorder order or owner) to the specified window.
GetWindowLong	Retrieves information about the specified window. The function also retrieves the 32-bit (long) value at the specified offset into the extra window memory of a window.

TABLE 7.8 (continued): The AppShell API Functions

API Function	Description
GetWindowText	Copies the text of the specified window's title bar (if it has one) into a buffer. If the specified window is a control, the text of the control is copied.
GetWindowTextLength	Retrieves the length, in characters, of the specified window's title bar text (if the window has a title bar). If the specified window is a control, the function retrieves the length of the text within the control.
IsWindow	Determines whether the specified window handle identifies an existing window.
OpenProcess	Returns a handle of an existing process object.
PostMessage	Posts a message in the message queue associated with the thread that created the specified window and then returns without waiting for the thread to process the message. Messages in a message queue are retrieved by calls to the GetMessage or PeekMessage function.
WaitForSingleObject	Returns when the specified object is in the signaled state or when the time-out interval elapses.

The AppShell Code in Action

The AppShell project uses the API functions in Table 7.8 to help you develop Visual Basic applications that can do the following:

▶ Launch a new application

▶ Launch a new application and wait until it is terminated

▶ Terminate a running application

Code 7.12 highlights the interaction of the VB application and the API functions.

Code 7.12: Declarations, Types, and Constants in the AppShell Project

```
Public Const GW_HWNDFIRST = 0
Public Const GW_HWNDLAST = 1
Public Const GW_HWNDNEXT = 2
Public Const GW_HWNDPREV = 3
```

```
Public Const GW_CHILD = 5
Public Const GW_MAX = 5

Global Const NORMAL_PRIORITY_CLASS = &H20&
Global Const INFINITE = -1&

Public Const STILL_ACTIVE = &H103
Public Const PROCESS_QUERY_INFORMATION = &H400

Public Const GW_OWNER = 4
Public Const GWL_STYLE = -16
Public Const WS_DISABLED = &H8000000
Public Const WS_CANCELMODE = &H1F
Public Const WM_CLOSE = &H10

Public glCurrentHwnd

Type STARTUPINFO
  cb As Long
  lpReserved As String
  lpDesktop As String
  lpTitle As String
  dwX As Long
  dwY As Long
  dwXSize As Long
  dwYSize As Long
  dwXCountChars As Long
  dwYCountChars As Long
  dwFillAttribute As Long
  dwFlags As Long
  wShowWindow As Integer
  cbReserved2 As Integer
  lpReserved2 As Long
  hStdInput As Long
  hStdOutput As Long
  hStdError As Long
End Type

Type PROCESS_INFORMATION
  hProcess As Long
  hThread As Long
  dwProcessID As Long
  dwThreadID As Long
End Type
```

```
Declare Function OpenProcess Lib "kernel32" _
    (ByVal dwDesiredAccess As Long, ByVal bInheritHandle _
    As Long, ByVal dwProcessID As Long) As Long
Declare Function GetExitCodeProcess Lib "kernel32" _
    (ByVal hProcess As Long, lpExitCode As Long) As Long
Declare Sub Sleep Lib "kernel32" (ByVal dwMilliseconds As Long)
Declare Function CloseHandle Lib "kernel32" (hObject As Long) _
    As Boolean
Declare Function WaitForSingleObject Lib "kernel32" (ByVal _
    hHandle As Long, ByVal dwMilliseconds As Long) As Long
Declare Function CreateProcessA Lib "kernel32" _
    (ByVal lpApplicationName As Long, ByVal lpCommandLine As _
    String, ByVal lpProcessAttributes As Long, ByVal _
    lpThreadAttributes As Long, ByVal bInheritHandles As _
    Long, ByVal dwCreationFlags As Long, ByVal _
    lpEnvironment As Long, ByVal _
    lpCurrentDirectory As Long, lpStartupInfo As STARTUPINFO, _
    lpProcessInformation As PROCESS_INFORMATION) As Long
Declare Function IsWindow Lib "user32" (ByVal hwnd As Long) _
    As Long
Declare Function GetWindow Lib "user32" (ByVal hwnd As Long _
    , ByVal wCmd As Long) As Long
Declare Function PostMessage Lib "user32" Alias _
    "PostMessageA" (ByVal hwnd As Long, ByVal wMsg _
    As Long, ByVal wParam _
    As Long, ByVal lParam As Long) As Long
Declare Function GetWindowLong Lib "user32" Alias _
    "GetWindowLongA" (ByVal hwnd As Long, _
    ByVal nIndex As Long) As Long

Declare Function FindWindow Lib "user32" Alias "FindWindowA" _
    (ByVal lpClassName As String, ByVal lpWindowName _
    As String) As Long

Declare Function GetParent Lib "user32" (ByVal hwnd _
As Long) As Long
Declare Function GetWindowTextLength Lib "user32" Alias _
    "GetWindowTextLengthA" (ByVal hwnd As Long) As Long
Declare Function GetWindowText Lib "user32" Alias _
    "GetWindowTextA" (ByVal hwnd As Long, ByVal lpString _
    As String, ByVal cch As Long) As Long
```

Finding All the Windows and Their Handles   The LoadTaskList subroutine (see Code 7.13) loops through all the windows in memory and uses GetParent, GetWindowTextLength, and GetWindowText to write the Task Name and handle to the list box. This includes all Windows-level processes and applications. Table 7.9 lists the values for the GetWindow function.

Code 7.13: The LoadTaskList Subroutine

```
Sub LoadTaskList()
    Dim CurrWnd As Long
    Dim Length As Long
    Dim TaskName As String
    Dim Parent As Long

    List1.Clear
    CurrWnd = GetWindow(Form1.hwnd, GW_HWNDFIRST)

    While CurrWnd <> 0
      Parent = GetParent(CurrWnd)
      Length = GetWindowTextLength(CurrWnd)
      TaskName = Space$(Length + 1)
      Length = GetWindowText(CurrWnd, TaskName, Length + 1)
      TaskName = Left$(TaskName, Len(TaskName) - 1)
      If Length > 0 Then
        If TaskName <> Me.Caption Then
          List1.AddItem TaskName & Chr(9) & Chr(9) & _
            CurrWnd
        End If
      End If
      CurrWnd = GetWindow(CurrWnd, GW_HWNDNEXT)
      DoEvents
    Wend
End Sub
```

TABLE 7.9: The Values for the GetWindow Function

VALUE	DESCRIPTION
GW_CHILD	The retrieved handle identifies the child window at the top of the Zorder.
GW_HWNDFIRST	The retrieved handle identifies the window of the same type that is highest in the Zorder.
GW_HWNDLAST	The retrieved handle identifies the window of the same type that is lowest in the Zorder.
GW_HWNDNEXT	The retrieved handle identifies the window below the specified window in the Zorder.
GW_HWNDPREV	The retrieved handle identifies the window above the specified window in the Zorder.
GW_HWNDPREV	The retrieved handle identifies the window above the specified window in the Zorder.
GW_OWNER	The retrieved handle identifies the specified window's owner window, if any.

Part ii

Opening an Application and Continuing The ShellAndContinue subroutine uses the OpenProcess API and the Visual Basic Shell functions to launch the selected application (see Code 7.14). After it is open, the program monitors the state with GetExitCodeProcess. As soon as the value of GetExitCodeProcess is not equal to STILL_ACTIVE, you are notified through a message box. Table 7.10 lists the access values for the OpenProcess function.

Code 7.14: The ShellAndContinue Subroutine

```
Sub ShellAndContinue(ByVal AppToRun As String)
    Dim hProcess As Long
    Dim RetVal As Long
    Dim Msg, Style, Title, Response

    'The next line launches AppToRun,
    'captures process ID
    hProcess = OpenProcess(PROCESS_QUERY_INFORMATION, 1, _
    Shell(AppToRun, vbNormalFocus))
    Do
        'Get the status of the process
        GetExitCodeProcess hProcess, RetVal

        DoEvents
    'Loop while the process is active
    Loop While RetVal = STILL_ACTIVE

    'Define message
    Msg = AppToRun & " Terminated by user"
    'Define buttons
    Style = vbOKOnly + vbInformation
    'Define title
    Title = "Termination Notice"
    'Display message
    Response = MsgBox(Msg, Style, Title)

End Sub
```

TABLE 7.10: The OpenProcess Access Values

ACCESS	DESCRIPTION
PROCESS_ALL_ACCESS	Specifies all possible access flags for the process object
PROCESS_CREATE_PROCESS	Used internally

TABLE 7.10 (continued): The OpenProcess Access Values

ACCESS	DESCRIPTION
PROCESS_CREATE_THREAD	Enables using the process handle in the CreateRemote-Thread function to create a thread in the process
PROCESS_DUP_HANDLE	Enables using the process handle as either the source or target process in the DuplicateHandle function to duplicate a handle
PROCESS_QUERY_INFORMATION	Enables using the process handle in the GetExitCode-Process and GetPriorityClass functions to read information from the process object
PROCESS_SET_INFORMATION	Enables using the process handle in the SetPriority-Class function to set the priority class of the process
PROCESS_TERMINATE	Enables using the process handle in the Terminate-Process function to terminate the process
PROCESS_VM_OPERATION	Enables using the process handle in the Virtual-ProtectEx and WriteProcessMemory functions to modify the virtual memory of the process
PROCESS_VM_READ	Enables using the process handle in the ReadProcess-Memory function to read from the virtual memory of the process
PROCESS_VM_WRITE	Enables using the process handle in the WriteProcess-Memory function to write to the virtual memory of the process
SYNCHRONIZE	Windows NT only: Enables using the process handle in any of the wait functions to wait for the process to terminate

Part ii

Opening an Application and Waiting until the User Terminates It

The ShellAndWait subroutine uses the API function CreateProcess to launch the application passed in the AppToRun parameter. This process also uses the function WaitForSingleObject to "freeze" the VB program until the new process is terminated; it then uses the CloseHandle function to close the handle to the process and free the VB project.

Code 7.15: The ShellAndWait Subroutine

```
Public Sub ShellAndWait(AppToRun)
    Dim NameOfProc As PROCESS_INFORMATION
    Dim NameStart As STARTUPINFO
    Dim rc As Long
```

```
            NameStart.cb = Len(NameStart)
            rc = CreateProcessA(0&, AppToRun, 0&, 0&, 1&, _
              NORMAL_PRIORITY_CLASS, _
              0&, 0&, NameStart, NameOfProc)
            rc = WaitForSingleObject(NameOfProc.hProcess, INFINITE)
            rc = CloseHandle(NameOfProc.hProcess)
        End Sub
```

Terminating an Application   The EndTask subroutine first checks
with the IsWindow function to make sure you do not close the AppShell
program. Next, the GetWindowLong function finds the state of the window you want to close. If it is disabled, you don't close it. If the selected
window is not the current window and it is not disabled, use the Post-
Message API to cancel and close the handle to the window.

Code 7.16:   The EndTask Subroutine

```
    Function EndTask(TargetHwnd As Long) As Long
       Dim rc As Integer
       Dim ReturnVal As Integer
       If TargetHwnd = Form1.hwnd Or GetWindow(TargetHwnd, _
           GW_OWNER) = Form1.hwnd Then
          End
       End If
       If IsWindow(TargetHwnd) = False Then
          GoTo EndTaskFail
       End If
       If (GetWindowLong(TargetHwnd, GWL_STYLE) And _
       WS_DISABLED) Then
          GoTo EndTaskSucceed
       End If

       If IsWindow(TargetHwnd) Then
          If Not (GetWindowLong(TargetHwnd, GWL_STYLE) And _
       WS_DISABLED) Then
          rc = PostMessage(TargetHwnd, WS_CANCELMODE, 0, 0&)
          rc = PostMessage(TargetHwnd, WM_CLOSE, 0, 0&)
           DoEvents
          End If
       End If
       GoTo EndTaskSucceed

    EndTaskFail:
       ReturnVal = False
       GoTo EndTaskEndSub
```

```
EndTaskSucceed:
   ReturnVal = True
EndTaskEndSub:
   EndTask = ReturnVal
End Function
```

As you can see, APIs are handy for helping VB open applications, create processes, find all the currently running processes, and even terminate processes. Now with everything in place, let's take the AppShell program through its paces.

Give AppShell a Try

Press F5 to start the AppShell application (shown in Figure 7.8, earlier in this chapter), and then follow these steps:

1. Click the Shell and Continue button to open a standard Open dialog box in which you can select an application.

2. Select an EXE file to run. You will notice that you still have control of the AppShell program.

3. Now, close the new application. A message box notifies you that the application has terminated.

4. Click the Process and Wait button, and choose an application. Notice that this time you do not retain control of the AppShell program.

5. Close the new application and control is returned to the AppShell program.

6. Clicking the Terminate App button terminates the application selected in the list box. Be careful with this one; it terminates any application that you select. Test it on an application such as Notepad.

7. Click the Refresh List Box button to refresh the list box with the name and handle of all open processes (see Figure 7.9).

Being able to control applications from within your Visual Basic program is really a plus. It's important to be able to start, monitor, and terminate applications running concurrently with your applications. Just as important to the VB developer is having a way to spy on an application's menu structure and having the power to activate a menu option automatically. The next section examines the API function and procedures necessary to pull this off.

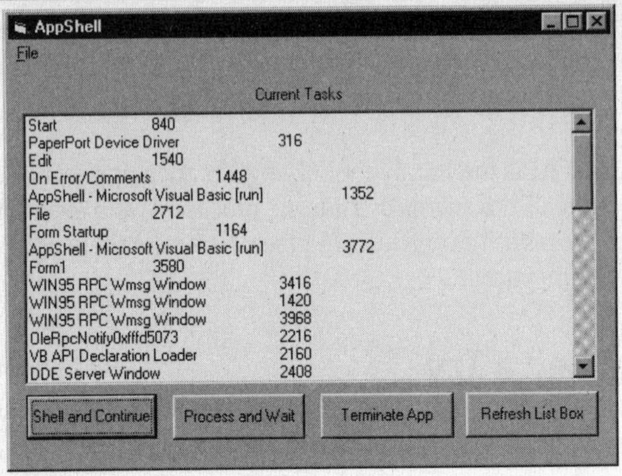

FIGURE 7.9:   The AppShell application at work

Analyzing an Application's Menu Structure

Most applications we write and encounter have some sort of menu structure. A menu can be a simple one-level structure that includes File and Exit options, or it can be complex, as is the menu structure for Visual Basic 6. With the aid of API functions, you can analyze an application's menu structure and trigger a menu option in another application.

You can use the FindWindow function to get the handle to an application if you already know its name. Once you have the handle, the function GetMenuItemCount returns the number of top-level menu entries. Top-level items are the menu options visible at the top of an application. In Visual Basic, for example, the top-level menus include File, Edit, View, Project, and Format. After you have the top-level menu items, use the function GetMenuItemInfo to retrieve information about the menu, and then use GetSubMenu to obtain information about the pop-up menus.

After you analyze all the top-level and submenus, it is easy to call the SendMessage function and trigger one of the menu options.

The AnalyzeMenu Project

The AnalyzeMenu project, shown in Figure 7.10, reads the menu structure of Notepad, Calculator, WordPad, and Paint. You can easily adjust it to analyze the menu structure of any application by using the techniques we discuss in this chapter.

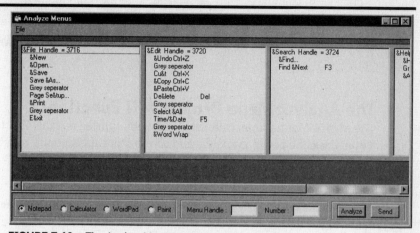

FIGURE 7.10:   The AnalyzeMenu project analyzing Notepad

As the program reads through the menu structure, it creates a new List Box control for each top-level menu item. Using the List Box's AddItem method, it adds the menu items to the list box. Each menu item and its sub items end up in their own list box. An OptionButton is provided for each of the four sample applications. Two Command Buttons and two Text Box controls are included:

The Analyze button   When you click this button, it loops through the application's menu structure and creates and loads a List Box control with the options for each top-level menu. Each top-level menu and its sub- and pop-up menus are placed in a separate list box with the caption of the menu option. The handle to the menu is also provided for all top- and sub-level menu options.

The Send button   Clicking this button triggers the selected menu option with the SendMessage API function.

The Menu Handle text box   Here, the handle of the menu is inserted when you click a menu. Optionally, you can enter the handle of the menu you want to activate.

The Number text box   Here, the menu number is inserted as you click the menu options. Optionally, you enter the number of the menu item to be triggered. Menu items start with zero and advance until you encounter another menu option with a handle.

NOTE

You'll find the AnalyzeMenu project in this book's section of the Sybex Web site.

The AnalyzeMenu Project API Functions

The AnalyzeMenu project calls the API functions listed in Table 7.11 to give Visual Basic the power to analyze and access other applications' menus.

NOTE

You'll find a complete description of these API functions in the Function Reference at the end of this book.

TABLE 7.11: The API Functions in the AnalyzeMenu Project

API FUNCTION	DESCRIPTION
FindWindow	Retrieves the handle to the top-level window whose class name and window name match the specified strings. This function does not search child windows.
GetMenu	Retrieves the handle of the menu assigned to the given window.
GetMenuItemCount	Determines the number of items in the specified menu.
GetMenuItemID	Retrieves the menu item identifier of a menu item located at the specified position in a menu.
GetMenuState	Retrieves the menu flags associated with the specified menu item. If the menu item opens a submenu, this function also returns the number of items in the submenu.
GetMenuString	Copies the text string of the specified menu item into the specified buffer.
GetSubMenu	Retrieves the handle of the drop-down menu or submenu activated by the specified menu item.
SendMessage	Sends the specified message to a window or windows. The function calls the window procedure for the specified window and does not return until the window procedure has processed the message.

The AnalyzeMenu Code in Action

Using the API functions in Table 7.11, the code in the AnalyzeMenu project (see Code 7.17) demonstrates how Visual Basic, with the help of API calls, can spy on the menu structure of other applications and activate menu options.

Code 7.17: Declarations, Types, and Constants in the Analyze-Menu Project

```
'Public Constants
Global hwndHold As Long
Global glSpaces As String
Global Const WM_COMMAND = &H111
Global glApplicationName As String   'hold the window to analyze
Public Const MF_BYPOSITION = &H400&
Public Const MF_BYCOMMAND = &H0&


'API Declarations
Declare Function FindWindow Lib "user32" Alias _
  "FindWindowA" (ByVal lpClassName As String, ByVal _
  lpWindowName As String) As Long
Declare Function GetMenu Lib "user32" (ByVal hwnd _
  As Long) As Long
Declare Function GetSubMenu Lib "user32" (ByVal hMenu _
  As Long, ByVal nPos As Long) As Long
Declare Function GetMenuItemCount Lib "user32" (ByVal _
  hMenu As Long) As Long
Declare Function GetMenuItemID Lib "user32" (ByVal _
  hMenu As Long, ByVal nPos As Long) As Long
Declare Function GetMenuString Lib "user32" Alias _
  "GetMenuStringA" (ByVal hMenu As Long, ByVal wIDItem _
  As Long, ByVal lpString As String, ByVal nMaxCount _
  As Long, ByVal wFlag As Long) As Long
Declare Function GetMenuState Lib "user32" (ByVal hMenu _
  As Long, ByVal wID As Long, ByVal wFlags As Long) As Long
Declare Function SendMessage Lib "user32" Alias _
  "SendMessageA" (ByVal hwnd As Long, ByVal wMsg As _
  Long, ByVal wParam As Long, lParam As Any) As Long
```

Analyzing the Top-Level Menu Structure The AnalyzeTopLevel-Menus subroutine shown in Code 7.18 loops through the menu structure of the main window and writes the menu text and handle to an array. Figure 7.11 shows the top-level menus for Visual Basic, which include File, Edit, View, and Project. You use the GetMenuItemCount function to get the number of top-level menus for this window. Then, you call the Get-SubMenu function to get the handle for the menus. The AnalyzeMenu subroutine uses this handle to determine when to start a new menu. Each time a top-level menu is found, the size of the main Form is increased, and a List Box control is added. This list box holds the menu structure that is found later in the AnalyzeMenu subroutine. Additionally, the value of the menu's handle is stored in the Tag property of the List Box. This handle is used later in the Click Event of the lstMenu list box to populate the txtHandle field.

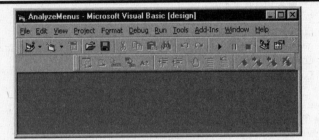

FIGURE 7.11: Top-level Visual Basic menus

Code 7.18:   The AnalyzeTopLevelMenus Subroutine

```
Public Sub AnalyzeTopLevelMenus(ByVal menuhnd)

    Dim slMenuCounter As Integer
    Dim slNumberOfMenus As Integer

    Dim slMenu As Integer
    Dim slMenuID As Long
    Dim slPopupMenu As Integer

    Dim slMenuInfo As Integer
    Dim slMenuFlags As Integer

    Dim menustring(128) As Byte
    Dim menustring2 As String * 128
    Dim context&

    'This routine can analyze up to 32 popup sub-menus
    Dim trackpopups&(32)

    Dim slXcnt As Integer

    'Find out how many entries are in the menu.
```

```
slNumberOfMenus = GetMenuItemCount(menuhnd)

'set the number of top level menus
ReDim aryTopLevel(Str$(slNumberOfMenus))

'Find out how many entries are in the menu.
slNumberOfMenus = GetMenuItemCount(menuhnd)

For slMenu = 0 To slNumberOfMenus - 1
  'Get the ID for this menu
  'It's a command ID, -1 for a popup, 0 for a separator
  slMenuID = GetMenuItemID(menuhnd, slMenu)
  Select Case slMenuID
    Case 0 'It's a separator

    Case -1 'It's a popup menu
      slMenuInfo = GetMenuString(menuhnd, slMenu, _
        menustring2, 127, MF_BYPOSITION)
      slMenuFlags = GetMenuState(menuhnd, slMenu, _
        MF_BYPOSITION)
      Debug.Print glSpaces & Left$ _
      (menustring2, slMenuInfo) _
      & " Handle = " & GetSubMenu(menuhnd, slMenu)
      'store the handle to this menu in the array
      aryTopLevel(slMenu) = _
      (GetSubMenu(menuhnd, slMenu))

      'add a list box for each menu and
      'increase the size of the form
      If slMenu > 0 Then
        Load Form1.lstMenu(slMenu)
        Form1.Width = Form1.Width + 3450
        Form1.lstMenu(slMenu).Left = Form1.lstMenu _
          (slMenu - 1).Left + Form1.lstMenu _
          (slMenu - 1).Width + 100
        Form1.lstMenu(slMenu).Visible = True
      End If
      'Store the handle for the menu in the Tag property
      'to use in the Click Event of the listbox to populate
      'the txtHandle and txtNumber fields.
      Form1.lstMenu(slMenu).Tag = GetSubMenu(menuhnd, _
          slMenu)
  End Select
Next slMenu

End Sub
```

Part ii

Analyzing the Menu Structure   The AnalyzeMenus subroutine uses the GetMenuItemCount function to return the number of menu items. The GetMenuItemID function tells us if the menu is a separator or a pop-up menu. Figure 7.12 shows the top-level menu of Notepad with the File submenu exposed. New, Open, Save, and Save As are pop-up menus, and the gray line below Save As is a separator.

The AnalyzeMenus subroutine (see Code 7.19) loops through the items in a menu and adds each item with the GetMenuString function; it then uses the GetSubMenu function to add the handle to a list box. Each top-level menu is added to a separate List Box control. The items are indented to mimic the look of the menu. This subroutine is a good example of API calls and Visual Basic loops. Figure 7.10, earlier in this chapter, shows the menus of Notepad analyzed.

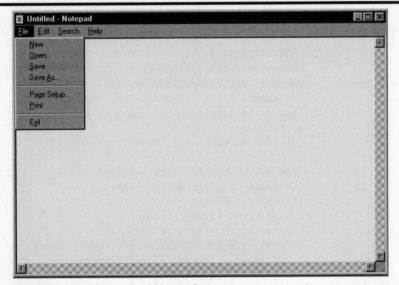

FIGURE 7.12:   The top-level Notepad menus

Code 7.19:   The AnalyzeMenus Subroutine

```
Public Sub AnalyzeMenus(ByVal menuhnd)

    Dim slMenuCounter As Integer
    Dim slNumberOfMenus As Integer

    Dim slMenu As Integer
    Dim slMenuID As Long
```

```
Dim slPopupMenu

Dim slMenuInfo As Integer
Dim slMenuFlags As Integer

Dim menustring(128) As Byte
Dim menustring2 As String * 128

'This routine can analyze up to 32 popup sub-menus
Dim trackpopups&(32)

Dim slXcnt As Integer

slPopupMenu = 0

'Find out how many entries are in the menu.
slNumberOfMenus = GetMenuItemCount(menuhnd)

For slMenu = 0 To slNumberOfMenus - 1
  'Get the ID for this menu
  'It's a command ID, -1 for a popup, 0 for a separator
  slMenuID = GetMenuItemID(menuhnd, slMenu)
  Select Case slMenuID
    Case 0 'It's a separator
      Form1.lstMenu(lstNum).AddItem glSpaces & _
        "Grey separator"
    Case -1 'It's a popup menu
      'Save it in the list of popups
      trackpopups&(slPopupMenu) = slMenu
      slPopupMenu = slPopupMenu + 1

      slMenuInfo = GetMenuString(menuhnd, slMenu, _
        menustring2, 127, MF_BYPOSITION)

      'Set the listbox according to the top level menu
      For slMenuCounter = 0 To UBound(aryTopLevel)
        If aryTopLevel(slMenuCounter) = (GetSubMenu _
          (menuhnd, slMenu)) Then
          lstNum = slMenuCounter
          'reset the indention
          glSpaces = ""
        End If
      Next

      slMenuFlags = GetMenuState(menuhnd, slMenu, _
        MF_BYPOSITION)
```

```
            Form1.lstMenu(lstNum).AddItem glSpaces _
            & Left$(menustring2, slMenuInfo) _
            & " Handle = " & GetSubMenu(menuhnd, slMenu)

            'At least one popup was found
            If slPopupMenu > 0 Then
              For slXcnt = 0 To slPopupMenu - 1
                slMenuID = trackpopups&(slXcnt)
                glSpaces = glSpaces & "  "
                AnalyzeMenus GetSubMenu(menuhnd, _
                slMenuID)
              Next slXcnt
              slPopupMenu = 0
              glSpaces = "  "
            End If

          Case Else 'A regular entry
            slMenuInfo = GetMenuString(menuhnd, slMenuID, _
              menustring2, 127, MF_BYCOMMAND)
            Form1.lstMenu(lstNum).AddItem glSpaces & _
              Left$(menustring2, slMenuInfo)
            slMenuFlags = GetMenuState(menuhnd, slMenuID, _
              MF_BYCOMMAND)
        End Select
      Next slMenu
      glSpaces = ""

  End Sub
```

Activating a Menu Option   The subroutine cmdSend uses the handle and menu number from the main Form and calls the API function Send-Message to activate a menu option (see Code 7.20).

Code 7.20:   The cmdSend Subroutine

```
Private Sub cmdSend_Click()
  Dim hwnd As Long
  Dim hMainMenu As Integer
  Dim hMenu As Integer
  Dim slMenuID As Long
  Dim rc
  Dim X As Long

  slMenuID = GetMenuItemID(txtHandle, txtNumber)

  rc = SendMessage(hwndHold, WM_COMMAND, slMenuID, 0&)

End Sub
```

The ability to activate a menu option from other applications adds a new dimension to the power and flexibility of Visual Basic. As you can see, you can program VB to do the following:

- ▶ Open a help file from another application
- ▶ Print a report
- ▶ Open a file
- ▶ Change properties such as font, color, and format
- ▶ Access any menu option

Testing the AnalyzeMenu Program

The AnalyzeMenu program is designed to analyze the menu structure of Notepad, Calculator, WordPad, or Paint. You could easily adapt it to analyze the menu structure of any application. For this test, we will analyze the menus of Notepad. Follow these easy steps:

1. Start and minimize the Notepad application.

2. Press F5 to start the AnalyzeMenu program.

3. Select the Notepad button.

4. Click the Analyze button. The top part of the Form will be filled with five list boxes, similar to what you see in Figure 7.10, earlier in this chapter. Each list box contains a top-level menu option and all the submenus and pop-up menus under it.

5. In the MenuHandle text box, enter the handle number for the &Help menu.

6. Enter the number zero into the Number text box. This tells the program that you want to trigger the first option, &Help Topics (remember that menu numbers start with zero).

7. Click the Send button to display the Notepad help file.

Menus are an integral part of Windows applications. By employing the API functions and procedures we looked at in this section, you can program Visual Basic to unlock the power of menus in other applications.

Part II

NOTE

If you use the AnalyzeMenu application to activate a menu option that displays a Dialog Box, such as Help About or a Print Setup, keep in mind that the Dialog Box will be displayed behind the AnalyzeMenu application. To access the dialog box, use Alt+Tab to make the dialog box active.

THE BITMAPS AND GRAPHICS API FUNCTIONS

In visual programming environments such as Visual Basic and Windows, bitmaps and graphics are important. Graphics and bitmaps are used in almost every part of a Visual Basic application—from the menu to the forms that make up the user interface. Visual Basic does not provide a lot of support for graphics; fortunately, API functions can fill the void. The Win32 API includes a vast array of API functions that can be employed in Visual Basic to do the following:

- ► Create bitmaps
- ► Copy bitmaps
- ► Flood a container with color
- ► Add bitmaps to menus

And the list goes on and on. One common thread is a bitmap.

Understanding Bitmaps

A bitmap is an object in Windows that holds an image. The two types of bit-maps are:

- ► Device-dependent bitmaps (DDB)
- ► Device-independent bitmaps (DIB)

Device-Dependent Bitmaps

All bitmaps in Windows are device-dependent unless otherwise noted. DDBs are described in a single structure, the BITMAP structure. The BITMAP structure defines the type, width, height, color, format, and bit values of a bitmap. Table 7.12 lists and describes the members of a BITMAP structure.

TABLE 7.12: The Members of a BITMAP Structure

MEMBER	DESCRIPTION
bmType	Specifies the bitmap type. This member must be zero.
BmWidth	Specifies the width, in pixels, of the bitmap. The width must be greater than zero.
BmHeight	Specifies the height, in pixels, of the bitmap. The height must be greater than zero.
BmWidthBytes	Specifies the number of bytes in each scan line.
BmPlanes	Specifies the count of color planes.
BmBitsPixel	Specifies the number of bits required to indicate the color of a pixel.
BmBits	Points to the location of the bit values for the bitmap.

Part ii

Copying and displaying a DDB is much faster than copying and displaying a DIB. All Windows needs to do to move a DDB is to copy memory. You can use the function BitBlt to do this. The key to using DDBs is compatibility. The easiest way to determine if a bitmap is compatible with a device is to use the CreateCompatibleBitmap function. On the other hand, you can use device-independent bitmaps to copy or display bitmaps across devices.

Device-Independent Bitmaps

A device-independent bitmap is a color bitmap in a format that eliminates the problems that occur in transferring DDBs to devices that have a different bitmap format. DIBs provide bitmap information that any display or printer driver can translate. The main purpose of DIBs is to allow bitmaps to be moved from one device to another.

Transferring bitmaps from one device to another was not possible in Microsoft Windows prior to version 3. Now, with DIBs, every device can display a bitmap to the extent of its color resolution. An application can store and display a bitmap regardless of the output device.

A bitmap file consists of a BITMAPFILEHEADER structure and the DIB itself. Table 7.13 lists the members of this structure.

TABLE 7.13: The Members of the BITMAPFILEHEADER Structure

FIELD	DESCRIPTION
bfType	WORD that defines the type of file. It must be BM.
BfSize	A DWORD that specifies the size of the file in bytes.
bfReserved1, bfReserved2	WORDs that must be set to zero.
BfOffBits	A DWORD that specifies the offset from the beginning of the BITMAPFILEHEADER structure to the start of the actual bits.

The BITMAPINFOHEADER structure follows immediately after the BITMAPFILEHEADER structure. Table 7.14 lists and describes the members of the BITMAPINFOHEADER structure. The header is made up of two parts: the header and the color table. They are combined in the BITMAPINFO structure, which is what all DIB APIs expect.

TABLE 7.14:
The Members of the BITMAPINFOHEADER Structure

FIELD	DESCRIPTION
BiSize	Should be set to the size of (BITMAPINFOHEADER). This field defines the size of the header (minus the color table).
biWidth, biHeight	Define the width and the height of the bitmap in pixels.
BiPlanes	Should always be 1.
BiBitCount	Defines the color resolution (in bits per pixel) of the DIB. Only four values are valid for this field: 1, 4, 8, and 24.
BiCompression	Specifies the type of compression. Can be one of three values: BI_RGB, BI_RLE4, or BI_RLE8.
BiSizeImage	Should contain the size of the bitmap proper in bytes.
biXPelsPerMeter biYPelsPerMeter	Define application-specified values for the desirable dimensions of the bitmap.
BiClrUsed	Provides a way for getting smaller color tables. When this field is set to 0, the number of colors on the biBit-Count field should be set to one of the following values: 1 indicates 2 colors, 4 indicates 16, 8 indicates 256, and 24 indicates no color table.
BiClrImportant	Specifies that the first x colors of the color table are important to the DIB.

The color table follows the header information. The number of entries in the color table matches the number of colors supported by the DIB except for a 24-bit color bitmap that does not have a color table. Table 7.15 shows the structure of a color table for a 16-color DIB.

TABLE 7.15: Color Structure

FIELD	DESCRIPTION
bmiHeader	BITMAPINFOHEADER information
BmiColors(15)	Colors

The ScreenCapture Project

The ScreenCapture project (shown in Figure 7.13) demonstrates how to use some of the most popular bitmap API functions.

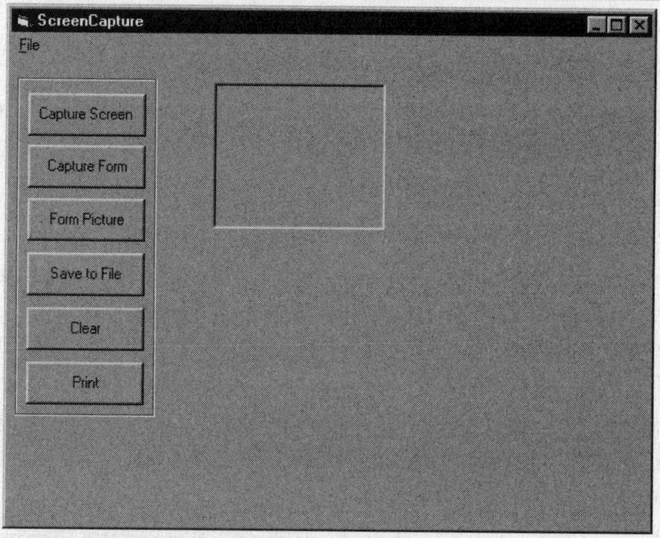

FIGURE 7.13: The ScreenCapture project

You can use a bitmap to do the following:

▶ Capture an image

▶ Store an image in memory

▶ Display an image at a different location or on a different device

To store an image temporarily, you can call the CreateCompatibleDC function to create a device context that is compatible with the current window device context. After you create the compatible device context, you can create a bitmap with the appropriate dimensions by calling the CreateCompatibleBitmap function. You can then call SelectObject to select it into the newly created device context.

After the compatible device context is created and the bitmap is selected into it, you can use the BitBlt function to capture an image. The BitBlt function performs a bit block transfer. It copies data from a source bitmap into a destination bitmap of the same size. The BitBlt function receives handles that identify two device contexts and copies the bitmap data from a bitmap selected into the source device context into a bitmap selected into the target device context. The target device context is a compatible device context; so when BitBlt completes the transfer, the image is copied into memory. You use the OleCreatePictureIndirect function to redisplay the image.

The ScreenCapture project has six Command Buttons:

Capture Screen   Clicking this button captures the screen and places an image of it in a picture box.

Capture Form   Clicking this button captures the Form and places an image of it in a picture box.

Create Form Picture   Clicking this button, after you capture an image, sets the Picture property of form2 to the captured image. This is an example of how to copy a bitmap into memory and then use it on a Form.

Save to File   Clicking this button opens a standard File Save dialog box, in which you can set the file name and location and save the picture to a file.

Clear   Clicking this button clears the contents of the Picture-Box control.

Print   Clicking this button prints the contents of the picture box on the default printer.

NOTE
You'll find the ScreenCapture project in this book's section of the Sybex Web site.

The ScreenCapture API Functions

The ScreenCapture project calls on the API functions listed in Table 7.16 to help Visual Basic perform bitmap functions.

TABLE 7.16: The ScreenCapture API Functions

FUNCTION	DESCRIPTION
BitBlt	Performs a bit-block transfer of the color data corresponding to a rectangle of pixels from the specified source device context into a destination device context.
CreateCompatibleBitmap	Creates a bitmap compatible with the device that is associated with the specified device context.
CreateCompatibleDC	Creates a memory device context that is compatible with the specified device.
CreatePalette	Creates a logical color palette.
GetDesktopWindow	Returns the handle of the Windows Desktop window. The Desktop window covers the entire screen. The Desktop window is the area on top of which all icons and other windows are painted.
GetDeviceCaps	Retrieves device-specific information about a specified device.
GetForegroundWindow	Returns the handle of the foreground window (the current window). The system assigns a slightly higher priority to the thread that creates the foreground window than it does to other threads.
GetSystemPaletteEntries	Retrieves a range of palette entries from the system palette that is associated with the specified device context.
GetDC	Retrieves a handle of a display device context for the client area of the specified window. The display device context can be used in subsequent GDI functions to draw in the client area of the window.

Part ii

TABLE 7.16 (continued): The ScreenCapture API Functions

FUNCTION	DESCRIPTION
GetWindowDC	Retrieves the device context for the entire window, including the title bar, menus, and scroll bars. A window device context permits painting anywhere in a window, because the origin of the device context is the upper-left corner of the window instead of the client area. The GetWindowDC function assigns default attributes to the window device context each time it retrieves the device context. Previous attributes are lost.
OleCreatePictureIndirect	Creates a new picture object initialized according to a PICT-DESC structure.
RealizePalette	Maps palette entries from the current logical palette to the system palette.
ReleaseDC	Releases a device context, freeing it for use by other applications. It frees only common and window device contexts and has no effect on class or private device contexts.
SelectObject	Selects an object into the specified device context. The new object replaces the previous object of the same type.
SelectPalette	Selects the specified logical palette into a device context.

The ScreenCapture Code in Action

Let's put these functions to work with VB to see how a bitmap can be used to capture a screen and part of a Form and how it can be used as the Picture property of a Form (see Code 7.21).

Code 7.21: Declarations, Types, and Constants in the ScreenCapture Project

```
Global Const INVERSE = 6
Const SOLID = 0
Const DOT = 2

Global HoldX As Single
Global HoldY As Single
Global StartX As Single
Global StartY As Single
Global SavedDrawStyle
Global SavedMode
```

```
Option Base 0

Private Type PALETTEENTRY
peRed As Byte
peGreen As Byte
peBlue As Byte
peFlags As Byte
End Type

Private Type LOGPALETTE
palVersion As Integer
palNumEntries As Integer
palPalEntry(255) As PALETTEENTRY ' Enough for 256 colors
End Type

Private Type GUID
Data1 As Long
Data2 As Integer
Data3 As Integer
Data4(7) As Byte
End Type


Private Const RASTERCAPS As Long = 38
Private Const RC_PALETTE As Long = &H100
Private Const SIZEPALETTE As Long = 104

Private Type RECT
  Left As Long
  Top As Long
  Right As Long
  Bottom As Long
End Type

Private Type PicBmp
  Size As Long
  Type As Long
  hBmp As Long
  hPal As Long
  Reserved As Long
End Type

Private Declare Function BitBlt Lib "GDI32" ( _
  ByVal hDCDest As Long, ByVal XDest As Long, _
  ByVal YDest As Long, ByVal nWidth As Long, _
  ByVal nHeight As Long, ByVal hDCSrc As Long, _
```

```
         ByVal XSrc As Long, ByVal YSrc As Long, ByVal dwRop As Long) _
         As Long
Private Declare Function CreateCompatibleBitmap Lib _
    "GDI32" (ByVal hDC As Long, ByVal nWidth As Long, _
    ByVal nHeight As Long) As Long
Private Declare Function CreateCompatibleDC Lib "GDI32" ( _
    ByVal hDC As Long) As Long
Private Declare Function CreatePalette Lib "GDI32" ( _
    lpLogPalette As LOGPALETTE) As Long
Private Declare Function DeleteDC Lib "GDI32" ( _
    ByVal hDC As Long) As Long
Private Declare Function GetDesktopWindow Lib "USER32" () As Long
Private Declare Function GetDeviceCaps Lib "GDI32" ( _
    ByVal hDC As Long, ByVal iCapabilitiy As Long) As Long
Private Declare Function GetForegroundWindow Lib "USER32" () _
    As Long
Private Declare Function GetSystemPaletteEntries Lib _
    "GDI32" (ByVal hDC As Long, ByVal wStartIndex As Long, _
    ByVal wNumEntries As Long, lpPaletteEntries _
    As PALETTEENTRY) As Long
Private Declare Function GetWindowDC Lib "USER32" ( _
    ByVal hWnd As Long) As Long
Private Declare Function GetDC Lib "USER32" ( _
    ByVal hWnd As Long) As Long
Private Declare Function GetWindowRect Lib "USER32" ( _
    ByVal hWnd As Long, lpRect As RECT) As Long
Private Declare Function OleCreatePictureIndirect _
    Lib "olepro32.dll" (PicDesc As PicBmp, RefIID As GUID, _
    ByVal fPictureOwnsHandle As Long, IPic As IPicture) As Long
Private Declare Function RealizePalette Lib "GDI32" ( _
    ByVal hDC As Long) As Long
Private Declare Function ReleaseDC Lib "USER32" ( _
    ByVal hWnd As Long, ByVal hDC As Long) As Long
Private Declare Function SelectObject Lib "GDI32" ( _
    ByVal hDC As Long, ByVal hObject As Long) As Long
Private Declare Function SelectPalette Lib "GDI32" ( _
    ByVal hDC As Long, ByVal hPalette As Long, _
    ByVal bForceBackground As Long) As Long
```

Capturing the Screen   The CaptureScreen function (shown in Code 7.22)
uses the GetDesktopWindow API function to retrieve a handle to the
Desktop. After the handle is retrieved, the VB function CaptureWindow
is called to copy the bitmap into memory. The screen resolution is passed
as well as the handle.

Code 7.22:   The CaptureScreen Function

```
Public Function CaptureScreen() As Picture
  On Error GoTo ErrorRoutineErr

  Dim hWndScreen As Long

  'Get a handle to the desktop window
  hWndScreen = GetDesktopWindow()

  'Call CaptureWindow to capture the entire desktop,
  'give the handle and return the resulting Picture object
  Set CaptureScreen = CaptureWindow(hWndScreen, 0, 0, _
  Screen.Width \ Screen.TwipsPerPixelX, _
  Screen.Height \ Screen.TwipsPerPixelY)

ErrorRoutineResume:
  Exit Function
ErrorRoutineErr:
  MsgBox "Project1.Module1.CaptureScreen" & Err & Error
  Resume Next
End Function
```

Part ii

Capturing the Form   The CaptureForm function (shown in Code 7.23) is similar to the CaptureScreen function except that it uses the Visual Basic Handle property hWnd to retrieve the handle to Form1. After the handle is retrieved, the VB function CaptureWindow is called to copy the bitmap into memory. The screen resolution is passed as well as the handle.

Code 7.23:   The CaptureForm Function

```
Public Function CaptureForm(frmSrc As Form) As Picture
  On Error GoTo ErrorRoutineErr

  'Call CaptureWindow to capture the entire form
  'given it's window
  'handle and then return the resulting Picture object
  Set CaptureForm = CaptureWindow(frmSrc.hWnd, 0, 0, _
  frmSrc.ScaleX(frmSrc.Width, vbTwips, vbPixels), _
  frmSrc.ScaleY(frmSrc.Height, vbTwips, vbPixels))

ErrorRoutineResume:
  Exit Function
ErrorRoutineErr:
  MsgBox "Project1.Module1.CaptureForm" & Err & Error
  Resume Next
End Function
```

Processing the CaptureWindow Actions   A lot of work is performed in this function (see Code 7.24). First, the API function GetWindowDC gets the device context for the screen or window. Next, CreateCompatibleDC creates a memory device context for the copy process, and then a bitmap is created with the CreateCompatibleBitmap function and placed into memory with the SelectObject function.

The next task is to get the screen properties. To accomplish this, we use the GetDeviceCaps function to find the raster capabilities and the palette size. If the screen has a palette, we need to copy it and select it into memory. We get the palette with the GetSystemPaletteEntries API function, create a copy of it with CreatePalette, and, finally, select it into memory with SelectPalette.

Now that we are finished with the preliminaries, we can use BitBlt to copy the image into the memory device context. If the screen has a palette, get it back with the SelectPalette function. With the bitmap and palette copied into memory, we can clean up a bit. We use the functions DeleteDC and ReleaseDC to release the device context resources back to the system. The last task is to call the function CreateBitmapPicture and create the picture object with the API function OleCreatePictureIndirect.

Code 7.24:   The CaptureWindow Function

```
Public Function CaptureWindow(ByVal hWndSrc As Long, _
    ByVal LeftSrc As Long, _
    ByVal TopSrc As Long, ByVal WidthSrc As Long, _
    ByVal HeightSrc As Long) As Picture

    On Error GoTo ErrorRoutineErr

    Dim hDCMemory As Long
    Dim hBmp As Long
    Dim hBmpPrev As Long
    Dim rc As Long
    Dim hDCSrc As Long
    Dim hPal As Long
    Dim hPalPrev As Long
    Dim RasterCapsScrn As Long
    Dim HasPaletteScrn As Long
    Dim PaletteSizeScrn As Long

    Dim LogPal As LOGPALETTE

    'Get device context for the window
```

```
hDCSrc = GetWindowDC(hWndSrc)

'Create a memory device context for the copy process
hDCMemory = CreateCompatibleDC(hDCSrc)
'Create a bitmap and place it in the memory DC
hBmp = CreateCompatibleBitmap(hDCSrc, WidthSrc, HeightSrc)
hBmpPrev = SelectObject(hDCMemory, hBmp)

'Get screen properties
'Raster capabilities
RasterCapsScrn = GetDeviceCaps(hDCSrc, RASTERCAPS)
'Palette support
HasPaletteScrn = RasterCapsScrn And RC_PALETTE
'Size of palette
PaletteSizeScrn = GetDeviceCaps(hDCSrc, SIZEPALETTE)

'If the screen has a palette, make a copy
If HasPaletteScrn And (PaletteSizeScrn = 256) Then
  'Create a copy of the system palette
  LogPal.palVersion = &H300
  LogPal.palNumEntries = 256
  rc = GetSystemPaletteEntries(hDCSrc, 0, 256, _
      LogPal.palPalEntry(0))
  hPal = CreatePalette(LogPal)
  'Select the new palette into the memory
  'DC and realize it
  hPalPrev = SelectPalette(hDCMemory, hPal, 0)
  rc = RealizePalette(hDCMemory)
End If

'Copy the image into the memory DC
rc = BitBlt(hDCMemory, 0, 0, WidthSrc, HeightSrc, _
hDCSrc, LeftSrc, TopSrc, vbSrcCopy)

'Remove the new copy of the on-screen image
hBmp = SelectObject(hDCMemory, hBmpPrev)

'If the screen has a palette get back the palette that was
'selected in previously
If HasPaletteScrn And (PaletteSizeScrn = 256) Then
hPal = SelectPalette(hDCMemory, hPalPrev, 0)
End If

'Release the device context resources back to the system
rc = DeleteDC(hDCMemory)
rc = ReleaseDC(hWndSrc, hDCSrc)
```

Part ii

```
'Call CreateBitmapPicture to create a picture
'object from the bitmap and palette handles.
'Then return the resulting picture object.
Set CaptureWindow = CreateBitmapPicture(hBmp, hPal)

ErrorRoutineResume:
   Exit Function
ErrorRoutineErr:
   MsgBox "Project1.Module1.CaptureWindow" & Err & Error
   Resume Next
End Function
```

Constructing a New Picture Object   The CreateBitmapPicture function (shown in Code 7.25) takes the handles of the bitmap and palettes that were placed into memory in the CaptureWindow function, adds the GUID structure and Pic parts, and with the OleCreatePictureIndirect API, creates a bitmap picture that can be placed in our PictureBox control on Form1.

Code 7.25:   The CreateBitmapPicture Function

```
Public Function CreateBitmapPicture(ByVal hBmp As Long, _
   ByVal hPal As Long) As Picture

   On Error GoTo ErrorRoutineErr

   Dim r As Long
      Dim Pic As PicBmp
   'IPicture requires a reference to "Standard OLE Types"
   Dim IPic As IPicture
   Dim IID_IDispatch As GUID

   'Fill in with IDispatch Interface ID
   With IID_IDispatch
      .Data1 = &H20400
      .Data4(0) = &HC0
      .Data4(7) = &H46
   End With

   'Fill Pic with necessary parts
   With Pic
      'Length of structure
      .Size = Len(Pic)
      'Type of Picture (bitmap)
      .Type = vbPicTypeBitmap
      'Handle to bitmap
```

```
        .hBmp = hBmp
        'Handle to palette (may be null)
        .hPal = hPal
    End With

    'Create Picture object
    r = OleCreatePictureIndirect(Pic, IID_IDispatch, 1, IPic)

    'Return the new Picture object
    Set CreateBitmapPicture = IPic

ErrorRoutineResume:
    Exit Function
ErrorRoutineErr:
    MsgBox "Project1.Module1.CreateBitmapPicture" & Err & Error
    Resume Next
End Function
```

As you can see, creating a bitmap in memory involves several steps. Without the help of the Win32API, Visual Basic would never be able to pull it off. Now, it's time to take the ScreenCapture project for a test run.

Testing the ScreenCapture Program

You can use the ScreenCapture project to capture a screen or a form with the aid of API calls and then use the bitmap as the Picture property of a Form. You can create a permanent copy of the bitmap by copying it to a file, and you can print the bitmap to the default printer. To test Screen-Capture, follow these steps:

1. Start the ScreenCapture project from within Visual Basic.

2. Click the Capture Screen button to capture the Desktop to the PictureBox control. Figure 7.14 shows the ScreenCapture project with the Desktop captured.

3. Click the Clear button to clear the picture box.

4. Click the Capture Form button to capture the ScreenCapture Form to the picture box.

5. If you want to save the bitmap to a file, click the Save to File button to open a standard Save As dialog box, in which you can select a path and file name and save the file.

6. Click the Print button to print the contents of the picture box on the default printer.

You can create bitmaps from almost any source, and this project demonstrates only the tip of the iceberg. By combining the techniques in the other sections of this chapter, you can really make APIs and bitmaps work for you to create some unique projects.

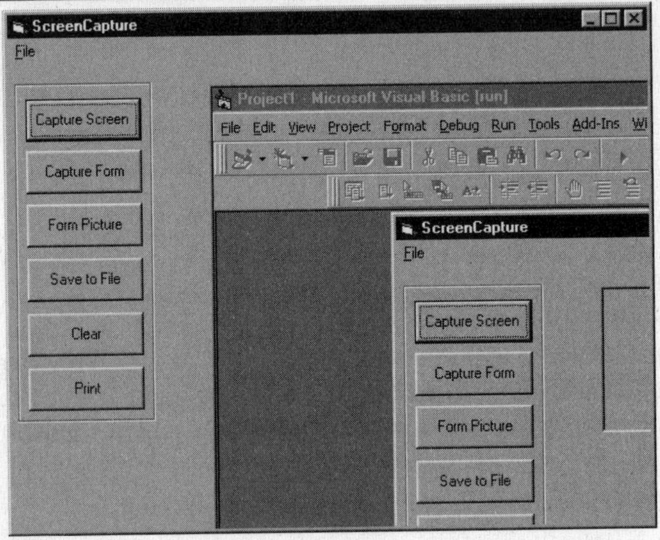

FIGURE 7.14: The Desktop captured

THE SYSTEM API FUNCTIONS

Visual Basic can tell you a lot about a computer's environment, but as developers we really need even more information. For example, when you get a support call, it's important to know the makeup of the user's system. Many times the problem is simply that the machine running the program does not meet the minimum hardware requirements.

If a computer is running an application that uses a few API functions, developers can have access to information about the following:

▶ Memory statistics

▶ Total and free disk space

▶ Number of colors

▶ Operating system

▶ Processor type

You can use the GlobalMemoryStatus API function to investigate the system and report the amount of memory. The GetFreeDiskSpace API returns, among others, the total disk space and the total free disk space. If your application needs to know the number of colors supported, call the GetDeviceCaps function.

You can use the GetVersionEx function to find out the major version, the minor version (such as NT version 4), the build number, and the service pack level for Windows NT. This last bit of information is especially important for NT users. Most applications written today require at least Service Pack 2 for NT.

Another must in today's programming environment is knowing the type of processor currently running. You can find this information with the GetSystemInfo API function. And if the user is signed on to a network, you can retrieve the user's name with the GetUserName function.

The Statistics Project

We will use the Statistics project (shown in Figure 7.15) to demonstrate some of the API functions you can use to get information about a computer's environment. When the application starts, it makes several API calls to catalog the current environment.

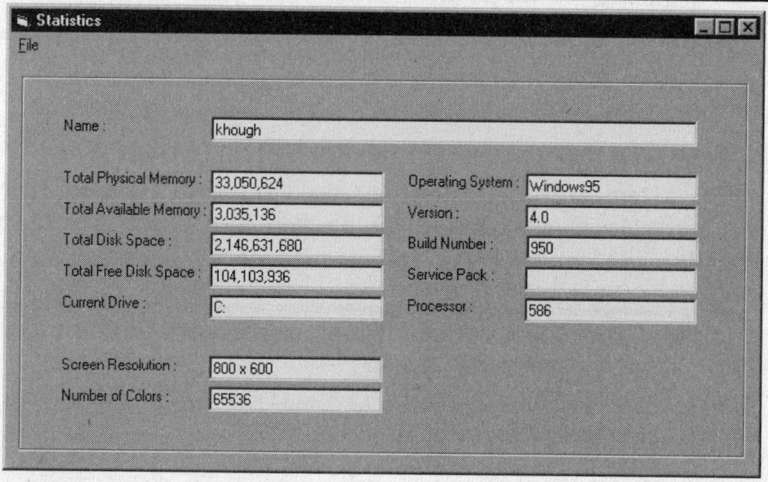

FIGURE 7.15: The Statistics project

The Statistics Project API Functions

Table 7.17 lists and describes the API functions in the Statistics project.

TABLE 7.17: The Statistics API Functions

FUNCTION	DESCRIPTION
GetDeviceCaps	Retrieves device-specific information about a specified device.
GetDiskFreeSpace	Retrieves information about the specified disk, including the amount of free space on the disk.
GlobalMemoryStatus	Retrieves information about current available memory. The function returns information about both physical and virtual memory. This function supersedes the GetFreeSpace function.
GetUserName	Retrieves the user name of the current thread. This is the name of the user currently logged on to the system.
GetVersionEx	Obtains extended information about the version of the operating system that is currently running.
GetSystemInfo	Returns information about the current system.

The Statistics Project Code in Action

The system statistic API functions listed in Table 7.17 can really give you a head start when it comes to troubleshooting application problems. Let's take a look at Code 7.26 to examine the functions in some code.

Code 7.26: Declarations, Types, and Constants Used in the Statistics Project

```
Global SectorsPerCluster As Long
Global BytesPerSector As Long
Global NumberOfFreeClustors As Long
Global TotalNumberOfClustors As Long
Global BytesFree As Long
Global BytesTotal As Long
Global PercentFree As Long
```

```
Public Const VER_Processor_WIN32_NT& = 2
Public Const VER_Processor_WIN32_WINDOWS& = 1

Public Const PROCESSOR_INTEL_386 = 386
Public Const PROCESSOR_INTEL_486 = 486
Public Const PROCESSOR_INTEL_PENTIUM = 586
Public Const PROCESSOR_MIPS_R4000 = 4000
Public Const PROCESSOR_ALPHA_21064 = 21064

Type MEMORYSTATUS
   dwLength As Long
   dwMemoryLoad As Long
   dwTotalPhys As Long
   dwAvailPhys As Long
   dwTotalPageFile As Long
   dwAvailPageFile As Long
   dwTotalVirtual As Long
   dwAvailVirtual As Long
End Type

Public Type SYSTEM_INFO
    dwOemID As Long
    dwPageSize As Long
    lpMinimumApplicationAddress As Long
    lpMaximumApplicationAddress As Long
    dwActiveProcessorMask As Long
    dwNumberOfProcessors As Long
    dwProcessorType As Long
    dwAllocationGranularity As Long
    wProcessorLevel As Integer
    wProcessorRevision As Integer
End Type

Public Type OSVersionInfo
    dwOSVersionInfoSize As Long
    dwMajorVersion As Long
    dwMinorVersion As Long
    dwBuildNumber As Long
    dwProcessorId As Long
    szCSDVersion As String * 128
End Type

' Holder for version information. Set on form load
Global myVer As OSVersionInfo
Declare Function GetDeviceCaps Lib "gdi32" (ByVal _
  hdc As Long, ByVal nIndex As Long) As Long
```

Part ii

```
Declare Function GetDiskFreeSpace Lib "kernel32" Alias _
    "GetDiskFreeSpaceA" (ByVal lpRootPathName As String, _
    lpSectorsPerCluster As Long, lpBytesPerSector As Long, _
    lpNumberOfFreeClusters As Long, lpTtoalNumberOfClusters _
    As Long) As Long
Declare Sub GlobalMemoryStatus Lib "kernel32" _
    (lpBuffer As MEMORYSTATUS)
Declare Function GetUserName Lib "advapi32.dll" Alias _
    "GetUserNameA" (ByVal lpBuffer _
    As String, nSize As Long) As Long
Declare Function GetVersionEx Lib "kernel32" Alias _
    "GetVersionExA" (lpVersionInformation As OSVersionInfo) _
    As Long
Declare Sub GetSystemInfo Lib "kernel32" _
    (lpSystemInfo As SYSTEM_INFO)
```

Getting the User's Name   A call to GetUserName returns the network logon name of the person currently logged on (see Code 7.27). You can use this name to send mail, verify access levels, mark records for history, and—well you get the idea.

Code 7.27:   The UserName Subroutine

```
Public Sub UserName()
    On Error GoTo ErrorRoutineErr

    Dim st As String
    Dim slCnt As Long
    Dim slDL As Long
    Dim slPos As Single
    Dim slUserName As String

    'Get the users name
    slCnt = 199
    st = String(200, 0)
    slDL = GetUserName(st, slCnt)
    slUserName = Left(st, slCnt) & slCnt
    slPos = InStr(1, slUserName, Chr(0))
    If slPos > 0 Then
        txtUserName = Left(slUserName, slPos - 1)
    End If

ErrorRoutineResume:
    Exit Sub
ErrorRoutineErr:
    MsgBox "Stats.Form1.UserName" & Err & Error
End Sub
```

Getting System Information The APIs in this section retrieve a lot of valuable system information. The GlobalMemoryStatus function retrieves and reports on the system's memory position–the total available memory and the total memory (see Code 7.28). After that, a call to GetDeviceCaps gets the number of colors supported. The function Get-FreeDiskSpace gets the total disk space and the total free disk space.

Code 7.28: The SystemInformation Subroutine

```
Public Sub SystemInformation()

    On Error GoTo ErrorRoutineErr

    Dim ms As MEMORYSTATUS
    Dim slDriveType
    Dim slDL As Long
    Dim slDrive
    Dim slPosition As Integer
    Dim slFreeBytes As Long
    Dim slTotalBytes As Long

    ms.dwLength = Len(ms)
    GlobalMemoryStatus ms

    'Get memory
    txtTotalPhysicalMemory = Format(ms.dwTotalPhys, "0,000")
    txtTotalAvailableMemory = Format(ms.dwAvailPhys, "0,00")

    'Screen resolution and colors
    txtScreenResolution = Screen.Width \ Screen.TwipsPerPixelX _
      & " x " & Screen.Height \ Screen.TwipsPerPixelY
    txtColors = DeviceColors((hdc))

    'Current drive
    slDrive = Left(App.Path, 2)
    slPosition = InStr(slDrive, " ")
    If slPosition > 0 Then
      slDrive = Left$(slDrive, slPosition - 1)
    End If
    If Right$(slDrive, 1) <> "\" Then slDrive = slDrive & "\"
    txtCurrentDrive = Left(slDrive, 2)

    'Total free disk space
    slDL = GetDiskFreeSpace(slDrive, SectorsPerCluster, _
      BytesPerSector, NumberOfFreeClustors, _
      TotalNumberOfClustors)
      slTotalBytes = TotalNumberOfClustors * _
      SectorsPerCluster * BytesPerSector
```

```
                    txtTotalDiskSpace = Format(slTotalBytes, "#,0")
                    slFreeBytes = NumberOfFreeClustors * _
                    SectorsPerCluster * BytesPerSector
                    txtTotalFreeDiskSpace = Format(slFreeBytes, "#,0")

          ErrorRoutineResume:
            Exit Sub
          ErrorRoutineErr:
            MsgBox "Stats.Form1.SystemInformation" & Err & Error
          End Sub
```

Getting Version Information   The GetVersionEx function finds out
the type of operating system and also gets the major version, the minor
version (such as NT version 4), the build number, and the service pack
level for Windows NT. Among other information, GetSystemInfo can tell
us the type of processor on which our application is currently running.
See both of these functions in Code 7.29.

Code 7.29:   The VersionInformation Subroutine

```
Public Sub VersionInformation()
  On Error GoTo ErrorRoutineErr
  Dim flagnum&
  Dim dl&, s$

  Dim vernum&, verword%
  Dim mySys As SYSTEM_INFO

  ' Get the windows flags and version numbers
  myVer.dwOSVersionInfoSize = 148
  dl& = GetVersionEx&(myVer)

  'Get the processor
  If myVer.dwProcessorId = VER_Processor_WIN32_WINDOWS Then
    txtOperatingSystem = "Windows95 "
  ElseIf myVer.dwProcessorId = VER_Processor_WIN32_NT Then
    txtOperatingSystem = "Windows NT "
  End If

  'Get the version, build, and service pack
  txtVersion = myVer.dwMajorVersion & "." _
    & myVer.dwMinorVersion
  txtBuildNumber = (myVer.dwBuildNumber And &HFFFF&)
  txtServicePack = LPSTRToVBString(myVer.szCSDVersion)

  GetSystemInfo mySys
```

```
Select Case mySys.dwProcessorType
  Case PROCESSOR_INTEL_386
      txtProcessor = "386"
  Case PROCESSOR_INTEL_486
      txtProcessor = "486"
  Case PROCESSOR_INTEL_PENTIUM
      txtProcessor = "586"
  Case Else
     txtProcessor = "586"
  End Select
ErrorRoutineResume:
  Exit Sub
ErrorRoutineErr:
  MsgBox "Stats.Form1.VersionInformation" & Err & Error
End Sub
```

Testing the Statistics Program

Testing the Statistics program is simple. Since all the major calls are in the Form Load procedure, all you have to do is start it up. As you can see in Figure 7.16, the Form is filled with information about the current environment.

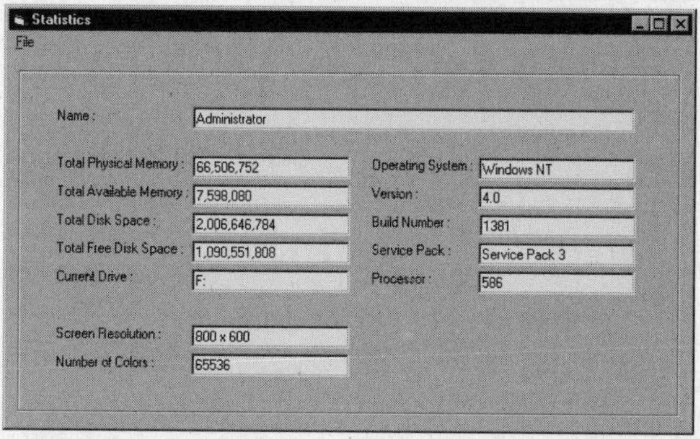

FIGURE 7.16: The Statistics project in action

WHAT'S NEXT?

Now that you know something about using API functions, you're ready for the projects in the next chapter: creating a screen saver and putting your own icon in the system tray. You'll also learn how to access the Windows Registry to enhance your VB applications.

Chapter 8

MAKING VISUAL BASIC DO WHAT YOU WANT

Visual Basic is my tool of choice when programming in Windows. With version 6, there are very few things you can't do in Visual Basic, especially if you use the Win32 API functions.

In this chapter, I'm going to build a few programs that take Visual Basic into areas that you may not have thought possible. I'll go through the ten steps necessary to build your own screen saver. Then I'm going to show you a goodie that Microsoft put on your CD-ROM and didn't bother to tell you about—the Systray control, which lets you add your own icon in the system tray. You should take a few minutes to look at the source code for this ActiveX control. Finally, I'll show you how easy it is to access information in the Windows Registry.

Adapted from *Expert Guide to Visual Basic 6*
by Wayne S. Freeze
ISBN 0-7821-2349-X   944 pages $49.99

BUILDING SCREEN SAVERS

Have you ever wanted to write your own screen saver program? Maybe you had something simple in mind, like a slide show program where you slowly scroll through a set of pictures. It turns out that building a screen saver program is a lot easier than you might think. Windows takes care of all the hard stuff, such as determining when to run the screen saver. All you need to do is to display the pretty graphics whenever Windows tells you to.

A screen saver is simply a normal program that has a file type of .SCR and responds to two different command-line arguments:

- ▶ /c is used to configure the screen saver.

- ▶ /s is used to start the screen saver.

Determining when to start the screen saver is Windows' responsibility; you just need to indicate when to end it. To help you build your own screen saver, I've put together a ten-step process, complete with source code and commentary:

1. Start a new Visual Basic project.

2. Create the display part of the screen saver.

3. Display the form in full-screen mode without a title bar.

4. Unload the form on any user-initiated mouse or keyboard events.

5. Add a second form to configure the screen saver.

6. Add a module to your project.

7. Add a Sub Main routine to control the screen saver.

8. Adjust the program's properties.

9. Install your program into the \Windows directory.

10. Configure your screen saver.

Step 1 is simple. In fact, you don't really have to start with a blank Visual Basic project, but you do need to create a copy of the program you can edit and change. The other steps require a bit more explanation.

Creating the Display Portion

The display portion of the screen saver is an intentional infinite loop. It should display a set of pictures or draw a set of graphics and then loop around and start all over again. It should be designed to be self-scaling; in other words, it should adapt itself to any display size. In the case of a slide show, you might center the pictures if they are too small to fill the whole screen. A graphics program would be scaled so that the whole screen is used.

Since the display part of the screen saver is separate from the configuration part, you should retrieve any configuration information from the Windows Registry using the GetSetting routine.

Declaring Module-Level Variables

NOTE

The complete code for the programs discussed in this chapter—the Screen Saver, Scheduler, and RegTool programs—can be found at the Sybex Web site (www.sybex.com). Once there, go to the Catalog page and enter 2469 (the first four digits of the last five in the book's ISBN) into the search engine. Follow the link for this book that comes up, and then click the Downloads button, which will take you to a list of files organized by chapter.

For my screen saver program, I decided to use a modified version of the StarSX program, which I talked about in Chapter 6. Listing 8.1 shows the module-level variables I use.

Listing 8.1: Module-Level Variables for ScreenSaver's Pic Form

```
Option Explicit

Dim AngleStep As Single
Dim Color As Long
Dim ColorIncrement As Long
Dim Delta As Single
Dim RadiusDecrement As Single
Dim TimeDelay As Long

Dim CenterX As Long
Dim CenterY As Long
Dim Radius As Single
Dim Theta As Single
```

Part ii

I will retrieve the first group of values (AngleStep, ColorIncrement, Delta, RadiusDecrement, and TimeDelay) from the Registry. The rest I will initialize when I begin drawing the figure.

Drawing the Star

The DrawArc routine, shown in Listing 8.2, is the same as the one in Chapter 6, except for some minor details. Rather than use a Timer control, I now use the Sleep Win32 API function to slow down the drawing process. I also rewrote the method that I used to increment color and created a separate subroutine that can be used by both the Pic form and the Config form. The revised logic lets me keep just one variable for color, and I break out the RGB (Red, Green, and Blue) components to create the color I display. Because of the way the logic works, the value for Color now ranges from 0 to 1535 (256 color levels times six different color bands minus one, since I'm starting at zero).

Listing 8.2: DrawArc Routine for ScreenSaver's Pic Form

```
Private Sub DrawArc()

Static OldX As Single
Static oldY As Single

Dim NewX As Single
Dim NewY As Single

Dim r As Integer
Dim g As Integer
Dim b As Integer

NewX = CenterX + Sin(Theta) * Radius
NewY = CenterY + Cos(Theta) * Radius

ColorToRGB r, g, b, Color

Pic.Line (OldX, oldY)-(NewX, NewY), RGB(r, g, b)
Pic.DrawMode = vbCopyPen

OldX = NewX
oldY = NewY

Theta = Theta + AngleStep
Radius = Radius - RadiusDecrement
Color = (Color + ColorIncrement) Mod 1535
```

```
DoEvents
Sleep TimeDelay

End Sub
```

The `DrawStarSx` routine, shown in Listing 8.3, is called to display a single StarSX image. It acquires the parameters from the Windows Registry using the `GetSetting` function. I then initialize the rest of the module-level variables and call the `DrawArc` routine until the `Radius` value is less than the specified value for `Delta`. Note that I use the form's `Height` and `Width` properties to determine the values that depend on the screen size, such as the center of the form (`CenterX` and `CenterY`) and the initial radius of the circle (`Radius`).

Listing 8.3: DrawStarSx Routine for ScreenSaver's Pic Form

```
Public Sub DrawStarSx()

Color = CInt(GetSetting("StarSX", "Pic", "Color", "1"))
TimeDelay = CLng(GetSetting("StarSX", "Pic", "TimeDelay", "50"))
AngleStep = CSng(GetSetting("StarSX", "Pic", "AngleStep", _
    "3.00"))
ColorIncrement = CLng(GetSetting("StarSX", "Pic", _
    "ColorIncrement", "2"))
Delta = CSng(GetSetting("StarSX", "Pic", "Delta", "10"))
RadiusDecrement = CSng(GetSetting("StarSX", "Pic",
    "RadiusDecrement", "10"))

Pic.DrawMode = vbNop
CenterX = Me.Width / 2
CenterY = Me.Height / 2
Radius = 0.95 * IIf(CenterX < CenterY, CenterX, CenterY)
Theta = 0

Do While Radius > Delta
  DrawArc
Loop

End Sub
```

TIP

Don't limit yourself: You can make your program a true multimedia experience by playing background music or other sounds to accompany your screen saver's display. Use the Visual Basic Multimedia control (MCI) to play background MIDI tunes or various .WAV files to coincide with the graphic presentation.

Part ii

Loading the Form

The first step the Form_Load event, shown in Listing 8.4, performs is to show itself when it first loads. Then it performs an infinite loop that clears the form and displays a StarSX picture. This is one of the few cases where you really want to use a Do While True statement, since the resulting infinite loop ensures that the screen saver will not end until it is interrupted by another process.

Listing 8.4:   Form_Load Event for ScreenSaver's Pic Form

```
Private Sub Form_Load()

Me.Show

Do While True
  Me.Cls
  DrawStarSX

Loop

End Sub
```

I didn't discuss the Form_Unload event, since it contains only a single statement, End. This ensures that whenever I unload this form for whatever reason, the program will stop completely.

Displaying the Form in Full-Screen Mode

It's very easy to maximize a form in Visual Basic. You just set the form's WindowState property to 2 (vbMaximized). However, this leaves the title bar in place, which would look rather dumb on a screen saver. You also might want to set the screen's background to black to make the graphics stand out better.

To prepare the form for the screen saver, you need to set the following properties:

Property	Setting
Caption	" "
ControlBox	False
MaxButton	False
MinButton	False
WindowState	vbMaximized

The first four values disable the title bar, and the last property runs the form in full-screen mode. You can set these values dynamically in your program, or you can set them as part of the form's design-time properties. I choose to do it at design time, since I can set `WindowState` to `vbNormal` while testing the program and then change it to `vbMaximized` when I'm ready to compile a real test version of the program.

TIP

Should a screen saver save screens? The original concept behind a screen saver was to minimize the burn-in effect on computer monitors. If the same screen is shown for a long period of time, the images begin to burn into the phosphor. A screen saver prevents this by displaying a moving image on the screen. Technological advances in modern computer monitors have minimized the burn-in effect, so a screen saver is no longer necessary. Today, screen savers are used primarily because of their entertainment value.

Unloading the Form on User-Initiated Events

A typical screen saver will stop the program if the user presses any key, moves the mouse, or clicks either mouse button. The way to stop the screen saver program is to simply unload the form. The `Form_Unload` event will execute the End statement, ensuring that the program is stopped properly.

Simply putting the `Unload Me` statement in the `MouseDown` and `KeyDown` events will take care of stopping the screen saver. You also need the `Unload Me` statement in the `MouseMove` event. Visual Basic sometimes moves the mouse as part of loading and displaying a form. To ensure that Visual Basic doesn't stop your screen saver before it starts, use the code in Listing 8.5 to ignore the first two mouse movements and end the program on the third.

Listing 8.5:   Form_MouseMove Event for ScreenSaver's Pic Form

```
Private Sub Form_MouseMove(Button As Integer, Shift As Integer, _
   X As Single, Y As Single)

Static c As Integer

If c > 2 Then
```

Part ii

```
    Unload Me

Else
  c = c + 1

End If

End Sub
```

TIP

Screen saver hot spots: A traditional screen saver ends whenever someone moves the mouse, clicks a mouse button, or presses a key. This doesn't mean that you have to be traditional. You could ignore mouse movements and instead create a hot spot on your screen where the user could click a mouse button. A mouse click on the hot spot could either display a pop-up menu or launch the configuration form without stopping the screen saver.

Adding a Configuration Form

The first form takes its startup parameters from the Windows Registry, so you need a method to put those values in the Registry in the first place. It doesn't really matter how this form looks, although you do need to make it easy to use.

Since StarSX the screen saver was built from StarSX the toy, I simply reused the same controls I used in the original StarSX program. Of course, I took a little time to make them look a little nicer, because I'm not sharing the form with the graphics anymore. Figure 8.1 shows the StarSX configuration settings.

I added three buttons to the form:

▶ The OK button saves the current settings to the Registry and closes the window.

▶ The Apply button merely saves the current settings to the Registry.

▶ The Cancel button closes the window without making any changes.

TIP

If you don't know, cheat: Sometimes the best way to design an application is to look at other applications that perform similar functions. In this case, I looked at some other screen saver dialog boxes to see how best to lay out my own screen saver.

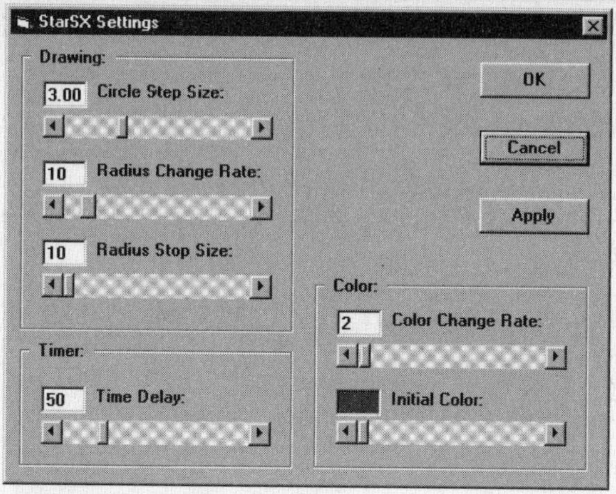

FIGURE 8.1: Configuring StarSX

Adding a Module and a Sub Main Routine

Visual Basic can launch a program by loading a form or by calling the `Main` subroutine. While you can use either in this program, I choose the `Main` subroutine because it offers a cleaner interface to start either the `Config` form or the `Pic` form. However, to use a `Sub Main`, you need to add a module to your program.

TIP

Use Sub Main to start your program: A `Main` subroutine will run before any forms are shown. This way, it is easy to decide which form you want to show at the start of the program. You might want to show the last form used in a database application or select the appropriate form based on someone's user name. This is also useful if you want to display a splash screen before you load the main form.

I start the `Main` subroutine by checking to see if there was a previous copy of this program already running. If so, I end the program since there is no reason to run two screen saver programs at the same time. I then start the `Config` form or the `Pic` form, depending on what command-line value is supplied by Windows. Listing 8.6 shows this subroutine

Listing 8.6:   Main Subroutine in ScreenSaver

```
Public Sub Main()

If App.PrevInstance Then
    End

ElseIf Left(LCase(Command()), 2) = "/c" Then
    Config.Show

ElseIf Left(LCase(Command()), 2) = "/s" Then
    Pic.Show

End If

End Sub
```

Adjusting the Program's Properties

You need to set a few program properties before you can compile your program. Figure 8.2 shows the Project Properties dialog box for StarSX.

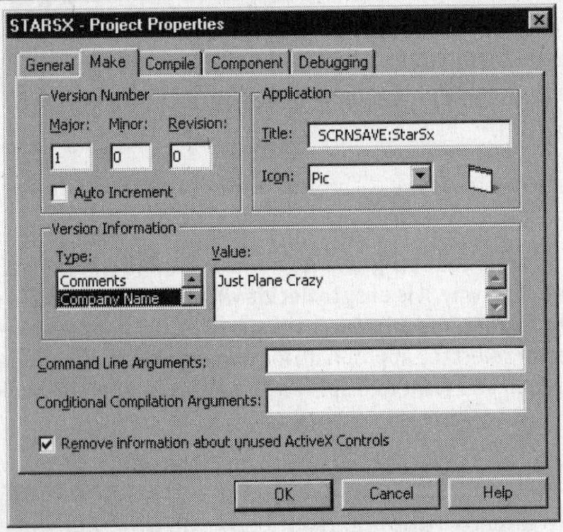

FIGURE 8.2: Setting the Application Title property

The Application Title property must be set to SCRNSAVE: followed immediately by the title of your program. It is important that SCRNSAVE be in all uppercase letters; otherwise, Windows will not recognize your program as a screen saver.

You also need to set the startup object to Sub Main to start that subroutine. Assuming that you are ready to try out your screen saver, you can compile the program into an .EXE file.

Installing and Configuring Your Screen Saver

Once you've compiled your program, you're ready to install it. The .EXE file must be renamed to .SCR and moved to the Windows directory (typically \Windows on Windows 95/98 and \WinNT on NT workstation).

To use your new screen saver, open the Control Panel and select the Display applet. Then select the Screen Saver tab. Click on the combo box's drop-down arrow and select the name of your screen saver, as shown in Figure 8.3.

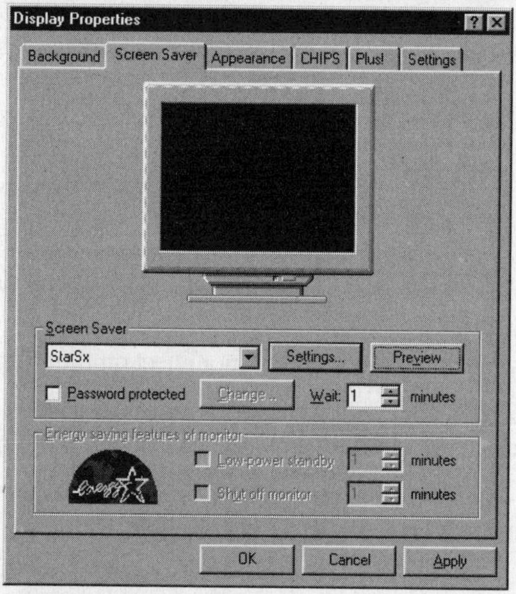

FIGURE 8.3: Selecting your screen saver in the Screen Saver tab of the Display Properties dialog box

The screen saver has six different parameters. Each of these parameters controls the image displayed on the screen. There are two parameters that control the basic image generated: Circle Step Size and Radius Change Rate. These parameters correspond to the variables AngleStep and

RadiusDecrement. Changing these values only slightly will often result in radically different pictures. Some interesting values for these two parameters are listed in Table 8.1.

TABLE 8.1: Selected Values for Circle Step Size and Radius Change Rate

CIRCLE STEP SIZE	RADIUS CHANGE RATE
4.00	10
4.00	1
3.25	2
3.14	1
2.90	8
2.70	7
2.00	6
1.58	3
1.57	1
0.80	10
0.70	2
0.50	2
0.04	1

The remaining parameters have a more minor effect on the image:

▶ Radius Stop Size stops the picture when the size center goes below this value. The larger the value, the quicker the picture will stop.

▶ Color Change Rate controls how quickly the colors change. A value of zero means that the color will never change.

▶ Initial Color is self-explanatory. However, note that even in a 24-bit color environment, only 1536 colors will be used (see the Color-ToRGB routine in this program on the CD-ROM for more details).

▶ Time Delay is also self-explanatory—the smaller the value, the quicker the drawing will be completed. Note that the accuracy of this value is limited to about 55, due the accuracy of the Windows clock. A value of zero disables the timer and will draw most pictures in less than a second.

The program will automatically configure itself for the default values you saw earlier in Figure 8.1. These values will generate a screen much like the one shown in Figure 8.4.

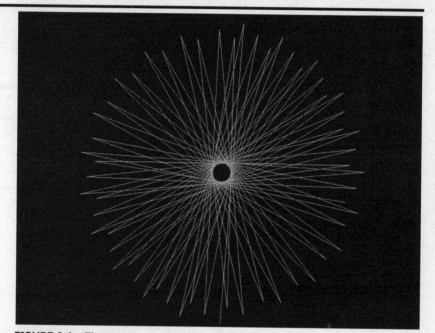

FIGURE 8.4:   The screen saver display with its default settings

Displaying an Icon in the System Tray

Have you ever looked at the system tray over in the right corner of the Windows Taskbar and wondered what it would take to use it in your own programs? I have. When I started writing this book, I planned to go through how to use the Win32 API to display my own icon in the system tray. However, when I looked through the Visual Basic CD-ROMs, I found the source code for an ActiveX control, called Systray, that did everything I wanted. So I changed my mind and decided to use it rather than write my own program (remember, the lazy programmer doesn't mind reusing code whenever possible).

Adding the Systray Control

Table 8.2 lists the properties of the Systray control. The `Index`, `Name`, `Object`, `Parent`, and `Tag` properties have the same meanings as in other ActiveX controls. The `TrayIcon` property holds the icon that will be displayed in the system tray. The `TrayTip` property holds a string of text that will be displayed above the icon in the toolbar when the mouse pointer hovers over the icon for about a second or so.

TABLE 8.2: Systray Control Properties

PROPERTY	DESCRIPTION
Index	Contains a number that uniquely identifies the control in a control array
InTray	When set to `True`, means that `TrayIcon` is shown in the system tray; when set to `False`, means that the icon is not displayed
Name	Specifies the name of the control
Object	Returns an object reference to the control
Parent	Returns an object reference to the control's container
Tag	Contains user-supplied information
TrayIcon	Specifies the icon to be displayed
TrayTip	Specifies the ToolTip text that will be displayed when the mouse pointer is held over the icon in the system tray

The `InTray` property is used to enable and disable the Systray icon. When `InTray` is `False`, the control is inactive. Setting `InTray` to `True` displays the icon in the system tray, and the control will trap the mouse events listed in Table 8.3.

WARNING

Don't stop too quickly: Ending a program while the `InTray` property is still True may leave the icon in the system tray while in the Visual Basic IDE. This can cause Visual Basic to crash or other nasty things. Be sure to set `InTray` to False before stopping your program.

TABLE 8.3: Systray Control Events

Event	Description
MouseDblClick	Occurs when the mouse is double-clicked on the icon in the system tray
MouseDown	Occurs when one or more mouse buttons are pressed while the mouse cursor is over the icon in the system tray
MouseMove	Occurs when the mouse cursor is moved over the icon in the system tray
MouseUp	Occurs when one or more mouse buttons are released while the mouse cursor is over the icon in the system tray

Programming the Systray Control

Only a few programs can benefit from the Systray control. These tend to be long-running programs that need very little interaction with the user. A minimized program takes space on the Taskbar, which is often at a premium on a busy system. Using a system tray icon to anchor a program requiring little user interaction allows you easy access to the program when necessary, without taking up a valuable amount of real estate elsewhere on the Taskbar.

A program that would benefit from the Systray control is a job scheduler, and that's the program I wrote. Basically, this program starts tasks at a specified time and automatically reschedules them for their next execution. Since this is a long-running program, there is no need for it to occupy space on the Taskbar. When you want to check the status of existing tasks, you can click on the program's icon in the system tray to see a window like the one shown in Figure 8.5. You also can easily add new tasks or change existing tasks by right-clicking on the scheduled tasks box. Figure 8.6 shows the dialog box that appears.

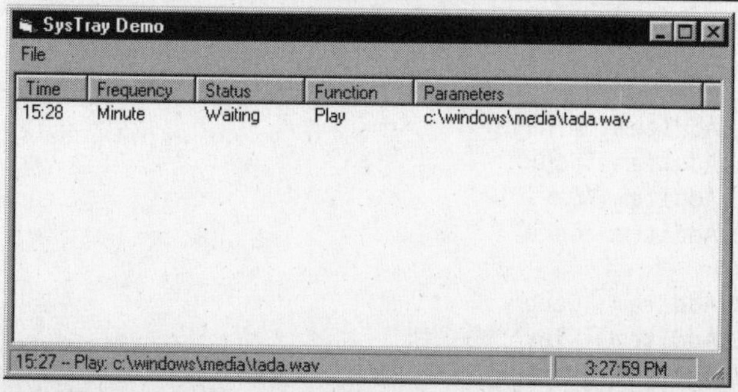

FIGURE 8.5: The Scheduler program's schedule display

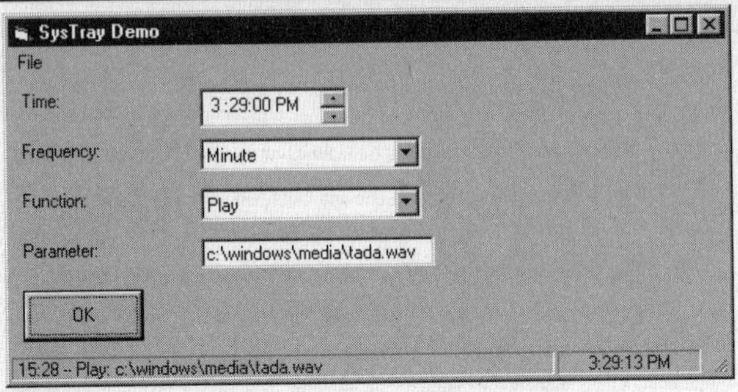

FIGURE 8.6:   Adding or editing a schedule entry

NOTE

Special note to Jill: After losing almost a whole chapter due to a system crash, my wife asked me why I couldn't write a little program that would copy my working files to our LAN server every hour or so. This is that program. Thanks, Jill.

Starting the Scheduler

The Scheduler program begins by initializing both combo boxes on the main form, as shown in Listing 8.7. I load the information about the currently active schedules. I get the number of entries from the Scheduler\ Main\Count key and then use a For/Next loop to load each individual entry.

Listing 8.7:   Form_Load Event in Scheduler

```
Private Sub Form_Load()

Dim c As Integer
Dim l As ListItem

Combo1.AddItem "Minute"
Combo1.AddItem "Hour"
Combo1.AddItem "Day"
Combo1.AddItem "Once"

Combo2.AddItem "Beep"
Combo2.AddItem "Play"
Combo2.AddItem "Run"
```

```
c = GetSetting("Scheduler", "Main", "Count", "0")

For CurrentEvent = 1 To c
  Set l = ListView1.ListItems.Add(, "x" &
FormatNumber(CurrentEvent, 0), _
    GetSetting("Scheduler", FormatNumber(CurrentEvent, 0), _
    "Time", ""))
  l.SubItems(1) = GetSetting("Scheduler", _
    FormatNumber(CurrentEvent, 0), _
    "Frequency", "")
  l.SubItems(2) = GetSetting("Scheduler", _
    FormatNumber(CurrentEvent, 0), _
    "Status", "")
  l.SubItems(3) = GetSetting("Scheduler", _
    FormatNumber(CurrentEvent, 0), _
    "Function", "")
  l.SubItems(4) = GetSetting("Scheduler", _
    FormatNumber(CurrentEvent, 0), _
    "Parameter", "")
Next CurrentEvent

ListView1.ZOrder 0

CurrentIcon = 1
Set cSysTray1.TrayIcon = ImageList1.ListImages(1).ExtractIcon
cSysTray1.InTray = True
Timer1.Interval = 1000
Timer1.Enabled = True
Me.Hide


End Sub
```

Part ii

After I load the scheduling information, I grab the icon to be displayed in the system tray from ImageList1. Then I set cSysTray1.InTray to True, which displays the icon in the tray and enables the mouse movements. Note that I could have assigned the TrayIcon value at design time; however, I decided to be cute, as you'll see in a moment.

I end this routine by setting a Timer control to interrupt every second. For a serious scheduling program, this time interval may be too small. Setting it to five or even thirty seconds may be more acceptable. However, setting the interval to one second lets me more accurately track what is happening in the program. It also simplifies the programming, since I don't need to worry about the clock drifting or restarting the program exactly on the minute boundary.

Controlling Program Flow

The Timer routine, shown in Listing 8.8, controls the flow of this program. Every time the clock ticks, I check the ListView control to see if there are any tasks to be run. If there is one, I call the RunMe subroutine with the appropriate information.

Listing 8.8:   Timer1_Event in Scheduler

```
Private Sub Timer1_Timer()

Dim 1 As ListItem

Set cSysTray1.TrayIcon =
ImageList1.ListImages(CurrentIcon).ExtractIcon
CurrentIcon = CurrentIcon Mod 8 + 1
StatusBar1.Panels(2) = FormatDateTime(Now, vbLongTime)

For Each 1 In ListView1.ListItems
  If 1.Text = FormatDateTime(Now, vbShortTime) And _
    1.SubItems(2) = "Waiting" Then
   RunMe 1.SubItems(3), 1.SubItems(4)
   UpdateStatus 1
  End If
Next 1

End Sub
```

Note that the first thing I do in this routine is to switch the icon displayed in the Taskbar to the next one in the ImageList control. Since I have eight icons I can loop through, I compute the current icon by taking the remainder after dividing the value by eight (using the Mod operator) and adding one. This will always give me a value between one and eight.

Running the Program

Listing 8.9 shows the RunMe subroutine for the Scheduler program.

Listing 8.9:   RunMe Routine in Scheduler

```
Private Sub RunMe(c As String, p As String)

StatusBar1.Panels(1).Text = FormatDateTime(Now, _
  vbShortTime) & " -- "
  & c & ": " & p

cSysTray1.TrayTip = StatusBar1.Panels(1).Text
```

```
If c = "Beep" Then
  Beep

ElseIf c = "Play" Then
  MMControl1.FileName = p
  MMControl1.Command = "Open"
  MMControl1.Wait = True
  MMControl1.Command = "Play"
  MMControl1.Command = "Close"

ElseIf c = "Run" Then
  StartMeUp p

End If

End Sub
```

NOTE

Beeps versus tadas: When I originally wrote this program, the RunMe routine played a beep. I tested with a schedule that called this routine once each minute. After my wife complained about the constant beeping (her desk is right next to mine), I decided to play a .WAV file instead. She later remarked that hearing tada.wav played every minute was probably worse than hearing the beeps.

Displaying a Pop-Up Menu

One of the simplest routines in this program is shown in Listing 8.10. This routine displays a pop-up menu whenever the right mouse button is clicked.

Listing 8.10: cSysTray1_MouseDown Event in Scheduler

```
Private Sub cSysTray1_MouseDown(Button As Integer, Id As Long)

If Button = 2 Then
  PopupMenu MenuTray
End If

End Sub
```

The fact that this routine is controlled by the cSysTray1 control isn't really important. You use the same code that you would use anywhere else in your program.

ACCESSING THE WINDOWS REGISTRY

When Microsoft released Windows 95, it included a replacement for .INI files called the Windows Registry. All kinds of useful information is kept in the Registry, including your system's hardware configuration, operating system details, and information about your applications. It's a useful repository of information, but using it can be dangerous, so I'll begin this discussion with a warning.

If you really want to write a program that manipulates the Registry, don't do it on a production machine. All of the backups in the world may not be enough to allow you to completely recover your system. Always test your program on a machine that you can afford to destroy. If you can, link your computers together over a network and keep copies of your program and any other important information on the other computer. Only when you are satisfied that your program is stable should you think about testing it somewhere else. And even then, you should take all of the recommended precautions before trying your program.

SAFETY IN NUMBERS

There are many ways to access the Registry. Probably the safest is to use standard Windows tools:

▶ Windows Explorer can manage all of the file type associations that make a function like ShellExecute so powerful.

▶ The Control Panel provides ways to configure your hardware.

▶ The Policy Editor is used establish rules and default values for your Desktop settings and system configuration options.

Using these tools ensures that the Registry is updated properly and helps to prevent problems.

Back Up Your Windows Registry

Remember those startup disks you didn't create when you installed Windows? Or perhaps you lost that envelope containing the emergency boot disks that came with your system. Find them now or create new ones. You will need them if you accidentally corrupt the Registry.

The safest way to ensure that you can recover from a Registry failure is to back up your entire system. The most common way is to back up your system to tape using a standard backup package. Just make sure that you understand how to recover your system from the backup tape.

TIP

Emergency repair utility: Your Windows 95 CD-ROM contains a program that you can use to create a backup copy of your critical files and restore those files from a DOS prompt. Check \Other\Misc\ERU on the CD-ROM for more details. Microsoft has improved how the Registry is managed in Windows 98. Select Start ➢ Accessories ➢ System Tools ➢ System Information and select the Registry Checker from the Tools menu. The Registry Checker program is run automatically each time the system is started, and it will automatically restore the Registry from a backup copy.

Another option is to back up your system to another disk drive. You can't just copy all of the files on your C: drive and expect it to work properly. However, there are several third-party tools that will create a backup copy of your disk drive on another disk drive.

While there is a great deal of information in common between the Windows 95/98 Registry and the Windows NT Registry, there is a lot of information that is unique to each operating system, and the structures to hold the information are different. These differences affect your backups.

Backing Up the Windows 95 or 98 Registry

Windows 95 and 98 store the Registry in two files, called SYSTEM.DAT and USER.DAT. These files are stored in the \Windows directory and marked as System, Hidden, and Read-Only. Each time Windows is started successfully, the current version of the Registry is copied to a backup file ending with .DA0. Even through Windows creates these backups, you should create your own backups. You can simply copy the DAT files to DA1, DA2, and so on to preserve the data.

WARNING

I lost all my settings: Remember that if you need to restore a backup copy of the Registry, all your settings will revert to the values in that copy.

Using your DOS boot disk, you can rename the current Registry files with temporary names. Then you can rename your backup copies of the Registry using their proper names. Use the ATTRIB command to verify that the files are System, Hidden, and Read-Only. Then try to reboot your system. If all goes well, you can delete the old copies of the Registry.

Backing Up the Windows NT Registry

In Windows NT, the Registry is stored as a series of files called *hives*. Each hive represents a real root key in the Registry. Hives are stored in the \WinNT\System32\ Config directory as files without a file type. Information for a particular user is stored in the \WinNT\Profiles\ *User* directory where *User* is a valid username.

Windows NT is a secure operating system, which means that you can't just go around copying Registry files as you can in Windows 95 or 98 and expect them to work properly. You could boot a DOS system and access the files if you have formatted the system drive as FAT, or you can use the Repair Disk Utility. This utility creates recovery information and a boot disk that you can use to try to recover your system.

Recovering Your Registry

Knowing how your backup and recovery process works is very important. You need to understand the risks when you change the Registry. I'm not trying to be all doom and gloom here, but unlike a database or a flat file, making a change to the Registry can affect your system's stability. Anyone who has had a corrupted Registry will acknowledge that. There's a big difference between knowing that you can recover and actually performing the recovery process.

You should test your recovery process at some point to make sure that it will work and that you know how it works. I've been in situations where a system I was responsible for became corrupted and I had to go through the recovery process. The recovery almost worked correctly. With a lot of hard work and even more luck, I was able to get the system running again, but I was cleaning up minor problems for weeks afterward. Once I modified the backup process slightly, I was able to recover without a glitch.

TIP

Reinstalling Windows again and again and again: After reinstalling Windows four times in four weeks while testing some beta code, I decided that there had to be a better way. On the average, it took about half a day to reinstall Windows with all of my usual applications. Using DriveImage from PowerQuest, I was able to create "standardized" Windows that included a complete Windows system, with all of the proper drivers, my usual applications, and my normal settings. It now takes me less than half an hour to restore my system from the backup file.

Understanding the Registry Structure

The Windows Registry contains a series of multiple-part keys that represents a hierarchical structure. Associated with each key are one or more values. Each value consists of a name and data pair. Every key always has a value with Null for the name. This is often displayed as (Default). This name may or may not have a value associated with it.

NOTE

Null is not nothing: There is a difference between a data value not having a value and a data value having a Null value.

Registry Data Types

Each data element associated with a name has a data type, as listed in Table 8.4. Windows NT supports all of the listed data types; only the first three types are supported by Windows 95 and 98. Also, Windows 95 and 98 Registry values are limited to 64KB bytes of storage. Windows NT data elements may be as large as 1MB.

TABLE 8.4: Windows Registry Data Types

DATA TYPE	SIZE LIMIT	DESCRIPTION
String/REG_SZ	95/98: 64KB; NT: 1MB	A sequence of text characters
Binary/REQ_BINARY	95/98: 64KB; NT: 1MB	A string of binary characters
DWORD/REG_DWORD	32 bits	A Long integer
na/REG_EXPAND_SZ	1MB	An expandable string (NT only)
na/REG_MULTI_SZ	1MB	Multiple strings (NT only)

Part ii

Registry Keys

The Registry contains a series of root keys that are used to reference information in the Registry:

► The HKEY_CLASSES_ROOT key is an alias of HKEY_LOCAL_ MACHINE\Software\ Classes that refers to the associations between file types and programs.

► The HKEY_CURRENT_USER key is an alias of HKEY_USERS\ username that contains information about the current user specified by *username*.

► The HKEY_LOCAL_MACHINE key contains information about the machine's hardware and software configuration. I'll go into a bit more detail about this key in a moment.

► The HKEY_CURRENT_CONFIG key is an alias of HKEY_LOCAL_ MACHINE\Config\ *config#* where *config#* represents 0001, 0002, and so on—the current configuration number.

► The HKEY_DYN_DATA key isn't a real key, nor is it an alias. It also doesn't exist in Windows NT. This is a temporary key that doesn't exist on disk and is used to hold information about the current Windows session.

► The HKEY_USERS key contains information about each user on your system. This is another key of interest, like HKEY_LOCAL_MACHINE, which I'll describe in more detail.

Note that not of these keys are available on both Windows 95/98 and Windows NT. Also, some the root keys provide shortcuts or aliases to other keys in the Registry.

Contents of HKEY_LOCAL_MACHINE

Only information that is common to all users will be stored here. While this key exists on both Windows 95/98 and Windows NT systems, much of the information stored here is different between the two machines. The HKEY_LOCAL_MACHINE key contains the following subkeys:

Config This subkey exists only on Windows 95/98 systems and contains a series of hardware configuration profiles. Each profile is a four-digit number beginning with 0001. Information is kept about the devices that are part of that configuration.

Enum   This subkey also exists only on Windows 95/98 systems and contains information about every piece of hardware that has ever been installed on the system.

Hardware   This subkey is used by Windows NT to describe the hardware configuration. This list is updated each time Windows NT is started. This subkey is also available in Windows 95/98, but not much information is stored here.

Network   This is a Windows 95/98 subkey that contains information about the currently logged-on user.

SAM   This subkey is found only on Windows NT. It contains security information about each user, group, and domain in Windows NT Server.

Security   This subkey contains information about shared resources and open network connections on a Windows 95/98 system. On a Windows NT system, this subkey contains information about the local security policy. Note you will be prevented from accessing this key using the Registry Editor in Windows NT.

Software   The subkey contains information about software installed on the system and that applies to all users. It contains information similar to that in \HKEY_USERS\username\ Software, except that the \HKEY_USERS key contains information that is specific to the user. This subkey is important to application developers, and I'll talk a bit more about it after the System subkey description.

System   This subkey contains configuration information about which devices and operating system services are loaded and started. In Windows 95/98, information is stored only under the CurrentControlSet subkey. Windows NT stores the information in several different subkeys, including Clone, ControlSet001 to ControlSet003, CurrentControlSet, Select, and Setup.

You can use the Software subkey to store settings about your application that are independent of the particular user, such as paths to directories, installed features, and so on. The Software key is typically formatted as

\HKEY_LOCAL_MACHINE\Software\Company\Product\Version\

where Company is the name of the company that has released the software, Product is the name of the software product, and Version is the version number of the product. For example, the following key contains information about Microsoft Word:

```
\HKEY_LOCAL_MACHINE\Software\Microsoft\Office\8.0\Word\ _
InstallRoot
```

Note that not all vendors (including Microsoft) always include Version as part of the key. Other types of information, such as file type associations (which are stored in Classes) and ODBC driver information, are also stored here.

Contents of HKEY_USERS   In this subkey, a special username called .Default contains the settings that will be used by the default user on your system. Within each user name is a set of subkeys that refer to various characteristics of a user:

AppEvents   This subkey contains information about various events in the system and the sounds that should be played when events occur.

Console   This is a Windows NT-only subkey that contains information about how to display character-based applications. It includes information such as window size, color, fonts, and so on.

Control Panel   This subkey contains information about various settings that the user can change using the Control Panel. Subkeys include Accessibility, Appearance, Colors, Cursors, Desktop, International, and Mouse. Note that some of these subkeys may be present only if changes to the default value have been made through the Control Panel.

Environment   This is a Windows NT-only subkey containing information about a user's environment variables.

InstallLocationsMRU   This is a Windows 95/98-only subkey that contains path information that is used to install Windows and make subsequent changes to its configuration.

Keyboard Layout   This subkey contains information about the keyboard.

Network   This is a Windows 95/98-only subkey that contains information about mapped disk drives and network-attached disk drives that have been recently used.

RemoteAccess   This is a Windows 95/98-only subkey that contains information about dial-up networking connections to other systems.

Software   This subkey contains user-specific information about software packages installed on a system. This is similar in function to the \HKEY_ LOCAL_MACHINE\Software key and follows the same suggested key-naming conventions. Of particular note is the VB and VBA Program Settings sub-key, which contains the information from the GetSetting and SaveSetting routines. You can use the Software sub-key to store settings about your application that apply only to a particular user, such as screen locations, color information, recently used files, and so on.

Using the Registry Editor

Microsoft supplies a tool called the Registry Editor (the RegEdit program) with Windows. This tool allows you to browse and edit items in the Registry. In Windows 95 and 98, there are essentially no restrictions on the changes you can make. If you are Administrator on a Windows NT system, you don't have as much freedom as you do under Windows 95/98 (which has no security restrictions), but you still can edit most of the entries in the Registry. Regular Windows NT users have even less freedom in the Registry than the Administrator user.

WARNING

Use RegEdt32 on Windows NT: Microsoft recommends that you use RegEdt32 on Windows NT rather then RegEdit. This is because RegEdit does not support the data types that are specific to Windows NT.

The Registry Editor presents a two-panel view of the Registry, as shown in Figure 8.7. On the left side is a list of Registry key values. A list of name and data pairs is on the right side.

WARNING

Reg Alert, Reg Alert, Reg Alert: The Registry Editor allows you direct access to the Registry. You can insert new keys and values, change existing values, and delete keys and their values. You can destroy your operating system. Use this program with extreme caution.

Part ii

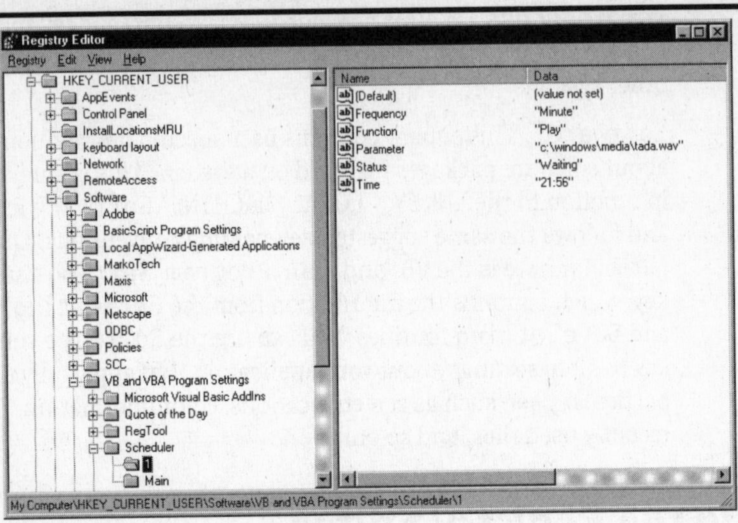

FIGURE 8.7: The Registry Editor

You can change the value of an existing value by clicking on its name. Figure 8.8 shows the Edit String dialog box that appears. Right-clicking on a value displays a pop-up menu that allows you to delete the value, rename it, or modify its contents. You can also use the regular menus to insert a new key or a new value with the specified data type. The only way to change the data type of a value is to delete the value and enter a new value.

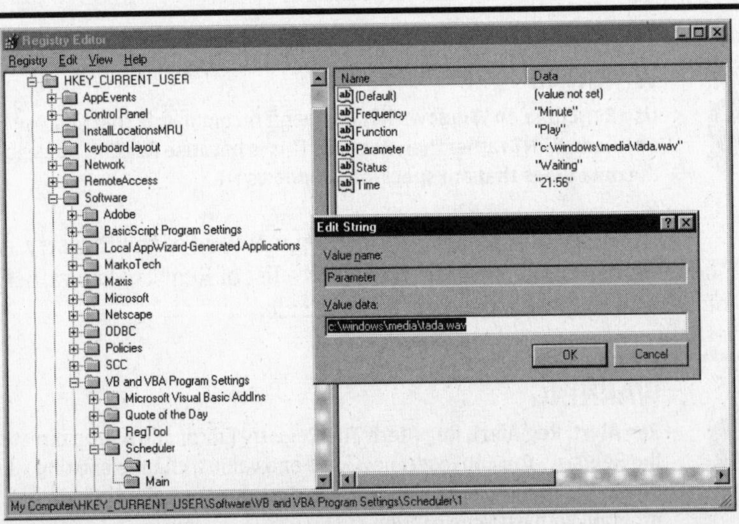

FIGURE 8.8: Editing a value in the Registry Editor

TIP

No need to write: Use the Registry Editor to look at entries in the Registry that were created with SaveSetting. This is the easiest way to verify that you wrote your data correctly.

Accessing the Registry from Visual Basic

After reading Chapter 7, you should have a good understanding of what it takes to use the Win32 API. Accessing the Registry is just as easy (or difficult) as using any of the routines you've seen so far. Listing 8.11 contains the header information you need in a program that accesses the Registry functions.

TIP

It's okay to be afraid: By now, I've probably scared you to the point where you are afraid to touch the Registry. This fear is good protection. It will prevent you from doing something stupid like deleting an item from your hardware configuration. Reading is the absolutely safest thing you can do with the Registry. Updating information is also safe when you're changing your own information.

Listing 8.11:   Windows Registry Access Header Information in RegTool

```
Option Explicit

' ================================================================
' = Windows Registry                           =
' ================================================================

Public Const ERROR_SUCCESS = 0&
Public Const ERROR_NO_MORE_FILES = 18&
Public Const ERROR_MORE_DATA = 234

Public Const READ_CONTROL = &H20000
Public Const STANDARD_RIGHTS_ALL = &H1F0000
Public Const STANDARD_RIGHTS_EXECUTE = (READ_CONTROL)
Public Const STANDARD_RIGHTS_READ = (READ_CONTROL)
Public Const STANDARD_RIGHTS_REQUIRED = &HF0000
Public Const STANDARD_RIGHTS_WRITE = (READ_CONTROL)
Public Const SYNCHRONIZE = &H100000
```

Part ii

```
Public Const HKEY_CLASSES_ROOT = &H80000000
Public Const HKEY_CURRENT_CONFIG = &H80000005
Public Const HKEY_CURRENT_USER = &H80000001
Public Const HKEY_DYN_DATA = &H80000006
Public Const HKEY_LOCAL_MACHINE = &H80000002
Public Const HKEY_PERFORMANCE_DATA = &H80000004
Public Const HKEY_USERS = &H80000003


Public Const KEY_CREATE_LINK = &H20
Public Const KEY_CREATE_SUB_KEY = &H4
Public Const KEY_ENUMERATE_SUB_KEYS = &H8
Public Const KEY_EVENT = &H1
Public Const KEY_NOTIFY = &H10
Public Const KEY_QUERY_VALUE = &H1
Public Const KEY_SET_VALUE = &H2
Public Const KEY_WRITE = ((STANDARD_RIGHTS_WRITE Or _
  KEY_SET_VALUE Or KEY_CREATE_SUB_KEY) And (Not SYNCHRONIZE))
Public Const KEY_ALL_ACCESS = ((STANDARD_RIGHTS_ALL Or _
  KEY_QUERY_VALUE Or KEY_SET_VALUE Or _
  KEY_CREATE_SUB_KEY Or KEY_ENUMERATE_SUB_KEYS Or _
  KEY_NOTIFY Or KEY_CREATE_LINK) And (Not SYNCHRONIZE))
Public Const KEY_READ = ((STANDARD_RIGHTS_READ Or _
  KEY_QUERY_VALUE Or KEY_ENUMERATE_SUB_KEYS Or KEY_NOTIFY) _
  And (Not SYNCHRONIZE))
Public Const KEY_EXECUTE = ((KEY_READ) And (Not SYNCHRONIZE))


Public Const REG_BINARY = 3
Public Const REG_CREATED_NEW_KEY = &H1
Public Const REG_DWORD = 4
Public Const REG_DWORD_BIG_ENDIAN = 5
Public Const REG_DWORD_LITTLE_ENDIAN = 4
Public Const REG_EXPAND_SZ = 2
Public Const REG_FULL_RESOURCE_DESCRIPTOR = 9
Public Const REG_LINK = 6
Public Const REG_MULTI_SZ = 7
Public Const REG_NONE = 0
Public Const REG_NOTIFY_CHANGE_ATTRIBUTES = &H2
Public Const REG_NOTIFY_CHANGE_LAST_SET = &H4
Public Const REG_NOTIFY_CHANGE_NAME = &H1
Public Const REG_NOTIFY_CHANGE_SECURITY = &H8
Public Const REG_OPENED_EXISTING_KEY = &H2
Public Const REG_OPTION_BACKUP_RESTORE = 4
Public Const REG_OPTION_CREATE_LINK = 2
Public Const REG_OPTION_NON_VOLATILE = 0
Public Const REG_OPTION_RESERVED = 0
Public Const REG_OPTION_VOLATILE = 1
```

```
Public Const REG_REFRESH_HIVE = &H2
Public Const REG_RESOURCE_LIST = 8
Public Const REG_RESOURCE_REQUIREMENTS_LIST = 10
Public Const REG_SZ = 1
Public Const REG_WHOLE_HIVE_VOLATILE = &H1
Public Const REG_LEGAL_CHANGE_FILTER = _
  (REG_NOTIFY_CHANGE_NAME Or _
  REG_NOTIFY_CHANGE_ATTRIBUTES Or REG_NOTIFY_CHANGE_LAST_SET _
  Or REG_NOTIFY_CHANGE_SECURITY)
Public Const REG_LEGAL_OPTION = (REG_OPTION_RESERVED Or _
  REG_OPTION_NON_VOLATILE Or REG_OPTION_VOLATILE Or _
  REG_OPTION_CREATE_LINK Or REG_OPTION_BACKUP_RESTORE)

Public Type ACL
    AclRevision As Byte
    Sbz1 As Byte
    AclSize As Integer
    AceCount As Integer
    Sbz2 As Integer
End Type

Public Type FILETIME
    dwLowDateTime As Long
    dwHighDateTime As Long
End Type

Public Type SECURITY_ATTRIBUTES
    nLength As Long
    lpSecurityDescriptor As Long
    bInheritHandle As Long
End Type

Public Type SECURITY_DESCRIPTOR
    Revision As Byte
    Sbz1 As Byte
    Control As Long
    Owner As Long
    Group As Long
    Sacl As ACL
    Dacl As ACL
End Type

Public Declare Function RegCloseKey Lib "advapi32.dll" _
    (ByVal hkey As Long) As Long
```

Part ii

```vb
Public Declare Function RegConnectRegistry Lib "advapi32.dll" _
    Alias "RegConnectRegistryA" (ByVal lpMachineName As String, _
    ByVal hkey As Long, phkResult As Long) As Long

Public Declare Function RegCreateKey Lib "advapi32.dll" _
    Alias "RegCreateKeyA" _
    (ByVal hkey As Long, ByVal lpSubKey As String, _
    phkResult As Long) As Long

Public Declare Function RegCreateKeyEx Lib "advapi32.dll" _
    Alias "RegCreateKeyExA" (ByVal hkey As Long, _
    ByVal lpSubKey As String, ByVal Reserved As Long, _
    ByVal lpClass As String, ByVal dwOptions As Long, _
    ByVal samDesired As Long, _
    lpSecurityAttributes As SECURITY_ATTRIBUTES, _
    phkResult As Long, lpdwDisposition As Long) As Long

Public Declare Function RegDeleteKey Lib "advapi32.dll" _
    Alias "RegDeleteKeyA" (ByVal hkey As Long, _
    ByVal lpSubKey As String) As Long

Public Declare Function RegDeleteValue Lib "advapi32.dll" _
    Alias "RegDeleteValueA" (ByVal hkey As Long, _
    ByVal lpValueName As String) As Long

Public Declare Function RegEnumKey Lib "advapi32.dll" _
    Alias "RegEnumKeyA" (ByVal hkey As Long, _
    ByVal dwIndex As Long, ByVal lpName As String, _
    ByVal cbName As Long) As Long

Public Declare Function RegEnumKeyEx Lib "advapi32.dll" _
    Alias "RegEnumKeyExA" (ByVal hkey As Long, _
    ByVal dwIndex As Long, ByVal lpName As String, _
    lpcbName As Long, ByVal lpReserved As Long, _
    ByVal lpClass As String, lpcbClass As Long, _
    lpftLastWriteTime As FILETIME) As Long

Public Declare Function RegEnumValue Lib "advapi32.dll" _
    Alias "RegEnumValueA" (ByVal hkey As Long, _
    ByVal dwIndex As Long, ByVal lpValueName As String, _
    lpcbValueName As Long, ByVal lpReserved As Long, _
    lpType As Long, lpData As Byte, lpcbData As Long) As Long

Public Declare Function RegFlushKey Lib "advapi32.dll" _
    (ByVal hkey As Long) As Long
```

```
Public Declare Function RegGetKeySecurity Lib "advapi32.dll" _
    (ByVal hkey As Long, ByVal SecurityInformation As Long, _
    pSecurityDescriptor As SECURITY_DESCRIPTOR, _
    lpcbSecurityDescriptor As Long) As Long

Public Declare Function RegLoadKey Lib "advapi32.dll" _
    Alias "RegLoadKeyA" (ByVal hkey As Long, _
    ByVal lpSubKey As String, ByVal lpFile As String) As Long

Public Declare Function RegNotifyChangeKeyValue Lib _
    "advapi32.dll" _
    (ByVal hkey As Long, ByVal bWatchSubtree As Long, _
    ByVal dwNotifyFilter As Long, ByVal hEvent As Long, _
    ByVal fAsynchronus As Long) As Long

Public Declare Function RegOpenKey Lib "advapi32.dll" _
    Alias "RegOpenKeyA" (ByVal hkey As Long, _
    ByVal lpSubKey As String, phkResult As Long) As Long

Public Declare Function RegOpenKeyEx Lib "advapi32.dll" _
    Alias "RegOpenKeyExA" (ByVal hkey As Long, _
    ByVal lpSubKey As String, ByVal ulOptions As Long, _
    ByVal samDesired As Long, phkResult As Long) As Long

Public Declare Function RegQueryInfoKey Lib "advapi32.dll" _
    Alias "RegQueryInfoKeyA" (ByVal hkey As Long, _
    ByVal lpClass As String, lpcbClass As Long, _
    ByVal lpReserved As Long, lpcSubKeys As Long, _
    lpcbMaxSubKeyLen As Long, lpcbMaxClassLen As Long, _
    lpcValues As Long, lpcbMaxValueNameLen As Long, _
    lpcbMaxValueLen As Long, lpcbSecurityDescriptor As Long, _
    lpftLastWriteTime As FILETIME) As Long

Public Declare Function RegQueryValue Lib "advapi32.dll" _
    Alias "RegQueryValueA" (ByVal hkey As Long, _
    ByVal lpSubKey As String, ByVal lpValue As String, _
    lpcbValue As Long) As Long

Public Declare Function RegQueryValueEx Lib "advapi32.dll" _
    Alias "RegQueryValueExA" (ByVal hkey As Long, _
    ByVal lpValueName As String, ByVal lpReserved As Long, _
    lpType As Long, lpData As Any, lpcbData As Long) As Long

Public Declare Function RegQueryValueExString Lib "advapi32.dll" _
    Alias "RegQueryValueExA" (ByVal hkey As Long, _
    ByVal lpValueName As String, ByVal lpReserved As Long, _
```

```
        lpType As Long, ByVal lpData As String, lpcbData As Long) _
        As Long

    Public Declare Function RegReplaceKey Lib "advapi32.dll" _
        Alias "RegReplaceKeyA" (ByVal hkey As Long, _
        ByVal lpSubKey As String, ByVal lpNewFile As String, _
        ByVal lpOldFile As String) As Long

    Public Declare Function RegRestoreKey Lib "advapi32.dll" _
        Alias "RegRestoreKeyA" (ByVal hkey As Long, _
        ByVal lpFile As String, ByVal dwFlags As Long) As Long

    Public Declare Function RegSaveKey Lib "advapi32.dll" _
        Alias "RegSaveKeyA" (ByVal hkey As Long, _
        ByVal lpFile As String, _
        lpSecurityAttributes As SECURITY_ATTRIBUTES) As Long

    Public Declare Function RegSetKeySecurity Lib "advapi32.dll" _
        (ByVal hkey As Long, ByVal SecurityInformation As Long, _
        pSecurityDescriptor As SECURITY_DESCRIPTOR) As Long

    Public Declare Function RegSetValue Lib "advapi32.dll" _
        Alias "RegSetValueA" (ByVal hkey As Long, _
        ByVal lpSubKey As String, ByVal dwType As Long, _
        ByVal lpData As String, ByVal cbData As Long) As Long

    Public Declare Function RegSetValueEx Lib "advapi32.dll" _
        Alias "RegSetValueExA" (ByVal hkey As Long, _
        ByVal lpValueName As String, ByVal Reserved As Long, _
        ByVal dwType As Long, lpData As Any, _
        ByVal cbData As Long) As Long

    Public Declare Function RegSetValueExString Lib "advapi32.dll" _
        Alias "RegSetValueExA" (ByVal hkey As Long, _
        ByVal lpValueName As String, ByVal Reserved As Long, _
        ByVal dwType As Long, ByVal lpData As String, _
        ByVal cbData As Long) As Long
```

Creating and Opening Keys

The RegCreateKey function creates a new key in the Registry and returns
a handle to it. If the specified key value already exists, a handle to it is
returned. The RegCreateKeyEx function works just like RegCreateKey,
but it includes a few extra parameters that specify security attributes and
object types.

The RegOpenKey function returns a handle to an existing key in the Registry. The RegOpenKeyEx function works like RegOpenKey, but it includes additional parameters that allow you to provide security and access information. You close the key using the RegCloseKey function.

TIP

Don't keep the handle open for too long: Handles should be closed as quickly as possible. You can always reopen a handle again later.

Getting, Setting, and Deleting Registry Information

The RegQueryInfoKey function returns a lot of information about a key and its subkeys. The ReqQueryValue function returns the data associated with a key's default value. The ReqQueryValueEx function returns the data for the specified value name. If there isn't sufficient space for the return value, ERROR_MORE_DATA will be returned.

TIP

Call me twice: You can determine the size of a value by passing a binary zero in place of the string reference (lpData) and passing a nonzero value for size of the return buffer (lpcbData). Then you can preallocate sufficient space for the return value and avoid the ERROR_MORE_DATA error.

The RegSetValue function is used to set the data part of a value with a Null name. The RegSetValueEx function will assign a value to the data part of a value for the specified name.

The RegDeleteKey function deletes a key and all of its subkeys and values from the Registry. The RegDeleteValue function deletes a value from the Registry. Both of these functions require an open key handle. Note that the handle still needs to be closed, even after the key has been deleted.

Iterating through the Registry

The RegEnumKeyEx function is used to iterate through a set of subkeys. The RegEnumKey function should not be used in a Visual Basic program. It exists for compatibility reasons and has been superceded by the RegEnumKeyEx function. To use this RegEnumKeyEx function, you should set the dwIndex parameter to zero for the first call, increment dwIndex, and repeat the call until the function returns ERROR_NO_MORE_ITEMS. You should not make any changes to any of the subkeys until you have finished the processing. The key handle must have been opened with the KEY_ENUMERATE_SUB_KEYS access option, which is included with the KEY_READ access option.

The RegEnumValue function is used to iterate through a set of values specified by the current key handle. You must have opened the key handle with the KEY_ QUERY_VALUE access option. It works just like the RegEnumKeyEx function. You set dwIndex to zero for the first call and increment it each time afterwards until a response of ERROR_NO_MORE_ITEMS is received.

Getting Notice of Changes

The RegNotifyChangeKey value establishes a callback function that will be triggered whenever a change is made to the specified key or any of its subkeys. With this function, you need to use the AddressOf operator to pass the address of the function that will be called.

Closing Registry Keys

The RegCloseKey function closes the handle to a Registry key. A value of ERROR_ SUCCESS will be returned if the call is successful. Use the RegFlushKey function to post any changes made to the Registry to disk when you need to be absolutely certain that the changes are written to disk. The RegCloseKey function posts the changes to disk using its lazy flusher.

WARNING

Flush only when you need to: Calling RegFlushKey can have a negative impact on your system's performance. You should call it only when you absolutely must have the most recent changes posted to disk.

Changing Key Security

The RegSetKeySecurity function will change the security of the specified key. This function requires the WRITE_OWNER permission or the SE_TAKE_OWNERSHIP_ NAME privilege.

Loading, Replacing, and Saving Keys

The RegLoadKey function creates a new key in the Registry under the HKEY_USER or HKEY_LOCAL_MACHINE key and loads the contents of a hive file into that subkey. The RegReplaceKey function switches one file containing the Registry with another. The change takes place the next time the system is restarted.

The RegSaveKey creates a file containing the contents of the specified key and all of its subkeys. The RegRestoreKey replaces a key and subkeys with the contents of the specified file.

Accessing Remote Computers and Multiple Values

The RegConnectRegistry function returns a key handle that can be used to access a Registry on a remote computer.

The ReqQueryMultipleValues function returns information about one or more values of a key. However, it does not work in Visual Basic, because there is no way to pass an array of user-defined types to a function.

Writing Registry Programs

You can make your installation program look more professional by retrieving the user's name and organization from the Registry and asking the user if that information is correct. You can also use the Win32 API Registry calls to interact with the GetSetting, DeleteSetting, and SaveSetting routines in Visual Basic.

I wrote the RegTool program to demonstrate how to get and set Registry values with Visual Basic. Figure 8.9 shows its window.

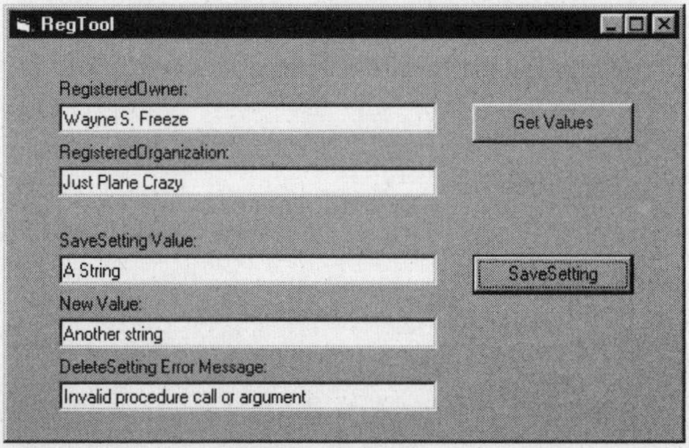

FIGURE 8.9: The RegTool program

Retrieving Registry Information

Listing 8.12 shows how easy it is to retrieve that information from the Registry. You begin by getting a handle to the Registry key Software\ Microsoft\Windows\ CurrentVersion. This key holds a lot of interesting information about Windows. Note that this key works only for Windows 95/98. For Windows NT, use Software\ Microsoft\Windows NT\CurrentVersion as the key.

Listing 8.12:   Command1_Click Event in RegTool

```
Private Sub Command1_Click()

Dim hkey As Long
Dim c As Long
Dim r As Long
Dim s As String
Dim t As Long

r = RegOpenKeyEx(HKEY_LOCAL_MACHINE, _
  "Software\Microsoft\Windows\CurrentVersion", 0, KEY_READ, _
  hkey)

If r = 0 Then
  c = 255
  s = String(c, Chr(0))
  r = RegQueryValueExString(hkey, "RegisteredOwner", 0, t, _
  s, c)
  If r = 0 And c > 0 Then
   Text1.Text = Left(s, c - 1)
  End If

  c = 255
  s = String(c, Chr(0))
  r = RegQueryValueExString(hkey, "RegisteredOrganization", _
  0, t, s, c)
  If r = 0 And c > 0 Then
   Text2.Text = Left(s, c - 1)
  End If

End If

r = RegCloseKey(hkey)

End Sub
```

I begin by opening a handle to the key containing the information I want. I specify a value of KEY_READ since I don't plan to update any information. If I get a successful return code (= 0), then I pad a string with 255 Null characters and retrieve the data associated with the name "RegisteredOwner". If I get another successful return code and have at least one character in the return buffer, I display it in the Text3 text box. Note that the length returned in c includes the Null character at the end of the string, so the actual number of characters in s is one less. Then I repeat the same process over again to retrieve the information for "RegisteredOrganization" and display it in the Text2 text box.

Managing Information with the Win32 API

Listing 8.13 demonstrates that the information managed by the SaveSetting, GetSetting, and DeleteSetting routines can also be managed by the Win32 API routines.

Part ii

Listing 8.13: Command2_Click Event in RegTool

```
Private Sub Command2_Click()

Dim hkey As Long
Dim c As Long
Dim r As Long
Dim s As String
Dim t As Long

SaveSetting "RegTool", "Main", "TestValue1", "A String"

r = RegOpenKeyEx(HKEY_CURRENT_USER, _
  "Software\VB and VBA Program Settings\RegTool\Main", _
  0, KEY_ALL_ACCESS, hkey)

If r = 0 Then
  c = 255
  s = String(c, Chr(0))
  r = RegQueryValueExString(hkey, "TestValue1", 0, t, s, c)
  If r = 0 And c > 0 Then
   Text3.Text = Left(s, c - 1)
  End If

  s = "Another string"
  r = RegSetValueExString(hkey, "TestValue1", 0, REG_SZ, s, _
  Len(s) + 1)
  If r = 0 Then
```

```
            Text4.Text = GetSetting("RegTool", "Main", "TestValue1", _
            "Error")
        End If

        r = RegDeleteValue(hkey, "TestValue1")
        If r = 0 Then
         On Error Resume Next
         DeleteSetting "RegTool", "Main", "TestValue1"
         If Err.Number <> 0 Then
           Text5.Text = Err.Description
         Else
           Text5.Text = "Value not deleted!"
         End If
        End If

      End If

      r = RegCloseKey(hkey)

    End Sub
```

I begin by creating an entry under RegTool\Main in the Registry
using the SaveSetting statement. Next, I open a key to the information by using the full key HKEY_CURRENT_USER\Software\VB and
VBA Program Settings\RegTool\ Main. I use this key to retrieve
the value I inserted with the SaveSetting statement.

I continue by using the RegSetValueEx function to change the data
associated with "TestValue1" to another string value. Then I use the
GetSetting function to verify that it really worked.

Then I use the RegDeleteValue function to delete the value from
the Registry and verify that is was deleted by using the DeleteSetting
statement. Note that the DeleteSetting statement should fail, so an
error message is actually okay. Finally I can close the handle to the Registry key and exit the routine.

FINAL THOUGHTS

Building a screen saver is a relatively easy process once you know the
tricks. But I know people who have spent twenty dollars just to buy a
screen saver that shows a series of images. After reading through the ten
steps, you should be able to create your own slide show screen saver in
the matter of a few hours.

In the case of the StarSX screen saver, drawing the same picture over and over again will get rather boring. However, it wouldn't be hard to rotate through some other pictures. You could modify the configuration form to save the set of parameters under a particular name in the Registry. Then you could use a combo box to display the list of parameter sets and to select the sets that should be shown. The picture part of the program could randomly select an entry and display that picture.

The Systray control serves a more useful purpose. Nearly any long-running program that doesn't often interact with a user could benefit from this control. For example, you might use it to track what is happening inside an ActiveX EXE program while the program is running as a server. Another idea is to use it to periodically check for mail using the Collaboration Data Objects and pop up a message when some arrives.

The Scheduler program I built is rather basic. You can specify when a function should start and how often it should be run after that, but you can't start something immediately unless you specify the time. When I load the schedule from the Registry, I don't allow you to immediately start processing those tasks that were in the schedule. It would be nice if I marked the time the various tasks completed. To do this, I would need to use a modified form of the WaitProg routine from the previous chapter, since I would like to track more than one task at a time. Maintaining a log file with the various events as they occur would also be beneficial. This would help the user look further back than the previous time the task executed.

Using the Win32 API Registry calls gives you the opportunity to get information about the system that Visual Basic doesn't provide. Although they also allow you to add and change information in the Registry, why bother? With the SaveSetting and GetSetting functions, you can save application-specific information without the potential risks.

You should note that there are many of Win32 API calls that will allow you to get information from the Registry without needing to search through it. For example, while all of the file type and associated program information is available in the Registry, the FindExecutable function performs the task without requiring you to build your own search logic.

One thing is clear—you should not assume that the material covered in this chapter is sufficient to teach you everything you need to know about the Registry and how to access it. There are several books available that cover the Registry in-depth, including how the information is arranged and how it should be accessed. You also can learn about other tools for performing Registry updates. These tools may offer a better alternative to using Visual Basic to update the Registry.

What's Next?

You've now been exposed to many ways to add features to your VB applications. In the next chapter, you'll be introduced to scripting, which will allow your users to customize and augment your applications themselves.

PART iii

INTRODUCTION TO VISUAL BASIC SCRIPTING AND THE INTERNET

Chapter 9

ADDING SCRIPTING SUPPORT TO YOUR APPLICATION

Do you want to allow your users to customize their copies of your application? Would you like to let your users automate repetitive tasks? Is there a need for a scripting language in your application? Are you interested in putting a really cool feature in your application? If you answered yes to any of these questions, then your application really needs MSScript.

MSScript began life as VBScript—a lightweight version of Visual Basic designed to compete with JavaScript in Web browsers. Today, the MSScript ActiveX control is used to provide general-purpose scripting services within an application. The MSScript control supports both VBScript and JavaScript scripting languages. Since I'm somewhat biased, I'm going to focus on how to use VBScript and not bother with JavaScript.

Adapted from *Expert Guide to Visual Basic 6*
by Wayne S. Freeze
ISBN 0-7821-2349-X   944 pages $49.99

The same techniques I discuss here apply to JavaScript as well. Only the actual scripting code used will differ.

In this chapter, I will build two new programs: a simple program that allows you to test functions in VBScript and a really programmable calculator. I'm also going to revisit the Charter program and add the ability to perform simple calculations using the MSScript control (also known as the ScriptControl).

NOTE

VBScript is not Visual Basic for Applications. It is important not to confuse VBScript and Visual Basic for Applications (VBA). VBA is included with products like Microsoft Word and Microsoft Excel, and it is a much richer language than VBScript. VBA has a more sophisticated development environment than VBScript. It is possible to develop complete applications using VBA. VBScript, on the other hand, is designed primarily as a macro language and is not very suitable for developing applications.

Using the ScriptControl

Using the ScriptControl is merely a matter of adding the control to your program, defining the objects the script programs can access, and then running the scripts as needed.

Before we go any further, I should warn you that using the ScriptControl is not for everyone. The ScriptControl is one of the least-documented controls available in Visual Basic. Most of the documentation for MSScript and VBScript was developed for people building Web applications. You can incorporate the ScriptControl into your own programs, but expect to spend some time getting the feel of this control and its quirks. Also, be sure to save your programs (both Visual Basic and VBScript) often.

Adding a ScriptControl

If you have tried the ScriptControl already, you may have had trouble finding information about it because Microsoft's documentation is really hidden. To find the documentation for this control, type **WinHelp MSScript** from a DOS session, or choose Start ➤ Run from the Taskbar.

Table 9.1 lists the key properties associated with the ScriptControl.

TABLE 9.1: Selected ScriptControl Properties

PROPERTIES	DESCRIPTION
AllowUI	When set to True, means that the script program can display user interface (UI) elements such as a MsgBox
CodeObject	Returns the set of objects that were created with the AddObject method using the script name for the object
Error	Returns an Error object containing information about the script error
Language	Contains either VBScript or JScript
Modules	Contains a collection of Module objects
Procedures	Contains a collection of Procedure objects
SitehWnd	Contains a reference to a hWnd that will be used to display GUIs
State	Describes how events of objects added with the AddObject method will be handled
Timeout	Specifies the maximum number of milliseconds the script will run before an error will be generated
UseSafeSubset	Prevents access to selected objects and procedures that can compromise an application's security

The Language property determines whether you use VBScript or JavaScript. The default value is VBScript, and if you are a Visual Basic advocate like me, no other option really exists. The AllowUI property determines if your script program can display visual elements like Input-Box and MsgBox.

The Modules and Procedures properties return object references to the Modules and Procedures collections. The Modules collection contains the name and object reference for each module available in the Script-Control. There is always at least one module in every ScriptControl called the Global module. Within each module is a collection of Procedures and a collection of object references (CodeObject) available to the procedures in that module. The Procedures collection contains the name, number of arguments, and whether the procedure returns a value or not for each procedure in the module.

The CodeObject property contains all of the routines defined with the AddCode method. The objects are referenced using the name of the subroutine or function; however, you must know the name of the routine at design time.

TIP

Don't hard-code: Although you can hard-code references to your script programs using the CodeObject property, you probably shouldn't bother. One of the reasons for using the ScriptControl is to allow the user to change the application without recompiling the application. Given the dynamic nature of script programs, you will be better served using the Run and Execute methods.

The Timeout property offers a safety shield to prevent a script program from going into an infinite loop and locking up the system. You can specify the maximum amount of time that a script can run before a warning message is displayed (if the AllowUI property is True). If the user chooses the End option, the Timeout event will occur. If you specify a value of −1, no timeouts will occur. A value of 0 means that the ScriptControl will monitor the execution of the script and will trigger the Timeout event if it determines that the script is hung.

Using ScriptControl Methods

The ScriptControl contains methods to execute code, add code and objects to the scripting engine, and reset the scripting engine to its initial state. Table 9.2 lists the ScriptControl methods. These methods apply to either the global module or any of the local modules that may be defined.

TABLE 9.2: ScriptControl Methods

METHODS	DESCRIPTION
AddCode	Adds a subroutine to the ScriptControl
AddObject	Makes an object available for the script programs
Eval	Evaluates an expression
ExecuteStatement	Executes a single statement
Reset	Reinitializes the scripting engine
Run	Executes a subroutine

There are four different ways to execute a program using the ScriptControl. The simplest way is with the `Eval` method. This method returns the value of the specified expression. For instance x = `ScriptControl1.Eval` `"1+2"` will assign a value of 3 to the variable x. The `Eval` method can also reference functions and variables that are defined in either the global module or the local module, if the method was invoked from a local module. It also can access any resource declared as public in any module.

NOTE

Wait for me to finish: When you run a script using the ScriptControl, you can't change most of the properties or use any of the methods until the script has finished. Trying to do so will result in the error "Can't execute; script is running."

You can also execute a single statement by using the `Execute-Statement` method, as in the following:

```
ScriptControl1.ExecuteStatement "MsgBox ""VBScript is fun"""
```

This method works just like the `Eval` method and can access resources in the module it was declared, in public variables declared in any module, and in the global module.

Another way to execute script code is to use the `Run` method. This method allows you to execute any subroutine declared in the ScriptControl. The subroutine may call any other subroutine or access any objects according to the rules that are used to create modules. You also can specify an array containing the parameters to be passed to the subroutine.

The `AddCode` method adds a block of code to the ScriptControl. During this process, the syntax of the code is checked, and the first error found will trigger the `Error` event.

WARNING

One-way street: Be sure to keep a separate copy of the code to which you added the ScriptControl. There is no way to retrieve code from the control once it has been added.

Using ScriptControl Events

Table 9.3 lists the only two events that are available with the ScriptControl. The `Timeout` event occurs after the user chooses End from the dialog box, after the script program has timed out. The `Error` event occurs whenever an error is encountered in the script program. You should use the `Error` object, described next, to determine the cause of the error and take the appropriate action.

TABLE 9.3: ScriptControl Events

Event	Description
Error	Occurs when the scripting engine encounters an error condition
Timeout	Occurs in timeout conditions when the user selected End from the dialog box

WARNING

No runs, no hits, no `Error` event: If you don't have an `Error` event in your application, any errors found by MSScript will trigger a runtime error in your application. Even a little syntax error while trying to add a script to a module can cause your application to end with a runtime error.

Getting Error Information

The `Error` object contains information about error conditions that arise while using the ScriptControl. Table 9.4 lists the properties and methods for the `Error` object.

TABLE 9.4: Error Object Properties and Methods

Property/Method	Description
Clear method	Clears the script error
Column property	Contains the source code column number where the error occurred
Description property	Describes the error
HelpContext property	Contains a help context reference describing the error
HelpFile property	Contains a help filename containing the help file context
Line property	Contains the source code line number where the error occurred

TABLE 9.4 (continued): Error Object Properties and Methods

PROPERTY/METHOD	DESCRIPTION
Number property	Contains the error number
Source property	Describes the general type of error
Text property	Contains the line of source code where the error occurred

The Source property describes the error as a runtime or compile-time error and the language as VBScript or JScript. The Text property contains the line of source code where the error condition was found. The Line and Column properties contain the exact location of the error in the script. The actual error number is available in the Number property, and the standard description of the error is in the Description property.

If you want to provide your users with a more detailed explanation, you can use the CommonDialog control with the HelpContext and HelpFile properties to display the Visual Basic help page for that error. (Note that you will need to install the associated help file on your system for this to work.)

The Clear method is used to reset the Error object. Using the Add-Code, Eval, ExecuteStatement, or Reset methods will also clear the Error object before these methods begin processing.

PROGRAMMING WITH VBSCRIPT

Writing VBScript programs is as easy as writing Visual Basic programs. The same basic (yes, the pun was intended) language is at the heart of both. However, just because VBScript looks like Visual Basic doesn't mean that anything you can do in Visual Basic you can do in VBScript.

Following Data Type Rules

First of all, VBScript supports only the Variant data type. Thus, the only reason you would use a Dim statement is to declare an array. VBScript doesn't support all of the features of the Dim, Public, and Private statements used to declare variables.

You can continue to use variables with different data types. You can still create Date values, String values, and Double values, but they must be created according to the rules of the Variant data type.

Part iii

Using VBScript Statements

Data types aren't the only things missing. VBScript also lacks several statements. It's missing all of the statements related to file I/O, such as Open, Close, Read, and Input. Other statements that are not available are Write. GoSub, On GoSub, On GoTo, On Error, and DoEvents. Table 9.5 contains a complete list of all of the available VBScript statements.

TABLE 9.5: Statements Supported in VBScript

STATEMENT	DESCRIPTION
Call	Invokes a subroutine
Const	Declares a constant value
Dim	Declares variables
Do/Loop	Executes a loop until a condition or while a condition is True
Erase	Reinitializes the contents of a fixed-size array and frees all of the memory allocated to a variable-sized array
For/Next	Executes a loop while iterating a variable
For Each/Next	Executes a loop while iterating through a collection of objects
Function/End Function	Declares a routine that will return a value
If/Then/Else/End If	Conditionally executes one set of statements or another
On Error	Takes the specified action if an error condition arises
Option Explicit	Requires that all variables must be declared before their use
Private	Declares private variables
Public	Declares public variables
Randomize	Initializes the random-number generator
ReDim	Changes the size of an array
Select Case/End Select	Chooses a single condition from a list of possible conditions
Set	Assigns a reference to an object or creates a new object
Sub	Declares a subroutine
While/Wend	Executes a loop while a condition is True

Using VBScript Functions

Not all functions are carried over to VBScript, just like not all of the statements are carried over. A complete list of functions available in VBScript is shown in Table 9.6.

TABLE 9.6: Functions Available in VBScript

FUNCTION	DESCRIPTION
Abs	Returns the absolute value of a number
Array	Returns a variant containing an array with the specified values
Asc/AscB/AscW	Returns the ASCII value of a character
Atn	Returns the arctangent of the argument
Chr/ChrB/ChrW	Returns a character for a specific ASCII value
Cbool	Converts a value to Boolean
Cbyte	Converts a value to Byte
Ccur	Converts a value to Currency
Cdate	Converts a value to Date
CDbl	Converts a value to Double
Cint	Converts a value to Integer
CLng	Converts a value to Long
Cos	Returns the cosine of the argument
CreateObject	Creates a new instance of the specified object
CSng	Converts a value to Single
Date	Returns the current date
DateSerial	Converts month, day, and year values to a Date value
DateValue	Returns a date part of a Date value
Exp	Returns the exponential of the argument
Filter	Returns a string array that meets the specified filter criteria
Fix	Returns the integer part of a number (Fix (1.2) = 1 and Fix(-1.2) = -1)
FormatCurrency	Formats a value as currency
FormatDateTime	Formats a value as a date or time
FormatNumber	Formats a number

TABLE 9.6 (continued): Functions Available in VBScript

FUNCTION	DESCRIPTION
FormatPercent	Formats a number as a percentage
GetObject	Returns a reference to an automation object
Hex	Returns a string containing the hexadecimal value of a number
InputBox	Displays a dialog box with a prompt for an input value
InStr/InStrB	Returns the starting position of the specified substring
InStrRev	Similar to InStr but starts at the end of the string.
Int	Returns an integer part of a number. (Fix (1.2) = 1 and Fix (-1.2) = -2)
IsArray	Returns True if the argument is an array
IsDate	Returns True if the argument contains a valid Date value
IsEmpty	Returns True if the argument has been initialized
IsNull	Returns True if the argument contains valid data
IsNumeric	Returns True if the argument contains a valid number
IsObject	Returns True if the argument contains an object
Join	Joins together a series of strings (opposite of Split)
Lcase	Converts a string to lowercase characters
Left/LeftB	Returns the leftmost part of a string or byte array
Len/LenB	Returns the length of a string or byte array
LoadPicture	Loads a picture object
Log	Returns the log of the argument
LTrim	Removes leading spaces from a string
Mid/MidB	Returns a substring from the middle of a string or byte array
MsgBox	Displays a dialog box with a message
Oct	Returns a string containing the octal value of a number
Replace	Replaces one substring with another substring the specified number of times
RGB	Returns a color based on values for red, green, and blue
Right/RightB	Returns the rightmost part of a string or byte array
Rnd	Returns the next random number from the random-number generator

TABLE 9.6 (continued): Functions Available in VBScript

FUNCTION	DESCRIPTION
Round	Rounds a value to the specified number of decimal places
Rtrim	Removes trailing spaces from a string
Sgn	Returns −1 if the argument is negative, 0 if it's zero, +1 if it's positive
Sin	Returns the sine of the argument
Space	Fills a string with the specified number of spaces
Split	Breaks apart a string into multiple strings based on a substring (opposite of Join)
Sqr	Returns the square root of the argument
StrComp	Compares strings
String	Fills a string with a specified character the specified number of times
StrReverse	Reverses the order of the characters in the string
Tan	Returns the tangent of the argument
Time	Returns the current time
TimeSerial	Converts hour, minute, and second values to a Date value
TimeValue	Returns the time part of a Date value
Trim	Removes leading and trailing spaces from a string
TypeName	Returns a string containing the name of the type of variable
VarType	Returns an integer containing the type of variable

Part iii

Using VBScript Objects

Unless you use the AddObject method to add more objects, VBScript knows about only a handful of objects, as listed in Table 9.7. If you set UseSafeSubset to True, then only the Err and Dictionary objects will be available. FileSystemObject and the other objects derived from it (Drive, Drives, File, Files, Folder, Folders, and Text-Stream) are considered unsafe, since they allow a script program direct access to disk files.

TABLE 9.7: Objects Available in VBScript

OBJECT	DESCRIPTION
Dictionary	Stores a collection of key and data values
Drive	Accesses information about a disk drive; part of FileSystemObject
Drives	Stores a collection of Drive objects; part of FileSystemObject
Err	Holds information about runtime errors
File	Accesses information about the files in a directory; part of FileSystemObject
Files	Stores a collection of File objects; part of FileSystemObject
FileSystemObject	Provides object-oriented access files and directories
Folder	Accesses folders; part of FileSystemObject
Folders	Stores a collection of Folder objects; part of FileSystemObject
TextStream	Accesses the contents of a file; part of FileSystemObject

BUILDING A SIMPLE MSSCRIPT PROGRAM

By now, you've probably noticed that the first thing I do when I want to try out a new feature in Visual Basic is to create a minimal program that can be easily modified to try out the new feature. That's exactly how the program shown in Figure 9.1 was built.

FIGURE 9.1: The MSScript Demo program

This program isn't pretty, but it allows you to test most of the major features of the ScriptControl. You can enter an expression, statement, or program into the large text window, and click on the Eval, ExecStmt, AddCode, or Run button to process your code. The Run button requires that you enter the name of the subroutine that you want to run in the small text box below the buttons.

The other buttons work as follows:

▶ The Reset button reinitializes the ScriptControl.

▶ The Load button copies a disk file into the text box.

▶ The Save button saves the text box into a disk file.

▶ The Exit button ends the program.

NOTE

The complete code for the programs discussed in this chapter—the MSScript Demo, Really Programmable Calculator, and Charter programs—can be found at the Sybex Web site (www.sybex.com). Once there, go to the Catalog page and enter **2469** (the first four digits of the last five in the book's ISBN) into the search engine. Follow the link for this book that comes up, and then click the Downloads button, which will take you to a list of files organized by chapter.

Adding Code to the Scripting Engine

There are two types of code you can add to the scripting engine: subroutines and module-level variable declarations. Figure 9.2 shows how you would add a global variable, and Figure 9.3 shows how to add a function. Note that you don't need to declare types for the variables or functions, because the only type available is Variant.

When you click the AddCode button, the event shown in Listing 9.1 is triggered. The AddCode method of the ScriptControl is used to add the contents of the large text box. This method will perform any necessary syntax checking, and it will make the code available for use with the Eval, ExecuteStatement, and Run methods. I use the On Error Resume Next statement to prevent compile-time errors in the script code from creating runtime errors in the main program.

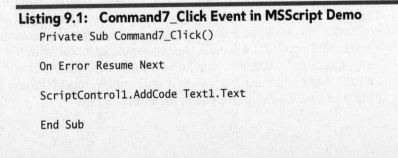

FIGURE 9.2: Adding a global variable

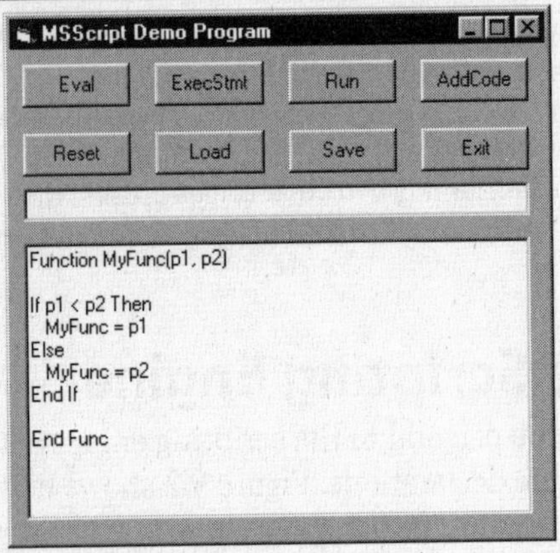

FIGURE 9.3: Adding a function

Listing 9.1: Command7_Click Event in MSScript Demo

```
Private Sub Command7_Click()

On Error Resume Next

ScriptControl1.AddCode Text1.Text

End Sub
```

TIP

All at once or a little at a time—the choice is yours: You can add all of your code in a single shot or load each declaration or routine separately. Which approach you choose should be based on how you plan to let your users edit the code. If they are supposed to edit each subroutine independently of the others, then you should probably load each routine separately. If you're planning to let users modify a series of declarations and routines, adding them all at one time is better.

Evaluating an Expression

In Figure 9.4, you see the results of evaluating a simple mathematical expression. Figure 9.5 shows that strings and functions can be included in the expression.

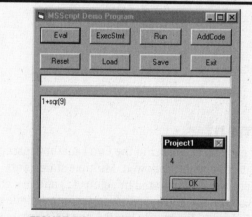

FIGURE 9.4: Evaluating a simple expression

FIGURE 9.5: Strings can be evaluated also.

Part iii

NOTE

Expressions need formatting, too: Expressions passed to the `Eval` method for processing must conform to the standard syntax rules for Visual Basic. The expression must fit on a single line, or each line but the last line must end with a blank followed by the underscore character.

The code in Listing 9.2 runs when the user clicks the Eval button. I use the `On Error Resume Next` statement to prevent runtime errors from occurring when I evaluate an expression. Then I simply call the `Eval` method and format the results. I used the `Format` function rather than one of the newer functions because it will format nearly any value; `Format-Number`, `FormatDateTime`, and the rest require specific data types.

Listing 9.2:   Command5_Click Event in MSScript Demo

```
Private Sub Command5_Click()

On Error Resume Next

MsgBox Format(ScriptControl1.Eval(Text1.Text))

End Sub
```

Executing a Statement

The `ExecuteStatement` method is similar to the `Eval` method, except that a complete Visual Basic statement is allowed. Multiple statements are permitted, provided that they are separated by colons (`:`) and placed on a single line (although you can use the space/underscore technique to split the text across several physical lines). Figures 9.6 and 9.7 show how to use the `ExecuteStatement` statement to perform functions that require more than one statement.

Are you beginning to see a pattern here? After setting the `On Error` statement, I simply use the `ExecuteStatement` method of the Script-Control to execute the statement in the `Text1` text box. Listing 9.3 shows the routine that runs when the user clicks the ExecStmt button.

Listing 9.3:   Command4_Click Event in MSScript Demo

```
Private Sub Command4_Click()

On Error Resume Next

ScriptControl1.ExecuteStatement Text1.Text

End Sub
```

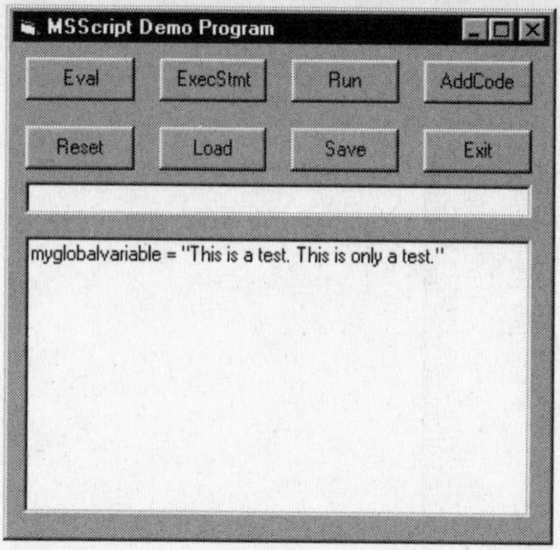

FIGURE 9.6:   Assigning values to a module-level variable

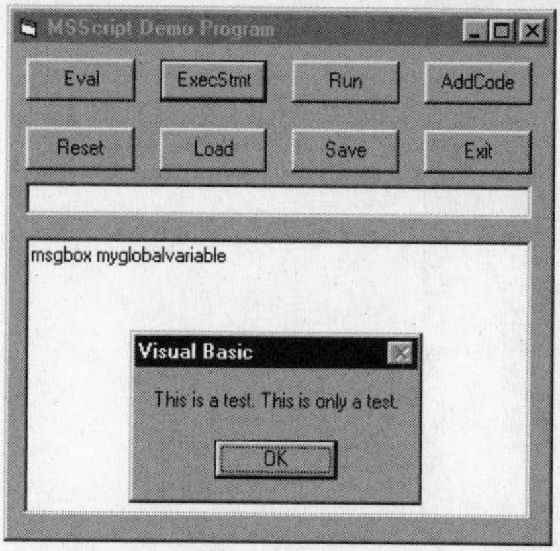

FIGURE 9.7:   Displaying a value from a module-level variable

Running a Program

The Run method differs from the Eval and ExecuteStatement methods in that the code must be added using the AddCode method before you can use the Run method. The code you add must be a complete subroutine or function, and it can even accept parameters. Figure 9.8 illustrates adding a subroutine, and Figure 9.9 shows the results of running that subroutine.

Part iii

FIGURE 9.8: Adding a subroutine

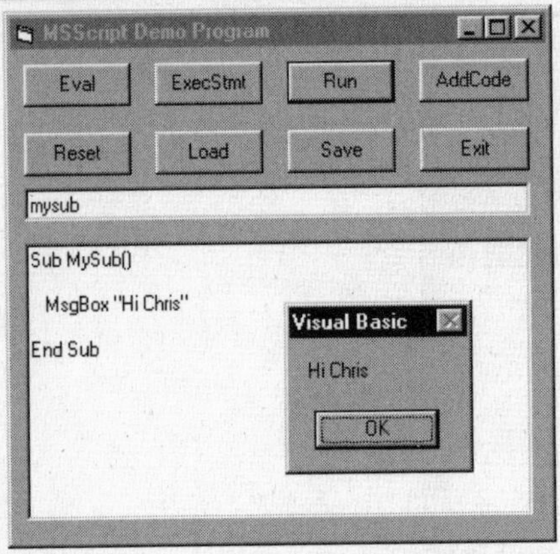

FIGURE 9.9: Running the subroutine

Listing 9.4 shows how to run your subroutine. This time, rather than passing the actual code itself to the Run method, I merely pass the name of the subroutine I want to run.

Listing 9.4:   Command1_Click Event in MSScript Demo

```
Private Sub Command1_Click()

On Error Resume Next

ScriptControl1.Run Text2.Text

End Sub
```

Handling Errors

Handling compile-time and runtime errors in the MSScript Demo program is really a two-step process. I've already pointed out the first step, which is to use an On Error statement with the AddCode, Eval, ExecuteStatement, and Run methods. This prevents a runtime error from stopping your application. The other step is to use the Error event to trap runtime and compile-time errors in your script program. Figure 9.10 shows a typical compile-time error that is trapped and reported to the user.

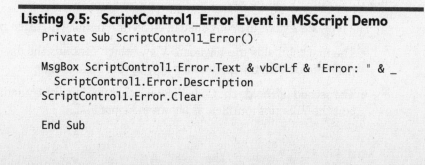

FIGURE 9.10: Trapping a compile-time error

The Error event is triggered when an error occurs in your script, either at compile-time or at runtime. The complete information about the error is contained in the Error object. As you can see in Listing 9.5, in this event, I choose to display the line that contains the error (Script-Control1.Error.Text) and the description of the error (Script-Control1.Error.Description). After I display the error message, I clear the error using the Clear method.

Listing 9.5: ScriptControl1_Error Event in MSScript Demo

```
Private Sub ScriptControl1_Error()

MsgBox ScriptControl1.Error.Text & vbCrLf & "Error: " & _
    ScriptControl1.Error.Description
ScriptControl1.Error.Clear

End Sub
```

Part iii

DESIGNING A CALCULATOR

As another example of using the ScriptControl, I developed a really programmable calculator—and that's what I called the program, as you can see in Figure 9.11. Every button triggers a VBScript routine. You can edit these routines and change the button captions to make the calculator do whatever you want. You can also save your code into a disk file and load it back again. The only problem is that you will need to do all of the work one keystroke at a time.

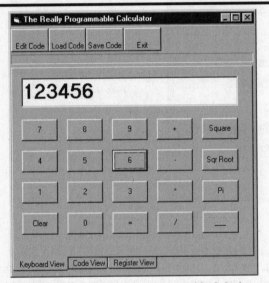

FIGURE 9.11: The Really Programmable Calculator program

The basic design of this program is relatively simple. The form contains a large display for the digits and a control array of command buttons that the user can click. Each of the command buttons calls a VBScript subroutine to perform the appropriate function.

The program's views are contained in an SSTab control with three tabs:

▶ The first tab holds the Keyboard View, which contains the display window and the calculator's keypad (see Figure 9.11).

▶ The second tab holds the Code View, which is used to display and edit the VBScript routines, as shown in Figure 9.12.

▶ The third tab shows the Register View, which holds some text boxes that can be used in intermediate calculations, as shown in Figure 9.13.

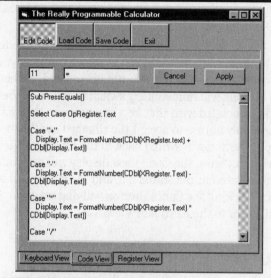

FIGURE 9.12: The Code View tab

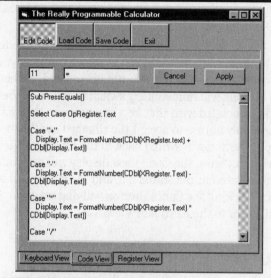

FIGURE 9.13: The Register View tab

Besides the three views, the calculator also includes a toolbar with a status bar beneath it. The toolbar is used to control some of the higher-level functions, such as editing the code assigned to a key, saving and loading the entire VBScript program, and shutting down the program. The status bar displays various error messages that may occur while the calculator is running.

The calculator has two modes: the normal mode and the edit mode. When the Edit Code button is not pressed, the calculator works as you would expect. However, when the Edit Code button is pressed, clicking on any of the keypad buttons will immediately switch to the Code View tab and show the code associated with that key. The user can then edit the code and click the Apply button to accept the changed code. Normally, clicking the Apply button will switch back to the Keyboard View. However, if there is a syntax error, the Code View display will remain, the error message will be displayed in the status bar, and the cursor will be positioned at the error. Clicking the Cancel button will discard any changes and return the user to the Keyboard View.

Handling KeyButton Events

Whenever the user clicks on one of the keys on the calculator's keypad, the KeyButton_Click event will occur. Listing 9.6 shows how I handle this event.

Listing 9.6:   KeyButton_Click Event in Programmable Calculator

```
Private Sub KeyButton_Click(Index As Integer)

On Error Resume Next

CurrentButton = Index
StatusBar1.Panels(1).Text = ""

If Toolbar1.Buttons.Item("EditCode").Value = tbrPressed Then
    CodeBlock.Text = Code(Index)
    CodeNam.Text = KeyButton(Index).Caption
    KeyPos.Text = CStr(Index)
    SSTab1.Tab = 1

Else
    If KeyButton(Index).Caption <> "___" Then
        ScriptControl1.Error.Clear
```

```
      ScriptControl1.Run CodeName(Index)
    End If
  End If

  End Sub
```

I start this routine by using the `On Error Resume Next` to prevent runtime errors from ending the program. Next, I save the `Index` of the currently pressed button and clear any messages that may be in the status bar.

Then I determine which mode the program is in by looking at the Edit Code button on the toolbar. If it's pressed, then I get the code for the key button and display it in the `CodeBlock` text box on the Code View tab. I save the name of the subroutine in the `CodeNam` text box, and save the index of the button in the `KeyPos` text box. Then I display the Code View tab (`SSTab1.Tab = 1`).

Updating the VBScript Routine

After making changes to the VBScript code in the Code View tab, the user can click the Apply button to save the changes. This will trigger the code shown in Listing 9.7.

Listing 9.7: Set_Click Subroutine in Programmable Calculator

```
Private Sub Set_Click()

Dim i As Integer
Dim k As Integer

On Error Resume Next

If Toolbar1.Buttons("EditCode").Value <> tbrPressed Then
  Exit Sub
End If

k = CInt(KeyPos.Text)
If Err.Number = 0 Then
  If k >= 0 And k <= MaxButtons - 1 Then
    ScriptControl1.AddCode CodeBlock.Text & vbCrLf
    If ScriptControl1.Error.Number = 0 Then
      Code(k) = CodeBlock.Text
      i = InStr(4, CodeBlock.Text, "()", vbTextCompare)
      CodeName(k) = Mid(CodeBlock.Text, 5, i - 5)
```

Part iii

```
       KeyButton(k).Caption = CodeNam.Text
       SSTab1.Tab = 0
     End If
    End If
   End If

   End Sub
```

I begin this routine by using the `On Error Resume Next` statement to prevent runtime errors from crashing my program. Next, I put in a safety check that ensures that I'm in edit mode when I attempt to save the changes, since it is possible to switch to this display without being in edit mode.

The real meat of this routine begins by converting the value in the button number field (`KeyPos.Text`) to the variable k. Then I verify that the data is valid by checking the `Number` property of the `Err` object and checking to see if it contains a valid `KeyButton` index.

If everything is correct so far, I use the `Add` method to add the code to the ScriptControl. If there are no syntax errors, I save the code into the Code array and extract the name of the subroutine, then save it in the CodeName array. Next, I update the caption displayed on the button from the `CodeNam.Text` field. Finally, I switch back to the Keyboard View by setting the `SSTab1.Tab` property to 0.

Note that I don't have any code to handle the error condition. That's because the code in the ScriptControl's `Error` event will take care of displaying the error message and positioning the cursor at the place where the error was detected. This handling is described next.

Trapping Script Errors

All script errors, whether they are compile-time or runtime errors, will cause the `Error` event to be triggered. In Listing 9.8, I handle both types of errors. Unlike the error handling in the MSScript Demo program (Listing 9.5), here I help the user identify and correct the error in a more user-friendly fashion.

Listing 9.8:   ScriptControl1_Error Event in Programmable Calculator

```
Private Sub ScriptControl1_Error()

Dim i As Integer
```

```
Dim k As Integer

If SSTab1.Tab <> 1 Then
   SSTab1.Tab = 1
   CodeBlock.Text = Code(CurrentButton)
End If

k = 1
For i = 1 To ScriptControl1.Error.Line - 1
   k = InStr(k, CodeBlock.Text, vbCrLf)
Next i

CodeBlock.SetFocus
CodeBlock.SelStart = k + 2 + ScriptControl1.Error.Column
k = InStr(CodeBlock.SelStart, CodeBlock.Text, vbCrLf)
CodeBlock.SelLength = k - CodeBlock.SelStart

StatusBar1.Panels(1).Text = ScriptControl1.Error.Description
ScriptControl1.Reset
Beep

End Sub
```

I begin the routine by seeing if the Code View tab is already visible. If it is not, then I make it visible and load the code related to the current button. Next, I use a For/Next loop to find the line containing the error. I scan the text box looking for carriage return/line feed pairs (vbCrLf). Since each line ends with a carriage return/line feed pair, I look for the line before the error, knowing that two characters after that is the start of the line I want.

Once I have the character offset to the start of the line with the error, I can find the starting position of the error by simply adding the Error object's Column property. By setting the text box's SelStart property, the cursor will be placed in front of that character. Then I can highlight the rest of the line of code by setting the SelLength property to the number of characters left in the line. I do this by searching for the position of the next carriage return/line feed pair and subtracting the current value of the SelStart property.

I finish this routine by copying the error's description into the status bar. Then I clear the error condition by using the Reset method. Finally, I provide a multimedia beep to let the user know something isn't right.

Part iii

Defining Objects for the VBScript Program

My Really Programmable Calculator program defines several objects that can be used in the VBScript program. I do this when I load the calculator form, as you can see in Listing 9.9. I also set the SSTab control to the Keyboard View, initialize the FileSystemObject, and call the Load-Code routine to load the default script program.

Listing 9.9: Form_Load Event in Programmable Calculator

```
Private Sub Form_Load()

ScriptControl1.AddObject "Display", Display
ScriptControl1.AddObject "XRegister", XRegister
ScriptControl1.AddObject "YRegister", YRegister
ScriptControl1.AddObject "ZRegister", ZRegister
ScriptControl1.AddObject "OpRegister", OpRegister

SSTab1.Tab = 0

Set fso = New FileSystemObject

LoadCode

End Sub
```

Defining the objects is a very simple process. All you need to do is call the AddObject method and specify the object's script name and real name. Inside your script program, you will refer to the object by its script name, while you will continue to refer to the object by its real name in your Visual Basic 6 application.

Loading the VBScript Program

Here's a quick hack job that lets me load the calculator's VBScript code from a disk file. As you can see in Listing 9.10, it isn't very pretty, but it works.

Listing 9.10: LoadCode Script Routine in Programmable
Calculator

```
Private Sub LoadCode()

Dim i As Integer
Dim j As Integer
```

```
Dim k As Integer
Dim s As String
Dim t As TextStream
Dim x() As String

On Error Resume Next

Set t = fso.OpenTextFile(App.Path & "\calc.mod")
s = t.ReadAll
t.Close

x = Split(s, "'~")

For i = 0 To MaxButtons - 1
   KeyButton(i).Caption = Trim(Mid(x(i + 1), 9, 10))
   j = InStr(1, x(i + 1), "Sub ", vbTextCompare)
   Code(i) = Mid(x(i + 1), j, Len(x(i + 1)) - j + 1)
   k = InStr(j + 4, x(i + 1), "()", vbTextCompare)
   CodeName(i) = Trim(Mid(x(i + 1), j + 4, k - j - 4))
   ScriptControl1.AddCode Code(i)
Next i

End Sub
```

I start this routine by declaring a bunch of local variables and inserting my usual On Error Resume Next statement. As I did with the VBScript updating routine, I'm going to let the Error event perform the work if an error arises.

I open the "calc.mod" file (the beginning of this file is shown in Listing 9.11) using the OpenTextFile method of the FileSystemObject and load the file into a memory with a ReadAll method. This is followed by a call to the Split function to split the contents of the file into individual subroutines using the array x. Each subroutine is separated by a marker consisting of an apostrophe followed by a tilde ('~). This is a valid comment in Visual Basic, so it doesn't hurt if it is included as part of the program.

Listing 9.11:   Start of the Calc.mod File

```
' Revised: 6/14/98 3:01:11 PM
'~

'Key:    7
Sub Press7()

Display.Text = Display.Text & "7"
```

```
End Sub
'~

'Key:    4
Sub Press4()

Display.Text = Display.Text & "4"

End Sub
'~
```

The section before the first marker I call the file's header. Basically, I throw this information away when I load the file; however, it is useful to have when looking at the raw file. This information will be loaded into x(0). Immediately following the marker is the information for the first button, KeyButton(0). Then the next marker will appear, followed by the next block of code. This will continue in the same order as the buttons until all 20 buttons have been defined.

The information associated with a single button has some strict formatting requirements. The marker is on a line by itself. A line containing the text to be displayed as the button's caption immediately follows the marker. The characters in positions nine through eighteen will be used as the key's caption.

The next line of the file contains the subroutine definition. The format is the typical definition Visual Basic subroutine definition like sub xxx(). To parse this line, I look for the keyword sub then I look for the empty parentheses (). The characters in between (xxx) are the name of the subroutine.

Once I have collected all of this information, I simply use the AddCode method to install the entire block of code into the scripting engine. The scripting engine ignores the lines of comments, which is why I formatted the additional information as comments.

NOTE

One little, two little, three little subroutines: After a little experimenting, I found that the AddCode and the ExecuteStatement methods are relatively insensitive to the amount of code processed. Each line of code must end in a carriage return/line feed pair, including the last. Beyond that, the number of subroutines or statements doesn't appear to matter when using the ScriptControl.

Writing the Calculator Script Program

The calculator script program is relatively straightforward. As buttons on the calculator's keypad are clicked, data is entered into the display register or a task is processed. When one of the keys from 0 to 9 is clicked, the digit is appended to the Display text box. Listing 9.12 shows the code run when the numeral 1 key is clicked.

Listing 9.12:   Press1 Script Routine in Programmable Calculator

```
'Key:      1
Sub Press1()

Display.Text = Display.Text & "1"

End Sub
```

Clicking the plus (+) key causes the code in Listing 9.13 to be run. The code executes the PressEquals routine if a mathematical operator was saved in OpRegister. Then it saves the current mathematical operator in OpRegister. It also saves the Display register in the XRegister before clearing the Display register. The code for the other mathematical operators (−, *, and /) works in the same way.

Listing 9.13:   PressAdd Script Routine in Programmable Calculator

```
'Key:      +
Sub PressAdd()

If Len(OpRegister.Text) > 0 then
   PressEquals
End If

OpRegister.Text = "+"
XRegister.Text = Display.Text
Display.Text = ""

End Sub
```

Pressing the equal sign (=) completes the calculation process and displays the results. As shown in Listing 9.14, the code selects the appropriate mathematical operation and performs it based on the current value of OpRegister. The result is saved in the Display register, and the XRegister and the OpRegister are both cleared at the end of this routine.

Listing 9.14:   PressEquals Script Routine in Programmable Calculator

```
'Key:     =
Sub PressEquals()

Select Case OpRegister.Text

Case "+"
  Display.Text = FormatNumber(CDbl(XRegister.text) + _
CDbl(Display.Text))

Case "-"
  Display.Text = FormatNumber(CDbl(XRegister.Text) - _
CDbl(Display.Text))

Case "*"
  Display.Text = FormatNumber(CDbl(XRegister.Text) * _
CDbl(Display.Text))

Case "/"
  Display.Text = FormatNumber(CDbl(XRegister.Text) / _
CDbl(Display.Text))

End Select

XRegister.Text = ""
OpRegister.Text = ""

End Sub
```

CALCULATING EQUATIONS IN A SPREADSHEET

Of all the programs I've written for this book, I felt that the Charter program could benefit the most from using the ScriptControl. The ability to evaluate expressions in the grid part of the program could add significant value to this simple spreadsheet program. Figure 9.14 shows how I can enter an equation into a cell.

Adding this capability requires modifying many of the existing functions because of a new global variable called Equations. The Equations variable is a string array, where each element in the string array corresponds to a cell on the grid. Rather than go through every routine that was changed, I'm just going to cover those that are related to using the ScriptControl.

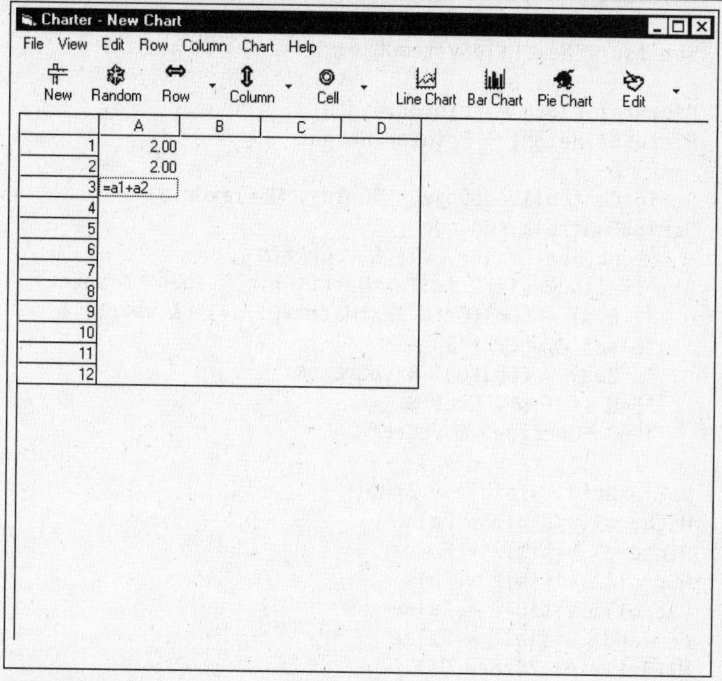

FIGURE 9.14:   Entering an equation into Charter

Initializing the ScriptControl

As you've seen elsewhere in this chapter, you need to initialize some aspects of the ScriptControl before you can use them. In this case, since I want to be able to access the grid from the ScriptControl, I need to create a reference to the MSFlexGrid control using the AddObject method. Since this needs to be done only once, I do it in the Form_Load event, as shown in Listing 9.15. Note that there is no requirement for the name inside the scripting engine to be the same as the name of the real object, so this time I called the internal name Grid rather than typing all of those characters.

Listing 9.15:   Form_Load Event in Charter

```
Private Sub Form_Load()

NewChart

Set fso = New FileSystemObject

Picture1.Width = Printer.Width
Picture1.Height = Printer.Height

ScriptControl1.AddObject "Grid", MSFlexGrid1
ScriptControl1.AddCode _
    "Function Eval(r, c)" & vbCrLf & _
    "If IsNumeric(Grid.TextMatrix(r,c)) Then" & vbCrLf & _
    " Eval = CDbl(Grid.TextMatrix(r,c))" & vbCrLf & _
    "Else" & vbCrLf & _
    " Eval = CDbl(0)" & vbCrLf & _
    "End If " & vbCrLf & _
    "End Function" & vbCrLf

MSFlexGrid1.Visible = True
MSChart1.Visible = False
Picture1.Visible = False
HScroll1.Visible = False
VScroll1.Visible = False
Command1.Visible = False
MSFlexGrid1.ZOrder 0

End Sub
```

The other thing I want to do when the program first starts is to create a short function that will allow me to access the contents of a cell as a Double. This function will also return a value of 0 if the cell is empty or contains a non-numeric value.

Entering an Equation into a Cell

Entering an equation into a single cell is as simple as typing an equal sign and then typing the equation. The equation will continue to be displayed in the cell until the user moves the cursor to another cell; then the LeaveCell event will occur. Listing 9.16 shows the code to achieve this.

Listing 9.16:   MSFlexGrid1_LeaveCell Event in Charter

```
Private Sub MSFlexGrid1_LeaveCell()

If Left(MSFlexGrid1.Text, 1) = "=" Then
  Equations(MSFlexGrid1.Row, MSFlexGrid1.Col) =
Mid(MSFlexGrid1.Text, 2)
  MSFlexGrid1.Text = Compute(Equations(MSFlexGrid1.Row,
MSFlexGrid1.Col))
End If

Recalculate

End Sub
```

The LeaveCell event contains the code that will save contents of the cell into Equations array if the first character of the cell is an equal sign. If so, then it computes a new value for the cell using the Compute function and saves the result in the cell.

Finally, I recalculate the contents of the entire grid using the Recalculate routine. This is done even if there wasn't an equation in the cell. It's possible that someone simply typed a new number into the cell, and the cell might be used in an equation somewhere else in the grid. Without recalculating the entire spreadsheet, any cells that use this value in their calculations would display an incorrect value.

Computing the Value of a Cell

The function shown in Listing 9.17 translates the equation that the user typed in into one that the scripting engine can evaluate. The basic problem this function has to handle is to translate cell references of the form <letter><number> into Eval(<row>, <column>). For example, a reference to A1 must be converted to Eval(1,1), and a reference to B7 must be converted to Eval(7,2).

Listing 9.17:   Compute Function in Charter

```
Private Function Compute(e As String) As String

Dim i As Integer
Dim j As Integer
Dim s As String
Dim t As String
```

```
On Error Resume Next

t = UCase(e)

For i = 1 To MSFlexGrid1.Cols - 1
  For j = 1 To MSFlexGrid1.Rows - 1
    s = Chr(j + 64)
    s = s & FormatNumber(i, 0)
    t = Replace(t, s, "Eval(" & FormatNumber(i, 0) & "," & _
      FormatNumber(j, 0) & ")")
  Next j
Next i

Compute = FormatNumber(ScriptControl1.Eval(t), 2)

End Function
```

There are basically two ways to handle this process. The first way is to parse the equation and determine which values are cell references and which values are not. This is the way that Microsoft Excel works. It's also the way I probably would have done it, except that it would have taken a lot more code to accomplish, and it really wouldn't make much of a difference given the size of the grids I'm using in this program.

So I chose to use the second way—a brute-force approach. I search the equation for every possible cell reference and replace that cell reference with the corresponding reference to the `Eval` function. I compute the letter part of the cell reference by adding 64 to the column number and converting the sum to a character. (Note that a value of 65 corresponds to an *A*, 66 corresponds to a *B*, and so forth.) Then I append the row number to create the cell reference. Finally, I use the `Replace` function to replace every occurrence of the cell reference with the corresponding call to the `Eval` function.

After I've processed all possible call references, I use the scripting engine's `Eval` method to compute a new value for the cell. Then I format the result and return it as the value of the function.

Recalculating the Grid

The last major step of this process is to loop through each cell in the grid and update the cell's displayed value. That's exactly what happens in Listing 9.18. I set up a loop to check every cell, and if the cell has an equation, then I update the value in the cell by using the `Compute` function.

Listing 9.18: Recalculate Routine in Charter

```
Private Sub Recalculate()

Dim i As Integer
Dim j As Integer

For i = 1 To MSFlexGrid1.Rows - 1
  For j = 1 To MSFlexGrid1.Cols - 1
    If Len(Equations(i, j)) > 0 Then
      MSFlexGrid1.TextMatrix(i, j) = Compute(Equations(i, j))
    End If
  Next j
Next i

End Sub
```

USING THE SCRIPTCONTROL IN YOUR OWN PROGRAMS

The hardest part about using the ScriptControl is finding the right situation in which to add it. Here, I'll offer some suggestions of when you might want to use it.

Many business applications have rules that are unique to a particular business. Using the ScriptControl allows you to customize your application without recompiling for each business. All you need to do is to code the business-specific rules in VBScript for each organization. Then they could be loaded at run time. A good example of this is computing sales tax for a particular state. Some items are taxable, and some are not. Even the tax rate may vary depending on the item. Using VBScript allows you to easily write a specific program for a state and quickly change it whenever the state changes its laws related to computing sales tax.

Another place where you might consider using the ScriptControl is in game playing. Many games, such as SimCity and Civilization, are rather complex and often involve tedious tasks that can follow a specific strategy. For instance, an advanced Civilization game player could benefit from a VBScript program that would automatically choose the next advance based on the advance just completed and the advances achieved by the other players.

Part iii

Yet another place where VBScript might prove valuable is to create a batch-processing facility. Suppose you have a tool like Photoshop, where you can perform various tasks based on keyboard and/or mouse movements. Then suppose that you need to apply that same transformation ten or fifty times. Rather than doing it by hand, it might be useful to write a little VBScript program that would allow you to repeat the transformation as many times as needed. This would not only save time, but it could also reduce mistakes.

Final Thoughts

I really consider the MSScript Demo program I talked about at the beginning of this chapter as a throwaway program because it isn't intended to perform a useful function other than testing. Including a new feature like a ScriptControl into an existing application can be confusing when problems arise. The most powerful feature of Visual Basic is its ability to add small amounts of code to your program and see how it works immediately.

When I wrote the MSScript Demo program, I didn't just type in all of the code and press F5. If you take a close look at the names of the command buttons, you can see how this program evolved as I experimented with the features. Originally, the Command1 command button performed both the AddCode and the Run functions in the same routine. I added the Command2 and Command3 buttons to allow me to load and save my scripts (I didn't show this in the text, so check the full program on the Sybex Web site) because I got tired of retyping my scripts each time the program died.

The Command4 and Command5 buttons showed up because I wanted to try the ExecuteStatement and Eval methods. About this time, I added the Error event to provide a little diagnostic information about why the script failed. The Command6 and Command7 buttons were added when I wanted to test the AddCode method separately from the Run method. Specifically, I wanted to create global variables to see how they worked with the Eval and ExecuteStatement methods. Finally, I added the Exit button (Command8) because I had an empty space on the form and couldn't think of anything better to add. I highly recommend using the technique of adding a section of code at a time whenever you need to try something new and don't have a good feel for how it works.

The Calculator program would need a lot of work before I would let non-programmer types use it. Little things like being able to specify a filename to load or save and simplifying the file format that I use to save the VBScript code need to be revisited and changed. I might even change the routine so that it worked more like a Visual Basic event, where I passed the caption of the button that was pressed rather than associating a different subroutine with each key. I could also use a Load event to initialize the calculator, add methods that could be used to change the layout of the existing buttons, and even create new buttons on the fly.

The Charter program is the kind of program that is easy to build if you use the right tools. The three major controls I use in this program—MSScript, MSChart, and MSFlexGrid—represent over 2.5MB of code that I didn't have to write. With these controls, it's no wonder why it is easy and fast to develop complex projects in Visual Basic!

What's Next?

Your scripting knowledge will grow in the following chapter. You'll learn about the FileSystemObject and Shell objects, the Script control, and the Windows scripting host. Using these tools, along with the many others you've gained, will give you a wide array of options when you're creating your applications.

Chapter 10
SCRIPTING OBJECTS

VBScript was introduced to script Web pages and harness the computing power of the client. Scripts are simple programs that are downloaded in text format and executed on the client computer. VBScript itself is the core of a programming language. On its own, VBScript can do very little. The real power in scripting comes from the way that VBScript can access the objects exposed by the browser. If you ignore the objects that can be manipulated through VBScript (such as the <DIV> tags or the intrinsic and ActiveX controls), what's left? A language that can create variables and assign values to them, perform basic operations on these variables, evaluate logical expressions, and repeat several loop structures. If you had a mechanism to perform these operations, you'd be able to build a custom programming language, wouldn't you?

Adapted from *Mastering Visual Basic 6*
by Evangelos Petroutsos
ISBN 0-7821-2272-8   1,312 pages $49.99

In principle, you can create a custom language and embed it in your applications. All you need is the engine that interprets and executes VBScript code. Add a few objects that expose properties and methods, and you have your own, custom language. DHTML and Internet Explorer expose a number of objects that can be manipulated with VBScript. Later in this chapter, you'll learn how to embed VBScript in your applications and allow users to program your application.

The same technology can also be embedded in other products, including Windows itself. As you probably know, you can automate Windows 98 operations with scripts, which are the equivalents of the old DOS batch files. Windows 98 includes the *Windows Scripting Host (WSH)*, an engine that interprets and executes VBScript code and exposes a few objects needed to script the operating system. One of the objects exposed by the WSH is the Environment object, which gives you access to the environment variables. Another WSH object is the Network object, which gives you access to the network's resources. I'll discuss these objects later in this chapter. For now, keep in mind that the language for scripting the Windows 98 operating system is VBScript, and you can easily apply your programming skills to another scripting area.

In the following section, we are going to look at a very useful object introduced with VBScript, the FileSystemObject object. It gives you access to the host computer's file system and was lacking in Visual Basic. We'll then explore the Script control, which lets you add scripting capabilities to your VB applications. Yes, it is possible to script your own applications with VBScript and make them much more flexible. In the last section of this chapter, you'll see how you can use VBScript to script Windows itself.

THE FILESYSTEMOBJECT OBJECT

VBScript introduced several new objects that are also available from within Visual Basic. The most important (from a VB programmer's point of view, at least) is the FileSystemObject object, which gives you access to the host computer's file system. Visual Basic provides a small number of functions and statements for accessing and manipulating the file system, but the *FileSystemObject* object is a very flexible object that provides methods and properties for accessing every folder and file on the host computer's disks.

To gain access to your computer's file system, you create a FileSystem-Object variable with the CreateObject() function:

```
Set FSys = CreateObject("Scripting.FileSystemObject")
```

The variable *FSys* represents the file system, and it must be declared as Object:

```
Dim FSys As Object
```

To access text files on the computer's disk, you use the FileSystem-Object object's methods, which I'll describe next.

This is how you can access the host computer's file system from within a Windows script. With Visual Basic there's a better method, which exploits early binding to speed up your application. You can add a reference to the Microsoft Scripting Runtime object by choosing Project ➤ References to open the References dialog box. Select the Microsoft Scripting Runtime item, and click OK. Once the reference is added to the project, you can declare the *FSys* variable as follows:

```
Dim FSys As New Scripting.FileSystemObject
```

Or you can simply declare it in the following way:

```
Dim FSys As New FileSystemObject
```

In the Code window, as soon as you type the name of the *FSys* variable and the following period, the components of the Scripting object appear in a list, and you can select the desired object. You can then use the *FSys* variable in your code without the CreateObject() function.

Let's exercise the FileSystemObject object. Start a new project and place a Command button on it. In the Form's Code window, enter the following declaration:

```
Dim FSys As New Scripting.FileSystemObject
```

Then enter the following statement in the Command button's Click event handler:

```
Debug.Print FSys.FileExists("C:\AUTOEXEC.BAT")
```

If the file C:\AUTOEXEC.BAT exists, the string "True" will appear in the Immediate window. The FileExists member of the *FSys* variable is a method, which returns True if the specified file exists; otherwise, it returns False.

The FileSystemObject object provides a number of properties and methods for manipulating the file system, as well as for creating new text files (and opening existing ones), to read from or write to. Visual Basic provides its own statements for accessing text files (as well as binary files), so this subset of the FileSystemObject object is not particularly useful to VB programmers. The members of the FileSystemObject object that allow you to open and read from or write to text files are very useful for developing Windows scripts, so I will present them here. This chapter is addressed to

Part iii

programmers, so I won't discuss them in much detail. Later, I will discuss the members of the FileSystemObject object that are just as useful for developing VB applications as they are for developing Windows scripts.

Being able to write information to text files and read from them is a basic operation in scripting. Many scripts save their results to text files or read their arguments from text files (scripts that process a large number of files, for instance). The methods of the FileSystemObject object for manipulating text files can also be used from within scripts in Visual Basic applications (see the StatClss example later in this chapter).

The CreateTextFile Method

This method creates a new text file and returns a *TextStream* object that can be used to read from or write to the file. The syntax of the Create-TextFile method is:

```
Set TStream = FSys.CreateTextFile(filename, overwrite, unicode)
```

The *filename* argument specifies the name of the file to be created and is the only required argument. *Overwrite* is a Boolean value that indicates whether you can overwrite an existing file (if True) or not (if False). If you omit the *overwrite* argument, existing files are not overwritten. The last argument, *unicode*, indicates whether the file is created as a Unicode or an ASCII file. If the *unicode* argument is True, the new file is created as a Unicode file; otherwise, it is created as an ASCII file. If you omit the *unicode* argument, an ASCII file is assumed.

To create a new text file, create a *FileSystemObject* object variable and then call its CreateTextFile method as follows:

```
Set TStream = FSys.CreateTextFile("c:\testfile.txt")
```

The *TStream* variable represents a TextStream object, whose methods allow you to write to or read from the specified file. (I'll discuss these methods in "The TextStream Object" section, later in this chapter.)

The OpenTextFile Method

In addition to creating new text files, you can open existing files with the OpenTextFile method, whose syntax is

```
FSys.OpenTextFile(filename, iomode, create, format)
```

The OpenTextFile method opens the specified file and returns a Text-Stream object that can be used to read from or write to the file. The *filename* argument is the only required one. The value of the *iomode* argument is one of the constants shown in Table 10.1.

TABLE 10.1: The Values of the OpenTextFile Method's *iomode* Argument

CONSTANT	VALUE	DESCRIPTION
ForReading	1	The file is opened for reading existing data.
ForAppending	2	The file is opened for appending new data.

The optional *create* argument is a Boolean value that indicates whether a new file can be created if the specified filename doesn't exist. If it's True, a new file is created. The last argument, *format*, is also optional and can be True (the file is opened in Unicode mode) or False (the file is opened in ASCII mode). If you omit the *format* argument, the file is opened using the system default (ASCII).

To open a TextStream object for reading, use the following statements:

```
Set TStream = FSys.OpenTextFile("c:\testfile.txt", ForReading)
```

Like the CreateTextFile method, the OpenTextFile method returns a TextStream object, whose methods allow you to write to or read from the specified file.

Now that you have seen how the FileSystemObject is used to open and create files, we are ready to look at the TextStream object, which lets you read from and write to files. The FileSystemObject object has more methods, which allow you to access the various drives, copy and delete files or entire folders, and more. I'll come back to the methods of the FileSystemObject object, but first let's see how you can manipulate text files through the TextStream object.

The TextStream Object's Methods

After you create a TextStream object with the CreateTextFile or the OpenTextFile method of the FileSystemObject object, you can use the following methods to read from and write to the file.

NOTE

As its name implies, the TextStream object applies only to text files.

Read   This method reads a specified number of characters from a TextStream object. Its syntax is

```
TStream.Read(characters)
```

in which *characters* is the number of characters to be read from and *TStream* is a TextStream variable.

ReadAll   This method reads the entire TextStream (text file) and returns the text as a string variable. Its syntax is

```
fileText = TStream.ReadAll
```

in which *fileText* is a string (or variant) variable.

ReadLine   This method reads one line of text at a time (up to, but not including, the newline character) from a text file and returns the resulting string. Its syntax is

```
fileText = TStream.ReadLine
```

Skip   This method skips a specified number of characters when reading a text file. Its syntax is

```
TStream.Skip(characters)
```

in which *characters* is the number of characters to be skipped.

SkipLine   This method skips the next line of the text file, and its syntax is

```
TStream.SkipLine
```

The characters of the skipped line are discarded, up to and including the next newline character.

Write   This method writes the specified string to a TextStream file. Its syntax is

```
TStream.Write(string)
```

in which *string* is the string (literal or variable) to be written to the file. Strings are written to the file with no intervening spaces or characters between each string. Use the WriteLine method to write a newline character or a string that ends with a newline character.

WriteLine   This method writes the specified string followed by a newline character to the file. Its syntax is

```
TStream.WriteLine(string)
```

in which *string* is the text you want to write to the file. If you call the Write-Line method without an argument, a newline character is written to the file.

WriteBlankLines This method writes a specified number of blank lines (newline characters) to the file. Its syntax is

```
TStream.WriteBlankLines(lines)
```

in which *lines* is the number of blank lines to be inserted in the file.

The TextStream Object's Properties

Besides its methods, the TextStream object provides a number of properties, which allow your code to know where the pointer is in the current TextStream.

AtEndOfLine This is a read-only property that returns True if the file pointer is at the end of a line in the TextStream object; otherwise, it returns False. The AtEndOfLine property applies to files that are open for reading. You can use this property to read a line of characters, one at a time, with a loop similar to the following:

```
Do While TSream.AtEndOfLine = False
    newChar = TStream.Read(1)
    {process character newChar}
Loop
```

This loop scans the file represented by the TStream object, and until it reaches the end of the current line, it reads and processes another character.

AtEndOfStream This is another read-only property that returns True if the file pointer is at the end of the TextStream object. The AtEndOf-Stream property applies only to TextStream files that are open for reading. You can use this property to read an entire file, one line at a time, with a loop such as the following:

```
Do While TStream.AtEndOfStream = False
    newLine = TStream.ReadLine
    {process line}
Loop
```

Column This is another read-only property that returns the column number of the current character in a TextStream line. The first character in a line is in column 1. Use this property to read data arranged in columns, without tabs or other delimiters.

Line This property is another read-only property that returns the current line number in the TextStream. The Line property of the first line in a TextStream object is 1.

VB6 at Work: The MakeFile Project

The MakeFile project (see Figure 10.1) demonstrates several of the Text-Stream object's methods. This application creates a text file and saves the contents of a TextBox control in it. It then opens the file, reads the text lines, and displays them on the same TextBox control.

To design the application, follow these steps:

1. Start a new Standard EXE project.

2. Add a reference to the FileSystemObject component.

3. Open the References dialog box, and select the Microsoft Scripting Runtime component.

4. Now, insert the following declaration in the Form's Code window:

   ```
   Dim FSys As New FileSystemObject
   ```

   The *FSys* variable is declared on the Form level so that all procedures can access it.

5. Place the controls shown in Figure 10.1 on the Form, and insert the code shown in Code 10.1 in the two Command buttons' Click events.

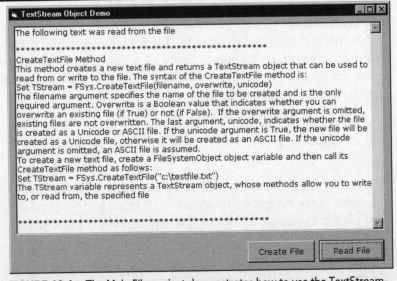

FIGURE 10.1: The MakeFile project demonstrates how to use the TextStream-Object to access a text file.

The Create File button reads the text on the TextBox control and saves it to the C:\TEXTFILE.TXT file in the application's folder. The code creates a TextStream object and uses it to write the text to the file.

Code 10.1:   The Create File Button

```
Private Sub bttnCreateFile_Click()
Dim OutStream As TextStream

    TestFile = App.Path & "\textfile.txt"
    Set OutStream = FSys.CreateTextFile(TestFile, True, False)
    OutStream.WriteLine Text1.Text
    Set OutStream = Nothing
End Sub
```

The second button reads the contents of the same file through another TextStream object. In addition to the text read from the file, it displays a few additional lines to delimit the text read from the file.

Code 10.2:   The Read File Button

```
Private Sub bttnReadFile_Click()
Dim InStream As TextStream

    TestFile = App.Path & "\textfile.txt"
    Set InStream = FSys.OpenTextFile(TestFile, 1, False, False)
    While InStream.AtEndOfStream = False
      TLine = InStream.ReadLine
      txt = txt & TLine & vbCrLf
    Wend
    Text1.Text = "The following text was read from the file" _
& vbCrLf
    Text1.Text = Text1.Text & vbCrLf & String(50, "*")
    Text1.Text = Text1.Text & vbCrLf & txt
    Text1.Text = Text1.Text & vbCrLf & String(50, "*")
    Set InStream = Nothing
End Sub
```

The *FSys* variable represents the file system. *InStream* and *OutStream* are two TextStream objects whose WriteLine and ReadLine methods are used to write and read individual lines to the file. After the desired lines have been written to the file, we set both object variables to Nothing to release the resources allocated to it (in effect this statement closes the file).

Part iii

The file's lines are read with a While...Wend loop, which examines the value of the TextStream object's AtEndOfStream property to find out how many lines to read from the file:

```
While InStream.AtEndOfStream = False
    TLine = Instream.ReadLine
    {process Tline variable}
Wend
```

At each iteration of the loop, the *TLine* variable holds the next line of text in the file.

Accessing Folders and Files

In the previous sections, we looked at the methods of the FileSystem-Object object, which allow you to access files on the local disk(s). The FileSystemObject object supports many more methods that apply to files and folders—methods that allow you to copy and delete files or folders, which are much more useful to a VB programmer than the methods for accessing text files. Although there are Visual Basic statements and functions to access the file system, the FileSystemObject object gives you a consistent, hierarchical view of the file system, and you should use it instead.

 NOTE
In order to access the file system from within scripts, you can only use the FileSystemObject object.

CopyFile   This method copies one or more files from one folder to another, and its syntax is

```
FSys.CopyFile source, destination, overwrite
```

The *source* argument is the path of the file to be moved and can contain wildcard characters (for copying multiple files). The *destination* argument is the path of the destination folder to which the file(s) will be copied. The *destination* argument may not contain wildcard characters. The last argument, *overwrite*, is optional, and it's a Boolean value (True/False) that indicates whether existing files are to be overwritten. The CopyFile method produces a runtime error if the destination file has its read-only attribute set, regardless of the value of the *overwrite* argument. See the discussion of the Attributes property for an example of how to overwrite read-only files.

CopyFolder   This method copies a folder from one location to another, including the subfolders (this is called *recursive* copying). The syntax of the CopyFolder method is

```
FSys.CopyFolder source, destination, overwrite
```

in which *source* is the path of the source folder (where files will be copied from) and may include wildcard characters, in case you want to copy selected files. The *destination* argument is the path of the destination folder (where the files will be copied to), and it may not contain wildcard characters. The last argument, *overwrite*, is optional, and it's a Boolean value that indicates whether existing folders can be overwritten. If it's True, the destination files can be overwritten, if they exist. To protect existing files in the destination folder, set it to False.

To copy all the DOC files from the folder MyDocuments to the folder WorkDocs\February, use the following statement

```
FSys.CopyFolder "c:\MyDocuments\*.DOC", "c:\WorkDocs\February"
```

in which *FSys* is a properly declared FileSystemObject object variable.

WARNING

The CopyFolder method stops when it encounters the first error. This means that some files have been copied and some have not. The CopyFolder method won't move the copied files back to their source folder, nor will it continue with the remaining files.

DeleteFile   This method deletes one or more files, and its syntax is

```
FSys.DeleteFile filespec, force
```

in which *filespec* is the name of the file(s) to delete and may contain wildcard characters. The *force* argument is optional, and it's a Boolean value that indicates whether read-only files will be deleted (if True) or not (if False). Like the CopyFile method, the DeleteFile method stops on the first error it encounters.

DeleteFolder   This method deletes a specific folder and its contents, including its subfolders and their files. Its syntax is identical to the syntax of the DeleteFile method:

```
FSys.DeleteFolder folderspec, force
```

Here, *folderspec* is the name of the folder to delete. The specified folder is deleted, regardless of whether it contains files (unlike the RMDIR DOS command). The *force* argument has the same meaning as it has with the DeleteFile method.

MoveFile   This method moves one or more files from one folder to another, and its syntax is

```
FSys.MoveFile source, destination
```

in which *source* is the path of the file(s) to be moved and *destination* is the path to which the file(s) will be moved. The MoveFile method works identically to the Copy method, but the original files are deleted after they are copied. The *source* argument string can contain wildcard characters to move multiple files, but the *destination* argument can't contain wildcard characters. If you're copying a single file, the *destination* argument can be either a filename or a folder name (in which case, the file is moved to the specified folder). If you're copying multiple files, the destination must be a folder's path, to which the files will be moved. If the *destination* is an existing file's name or an existing folder's name, an error occurs.

MoveFolder   This method moves a folder to another location. Its syntax is

```
FSys.MoveFolder source, destination
```

in which *source* and *destination* are the specifications of the source and destination folders.

FileExists, FolderExists   These two methods return True if the specified file or folder exists. Use them to make sure a file or folder exists before attempting to use it from within your script. Their syntax is

```
FSys.FileExists(fileSpec)
```

and

```
FSys.FolderExists(folderSpec)
```

GetFile, GetFolder   These methods return a File and Folder object, which represent a specific file or folder.

NOTE
The GetFile method doesn't return the entire file, nor does it return the name of the file. It's a reference to a file through which you can access the file's properties. I'll discuss the File and Folder objects later in this chapter.

To create a *File* object variable with the GetFile method, you first create a *FileSystemObject* object variable and then call its GetFile method:

```
Set thisFile = FSys.GetFile("c:\autoexec.bat")
```

The variable *thisFile* represents the file AUTOEXEC.BAT, and you can use its properties and methods to manipulate the file. For example, you can use its Size property to find out the file's size, its DateCreated property to find out when the file was created, and so on. I'll discuss the properties and methods of the File object in the "The File Object" section, later in this chapter.

The GetFolder method is quite similar to the GetFile method, only it returns a Folder object. The argument of the GetFolder method must be an absolute or relative path name:

```
Set thisFolder = FSys.GetFolder("c:\windows\desktop")
```

The variable *thisFolder* represents the Desktop, and you can use its properties and methods to manipulate the Desktop folder. For example, you can use its Size property to find out the size of a folder (including its subfolders), its DateCreated property to find out when the folder was created, and so on. I'll describe the properties and methods of the Folder object in "The Folder Object" section, later in this chapter.

GetFileName   This method returns the last component of specified path, which is a filename with its extension. The GetFileName method is usually called with a File object as an argument, to retrieve the filename. Without the GetFileName method, you'd have to provide your own routine for parsing the path name.

NOTE

The GetFileName method works on its argument, regardless of whether such a path exists.

The Files Collection

The Files Collection contains a File object for each file in a folder. The following script iterates through the files of a specific folder using the For Each...Next statement:

```
Set ThisFolder = FSys.GetFolder(folderName)
Set AllFiles = ThisFolder.Files
For Each file in AllFiles
    {process current file}
Next
```

In the loop's body, you can access the properties of the current file. Its name is file.Name, its creation date is file.DateCreated, and so on. In the following sections, we'll look at the properties and methods of the File object.

The File Object

The File object represents a file and provides properties, which represent the properties of the actual file, and methods, which let you copy, move, and delete files.

To obtain a File object and examine its properties, follow these steps:

1. Create a *FileSystemObject* variable either by declaring it,

    ```
    Dim FSys As New FileSystemObject
    ```

    or by calling the CreateObject() function:

    ```
    Set FSys = CreateObject("Scripting.FileSystemObject")
    ```

2. Use the *FSys* variable to obtain an object that represents a specific file,

    ```
    Set file = FSys.GetFile(fileName)
    ```

    in which *fileName* is the file's path name (c:\Images\ Sky.bmp, for example).

3. Now, access the file's properties through the *file* object variable:

    ```
    FName = file.Name
    FDate = file.DateCreated
    FSize = file.Size
    ```

Next, we are going to look at the properties of the File object.

The File Object's Properties

The File object provides the following properties. Many of these properties apply to the Folder object as well, which is discussed in "The Folder Object" section, later in this chapter.

Attributes   You use this property to read or set a file's attributes. To read the attributes of a file, use the syntax

```
thisFile.Attributes
```

You can also set selected attributes using the syntax

```
thisFile.Attributes = thisFile.Attributes Or new_attribute
```

The *new_attribute* variable can have any of the values shown in Table 10.2. To change multiple attributes, combine the corresponding values with the logical OR operator. The statement

```
thisFile.Attributes = new_attribute
```

will turn on a specific attribute, but it will clear all other attributes. If a file is read-only and hidden, its Attributes property is 3 (1+2 according to Table 10.2). If you attempt to turn on the Archive attribute by setting its Attributes property to 32, the other two attributes will be cleared. By combining the new attribute (32) and the existing attributes with the OR operator, the file will be Read-only, Hidden, and Archive.

Table 10.2: The Values of the *new_attribute* Variable

CONSTANT	VALUE	DESCRIPTION
Normal	0	Normal file
ReadOnly	1	Read-only file
Hidden	2	Hidden file
System	4	System file
Volume	8	Disk drive volume label
Directory	16	Folder or directory
Archive	32	File has changed since last backup
Alias	64	Link or shortcut
Compressed	128	Compressed file

To find out whether a file is read-only, use this statement:

```
If thisFile.Attributes and 32 Then
    MsgBox "Read-only file"
End If
```

You can also use the MsgBox() function to prompt the user to change the read-only attribute:

```
If thisFile.Attributes And 32 Then
    reply = MsgBox("This is a read-only file. _
        Delete it anyway?", vbYesNo)
    If reply = vbYes Then
        thisFile.Attributes = thisFile.Attributes + 32
Else
    thisFile.Delete
End If
```

Part iii

Delete is a method of the File object, which deletes the specific file. See the "Delete" section later in this chapter for its syntax.

Normally, when you set a file's attributes, you don't reset its existing attributes. For example, you can choose to add the Hidden attribute from a file that has its ReadOnly attribute set. To turn on the Hidden attribute without affecting the other attributes, use a statement such as

```
thisFile.Attributes = aFile.Attributes + 2
```

or

```
thisFile.Attributes = aFile.Attributes Or 2
```

To remove a specific attribute, first find out whether this attribute is already set, and then subtract its value for the Attributes property's value. To remove the Hidden attribute, use a structure like the following:

```
If thisFile.Attributes And 2 Then
   thisFile.Attributes = thisFile.Attributes - 2
End If
```

DateCreated   This property returns the date and time that the specified file or folder was created, and it's read-only. To retrieve the date a specific file was created, use the syntax

```
thisFile.DateCreated
```

The following code segment calculates the age of a file in days. You can calculate the file's age in any other time interval by multiplying or dividing the file's age in days by the appropriate constant.

```
Set thisFile = FSys.GetFile("c:\windows\Explorer.exe")
DateCreated = thisFile.DateCreated
MsgBox Int(Now() - DateCreated)
```

To express this difference in hours, divide the difference by 24.

DateLastAccessed   This property returns the date and time that the specified file or folder was last accessed. The DateLastAccessed property is identical in its use to the DateCreated property.

DateLastModified   This property returns the date and time that the specified file or folder was last modified. The DateLastModified property is identical in its use to the DateCreated property.

NOTE

The DateCreated, DateLastAccessed, and DateLastModified properties are read-only. Sometimes, we need to "touch" the files in a folder (change the DateLast-Accessed property). If you are using scripts or another automated mechanism for deleting or moving old files, touching them will enable you to exclude certain files from an automatic deletion operation. It would be convenient to touch a file by changing the value of its DateLastAccessed property, but this is impossible. To change the DateLastAccessed property, you should copy the file, delete the original, and then rename the copied file back to the name of the original file.

Drive   This property returns the drive letter of the drive on which the specified file or folder resides. It's read-only, and its syntax is

```
object.Drive
```

in which *object* is always a File or Folder object.

Name   This property returns or sets the name of a file or folder (the last part of the path). To find out the name of a file, use the following statement:

```
FileObject.Name
```

To rename an existing file (or folder), use the following syntax

```
FileObject.Name = new_name
```

in which *newname* is the new name of the file represented by the *File-Object* variable (or the corresponding *Folder object variable)*.

ParentFolder   This property returns a Folder object, which represents the parent folder of the specified file or folder. The ParentFolder property is read-only.

Path   This property returns the path for a specified file or folder. If the file resides in the root folder, the backslash character (\)is not included. In other words, the path for the file C:\Autoexec.bat is "C:" and not "C:\".

If the *FileObject* object variable represents the file c:\windows\desktop\TOC.doc, the expression FileObject.Path returns the string "c:\windows\desktop", and the expression FileObject.Name returns the string "TOC.doc".

ShortName   This property is similar to the Name property, but it returns the short name (8.3 convention) of the specified file or folder.

Size   When applied to File objects, this property returns the size, in bytes, of the specified file. For folders, it returns the size, in bytes, of all files and subfolders contained in the folder.

Type   This property returns information about the type of a file or folder. For example, for files ending in .TXT, the string "Text Document" is returned.

The File Object's Methods

The File object provides a number of methods for moving files around, and they are similar to the methods of the FileSystemObject object. The difference between the methods of the FileSystemObject object and those of the File object is that you can't operate on multiple files at once with the File object's methods. Each method applies to a specific file only.

Copy   This method copies a file (or folder) from one location to another. Its syntax is

```
FileObject.Copy destination, overwrite
```

in which *destination* is the new name or folder of the file and may not contain wildcard characters. The second argument, *overwrite*, is optional, and it's a Boolean value that indicates whether existing files or folders are to be overwritten (if True) or not (if False).

Delete   This method deletes a file (or folder). Its syntax is the following:

```
FileObject.Delete force
```

The *force* argument is optional and indicates whether files with their read-only attributes should be deleted anyway (if True) or not (if False). Unlike the DOS RMDIR command, the Delete method removes a folder regardless of whether it contains files or subfolders.

Move   This method moves a file to a new location (it's equivalent to copying the file to a new location and then deleting the original file). Its syntax is

```
FileObject.Move destination
```

in which *destination* is the path to which the file is moved. If the *destination* argument is a folder name, the file is moved to the specified folder with the same name. If the *destination* argument also contains a filename, the file is moved and renamed. You can call the Move method with a different filename to simply rename the original file.

OpenAsTextStream This method opens a specified file and returns a TextStream object that can be used to read from or write to the file. Its syntax is the following:

```
FileObject.OpenAsTextStream(iomode, format)
```

Both arguments are optional. The *iomode* argument specifies whether the file will be opened as input, output, or appending, and it can have one of the values shown in Table 10.3.

TABLE 10.3: The Settings of the *iomode* Argument of the OpenAsTextStream Method

CONSTANT	VALUE	DESCRIPTION
ForReading	1	Opens a file for reading only; you can't write to this file
ForWriting	2	Opens a file for writing; if a file with the same name exists, its previous contents are overwritten
ForAppending	8	Opens a file and writes to the end of the file

The second argument, *format,* indicates whether the file should be opened as Unicode or ASCII, and it can have one of the values shown in Table 10.4.

The OpenAsTextStream method does the same thing as the Open-TextFile method of the FileSystemObject object. They both prepare a file for input or output. Use the OpenAsTextStream method when you have an object variable that represents the file you want to open. If you know the name of the file, use the OpenTextFile method of the FileSystem-Object object.

TABLE 10.4: The Settings of the *format* Argument of the OpenAsTextStream Method

VALUE	DESCRIPTION
–2	Opens the file using the system default
–1	Opens the file as Unicode
0	Opens the file as ASCII

Part iii

VB6 at Work: The FileMover Project

The FileMover project demonstrates how to manipulate multiple files using the FileSystemObject object's methods.

NOTE

The FileMover project, along with other projects and scripts discussed in this chapter, can be found at the Sybex Web site (www.sybex.com). Once there, go to the Catalog page and enter **2469** (the first four digits of the last five in the book's ISBN) into the search engine. Follow the link for this book that comes up, and then click the Downloads button, which will take you to a list of files organized by chapter.

On the Form in Figure 10.2, the user can select any folder on any disk and see its files in the FileListBox control. Any file can be dragged to the ListBox at the bottom of the Form. This list can be populated with filenames from multiple folders, since it stores the full path names of the files. After selecting the files in the ListBox control, the user can copy them with the Copy Selected Files button.

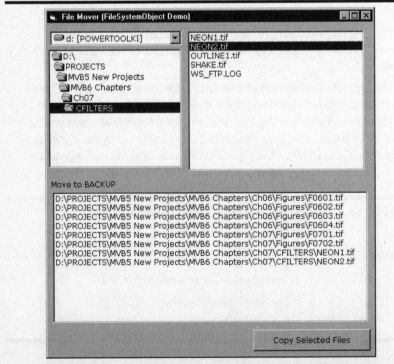

FIGURE 10.2:   The FileMover project uses the FileSystemObject object to move the selected files to the same folder.

Each time the user drags an item from the FileListBox control, the program drags the outline of a small TextBox control that matches the size of a single item in the list. At all other times, the TextBox control remains hidden. You can open the project in the Visual Basic IDE and examine the application's code. This is another situation where you can't use the Common Dialogs control; you must build your own Form with the FileSystem controls.

The Command button copies the files stored in the ListBox control to the folder D:\BACKUP. The name of the destination folder is hardcoded in the project, so you must edit this subroutine before testing the application.

Code 10.3: Moving the Selected Files

```
Private Sub Command1_Click()
Dim FSys As New FileSystemObject
Dim thisFile As File
Dim i As Integer

   For i = 0 To TEMPList.ListCount - 1
     Set thisFile = FSys.GetFile(TEMPList.List(i))
' NOTICE: THE FOLDER D:\backup MUST EXIST!
     If Not (thisFile Is Nothing) Then
        thisFile.Copy "D:\BACKUP\" & thisFile.Name
     End If
   Next
End Sub
```

The code scans all the files in the list and uses the GetFile method to create the *thisFile* object variable that references the current file. The GetFileMethod accepts the path name of a file and returns a reference to this file. Notice that the GetFile method returns a reference to a file, not the file's name or its contents. Through the *thisFile* variable, we can manipulate the file. The FMover project copies the selected files, since this is the least dangerous operation for testing purposes.

You can move or delete the file, by calling a different method of the variable *thisFolder*. Or, you can further process the file based on its type, date stamp, and other attributes. For example, you can create a new folder for each ZIP file and call the PKUNZIP application to extract the contents of the ZIP file to the folder by the same name. (To start another application from within your VB code, call the Shell() function, which is described in the Language Reference at the end of this book.)

The Folders Collection

The Folders collection contains a Folder object for each subfolder in a folder. The following script iterates through the subfolders of a specific folder using the For Each...Next statement:

```
Set FSys = CreateObject("Scripting.FileSystemObject")
Set ThisFolder = FSys.GetFolder(folderName)
Set AllFolders = ThisFolder.SubFolders
For Each folder in AllFolders
  {process current folder}
Next
```

In the loop's body you can access the properties of the current folder. Its name is folder.Name, its creation date is folder.DateCreated, and so on.

The various properties of the Folder object are described next. But first, let's look at the AddFolder method, the Folder object's single method.

AddFolder   This method adds a new Folder object to a Folders collection, and its syntax is

```
FolderObject.AddFolders folderName
```

in which *folderName* is the name of the new folder to be added.

The Folder Object

This object represents a folder on a disk; it allows you to manipulate the actual folders on your disk through its properties and methods. To create a Folder object, you first create a *FileSystemObject* object variable, and then you call its GetFolder method, using the folder's path as an argument:

```
Set FSys = CreateObject("Scripting.FileSystemObject")
Set thisFolder = FSys.GetFolder("c:\windows\desktop")
```

After these lines execute, the variable *thisFolder* represents the folder c:\windows\desktop, and you can manipulate the folder through the variable's properties and objects.

I'll discuss the Folder object's properties next. Since many of these properties are quite similar to corresponding properties of the File object, I'll just mention them briefly and focus on the unique properties of the Folder object.

Attributes   This property returns or sets the attributes of files or folders. See the discussion of the Attributes property of the File object for more information on using this property.

DateCreated   This property returns the date and time that the specified file or folder was created, and it's read-only.

DateLastAccessed, DateLastModified   These properties return the date and time that the specified file or folder was last accessed or modified, and they are read-only.

Drive   This property returns the letter of the drive on which the specified file or folder resides, and it's read-only.

ParentFolder   This property returns the parent folder of a Folder object. See the discussion of the IsRootFolder property for an example.

IsRootFolder   This property returns True if the specified folder is the root folder; otherwise, it returns False. There is no equivalent property for the File object. You can use the RootFolder property to calculate the depth of a folder, with a subroutine such as the following:

```
Sub GetDepth(FolderObject)
If FolderObject.IsRootFolder Then
    MsgBox "The specified folder is the root folder."
Else
  Do Until FolderObject.IsRootFolder
    Set FolderObject = FolderObject.ParentFolder
    fdepth = fdepth + 1
  Loop
  MsgBox "The specified folder is " & fdepth & " levels
deep."
End If
End Sub
```

Name   This property returns the name of a specified file or folder (the last part of the folder's path name). See the Name property of the File object for details on using this property.

Path   This property returns the path of a specified file or folder (the folder's path name without the last part). See the Path property of the File object for details on using this property.

ShortName   This property returns the short folder name (8.3 convention) of a Folder or File object.

ShortPath   This property returns the short path name (8.3 convention) of a Folder or File object.

Size   Size is a property of both files and folders, and it returns the size (in bytes) of a file, or it returns the total size of all the files in a folder and its subfolders. To find out the size of a file or a folder, you first create the appropriate File or Folder object variable and then read the variable's Size property:

```
Set FSys = CreateObject("Scripting.FileSystemObject")
Set thisFile = FSys.GetFile("c:\windows\desktop\Message.doc")
MsgBox "The MESSAGE.DOC file is " & _
    thisFile.Size & " bytes long."
Set thisFolder = FSys.GetFolder("c:\windows\")
MsgBox "The WINDOWS folder's size is " & _
    thisFolder.Size \ (1024*1024) & " MB."
```

The Subfolders Collection

The Subfolders property returns a Subfolders collection, which contains all the subfolders of a specific folder. To obtain the collection of subfolders in the folder C:\WINDOWS, create a *FileSystemObject* variable, use its GetFolder method to obtain a reference to the specific folder, and then create a Collection with its subfolders, using the SubFolders property, as shown in the following statements:

```
Set FSys = CreateObject("Scripting.FileSystemObject")
Set thisFolder = FSys.GetFolder("c:\windows")
Set allFolders = aFolder.SubFolders
For Each subFolder in allFolders
  {process folder subFolder}
Next
```

To scan the subfolder under the specified folder, use a For Each...Next statement, as shown in the above listing. The current folder's name in the loop's body is subFolder.Name. The processing of the current folder could be to examine its files, and this is exactly what we are going to do next.

Scanning a Folder Recursively

Scanning a folder recursively (that is, scanning the folder's files and its subfolders' files to any depth) is a common operation in programming the file system. (This is accomplished with the standard File System controls—the DriveListBox, DirectoryListBox, and FileListBox controls.) An application can populate a TreeView control with the contents of a drive or a folder. The tree structure is ideal for representing a folder because the folder itself has a tree structure.

In this section, I'm going to discuss the FSystem application, which populates a TreeView control with the folders of the C: drive. Change the name of the root directory in the code to map any drive or folder. The Form of the FSystem application is shown in Figure 10.3. Run the application, and click the Populate Tree button to map the folder structure of drive C: on the TreeView control. How long the application takes to map the entire drive depends on how many folders exist in your root drive. So, be patient, or change the code to map a smaller section of the drive.

To help you follow the code and experiment with it, I will start with a simpler version of the application, which prints the folder names in the Immediate window. We'll then replace the Debug.Print statements with the appropriate statements to add the folder names to the TreeView control.

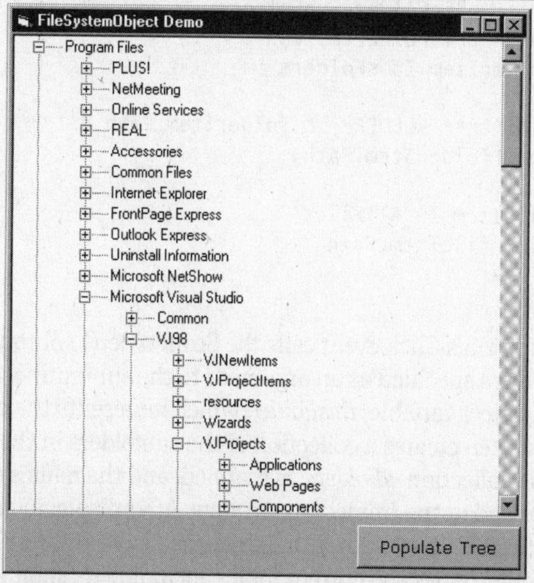

FIGURE 10.3: The FSystem application demonstrates some of the FileSystemObject object's methods and the TreeView control.

Part iii

Code 10.4:   Scanning a Drive with the FileSystemObject Object

```
Dim FSys As New Scripting.FileSystemObject

Private Sub Command1_Click()
Dim folderSpec As String

  Set FSys = CreateObject("Scripting.FileSystemObject")
  ' Specify the folder you wish to map in the following line
  folderSpec = "C:\"
  ScanFolder (folderSpec)
  Debug.Print "*** END OF DIRECTORY LISTING ***"
End Sub

Sub ScanFolder(folderSpec As String)
Dim thisFolder As Folder
Dim sFolders As Folders
Dim fileItem As File, folderItem As Folder
Dim AllFiles As Files

  Set thisFolder = FSys.GetFolder(folderSpec)
  Set sFolders = thisFolder.SubFolders
  Set AllFiles = thisFolder.Files
  For Each folderItem In sFolders
    Debug.Print
    Debug.Print "*** FOLDER " & folderItem.Path & "***"
    ScanFolder (folderItem.Path)
  Next
  For Each fileItem In AllFiles
    Debug.Print fileItem.Path
  Next
End Sub
```

The Command button's Click event calls the ScanFolder() subroutine to scan the folder that's specified as an argument to the subroutine. ScanFolder() creates an object variable, *thisFolder*, which represents the current folder. The program then creates a collection of the subfolders in the folder being scanned. This collection, *sFolders*, is scanned, and the names of the subfolders are displayed in the Immediate window. After displaying each folder's name, the ScanFolder() subroutine calls itself to scan the subfolders of the current folder. After the current folder, including its subfolders, has been scanned, the program goes ahead and displays the files in the current folder by iterating through the *AllFiles* collection.

In the version of the FSystem application you'll find on the Sybex Web site, I've commented out the statements that display in the Immediate window and added the statements to add the names of the folders and files to the TreeView control.

Code 10.5: Populating the TreeView Control

```
Dim FSys As New Scripting.FileSystemObject

Private Sub Command1_Click()
Dim folderSpec As String

  Set FSys = CreateObject("Scripting.FileSystemObject")
  ' Specify the folder you wish to map in the following line
  folderSpec = "C:\wind"
  folderSpec = UCase(folderSpec)
  TreeView1.Nodes.Add , , folderSpec, folderSpec
  Screen.MousePointer = vbHourglass
  ScanFolder (folderSpec)
  Screen.MousePointer = vbDefault
  TreeView1.Nodes(1).Expanded = True
  MsgBox "File List created"
End Sub


Sub ScanFolder(folderSpec As String)
Dim thisFolder As Folder
Dim sFolders As Folders
Dim fileItem As File, folderItem As Folder
Dim AllFiles As Files

  Set thisFolder = FSys.GetFolder(folderSpec)
  Set sFolders = thisFolder.SubFolders
  Set AllFiles = thisFolder.Files
  For Each folderItem In sFolders
    TreeView1.Nodes.Add folderItem.ParentFolder.Path, _
        tvwChild, folderItem.Path, folderItem.Name
    ScanFolder (folderItem.Path)
  Next
  For Each fileItem In AllFiles
    TreeView1.Nodes.Add fileItem.ParentFolder.Path, _
        tvwChild, fileItem.Path, fileItem.Name
  Next

End Sub
```

Notice how the Add method of the TreeView control adds the folder and filenames to the proper location in the tree. Each folder node is a child of the parent folder's node. The expression `folderItem.ParentFolder.Path` is the path name of the folderItem node's parent node. Likewise, the expression `fileItem.Path` is the current file's path name and it's used as the node's key. In other words, each item's key is its path name, so the keys of identically named files in different folders will end up in the proper place in the tree.

You can easily modify the code of the FSystem project to populate the TreeView control not with all filenames but with only the names of selected files. The selection can be based on the attributes of the files, such as their size, type, date stamp, and so on. For example, you can select only image files whose size exceeds 100Kb. Or you can select text files that haven't been accessed in a month, and so on.

THE SCRIPT CONTROL

In addition to scripting Web pages, you can use VBScript to script Visual Basic applications. You can embed the functionality of VBScript in your applications with the help of the Script control, which was released several months before Visual Basic 6. For the purposes of this book, I downloaded the Script control from Microsoft's Web site, at `http://www.microsoft.com/scripting`. At the same URL, you will find additional documentation on the control and samples. As of this writing, the documentation is sketchy, and the control itself has a few quirks, but scripting Visual Basic applications is an exciting new development, which I couldn't ignore.

So, what can the Script control do for your applications? To begin with, it can evaluate expressions at runtime. Since the Script control can be manipulated from within your application's code, these expressions can be created at runtime (something you can't do with your application's code).

Let's say you want to develop a math calculator that evaluates math expressions. Visual Basic can evaluate any math expression, as long as the expression is entered at design time. Let's say the user of your application needs to evaluate a math expression such as `99.9/log(2.5)` at runtime or plot an expression such as `9*sin(x)/cos(x)`. How would you handle this situation with Visual Basic? Unless you're willing to duplicate the expression evaluation capabilities of Visual Basic (in other words implement your own component that evaluates expressions), not much.

Later in this chapter, we'll revise the Graph application so that it can plot any function supplied by the user at runtime. This is the type of functionality the Script control can bring to your application. It allows you to furnish a math expression and ask it to evaluate the expression and return the result. The Script control can evaluate more than math expressions. It can evaluate logical expressions, adjust its course of action based on the result, and execute statements repeatedly. You can use the entire repertoire of VBScript statements and functions with the Script control. For example, you might want to plot the envelope of two functions (evaluate both functions and plot the maximum value at each point). Here's the VBScript code that evaluates the maximum of two functions:

```
Val1= sin(x)/cos(x)
Val2 = cos(x)/atn(1/x)
If Val1 > Val2 Then
    Envelope = Val1
Else
    Envelope = Val2
End If
```

The program will use the value *Envelope* to generate the plot. The user can enter the above code at runtime, and it need not be embedded in the application's source code.

If your application exposes an object model (something like Word's or Excel's objects, which let you manipulate the application behind the scenes), users can script the application by supplying the appropriate VBScript statements. Office applications are programmed with VBA, but VBA is a full-blown language, can't be easily incorporated in an application, and is very costly. Although very few applications incorporate VBA, a host of applications come with their own scripting languages, which users can deploy to automate operations. The problem with these applications is the multitude of scripting languages. With VBA and VBScript or JavaScript, manufacturers will probably standardize the scripting capabilities of their products and even small applications will be scriptable.

According to the documentation, VBScript is recommended for moderately sized applications (1 to 2MB) and only if you are willing to trade some performance for simplicity. VBScript is an interpreted language and can't match the speed of compiled VB applications. Even worse, VBScript is a typeless language, which means that all its variables are stored internally as variants. This entails a considerable performance penalty, as all variables must be converted to the proper type before they can be used in calculations. Another ramification of a typeless language is that objects can't be early-bound. So, VBScript is not for performance; it's for your convenience only. As you'll see, deploying VBScript with the Script control is straightforward and far simpler than VBA.

Using the Script Control

The Script control has a very simple design philosophy: it stores procedures and can execute any of them at any time. In addition, it can evaluate isolated expressions and return the result. Let's exercise the Script control with a few simple examples.

To use the Script control in a project, you must first add it to the Toolbox. Follow these steps:

1. Start a new project.

2. Right-click the Toolbox, and from the shortcut menu, select Components to open the Components dialog box.

3. Check the Microsoft Script Control 1.0 option (or a newer version, should one become available by the time VB6 is released) and click OK.

4. Once the control is added to the Toolbox, place an instance of the control on the Form.

Let's start by listing the most important members of the Script control, which we'll use momentarily in the examples.

The ExecuteStatement Method

This method executes a single statement and returns the result. It accepts a single argument, which is the statement to be executed. Here's a valid VBScript statement:

```
MsgBox "Programmers of the world unite!"
```

To execute it (and display the string in a message box), you pass the entire statement to the ExecuteStatement method:

```
statement = "MsgBox " & Chr(34) & _
        "Programmers of the world unite!" & Chr(34)
ScriptControl1.ExecuteStatement statement
```

The expression Chr(34) inserts a double quote into a string variable. Another technique is to use two consecutive double quote characters and combine the two statements into one:

```
ScriptControl1.ExecuteStatement _
        "MsgBox ""Welcome to VBScript!"""
```

ExecuteStatement isn't limited to a single function call. Similar to Visual Basic, VBScript lets you place multiple statements in a single line, as long as you separate them with colons. Here's a short VBScript code segment (which is also a VB code segment):

```
X=InputBox("Enter a value from 0 to 5")
If X=3 Then
   X=X+1
Else
   X=X-1
End If
MsgBox "The value of X is: " & X
```

If you execute this VBScript code, you'll be prompted to enter a numeric value. The code will display a new value that is 1 smaller than the value you enter, unless the original value is 3, in which case the value 4 will be displayed. To insert all the statements and execute them with the ExecuteStatement method, place a new Command button on the Form and enter the following code in its Click event handler:

```
Private Sub Command2_Click()
   ScriptControl1.ExecuteStatement "X=InputBox(""Enter a _
      value from 0 to 5""):If X=3 Then X=X+1: Else _
      X=X-1: End If: MsgBox ""The value of X is: "" & X "
End Sub
```

The ExecuteStatement method's argument is created by appending consecutive statements and separating them with a colon. You must enclose the entire argument in double quotes, and you must replace the double quotes in the code with two consecutive double quote characters.

Obviously, this is not the best method for passing long statements to be executed to the Script control. It's best to create a string variable with the statement to be executed and then pass a string variable to the Execute-Statement method. Here's a clearer coding of the last example:

```
Private Sub Command2_Click()
   script = ""
   script = script & "X=InputBox(""Enter a value _
      from 0 to 5""):"
   script = script & " If X=3 Then X=X+1:"
   script = script & " Else X=X-1:"
   script = script & "End If: "
   script = script & "MsgBox ""The value of X _
      is: "" & X "
   ScriptControl1.ExecuteStatement script
End Sub
```

Part iii

The AddCode and Run Methods

Executing simple statements with the Script control is an interesting exercise, but in a practical situation you need to execute more than a simple statement. The Script control can store large segments of code, similar to a Code Module of a Visual Basic project, and execute them at will.

To add one or more procedures to the Script control, use the AddCode method, which accepts a string argument with the code. The code you add to the control may contain Modules (subroutines and functions), and you can later call one of them by name, with the Run method. Here's a simple script that contains a subroutine, which in turn calls a function:

```
Sub Main()
   MsgBox "28908 in hexadecimal notation is " &
IntToHex(28908)
End Sub

Function IntToHex(Decimal)
   IntToHex=Hex(Decimal)
End Function
```

The Main() subroutine calls the IntToHex() function to convert a decimal value to hexadecimal notation and display the results in a message box.

There's no need to write a separate function to convert decimal values to hexadecimal notation because this is a simple example meant to demonstrate the Script control's methods. You can provide your own routines to convert temperatures, if you haven't developed an allergy to the temperature conversion example yet. Place a third Command button on the Form and enter the following code in its Click event's handler:

```
Private Sub Command3_Click()
script = "Sub Main()" & vbCrLf & _
   " MsgBox ""28908 in hexadecimal notation is "" & _
    IntToHex(28908)" & vbCrLf & _
   "End Sub" & vbCrLf & _
   "Function IntToHex(Decimal)" & vbCrLf & _
   " IntToHex=Hex(Decimal)" & vbCrLf & _
   "End Function" & vbCrLf
ScriptControl1.AddCode script
ScriptControl1.Run "Main"
End Sub
```

Run the project, click the third Command button, and you'll see the value 70EC in a message box. The statement `ScriptControl1.AddCode` adds the code segment to the control (it's stored internally in a format that you don't have to know). Then, the Run method calls the Main() subroutine by name. The syntax of the Run method is

```
ScriptControl1.Run procedure_name, param_array()
```

in which *procedure_name* is the name of the procedure you want to invoke, and *param_array* is an array that holds the parameters to be passed to the procedure. The second argument is optional, as in the case of the above example.

You can also invoke the IntToHex() function directly with the Run method. Comment out the line that invokes the Run method in the last example, and enter the following one:

```
ScriptControl1.ExecuteStatement "MsgBox IntToHex(3432)"
```

The value D68 will appear in a message box (the hexadecimal equivalent of the integer 3432).

As you may have guessed, the best way to add procedures to a Script control is to enter the statements in a TextBox control and then add the TextBox control's Text property to the Script control. Later in this chapter, we are going to build an application that lets the user enter scripts with the help of a TextBox control and execute them. But first, let's see some of the Script control's simpler, yet extremely valuable applications.

VB6 at Work: The Graph Project

To demonstrate the Script control, we'll revise an application—the Graph application—I've developed. The Graph application, shown in Figure 10.4, draws one or both of the two functions whose definitions appear at the top of the Form. The original Graph application always plots the same two functions, whose definitions are hardcoded into the application. The revised Graph application allows the user to specify the functions to be plotted. (Both versions of the Graph application can be downloaded from the Sybex Web site.)

Open the original Graph application, and save its Form and the project itself to a new folder. After the Script control is added to the project, place an instance of the control on the Form. It doesn't make any difference where you place the control on the Form or its size, because the Script control remains invisible at runtime.

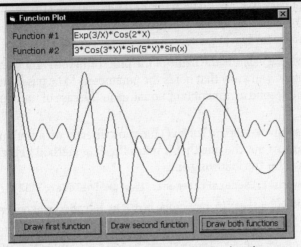

FIGURE 10.4:   The revised Graph application lets the user specify the functions to be plotted at runtime.

The code behind the buttons plots the corresponding functions by calling the functions FunctionEval1() and FunctionEval2(). These functions return the value of the two functions shown at the top of the Form for a specific value of *X*. If you replace the definitions of these function with the following code, you can plot any user-supplied function.

Code 10.6:   Evaluation Math Expressions at Runtime

```
Function FunctionEval1(ByVal X As Double) As Double
    ScriptControl1.ExecuteStatement "X=" & X
    FunctionEval1 = ScriptControl1.Eval(Trim(Text1.Text))
End Function
Function FunctionEval2(ByVal X As Double) As Double
    ScriptControl1.AddCode "X=" & X
    FunctionEval2 = ScriptControl1.Eval(Trim(Text2.Text))
End Function
```

The revised functions can evaluate any expression entered by the user in the TextBox controls at the top of the Form. The remaining code, which I will not repeat here, plots these expressions.

Notice that the FunctionEval1() and FunctionEval2() functions do not contain error handlers. Even if you caught an error in these functions, what could you do? The rest of the code would keep calling them anyway (the code that plots the first expression calls the FunctionEval1() function once for each point along the x axis). The error trap is in the code that actually plots the functions. Errors don't need to be caught as soon as they occur. If the procedure in which an error occurs doesn't trap the error, the procedure that called it may trap it with its own error handler.

If you open the Graph project and examine its code, you'll see that I've inserted an error trap in the Click event handlers of the Command buttons with the statement:

```
On Error GoTo FncError
```

The FncError error handler displays a message indicating that an error occurred and exits:

```
FncError:
    MsgBox "There was an error in evaluating the function"
    Screen.MousePointer = vbDefault
```

This error handler allows us to break the loop that plots the function. Had I caught the error in the FunctionEval1() function, for example, I wouldn't be able to stop the plotting, and the same error would probably come up for all consecutive points.

VB6 at Work: The Script Editor Project

The Script Editor project (available on the Sybex Web site) consists of a single Form with two TextBox controls on it (see Figure 10.5). In the upper box, the user can enter VBScript code and execute it by clicking the Execute Script button. The script must contain a Main() subroutine, which is invoked with the Script control's Run method. The Main() subroutine may call any other procedure.

The script can communicate with the user through the usual message boxes or through the lower textbox. To display something on this textbox, use the Show method, whose syntax is

```
Show "The file's size is " & Fsize & " bytes"
```

You'll see shortly how the Show method is implemented. In the meantime, you can simply use it to place information in the lower textbox, just like Visual Basic's Debug.Print method.

The code behind the Execute Script button adds the code in the upper textbox to the Script control with the AddCode method and then executes the script by calling the Main procedure.

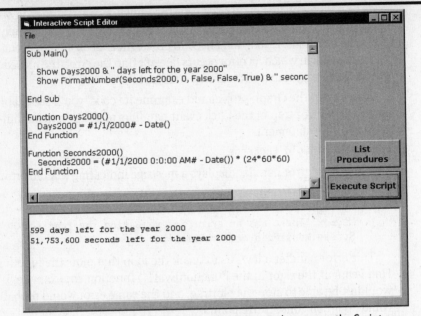

FIGURE 10.5: The SEditor application demonstrates how to use the Script control to add scripting capabilities to your applications.

Code 10.7: The Execute Script Button

```
Private Sub bttnExecute_Click()
On Error GoTo CodeError
   ScriptControl1.AddCode Text1.Text
   ScriptControl1.Run "Main"
   Exit Sub
CodeError:
   If ScriptControl1.Error.Number <> 0 Then
     msg = ScriptControl1.Error.Description & bvcrlf
     msg = msg & "In line " & ScriptControl1.Error.Line _
        & ", column " & ScriptControl1.Error.Column
     MsgBox msg, , "Error in script"
   Else
     MsgBox "ERROR # " & Err.Number & vbCrLf & Err.Description
   End If
End Sub
```

The code that executes the script consists of two simple statements. The error-handling code is longer, but I'll cover the topic of error handling during script execution later in this chapter (see the section "Handling Errors").

Error handling is the Script control's weakest point. Only a few syntax errors will be identified correctly. For example, if you enter a statement such as

```
Limit == 99
```

you'll get a descriptive error message:

```
Syntax errror in Line 2, column 7
```

Most errors, however, generate a general automation error message, and there is no way to extract more information about the line where the error occurred. If you call a nonexistent function, such as Dates() instead of Date(), or if you call a function with the wrong number of arguments, you will see the message "Automation error", because this is all the information the Script control provides.

Run the SEdit application, and execute a few simple scripts by inserting the proper code between the Sub Main() and End Sub statements.

WARNING

When it comes to debugging, you're literally on your own.

To experiment with the Script control, I've included a few scripts with the SEditor application, and you can load them by choosing File ➢ Load after you've downloaded them. You can also save your scripts to disk by choosing File ➢ Save. The Excel script, for example, contacts Excel to perform a calculation and demonstrates how to contact other applications from within VBScript and automate them. Here's the Excel script's code. To contact an OLE server, you must first create an object variable with the CreateObject() function, and then you call the variable's methods and properties to contact the server.

Part iii

Code 10.8:   Contacting Excel from a Script

```
Sub Main()

    Set EXL = CreateObject("Excel.Application")
    Show EXL.Evaluate("Log(99)")
    Set EXL = Nothing
End Sub
```

Scripting ActiveX Objects

The most powerful feature of the Script control, which makes it possible to use this control to add scripting capabilities to an application, is its ability to manipulate ActiveX components. In the example in the last section, you saw how to create object variables to access OLE servers such as Excel. If your application uses Classes, it is possible to access them with a VBScript control. All you have to do is create an instance of the Class (or multiple Classes) and store them in the Script control. Then, the properties and methods of the Class can be accessed through an object variable, as if they were VBScript commands.

To add an object to the Script control, use the *AddObject* method, whose syntax is shown here:

```
ScriptControl1.AddObject Name, Object, members
```

The first argument, *Name*, is the name by which the Class can be accessed from within the script, and it's a string variable. The second argument, *Object*, is the actual name of the Class. Let's say your application exposes the DisplayClass Class. To add this Class to a Script control, create an object variable such as the following:

```
Private Display As New DisplayClass
```

Then use a statement like this:

```
ScriptControl1.AddObject "Output", Display
```

After the execution of this statement (which usually appears in a Form's Load event), the script can access the members of the Display-Class Class through the *Output* object variable. If the Display Class exposes a Show method, any script can access this method as

```
Output.Show "some message"
```

(The Show method displays a message in the Form's lower textbox.)

The last (optional) argument, *members*, is a Boolean value that indicates whether the members of the Class should be accessed through an object variable. Class members are always accessed through an object variable. If you set the *members* argument to True, the members of the Class can be accessed by name, as if they were VBScript functions. If you add the Display Class to a Script control with the following statement,

```
ScriptControl1.AddObject "Output", Display, True
```

you can access the Show method of the Class from within the script without the object variable's name:

```
Show "some message"
```

VB6 at Work: The Display Class

One of the limitations of VBScript is that it doesn't support input/output functions. This isn't really a limitation, since VBScript is a scripting language, and scripting languages by definition, lack a user interface. If you want to develop applications with visual interfaces, use Visual Basic. In programming, however, especially in the design and testing phase, we need a mechanism to display intermediate results.

The SEditor project's Form has a window in which the script can place its output (similar to the Immediate window). This feature is implemented with the help of the DisplayClass. The DisplayClass exposes two methods:

▶ The Show method, which prints a string in the lower TextBox control at the bottom of the Form

▶ The Clear method, which clears the contents of the lower TextBox control

The DisplayClass Class Module is implemented with a few lines of code.

Code 10.9: The Display Class

```
Public Sub Show(message)
  ScriptForm.Text2.Text = ScriptForm.Text2.Text _
        & vbCrLf & message
End Sub
Public Sub Clear()
  ScriptForm.Text2.Text = ""
End Sub
```

To use the DisplayClass's members from within a script without having to register the Display DLL and create an object variable with the CreateObject() function, you add the Display object to the Script control. Insert the following statement in the ScriptForm's Load event:

```
Private Sub Form_Load()
  ScriptControl1.AddObject "Output", display, True
End Sub
```

Notice that the last argument of the AddObject method is True, so the Show and Clear methods can be accessed by name, as if they were VBScript commands.

The SEditor project is a simple application that lets you experiment with VBScript. You can develop really complicated applications, as long as they don't require extensive I/O capabilities (besides the MsgBox()

Part iii

function and the Show method), and you can live with a simple editor. You can't count on this editor to display the members of an object variable or do syntax checking as you type.

Handling Errors

The Script control provides the Error event, which is triggered every time an error occurs. The error may be due to the control (calling a method with the wrong arguments or attempting to set a nonexistent property) or to the script itself. A trappable error is also triggered in the host application, but not before the user is prompted to use the Script Debugger. While you're developing and testing your scripts, let Visual Basic start the debugger and help you debug the script. When you distribute the application, however, you may not want users of your application to see this prompt.

It seems there is no way to suppress this dialog box in the current version of the control, and this makes it difficult to distribute the application. Users may not have the Script Debugger installed, and this prompt will confuse them. The Script control is still rough around the edges, but I hope the next version will be more flexible, and it may even come with a programmer's editor.

In the meantime, you'll have to live with the limitations and the quirks of the Script control. To handle the error, use the *Error* object, which is a property of the Script control, and it's a different object from Visual Basic's Err object. The Error object provides two properties, which identify the location of the error in the script:

▶ *Line*, which is the number of the line where the error occurred

▶ *Column*, which is the location of the first character of the offending statement in the error line

You can use these two properties to place the pointer at the location of the error. When you use a TextBox control as an editor, moving to a specific character of a specific line in the control's text isn't simple; there are no methods or properties to take you directly to the specified location in the text.

The Script control's Error object provides additional properties, which are listed in Table 10.5.

TABLE 10.5: Additional Properties of the Script Control's Error Object

PROPERTY	DESCRIPTION
Number	The error's number
Description	The error's description
Text	A string with the offending statement
Source	The procedure or Class name where the error took place

Finally, after processing an error, you must call the Error object's Clear method to reset the error.

Let's look at the error handler of the Execute Script button. If the Script-Control generates a runtime error and the ScriptControl1.Error.Number property is nonzero, we can use the Script control's Error property to extract information regarding the offending statement. In most cases, however, the Script control produces an automation error and doesn't set its Error object. The error handler simply displays the error in a message box.

```
CodeError:
  If ScriptControl1.Error.Number <> 0 Then
    msg = ScriptControl1.Error.Description & bvcrlf
    msg = msg & " In line " & ScriptControl1.Error.Line _
        & ", column " & ScriptControl1.Error.Column
    MsgBox msg, , "Error in script"
  Else
    MsgBox "ERROR # " & Err.Number & vbCrLf & Err.Description
  End If
```

The most common source for errors is the call of invalid methods or object variables. The following statements, for example, invoke Excel and call its Evaluate method:

```
Set EXL = CreateObject("Excel.Application")
MsgBox "The logarithm of 99 is " & EXL.Evaluate("Log(99)")
```

If you misspell the name of the *EXL* variable or if Excel doesn't exist on the host computer, you'll get the same error message, which is an automation error. This simply means that the script couldn't contact the object. If you call the InStr() function with an invalid argument (or the incorrect number of arguments), you'll get the same error message. In fact, only simple syntax errors in your script set the Script control's Error object and can be spotted easily. When working with objects, the Script control can't provide any substantial help.

Retrieving the Procedure Names

The *AddCode* method of the Script control allows you to add many procedures to the control. At some point, you may want to list the names of the procedures in the control. The *Procedures* property is a collection that contains all the procedures you have added to the Script control. As a collection, it has a *Count* property, which returns the number of procedures, and an *Item* property, which returns a specific procedure. The following loop scans all the procedures stored in the Procedures collection:

```
For i = 1 To ScriptControl1.Procedures.Count
   {process element ScriptControl1.Procedures(1)}
Next
```

Each item in the Procedures collection has a *Name* property, which is the corresponding procedure's name, and a *HasReturnValue* property, which returns True if the procedure returns a result (in other words, HasReturnValue returns True if the procedure is a function). The List Procedures button on the ScriptForm of the SEdit project lists the names and types of all procedures in the lower textbox.

Code 10.10:   Listing the Script Control's Procedures

```
Private Sub Command2_Click()
On Error GoTo CodeError
   ScriptControl1.AddCode Text1.Text
   For i = 1 To ScriptControl1.Procedures.Count
      If ScriptControl1.Procedures(i).HasReturnValue Then
         Text2.Text = Text2.Text & vbCrLf & "Function  " _
            & ScriptControl1.Procedures(1).Name
      Else
         Text2.Text = Text2.Text & vbCrLf & "Subroutine " _
            & ScriptControl1.Procedures(1).Name
      End If
   Next
   Exit Sub
CodeError:
   MsgBox Err.Description
End Sub
```

Notice how the code classifies a procedure as a function or a subroutine based on the value of the HasReturnValue property.

TIP

You'd expect the Procedures collection to have a Code or similarly named property that would return the procedure's listing. Unfortunately, such a property doesn't exist. You simply can't extract the listing of an individual procedure. Moreover, the Script control lacks a method to remove an individual procedure. You can use the control's Reset method to remove all the procedures and then add all but the ones you want to exclude, provided you keep the listings of the control in another control (such as a TextBox control). Even so, the process of removing individual procedures isn't simple. In the SEdit project, for example, you'd have to parse the contents of the top TextBox and extract each individual procedure.

Scripting an Application

If your application exposes Classes, you can add a Script control on a separate Form, such as the ScriptForm, and allow the users of the application to script it. Let's say you have an application that allows the user to open image files and save them in different formats (TIF, JPEG, NPG, and so on). Users that want to convert numerous image files need not open and save each file individually. They would rather write a script that opens a file at a time, converts it, and then saves it to disk with a different filename.

This Class should expose a small number of methods, such as an *Open(filename)* method to open the image file, a *Convert(format1, format2)* method that converts between two formats, and a *SaveAs(filename)* method that saves the image in the new format. The code for converting image file formats is quite complicated, but it has been published in several books, and you should be able to convert the procedures into methods and attach them to a Class.

THE WINDOWS SCRIPTING HOST

You can also use VBScript, including its FileSystemObject object, to script Windows itself. In this section, you'll learn how to create scripts that run under Windows 98 and automate many common tasks, such as connecting to printers and network drives, cleaning up your folders, and even processing a large number of files in batch mode.

For those of you who are totally unfamiliar with DOS batch files, here's a simple example. Let's say you use two folders (directories in the DOS terminology), the C:\TMP and C:\DOCS\TEMP, where you store temporary files, which should be deleted at the end of the day or every so often. To delete these files, you would execute the following commands:

```
CD C:\TMP
DEL *.*
CD C:\DOCS\TEMP
DEL *.*
```

The CD command (Change Directory) switches to another directory, and the DEL *.* command deletes all the files in the current directory. If the two directories contain subdirectories, the DEL *.* command will not remove them. You must use the DELTREE command instead.

The syntax of DOS batch files is peculiar too. For example, there are no commands to write data to files (or read data from existing files). To send the output of a batch file to a text file, you have to use the redirection symbol (>). To save the (possible) error messages generated by the previous batch file to a text file, you would use the following syntax (assuming that the name of the batch file is DELTEMP.BAT):

```
DELTEMP > ERRMSG.TXT
```

You would then open the ERRMSG.TXT file with a text editor to read the error messages.

If you are familiar with DOS, you probably know the type of operations you can automate with batch files. You can initialize printers, establish network connections, process files en masse, and so on. Any operation that can be carried out with DOS commands from the prompt line can be coded as a batch file.

You can do the same and more with Windows 98. Earlier versions of the Windows operating system didn't support a batch, or scripting, language, and many people wished for a way to automate batch operations. The scripting language of Windows 98 is VBScript, which means you can take advantage of this aspect of the operating system without any additional effort. As a VB programmer, you're ready to develop Windows scripts.

In this chapter, you will learn how to use VBScript to write useful scripts to automate your daily tasks. You will find a number of examples that demonstrate the operations you can automate with scripts and that can become starting points for your own, custom scripts. First, you'll learn how to write simple scripts and execute them. Then, you'll learn about the objects exposed by Windows Scripting Host, and this is all the information you really need.

Writing and Executing a Script

Let's start by building a script that does something and run it. A script is a text file with VBScript commands, which accomplishes a specific task. We'll write a script that displays the number of days left to the end of the century. Start Notepad and enter the lines in Code 10.12.

Code 10.12: The YEAR2000.VBS Script

```
DaysLeft = #1/1/2000# - Date()
Message = DaysLeft & " days left for the year 2000"
MsgBox(Message)
```

Then save the file with the name YEAR2000.VBS on your disk. When saving the file with Notepad, don't forget to select All Files in the Save As Type drop-down list in the File Save dialog box. If you don't select this option, the file will be saved as 2000.VBS.TXT.

The expression #1/1/2000# is a date. In VBScript, dates are enclosed with pound signs. Text is enclosed in double quotes. Date() is another VBScript function that returns the current date. The value returned by the Date() function (a value such as 10/04/1998) is subtracted from the first day of the year 2000, and the result is assigned to the variable *DaysLeft*.

To run this script, locate the file YEAR2000.VBS on the Desktop (or whatever folder you stored it in), and double-click its icon. You will see this dialog box:

```
┌─────────────────────────────┐
│ Visual Basic            [X]  │
├─────────────────────────────┤
│  599 days left for the year 2000 │
│                             │
│       ┌──────────┐          │
│       │   OK     │          │
│       └──────────┘          │
└─────────────────────────────┘
```

Click OK to close the dialog box.

In the following sections, I'm going to discuss the basics of VBScript: variables, functions, and control flow statements. These sections don't contain any practical examples. Unfortunately, you'll have to learn the basic mechanisms of the language before you'll be able to write any practical scripts.

Running Scripts with WSCRIPT.EXE

Double-clicking the icons of a script is the quickest way to run a script, but this method precludes the use of arguments. Since scripts don't have a visible interface, the only way to alter their behavior is by passing one or more initial arguments to them. To run a script and pass arguments to it, you must invoke the WSCRIPT.EXE application.

Choose Start ➤ Run to open the Run dialog box. Enter the name of the WSCRIPT.EXE application, followed by the name of the script you want to execute. For example, if you have saved the FILEDTR.VBS script in the SCRIPTS folder on the Desktop, enter this line:

```
WSCRIPT C:\WINDOWS\DESKTOP\SCRIPTS\FILEDTR.VBS
```

This command starts the WSCRIPT.EXE program, which executes the script FILEDTR.VBS. If the path contains spaces, enclose the script's path name with double quotes, as shown here:

```
WSCRIPT "C:\WINDOWS\DESKTOP\SAMPLE SCRIPTS\FILEDTR.VBS"
```

You can also pass arguments to a script that's executed with the WSCRIPT.EXE program from the command line, by separating them from the name of the script with spaces:

```
WSCRIPT C:\WINDOWS\DESKTOP\SCRIPTS\FILEDTR.VBS arg1 arg2
```

The two arguments are *arg1* and *arg2*. (You can't test the argument-passing mechanisms right now. You must first learn how to process them from within your script.)

NOTE

Multiple arguments are separated by a space (or multiple spaces). If you use commas, they will be treated as part of the arguments.

Besides providing an environment for executing the scripts, WSCRIPT .EXE provides a few objects, which let you access special features of the Windows shell that you can't access through VBScript. Practically speaking, you can think of the objects of Wscript as an extension to VBScript. I will start the presentation of the Wscript object with the Arguments collection, which contains the arguments passed to the script. In the following section, you'll learn how to access the arguments to a script and modify the script's behavior based on the values of the arguments.

NOTE

If you want to pass a large number of arguments to a script (which is a rather common situation), implement the script so that it reads its arguments from a text file, as discussed earlier in this chapter. Users will find it easy to enter the names of a dozen files to a text file and edit it, before using it with a script. Don't expect the users of your scripts to type long path names and get them right the first time.

Using Arguments

So far, you've seen how to build and execute scripts and how to pass arguments to them, but not how to process them from within the script's code. VBScript can't handle arguments on its own. The Arguments property of the Wscript object lets your script read the arguments passed to it. To access the actual arguments, you must create an object variable with the statement:

```
Set Args = Wscript.Arguments
```

The *Args* variable is a collection that provides the Item and Count properties. To iterate through the collection's items, you can use a For...Next loop, such as the following one,

```
For i = 0 to Args.Count - 1
   {process each argument}
Next
```

or a For Each...Next loop, such as this:

```
For Each arg In Args
   {process each argument}
Next
```

In the case of the For...Next loop, you can access each argument with the expression Args(i), and in the case of the For Each...Next loop, you can access them through the variable *arg*. The ARGS1.VBS and ARGS2.VBS scripts demonstrate how to access the script's argument with both methods.

Code 10.13: The ARGS1.VBS Script

```
Set Args = Wscript.Arguments
For i=0 to Args.Count - 1
   txt = txt & Args(i) & vbCrLf
Next
MsgBox txt
```

Each argument is a member of the collection *Args,* and the elements appear in the order in which they were passed to the script.

Code 10.14: The GS2.VBS Script

```
Set Args = Wscript.Arguments
For Each arg In Args
   txt = txt & arg & vbCrLf
Next
MsgBox txt
```

To pass one or more arguments to a script, you execute it with the Run command of the Start menu. Open the Start menu (press Ctrl+Escape), and from the menu, select Run. In the Run dialog box enter this string:

```
WSCRIPT "C:\SCRIPTS\ARGS1.VBS" John Doe 33.5
```

You must modify the path to the script ARGS1.VBS according to your hard disk's structure. The name of the script is enclosed in double quotes because long path names in Windows 98 can contain spaces. After the script's name, supply the arguments using the space as separator. If you call either script with these arguments, the arguments will appear in a message box, as shown in Figure 10.6.

FIGURE 10.6:   The ARGS1.VBA and ARGS2.VBA scripts display their arguments in a message box.

Do not use the comma to separate the arguments of your script. The comma will be attached to the argument that precedes it. If you supply the arguments,

```
WSCRIPT "C:\SCRIPTS\ARGS1.VBS" 1, 2, string
```

the script will display its arguments, as shown in Figure 10.7. The comma is treated like any other character; only the space character is treated differently.

FIGURE 10.7:   Script arguments should not be delimited with the comma character.

If any of the arguments include spaces, you must enclose them in double quotes. For example, if the last argument in our example was a string with a space in it, like the one shown here without the double quotes,

```
WSCRIPT "C:\SCRIPTS\ARGS1.VBS" 1, 2, "string variable"
```

the Arguments collection would contain four arguments: 1, 2, "string", and "variable" (the double quotes themselves are not included in the argument).

The Wscript Object's Properties

The Wscript object provides other properties in addition to the Arguments property. They relate to the Scripting Host (the WSCRIPT.EXE executable) and the script being executed.

Application This property returns the friendly name of the Wscript object, which is the string "Windows Scripting Host" (the same value is also returned by the property Name).

FullName This property returns the path and file name of the executable file of the Windows Scripting Host (WSCRIPT.EXE).

Name This property returns the friendly name of the Wscript object, which is the string "Windows Scripting Host."

Path This property returns the name of the folder where WSCRIPT.EXE or CSCRIPT.EXE resides (usually c:\windows).

ScriptFullName This property returns the path and filename of the script being executed by the Windows Scripting Host.

Version This property returns the version of the Windows Scripting Host (WSCRIPT.EXE). The version that ships with Windows 98 is 5.

ScriptName This property provides the filename of the script being executed by the Windows Scripting Host. The script WSCRIPT.VBS demonstrates several of the properties of the Wscript object. Figure 10.8 shows the output.

Part iii

Code 10.15: The WSCRIPT.VBS Script

```
msg ="Script File Name    " & _
    Wscript.ScriptName & vbCrLf
msg = msg & "Script Path Name    " & _
    Wscript.ScriptFullName & vbCrLf
msg = msg & "Executed by       " & _
    Wscript.Application & " (version " & _
    Wscript.Version & ")" & vbCrLf
MsgBox msg
```

Visual Basic

Script File Name   WSCRIPT.VBS
Script Path Name   D:\PROJECTS\MVB5 New Projects\MVB6 Chapters\Ch20\Projects\Scripts\WSCRIPT.VBS
Executed by   Windows Scripting Host (version 5.0)

OK

FIGURE 10.8:   The output of the WSCRIPT.VBS script

The Wscript Object's Methods

The Wscript object provides a number of methods, most of which have an equivalent VBScript function. The most important methods are the Create-Object and GetObject methods, which are identical to the VBScript functions by the same name. Let's start with the simpler methods of the Wscript object.

Echo   This method displays one or more values in a message box. You can display the friendly name of the Windows Scripting Host with the Echo method on a message box, which is identical to the box displayed by the MsgBox() function:

```
Wscript.Echo Wscript.Name
```

You can display multiple values, as long as they are delimited by a comma character. Multiple values are displayed next to each other with a space between them. The following statement will display the message box shown in Figure 10.9:

```
Wscript.Echo "string argument", Wscript.Name, 98.9+1
```

Notice that the Name property is replaced by its value, and the expression 98.9+1 is calculated and substituted by its result.

Windows Scripting Host

string argument Windows Scripting Host 99.9

OK

FIGURE 10.9:   The Echo method can display multiple values next to each other.

Echo is a simple method and is provided as a primitive debugging tool. The MsgBox() function and the Pop-up method (described next) provide many more options and should be preferred.

Quit   This method quits the execution of the script and, optionally, returns an error code. Its syntax is:

```
Wsript.Quit errorCode
```

The optional argument *errorCode* is the error code to be returned. If omitted, the Quit method returns the error code zero. You can use the error code to specify whether the script ended its execution normally or to specify the error that prevented the script from completing its execution.

THE SHELL OBJECT

The Shell object is a property of the Wscript object, which gives your script access to special items such as the environment variables and the special folders, as well as a number of methods for manipulating the Registry. Let's start with the Shell object's properties. Before you can access the Shell object's properties, you must create a *Shell* object variable, with this statement:

```
Set wShell = Wscript.CreateObject("Wscript.Shell")
```

The Environment Collection

The Environment property returns a collection with the environment variables. To iterate through the environment variables, create a Shell object and then request its Environment collection:

```
Set WShell = Wscript.CreateObject("Wscript.Shell")
Set AllVars = WShell.Environment
For Each evar In AllVars
  txt = txt & evar & vbcrlf
Next
Msgbox txt
```

The *evar* variable represents an environment variable in this form:

```
Variable = setting
```

The output of the ENVVARS.VBS script is shown in Figure 10.10. To access the values of specific environment variables, you can use the Environment object, which is described later in this chapter.

Part iii

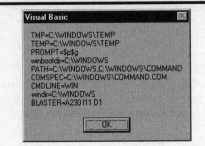

FIGURE 10.10: The ENVVARS.VBS script displays the names and values of the environment variables.

The variables that the Environment method returns by default are the PROCESS environment variables. These are built-in variables, such as Win-Dir and WinBootDir, as well as variables created with the SET command (this is a DOS command that appears several times in the AUTOEXEC.BAT file). These variables are shown in Table 10.6 (not all of these variables need to exist on every system).

Optionally, you can pass an argument to the Environment method, which causes it to return a different set of environment variables. Windows NT supports several sets of environment variables. Windows 98 supports only the PROCESS and the VOLATILE sets. The VOLATILE environment variables are the ones you set through your scripts, as you will see shortly. Your scripts can use VOLATILE environment variables to communicate with each other. You can dynamically declare and delete VOLATILE environment variables.

TABLE 10.6: The Names of the Environment Variables

NAME	DESCRIPTION
NUMBER_OF_PROCESSORS	Number of processors running on the machine
PROCESSOR_ARCHITECTURE	Processor type of the user's workstation
PROCESSOR_IDENTIFIER	Processor ID of the user's workstation
PROCESSOR_LEVEL	Processor level of the user's workstation
PROCESSOR_REVISION	Processor version of the user's workstation
OS	Operating system on the user's workstation
COMSPEC	Executable for command Command Prompt (typically CMD.EXE)
HOMEDRIVE	Primary local drive (typically the C: drive)

TABLE 10.6 (continued): The Names of the Environment Variables

NAME	DESCRIPTION
HOMEPATH	Default directory for users (on Windows NT this is typically \users\default)
PATH	PATH environment variable
PATHEXT	Extensions for executable files (typically .COM, .EXE, .BAT, or .CMD)
PROMPT	Command prompt (typically PG)
SYSTEMDRIVE	Local drive on which the system directory resides
SYSTEMROOT	System directory (for example, c:\winnt); this is the same as WINDIR
WINDIR	System directory (for example, c:\winnt); this is the same as SYSTEMROOT
TEMP	Directory for storing temporary files (for example, c:\temp)
TMP	Directory for storing temporary files (for example, c:\temp)

The SpecialFolders Collection

The SpecialFolders property gives your script access to the special folders on your system. The special folders include the Desktop folder, the Start menu folder, and the personal document folder.

Part iii

NOTE

The SpecialFolders property returns the path name of the Desktop folder (for example, c:\windows\desktop) and not a Folder object. To access the files and subfolders of the Desktop folder, you must first create a *Folder* object variable with the GetFolder method of the FileSystemObject object, as shown in the example that follows.

Use the SpecialFolders collection to create new shortcuts on the Desktop or to place new applications in the Start menu folder. The following script displays the names of the files on the Desktop, along with their type. This script (it's called DTOP.VBS, and you'll find it on the Sybex Web site) uses the FileSystemObject object to iterate through the files of the Desktop folder.

Code 10.16: The DTOP.VBS Script

```
' This script displays all files on the desktop,
' along with their types
Set FSys = CreateObject("Scripting.FileSystemObject")
Set WShell = Wscript.CreateObject("Wscript.Shell")
DTOPfolder = WShell.SpecialFolders("Desktop")
Set Desktop = FSys.GetFolder(DTOPfolder)
Set DesktopFiles = Desktop.Files
For Each file in DesktopFiles
   txt = txt & file.Name & " (" & file.Type & ")" & vbCrLf
Next
MsgBox txt
```

This script creates an object variable that references the Desktop folder, by calling the SpecialFolders method of the Shell object. It then retrieves all files on the desktop and stores them to a collection, the DesktopFiles collection, and scans all the items in this collection with a For Each...Next loop. At each iteration of the loop, it can access the current file's properties through the *file* object variable.

You can also access all the special folders on the computer using the SpecialFolders Collection. The following script iterates through the computer's special folders and displays their names. The script is called SPFOLDER.VBS, and you will find it on the Sybex Web site.

Code 10.17: The SPFOLDER.VBS Script

```
' List all special folders on the host computer
Set WShell = Wscript.CreateObject("Wscript.Shell")
For Each Folder In WShell.SpecialFolders
   msg = msg & Folder & vbCrLf
Next
MsgBox msg
```

If you execute this script, it will display the path names of the following folders:

Application Data	MyDocuments	Recent	Startup
Desktop	NetHood	SendTo	Templates
Favorites	PrintHood	ShellNew	
Fonts	Programs	StartMenu	

The Pop-Up Method

This method displays a message box, similar to VBScript's MsgBox function. It has the same syntax, and the only advantage to using this method is that it allows you to specify how many seconds it will remain active on the screen before it shuts itself down. The syntax of the method is

```
Popup(msg, seconds, title, type)
```

in which *msg* is the message to be displayed; this is the only mandatory argument. If the second argument, *seconds*, is supplied, the message box automatically closes after so many seconds. The argument *title* is the message box's title, and the last argument, *type*, is the same as in the MsgBox() function. It determines which buttons and icons appear in the message box. Its possible values are shown in Tables 10.7 and 10.8.

TABLE 10.7: The Button Combinations You Can Display in a Pop-Up Window

VALUE	BUTTON(S)
0	OK
1	OK and Cancel
2	Abort, Retry, and Ignore
3	Yes, No, and Cancel
4	Yes and No
5	Retry and Cancel

The icon is specified by one of the values in Table 10.8, which must be added to the value specifying the button to appear in the message box.

TABLE 10.8: The Icons You Can Display in a Pop-Up Window

VALUE	ICON
16	Stop mark
32	Question mark
48	Exclamation mark
64	Information mark

Part iii

Depending on which button on the message box was clicked, the Pop-up method returns a value, which is one of those shown in Table 10.9.

TABLE 10.9: The Values Returned by the Pop-Up Method

VALUE	DESCRIPTION
1	OK button
2	Cancel button
3	Abort button
4	Retry button
5	Ignore button
6	Yes button
7	No button

The following script displays a pop-up dialog box and waits for 10 seconds. If the user doesn't click on a button during this interval, the dialog box closes, and the program resumes.

Code 10.18:   The POPUP.VBS Script

```
Set WShell = Wscript.CreateObject("Wscript.Shell")
Reply = WShell.Popup("Display long file names?", 10, _
    "Timed Dialog Box", 4+64)
If Reply = 6 Then
  Wscript.Echo "OK, here are a few long file names..."
Else
  If Reply = 7 Then
    Wscript.Echo "OK, here are a few short file names..."
  Else
    Wscript.Echo "I selected long file names for you"
  End If
End If
```

The dialog box expires after 10 seconds. In this case, the Pop-up method returns the value -1, and the script makes the default selection (as though the Yes button was clicked). After a Pop-up dialog box expires, there is no reason to display a message box as I have done (for demonstration purposes) in the example.

The CreateShortcut Method

The CreateShortcut method of the WshShell object creates a Shortcut or a URLShortcut object. A *URLShortcut* object is a link to a URL instead of a file on the local disk. When you click URLShortcut, the corresponding page is opened with Internet Explorer.

Creating an actual shortcut on the Desktop is a bit more complicated than using the CreateShortCut method, since you must specify the properties of the shortcut (its name, icon, target, and so on) and then save it. The first step in creating a shortcut, however, is to create a Shortcut object and then use it to set its properties. The process of creating shortcuts is described later in this chapter, but here is a short script that creates a shortcut:

```
Set WShell = Wscript.CreateObject("Wscript.Shell")
Set ShellLink = WShell.CreateShortcut("Run Any Script.lnk")
ShellLink.TargetPath = "WSCRIPT.EXE"
ShellLink.Save
```

Placing these lines in a VBS file and executing them creates a shortcut on the Desktop. The shortcut's icon will be the icon of the WSCRIPT application. This shortcut starts the WSCRIPT.EXE application. Not a very useful shortcut, unless you drop a script on it, in which case it executes the script, as though you'd double-clicked the script's icon.

The *ShellLink* variable is a Shortcut object, which has its own properties and methods (like the TargetPath property and Save method we used in the last example). The Shortcut object's properties are described in the following section.

The WshShortcut Object

The WshShortcut object represents a shortcut and lets you manipulate the properties of an existing shortcut or create a new shortcut. To create a WshShortcut, use these statements:

```
Set WShell = Wscript.CreateObject("Wscript.Shell")
strDesktop = WShell.SpecialFolders("Desktop")
Set aShortcut = WShell.CreateShortcut(strDesktop & _
    "\Encrypt.lnk")
```

If the Encrypt.lnk file exists, the *aShortcut* variable represents the shortcut on the Desktop. If no such shortcut exists, a new one is created.

NOTE
The new shortcut will not appear on the Desktop until you save it with the Save method.

The properties of the WshShortcut object and its Save method are explained in the following sections. In effect, they are the parameters you can set in the Shortcut tab of the shortcut's Properties window, which is shown in Figure 10.11.

Shortcut to Projects Properties

General | Shortcut |

Shortcut to Projects

Target type: File Folder

Target location: D:\

Target: D:\PROJECTS

Start in:

Shortcut key: None

Run: Normal window

Find Target...   Change Icon...

OK   Cancel   Apply

FIGURE 10.11: A shortcut's Properties window displays the properties of a shortcut.

Arguments   This property specifies the arguments to be passed to the shortcut represented by the variable.

Description   This property specifies the description of a shortcut.

FullName   This property specifies the full path name of the shortcut.

Hotkey   This property provides the *hotkey* of a shortcut, which is a keyboard shortcut to start or switch to a program. The hotkey consists of a modifier and a key and has the form Alt+E or Ctrl+Shift+A. The available modifiers are:

ALT+ CTRL+ SHIFT+ EXT+

You can use the following keys in hotkey combinations:

▶ The characters A–Z

▶ The digits 0–9

▶ The special keys:

Back	Tab	Clear	Return
Escape	Space	PgUp	PgDn
Home	End	F1 through F12	

To assign a hotkey combination to the shortcut represented by the variable *myShortCut*, use this statement:

```
myShortCut.Hotkey = "ALT+SHIFT+F"
```

IconLocation   This property specifies the location of the icon to be used for a shortcut. Usually, multiple icons are stored in the same file, and the format of the IconLocation property is *Path,index*. If you look for the key Icon in the Registry, you will find values such as the following:

```
C:\Program Files\NetMeeting\conf.exe, 1
```

Here, the icon to be used with NetMeeting is the first one in the CONF.EXE file.

TargetPath   This property specifies the target path of a shortcut object (the object it refers to).

WindowStyle   This property specifies the window style of a shortcut object. This is the style of the window when the referenced application starts, and it can have one of the values shown in Table 10.10.

TABLE 10.10: Possible Values for the WindowStyle Property

VALUE	DESCRIPTION
0	Normal
1	Minimized
2	Maximized

Part iii

WorkingDirectory   This property specifies the working directory of a shortcut object.

Save   This method saves the shortcut object to the location specified by the FullName property.

The WshNetwork Object

The WshNetwork object provides the properties and methods you need to manipulate the shared devices (drives and printers) on the network, as well as the properties of the local computer on the network (its name, domain name, and so on). For information on using the WshNetwork object and the objects it exposes, visit the Web site `http://msdn` `.microsoft.com/scripting`.

WHAT'S NEXT?

Visual Basic can be used to merge aspects of the Web with your applications. In Chapter 11, you'll learn about Web Browsing objects, the Web-Browser control and InternetExplorer object, using hyperlinks in Visual Basic applications, the Internet Explorer scripting model, and building Internet-enabled controls.

Chapter 11

VISUAL BASIC AND THE WEB

So far, you have seen how to apply Visual Basic to the Web by means of scripting Web pages with VBScript. This chapter demonstrates the merging of the desktop and the Web and includes the related objects and examples. The first topic I'll discuss is the WebBrowser control, which lets you display HTML documents in your VB applications. With this control, you can design a Form that connects the user to your Web site (or a specific page depending on what he or she is doing at the moment) and displays your home page, as if it were viewed with Internet Explorer. Because the WebBrowser control doesn't provide any navigational tools, you can limit the user to your own Web site (unless the site contains hyperlinks to other sites).

Adapted from *Mastering Visual Basic 6*
by Evangelos Petroutsos

ISBN 0-7821-2272-8   1,312 pages $49.99

In a corporate environment, you can design Forms that display announcements, special instructions, and all types of information that change frequently. The user doesn't have to start the browser to view this information. The WebBrowser control enables you to push information to your users from within applications they use daily.

The WebBrowser control, just like Internet Explorer, can display HTML pages, which must be authored ahead of time and reside on a server (or even on your hard disk). It is also possible to manipulate the document in the control directly, through the IE Scripting Object Model. Through the objects of the IE Scripting Object Model, you can write VB applications that generate HTML code and place it on the WebBrowser control. In other words, it is possible to develop VB applications that generate HTML documents on the fly and display them in the WebBrowser control. It's an exciting capability, especially for authoring interactive tutorials.

The last topic I will discuss in this chapter is how it is possible to develop ActiveX controls that can take advantage of the host computer's connection to the Internet and download information from the network. These controls are called *Internet-enabled*, and I expect that many of you will develop custom controls whose primary function is to connect to servers and download information on demand.

WEB BROWSING OBJECTS

The two objects you need in order to add Web techniques and hyper-linked documents to your Visual Basic applications are

▶ The WebBrowser control

▶ The InternetExplorer object

The WebBrowser is an ActiveX control that can display HTML documents on Visual Basic Forms. InternetExplorer is an OLE Automation object that you can use to control Microsoft Internet Explorer (and the WebBrowser control) from within your code. The two objects have many common members, and I will discuss them together. The emphasis will be on the WebBrowser control, which VB programmers will find more useful.

The WebBrowser Control

Simply put, the WebBrowser control is Internet Explorer's window. Any HTML document that can be displayed in Internet Explorer can also be displayed in the WebBrowser control. In other words, the WebBrowser control adds browsing capabilities to your Visual Basic applications. It allows the user to browse sites on the World Wide Web, local files, or ActiveX documents, such as Word or Excel documents—all from within a Visual Basic application.

Because the WebBrowser is an ActiveX control, you can place it on any Visual Basic Form. Before you can use it, however, you must add it to the Toolbox. Follow these steps:

1. Right-click the Toolbox, and from the shortcut menu, select Components to open the Components dialog box.

2. Select Microsoft Internet Controls, and then click OK. Two new icons will appear on the Toolbox—the WebBrowser control's icon and the ShelFolderViewOC control's icon.

3. Select the WebBrowser control's icon and draw an instance of the control on the Form.

When you place a WebBrowser control on a Form, it's a borderless rectangle that you can size in any way you like. Because the control can't be resized by the user at runtime, you should try to adjust its size according to the size of its container, which is a Visual Basic Form. When the user resizes the Form, the WebBrowser control should be resized also so that it covers most of the Form.

To display a Web page in the WebBrowser control, use the Navigate method. You can also move through the list of URLs that have been displayed already with the GoBack and GoForward methods. The WebBrowser control automatically maintains the list of visited URLs. We'll look at the control's properties, methods, and events later. Let's start by developing a simple application that demonstrates the basic features of the control.

VB6 at Work: The Browser Project

In this section, we'll develop an application based on the WebBrowser control that demonstrates how to add Web-browsing capabilities to your Visual Basic applications. The project is called Browser.

NOTE

You'll find this chapter's projects on the Sybex Web site (www.sybex.com). Once there, go to the Catalog page and enter **2469** (the first four digits of the last five in the book's ISBN) into the search engine. Follow the link for this book that comes up, and then click the Downloads button, which will take you to a list of files organized by chapter.

Figure 11.1 shows the Browser application displaying the Sybex Web site. The user can select a URL from the ComboBox control or select a local HTML file by clicking the Open HTML File button.

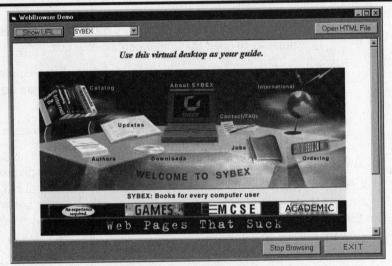

FIGURE 11.1: The Browser application shows how to add Web-browsing capabilities to a Visual Basic application.

To build the application, follow these steps:

1. Start a new Standard EXE project, and add the WebBrowser control to the Toolbox, as shown earlier in this chapter.

2. Widen the Form and then place an instance of the WebBrowser control on it. Make the control large enough to cover most of the Form's area.

3. Now, place the other controls you see in Figure 11.1 on the Form. In addition to the visible controls (the Command buttons and the ComboBox), there is a Common Dialog control,

which will be used to display the Open dialog box and in which the user can select local HTML files to display on the Web-Browser control.

4. Enter the following lines to initialize the ComboBox control when the Form is loaded:

```
Private Sub Form_Load()
  Combo1.AddItem "Microsoft"
  Combo1.AddItem "SYBEX"
  Combo1.AddItem "Infoseek"
  Combo1.AddItem "Excite"
  Combo1.AddItem "RealAudio"
  Combo1.ListIndex = 0
End Sub
```

You can add your favorite URLs here, as long as the name displayed in the box is the name of a commercial Web server. When the user selects the *ServerName* entry in the Combo-Box, the program connects to the following URL:

```
http://www.ServerName.com
```

5. The Show URL button creates a complete URL from the computer's name and uses it with the Navigate method to display the specified URL on the WebBrowser control.

Code 11.1:   The Show URL Button

```
Private Sub Command1_Click()
  WebBrowser1.Navigate "http://www." & Combo1.Text & ".com"
End Sub
```

The Open HTML File button is quite similar, but instead of displaying a remote URL, it prompts the user to select a local HTML file with the File Open dialog box and then renders it on the WebBrowser control.

Code 11.2:   The Open HTML File Button

```
Private Sub Command2_Click()
  CommonDialog1.CancelError = True
  On Error GoTo CancelOpen
  CommonDialog1.Filter = "HTML Files|*.HTM|Text Files| _
          *.TXT|All Files|*.*"
  CommonDialog1.ShowOpen
  If CommonDialog1.filename <> "" Then
    WebBrowser1.Navigate CommonDialog1.filename
  End If
```

Part iii

```
      Exit Sub

   CancelOpen:
      Exit Sub
   End Sub
```

Run the Browser application and check it out. Visit various pages on the World Wide Web, and open HTML files on your local disk (try loading the Web pages developed in the previous chapter). Figure 11.2 shows the Calendar.htm document (which we'll develop later in this chapter) opened with the Browser application. You can also open other types of documents (images, Word documents, Excel spreadsheets, and so on), as long as the browser can handle them.

			May 1998				
Sun	Mon	Tue	Wed	Thu	Fri	Sat
					1	2
3	4	5	6	7	8	9
10	11	12	13	14	15	16
17	18	19	20	21	22	23
24	25	26	27	28	29	30
31						

FIGURE 11.2: The Calendar.htm page viewed with the Browser application

WARNING

If you open a Word document, you will see it as it appears in Word, but you won't see Word's menu and toolbar—which makes it impossible to edit from within the WebBrowser control.

The InternetExplorer Object

The InternetExplorer object allows you to start an instance of Internet Explorer from within your application and manipulate it through OLE

Automation. The InternetExplorer object supports the same properties and methods as the WebBrowser control, plus a few more. We will look at the object's properties and methods shortly, but first let's build an application that controls Internet Explorer. It's called IExplore, and you will find it on the Sybex Web site.

VB6 at Work: The IExplore Project

To reference Internet Explorer from within your project, you must first add a reference to the InternetExplorer object. Follow these steps:

1. Start a new project and select Standard EXE as the project type.

2. Choose Project ➢ References to open the References dialog box.

3. Check the Microsoft Internet Controls checkbox.

This time, you won't see a new icon in the Toolbox. But if you open the Object Browser window, you will see that the InternetExplorer Class has been added to the project. In the Members window, you will see the properties and methods exposed by the InternetExplorer Class, and through these members you can OLE automate the Internet Explorer application.

Let's build an application that will control one or more instances of Internet Explorer. The application is shown in Figure 11.3. The user can select a destination in the ComboBox control in the Visual Basic window and click the Show URL button to start an instance of Internet Explorer, in which the selected URL is displayed.

To continue building the application, follow these steps:

4. Design a Form like the one shown in Figure 11.3.

5. Declare a Form-wide object variable, though which you'll be accessing the members of the InternetExplorer Class:

```
Dim IE As New InternetExplorer
```

6. Now, add the following initialization code in the Form's Load event:

```
Private Sub Form_Load()
  List1.AddItem "microsoft"
  List1.AddItem "sybex"
  List1.AddItem "infoseek"
  List1.AddItem "realaudio"
End Sub
```

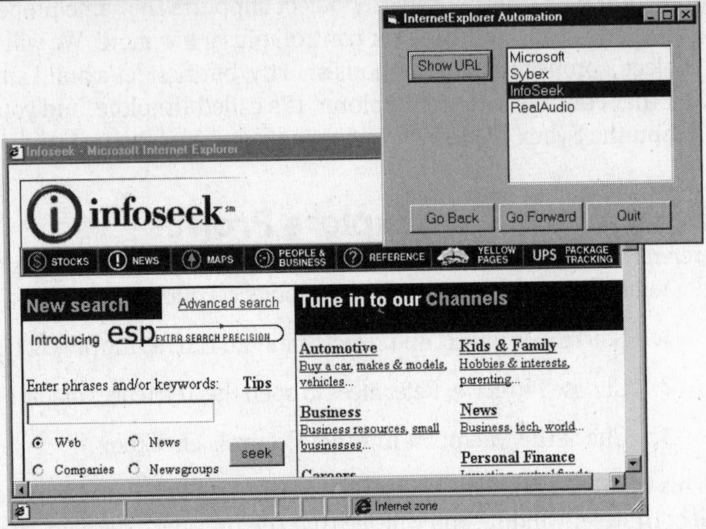

FIGURE 11.3:   Use the IExplore application to OLE automate Internet Explorer.

The most interesting part of this application is the code behind the Show URL Command button, which loads an instance of Internet Explorer and opens the selected URL in its window.

Code 11.3:   The Show URL Button

```
Private Sub Command1_Click()
   IE.ToolBar = False
   IE.MenuBar = False
   IE.Visible = True
   IE.Navigate "http://www." & List1.Text & ".com"
End Sub
```

The ToolBar and MenuBar properties determine whether the toolbar and menu bar of Internet Explorer will be visible. Notice that the Internet Explorer window shown in Figure 11.3, earlier in this chapter, has neither a toolbar nor a menu bar. The Navigate method opens the specified document and displays it in the browser's window. (I'll discuss the properties and the methods of the InternetExplorer object and the Web-Browser control in the next section.)

The Back and Forward buttons are implemented with two methods of the InternetExplorer object, GoBack and GoForward.

Code 11.4: The GoBack and GoForward Methods

```
Private Sub BackBttn_Click()
On Error GoTo NoBack
  IE.GoBack
  Exit Sub

NoBack:
  MsgBox "There are no URL in the History List"
End Sub

Private Sub ForwardBttn_Click()
On Error GoTo NoForward
  IE.GoForward
  Exit Sub

NoForward:
  MsgBox "There are no URLs in the History List"
End Sub
```

NOTE

We use error-trapping code to prevent runtime errors that will be generated if the user attempts to move in front of or past the history list.

THE PROPERTIES OF THE WEBBROWSER CONTROL AND THE INTERNETEXPLORER OBJECT

In this and the following two sections, we will look at the most common properties, methods, and events of the WebBrowser control and the InternetExplorer object. Most members apply to both, but the following sections focus on the members of the WebBrowser control.

TIP

The InternetExplorer object has a few additional members, which I won't discuss here. For complete documentation, visit the following site: http://www.microsoft.com/intdev/sdk/docs/scriptom.

Part iii

Application   This property returns the automation object where HTML documents are displayed (the WebBrowser control or the InternetExplorer object).

Busy   This property returns a True/False value specifying whether the control is navigating to a new URL or is downloading a Web page. If the control's Busy property is True for an unusually long time, call the Stop method to cancel the navigation or the download of a document.

Container   This property returns an object that evaluates to the container of the WebBrowser control, if any. To find out the name of the container, use a statement such as the following:

```
WebBrowser1.Container.Name
```

This expression will return the name of the Form that contains the control.

Document   This property returns the automation object of the active document, if any. This is not the Document object of the Scripting Model (which is covered later in this chapter). To access the document displayed on the control, you use the following expression:

```
WebBrowser1.Document.Script.Document
```

This expression accesses the active document through the script property of the automation object. Later in this chapter, in the section "The IE Scripting Object Model," you'll learn how to manipulate the document from within your code (access its hyperlinks, for example, or even create a new document on the fly and display it on the WebBrowser control).

Height, Width   These two properties return the dimensions, in pixels, of the control that contains the WebBrowser control.

Top, Left   These two properties return the location, in pixels, of the control's upper-left corner on the Desktop.

LocationName   This property returns the title of the Web page displayed on the WebBrowser control.

LocationURL   This control returns the URL of the page displayed on the WebBrowser control. The LocationName and LocationURL properties retrieve information about the location of the displayed document. If the location is an HTML page on the World Wide Web, LocationName retrieves the page's title, and LocationURL retrieves the URL of that page. If the document displayed is a local file, both LocationName and LocationURL retrieve the full path of the file (or its UNC, if it's located on a network).

Type This property returns a string that determines the type of the contained document object. The type for HTML documents is Windows HTML Viewer.

THE METHODS OF THE WEBBROWSER CONTROL AND THE INTERNETEXPLORER OBJECT

The methods of the WebBrowser control and the InternetExplorer object let you navigate to new URLs or to URLs already visited.

GoBack, GoForward These two methods navigate backward or forward one item in the history list, which is maintained automatically by the Web-Browser control or the InternetExplorer object. Attempting to move after the most recent URL or before the first URL in the list generates a runtime error. To prevent this, you must include some error-trapping code, similar to the code you saw in the IExplore application, earlier in this chapter.

GoHome, GoSearch The GoHome method navigates to the current home page; the GoSearch method navigates to the search page, as specified in the Internet Explorer Options dialog box.

Navigate This method navigates to a URL or opens an HTML file, as specified in the method's first argument. This method has the following syntax:

```
Navigate URL [Flags,] [TargetFrameName,] [PostData,] [Headers]
```

All the arguments except the first are optional. The *URL* argument is the URL of the resource to be displayed on the control. The *Flags* argument is a constant or a value that specifies whether to add the resource to the history list, whether to read from or write to the cache, and whether to display the resource in a new window. It can be a combination of the values shown in Table 11.1.

TABLE 11.1: The Values of the *Flags* Argument

CONSTANT	VALUE	DESCRIPTION
NavOpenInNewWindow	1	Opens the resource or file in a new window
NavNoHistory	2	Does not add the resource or filename to the history list
NavNoReadFromCache	4	Does not read from the disk cache for this navigation
NavNoWriteToCache	8	Does not write the results of this navigation to the disk cache

The *TargetFrameName* argument is the name of a frame in which the document will be displayed. If the document displayed on the Web-Browser control contains frames, you can display the new document in one of the existing frames.

The *PostData* argument is a string to be sent to the server during the HTTP POST transaction. The POST transaction is used to send data gathered on an HTML Form. If this parameter does not specify any post data, the Navigate method issues an HTTP GET transaction (it simply retrieves a document). This parameter is ignored if *URL* is not an HTTP URL (one whose protocol is http).

The *Headers* argument is a value that specifies additional HTTP headers to be sent to the server. These headers are added to the default Internet Explorer headers, and they can specify such things as the action required of the server, the type of data being passed to the server, or a status code. This parameter is ignored if *URL* is not an HTTP URL.

Refresh   This method reloads the page currently displayed on the Web-Browser control.

Refresh2   This method is similar to Refresh, but it lets you specify the refresh level. It has the following syntax:

```
WebBrowser1.Refresh2 level
```

The *level* argument can have one of the values shown in Table 11.2.

TABLE 11.2: The Values of the *level* Argument

CONSTANT	VALUE	DESCRIPTION
REFRESH_NORMAL	0	Performs a quick refresh that does not include sending the HTTP "pragma: nocache" header to the server
REFRESH_IFEXPIRED	1	Performs a quick refresh if the page has expired
REFRESH_COMPLETELY	3	Performs a full refresh by downloading the entire page from the server

In addition, you can prevent the control from using the cache by specifying the *navNoReadFromCache* and *navNoWriteToCache* flags when calling the Navigate method.

Stop   This method cancels any pending navigation or download operation and stops playback of multimedia elements such as background sounds and animations.

The Events of the WebBrowser Control and the InternetExplorer Object

The events of the WebBrowser control and the InternetExplorer object are triggered each time the user moves to another URL with Internet Explorer's navigation buttons or the WebBrowser control's navigation methods. They also monitor the progress of each download and let your application know when the download of a page is finished.

BeforeNavigate2   This event occurs when the WebBrowser control is about to navigate to a different URL. It can be caused by external automation (by calling its Navigate method) or by internal automation from within a script or when the user clicks a hyperlink in the current document. Your application has an opportunity to cancel the navigation by setting the method's Cancel argument to True.

TIP

The BeforeNavigate2 event isn't issued unless the hyperlink is valid. In other words, the control first contacts the Web server and then navigates to the specified document.

The BeforeNavigate2 method has the following declaration:

```
Private Sub WebBrowser1_BeforeNavigate2(ByVal pDisp As _
    Object, URL As Variant, Flags As Variant, _
    TargetFrameName As Variant, PostData As Variant, _
    Headers As Variant, Cancel As Boolean)
```

The first argument, *pDisp*, represents the object on which the document is displayed. Since this object is usually the WebBrowser control, you can use this argument to access the properties of the control. *pDisp.Name* is its name, *pDisp.Width* and *pDisp.Height* are the control's dimensions, and so on.

The *URL* argument is the destination URL (specified by the Navigate method or in the hyperlink that was clicked), and *Flags* is a reserved argument. The *TargetFrameName* argument is the name of the frame in which to display the specified document, or it is NULL if the document is to appear on the control, outside any frames. The *PostData* and *Header* arguments are the same as for the Navigate method.

The application can set the *Cancel* argument (notice that it's passed by reference) to cancel the navigation process. If you set this argument to True, the navigation won't even start. To stop a navigation process in progress, use the Stop method.

NavigateComplete   This event occurs after the control has successfully navigated to the new location. Some of the document's resources may still be downloading (a large image, for instance, may take quite a while), but at least part of the document has been received from the server, and progressive rendering has started already. To interrupt this process, you must call the Stop method.

The NavigateComplete event has the following declaration:

```
Sub WebBrowser1_NavigateComplete(ByVal URL As String)
```

The *url* variable is the URL of the document being downloaded.

DownloadBegin   This event occurs when a navigation operation is beginning. It's triggered shortly after the BeforeNavigate event (unless the navigation was canceled), and it signals your application to display a busy message or change the pointer's shape. The DownloadBegin event has the following declaration:

```
Sub WebBrowser1_DownloadBegin ()
```

DownloadComplete   This event occurs when a navigation operation is finished, halted, or failed. Unlike NavigateComplete, which may not be triggered if the navigation doesn't complete successfully, this event is always triggered after a navigation starts. Any busy indication by your application must end from within this event. The DownloadComplete event has the following declaration:

```
Sub WebBrowser1_DownloadComplete ()
```

ProgressChange   The WebBrowser control tracks the progress of a download operation and periodically issues the ProgressChange event to inform your application of the progress. The ProgressChange event has the following declaration:

```
Sub WebBrowser1_ProgressChange(ByVal Progress As Long, _
    ByVal ProgressMax As Long)
```

Both arguments are long integers. The *Progress* argument is the amount of data downloaded so far, and *ProgressMax* is the total amount of data to be downloaded.

TIP

The percentage of data downloaded is *Progress/ProgressMax*, but you must always check the value of *ProgressMax*, because it can be zero (when the control doesn't know the total amount of data to be downloaded). Moreover, the ProgressChange event is triggered for each of the document's resources, and there is no way to know in advance the total size of the components you're downloading. As you have noticed, Internet Explorer displays the progress of each component's download, and not the progress of the entire document.

TitleChange   This event occurs when the title of the current document changes. The title of an HTML document can change; while the document is being downloaded, the URL of the document is also its title. After the real title (if one was specified with the TITLE tag) is parsed, the TitleChange event is triggered, and you can use it to update the Caption property on your Visual Basic Form. The TitleChange event has the following declaration:

```
Sub WebBrowser1_TitleChange(ByVal Text As String)
```

The *Text* argument is the string that appears in Internet Explorer's caption bar.

NewWindow   Although most hyperlinks result in updating the same window in which the document with the hyperlink is displayed, some hyperlinks specify that a new window be opened to display the destination document. When a new window is about to be created for displaying a new document, the NewWindow event is triggered.

This event can be also be triggered if the user holds down the Shift key and clicks the mouse while the cursor is over a hyperlink or if the user chooses New Window ➤ Open in the hyperlink's shortcut menu. The NewWindow event gives your application the opportunity to halt the creation of the new window. When this event is used with Internet Explorer, the new window is another instance of Internet Explorer.

When the NewWindow event is used with the WebBrowser control, however, your application must either create a new WebBrowser control and display the document there or request that the new document be displayed in the same window. If your application creates a new WebBrowser control, it must pass all the parameters from the NewWindow event directly to the Navigate method on the newly created WebBrowser control. If you decide to display the new document on the same control, you must again pass the parameters from this event to the Navigate method in the existing window.

The NewWindow event has the following declaration:

```
Sub WebBrowser_NewWindow (ByVal url As String, _
    ByVal Flags As Long, ByVal TargetFrameName As String, _
    PostData As Variant, ByVal Headers As String, _
    Processed As Boolean)
```

The arguments of the NewWindow event are identical to the arguments of the Navigate method, except for the last argument which is a True/False value indicating whether your application will create the new window (set it to True) or not (set it to False).

FrameBeforeNavigate, FrameNavigateComplete, FrameNewWindow   These three events are identical to the BeforeNavigate, NavigateComplete, and NewWindow events, except that they are triggered from within frames.

USING THE WEBBROWSER CONTROL

You can use the WebBrowser control to build customized Web browsers because it supports all the browsing functionality of Internet Explorer. You can implement the Back and Forward buttons of Internet Explorer with the GoBack and GoForward methods, capture the jumps to hyperlinks, control which sites the user of the application can visit, and so on.

Of course, the WebBrowser doesn't have all the features of Internet Explorer. The most important limitation is that it can't access the displayed document, and you can't save the current HTML document from within your code. The user, however, can invoke the document's shortcut menu and select View Source.

In the following two sections, we are going to look at two applications that demonstrate how to use the WebBrowser control from within Visual Basic. The first application is a custom Web browser. The second application demonstrates how to exploit the hypertext model of an HTML document from within Visual Basic applications and how to add hyperlink features to a user interface.

VB6 at Work: A Customized Web Browser

Figure 11.4 shows an interesting approach to customized browsers. The Form shown in this figure contains a TabStrip control, with several pages, each displaying a different URL. The URLs can be local files or pages on remote servers. You can use local help files for an application (step-by-step instructions), or you can connect your application's users to a Web server that has up-to-the-minute information.

To create the SuperBrowser application, follow these steps:

1. Start a new Standard EXE project, and add a TabStrip control to the Form. Make the Form larger than its default size, and stretch the TabStrip control to fill as much of the Form as possible. You may want to leave some space for a few command buttons, such as Back and Forward (which aren't implemented in this example).

2. If the Toolbox doesn't contain the WebBrowser icon, add it using the Components dialog box (select Internet Controls from the list of available components). You may have to add the TabStrip control to the Toolbox using the Components dialog box also.

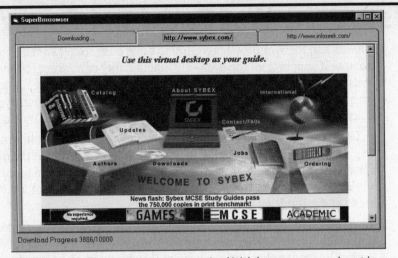

FIGURE 11.4: SuperBrowser is a customized Web browser you can insert in any Visual Basic application.

3. In the Toolbox, select the WebBrowser control, and place an instance of the control on each of the TabStrip's tabs. The WebBrowser control should cover nearly all the tab's area. The three WebBrowser controls are members of the control array WebBrowser1, and their Index values are 0, 1, and 2.

4. Double-click the Form to open its Code window.

5. In the Form's Load event, enter the following lines, which cause the three WebBrowser controls to navigate to three different Web sites:

```
Private Sub Form_Load()
  WebBrowser1(0).Navigate "http://home.microsoft.com"
  WebBrowser1(1).Navigate "http://www.sybex.com"
  WebBrowser1(2).Navigate "http://www.infoseek.com"
End Sub
```

As soon as the Form is loaded, the corresponding WebBrowser controls download the three pages and display them progressively. You can select the page to view by switching to the appropriate tab of the TabStrip control. All three pages continue downloading, as if you had opened three instances of Internet Explorer, each displaying a different document.

Let's add a few lines of code to display the URL of each page on the corresponding tab. Switch back to the Code window, and enter the following line in the WebBrowser control's BeforeNavigate2 event:

```
Private Sub WebBrowser1_BeforeNavigate2(Index As Integer, _
    ByVal URL As String, ByVal Flags As Long, _
    ByVal TargetFrameName As String, PostData As Variant, _
    ByVal Headers As String, Cancel As Boolean)
  SSTab1.TabCaption(Index) = URL
End Sub
```

This line displays the URL of the page that started downloading to the corresponding tab's caption area.

Once the page is downloaded, the WebBrowser control knows its title. At this point, you replace the URL with the actual title. Enter the code to do so in the NavigateComplete event:

```
Private Sub WebBrowser1_NavigateComplete(Index As Integer, _
    ByVal URL As String)
  SSTab1.TabCaption(Index) = WebBrowser1(Index).LocationName
End Sub
```

Now run the application and watch how the captions on the TabStrip control reflect the contents of each page.

Monitoring the Download Progress

This application provides a good opportunity to experiment with the download events. Switch back to the Code window, and enter the following code in the DownloadBegin and DownloadComplete events:

```
Private Sub WebBrowser1_DownloadBegin(Index As Integer)
  Debug.Print "Started Download for tab #" & Index
End Sub

Private Sub WebBrowser1_DownloadComplete(Index As Integer)
  Debug.Print "Completed download for tab #" & Index
End Sub
```

If you run the application now, you will see the following messages in the Immediate execution window (the order will be different on your computer):

```
Started Download for tab #0
Started Download for tab #1
Started Download for tab #2
```

Part iii

```
Completed download for tab #1
Completed download for tab #2
Started Download for tab #1
Started Download for tab #2
Completed download for tab #1
Completed download for tab #0
Started Download for tab #0
Completed download for tab #0
Completed download for tab #2
```

The WebBrowser control starts and completes several downloads for each page. These messages correspond to the downloads of the various elements of each page. If you want to display the progress as well, you must program the ProgressChange event.

To do so, place a Label control on the first tab of the TabStrip control, and enter the following lines in the WebBrowser control's Progress-Change event:

```
Private Sub WebBrowser1_ProgressChange(Index As Integer, _
     ByVal Progress As Long, ByVal ProgressMax As Long)
  If SSTab1.Tab = Index Then
    If Progress >= 0 Then
      Label1.Caption = "Download Progress " & _
         Progress & "/" & ProgressMax
    Else
      Label1.Caption = "Page downloaded"
    End If
  End If
End Sub
```

The outer If structure makes sure that only the progress of the selected tab is displayed. If the ProgressChange event reports the progress of a WebBrowser control other than the one on the currently active tab, the event is not processed.

TIP

If you have a fast connection to the server on which the documents reside, the messages are displayed for only an instant.

ADDING OTHER FEATURES TO YOUR CUSTOM BROWSER

Another interesting feature you can add to your custom browser is URL monitoring. For example, you can keep a list of URLs visited frequently by the user. When the user selects one of them, you ask whether the user wants to open the pages from the cache or download them again.

Or you can prevent the user from following links outside a given Web. This isn't as outrageous as it may sound in an intranet environment. In this case, you might want to limit certain users to the company's Web and not let them take the trip of the thousand clicks during business hours.

USING HYPERLINKS IN VISUAL BASIC APPLICATIONS

What makes Web pages tick is the hypertext model they use to connect to other pages anywhere on the World Wide Web. Although you can access the functionality of Web technology from within your Visual Basic applications with objects such as the WebBrowser and InternetExplorer, you still can't exploit this technology by making it an integral part of your Visual Basic application.

The WebBrowser controls make it possible to exploit the hyperlink model in your applications, and we'll present an example that uses hyperlinks as part of the user interface of a Visual Basic application.

VB6 at Work: The DemoPage Project

The DemoPage application is shown in Figure 11.5, and you will find it on the Sybex Web site. The DemoPage application consists of two Forms:

▶ VBForm

▶ WEBForm

The main Form is VBForm and is used for drawing simple shapes with Visual Basic methods. The WEBForm displays an HTML document that contains instructions on the Visual Basic drawing methods. The HTML document contains the instructions and a few hyperlinks. When either

Part iii

hyperlink is activated, it doesn't display another document. Instead, it draws a shape on the first Visual Basic Form.

Design the two Forms as shown in Figure 11.5. The main Form contains a Label control at the top, on which a command is displayed. The second Form (WEBForm) contains a WebBrowser control, on which the Demo.htm page is displayed.

When the first Form is loaded, it loads the second Form and displays the HTML document on the WebBrowser control. All the code in the VBForm Form is located in the Load event.

Code 11.5: The Load Event

```
Private Sub Form_Load()
Dim target
    target = App.Path & "\Demo.htm"
    WEBForm.WebBrowser1.Navigate target
    WEBForm.Show
End Sub
```

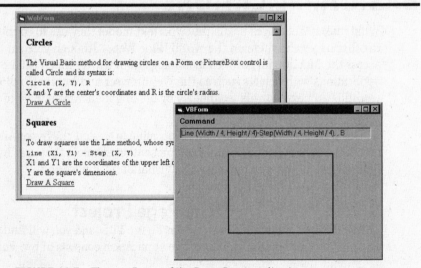

FIGURE 11.5: The two Forms of the DemoPage application

To avoid an absolute reference, the code assumes that the HTML document (the file Demo.htm) is stored in the same folder as the project. The complete Demo.htm page is shown in Figure 11.6.

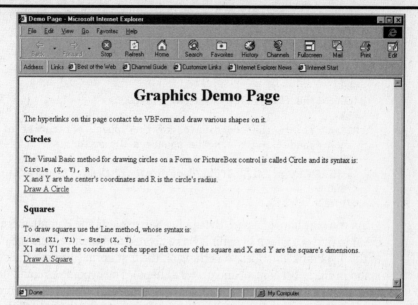

FIGURE 11.6: The entire Demo.htm as displayed by Internet Explorer

Code 11.6: The DemoPage Application

```
<HTML>
<TITLE>Demo Page</TITLE>

<BODY>
<CENTER>
<H1>Graphics Demo Page</H1>
</CENTER>

The hyperlinks on this page contact the VBForm and draw
various shapes on it.
<P>
<H3>Circles</H3>

The Visual Basic method for drawing circles on a Form or
PictureBox control is called Circle and its syntax is:
<BR>
<CODE>Circle (X, Y), R</CODE>
<BR>
X and Y are the center's coordinates and R is the circle's
radius.
<BR>
```

```
<A HREF="http://127.0.0.1/demo.htm#circle">Draw A Circle</A>
<BR>
<BR>
<H3>Squares</H3>
To draw squares use the Line method, whose syntax is:
<BR>
<CODE>Line (X1, Y1) - Step (X, Y)</CODE>
<BR>
X1 and Y1 are the coordinates of the upper left corner of the
  square and X and Y are the square's dimensions.
<BR>
<A HREF="http://127.0.0.1/demo.htm#box">Draw A Square</A>
</BODY>
</HTML>
```

As you may have guessed, the application exploits the BeforeNavigate2 event to find out which hyperlink was activated and then cancels the jump to this hyperlink and does something on the first Form (displays the command in the Label control and draws a shape). The hyperlinks could be fake; all we need is to know which one was clicked. However, the Before-Navigate2 event isn't triggered unless the destination of the hyperlink is a valid URL.

The definitions of the two hyperlinks are shown next. As you can see, the destinations of the hyperlinks include some information about the kind of shape to be drawn on the first Form.

```
<A HREF="http://127.0.0.1/demo.htm#circle">Draw A Circle</A>
<A HREF="http://127.0.0.1/demo.htm#box">Draw A Square</A>
```

The HTML document doesn't contain any anchors named "circle" and "box", and you don't really need them. The WebBrowser control generates an error message, but all you really need is the name of the anchor. The server address is the IP address of the local machine (127.0.0.1), which is always a valid server name. Let's see how the code of the Before-Navigate2 event causes some action to take place on the other Form.

Code 11.7:   The BeforeNavigate2 Event

```
Private Sub WebBrowser1_BeforeNavigate2(ByVal pDisp As Object,_
      URL As Variant, Flags As Variant, _
      TargetFrameName As Variant, PostData As Variant, _
      Headers As Variant, Cancel As Boolean)
Dim Position As Integer, Shape As String
On Error Resume Next

   If UCase(Right$(URL, 8)) <> "DEMO.HTM" Then Cancel = True
```

```
Position = InStr(URL, "#")
Shape = Mid$(URL, Position + 1)
If Shape = "circle" Then
  VBForm.Cls
  VBForm.Circle (VBForm.Width / 2, VBForm.Height / 2), _
         VBForm.Height / 3
  VBForm.Label1.Caption = "Circle (Width / 2, Height / 2), _
         Height / 3"
End If
If Shape = "box" Then
  VBForm.Cls
  VBForm.Line (VBForm.Width / 4, VBForm.Height / 4) _
       -Step(VBForm.Width / 2, VBForm.Height / 2), , B
  VBForm.Label1.Caption = "Line (Width / 4, Height / 4) _
       -Step(Width / 4, Height / 4), , B"
End If
End Sub
```

The first statement is an error-trapping statement; it tells Visual Basic to ignore errors and continue with the next statement. We know that an error will occur because the destinations of the two hyperlinks are invalid. We then cancel the navigation by setting the Cancel argument to True. The If statement makes sure that other (possibly valid) hyperlinks aren't canceled. The program then examines the last part of the hyperlink's destination URL (everything to the right of the pound sign). If this string is "circle", the program draws a circle on the VBForm Form and displays the command used to draw the circle in the Label control. If the string is "box", it draws a square on the Form and displays the corresponding command on the Label.

You can easily modify this application to accommodate more actions, place detailed instructions in the HTML document, and even create demos for your applications. The approach is rather clumsy, but hyperlinks are not yet part of the Visual Basic interface model. The application does, however, demonstrate how to incorporate the functionality of hyperlinks in your Visual Basic applications.

Part iii

THE IE SCRIPTING OBJECT MODEL

The Scripting Model is a hierarchy of objects through which you can access the properties of HTML documents displayed in the browser and the properties of the browser itself. The model's organization is similar to the organization of the Database Access objects. In the Scripting Model, each object has properties, which are themselves objects. As such, they have their own properties (some of them also being objects), methods, and events.

The top-level object in the Scripting Model is the Window object. The document is rendered within this object. Some basic properties of the Window object are its name (property Name) and the location of the document displayed (property URL). Before we look at these and other properties, though, let's look at the objects of the Scripting Model at large and see what they can do for your Web pages.

The most important property of the Window object is another object, the Document object. The Document object represents the HTML document displayed in the window, which in turn has its own properties, such as background color, title, and so on. A window can also contain frames, which in turn can contain documents. To access the document in a frame, you first access the appropriate frame object and then the document object of the specific frame.

The Properties of the Scripting Objects

The Window is the top-level object and is the container for all other objects. The Window object represents the browser's window, in which HTML documents are displayed. Its properties include the name of the Window and the message displayed in its status bar. To access the Name property of the Window object, use a statement such as the following:

```
win_new = Window.Name
```

You can use the variable *win_new* from within your code to address the window. For example, you can request that another document be displayed in the *win_new* window.

To display a welcome message in the browser's status bar, use a statement such as the following:

```
Window.Status = "Welcome to our Fabulous Site"
```

You can also include VBScript functions in the definition of the status string, such as the date and time functions:

```
Window.Status = "Welcome to our Fabulous Site" & "It is " & _
        date & " and the time is " & time
```

The most important property of the Window object is another object, the Document object. Through the Document object, you can access the properties and methods of the document displayed in the browser's window. Two common properties of the Document object are its background color (property bgColor) and its foreground color (fgColor). To change the document's background color to white, for example, you use the following statement:

```
Window.Document.bgColor = white
```

Just as some of the Window object's properties are objects, the Document object has properties that are themselves objects. One of these objects is the Location object, with which you access the properties of the location of the document. The URL of the document in the browser's window is given by the hRef property of the Location object. You can find out the current document's URL or set this property to the URL of another document. The hHef property is a property of the Location object, and you access it with the following expression:

```
Location.href
```

The Location object is a property of the Document object, and it must be accessed as follows:

```
Document.Location.href
```

Finally, because the Document object is a property of the Window object, the complete expression for accessing the document's URL is the following:

```
Window.Document.Location.href
```

This expression is long, but it's easy to understand. The first-level object is the Window object. The following objects are more specific, and you can step down this hierarchy to reach the desired property. The organization of the scripting objects in a hierarchy simplifies the syntax of its methods and properties.

A window can also contain frames. Frames are accessed though the Frames object, which is an array of objects. The first frame is Frames(0), the second one Frames(1), and so on. To access the document in a specific frame, you start with the Window object and specify the frame whose document you want to access. For example, if you want to access the second frame, you specify the following:

```
Window.Frames(1)
```

Each frame displays a different document and therefore has its own Document property. To access the properties of the document on the second frame, use the following expression:

```
Window.Frames(1).Document
```

What would the background color of this document be? Simply tack on the bgColor property name at the end of the previous expression, and you have it:

```
Window.Frames(1).Document.bgColor
```

As you can see, the same property can be attached to multiple objects. The window has its own Document object, and the document has a Location property. But, if the window contains frames, each frame in the window has its own Location property. You may find this behavior confusing at first, but you'll soon get the hang of it.

The Methods of the Scripting Objects

The scripting objects also have methods. The Document object, for example, provides the Write method, which lets your script place text directly on the Web page. In other words, with the Write method you can create Web pages on the fly.

The Write method displays a string on the current page. The following statement displays the current date on the page:

```
Document.Write Date()
```

If you use HTML instead, you must hardcode the date and consequently update the document daily. The VBScript Date() function returns the current date, but VBScript doesn't provide any methods for actually displaying the date on the page. To display something on a page from within its script, you use the objects of the Scripting Model.

Let's look at an example. Here's a simple HTML document:

```
<HTML>
<BODY BGCOLOR="#H00FF00">
<H1>Welcome to Visual Basic and the Web</H1>
</BODY>
</HTML>
```

This document displays a page with a green background and a level 1 heading. You can create the same page with the following VBScript code:

```
<HTML>
<SCRIPT LANGUAGE="VBScript">
Document.bgColor = "#H00FF00".
Document.Write "<H1> Welcome to Visual Basic and the
Web</H1>"
</SCRIPT>
</HTML>
```

What's the benefit of using the Write method to generate the page? Flexibility. This page is actually generated on the client computer. If you want to display the date and the time this page was opened, you can add the following line of VBScript code:

```
Document.Write "This page was opened on " & date() & _
        ", at " & time()
```

The Write method provides even more flexibility. You can write complicated VBScript code to produce elaborate pages on the fly. For example, you can prompt the user for his or her name and personalize a Web page as follows:

```
UserName = InputBox("Please enter your name")
Document.Write "<H1>Welcome to our Active Pages, " & _
UserName & "</H1>"
```

The actual heading will be different on each client computer, depending on the user's response to the prompt. Figure 11.7 shows a typical page generated on the fly with VBScript code that manipulates the IE Scripting Objects.

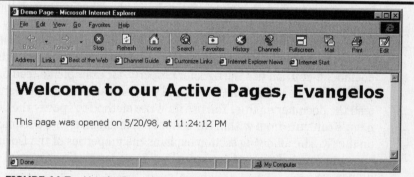

FIGURE 11.7: Use the Document object's Write method to create HTML documents on the fly.

Here is the HTML file that produced the page shown in Figure 11.7:

```
<HTML>
<HEAD>
<TITLE>Demo Page</TITLE>
<SCRIPT LANGUAGE="VBSCRIPT">
UserName = InputBox("Please enter your name")
Document.Write "<H1>Welcome to our Active Pages, " _
        & UserName & "</H1>"
Document.Write "<BR>"
```

Part iii

```
Document.Write "This page was opened on " & date() & _
        ", at " & time()
</SCRIPT>
</HEAD>
<BODY>

</BODY>
</HTML>
```

Notice that this document doesn't contain any HTML tags in its BODY section. The entire document was generated from within the page's script section with VBScript commands.

In the following sections, we are going to explore the Document object of the Scripting Model, since this is the most important one from a VB programmer's point of view.

THE DOCUMENT OBJECT

From a programming point of view, the Document object is probably the most important object in the scripting hierarchy. The Document object represents the HTML document displayed in the browser's window or in one of its frames. Through the Document object's properties and methods, you can manipulate the appearance and even the contents of the document. You can use the bgColor property, for example, to read or set the document's background color, and you can use the Title property to read the document's title. You use its Write method to specify the document's contents from within the script and, in effect, create documents on the fly. The following section explains the properties of the Document object and provides short examples that demonstrate the syntax of the properties.

The Properties of the Document Object

The Document object provides a few simple properties that let you set the document's background color, the color of the links, and so on. It also provides a few of the most advanced properties, such as the Cookie property, which lets your script store information on the client computer and read it the next time the document with the script is loaded.

linkColor, aLinkColor, vLinkColor   These properties return or set the color of the links in the document. The linkColor property is the default color of the hyperlinks in the document, aLinkColor is the color of the active hyperlink, and vLinkColor is the color of the hyperlinks already visited. These properties accept color values that can be expressed as hexadecimal numbers or as color names:

```
Window.Document.vLinkColor = #00FFFF
Window.Document.linkColor = blue
```

bgColor, fgColor   These properties return or set the document's background color and foreground color. The foreground color is the color used for rendering text if the HTML code doesn't overwrite this setting. Likewise, the background property can be overwritten by the document if it uses a background image. These properties accept color values.

Title   This property returns the current document's title. This is a read-only property and can't be used to change the document's title at runtime.

Cookie   As you know, scripts written in VBScript are executed on the client computer. VBScript, therefore, had to be a safe language. There is no way for VBScript to access the file system of the client computer and tamper with it. That's why VBScript lacks the file I/O commands of Visual Basic. A language that can't store information locally is rather limited. Scripts can't even open or save a few bytes of data on a local file, and for many applications, this is a serious limitation.

TIP

In the last chapter we discussed the FileSystemObject object, which gives VBScript access to the computer's file system. If you attempt to access the host computer's file system, however, Internet Explorer will not execute the script. Statements that can harm the host computer's system are not considered safe, and Internet Explorer is smart enough to ignore these scripts. If you're using VBScript to script applications or Windows itself, you can access the computer's file system, just as you would access it with Visual Basic statements.

The solution to this problem is to use cookies. A cookie is a property of the Document object and is a string that can be stored on the client computer. Cookies are quite safe, though, because they are text files written and read to and from the disk by the browser, and they live in a specific folder. They are not executable files (they present no threat to the rest of the file system), and they can be accessed only by the browser. Cookies can't be considered a substitute for file I/O, but they can save a piece of information on the client computer so that the next time the script is executed, it will find the information there.

The information stored on the client computer by means of cookies is limited. You can't store large files with text or numbers. But you can store customization information such as the user's name and preferences so that the next time the user requests the same page, the script can find the values it stored on the client computer the last time and customize itself for the user.

NOTE

The most common use for cookies is for storing customization data.

Another practical reason for using cookies is to share information among pages. The shopping basket is a typical example. As you know, a script is limited to a single page. If the page with the script loads another page, the original script ceases to exist. The script (if any) on the newly loaded page takes over. Some sites let viewers select items to purchase on various pages, and they keep track of the items in the user's shopping basket. If each page is a separate entity and the pages can't share information, how is this done?

The answer is the Cookie property of the Document object. When a page wants to pass some information to other pages, it can leave a cookie on the client computer. The page that needs the information can read it. To the viewer, it appears that the various pages are communicating as if they were Forms of an application, to use a Visual Basic analogy.

VB6 at Work: The Cookie Page

To store a string on the client computer's system and access it from another page or to access it the next time the page is opened, use the Cookie property, as outlined in the Cookie page. The Cookie page, shown in Figure 11.8, is a revision of the Page1 page. This time we prompt the user for his or her name, and then we store it in the Document object's Cookie property. The next time you open this page, the user's name appears automatically.

To test the Cookie page, you must have a Web server installed. Opening the Cookie page with Internet Explorer won't do the trick. Cookies are saved on the client computer by the browser and only if they are furnished by a server. You can use any Web server, including the FrontPage Web server or the Personal Web Server.

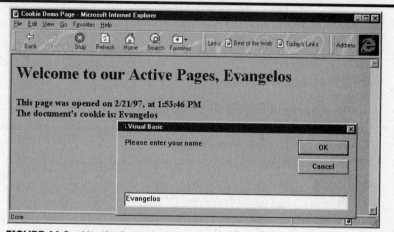

FIGURE 11.8: Use the Document object's Cookie property to customize your pages.

TIP

The Personal Web Server is part of FrontPage and Internet Explorer 4. It is also available from Microsoft's Web site (http://www.microsoft.com/sitebuilder).

I used the FrontPage Web server to test this example (which works just like the Personal Web Server). Here are the steps to follow to experiment with the Cookie property:

1. Download the Cookies.htm file from the Sybex Web site to the Cookie folder under the Web server's root folder.

2. Rename it to Index.htm.

3. Start the FrontPage Web server or any other server you have installed on your system (if it's not already running).

4. Start Internet Explorer and connect to the following URL:
   http://127.0.0.1/Cookie

   The numerals 127.0.0.1 constitute the IP address of the local server, and Cookie is the name of the folder to which the site has been copied (this site contains a single page).

5. When prompted, enter your name. The script displays it on the page and saves it in the Document object's Cookie property.

6. Connect to another URL by entering it in the browser's Address box.

7. Click Back to return to the Cookie page. This time you won't be prompted for your name. It's already stored in the Cookie property.

Now, let's look at the script of the Cookies.htm page.

Code 11.8:   The Cookies.htm Document

```
<HTML>
<HEAD>
<TITLE>Cookie Demo Page</TITLE>
<SCRIPT LANGUAGE="VBSCRIPT">
If Document.Cookie = "" Then
  UserName = InputBox("Please enter your name")
  document.cookie=UserName
Else
  UserName = Document.Cookie
End If
Document.write "<H1>Welcome to our Active Pages, " &
  UserName & "</H1>"
Document.write "<BR>"
Document.write "This page was opened on " & date() & ",
  at " & time()
Document.write "<BR>"
Document.write "The document's cookie is: " & Document.cookie
</SCRIPT>
</HEAD>
<BODY>

</BODY>
</HTML>
```

The If structure of the script examines the value of the Cookie property. If this property has no value, it prompts the user to enter a name. It then stores the name entered by the user in the Cookie property.

The second time you connect to this page, the Cookie property has a value, and the Else clause executes, which assigns the cookie's value to the *UserName* variable. The rest of the code is the same as that for the Page1 page, with the exception of the last Write method, which displays the current value of the cookie on the page.

Using cookies in this way is slightly unorthodox. Cookies are usually stored as pairs of names and values, separated with a semicolon. A more reasonable cookie value is the following:

```
"UserName = Cibil; Age = 24; Browser=IE3.02"
```

As you can see, you can store many variable values in the cookie, but there are no methods for retrieving the value of a single variable. You must read the entire cookie and then use the string manipulation functions (the InStr(), Mid(), and other string manipulation functions) to isolate each pair and extract the name of the variable and its value.

COOKIES EXPIRE

Cookies have an expiration date. If you don't specify an expiration date (I didn't use an expiration date in the Cookie example), the cookie expires after the current session. To create a new session, shut down the Web server and start it again. Shutting down and restarting Internet Explorer won't start a new session.

To specify an expiration date, append a string like this one to the cookie:

```
expires = Thu, 01 Jan 1998 12:00:00 GMT
```

This string must be appended to the cookie as follows:

```
Document.cookie = UserName & " expires = Thu, 01 _
Jan 1998 12:00:00 GMT"
```

Cookies with expiration dates are actually stored on disk as text files, and you can view them with a text editor. Each Web site's cookies are stored in the Cookies folder under the Windows folder.

Anchor   Anchor is a property of the Document object, and like some other properties, it is also an object. The Length property of the Anchor object returns the number of anchors in the document. The individual anchors are stored in the Anchors array, whose elements can be accessed with an index. The name of the first anchor in the document is Anchors(0) (its value is the NAME attribute of the <A> tag that inserted the anchor in the document), Anchors(1) is the second anchor, and so on. The following statements display the number of anchors in the current document in a message box:

```
TotalAnchors = Document.Anchors.Length
MsgBox "The document contains "& TotalAnchors & "anchors"
```

You can also scan all the anchors in a document with a loop such as the following:

```
For i=0 to TotalAnchors-1
    ThisAnchor=Document.Anchors(i)
    {do something with this anchor}
Next
```

Scanning the anchors of the current document from within the same document's script section isn't practical. But you can open another document in a frame and access the anchors of the frame with the *Frame(1) .Document.Anchors* array. For another example, see the DocumentLinks example, later in this chapter.

Link   This property is similar to the Anchor property, but instead of representing the anchors, it represents the hyperlinks in the current document. Like the anchors array, the links array is a property of the Document object, which is the only object that can contain links. The basic property of the Link object is the Length property, which returns the number of links in the document.

Each link is a member of the *Links* array. The first link is Links(0), the second one is Links(1), and so on. Because the hyperlinks in a document are destinations, the Link object's properties are identical to the properties of the Location object, but they are read-only.

To obtain the number of links in the document displayed in the browser's window, use the following statement:

```
Window.Document.Links.Length
```

To scan the hyperlinks in the document and examine their destinations, use a loop such as the following:

```
For i=0 to Window.Document.Links.Length-1
    {process the hyperlink}
Next
```

At each iteration of the loop, the current hyperlink is given by the following expression:

```
Window.Dcument.Links(i).href
```

lastModified   This property returns the date the current document was last modified. You can use the lastModified property of the Document object to display the date and time it was last modified, without having to hardcode this information in the document itself.

Referrer   This property returns the URL of the referring document.

The Methods of the Document Object

The Document object supports a few methods as well, which let you manipulate its contents. The Document object's methods manipulate the contents of the current document.

Open   This method opens the document for output. The current document is cleared, and new strings can be placed on the document with the Write and WriteLn methods.

NOTE

The Open method of the Document object opens the current document for output and has nothing to do with the Open method of the Window object, which opens a new instance of Internet Explorer and displays a document in it.

Write string   This method writes the *string* variable to the document. The argument is inserted in the current document at the current position, but it doesn't appear until the document is closed with the Close method.

WriteLn string   This method writes the *string* variable into the current document with a newline character appended to the end. The newline character is ignored by the browser anyway, so the WriteLn string method is practically the same as the Write string method.

Close   This method closes the document and causes all the information written to it with the Write and WriteLn methods to be displayed, as if it were placed in an HTML document that is loaded in the browser's window.

Clear   This method clears the contents of the document.

Using the Document Object's Methods

In effect, these methods allow the programmer (or Web author) to create an HTML document from within the script, as the Page1.htm example of the next section demonstrates. The Document object's methods are usually called in the following order:

```
Document.open
Document.write string
. . .
Document.write string
Document.close
```

Part iii

The *string* variable, or literal, could be anything that normally appears in an HTML document (text, HTML tags, hyperlinks, and so on). Because the Write method's argument can contain HTML tags, you have the flexibility to create Web pages on the fly. The following statements display a level 1 header, centered on the page:

```
Document.write "<CENTER>"
Document.write "<H1>Welcome to our Active Pages</H1>"
Document.write "</CENTER>"
```

If you take the arguments of the Write methods and strip the quotes, you'll get the HTML document that would produce the same page.

The most common use of these methods is to create documents on the fly. The Write method is extremely flexible, and we are going to look at a couple of examples.

VB6 at Work: The Navigate Page

The `Navigate.htm` document, shown in Figure 11.9, contains a floating frame and two buttons. The first button displays a user-specified URL in the frame by calling the Window object's Navigate method. The second button also displays the user-specified URL in the frame, only this one uses the hRef property of the Location object.

The floating frame was inserted with the following statement:

```
<IFRAME SRC="http://www.sybex.com" WIDTH=600 HEIGHT=300">
```

When the page is first loaded, it displays the Sybex home page in the floating frame. To display another page, click one of the two command buttons. The document's body consists of the following lines:

```
<BODY>
<BR>
<CENTER>
    <INPUT TYPE=Button NAME='Button1' VALUE="Navigate URL">
    <INPUT TYPE=Button NAME='Button2' VALUE=" Set URL ">
    <BR>
    <H1>Welcome to the NAVIGATE page</H1>
    <IFRAME SRC="http://www.sybex.com" WIDTH=600 HEIGHT=300>
    </IFRAME>
    </CENTER>
</BODY>
```

The URLs must be complete, including their protocol part. To navigate to Microsoft's home page, enter the URL `http://home.microsoft.com`, and not just `home.microsoft.com`.

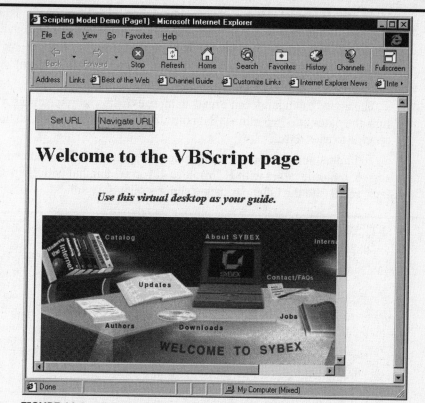

FIGURE 11.9: The Navigate.htm example demonstrates two methods for navigating to any URL.

The Command buttons were placed on the page with two <INPUT> tags, and their names are Button1 and Button2. The two buttons react to the onClick event with the following handlers. The first button's code sets the frame's destination to a user-specified URL and is as follows:

```
Sub Button1_onClick()
    newURL=InputBox("Please enter the URL you want to view")
    Call window.frames(0).navigate(newURL)
End Sub
```

The second button does the same, only this time by setting the Href property, which is equivalent to the Navigate method:

```
Sub Button2_onClick()
    newURL=InputBox("Please enter the URL you want to view")
    window.frames(0).location.href=newURL
End Sub
```

VB6 at Work: The Calendar.htm Page

The page shown in Figure 11.10 was created entirely from within a
script. The calendar is generated by VBScript code on the client's side
and displays the days of the current month. By specifying a different
date you can create any month's calendar.

The actual calendar doesn't react to mouse clicks, but you can easily
turn the dates into hyperlinks that point to documents with information
specific to each date.

To understand the code of this application, you need a basic knowledge of building tables with HTML tags. If you are familiar with these
tags, you'll find the Calendar page's script straightforward.

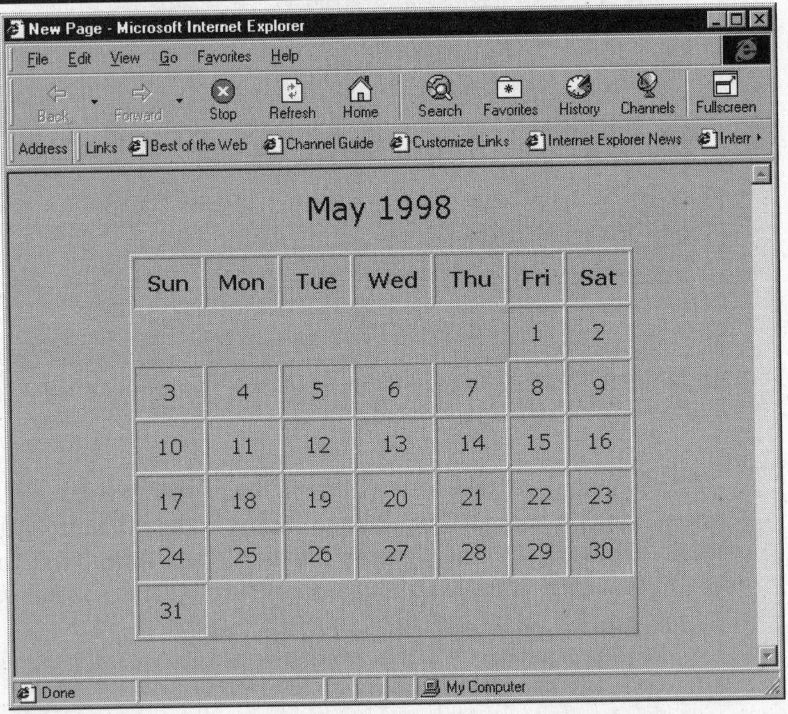

FIGURE 11.10: This calendar was generated with VBScript code.

Code 11.9: The Script for the Calendar Page

```
<HTML>
<HEAD>
<TITLE>New Page</TITLE>
```

```
<SCRIPT LANGUAGE="VBSCRIPT">
Dim imonth, thisdate, nextday, cday
imonth=month(date)

  document.bgcolor="#C0C0C0"
  document.write "<CENTER>"
  document.write "<FONT FACE='Verdana' SIZE=5>"
  document.write MonthName(Month(date)) & " " & Year(date)
  document.write "<P>"
  document.write "<TABLE CELLPADDING=10 BORDER><TR>"
  document.write "<TD><B>Sun<TD><B>Mon<TD><B>Tue<TD><B>Wed _
<TD><B>Thu<TD><B>Fri<TD><B>Sat"
  document.write "<TR>"
  thisdate=DateSerial(year(date), month(date), 1)
  nextday=1
  For cday=1 to 7
    If WeekDay(thisdate)>cday Then
      document.write "<TD></TD>"
    else
      document.write "<TD ALIGN=CENTER><FONT SIZE=3>" & _
nextday & "</TD>"
      nextday=nextday+1
      thisdate=DateSerial(year(date), imonth, nextday)
    End If
  Next
  document.write "<TR>"
  weekDays=1
  while month(thisdate)=imonth
    document.write "<TD ALIGN=CENTER><FONT SIZE=3>" & _
nextday & "</TD>"
    nextday=nextday+1
    weekDays=weekDays+1
    If weekDays>7 then
      WeekDays=1
      document.write "<TR>"
    End If
    thisdate=DateSerial(year(date), imonth, nextday)
  wend
  document.write "</TABLE>"
  document.write "</CENTER>"

</SCRIPT>
</HEAD>
<BODY>

</BODY>
</HTML>
```

Part iii

First, the script displays the week's days as headers of the table:

```
document.write _  "<TD><B>Sun<TD><B>Mon<TD><B>Tue<TD> _
<B>Wed<TD><B>Thu<TD><B>Fri
<TD><B>Sat"
```

Next, the program displays the days of the first week with a For...Next loop. The first week of the month is frequently incomplete, and the first few cells in the table are likely to be blank. This loop goes through the seven days in the week until it hits the first day in the month.

After the first day in the month is found, the program creates cells in which it places the value of the variable *nextday*, which is increased with every iteration (it goes from 1 to 31). The following string produces a cell with a number:

```
"<TD ALIGN=CENTER><FONT SIZE=3>" & nextday & "</TD>"
```

This is HTML code, and any references to variables are replaced with the actual value of the *nextday* variable. For example, if the value of the *nextday* variable is 24, the following line is actually written to the document:

```
<TD ALIGN=CENTER><FONT SIZE=3>24</TD>
```

After the first week of the calendar is displayed, the program continues with the following weeks. These weeks are complete, except for the last one, of course.

A While...Wend loop handles the remaining days of the month. At each iteration, the *nextday* variable is increased by one day, and the loop continues to the end of the month.

You can easily turn each day of the month into a hyperlink that points to a file on the server. If you maintain a separate document on the server for each day of the month, you can modify the application so that each day is a hyperlink to this date's file. Instead of writing the number of the day to the output, you can insert the appropriate <A> tags to turn the day number into a hyperlink. For example, if the current value of the *nextday* variable is 24, the following VBScript line

```
"<A HREF=" & imonth & "-" & nextday & ".htm>" & nextday _
& "</A>"
```

writes this string, which is indeed a hyperlink, to the document:

```
<A HREF=1-24.htm>24</A>
```

The names of the files specified in the hyperlinks must also exist on the server or in the same folder as the document that opened them.

VB6 at Work: The HTMLEditor Project

The HTMLEditor project is the simplest HTML editor you can imagine. It consists of two panes, which can be resized at runtime with the mouse (see Figure 11.11). The upper pane is a RichTextBox control, where you can enter HTML code. The lower pane is a WebBrowser control, where the HTML code is rendered. The HTMLEditor project (you'll find it on the Sybex Web site) is ideal for experimenting with HTML. There are many WYSIWYG HTML editors around, but in order to get exactly what you want, you must tweak the source HTML code. HTMLEditor combines the operations of HTML editing and rendering in the same window.

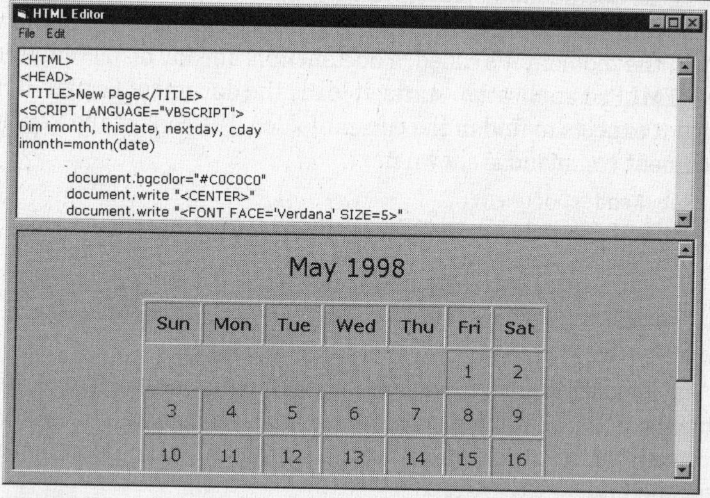

FIGURE 11.11: HTMLEditor may not be WYSIWYG, but it's quite convenient, and you can customize it according to your needs and preferences.

Part iii

I could have used a simple TextBox control for editing the HTML source code, but instead I used the RichTextBox control because its built-in features simplify the implementation of many custom editing features. It even allows the use of different colors for HTML tags or lets you convert them to uppercase.

The HTMLEditor can handle every document you could normally display in Internet Explorer, thanks to the WebBrowser control. The upper half of the Form is a simple editor. No HTML specific features were added to this editor, just the built-in editing features of the RichTextBox control. The Edit menu, which is also implemented as a context menu, contains the usual editing commands (Copy, Cut, Clear, Paste, and Select All) plus the Render Document command, which renders the current document on the WebBrowser control.

To access the document displayed in the WebBrowser control, you must first access the Script object of the WebBrowser control's Document property. If you wanted to clear the current document from within a script, you should have used the expression `Window.Document.Clear`. To clear the contents of the WebBrowser control from within your VB application, you use the following expression:

```
WebBrowser1.Document.script.Document.Clear
```

The Script object of the WebBrowser's Document property lets you access the document displayed on the control and manipulate it from within your VB code. But there's a catch here. This expression will work only if, the moment it's called, a document is already displayed. When the HTMLPad application starts, it loads the document `Empty.htm`, which it expects to find in the current folder. The code of the Render Document command is shown next:

```
Sub RenderDocument()
    HTMLEdit.WebBrowser1.Document.Script.Document.Clear
    HTMLEdit.WebBrowser1.Document.Script.Document.Write _
        HTMLPad.RichTextBox1.Text
    HTMLEdit.WebBrowser1.Document.Script.Document.Close
End Sub
```

The RenderDocument() subroutine is a short procedure that clears the contents of the WebBrowser control, opens the document, and then writes to it the HTML code of the RichTextBox control with the Document object's Write method.

Now that you know how to manipulate the document displayed on the WebBrowser control, you can access any page displayed on the control through your VB code. For example, you can use the *Links* array of the Scripting Model to access the hyperlinks in the document, examine which ones are images, and start another process to download them in the background. Or you can write an application that downloads a Web page and all the documents on the same Web that are referenced on the home page via hyperlinks.

Resizing the HTMLEditor Window

The HTMLEditor application wouldn't be nearly as functional if you couldn't resize its panes. When you're working with the HTML code, you need a large editor window. When you view the rendered document, you want to view as much of the document as possible. The code for resizing the application's window and its panes has nothing to do with the topics covered in this chapter, but because this is such an important feature of the application, I will discuss the code briefly.

First, you must provide the code that resizes and arranges the two controls on the Form. The HTMLEditor Form's Resize event is shown next:

```
Private Sub Form_Resize()
    RichTextBox1.Width = HTMLVal.Width - RichTextBox1.Left - 200
    WebBrowser1.Width = RichTextBox1.Width
    RichTextBox1.Height = 0.3 * HTMLVal.Height
    WebBrowser1.Move WebBrowser1.Left, RichTextBox1.Top + _
        RichTextBox1.Height + 120, WebBrowser1.Width, _
        HTMLVal.Height - RichTextBox1.Top - _
        RichTextBox1.Height - 940
    WebBrowser1.Navigate App.Path & "\empty.htm"
End Sub
```

Another feature of the HTMLEditor application is that the stripe between the two controls acts as a movable bar that lets you change the heights of the editor's and browser's areas. This allows you to give more space to one of them, depending on in which one you're working. To move the bar up or down, place the pointer over the stripe and press the left button. When the pointer turns into a double arrow, move the bar to the desired position, and then release the button.

To implement this feature, you must program the Form's mouse events. When the mouse is first pressed, the code changes the mouse pointer and saves the Y coordinate of the mouse to a Form variable, *DragStartY*. The *ResizeWindows* variable is also set to True to indicate that the two sections of the Form can be resized from within the Mouse-Move event. Here is the handler of the Form's MouseDown event:

```
Private Sub Form_MouseDown(Button As Integer, Shift As Integer, _
    X As Single, Y As Single)
  If Button = 1 And (Y > RichTextBox1.Top + _
      RichTextBox1.Height) And (Y < WebBrowser1.Top) Then
    Screen.MousePointer = vbSizeNS
    ResizeWindows = True
    DragStartY = Y
    WebHeight = WebBrowser1.Height
    HTMLHeight = RichTextBox1.Height
  End If
End Sub
```

In the MouseMove event, you must resize the two controls on the Form by changing their height, as well as the top coordinate of the Web-Browser control:

```
Private Sub Form_MouseMove(Button As Integer, _
        Shift As Integer, X As Single, Y As Single)
On Error Resume Next
  If ResizeWindows Then
    RichTextBox1.Height = HTMLHeight + (Y - DragStartY)
    WebBrowser1.Move WebBrowser1.Left, RichTextBox1.Top + _
        RichTextBox1.Height + 120, WebBrowser1.Width, _
        WebHeight - (Y - DragStartY)
    Form1.Refresh
  End If

End Sub
```

Finally, in the MouseUp event, you must reset the mouse pointer and the *ResizeWindows* variable:

```
Private Sub Form_MouseUp(Button As Integer, Shift As Integer, _
    X As Single, Y As Single)
  ResizeWindows = False
  Screen.MousePointer = vbDefault
End Sub
```

Loading and Rendering Files

The code of the HTMLEditor application has two more interesting procedures. The Save command on the File menu stores the contents of the RichTextBox control (the HTML source code) to a disk file with the Save-File method of the RichTextBox control. The HTML source code is saved as ASCII text with the following procedure:

```
Private Sub FileSaveAs_Click()
  CommonDialog1.DefaultExt = "htm"
  CommonDialog1.Filter = "HTML Documents|*.htm|All Files|*.*"
  CommonDialog1.ShowSave
  If CommonDialog1.filename = "" Then Exit Sub
  RichTextBox1.SaveFile CommonDialog1.filename, 1
  OpenFile = CommonDialog1.filename
End Sub
```

The Open command is a bit more involved, as it must handle various types of files other than HTML files. When an HTML file is opened, its source code must appear in the editor's box, and the document must be rendered on the WebBrowser control. If the document is an image (a JPG or GIF file), it must be rendered in the WebBrowser control, but the file's contents must not appear in the editor. If it's a sound, it must be played back, but the file's contents must not be displayed. The code of the Open command is:

```
Private Sub FileOpen_Click()
On Error Resume Next

    CommonDialog1.Filter = "HTML Documents|*.htm;*.html|ActiveX _
        Documents|*.vbd|All Files|*.*"
    CommonDialog1.ShowOpen
    If Trim(CommonDialog1.filename) = "" Then Exit Sub
    dPos = InStr(CommonDialog1.filename, ".")
    If dPos > 0 Then ext = Mid$(CommonDialog1.filename, dPos + 1)
    If UCase$(ext) = "HTM" Or UCase$(ext) = "HTML" _
        Or UCase$(ext) = "TXT" Then
      RichTextBox1.LoadFile CommonDialog1.filename, 1
      WebBrowser1.Navigate CommonDialog1.filename
      OpenFileName = CommonDialog1.filename
    End If
' The following lines handle non-HTML file types
' like sounds and images
    WebBrowser1.Navigate CommonDialog1.filename
End Sub
```

If the user selects an HTML or text file in the File Open dialog box, it's displayed in the editor, and the program attempts to render it on the Web-Browser control. If not, the WebBrowser control is navigated to this file. If it's a file that the browser can handle, it does so. If not, no error message is generated. This is a feature of browsers: when they run into information they can't handle, they process as much information as they can or ignore it altogether. But they won't generate any error messages. The error handler was included in case something goes wrong with the VB code.

THE HISTORY OBJECT

The History object provides methods for navigating through the browser's history. In other words, it lets you access the functionality of the browser's navigation buttons from within your code.

The Methods of the History Object

The History object of the Scripting Model maintains the list of sites already visited, and you can access them through the History object's methods, which are described next. The History object doesn't have its own properties or events.

Back *n*   This method moves back in the history list by *n* steps, as if the user has clicked the browser's Back button *n* times. To move to the most recently visited URL, use the following statement:

```
call Window.History.back(0)
```

Or simply use this statement:

```
call Window.History.back
```

Forward *n*   This method moves forward in the history list by *n* steps, as if the user has clicked the browser's Forward button *n* times.

Go *n*   This method moves to the *nth* item in the history list. The following statement takes you to the first URL in the list:

```
Window.History.go 1
```

THE NAVIGATOR OBJECT

The Navigator object returns information about the browser. One of the major problems you will face as a Web author is that the two major browsers (Netscape Navigator and Microsoft Internet Explorer) are not totally compatible. Each supports a few unique features that the other doesn't. The truth is, both Netscape and Microsoft try to catch up with each other instead of attempting to establish new standards.

Developing pages that will work on both browsers is not a trivial task, especially for those who design active pages. Even if you can't design a page that can be rendered on both browsers, you can at least have two sets of pages, one for each browser, and display the appropriate pages. Even for this crude technique to work, you must figure out from within a script which browser is opening the page.

The properties of the Navigator object are read-only, and they return information about the browser in which the document is viewed.

AppCodeName   This property returns the code name of the application. Internet Explorer returns "Mozilla."

AppName   This property returns the name of the application. Internet Explorer returns "Microsoft Internet Explorer."

AppVersion   This method returns the version of the application. Internet Explorer 4 under Windows 95 returns "4.0 (compatible; MSIE 4.01; Windows 95)." Future versions of Internet Explorer and Windows 98 may return a slightly different string.

UserAgent   This method returns the user agent of the application. Internet Explorer 4 returns "Mozilla/4.0 (compatible; MSIE 4.01; Windows 95)."

Suppose you have prepared an HTML page that can be viewed with any browser (in other words, a generic page), and you have prepared a more advanced version of the same page that includes features supported only by Internet Explorer 4. You can easily detect which browser is running at the client's side, and you can display the advanced page if the browser happens to be Internet Explorer 4 and display the generic HTML page for all other browsers.

To find out the values of the various properties of the Navigator object, run the HTMLEditor application (discussed earlier in this chapter), and create a small script like the following, in which *propName* is the actual name of a property of the Navigator object:

```
<SCRIPT LANGUAGE=VBScript>
  Document.Write Window.Navigator.propName
</SCRIPT>
```

Then render the document, and the property's value will appear in the lower pane of the HTMLEditor window.

THE LOCATION OBJECT

The Location object applies to the Window and Frames objects and provides information about the window's (or frame's) current URL. You've already seen examples of the Location object, but we haven't looked at all its properties yet. Here are all the properties of the Location object. The Location object's properties return information about the URL of the current document. By setting this object's properties, you can navigate to another document.

href   This property returns or sets the complete URL for the location to be loaded into the browser's window. Use this property to connect to another location through your VBScript code. To display the current document's URL, use a statement such as the following:

```
MsgBox "You are currently viewing " & document.location.href
```

You can also display another document in the window or frame with the following statement:

```
document.location.href="http://www.microsoft.com"
```

As you may recall from the discussion of URLs in the previous chapter, URLs have several parts. The properties shown in Table 11.3 return (or set) these parts.

TABLE 11.3: The Properties That Return or Set URL Parts

PROPERTY	WHAT IT DOES
Protocol	Returns or sets the protocol of the URL (usually http)
Host	Returns or sets the host and port of the URL. The host and port are separated with a colon, as in host:port. The port is optional and rarely used.
Hostname	Reads or sets the host of a URL, which can be either a name or an IP address
Port	Returns or sets the port of the URL (you rarely have to specify the port number in a WWW URL)
Pathname	Returns or sets the pathname of the URL. Use this property when you want to display a document other than the Web's root document.

THE LINKS OBJECT

Another invisible object is the Links object, which represents a link in an HTML document and exposes properties through which you can find out the destination of the link. The number of hyperlinks in the current document is given by the property Links.Length, and each hyperlink in the document is given by the *Links* array. The URL of the first hyperlink is links(0), links(1) is the URL of the second hyperlink, and so on up to links(Links.Length-1).

The *Links* array returns a Links object, which in turn provides information about a hyperlink's attributes. The Links object has the properties shown in Table 11.4.

TABLE 11.4: The Properties of the Links Object

PROPERTY	WHAT IT DOES
Href	Returns or sets the complete URL for the location to be loaded into the frame.
Protocol	Returns or sets the protocol of the URL (usually http).
Host	Returns or sets the host and port of the URL.
Hostname	Reads or sets the host of a URL, which can be either a name or an IP address.
Port	Returns or sets the port of the URL.
Pathname	Returns or sets the pathname of the URL.
Search	Returns or sets the search portion of the URL, if it exists.
Hash	Returns or sets the hash portion of the URL.
Target	The last property of the Frames object is the target that may have been specified in the <A> frame. The target of the link is the window or frame in which the destination object will be displayed.

WHAT'S NEXT?

In Part 4, you'll enter the world of Visual Basic for Applications. Chapter 12 will introduce you to VBA, discussing programming with objects, using the VBA Editor to create macros, automating Microsoft Office applications, and designing and using VBA Forms with Visual Basic.

Part iii

PART iV
INTRODUCTION TO VISUAL BASIC FOR APPLICATIONS

Chapter 12

AN INTRODUCTION TO VBA

F or several years, VBA (Visual Basic for Applications) was the programming language to use with Microsoft Office applications. VBA is a simple programming language that allows programmers (and power users as well) to do the following:

- ▶ Extend and automate Office applications
- ▶ Integrate Office applications and their data with other applications

The basic idea is really simple: Create a common language and programming environment for a number of applications so that people can customize applications and add capabilities to suit

Adapted from *Visual Basic 6 Developer's Handbook*
by Evangelos Petroutsos and Kevin Hough
ISBN 0-7821-2283-3   1,504 pages $49.99

their own environment. As such, VBA had to be simple. You can't use VBA to develop just any type of application you may need or think of. VBA provides only the basic control structures, math and string functions, and variable manipulation capabilities. The real power of VBA comes from the objects of the applications that support it.

With the introduction of VBA 5, Microsoft started licensing the language to manufacturers who wanted to add programmable features to their products—for example, Autodesk's AutoCAD. AutoCAD has been a programmable environment for many years, but its programming language was unique to AutoCAD and couldn't be shared with other applications. Many other manufacturers included scripting languages or other means of automating their software. But the need for a global language that would act as the glue in putting together the pieces of many applications was clear. Finally, Microsoft came up with a version of VBA that meets the needs of other manufacturers, and VBA is on its way to becoming a universal language for automating applications under Windows.

Most companies today use off-the-shelf software and need to customize it. More than half of the corporations in the United States use Microsoft Office products, and many of them use VBA to customize those applications to suit their business needs. This trend will continue and become stronger in the future. There is already a need not to simply customize applications, but to tie them together so that they can communicate. VBA does this too, and as a result, the need for VBA programmers will increase in the next few years.

Today's applications are so powerful and so feature-rich that it no longer makes sense to develop custom applications. Instead, it makes sense to customize existing applications and make them work together. Even the Office 97 applications are adequate for addressing most of the day-to-day computer operations of a typical corporation. With a host of third-party applications supporting VBA, you can easily guess its importance in corporate environments.

In this chapter, we'll introduce you to the parts and pieces of VBA and show you in general how you can use it with Visual Basic. The examples in this chapter assume that you have Word and Excel installed on your system. You can automate other applications with VBA, but we are going to focus on the primary Office applications, since most of the VBA code written today applies to them. Because VBA depends on the functionality and the objects exposed by each individual application, you can apply the information in this chapter to other applications.

PROGRAMMING WITH OBJECTS

The goal of VBA is to access the functionality of applications and either automate them (with macros—procedures made up of VBA commands) or control them from within other applications. And applications make their functionality available to other applications via objects. Applications expose objects, which represent their programmable entities. For instance,

▶ The Visual Basic IDE exposes the CommandBars collection, which represents the toolbars of the Visual Basic IDE.

▶ The DAO (Data Access Objects) exposes the Database object, which represents an entire database.

▶ Word exposes the ActiveDocument object, which represents the current document, the Selection object, which represents the current selection, and so on.

▶ Excel exposes a different set of objects, better suited for the type of data it can handle. Instead of the ActiveDocument object, it exposes the ActiveSheet object, which represents the active worksheet.

All of these objects have properties that are also objects or collections of objects. For instance, the Documents collection contains an item for each open document. Each Document object, in turn, contains a Paragraphs collection, which represents all the paragraphs in the document. You can access each paragraph of a DOC document, and as you will see, you can also access individual words and characters.

For example, to access the first paragraph of the document DevHandbook.doc, you use an expression such as the following:

```
Documents("DevHandbook.doc").Paragraphs(1)
```

To set the Bold attribute of this paragraph, you must use an even longer expression:

```
Documents("DevHandbook.doc").Paragraphs(1).Font.Bold
```

NOTE

Bold is a property of the Font object, as you may recall from Chapter 4.

Part iv

Expressions involving objects exposed by Office applications can get quite lengthy, but they are usually simple to build and understand. The object model of each application forms a hierarchy, which represents the structure of the documents each application can handle.

When an application is manipulated from within another, we say that the application is *automated*. You can't really program Word to do something it doesn't know how to or can't do. You must call functions already built into Word to access the objects exposed by Word itself. In essence, you are automating Word. You are telling Word to carry out an action that isn't implemented as a menu command, to carry out an action repeatedly on each paragraph, and so on. VBA is not a complete language. Instead, it relies on the functionality of the applications that support VBA and expose it via an object model.

The same object can also be used from within other applications. You can write Word macros that rely on Excel to retrieve data and then format them as DOC files. You can also borrow the functionality of Office applications from within your Visual Basic applications. You will see later in this chapter how to use Word's spell-checking capabilities to verify the spelling of a document from within a Visual Basic application and how to use Excel capabilities to evaluate a math expression from within your Visual Basic application.

THE NEW VBA EDITOR

VBA is not a new language; it's been around for several years, although limited to Office applications. And, as you probably know, the simplest way to program in VBA is to record a macro. Every operation you can perform with the keyboard and menu commands in Word or Excel can be recorded as a macro. Macros can be executed (played back) to perform the same operation on different data.

The most common use of macros is to assign formatting commands to keystrokes. Let's say you are using Word to prepare elaborate documents, with many formatting options. If your documents contain code segments, you probably want to format these segments in Courier New, 10 or 11 point, and indent their left edge more than the text. Instead of selecting every code segment in the document and then applying the formatting manually, you can record a macro that contains all the commands you must issue to apply the desired formatting. You can also assign these commands to a keystroke, such as Alt+C. Then, each time you want to format a section as a code segment, all you have to do is select the text and press Alt+C.

In older versions of VBA, macros were the only means of programming, or automating, Office applications. You could edit macros, but there were no debugging tools and no special editor (an editor with an Auto List Members features, for example). With VBA 5, a new editor was introduced that is nearly identical to the IDE editor of Visual Basic 5. As you type the name of an object variable, the editor displays the names of its members in a drop-down list, where you can select the desired member. The new VBA editor is a programmer's editor, and it simplifies the manual coding of macros as much as an editor can. VBA 5 comes with an integrated development and debugging environment, which was sorely missing from previous versions of VBA.

USING THE AUTO LIST MEMBERS FEATURE

If you're a seasoned programmer, you may find the Auto List Members feature a real annoyance. But you will find it extremely useful with VBA because Office applications expose their own objects and most VB programmers just aren't familiar with these objects. A reminder won't hurt.

If you want, you can turn off the Quick Tip feature and type the names of the members in lowercase. If the member is supported by the object, the VBA editor will adjust the spelling of the member's name the moment your pointer leaves the line.

For example, you can type the following:

Application.activeprinter

If the Application object supports the property ActivePrinter, the editor automatically changes the name of the property to Application.ActivePrinter when you press Enter (or move the pointer to another line).

Another limitation of previous versions of VBA was the lack of Forms. VBA macros were limited to the user interface of the application. You could add a few dialog boxes, but not elaborate Forms, such as the ones you can design with Visual Basic. VBA 5 has a Form Designer that lets you design Forms, just as you do with Visual Basic, and incorporate them in a macro. As you can see, with a proper editor, debugging tools, and a Form Designer window, VBA is no longer a macro language. It's a fully developed language with which you can write real applications in the environment of Office 97, not just customize applications.

Recording Macros

The example of a paragraph formatting macro is a trivial one, but you will see shortly how to develop more elaborate macros that behave like applications. But let's start with the simplest operation of all—recording a macro.

No matter how elaborate your VBA programs are, macros are indispensable. The Macro Recorder will generate most of the trivial code of your macro. As you will see, VBA is a verbose language, and the more code you can generate automatically, the better—less typing, fewer chances for mistakes, and less testing.

Let's start by looking at the VBA code of a common operation, searching for a string:

1. Start Word and open an existing file, or create a new one and enter some text.

2. Choose Tools ≻ Macro ≻ Record New Macro to open the Record Macro dialog box:

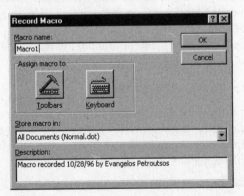

3. In the Macro Name box, enter the name of the new macro. You can click the Toolbars or the Keyboard button to assign the new macro to a keystroke or to the toolbar. (This is a simple

test, and you don't need to make the macro permanent. We'll delete it shortly anyway.)

4. The default macro name is Macro1, and if a macro by the same name exists, Word will ask you whether it should overwrite it.

5. Click OK, and you will see a small window on your screen, with two VCR-style buttons: Stop Recording and Pause Recording. Every action you perform on the current document with the keyboard or the mouse from now on will be recorded. To pause the recording of the commands (say you want to look up the Help files), click the Pause Recording button. To end the recording of the macro, click the Stop Recording button.

Now perform the following actions:

1. Press Ctrl+Home to move to the top of the document.

2. Choose Edit ➢ Find to open the Find and Replace dialog box.

3. In the Find What box, enter the string you want to look for (in this example, our text included the word *macro,* and we searched on that string), and click the Find Next button. Word locates and highlights the first instance of the word *macro* in the document. Because we did not check the Match Case box or the Find Whole Words Only box, it locates any instance of the word, regardless of case or whether the word is part of another word.

4. The macro is now recorded. Click the Stop Recording button.

Now let's open the macro to see its code. Follow these steps:

1. Choose Tools ➢ Macro ➢ Macros to open the window where all available macros are displayed.

2. Select the Macro1 entry (or whatever the macro's name is) and then click the Edit button to open the VB Editor window. You will see the listing of the Macro1 macro, as shown in Figure 12.1.

Part iv

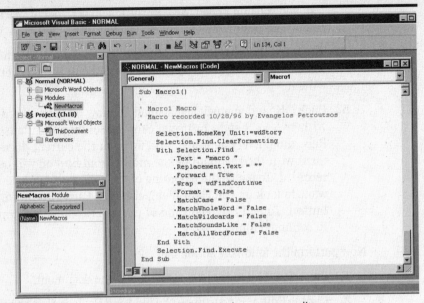

FIGURE 12.1: In the Visual Basic Editor window, you can edit any macro recorded in a Word session.

Code 12.1: The Macro1 Macro

```
Sub Macro1()
'
' Macro01 Macro
' Macro recorded 10/26/96 by Evangelos Petroutsos
'
    Selection.HomeKey Unit:=wdStory
    Selection.Find.ClearFormatting
    With Selection.Find
        .Text = "macro"
        .Replacement.Text = ""
        .Forward = True
        .Wrap = wdFindContinue
        .Format = False
        .MatchCase = False
        .MatchWholeWord = False
        .MatchWildcards = False
        .MatchSoundsLike = False
        .MatchAllWordForms = False
    End With
    Selection.Find.Execute
End Sub
```

The first line of code represents the Ctrl+Home keystroke, which took us to the beginning of the document. All the following lines represent the Find operation. Since we are not replacing the word we found, you can omit the following line:

```
.Replacement.Text = ""
```

To find another word, simply replace the string macro with any other string. If you want to perform a more elaborate search, use the macro recorder to capture the appropriate commands. Figure 12.2 shows the Find and Replace dialog box with the arguments of another, more complicated search operation. By specifying the word *replace* and checking the Find All Word Forms box, you're telling Word to find not only the instances of the word *replace*, but the words *replaced* and *replacing* as well. The new macro is identical to the previous one, except for the last option:

```
.MatchAllWordForms = True
```

FIGURE 12.2: The Find and Replace dialog box for a more complicated search

THE WITH STRUCTURE

You are probably familiar with the With structure. It's a shorthand notation for referencing objects' properties and methods. Objects can have really long names. The expression Selection.Find represents the Find dialog box, and each option in this dialog box is another property of this object. The expression Selection.Find.Text represents the text to search for.

CONTINUED ➡

Part iv

> Instead of repeating the object's name over and over (thus making the code harder to type and read), you can type the names of the properties within a With structure. The object name following the With keyword determines the object to which these properties apply.

Developing a "Real World" Word Macro

Let's look at a more meaningful example of automating Word. When preparing long documents with many figures, such as this chapter, we avoid inserting figures in the text. This would slow down many normal editing operations, not to mention that, in general, the figures are not available at the time of the writing or they must be revised later.

To make sure that we have all the figures we need for a chapter, we like to collect all the figure captions at the end of the chapter or in a separate file and use this file to capture the appropriate figures. When all figure captions, along with their numbers, are listed in the same order as they appear in the text, we can easily check whether we've skipped a figure number. This simple operation is done with the CollectCaptions macro we'll develop in this section.

NOTE   You'll find the CollectCaptions macro, along with the other files referred to in this chapter, at the Sybex Web site (www.sybex.com). Once there, go to the Catalog page and enter 2469 (the first four digits of the last five in the book's ISBN) into the search engine. Follow the link for this book that comes up, and then click the Downloads button, which will take you to a list of files organized by chapter.

The CollectCaptions macro is based on the one you recorded earlier, only it repeats the search as many times as necessary to extract all the captions from the text. Clearly, we must place the lines generated earlier by the Macro Recorder into a loop structure, which will repeat them as many times as there are captions in the document. The captions copied by the macro will be appended to a string variable, and, when done, we'll paste this variable at the end of the document.

To implement the new macro in the Visual Basic Editor of Word, follow these steps:

1. Start Word, and choose Tools ➤ Macro ➤ Visual Basic Editor to open the VB Editor window for Word, which looks a lot like the Visual Basic window.

2. Open the Code window and create a new subroutine and name it CollectCaptions. In other words, enter the following lines in the Code window:

    ```
    Sub CollectCaptions()
    End Sub
    ```

3. Copy the contents of the Macro1 macro and paste them in the new procedure's body.

The specification `.Wrap = wdFindContinue` tells Word to ask the user whether to continue searching the document from the beginning once it reaches the end. Since we are going to start the Find operation at the first character of the document, we don't need to display this prompt; so remove this line from the code or comment it out as we've done in the listing.

Next, we must decide how many times to loop. Since we don't know in advance how many captions the document contains, we must set up a While...Wend loop that will keep finding the next caption until a search operation ends unsuccessfully. When a Find operation ends unsuccessfully, the Found property of the Find object is False. Our code will examine the value of this property and end the loop by setting the value of the FindMore variable.

Code 12.2: The CollectCaptions Macro

```
Sub CollectCaptions()
'
' CollectCaptions Macro
' Macro recorded 10/25/96 by Evangelos Petroutsos
' This macro collects all figure captions in the text
' and appends them to the document.
' Captions are formatted with the Caption style, which is
' used to locate them in the text

Dim CaptionsText As String

' Move to beginning of document
Selection.HomeKey Unit:=wdStory
' Set up the Find & Replace dialog box's parameters
```

```
Selection.Find.ClearFormatting
Selection.Find.Style = ActiveDocument.Styles("Caption")
With Selection.Find
  .Text = ""
  .Replacement.Text = ""
  .Forward = True
  .Wrap = wdFindAsk
  .Format = True
  .MatchCase = False
  .MatchWholeWord = False
  .MatchWildcards = False
  .MatchSoundsLike = False
  .MatchAllWordForms = False
End With
' Now execute the Find operation
Selection.Find.Execute
CaptionsText = CaptionsText & Selection.Text
If (Not Selection.Find.Found) Or Selection.End Then
  FindMore = False
End If
FindMore = True
' Repeat the Find operation as long as there are more instances
' of the text being searched
While FindMore
  Selection.Find.ClearFormatting
  Selection.Find.Execute
' Stop searching if last find operation was not successful
  CaptionsText = CaptionsText & Selection.Text
  If (Not Selection.Find.Found) Then
    FindMore = False
  End If
Wend
' Insert spaces before the list of captions
CaptionsText = vbCrLf & vbCrLf & vbCrLf & "L I S T  O F  C A P
T I O N S" & vbCrLf & CaptionsText
' Append list of captions to text
Selection.EndKey Unit:=wdStory
Selection.Text = CaptionsText
' Set Normal style, or else it may be formatted in the
' document's last paragraph's style
Selection.Style = "Normal"
End Sub
```

Figure 12.3 shows the CollectCaptions macro being edited in Word's Visual Basic Editor. Notice that the Find object's properties need not be defined at each iteration. We can simply call the Execute method of the Find object. Each time a new caption is located in the text, we copy it and append it to the local variable *CaptionsText*. When the loop ends, we paste the variable *CaptionsText* at the end of the document. We move to the end of the document and paste the string as a Selection object. This highlights the new text so that we can apply the Normal format to it. If you don't reformat the pasted text, it will be formatted according to the format of the last paragraph in the document (which could be another caption, for all we know).

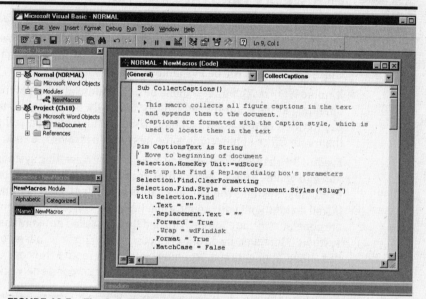

FIGURE 12.3: The CollectCaptions macro being edited in the VBA Editor

AUTOMATING OFFICE APPLICATIONS

In this section, we'll explore how you can automate Office applications from within your Visual Basic applications. The idea is to exploit the functionality of the various applications without having to rewrite the code. One of the things you can do so well with Word is spell-check your documents, but this feature is useful in the context of other applications. If you want to add spell-checking capabilities to a VB application, you can "borrow" the spell-checking capabilities of Word and incorporate them in your application. You can even hide Word, and users need not know you are contacting Word to do all the work. However, the Word application must be installed on the host system.

To access an Office application from within a VB application, you must first create an object variable that references the desired application. You declare this variable as Object, with the following statement (change the name of the variable according to the application you want to access):

```
Dim AppExcel As Object
```

RICH SERVICES AND THE OPERATING SYSTEM

Shouldn't basic services, such as document editing, spell-checking, charting, and so on, be part of the operating system? Right now, they are part of Office applications, and you can't assume that Office applications will be available on every system.

It would work much better if these basic features were part of the operating system, but these features are costly. Someone has to pay for their development, and Microsoft decided that including them with Office applications is the best way to recover the cost.

Eventually, all these services may end up in the operating system, and you will be able to expect that your applications will run on every host system. You can also purchase a spell-checker and install it along with your application. However, Office applications are popular, and you can expect to find them installed on many host systems. Moreover, by developing custom applications based on the Office applications, you may be able to justify the cost of installing Office on a stand-alone system or on a corporate network.

To actually instantiate the AppExcel, you use the CreateObject or the GetObject function. The CreateObject function creates a new instance of an object. To create a new instance of Excel from within your VB application, use this statement:

```
Set AppExcel = CreateObject("Excel.Application")
```

The string Excel.Application is the programmatic ID of the application that supplies the object. This variable references the application itself. The CreateObject function starts a new instance of the application (or ActiveX component), even if an instance of it is already running.

If one or more instances of the application is already running, you can contact this instance of the application instead of creating a new one. The obvious advantage of this technique is that no additional resources are required. To do so, use the GetObject function, whose syntax is

```
Set objectvariable = GetObject([pathname] [, progID])
```

The *pathname* argument can be the path to an existing file or to an empty string, or it can be omitted entirely. If you omit it, the *progID* argument is required. If you specify the path to an existing file, the GetObject function will create an object using the information stored in the file (it will start the application associated with this file). If it's a DOC file, for example, it opens the specified file in an existing instance of Word. If Word isn't running at the moment, it will be started, and the specified file will be opened in its main window. Using an empty string for the first argument causes GetObject to act like CreateObject—it creates a new object of the class whose programmatic identifier is *progID*.

To open the file SALES97.xls with Excel, you can use the statements

```
Dim XLObj As Object
Set XLObj = GetObject("C:\SALES\SALES97.xls")
```

When the second line executes, the file SALES97.xls either opens in a running instance of Excel or starts a new instance of Excel and opens the XLS file in it. When you supply the *pathname* argument (the filename of a document), you need not specify the *progID* argument.

If you omit the name of the file in the GetObject() function, the function returns a handle to the running instance of Excel or an error message if Excel isn't running. If you want to use the running instance of Excel to evaluate a math expression (an operation that doesn't entail any changes in the currently open document), you can contact a running instance of Excel, call its Evaluate method, and then release the object variable, as shown here:

```
Dim XLObj As Object
Set XLObj = GetObject(, "Excel.Application")
If Err.Number <> 0 Then
  ' Excel isn't running, you must start a new instance
  Set XLObj = CreateObject("Excel.Application")
End If
X = XLObj.Evaluate("3*sin(2/log(45.5))"
```

Object Variables and Early Binding

The object variables we created in the previous section are not of a specific type. Visual Basic doesn't have enough information about them at design or compile time to check the validity of their members. This means that the variables will be late bound; not only will the application be slower at run time, but any reference to nonexistent members will cause a run-time error. Whenever possible, declare object variables with specific types.

If you enter the following line in the Visual Basic Editor (not the VBA Editor), you would expect to see a variable type that matches the object you want to reference.

```
Dim AppWord As
```

Such a type doesn't appear in the drop-down list. Does this mean you can't use early binding with object variables that reference Office applications and/or their objects? Not at all. You don't see the Word or Excel object in the Auto List Members drop-down box because Visual Basic doesn't know that you want to reference another application from within your program. When the line that sets the object variable is reached during execution, Visual Basic locates the application you are referencing in the Registry and starts it in the background.

To be able to declare the *AppWord* and *AppExcel* variables with an explicit type (and not as Object type), you must first add a reference to the type library of the application you want to reference. To do so, follow these steps:

1. Choose Project ➢ References to open the References dialog box.

2. Check the boxes Microsoft Excel 8.0 Object Library and Microsoft Word 8.0 Object Library, as shown in Figure 12.4.

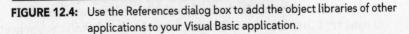

FIGURE 12.4: Use the References dialog box to add the object libraries of other applications to your Visual Basic application.

3. Now enter the same line in the Form's declaration section and scan the list of available variable types in the Auto List Members drop-down list box (shown in Figure 12.5).

```
VBAObjectsProject - VBAObjects (Code)
(General)                          (Declarations)
    Option Explicit
    Dim AppWord As Word.Application
    Dim AppExcel as Excel.
                        AddIn
                        AddIns
                        Adjustments
                        Application
                        Areas
                        AutoCorrect
                        AutoFilter
```

FIGURE 12.5: Add the object libraries of the applications you want to reference, and their types will appear in the Auto List Members box as you enter VB code.

The declarations of the object variables *AppExcel* and *AppWord* should be

```
Dim AppWord As Word.Application
Dim AppExcel As Excel.Application
```

These declarations are all the information Visual Basic needs to early bind the variables and check the validity of their members at design time.

THE VBAOBJECTS APPLICATION

Now that we have seen how to create object variables that represent the Office applications, let's build an application that demonstrates these techniques. The VBAObjects application lets you start a new instance of Excel or Word, create a new Word document or a new Excel worksheet, and manipulate it from within a Visual Basic application. The application's main Form is shown in Figure 12.6.

NOTE

You'll find the VBAObjects application at the Sybex Web site.

Part iv

When you run VBAObjects, all buttons are disabled except for the two buttons that reference Excel and Word. When these buttons are clicked, the program creates a new instance of Excel or Word and enables the remaining buttons on the Form. (We'll discuss the operation of these buttons later in this chapter.)

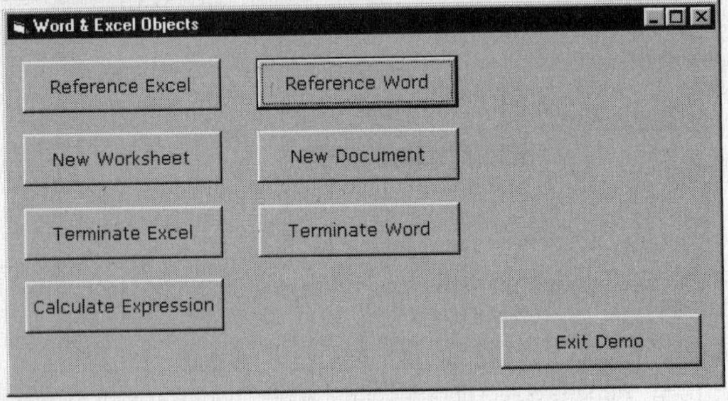

FIGURE 12.6: The main Form of the VBAObjects application

The object variables that represent the two applications are declared outside any procedure:

```
Dim AppWord As Word.Application
Dim AppExcel As Word.Excel
```

Both buttons create a new instance of the application, and they assign it to an object variable, which is used later by the other procedures in the program.

Code 12.3: The Click Event Handler of the Reference Excel Button

```
Private Sub Command1_Click()

    Screen.MousePointer = vbHourglass
    Set AppExcel = CreateObject("Excel.Application")
    Screen.MousePointer = vbDefault
    Command3.Enabled = True
    Command5.Enabled = True
    Command8.Enabled = True

End Sub
```

The code for the Reference Word button is similar, except that it passes the Class Word.Application to the CreateObject method.

We will examine the code behind the other buttons on the VBAObjects Form later, but you can run the application now. Instantiate the *AppExcel* and *AppWord* object variables, and then break the application and check out the members of the two object variables in the Immediate window. (In the examples below, the results displayed in the Immediate window are indented to the right.) You can find the names of the applications that these two variables reference.

```
Print AppExcel.Name
    Microsoft Excel
Print AppWord.Name
    Microsoft Word
```

Or you can ask Excel to evaluate math expressions:

```
Print AppExcel.Evaluate ("log(999.333)")
    2.99971022893117
```

You can use the AppWord object to find out whether a word is spelled correctly:

```
Print AppWord.CheckSpelling("Antroid")
    False
```

Or you can display the names of the fonts installed:

```
For i=1 To AppWord.FontNames.Count: Print
AppWord.FontNames(i):Next
    Times New Roman
    Arial
    Courier New
    {more font names}
```

Simply type the name of the object variable followed by a period and then select a member (property or method) from the drop-down list that appears automatically, as shown in Figure 12.7.

You might want to change the declarations of the *AppWord* and *App-Excel* object variables to generic object variables to see how they are going to affect the application at design time and at run time. The Auto List Members feature will be practically useless, and all references to the wrong members will cause run-time errors.

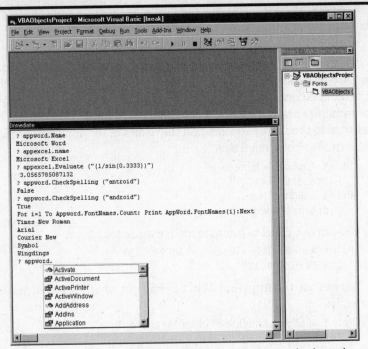

FIGURE 12.7:   Use the Visual Basic Immediate window to check out the members of the AppWord and AppExcel object variables.

The Application Object

When an application is executed in the background, you can access it via the Application object, which represents the running application and is common to all Office applications. You can think of the Application object as a container for the application's objects. Besides being your back door to the running application, the Application object has a few members of its own. Here are the most important:

ActivePrinter   Returns or sets the name of the active printer.

ActiveWindow   Returns the handle to the application window that has the focus.

Caption   Returns or sets the string that appears on the application window's title bar. You can use this property to find out whether a window contains a specific document.

DisplayAlerts   Normally, Office applications display dialog boxes to confirm certain actions (such as deleting a large amount of data) or irreversible actions (such as closing a document without saving it). If you are running the application in the background and you don't want users to see any dialog boxes other than the ones displayed by your application, set this property to False. When your procedure ends, the DisplayAlerts property is reset to True automatically.

ScreenUpdating   Normally, when a macro is executed, the application's window is updated after the completion of each command. This is usually unnecessary, as these actions take place too quickly and the user can't follow them anyway. In general, it's a good idea to turn off the updating of the screen from within your macros. To do so, set the ScreenUpdating property to False. When you are done, remember to turn it on again; this property isn't reset automatically.

Top, Left   These two properties return or set the position of the application's window.

Width, Height   These two properties return or set the dimensions of the application's window.

UsableWidth, UsableHeight   These properties return the dimensions of the document window within the application's window. Normally, they are the window's total width (or height), minus the space taken by scroll bars, menu bars, and toolbars.

Visible   Hides (if False) or displays (if True) the application's window.

Windows   This property is a collection of Window objects that represent the application's windows.

WindowState   This property returns or sets the state of the application's main window. The window's state can be

    Maximized   xlMaximized or wWindowStateMaximize

    Minimized   xlMinimized or wWindowStateMinimize

  Normal   xlNormal or wWindowStateNormal

The Application object supports a few methods as well, which are different depending on the application. You can use these methods to tap into the functionality unique to the application. Both Excel's and Word's Application objects provide the OnTime method, which executes a procedure at a specified time. Its syntax is

```
Application.OnTime when, name, tolerance
```

The argument When is a date and time expression indicating when the procedure will be invoked; Name is the name of the procedure that will be executed, and the Tolerance argument is the delay (in seconds) you are willing to tolerate, with respect to the argument When.

Another common method is the Move method, which repositions the window on the screen and is equivalent to changing the Top and Left properties. The methods that apply to all applications are more or less generic. However, a few methods expose unique functionality that you can access from within your applications. One of them is the Check-Spelling method, which can spell-check a word or an entire document. The CheckSpelling method is a member of the Application object and of the Selection object, which represents the current selection. When used as a method of the Application object, its syntax is

```
Application.SpellCheck(word, CustomDictionary, IgnoreUpperCase)
```

The Word argument is the word to be spelled, CustomDictionary is the filename of a custom dictionary, and *IgnoreUpperCase* specifies whether words in uppercase will be ignored. The SpellCheck method returns a True/False result, indicating whether the word is spelled correctly. The same method is also available with Excel's Application object.

In the following sections, we are going to look at the basic objects of Word and Excel, and we'll present a few examples.

WORKING WITH WORD VBA OBJECTS

Word provides numerous objects with which you can program any action that can be carried out with menu commands. Under the Application object is the Documents collection, which contains a Document object for each open document. Using an object variable of Document type, you can access any open document (or create and open a new document). The most important object that each document exposes is the Range object, which represents a contiguous section of text. This section can be words, part of a word, characters, or even the entire document. Using the Range object's methods, you can insert new text, format or delete existing text, and so on.

To address specific units of text, use the following collections:

- ► Paragraphs, which are made up of Paragraph objects
- ► Words, which are made up of Word objects
- ► Characters, which are made up of Character objects

These objects represent a paragraph, word, or character in the object to which they apply. For example, if you access the Paragraphs collection of a specific document, you retrieve all the paragraphs of the document. If you apply the same method to the current selection (represented by the Selection object), you retrieve all the paragraphs in the selected text.

The Documents Collection and the Document Object

The first object under the Word Application object hierarchy is the Document object, which is any document that can be opened with Word or any document that can be displayed in Word's window. All open documents are represented by a Documents collection that is made up of Document objects. Like all other collections, it supports the Count property (the number of open documents), the Add method, which adds a new document, and the Remove method, which closes an existing one. To access an open document, you can use the Item method of the Documents collection, specifying the document's index,

```
Application.Documents.Item(1)
```

or the document's name:

```
Application.Documents.Item("VBHandbook.doc")
```

Since Item is the collection default property, you can omit its name altogether:

```
Application.Documents(1)
```

To open an existing document, use the Documents collection's Open method, whose syntax is

```
Documents.Open(fileName)
```

The *fileName* argument is the document file's path name.

To create a new document, use the Documents collection's Add method, which accepts two optional arguments:

```
Documents.Add (template, newTemplate)
```

Part iv

The argument *template* specifies the name of a template file to be used as the basis for the new document. The *newTemplate* argument is a Boolean value. If it's set to True, Word creates a new template file.

Most of the operations you will perform on text apply to the active document, which is represented by the ActiveDocument object. This is the document in the active Word window. You can also make any document active by calling the Activate method of the Document object. To make the document MyNotes.doc active, use the following statement:

```
Documents("MyNotes.doc").Activate
```

After the execution of this statement, the MyNotes.doc document is active, and your code can refer to it through the object ActiveDocument.

Objects That Represent Text

The basic object for accessing text in a Word document is the Range object, which represents a contiguous segment of text. To extract some text from a document, you can use the Document object's Range method, which accepts as arguments the positions of the starting and ending characters in the text. The syntax of the Range method is

```
Document.Range(start, end)
```

The *start* and *end* arguments are two numeric values. Oddly enough, the first character's position in the document is zero. The statement

```
Range1 = Document.Range (0, 99)
```

extracts the first 100 character of the document represented by the *Document* object variable. These characters are assigned to the *Range1* object variable, which represents a Range object.

In the previous expressions, the *Document* variable must first be set to reference an existing object, with a statement such as the following:

```
Set Document = Documents(1)
```

You can also replace the variable *Document* with the built-in object App-Word.ActiveDocument, which represents the active document (the one you've set with the Activate method).

Words, sentences, and paragraphs are more meaningful units of text than characters. We mentioned these collections earlier in this chapter. The Word, Sentence, and Paragraph objects are better suited for text manipulation, and you commonly use these objects to access documents. These objects, however, don't support all the properties of the Range object. Therefore, in addition to the Range method, there is a Range property, which returns a Word, Sentence, or Paragraph object as a Range.

For example, the statement

```
Document.Paragraphs(3).Range
```

returns the third paragraph in the document as a Range object. You can then access the Range object's properties to manipulate the third paragraph. The Paragraph object doesn't have a Font property or a Select method. To change the appearance of the third paragraph in the document, you can use a statement such as the following:

```
Document.Paragraphs(3).Font.Bold = True
```

Document is a properly declared Document variable, or you can use the AppWord.ActiveDocument object.

The following statement selects (highlights) the same paragraph:

```
Document.Paragraphs(3).Select
```

Once a paragraph (or any other piece of text) is selected, you can apply all types of processing to it (edit it, move it to another location, format it, and so on).

The two methods of the Range object that you will use most often are

- ▶ InsertAfter, which inserts a string of text after the specified Range

- ▶ InsertBefore, which inserts a string of text in front of the specified Range

The following statements insert a title at the beginning of the document and a closing paragraph at the end:

```
AppWord.ActiveDocument.Select
AppWord.ActiveDocument.Range.InsertBefore "This is the _
document's title"
AppWord.ActiveDocument.Range.InsertAfter "This is the _
closing paragraph"
```

The Select method of the ActiveDocument object selects the entire text. The selected text is assigned to the Range object. The InsertBefore and InsertAfter methods place some text before and after the Range object.

Part iv

VBAObjects: Creating a New Document

Now we can examine the code behind the New Document button of the VBAObjects application, which we looked at earlier in this chapter. When this button is clicked, the program does the following:

- ▶ Connects to a new instance of Word
- ▶ Creates a new document
- ▶ Inserts some text and formats it
- ▶ Counts the paragraphs, words, and characters in the new document and displays them in a message box

These actions take place from within the Visual Basic application, and Word is running in the background. The user doesn't see Word's window, not even as an icon on the taskbar. Clicking the OK button in the message box opens the Word window and displays the newly created document, as shown in Figure 12.8. At this point you can edit the document or shut down Word.

The code behind the New Document button is straightforward. It uses the object AppWord.Documents(1).Range to manipulate the text (insert new paragraphs and format them). Notice how it changes the alignment of the first text paragraph with the Alignment property of the Paragraph object.

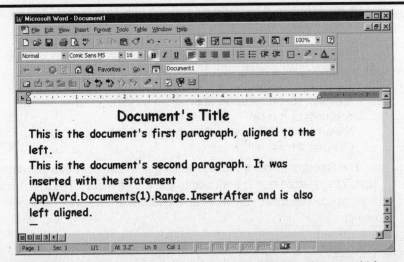

FIGURE 12.8: This document is created by a Visual Basic application, which manipulates the objects exposed by Word.

Code 12.4: The New Document Button

```
Private Sub Command4_Click()
Dim wDoc As Document
Dim tmpText As String
Dim parCount As Long, wordCount As Long, charCount As Long
Dim msg As String

    If AppWord.Documents.Count = 0 Then
        AppWord.Documents.Add
    End If
    AppWord.Documents(1).Range.InsertAfter "Document's _
Title" & vbCr
    AppWord.Documents(1).Range.Font.Bold = True
    AppWord.Documents(1).Range.Font.Size = 16
    AppWord.Documents(1).Range.Font.Name = "Comic Sans MS"
    AppWord.Documents(1).Range.InsertAfter "This the _
        document's first paragraph, aligned to the left." & vbCr
    AppWord.Documents(1).Range.InsertAfter "This the _
        document's second paragraph. "
    AppWord.Documents(1).Range.InsertAfter "It was inserted _
        with the statement "
    AppWord.Documents(1).Range.InsertAfter _
        "AppWord.Documents(1).Range.InsertAfter "
    AppWord.Documents(1).Range.InsertAfter "and is also left _
        aligned." & vbCrLf

    parCount = AppWord.Documents(1).Paragraphs.Count
    wordCount = AppWord.Documents(1).Words.Count
    charCount = AppWord.Documents(1).Characters.Count
    msg = "The new document contains " & vbCrLf
    msg = msg & parCount & " paragraphs" & vbCrLf
    msg = msg & wordCount & " words" & vbCrLf
    msg = msg & charCount & " characters"
    MsgBox msg

    AppWord.Documents(1).Paragraphs(1).Alignment = _
        wdAlignParagraphCenter
    AppWord.Visible = True

End Sub
```

The code behind the Terminate Word button is more interesting. To shut down Word, all you really need is the Quit method of the Application object. It would be quite simple if Word were running in the background only. But since we display Word's window, the user can close it before switching back to the VBAObjs application. If we attempt to close an application that has been closed already, we'll end up with a run-time error. To avoid a run-time error, the procedure that terminates Word uses an error handler.

The program closes Word with the Quit method and resumes with the next statement, if an error occurs. The next executable statement attempts to read the name of the application. If the error occurs because this particular instance of Word was already closed, an error will occur again, and the program will simply disable the New Document and Terminate Word buttons. If no error occurs, the two buttons are not disabled and the procedure ends.

Code 12.5: The Terminate Word Button

```
Private Sub Command6_Click()

    On Error Resume Next
    AppWord.DisplayAlerts = False
    AppWord.Quit
Dim wRunning As String
    wRunning = AppWord.Application.Name
    If Error Then
       Command4.Enabled = False
       Command6.Enabled = False
    End If
End Sub
```

Spell-Checking Documents

One of the most useful features of Word (and of every Office application) is the ability to spell-check a document. This functionality is also exposed by Word's VBA objects, and you can borrow it for use within your VB applications. This is not only possible; it's quite simple. To call upon Word's spell-checking routines, you need to know about two objects:

▶ The ProofreadingErrors collection

▶ The SpellingSuggestions collection

The ProofreadingErrors collection is a property of the Range object, and it contains the misspelled words in the specified Range. If you want Word to spell-check a range of text and populate the ProofreadingErrors collection, call the Range object's SpellingError method. This method returns a result that must be stored in an object variable of type *ProofreadingErrors*:

```
SpellCollection As ProofreadingErrors
Set SpellCollection = DRange.SpellingErrors
```

The second line populates the *SpellCollection* variable with the misspelled words. You can then set up a loop to read the words from the collection.

Besides locating spelling errors, Word can also suggest a list of alternate spellings or words that sound like the misspelled one. To retrieve the list of alternate words, you call the GetSpellingSuggestions methods of the Application object, passing the misspelled word as an argument. Notice that this is a method of the Application object, not the Range object you are spell-checking. The results returned by the GetSpelling-Suggestions method must be stored in a similar object variable, declared as SpellingSuggestions type:

```
Public CorrectionsCollection As SpellingSuggestions
Set CorrectionsCollection =
AppWord.GetSpellingSuggestions("antroid")
```

The second line retrieves the suggested alternatives for the word *antroid*. To scan the list of suggested words, you set up a loop that retrieves all the elements of the CorrectionsCollection collection. The example in the next section demonstrates the use of both methods from within a Visual Basic application.

THE SPELLDOC APPLICATION

In this section, we are going to look at the SpellDoc application (see Figure 12.9), a VB application that uses Word's methods to spell-check a document.

NOTE You'll find the SpellDoc application at the Sybex Web site.

The user can enter text in the multiline TextBox control (or paste it from another application) and then spell-check it by clicking the Check Document button.

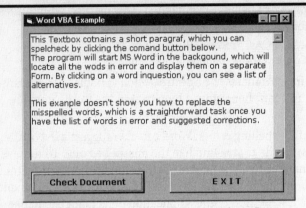

FIGURE 12.9:   The SpellDoc application's main Form

The results, which are the misspelled words, are displayed on a different Form, shown in Figure 12.10. The ListBox control on the left shows all the misspelled words returned by Word. Word can not only locate misspelled words, but suggest alternatives as well. To view the correct words suggested by Word for each misspelled word, click the corresponding entry in the list of misspelled words. The SpellDoc application doesn't replace the misspelled word in the document with the selected alternative, but this is straightforward code that manipulates strings. Once you have the list of misspelled words and the alternatives, you can design any number of interfaces that allow the user to correct the original document with point-and-click operations.

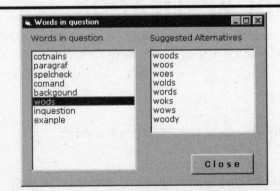

FIGURE 12.10:   This Form of the SpellDoc application displays the misspelled words and possible alternatives.

The program uses three public variables, which are declared as follows:

```
Public AppWord As Application
Public CorrectionsCollection As SpellingSuggestions
Public SpellCollection As ProofreadingErrors
```

The *SpellCollection* variable is a collection that contains all the misspelled words, and the *CorrectionsCollection* variable is another collection that contains the suggested alternatives. The *CorrectionsCollection* variable's contents are assigned every time the user clicks another misspelled word.

When the Check Document button is clicked, the program contacts the Word application. First, it attempts to connect to an existing instance of Word, with the GetObject function. If no instance of Word is currently running, it starts a new instance of Word.

Code 12.6: The Check Document Button

```
Set AppWord = GetObject("Word.Application")
  If AppWord Is Nothing Then
    Set AppWord = CreateObject("Word.Application")
    If AppWord Is Nothing Then
      MsgBox "Could not start Word. Application will end"
      End
    End If
  End If
```

After contact with Word is established, the program creates a new document and copies the text there, using the InsertAfter method of the Range object:

```
AppWord.Dcouments.Add
DRange.InsertAfter Text1.Text
```

Now comes the interesting part. The VB code calls the Range object's SpellingErrors method, which returns a collection of Word objects. The result of the SpellingErrors method is assigned to the object variable *SpellCollection*:

```
Set SpellCollection = DRange.SpellingErrors
```

The following lines add the words contained in the *SpellCollection* variable to the left list of the second Form, and then they display the Form.

Code 12.7: The Check Document Button

```
Private Sub Command1_Click()
Dim DRange As Range

  Me.Caption = "starting word ..."
```

```
On Error Resume Next
  Set AppWord = GetObject("Word.Application")
  If AppWord Is Nothing Then
    Set AppWord = CreateObject("Word.Application")
    If AppWord Is Nothing Then
      MsgBox "Could not start Word. Application will end"
      End
    End If
  End If
On Error GoTo ErrorHandler
  AppWord.Documents.Add
  Me.Caption = "checking words..."
  Set DRange = AppWord.ActiveDocument.Range
  DRange.InsertAfter Text1.Text
  Set SpellCollection = DRange.SpellingErrors
  If SpellCollection.Count > 0 Then
    SuggestionsForm.List1.Clear
    SuggestionsForm.List2.Clear
    For iWord = 1 To SpellCollection.Count
      SuggestionsForm!List1.AddItem
SpellCollection.Item(iWord)
    Next
  End If
  Me.Caption = "Word VBA Example"
  SuggestionsForm.Show
  Exit Sub

ErrorHandler:
  MsgBox "The following error occurred during the document's
  spelling" & vbCrLf & Err.Description
End Sub
```

On the second Form of the application, all the code is concentrated in the "Words in Question" list's Click event. Every time an entry in this List is clicked, the code calls the AppWord object's GetSpellingSuggestions method, passing the selected word as an argument. Notice that we add 1 to the List's ListIndex property to offset the fact that the indexing of the elements of a collection starts at one, while the indexing of the elements of a ListBox control starts at zero. The GetSpellingSuggestions method returns another collection, with the suggested words, which are placed in the list on the right.

Code 12.8:   The List's Click Event

```
Private Sub List1_Click()

Screen.MousePointer = vbHourglass
```

```
Set CorrectionsCollection = _
  AppWord.GetSpellingSuggestions(SpellCollection.Item _
  (List1.ListIndex + 1))
List2.Clear
For iSuggWord = 1 To CorrectionsCollection.Count
  List2.AddItem CorrectionsCollection.Item(iSuggWord)
Next
Screen.MousePointer = vbDefault

  End Sub
```

The SpellDoc application can become the starting point for many VB applications that require spell-checking but that don't need powerful editing features. This situation isn't common, but in some cases you might want to customize spelling. In a mail-aware application, for example, you can spell-check the text and exclude URLs and e-mail addresses. You first scan the words returned by the SpellingErrors method to check which ones contain special characters and omit them.

As you can see, tapping into the power of the Office applications isn't really complicated. Once you familiarize yourself with the objects of these applications, you can access the Office applications by manipulating a few properties and calling the methods of these objects.

WORKING WITH EXCEL VBA OBJECTS

The objects that Excel exposes have different names, but they form an equally sensible and structured hierarchy for accessing data stored in a tabular arrangement. Just as Word's basic unit of information is the text segment (not characters or words), Excel's basic unit of information is a Range. A Range object can contain a single cell or an entire worksheet (and everything in between).

The Application object represents an instance of Excel, and it supports most of the basic properties and methods of Word's Application object. In addition, it supports a few more methods that are unique to Excel. The most important methods of Excel's Application object are

▶ Calculate

▶ OnKey

▶ Evaluate

Part iv

The Calculate method recalculates all open worksheets. The OnKey method allows the programmer to specify a procedure to be executed each time the user presses a specific keystroke. The syntax of this method is

```
Application.OnKey(key, procedure)
```

The Key argument represents the keystrokes that will initiate a procedure, and the Procedure argument is the procedure that will be executed each time the specified key combination is pressed. Table 12.1 shows the strings you can use for the Key argument.

TABLE 12.1: The Settings of the OnKey Method's Key Argument

KEY	EXPRESSION
Arrow Dn	"{DOWN}"
Arrow Left	"{LEFT}"
Arrow Rt	"{RIGHT}"
Arrow Up	"{UP}"
Backspace	"{BACKSPACE}"
Break	"{BREAK}"
Caps Lock	"{CAPSLOCK}"
Delete	"{DELETE}", "{DEL}"
End	"{END}"
Enter	"{ENTER}", "{~}"
Esc	"{ESCAPE}", "{ESC}"
Home	"{HOME}"
Help	"{HELP}"
Insert	"{INSERT}"
Num Lock	"{NUMLOCK}"
PgDn	"{PGDN}"
PgUp	"{PGUP}"
Scroll Lock	"{SCROLLLOCK}"
Tab	"{TAB}"
F1–F12	"{F1}"–"{F12}"

The Evaluate method evaluates math expressions and returns the result. The statement

```
Application.Evaluate "cos(3/1.091)*log(3.499)"
```

returns a numeric value that is the value of the math expression passed to the Evaluate method as an argument. You can also use variables in your expressions, as long as you store their values in specific cells and use the addresses of these cells in the expression. The statement

```
Application.Evaluate "log(" & Application.Range("A1") & ")"
```

returns the logarithm of the numeric value stored in cell A1. The Range object represents one or more cells, depending on the address you supply. In this example, we addressed a single cell (A1). You will see how you can address and access specific cells in an Excel worksheet in the following two sections.

The Sheets Collection and the Sheet Object

Each workbook in Excel contains one or more worksheets. The Worksheets collection, which is similar to Word's Documents collection, contains a Worksheet object for each worksheet in the current workbook. To add a new worksheet, use the Add method, whose syntax is

```
Application.Worksheets.Add(before, after, count, type)
```

The Before and After arguments let you specify the order of the new worksheet in the workbook. You can specify one of the two arguments, and if you omit both, the new worksheet is inserted before the active worksheet. The Type argument specifies the type of the new worksheet and can have one of the following values:

xlWorksheet (the default value)

xlExcel4MacroSheet (a worksheet with Excel 4 macros)

xlExcel4IntlMacroSheet (a worksheet with Excel 4 international macros)

To access a worksheet, use the collection's Item method, passing the index or the worksheet's name as an argument. The following expressions are equivalent (if the second worksheet is named SalesData.xls):

```
Application.Worksheets.Item(2)
Application.Worksheets.Item("SalesData.xls")
```

Since Item is the collection default property, you can omit its name altogether:

```
Application.Worksheets(2)
```

Excel is an application for manipulating units of information stored in cells, but the basic object for accessing the contents of a worksheet is the Range object, which is a property of the Worksheet object. There are several ways to identify a Range, but here's the basic syntax of the Range method:

```
Worksheet.Range(cell1:cell2)
```

Here, *cell1* and *cell2* are the addresses of the two cells that delimit a rectangular area on the worksheet. They are the addresses of the upper-left and lower-right corners of the selection (which is always rectangular; you can't select disjointed cells on a worksheet). Of course, you can address cells in several ways, but we will not discuss them here. In this section, we are going to use the standard Excel notation, which is a number for the row and a letter for the column (for example, C3 or A103).

You can also retrieve a single cell as a Range object, with the Cells method, whose syntax is

```
Worksheet.Cells(row, col)
```

The *row* and *col* arguments are the coordinates of the cell as numbers. Finally, the Rows and Columns methods return an entire row or column by number. The two expressions

```
Worksheet.Rows(3)
Worksheet.Columns("D")
```

return the third row and the fourth column as Range objects.

The Range object is not a collection, but you can access individual cells in a Range object with the Cells method. The Cells method accepts a single argument, which is the index of the cells in the range. The index 1 corresponds to the upper-left cell in the range, the index 2 corresponds to the second cell of the first row, and so on up to the last cell in the first row. The next index corresponds to the first cell of the second row and so on up to the last row. The Text property returns the cell's contents as a string, and the Value property returns the cell's contents as a string (if it's text) or as a numeric value (if it's numeric).

Another way to work with cells is to make a selection and access the properties and methods of the Selection object. To create a Selection object (which represents the cells that are highlighted if you select them with the mouse), use the Range object's Select method:

```
Range("A2:D2").Select
```

This statement creates a new Selection object, which you can access by name. Because a worksheet has only one selection, you don't have to specify any arguments. To change the appearance of the selection, for instance, use the Font property:

```
Selection.Font.Bold = True
Selection.Font.Size = 13
```

Now that we've looked at the basic objects of Excel VBA, we can examine the code behind the New Worksheet button of the VBAObjs application.

VBAOBJECTS: CREATING A NEW WORKSHEET

The VBAObjs application's New Worksheet button demonstrates how to access a worksheet, populate it with data, and then format the data. The program starts by examining the number of open workbooks. If no workbook is open, the program creates a new one. If a workbook exists, the program assigns it to the *wBook* object variable:

```
Dim wSheet As Worksheet
Dim wBook As Workbook

If AppExcel.Workbooks.Count = 0 Then
    Debug.Print "Adding a new Workbook"
    Set wBook = AppExcel.Workbooks.Add
End If
Set wSheet = AppExcel.Sheets(1)
```

TIP

Before you run the VBAObjs application, be sure that you don't have an instance of Excel with useful data running. Or, add a new worksheet to the workbook, and give it a unique name (unless you don't mind overwriting the data of the open worksheet, of course).

The code then populates the first four cells on the first and second rows. Figure 12.11 shows the worksheet after it has been populated and formatted by the VBAObjs application. To populate the worksheet, the program uses the Cells object, as shown in the following lines:

```
wSheet.Cells(2, 1).Value = "1st QUARTER"
wSheet.Cells(3, 1).Value = 123.45
```

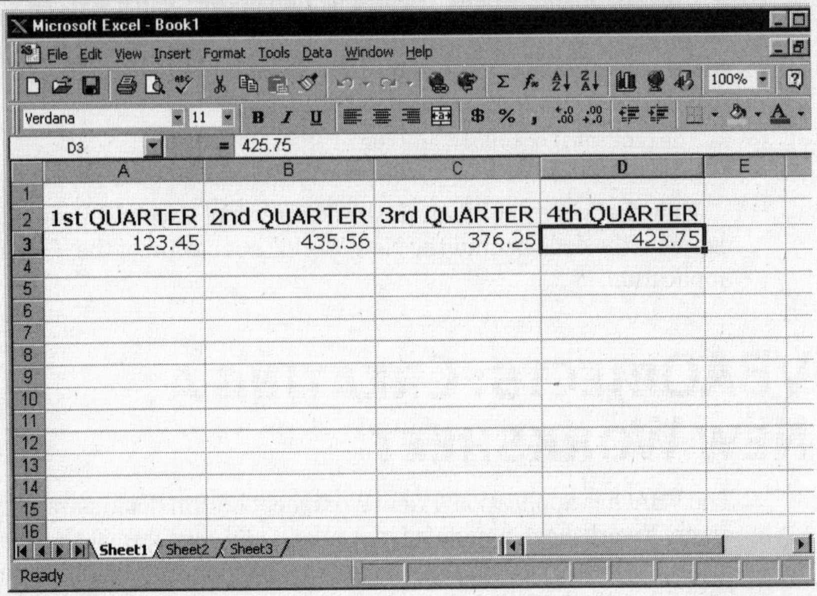

FIGURE 12.11: The VBAObjs application populated and formatted this worksheet.

To format a range of cells, the code uses the Select method of the Range object to create a selection and then manipulate the appropriate properties of the Selection object. The following lines format the headings of the worksheet shown in Figure 12.11:

```
Range("A2:D2").Select
With Selection.Font
  .Name = "Verdana"
  .FontStyle = "Bold"
  .Size = 12
End With
```

While the worksheet is being populated and formatted, Excel is running in the background. Users can't see Excel, although they will notice activity (the disk is spinning, and the pointer assumes an hourglass shape for several seconds). After all operations complete, the program displays Excel by setting its Visible property to True.

Code 12.9: The New Worksheet Button

```
Private Sub Command3_Click()
Dim wSheet As Worksheet
Dim wBook As Workbook
```

```
    If AppExcel.Workbooks.Count = 0 Then
       Debug.Print "Adding a new Workbook"
       Set wBook = AppExcel.Workbooks.Add
    End If
    Set wSheet = AppExcel.Sheets(1)
    wSheet.Cells(2, 1).Value = "1st QUARTER"
    wSheet.Cells(2, 2).Value = "2nd QUARTER"
    wSheet.Cells(2, 3).Value = "3rd QUARTER"
    wSheet.Cells(2, 4).Value = "4th QUARTER"
    wSheet.Cells(3, 1).Value = 123.45
    wSheet.Cells(3, 2).Value = 435.56
    wSheet.Cells(3, 3).Value = 376.25
    wSheet.Cells(3, 4).Value = 425.75

    Range("A2:D2").Select
    With Selection.Font
       .Name = "Verdana"
       .FontStyle = "Bold"
       .Size = 12
    End With

    Range("A3:D3").Select
    With Selection.Font
       .Name = "Verdana"
       .FontStyle = "Regular"
       .Size = 11
    End With

    Range("A2:D2").Select
    Selection.Columns.AutoFit
    Selection.ColumnWidth = Selection.ColumnWidth * 1.25
    Range("A2:E2").Select
    Selection.HorizontalAlignment = xlCenter

    AppExcel.Visible = True

    End Sub
```

VBAObjects: Using Excel as a Math Parser

In the section "Spell-Checking Documents," you saw how you could steal the spell-checking capabilities of Word. Now, we'll do something similar with Excel. Excel is a great tool for doing math. At the same time, Visual

Basic doesn't provide a function or a method for evaluating math expressions. With the little information on VBA programming we have presented so far, you can exploit this capability of Excel and use it as a background server to calculate math expressions.

To calculate a math expression such as

```
1/cos(0.335)*cos(12.45)
```

with Excel, all you have to do is enter the expression in a cell and let Excel calculate the cell. For Excel to recognize that the text you've entered is a formula and treat it accordingly, you must prefix the expression with the equals sign.

That's exactly what the Calculate Expression button does. It contacts Excel, builds a new worksheet (if needed), and then copies a user-assigned math formula to a cell. The formula is prefixed with the equals sign so that Excel will calculate the value of the expression and place it in the same cell. The value of this cell is then read back and displayed from within the VBObjs application (see Figure 12.12).

Code 12.10: The Calculate Expression Button

```
Private Sub Command8_Click()
Dim wSheet As Worksheet
Dim wBook As Workbook
Dim expression

    expression = InputBox("Enter math expression to evaluate _
(i.e., 1/cos(3.45)*log(19.004)")
    If Trim(expression) <> "" Then
      If AppExcel.Workbooks.Count = 0 Then
        Debug.Print "Adding a new Workbook"
        Set wBook = AppExcel.Workbooks.Add
      End If
      Set wSheet = AppExcel.Sheets(1)
      On Error GoTo CalcError
      wSheet.Cells(1, 1).Value = "=" & expression
      wSheet.Calculate
      MsgBox "The value of the expression " & expression & _
        vbCrLf & " is " & wSheet.Cells(1, 1).Value
    End If
    Exit Sub

CalcError:
    MsgBox "Error in evaluating expression"
End Sub
```

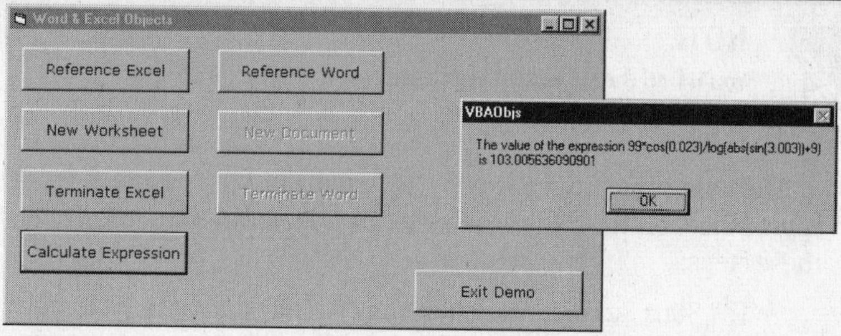

FIGURE 12.12: Using Excel's Evaluate method to evaluate math expressions

VBA AND FORM DESIGN

Besides the VB Editor, Office applications come with a Form Designer that is similar to the Form Designer in the Visual Basic IDE. With VBA 5, you can create Forms and display them from within your VBA applications. In the past, VBA programs were limited to the user interface of the Office application. A Word macro that called some of Excel's methods to streamline the transfer of data from Excel to Word and format them in Word could use the user interface of Word or Excel and display a few simple dialog boxes on its own, but not a real Form such as the ones you can build with Visual Basic. Custom Forms were not an option.

The situation has changed, and now you can design Forms similar to Visual Basic Forms, program their events, and display them from within your macros. This significant development was the next step in the evolution of Word and Excel applications to fully programmable environments. In the following sections, we'll describe how to design and use Forms with Excel's Visual Basic Editor and how to import these Forms into Visual Basic applications.

VBA Forms

We'll demonstrate the VBA Form Designer with a simple, but typical, example: the VBAExcel application. The Form shown in Figure 12.13 is displayed from within Excel. It summarizes the data shown on the Excel spreadsheet. You could just as easily process the data in Excel, but in some situations it is best to extract the information from a spreadsheet, process it, and display the results on a different Form.

NOTE
You'll find the VBAExcel application at the Sybex Web site

The data come from the NWIND database, but you won't find the spreadsheet on the Sybex Web site. To import the data into Excel, follow these steps:

1. Start Access, and open the NWIND database (you will find it in the VB folder).

2. In the Queries tab of the Database window, double-click the Order Details Extended box to display all the invoice details.

3. Select the data on the data grid (shown in Figure 12.13) and copy them.

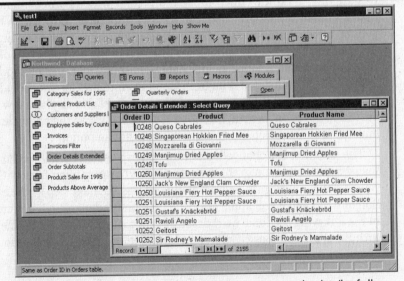

FIGURE 12.13: The Order Details Extended query returns the details of all invoices in the NWIND sample database.

4. Start Excel.

5. Paste the data from the clipboard into the first cell.

6. Select the following columns (by clicking their headings) and remove them from the grid by choosing Edit ➤ Delete:

   ▶ Product

▶ Unit Price

▶ Quantity

▶ Discount

What you now have on the spreadsheet are the details of all invoices recorded in the NWIND database. Your Excel window should look like the one shown in Figure 12.14. However, there are no totals for each invoice. The specific query returns the detail lines. Notice that the same invoice number is repeated on the spreadsheet as many times as there are lines in the invoice.

Assuming we are not interested in taxes or other charges, we can calculate the total for each invoice by running down the details and summing the Extended Prices for all lines with the same OrderID field. All it takes is a macro that loops through the spreadsheet's rows, compares the OrderID cell with the previous one, and adds the Extended Price to the running total. But how about displaying the totals? One approach is to insert a new row after each invoice's line. Another is to place the total in the cell next to each invoice's last Extended Price cell.

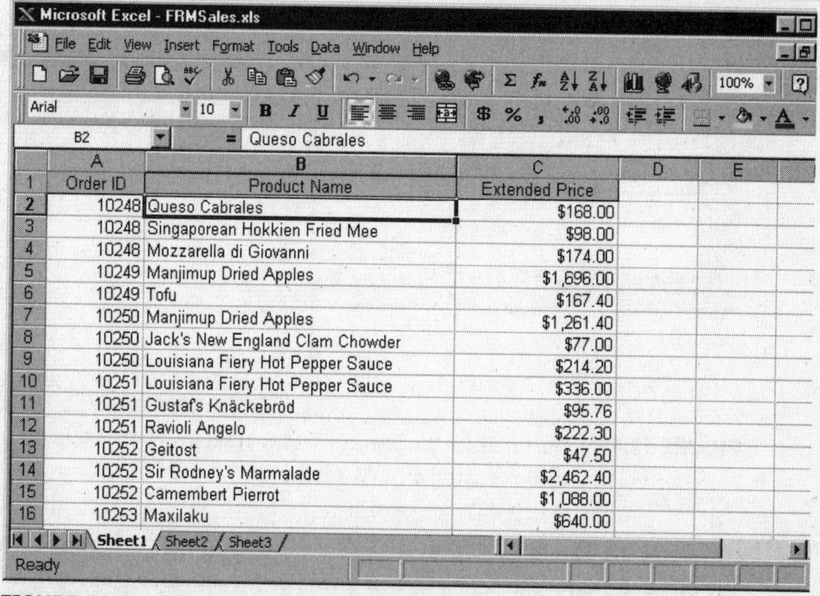

	A	B	C	D	E
1	Order ID	Product Name	Extended Price		
2	10248	Queso Cabrales	$168.00		
3	10248	Singaporean Hokkien Fried Mee	$98.00		
4	10248	Mozzarella di Giovanni	$174.00		
5	10249	Manjimup Dried Apples	$1,696.00		
6	10249	Tofu	$167.40		
7	10250	Manjimup Dried Apples	$1,261.40		
8	10250	Jack's New England Clam Chowder	$77.00		
9	10250	Louisiana Fiery Hot Pepper Sauce	$214.20		
10	10251	Louisiana Fiery Hot Pepper Sauce	$336.00		
11	10251	Gustaf's Knäckebröd	$95.76		
12	10251	Ravioli Angelo	$222.30		
13	10252	Geitost	$47.50		
14	10252	Sir Rodney's Marmalade	$2,462.40		
15	10252	Camembert Pierrot	$1,088.00		
16	10253	Maxilaku	$640.00		

FIGURE 12.14: The invoice details of the grid shown in Figure 12.13 in an Excel spreadsheet

To demonstrate the design of Forms, we are going to display the totals for each on a separate Form, as shown in Figure 12.15. This Form looks like an ordinary VB Form, but it was designed with Excel's Visual Basic Editor and displayed in Excel's environment. You don't even need to have Visual Basic installed to design and display this Form. In the next section, we are going to export this Form and use it with a VB application.

You may be wondering, Why deploy a new Form instead of using Excel's subtotaling features? Keep in mind that this is a simple example. The processing of the data may be more complicated, and it may not always be convenient to display the results on the same spreadsheet. This example does not demonstrate the need to deploy custom Forms, but everyone who's programmed Excel in the past will admit that they wished they could pop up a similar Form at one time or another.

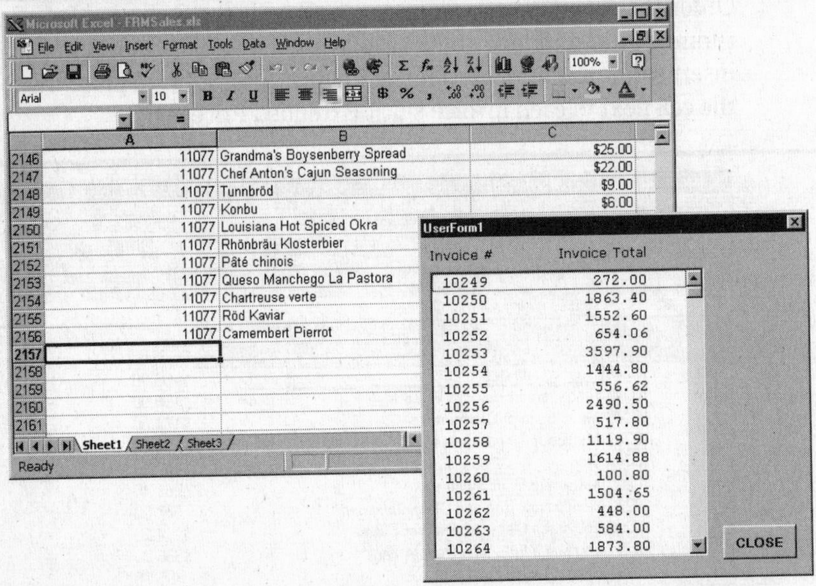

FIGURE 12.15: The totals for the invoices shown in Figure 12.14 displayed in a ListBox control on a VBA Form

Forms are the next step in Excel's evolution toward a fully programmable environment. Once you understand the structure of a spreadsheet and the objects that expose this structure to other applications, programming Excel will be no different from programming with Visual Basic, including

Form design. You can even "dress your application up" with Forms so that users will see very little Excel, and they may even think that the spreadsheet is another data-entry window in your application.

DESIGNING A FORM

To design a new VBA Form with Excel, open a new worksheet and choose Tools ➤ Macro ➤ Visual Basic Editor. You will see the window shown in Figure 12.16. To get the Form shown in Figure 12.16, open the VBA Editor and choose Insert ➤ UserForm. This window contains the usual Project, Properties, and Form panes, just like the Visual Basic Editor. The Project pane contains all the components of the Excel project, including the spreadsheets and the modules (recorded macros are stored in the project's main module). If you select the Form, you will see a Toolbox, similar to the one in the Visual Basic editor, except that it doesn't contain as many controls. If you don't see the Toolbox, click the Form to display it. When you are not designing a Form's interface, the Toolbox remains hidden.

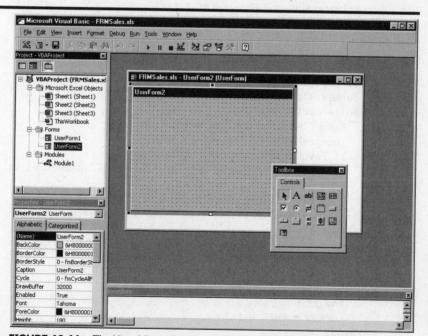

FIGURE 12.16: The Visual Basic Editor's window for a typical Excel project

Part iv

To design the Form shown in Figure 12.15 earlier in this chapter, place the ListBox control on it, add a Command Button to the right side of the control, and place two Label controls on top of the List control. The exact placement of the two labels depends on the size of the tab character between the two columns on the ListBox control, and the initial placement will be approximate.

The data should be loaded when the Form is initialized, which is signaled by the Initialize event. In this event's handler, we must set up a loop to scan all the rows of the spreadsheet and sum the prices while the OrderID field is the same. As each invoice is processed, the new total is added to the list. The OrderID fields are accessed by the expression

```
Range("A" & curRow)
```

in which *curRow* is the row's number, which is increased by one with every iteration. Many of the lines deal with formatting the numbers, and you can ignore them initially.

Code 12.11: The Initialize Event

```
Private Sub UserForm_Initialize()
Dim InvoiceValue As String

curRow = 2
Range("A" & curRow).Select
curInvoice = ActiveCell.Value
curRow = curRow + 1
While curInvoice <> ""
  Range("A" & curRow).Select
  InvoiceNumber = ActiveCell.Value
  If InvoiceNumber = curInvoice Then
    invoicetotal = invoicetotal + Range("C" & curRow).Value
  Else
    InvoiceValue$ = Format$(invoicetotal, "#.00")
    InvoiceValue$ = Space(12 - Len(InvoiceValue$)) & _
InvoiceValue
    ListBox1.AddItem InvoiceNumber & Chr(9) & Chr(9) & _
InvoiceValue$
    invoicetotal = Range("C" & curRow).Value
    curInvoice = InvoiceNumber
  End If
  curRow = curRow + 1
Wend
DoEvents
End Sub
```

The List's Font property is set to a monospaced font to simplify alignment. There are better ways to align multiple columns in a ListBox control, but for this example we want to keep the code's complexity to a minimum.

To display the Form, press F5, or choose Run ➤ Run Sub/User Form. The Form will be loaded, and a couple of seconds later the invoice totals will appear, as shown in Figure 12.15. The Close button simply hides the Form with the following statement:

```
Me.Hide
```

USING VBA FORMS WITH VISUAL BASIC

You can use the Forms and applications that you design with VBA with Visual Basic by making a few adjustments in the code. This means that you can start with VBA and move your designs to Visual Basic, or vice versa. Both the user interface and the code can be reused and shared by people in different environments.

To reuse a VBA Form in a Visual Basic application, first export it by choosing File ➤ Export.

NOTE

VBA Forms are saved automatically with the current project, and you don't have to save them separately. Every time you save the workbook, the Forms (and macros) you designed in the current session are also saved as part of the project.

Choosing File ➤ Export saves the current Form in an FRM file. You can then import this file into a Visual Basic project by choosing Project ➤ Add Form. Save the Form you designed in the last section and then start a new Visual Basic project.

Choose Project ➤ Add Form to add the VBA Form. Visual Basic creates a new folder in the Project window, the Designers folder, and places the VBA Form there. This folder contains Forms designed outside Visual Basic. The UserForm1 Designer is quite similar to a Visual Basic Form, but you can't add to it all the controls you can use with regular Visual Basic Forms. If you click UserForm1, you will see the same Toolbox as you see in the VBA Editor (see Figure 12.17). The Designer should be usable in the environment in which it was created, even after it's been edited with Visual Basic.

If you open the UserForm1 Form's Code window, you will see that it doesn't support all the events recognized by regular Forms. Most of the events are still present, and the code you entered in the VBA Editor is still there.

To complete the application VBExcel, add a new module (the Inv-Module) and enter the following lines:

```
Public appExcel As Object


Sub Main()
  On Error Resume Next
  Set appExcel = GetObject(App.Path & "\FRMSales.xls", _
  "Excel.Application")
  If appExcel Is Nothing Then
    Set appExcel = CreateObject("Excel.Application")
    appExcel.Workbooks.Open App.Path & "\FRMSales.xls"
  End If
  VBEXCEL.Show
End Sub
```

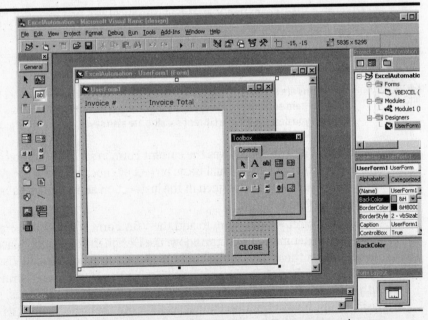

FIGURE 12.17: To adjust the interface of a Designer, you must use the same Toolbox as the application in which the Designer was created.

As you can guess, the code of the UserForm1 Form's code isn't going to work as is. When executed from within Excel's VB Editor, it can safely assume it's connected to an instance of Excel. This is no longer the case. The VB application must first establish a connection to an instance of Excel and then show the Form.

The code of the Main subroutine does exactly that. It instantiates the *appExcel* object variable, assigns the FRMSales spreadsheet to it, and then displays the VBExcel Form, shown in Figure 12.18. This Form simply waits for the user to click the Show Invoice Totals button or terminate the application. The project's Startup object is the subroutine Main (open the Project Properties window and select Sub Main in the Startup Object list).

The code of the Show Invoice Totals button's Click event doesn't do much. It simply loads and displays the UserForm1 Form with the statement

```
UserForm1.Show
```

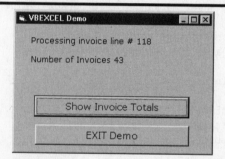

FIGURE 12.18: The VBExcel application's starting Form. As the program reads the invoice lines, it displays its progress on the Form.

When UserForm1 is loaded, its Initialize event is triggered, and the data are read from Excel. We must adjust the code of the Initialize event. The necessary corrections are quite simple. When this code is executed in Excel's environment, we don't have to tell it which spreadsheet to access. We can call the Range method to access the cells of the active spreadsheet. Now, however, the Range method isn't adequate. We must now tell Visual Basic to contact a server application (appExcel) and request data from the first worksheet ("Sheet1" or any other name you may have used in Excel). All instances of the methods called in the Initialize event handler must now be prefixed with the following string:

```
appExcel.Sheets("Sheet1")
```

To read the value of the active cell, for example, we use the expression

```
appExcel.ActiveCell.Value
```

The revised code of the UserForm1 object's Initialize event handler is shown next.

Code 12.12:   The UserForm1_Initialize Event Handler

```
Private Sub UserForm_Initialize()
Dim InvoiceValue As String

curRow = 2
appExcel.Sheets("Sheet1").Range("A" & curRow).Select
curInvoice = appExcel.ActiveCell.Value
curRow = curRow + 1
While curInvoice <> ""
  appExcel.Sheets("Sheet1").Range("A" & curRow).Select
  InvoiceNumber = appExcel.ActiveCell.Value
  If InvoiceNumber = curInvoice Then
    invoicetotal = invoicetotal + _
      appExcel.Sheets("Sheet1").Range("C" & curRow).Value
  Else
    InvoiceValue$ = Format$(invoicetotal, "#.00")
    InvoiceValue$ = Space(12 - Len(InvoiceValue$)) & _
      InvoiceValue
    ListBox1.AddItem InvoiceNumber & Chr(9) & Chr(9) & _
      InvoiceValue$
    invoicetotal = appExcel.Range("C" & curRow).Value
    curInvoice = InvoiceNumber
    InvCounter = InvCounter + 1
  End If
  VBEXCEL.Label1.Caption = "Processing invoice line # " & _
    curRow
  VBEXCEL.Label2.Caption = "Number of Invoices " & InvCounter
  curRow = curRow + 1
  VBEXCEL.Refresh
Wend
End Sub
```

If you load the VBExcel application, be sure that the FRMSales.xls file (the worksheet with the invoice details) has been prepared and resides in the same folder as the application. Moreover, you may have to change the addresses of the cells. In the project's code, we assume that the OrderID values are stored in the first column (A) and the prices in the third column (C). If you paste the data into a different location on the worksheet, adjust the references in the code accordingly. Figure 12.19 shows the Form being used within a VB application.

NOTE
The NWIND database contains more than 2,000 invoice lines, and processing them won't be instant, even on a fast machine.

This example concludes our introduction to the basic objects exposed by Excel and Word. You have now seen how you can build VB applications to control other applications that act as OLE servers by manipulating their objects. In the following chapters, you will find a complete discussion of all the objects exposed by Word and Excel and lots of examples.

VBEXCEL Demo

Processing invoice line # 2157

Number of Invoices 830

Show Invoice Total

EXIT Demo

UserForm1

Invoice #	Invoice Total
10249	272.00
10250	1863.40
10251	1552.60
10252	654.06
10253	3597.90
10254	1444.80
10255	556.62
10256	2490.50
10257	517.80
10258	1119.90
10259	1614.88
10260	100.80
10261	1504.65
10262	448.00
10263	584.00
10264	1873.80

CLOSE

FIGURE 12.19: A VBA Form being used from within a Visual Basic application

WHAT'S NEXT?

You now know the fundamentals of VBA. In the next chapter, you'll build on that foundation by learning about the Word object model and ways to use VBA more effectively.

Chapter 13

THE WORD OBJECT MODEL

I n this chapter, we'll look at the Word object model, which describes the theoretical architecture underlying Word. By understanding the Word object model, you can manipulate the objects from which Word is built and work quickly and effectively with VBA.

I should warn you at the outset that the Word object model is too complex to be dissected thoroughly in this chapter. Instead, my goal is to help you understand the general structure of Word's plethora of objects, learn to navigate the object model to find the objects you need, and manipulate them efficiently once you've gotten a hold of them.

Adapted from *Word 97 Macro & VBA Handbook*
by Guy Hart-Davis
ISBN 0-7821-1962-X   848 pages $44.99

WHAT IS THE WORD OBJECT MODEL?

VBA works mostly with *objects*. Objects are the elements that VBA uses to manipulate Word, ranging from the Application object that represents the whole of Word to Document objects that represent open documents and Character objects that represent individual characters within a document. When you need to perform a task in VBA, you usually end up working with a *property* of an object (for example, setting the FullName property of a document) or performing some action (a *method*) on an object. As a simple example of this, you've seen that to close the active document, you use the Close method on the ActiveDocument object:

```
ActiveDocument.Close
```

The *object model* is the structure that describes how the different objects in Word relate to each other. When you examine the object model, it begins to resemble a set of Chinese boxes: within each object is another object, which in turn contains other objects, inside each of which lurk still more objects. For example, a document object contains a number of word objects, which in turn contain a number of character objects. To use the object model, you open each box in turn until you reach the object you need, and then you start performing actions on it.

A VBA object that contains all the objects of a particular type is called a *collection*. The items in the collection are known as *members*; you refer to a particular member of a collection by using its name or its index number. You can also manipulate a collection as a single object. For example, the Documents collection contains all the documents that are currently open. By working with the Documents collection, you can manipulate all its members—all the open documents—at once. You could save and then close all the open documents by using the Save method and then the Close method on the Documents collection like this:

```
Documents.Save
Documents.Close
```

When you need to take action on all the open documents at the same time, working with the collection is much faster and much simpler than working with the individual documents. Likewise, you can work with collections of windows by using the Windows collection, with command bars by using the CommandBars collection, with words by using the Words collection, and so on.

The Application object is at the top level of the Word object model, which makes it a good place to start.

THE APPLICATION OBJECT

The Application object represents the Word application. Because you'll usually be working with Word in VBA, you seldom need to specify the Application object—in most cases it will be understood, although you can specify it if you want to. (You do need to specify the Application object when you're working with VBA in another application—Excel, for example—and you want to manipulate Word or vice versa.)

Figure 13.1 shows the Application object and the objects it contains. The plural names with singular names in parentheses indicate collections and the individual objects they contain, respectively: for example, the Addins collection comprises all Addin objects in the Application object, and the Documents collection contains all the open Document objects in the Application object. The arrows to the right of the Auto-Correct, Documents, Selection, Templates, and Windows objects indicate that these objects contain further objects (beyond the objects in the collections)—for example, the Documents collection and the Document object, which we'll look at in the next section, contain a number of objects (and collections) from Bookmarks through Words. We'll start looking at some of these later in this chapter.

You can refer to the objects contained within the Application object by specifying their names. For example, if you want to refer to the name of the first of the command bars within the application, you can use the Name property of the first item in the CommandBars collection within the Application object:

```
Application.CommandBars(1).Name
```

Again, it's not necessary to use the Application object here, because it's understood—you can get the same effect by using Command-Bars(1).Name instead.

The three most-used objects in the Application object are Documents, Windows, and Selection. By using these, you can manipulate the documents that are open, the windows that are open, and the current selection in the active document. Figure 13.2 shows some of the more important objects within each of these three objects.

Part iv

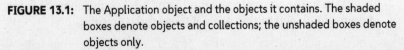

```
Application
    Addins (Addin)
    Assistant
    AutoCaptions (AutoCaption)
    AutoCorrect                                          ▶
    Browser
    CaptionLabels (CaptionLabel)
    CommandBars (CommandBar)
        CommandBarControls (CommandBarControl)
    Dialogs (Dialog)
    Dictionaries (Dictionary)
    Documents (Document)                                 ▶
    FileConverters (FileConverter)
    FileSearch
    FontNames
    KeysBoundTo (KeyBinding)
    KeyBindings (KeyBinding)
    Languages (Language)
        Dictionary
    ListGalleries (ListGallery)
        ListTemplates (ListTemplate)
            ListLevels (ListLevel)
    MailingLabel
        CustomLabels (CustomLabel)
    MailMessage
    Options
    RecentFiles (RecentFile)
    Selection                                            ▶
    SpellingSuggestions (SpellingSuggestion)
    SynonymInfo
    System
    Tasks (Task)
    Templates (Template)                                 ▶
    VBE
    Windows (Window)                                     ▶
```

FIGURE 13.1: The Application object and the objects it contains. The shaded boxes denote objects and collections; the unshaded boxes denote objects only.

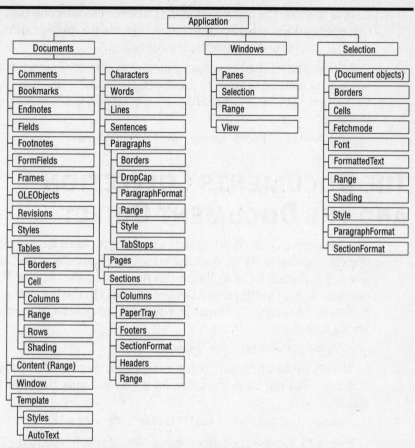

FIGURE 13.2: Part of the Word object model, showing the Documents collection, the Windows collection, and the Selection object under the Application object

As you can see in the figure, the Documents collection contains collections for Characters, Words, Lines, Sentences, Paragraphs, Pages, and Sections, among others; the Paragraphs and Sections collections each contain objects of their own. So to access one of the paragraphs in a document, you would specify the Document object in the Documents collection and then the Paragraph object in the Paragraphs collection inside it:

```
Documents(1).Paragraphs(2)
```

Part iv

This specifies the first object in the Documents collection (i.e., the first opened document) and the second object in the Paragraphs collection (i.e., the second paragraph in the document).

Once you've reached the object you want to refer to, you specify the property or method to apply to the object. In this case, you might specify the property Style = "Heading 1" to set the style of the paragraph to Heading 1:

```
Documents(1).Paragraphs(2).Style = "Heading 1"
```

THE DOCUMENTS COLLECTION AND THE DOCUMENT OBJECT

The Documents collection contains a Document object for each of the open documents in Word. You refer to the Document objects in the Documents collection by using their index numbers or their names. For example, to refer to the second Document object in the Documents collection and display its full name in a message box, you could use the following statement:

```
MsgBox Documents(2).FullName
```

To refer to the Document object named Quarterly Analysis.doc and display a Print Preview window for it, you could use the following statement:

```
Documents("Quarterly Analysis.doc").PrintPreview
```

Figure 13.3 shows the collections and objects contained in the Documents collection and the Document object.

Of the collections that the Documents collection and the Document object contain, you'll often find yourself needing to work with the Characters collection, the Words collection, the Sentences collection, and the Paragraphs collection. You use these collections to reference the objects in the document that you want to work with. For example, if you wanted to apply Arial font to the first sentence in the document named Promotion.doc, you could use a statement like this:

```
Documents("Promotion.doc").Sentences(1).Font.Name = "Arial"
```

If you wanted to apply the font to several consecutive sentences, you could create a range containing the sentences and then apply formatting to the range.

```
Documents (Document)
  ├ Bookmarks (Bookmark)
  ├ DocumentProperties (DocumentProperty)
  ├ Characters (Range)                    ▶
  ├ CommandBars (CommandBar)
  ├ Comments (Comment)
  ├ Endnotes (Endnote)
  ├ Envelope
  ├ Fields (Field)
  ├ Footnotes (Footnote)
  ├ FormFields (FormField)                ▶
  ├ Frames (Frame)
  ├ Hyperlinks (Hyperlink)
  ├ Indexes (Index)
  ├ InLineShapes (InLineShape)
  ├ LetterContent
  ├ ListParagraphs (Paragraph)
  ├ Lists (List)
  │   ├ ListParagraphs (Paragraph)
  │   └ Range
  ├ ListTemplates (ListTemplate)
  │   └ ListLevels (ListLevel)
  │       └ Font
  ├ Mailer
  ├ MailMerge
  │   ├ MailMergeDataSource
  │   └ MailMergeFields (MailMergeField)
  └ PageSetup
      ├ LineNumbering
      └ TextColumns (TextColumn)

  ├ Paragraphs (Paragraph)                ▶
  ├ ProofreadingErrors (Range)            ▶
  ├ Revisions (Revision)
  ├ Range                                 ▶
  ├ ReadabilityStatistics (ReadabilityStatistics)
  ├ RoutingSlip
  ├ Sections (Section)
  ├ Sentences (Range)                     ▶
  ├ Shapes (Shape)
  ├ StoryRanges (Range)                   ▶
  ├ Styles (Style)                        ▶
  ├ Subdocuments (Subdocument)
  ├ Tables (Table)                        ▶
  ├ TablesOfAuthoritiesCatagories (T.O.A.C.)
  ├ TablesOfAuthorities (TableOfAuthority)
  ├ TablesOfContents (TableOfContents)
  ├ TablesOfFigures (TableOfFigures)
  ├ Variables (Variable)
  ├ VBProject
  ├ Versions (Version)
  ├ Windows (Window)                      ▶
  └ Words (Range)                         ▶
```

FIGURE 13.3:   The collections and objects contained in the Documents collection and the Document object

THE SELECTION OBJECT

The Selection object enables you to work with the current selection. (You can only have one selection at a time in a Word session, so Selection is an object rather than a collection.)

Figure 13.4 shows the collections and objects contained in the Selection object.

As you can see, the Selection object contains collections that include, among others, Characters, Words, Sentences, and Paragraphs, enabling you to work directly with the objects inside the selection. For example, if you wanted to display a message box containing the first word of the current selection, you could use this statement:

```
MsgBox Selection.Words(1)
```

If you wanted to change the font size of the first word of the current selection to 50-point type, you could use the following statement:

```
Selection.Words(1).Font.Size = "50"
```

This statement sets the Size property of the Font object of the first object in the Words collection in the Selection object to 50-point type.

THE WINDOWS COLLECTION AND THE WINDOW OBJECT

The Windows collection object gives you access to the Window objects for all the available windows in the application. Figure 13.5 shows the collections and objects contained in the Windows collection object.

NOTE

There are two Windows collections—one for the application and one for the windows displaying the document with which you are working. The Windows collection for the Document object can be useful if you have multiple windows open for the same document (as you can do with the Window ➢ New Window command), but usually you'll want to use the Windows collection for the Application object.

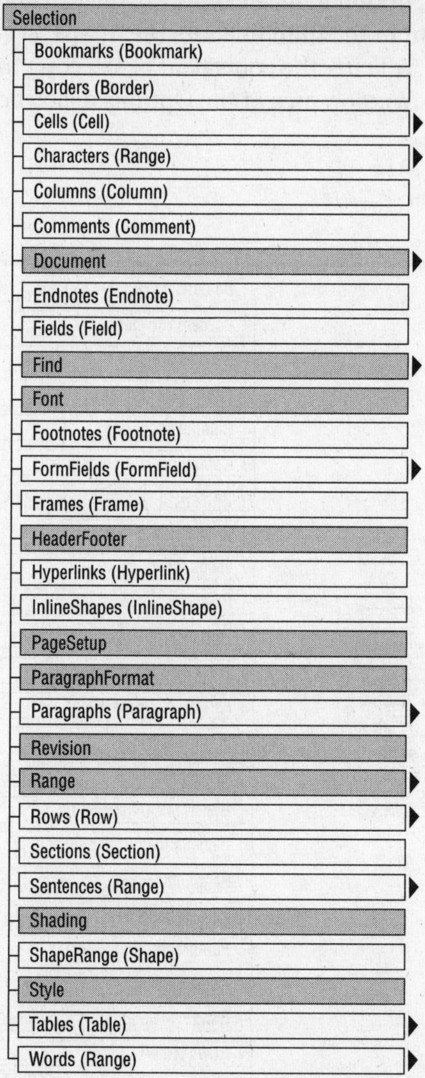

FIGURE 13.4: The collections and objects contained in the Selection object

If you want to manipulate the view of the windows currently displayed, you can use a For Each…Next statement with the Windows collection. Below, the statement in the second line sets the ShowAll property of the View object to False, the equivalent of clearing the All check box in the Nonprinting Characters area of the View tab of the Options dialog box, or

Part iv

of clicking the Show/Hide ¶ button to toggle off the display of nonprinting characters. The statement in the third line sets the `WrapToWindow` property of the `View` object to `True`, the equivalent of selecting the Wrap to Window check box in the Window area of the Options dialog box.

```
For Each Win In Windows
  Win.View.ShowAll = False
  Win.View.WrapToWindow = True
Next Win
```

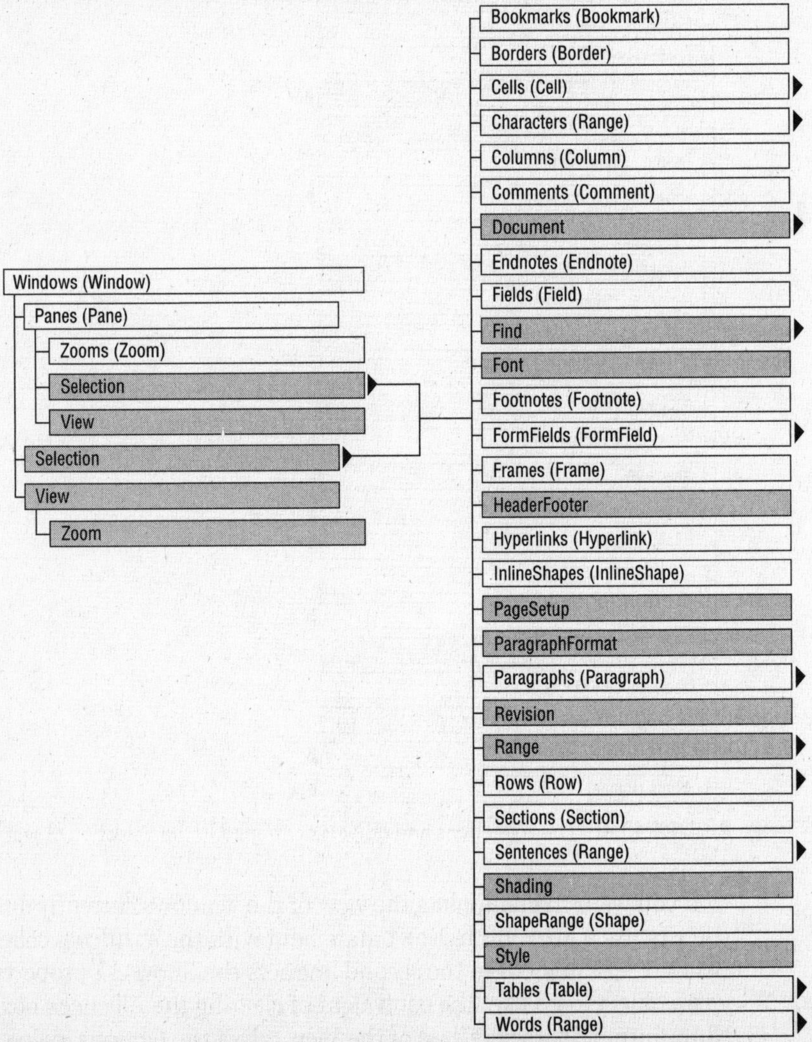

FIGURE 13.5: The collections and objects contained in the Windows object

NAVIGATING THE WORD OBJECT MODEL

The Visual Basic Editor provides a number of tools for navigating the Word object model:

- ▶ The macro recorder
- ▶ The Object Browser
- ▶ The online Help system, which has detailed pictures of the hierarchy of the Word object model
- ▶ The List Properties/Methods feature

Using the Macro Recorder to Record the Objects You Need

One of the best tools with which to start your exploration of the Word object model is the macro recorder. By recording the actions you perform, the macro recorder creates code that you can then work with in the code window of the Visual Basic Editor.

However, there are a couple of problems with using the macro recorder to navigate your way through the object model:

- ▶ First, you can't record all the actions that you might want. Say you want to create a statement that performed an action on a specified document in the Documents collection rather than on the active document, but with the macro recorder, you can only record actions performed on the active document. (This is because the macro recorder can record only those actions you can perform interactively in Word, and you can't work interactively with any document other than the active one.)

- ▶ Second, the macro recorder is apt to record statements that you don't strictly need, particularly when you're trying to record a setting in a dialog box.

As an example of the second point, try recording a quick macro to create an AutoCorrect entry: start the macro recorder, choose Tools ➤ AutoCorrect, enter the text to be replaced in the Replace box and the replacement text in the With box, click the OK button to close the AutoCorrect dialog box, and

Part iv

stop the macro recorder. Then open the resulting macro in the Visual Basic Editor. You'll probably see code something like this:

```
Sub Add_Item_to_AutoCorrect()
'
' Add_Item_to_AutoCorrect Macro
' Macro recorded 4/4/97 by Rikki Nadir
'
    AutoCorrect.Entries.Add Name:="reffs",Value:="references"
    With AutoCorrect
      .CorrectInitialCaps = True
      .CorrectSentenceCaps = True
      .CorrectDays = True
      .CorrectCapsLock = True
      .ReplaceText = True
    End With
End Sub
```

Here, you get eleven lines of padding around the one line you need:

```
AutoCorrect.Entries.Add Name:="reffs", Value:="references"
```

This line shows you that the object you need to work with to add an AutoCorrect entry is the `Entries` collection object in the `AutoCorrect` object. You use the `Add` method on the `Entries` collection to add an AutoCorrect entry to the list.

By removing the seven lines containing the `With...End With` statement from this recorded macro, you can reduce it to just the line it needs to contain (together with the comment lines, which you could also remove if you wanted):

```
Sub Add_Item_to_AutoCorrect()
'
' Add_Item_to_AutoCorrect Macro
' Macro recorded 4/4/97 by Rikki Nadir
'
    AutoCorrect.Entries.Add Name:="reffs",Value:="references"
End Sub
```

In spite of its limitations, the macro recorder does provide quick access to the objects you need to work with, and you can always adjust the resulting code in the Visual Basic Editor.

Using the Object Browser

The macro recorder is a good tool for recording the object you want to get a grip on, but the primary tool for navigating the Word object model is the Object Browser. In this section, you'll get to know the Object Browser better and will learn to use it to find the information you need on objects.

Components of the Object Browser

The Object Browser provides the following information on both built-in objects and custom objects you create:

- ▶ Classes (formal definitions of objects)

- ▶ Properties (the attributes of objects or aspects of their behavior)

- ▶ Methods (actions you can perform on objects)

- ▶ Events (for example, the opening or closing of a document)

- ▶ Constants (named items that keep a constant value while a program is executing)

Figure 13.6 shows the different components of the Object Browser. Here's what they do:

- ▶ The **Project/Library drop-down list** provides a list of object libraries available to the current project. (An *object library* is a reference file containing information on a collection of objects available to programs.) Use the drop-down list to choose the object libraries you want to view. For example, you might choose to view only objects in Word by choosing Word from the Project/Library drop-down list. Alternatively, you could stay with the default choice of <All Libraries>.

- ▶ In the **Search Text box**, enter the string you want to search for; either type it in, or choose a previous string in the current project session from the drop-down list. Then either press Enter or click the Search button to find members containing the search string.

TIP

To make your searches more specific, you can use wildcards such as ? (representing any one character) and * (representing any group of characters). You can also choose to search for a whole word only (rather than matching your search string with part of another word) by right-clicking anywhere in the Object Browser (except in the Project/Library drop-down list or in the Search Text box) and choosing Find Whole Word Only from the context menu. The Find Whole Word Only choice will have a check mark next to it in the context menu when it is active; to deactivate it, choose Find Whole Word Only again on the context menu.

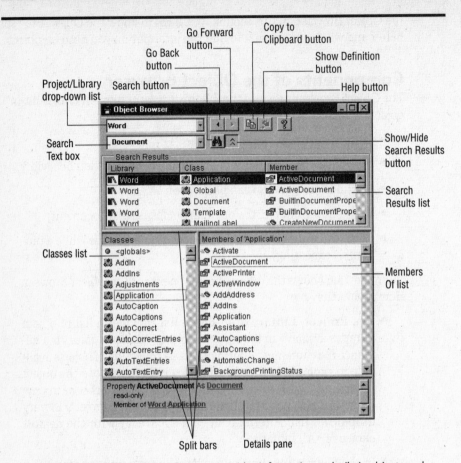

FIGURE 13.6: The Object Browser provides information on built-in objects and custom objects.

▶ Click the **Go Back button** to go back one by one through your previous selections in the Classes list and the Members Of list. Click the **Go Forward button** to go forward through your previous selections one by one. The Go Back button will become available when you go to a class or member in the Object Browser; the Go Forward button will become available only when you use the Go Back button to go back to a previous selection.

▶ Click the **Copy to Clipboard button** to copy the selected item from the Search Results box, the Classes list, the Members Of list, or the Details pane to the Clipboard so that you can paste it into your code.

▶ Click the **Show Definition button** to display a code window containing the code for the object selected in the Classes list or the Members Of list. The Show Definition button will be available (undimmed) only for objects that contain code, such as macros and userforms that you've created.

▶ Click the **Help button** to display any available Help for the currently selected item.

▶ Click the **Search button** to search for the term entered in the Search Text box. If the Search Results pane is not open, VBA will open it at this point.

▶ Click the **Show/Hide Search Results button** to toggle the display of the Search Results pane on and off.

▶ The **Search Results list** in the Search Results pane contains the results of the latest search you've conducted for a term entered in the Search Text box. If you've performed a search, the Object Browser will update the Search Results list when you switch to a different library by using the Project/Library drop-down list.

▶ The **Classes list** shows the available classes in the library or project specified in the Project/Library drop-down list.

▶ The **Members Of list** displays the available elements of the class selected in the Classes list. A method, constant, event, property, or procedure that has code written for it appears in boldface. For example, in the Members Of list shown in Figure 13.7, the procedures `Add_Item_to_AutoCorrect` and `Area_Code_from_Phone_Number` contain code and so appear in boldface. The Members Of list can display the members either grouped into their different categories (methods, properties, events, etc.) or ungrouped as an alphabetical list of all the members available. To toggle between grouped and ungrouped, right-click in the Members Of list and choose Group Members from the context menu; click to place a check mark (to group the members) or to remove the check mark (to ungroup the members).

▶ The **Details pane** displays the definition of the member selected in the Classes list or in the Members Of list. For example, if you select a macro in the Members Of list, the Details pane will display its name, the name of the module and template or document in which it is stored, and any comment lines you inserted at the beginning of the macro. The module name and template name will contain hyperlinks (jumps) so that you can quickly move to them.

▶ Drag the three **split bars** to resize the panes of the Object Browser to suit you. (You can also resize the Object Browser window.)

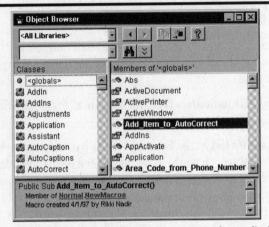

FIGURE 13.7:   Procedures that contain code are displayed in boldface in the Members Of list.

Adding and Removing Object Libraries

You can add and remove object libraries by using the References dialog box. By adding object libraries, you can make available additional objects to work with; by removing object libraries that you do not need to view or use, you can reduce the number of object references that VBA needs to resolve when it compiles the code in a project, thus allowing it to run faster.

You can also adjust the priority of different references by adjusting the order in which the references appear in the References dialog box. The priority of references matters when you use in your code an object whose name appears in more than one reference; VBA checks the order in the References list of the references that contain that object name and uses the first of them.

TIP

You probably won't want to mess with object libraries until you find that parts of your code are not working as you expect them to. For the moment, though, take a look at the references that appear in the References dialog box to make sure you're not loading a large number of object libraries that you don't need. My recommendation is to load the following object libraries in this order: Visual Basic for Applications; Microsoft Word 8.0 Object Library; OLE Automation; Microsoft Forms 2.0 Object Library; and Microsoft Office 8.0 Object Library. This forms a core group that will provide functionality for most operations in Word; if you're not using any of the Office functions, you might want to try unloading the Microsoft Office 8.0 Object Library, and if you think you're not using OLE Automation, you could remove that as well. But given the prevalence of OLE in Microsoft's applications, the OLE Automation object library is a good bet for most circumstances. If later on you wanted to work with objects from, say, Outlook, you could add the Microsoft Outlook 8.0 Object Model library. You can also add global templates to make their contents available to all open projects, and you can add references to open templates and documents so that you can use macros in them.

To add or remove object libraries:

1. In the Object Browser window, right-click in the Project/Library drop-down list (or in the Classes window or the Members window) and choose References from the context menu; alternatively, choose Tools ➤ References in the Visual Basic Editor; either action will display the References dialog box, shown in Figure 13.8.

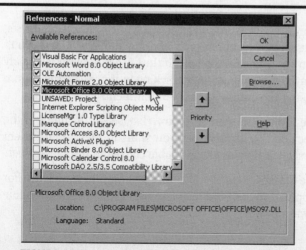

FIGURE 13.8: You can add and remove object libraries from the References dialog box.

2. In the Available References list box, select the check boxes for the references you want to have available, and clear the check boxes for the references you want to remove.

3. Adjust the priority of the references if necessary by selecting a reference and using the up- and down-arrow Priority buttons to move it up or down the list. Usually, you'll want to keep Visual Basic for Applications and the Microsoft Word 8.0 Object Library at the top of your list if you're working with VBA and Word.

TIP

You can add further reference libraries by clicking the Browse button to display the Add Reference dialog box, selecting the library file, and clicking the Open button.

4. Choose the OK button to close the References dialog box and return to the Object Browser.

Navigating with the Object Browser

Now that you've seen the components of the Object Browser, let's look at how to use them to browse the objects available to a project:

1. First, activate a code module by double-clicking it in the Project Explorer.

2. Display the Object Browser by choosing View ➤ Object Browser, by pressing the F2 button, or by clicking the Object Browser button on the Standard toolbar. (If the Object Browser is already displayed, make it active by clicking in it or selecting it from the list at the bottom of the Window menu.)

3. In the Project/Library drop-down list, select the name of the project or the library that you want to view. The Object Browser will display the available classes in the Classes list.

4. In the Classes list, select the class you want to work with. For example, if you chose a template in step 3, select the module you want to work with in the Classes list.

5. If you want to work with a particular member of the class or project, select it in the Members Of list. For example, if you're working with a template project, you might want to choose a specific macro or userform to work with.

Once you've selected the class, member, or project, you can take the following actions on it:

▶ View information about it in the Details pane at the bottom of the Object Browser window.

▶ View the definition of an object by clicking the Show Definition button. Alternatively, right-click the object in the Members Of list and choose View Definition from the context menu. (Remember that the definition of a macro is the code that it contains; the definition of a module is all the code in all the macros that it contains; the definition of a userform is the code in all the macros attached to it.) As I mentioned before, the Show Definition button will be available (undimmed) only for objects that contain code, such as macros and userforms that you've created.

▶ Copy the text for the selected class, project, or member to the Clipboard by clicking the Copy to Clipboard button or by issuing a standard Copy command (e.g., Ctrl+C, Ctrl+Insert).

Using Help to Find the Object You Need

VBA's Help system provides another easy way to access the details of the objects you want to work with. The Help files provide you with a hyperlinked reference to all the objects, methods, and properties in VBA, including graphics that show how the objects are related to each other.

The quickest way to access VBA Help is to activate the Visual Basic Editor and then press the F1 key. VBA will respond by displaying the Visual Basic Reference window (see Figure 13.9). If you've disabled the Office Assistant (as most people do after a while of suffering its merry pranks), you can also choose Help ➤ Microsoft Visual Basic Help; if you haven't disabled the Office Assistant, choosing Help ➤ Microsoft Visual Basic Help will display the Office Assistant.

TIP

To get help on a specific object, keyword, etc. referenced in your code, place the insertion point in the appropriate word before pressing the F1 key. VBA will display the Help for that topic.

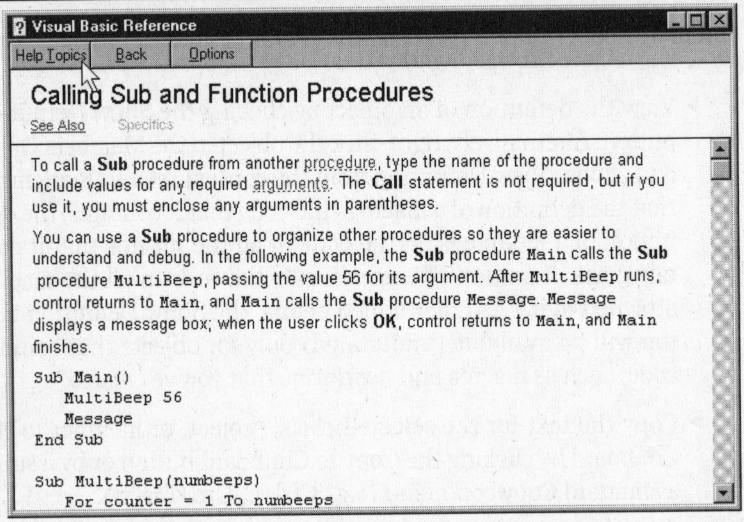

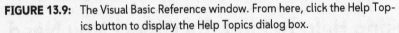

FIGURE 13.9: The Visual Basic Reference window. From here, click the Help Topics button to display the Help Topics dialog box.

Click the Help Topics button at the top-left corner of the Visual Basic Reference window to display the Help Topics dialog box, shown in Figure 13.10. Click the Index tab to display it if it isn't already displayed. In the top text box, start typing the name of the object about which you want to get information, and then select the appropriate entry in the list box and click the Display button to display the entry.

For example, if you display help on the Document object, you'll see a Help window like the one shown in Figure 13.11.

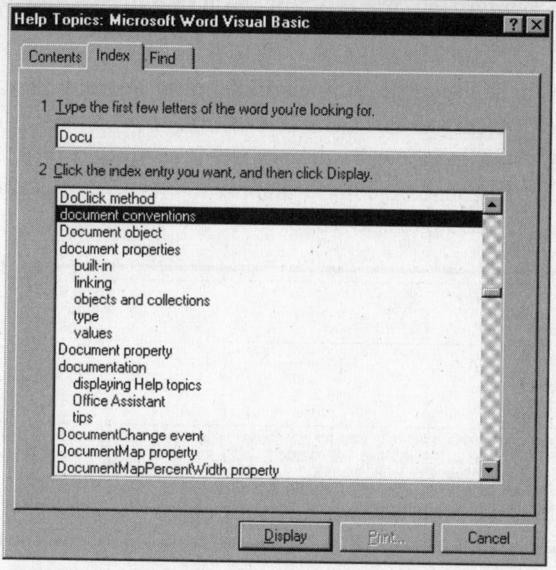

FIGURE 13.10:   Use the Index tab of the Help Topics dialog box to find the object about which you want to get information.

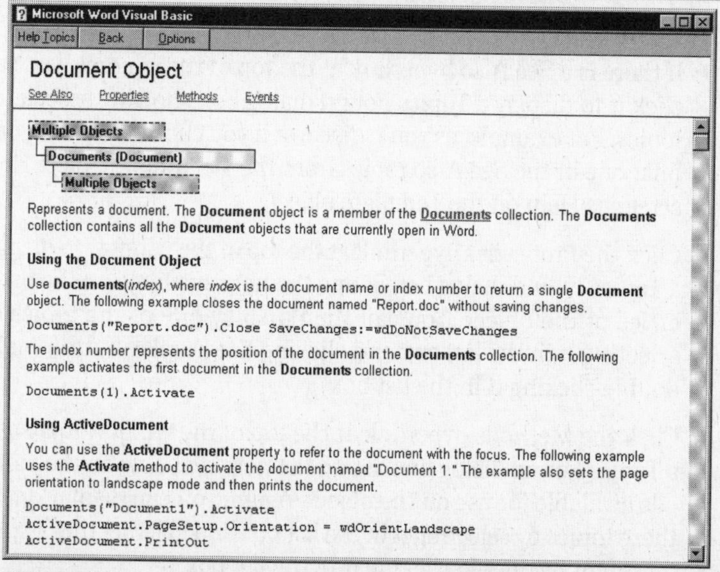

FIGURE 13.11:   Here's what you'll get if you search for help on the Document object.

Apart from the regular Help information you'll find in the Help window, there are a few items that deserve comment here:

▶ The graphic at the top of the Help listing shows the relationship of the current object (in this case, Document) to the object (or objects) that contain it and to the objects it contains. You can click on either of these objects to display a list of the relevant objects, as shown in Figure 13.12.

Document Object

See Also   Properties   Methods   Events

Multiple Objects
└ Documents (Document)
  └ Multiple Objects

Bookmarks, Characters, CommandBars, Comments, DocumentProperties, Endnotes, Envelope, Fields, Footnotes, s all
FormFields, Frames, HyperLinks, Indexes, InlineShapes, LetterContent, ListParagraphs, Lists, ListTemplates,
Mailer, MailMerge, PageSetup, Paragraphs, ProofreadingErrors, Range, ReadabilityStatistics, Revisions,
RoutingSlip, Sections, Sentences, Shapes, StoryRanges, Styles, Subdocuments, Tables, TablesOfAuthorities,
TablesOfAuthoritiesCategories, TablesOfContents, TablesOfFigures, Template, Variables, VBProject, Versions,
Windows, Words

`Documents("Report.doc").Close SaveChanges:=wdDoNotSaveChanges`

FIGURE 13.12: Click one of the objects in the graphic to see a list of the objects it contains. Here, you can see that the Document object contains a plethora of other objects from Bookmarks and Characters to Windows and Words.

▶ If there is a See Also hyperlink at the top of the window, you can click it to display a Topics Found dialog box showing associated topics. For example, as you'd discover if you clicked on the hyperlink, one of the See Also topics from the Document Object Help screen is Help on the Template object.

▶ Click the Properties hyperlink at the top of the window to display a Topics Found dialog box listing the help available on the properties of the object. You can then display one of the topics by selecting it in the list box and clicking the Display button (or by double-clicking it in the list box).

▶ Click the Methods hyperlink at the top of the window to display a Topics Found dialog box listing the help available on the methods available for use on the object. Again, you can display one of these topics by selecting it in the list box and clicking the Display button or by double-clicking it in the list box.

▶ Some objects also have one or more events associated with them. If the object has any events associated with it (as the Document object does here), you can access them by clicking the Events hyperlink at the top of the window to display a Topics Found dialog box.

Using the List Properties/Methods Feature

When you're entering a statement in the Visual Basic Editor and type the period at the end of the current object, the List Properties/Methods feature displays a list of properties and methods appropriate to the statement you've entered so far.

The List Properties/Methods feature provides a quick way of entering statements, but you need to know the object from which to start. Sometimes using this feature is a bit like finding your way through a maze and being given paradoxical directions that mostly consist of "You can't get there from here."

Once you know the object from which to start, though, it's clear sailing. For example, to put together the statement Application .Documents(1).Close to close the first document in the Documents collection, you could work as follows:

1. Place the insertion point on a fresh line in an empty macro (between the Sub and End Sub statements).

2. Type the word **Application**, or type **Appl** and press Ctrl+ spacebar to have the Complete Word feature complete the word for you.

3. Type the period after **Application**. The List Properties/ Methods feature will display the list of properties and methods available to the Application object.

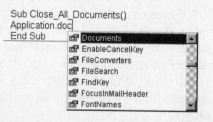

4. Choose the Documents item in the List Properties/Methods list. You can either scroll to it using the mouse and then double-click it to enter it in the code window, scroll to it by using the ↑ and ↓ keys and enter it by pressing Tab, or scroll to it by typing the first few letters of its name (as shown here) and then enter it by pressing Tab.

5. Type the **(1).** after **Documents**. When you type the period, the List Properties/Methods feature will display the list of properties and methods available to the Documents collection.

6. Choose the Close method in the List Properties/Methods list by scrolling to it with the mouse or with the ↑ and ↓ keys. Because this is the end of the statement, press the Enter key to enter the method and start a new line rather than pressing the Tab key (which would enter the method and continue the same line).

Using For Each...Next Loops with Collections

Earlier in this chapter, I touched briefly on how you can save time by working with the collections in the Word object model rather than working with the individual objects they contain. You can use a method on a collection to affect all the objects contained in it, such as closing all Document objects in the Documents collection, maximizing all Window objects in the Windows collection, and so on.

However, you don't need to take such sweeping actions: you could also use a For Each...Next loop with the Documents collection to work on each member of the collection in turn. For instance, you might want to search the contents of each document for a particular word or phrase and close each document that did not contain it. To do so, you could use code like that shown in Listing 13.1. One of the advantages of using the collection and the For Each...Next loop is that you do not need to know how many objects there are in the collection—you just tell VBA to repeat the loop for each object in the collection, and VBA handles the rest. (If there are no objects in the collection, VBA terminates the loop on the first iteration.)

Listing 13.1

```
1.   Sub Close_Documents_without_Specified_Text()
2.       Dim SearchText As String
3.       SearchText = InputBox("Enter the text to search for:",
         ƒ"Close Documents without Specified Text")
4.       For Each Doc in Documents
5            Selection.Find.Text = SearchText
6.           Selection.Find.Execute
7.           If Selection.Find.Found = False Then
             ƒDocuments(Doc).Close
8.       Next Doc
9.   End Sub
```

Analysis

Here, line 2 declares the string variable SearchText. Line 3 then prompts the user for the text for which to search and stores the result of the input box in SearchText.

Line 4 begins a For Each...Next loop that runs for each member of the Documents collection. Here, the counter variable for the Documents collection is named Doc; you could use any valid name for it. Line 5 sets Word to find SearchText, and line 6 executes the search. Line 7 uses an If...Then condition to verify whether the search was successful; if it was not—as specified by Selection.Find.Found = False—VBA closes the current document in the Documents collection. Line 8 completes the loop, and line 9 ends the macro.

USING WITH...END WITH STATEMENTS WITH OBJECTS OR COLLECTIONS

VBA's With statements let you simplify complex code that deals with the same object or collection. Instead of referring repeatedly to the same object, you can identify the object and then use a With...End With statement to perform a series of actions on it. The result is code that is easier to read and that runs faster.

The syntax for a With statement is as follows:

```
With object
    statements
End With
```

Here, `object` can be any object, including a collection.

As an example, consider the formatting you might want to apply to a paragraph to spice up its current style without applying a different style. Let's say you decided to apply a different font, a larger font size, and no underline, but still have the paragraph identified as a Heading 1 style. You could apply this formatting to it with the following three statements:

```
Selection.Font.Name = "Arial Black"
Selection.Font.Size = 24
Selection.Font.Underline = wdUnderlineNone
```

Alternatively, you could use a `With` statement to simplify the code:

```
With Selection.Font
    .Name = "Arial Black"
    .Size = 24
    .Underline = wdUnderlineNone
End With
```

Here, all the statements between the `With` statement and the `End With` statement apply to the object defined in the `With` statement, `Selection.Font`.

Likewise, you could use a `With` statement to apply paragraph formatting to the current selection. The statements below set the space before the paragraph to 0 points and the space after the paragraph to 12 points.

```
With Selection.ParagraphFormat
    .SpaceBefore = 0
    .SpaceAfter = 12
End With
```

Here, all the statements between the `With` statement and the `End With` statement apply to the `Selection.ParagraphFormat` object.

You could also combine these two `With` statements by using the object `Selection`, which is common to them both, as follows:

```
With Selection
    .Font.Name = "Arial Black"
    .Font.Size = 24
    .Font.Underline = wdUnderlineNone
    .ParagraphFormat.SpaceBefore = 0
    .ParagraphFormat.SpaceAfter = 12
End With
```

You can also nest `With` statements, as in the following example. In this case, the nesting is not strictly necessary (though it works fine), but in other cases, you may find it necessary:

```
With Selection
    With .Font
```

```
      .Name = "Arial Black"
      .Size = 24
      .Underline = wdUnderlineNone
   End With
   With .ParagraphFormat
      .SpaceBefore = 0
      .SpaceAfter = 12
   End With
End With
```

TIP

The easiest way to create a `With` statement when you're learning to use VBA is by using the macro recorder to record the method of accessing the objects you want to work with and the actions you want to perform on them. Once you've done that, edit the code in the Visual Basic Editor and create a `With` statement that uses a stripped-down version of the recorded code to perform the actions.

If you've reached this point in the chapter without skipping ahead, you're probably ready for a break. Take a walk, or some refreshment, or even get a good night's sleep.

WHAT'S NEXT?

This chapter explored the Word object model. The following chapter will conduct a similar exploration of the Access object model. You'll be introduced to the object hierarchies in Access and Jet, how to relate objects to one another, referring to objects and properties by name, and using the Expression Builder to create references.

Chapter 14
INTRODUCING THE ACCESS OBJECT MODEL

When you automate a database operation you create instructions that run when an object recognizes an event. You must understand which objects you can write instructions for, the events that an object recognizes, and how to write the instructions. This chapter focuses on specific objects: which objects are available, which properties can be changed, how the objects are related to each other, and how you identify an object when you write a program.

The Access object model is large and complex. The purpose of this chapter is to get you started with the model by introducing you to those objects and properties that are available in both macro and VBA programming.

Adapted from *Access 97 Macro & VBA Handbook*
by Susann Novalis
ISBN 0-7821-1977-8   1,104 pages $54.99

Relating Objects to Each Other

You are familiar with the Database window objects of interactive Access: the tables, queries, forms, and reports. We'll continue to use the word "object" informally and add a few more objects to our list: table fields, query fields, form controls, and report controls. When you work interactively with Access, you don't have to be concerned with how objects are related to each other; the Access user interface takes care of the relationships for you. However, to create programs that manipulate the objects, you need to understand how objects are related so you can use these relationships to refer to an object in a program.

Understanding groups of objects, whether the objects are people, celestial bodies, or database objects, means understanding how they are tied together in relationships. Two kinds of relationships are obvious: some objects are *similar* to other objects, and some objects *contain* other objects.

Grouping Similar Objects

It is natural to group objects with similar properties and behaviors together. For example, it is natural to group the forms in a database, to group command buttons, or to group text boxes. A group of similar objects is called a *collection*.

In Access, most of the objects are in collections. For example, a database has a single collection of tables that contains all of the tables in the database; each table has a collection of fields that contains all of the fields you have defined for the table; a database has a single collection of open forms; and each open form has a collection of controls that contains all of the controls you have placed on the form. Access begins the name of each type of object with a capital letter such as Form, Report, Control, and Field objects. Access names a collection by adding the letter "S" to the name of the object type in the collection; for example, the Controls collection of a specific form contains the Control objects placed on the form. Access treats the collection itself as an object; for example, a Controls collection is an object that contains the Control objects for a specific form or report.

Another example of collections involves the distinction between a form that is open and one that is closed. An open form is a Form object and the collection of open forms is the Forms collection. By contrast, a closed form is not a Form object and is not a member of the Forms collection—a closed form is just a closed form. Figure 14.1 depicts the Forms collection for the Expenses application when the Switchboard and the Expense Reports by Employee forms are the only open forms.

Objects that are not in collections are *singular objects*. There is, for example, an object named Application that represents the Access application and an object named DBEngine that represents the Jet database engine. Each of these is a singular object because Access has only one Application object and the Jet database engine has only one DBEngine object. A collection object is also a singular object; for example, there is only one Forms collection object in the application and each Form in the collection has only one Controls collection. Whether an object is a singular object or is in a collection becomes important when you refer to the object.

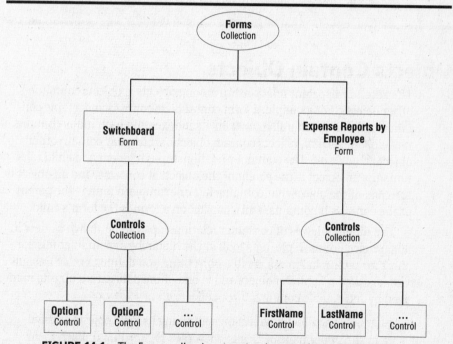

FIGURE 14.1: The Forms collection contains the open forms. Each open form has its own Controls collection containing the controls on the form.

CLASSES AND INSTANCES

Another way to look at groups of similar objects is to separate the definition of a group from the objects in the group.

We'll use the word *class* to refer to the definition of a group, for example, the class of forms or a class of text boxes. A class is a blueprint for its objects. As a simple example, you can think of table Design view as representing the class of tables. When you create a specific table by defining table fields and setting table properties, you are creating an *instance* of the class.

As another example, the Text Box tool in the toolbox represents the text box class. When you use the text box tool to create a text box with a specific set of properties, you are creating an instance.

So, when you think of a group of objects with similar properties and behaviors, there are really two parts: the definition of the group, that is, the class, and the objects themselves, that is, the instances.

Objects Contain Objects

The second important relationship among objects is objects containing other objects. For example, a form contains its controls and a table contains its fields. A table also contains its indexes and each index contains its fields. In general, objects contain objects, which may contain other objects, and so on. The container relationship is a parent and child relationship: an object is the *parent* of the objects it contains, and an object is the *child* of the object that contains it. For example, a form is the parent of the controls it contains, and a control on a form is the form's child.

The different levels of container relationships can be shown as tiers in a hierarchy. For example, let's look at the hierarchy of container relationships for tables. In Access, a table object that you define in table Design view is called a TableDef object and is one of the data access objects managed by Jet. A table contains three collections as follows:

- ▶ A table has a Fields collection containing its Field objects as listed in the upper pane of Design view (see Figure 14.2a). Each Field object has a Properties collection containing a Property object for each property listed in the lower pane of Design view.

▶ A table has an Indexes collection as listed in its Indexes dialog (see Figure 14.2b); each Index in the collection has a Properties collection containing a Property object for each property listed in the lower pane of the Indexes dialog. Each Index has a Fields collection containing the Field objects listed in the upper pane of the Indexes dialog (in this example, each Index object has a single field). Each Field object in an Index has a Properties collection containing Property objects for the Field.

▶ A table has a Properties collection containing Property objects as listed in the Table Properties dialog (see Figure 14.2c).

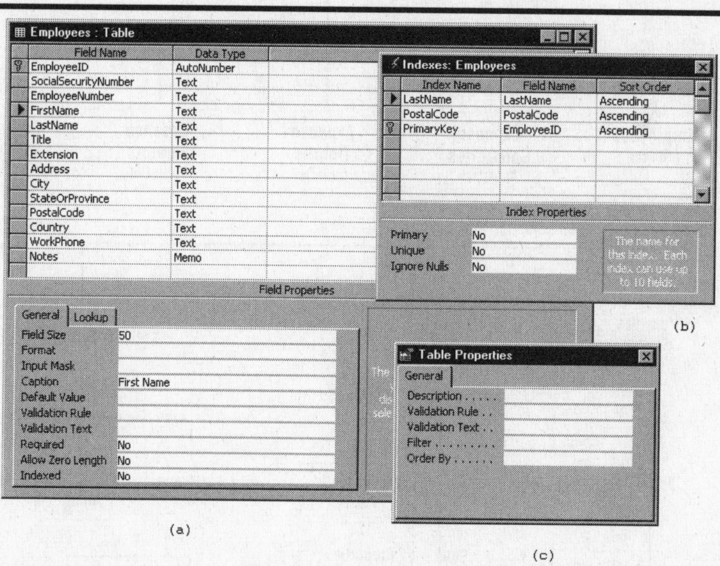

FIGURE 14.2: The Field objects for a table and the Property objects for a table Field (a). The Property objects and the Field objects for a table Index (b). The Property objects for a table (c).

Figure 14.3 shows a partially expanded view of the TableDefs collection for the Expenses database. In this figure, the Employees table is expanded to show its three collections, which are expanded to show some of their members. In each case, one of the collection members is expanded to show its collections, which are expanded to show their members, and so on. The property sheets that you are familiar with in Design view show only the design-time properties; each object also has many run-time properties. The expanded views of container relationships quickly become large and over-whelming; the important concept here is the structure of the hierarchy.

Figure 14.4 is a fully collapsed view of the table hierarchy that focuses on the structure: in this figure, each rectangle represents a collection and a representative member of the collection shown in parentheses. In looking at a collapsed view, keep in mind that each collection can be expanded to show its specific members.

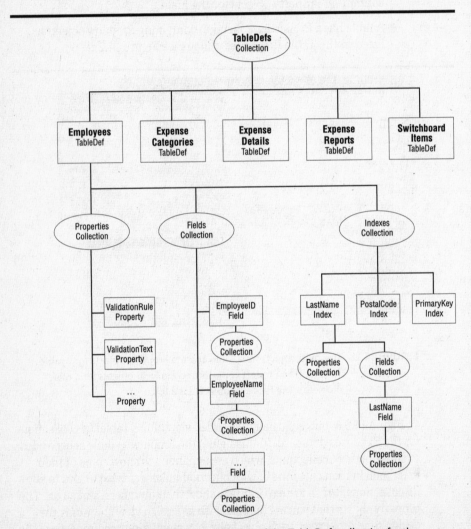

FIGURE 14.3: A partially expanded view of the TableDefs collection for the Expenses database

You need to know the container relationships for all of the objects in Access because when you write programs to manipulate the properties and behaviors of an object, you may have to refer to all of the objects that lie along a hierarchical path to the object.

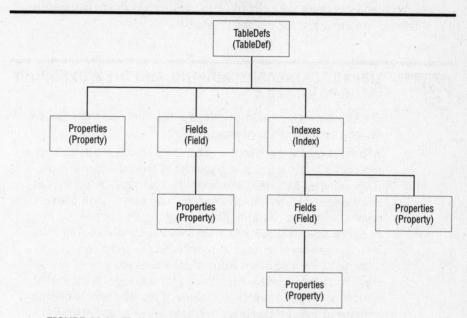

FIGURE 14.4:   The hierarchy of container relationships for tables

THE ARCHITECTURE OF ACCESS

When you install Access you actually install two major components: the Access Application layer and the Jet database engine.

The Application Layer

The Application layer consists of all the files necessary to control the user interface and all the files needed for writing and running macros and VBA procedures. The Application layer contains the menu bars, toolbars, and windows for creating and viewing Database window objects. When you create a database interactively, you work directly in the Application layer using the Design windows to create the individual tables, queries, forms, and reports as well as the macros and modules that fuse the objects into an application. Although you use the Application's interface to create all six Database window objects, only forms, reports, and modules are defined as Application objects. The tables and queries you create in the Access interface are Jet data access objects. Macros are not included in either object model because normally you don't write programs to manipulate macros, you write just the macros themselves.

LIBRARY DATABASES, ADD-INS, AND THE WORKGROUP INFORMATION FILE

The Application layer also includes a set of library databases, add-ins, and the workgroup information file.

A *library database* is a collection of database objects and procedures that you can use in any database you create. The convention in Access is to use the MDA and MDE extensions for library databases. You can use the built-in library databases or you can create your own. Access comes with five built-in library databases: `utility.mda`, `wzcnf80.mda`, `wzlib80.mde`, `wzmain80.mde`, and `wztool80.mde`. You can open any of these as a normal database except for `utility.mda`. `Utility.mda` opens automatically when you start Access, so if you try to open it within Access you get a message telling you the file is already open as a library database. If you want to work directly with the `utility.mda` library database, make a copy of `utility.mda` under another name, such as `myutility.mda`, before you open Access; after you open Access, you can open the copy. (A database with the MDE extension contains only a compiled version of code and does not contain a viewable and editable version.)

An *add-in* is a tool designed to accomplish a specific task. Add-ins can make a task easier to carry out or can introduce a new operation that isn't available in the basic product. There are several add-ins that are built-in, and you can also create your own add-ins. There are three kinds of add-ins:

▶ A *wizard* is a series of dialogs for guiding you through the process of creating an object. You design the object by entering your specifications in the dialogs. After collecting all the required information, the wizard creates the object for you. Examples of wizards include the Table, Query, Form, and Report Wizards.

CONTINUED ➡

▶ A *builder* is usually a single dialog for helping you through the process of creating items. There are builders for creating expressions and for setting properties. Later in this chapter we'll use the Expression Builder to create object references. Normally, builders are context sensitive—you summon a builder after selecting a specific property you need help with. For example, when you change one of the color properties, clicking the Build button to the right of the property box summons the Color builder.

▶ A *menu add-in* is a mini-application that performs some general function. Normally a menu add-in operates on several objects or on the entire application. You summon menu add-ins by selecting the Add-ins command on the Tools menu. Examples of built-in add-ins are the Switchboard Manager, the Database Splitter, the Linked Table Manager, and the Menu Builder. Additionally, the Add-in Manager is a menu add-in that you use to install your own menu add-ins. Several useful third-party utilities, such as the Find and Replace utility for propagating name changes, install as menu add-ins.

The *workgroup information file*, named system.mdw, stores information about the users, groups, and passwords that you set as part of your security model. You can specify security information in dialogs available by choosing the Security command in the Tools menu.

The Jet Database Engine

The Jet database engine consists of the files necessary to manage your data, to control access to the data in your database file, and to store objects that belong to the Application layer. Jet includes the internal programs for six basic database management functions:

Data definition and integrity   With Jet you can create and modify the objects that hold the data. You can use both the interface and VBA programming to create and modify the following Jet objects: databases, tables, fields, indexes, relations, and queries. Jet enforces the entity and referential integrity rules that you specify when you design tables and create relationships.

Data storage   Jet uses a method called the Indexed Sequential Access Method (ISAM) to store data in the file system. The basic characteristics of this method are data is stored in pages of size 2K containing one or more records, records have variable length, and records can be ordered using an index.

Data retrieval   Jet provides two ways to retrieve data. One way is to use Jet's powerful query engine, which uses Structured Query Language (SQL) to retrieve data. The second way is to access the data programmatically using the data access objects in VBA procedures.

Data manipulation   With Jet you can add new data and modify or delete existing data. You can manipulate data either using the Jet query engine with SQL action queries or using the data access objects in VBA procedures.

Security   Jet has two security models, including a database password model for simple password security to the entire database and a workgroup security model in which individual users and groups have permissions to individual database objects.

Data sharing   Jet enables multiple users to access and modify data in the same database. Jet locks the data on a given page when a record is being modified by a user: either Jet locks the page as soon as one user starts editing (*pessimistic locking*) and unlocks the page when the editing is completed, or Jet allows multiple users to edit a record and locks the page only when a user tries to save or commit the changes (*optimistic locking*).

JET'S EVOLUTION

In the first release of Access 1 in 1992, Jet 1 was packaged as a database management system specifically designed to support Access. For the most part, Jet was hidden; you worked directly with the Application layer and couldn't write programs to manipulate Jet's objects.

Through its versions 1.1, 2, 2.5, 3, and now 3.5 in Access 97, Jet has evolved into an application-independent database management system. Normally, you use another application such as Access or Excel to run Jet (the application that runs Jet is called the *host application*). Jet 3.5 can manage the data created by a large set of applications

CONTINUED ➡

including Word, Excel, Visual C++, FoxPro, and Visual Basic. Jet itself doesn't recognize the application-specific objects that these applications create. Jet does, however, provide storage for the objects that an application creates. The Access forms, reports, macros, and modules that you create in the Application are stored in your database file. Jet keeps track of such application-specific objects using Document and Container data access objects.

Jet 3.5 provides access to all of its objects through the Data Access Objects (DAO) language. This means that you can arrange for Jet to provide its database management services by writing and running VBA procedures in addition to the usual arrangements for services that you make through the Access interface when you work interactively with Access.

A new feature of DAO 3.5 is that you can establish a direct connection, called *ODBCDirect*, to an ODBC data source managed by another database management program such as Microsoft SQL Server. When you establish a direct connection to the data source, Access doesn't have to load the Jet database engine into memory. ODBCDirect is useful when you need the additional features that the other program can provide. When you use ODBCDirect, the Connection object is similar to the Database object that you use to connect to the Jet database engine. See *Access 97 Developer's Handbook* by Paul Litwin, Ken Getz, and Mike Gilbert (Sybex, 1997) for more information.

Object Hierarchies

You create macros and VBA procedures to manipulate objects. The objects that are available for manipulation are the built-in objects that the developers of Access and Jet have defined. (You can create your own objects in VBA programming but not in macro programming.) These built-in objects are grouped into their own collections and arranged into separate hierarchies. In each case, the top of the hierarchy is occupied by a singular object: the Application object sits at the top of the Access Application hierarchy and the DBEngine object sits at the top of the Jet engine hierarchy. The upper portion of Figure 14.5 shows the Application hierarchy that you use for programming in VBA. The lower portion of Figure 14.5 shows the Access VBA object hierarchy. Figure 14.6 shows the data access objects in the Jet database engine hierarchy that you use for manipulating the Jet engine using VBA programming. (The figure does not show the Properties collection and Property object contained in each object except for the Error object.) In these figures, singular objects that are not collection objects are shown in ovals. Collection objects are shown in rectangles with objects contained within the collection shown in parentheses.

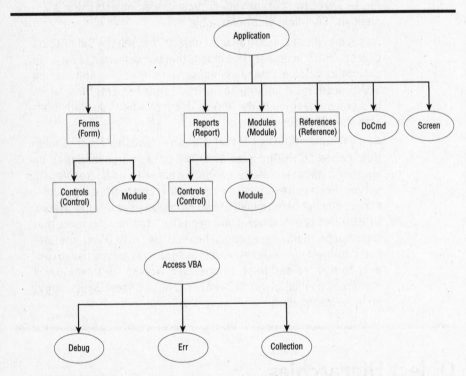

FIGURE 14.5: The Access Application hierarchy

NOTE

There is a separate object model for opening a connection to a database using ODBCDirect. See Microsoft Data Access Objects (DAO) in the Contents tab of online Help.

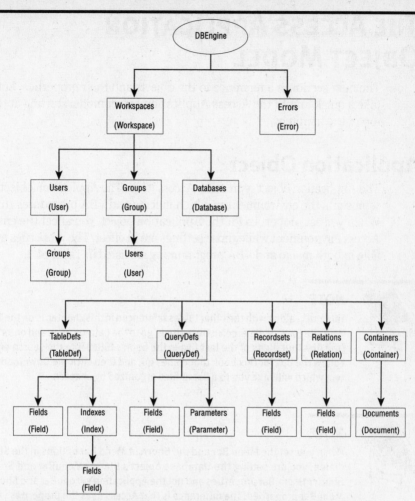

FIGURE 14.6: The Jet database engine hierarchy. Each object except the Error object also contains a Properties collection with Property objects for the built-in properties.

Every data access object except the Error object (and the Connection object in ODBCDirect) has a Properties collection containing separate Property objects for each built-in property. The Access Application hierarchy does not include separate Properties collection and Property objects because properties are treated differently in the Application and in Jet.

THE ACCESS APPLICATION OBJECT MODEL

The next section is a reference to the objects and their properties. Let's take a quick tour of the Access Application object model starting at the top of the hierarchy.

Application Object

The Application object represents Access itself. The Application object also represents the environment in which macros and VBA procedures run. When you set properties for the Application object, you affect the entire Access environment while those settings are in effect. The properties available in both macro and VBA programming are listed in Table 14.1.

NOTE

Table 14.1, along with the other tables referenced in this chapter, is on the Sybex Web site (www.sybex.com). Once there, go to the Catalog page and enter **2469** (the first four digits of the last five in the book's ISBN) into the search engine. Follow the link for this book that comes up, and then click the Downloads button, which will take you to a list of files organized by chapter.

NOTE

When you set the Menu Bar and the Shortcut Menu Bar options in the Startup dialog, you are setting the Database object's StartupMenuBar and Startup-ShortcutMenuBar properties and not the Application's MenuBar and Shortcut-MenuBar properties. The difference is that Access uses the properties you set in the Startup dialog when starting up the database. You can set the corresponding Application properties in a macro or VBA procedure that are run after the database starts up (and override the Startup dialog settings).

The Forms and Reports Collection Objects

When you first open a database, Access creates two collections; Forms is the collection of all open forms and Reports is the collection of all open reports. Access updates each collection as you open and close individual forms and reports. The Forms and Reports collections have the properties shown in Table 14.2, which is on the Sybex Web site.

The Form Object

The Form object refers to a specific open form. Form objects are members of the Forms collection. You can't add or delete a Form object from the Forms collection (except by opening or closing a form). There are more than 100 Form object properties that describe a form's appearance and behavior; you can set about 75 of the properties in the form's property sheet. The property sheet includes the 30 event properties that a form recognizes. Table 14.3 (on the Sybex Web site) is a list of some of the properties that are particularly useful in both macro and VBA programming; many of these properties are available only in macro and VBA programming and are not listed on the form's property sheet. The list includes the property's data type and how the property can be set.

The Report Object

The Report object refers to a specific open report. Report objects are members of the Reports collection. You can't add or delete a Report from the Reports collection (except by opening or closing a report). There are more than 100 Report object properties that describe a report's appearance and behavior; you can set about 50 of the properties in the report's property sheet. The list includes the seven event properties that a report recognizes. Table 14.4 (on the Sybex Web site) is a list of some of the properties that are particularly useful in both macro and VBA programming. The list includes the property's data type and how the property can be set.

The Controls Collection Object

Each form and each report has a Controls collection object that contains all of the controls on the form or report. The Controls collection has properties shown in Table 14.5 (on the Sybex Web site).

The Control Object

The Control object represents a control on a form or report. The controls on a form or report belong to the Controls collection for that form or report. You are familiar with the 17 types of built-in controls, including the new Tab Control, that appear on the toolbox (see Figure 14.7). In addition there is a built-in Chart Control that you can add to the toolbox. You can also use

Part iv

custom controls, called ActiveX controls, to provide your application with additional features. The Control object represents both built-in and custom controls.

FIGURE 14.7:   The built-in controls in the toolbox

Each type of control has its own set of properties, including event properties for the events that the control recognizes. For some types of controls there is a special property, called the *default property*, that is the most commonly used property for that type of control. The default property is the property that Access assumes when you refer to a control without specifying a property name. For example, when you refer to a text box, Access assumes you are referring to the Value property.

Data controls are controls that can hold data and can be bound to table fields. A data control has a ControlSource property to indicate the source of the data. The seven built-in data controls include text boxes, combo boxes, list boxes, check boxes, option buttons, toggle buttons, and option groups. Other controls may be associated with another object such as a form or report; such controls have a SourceObject property to indicate the object or a SourceDoc property to indicate the source of an embedded or linked file. As an example, subform and subreport controls have a SourceObject property that you use to specify the form or report that you want to display in the control. Some controls can display a picture and have a Picture property to indicate the source of the image; for example, command buttons and toggle buttons may display images. Table 14.6 (on the Sybex Web site) lists the built-in controls, their default properties, and whether each control is associated with data, another object or file, or an image.

Each individual type of control has its own set of properties, but all control types share a set of core properties. Table 14.7 (on the Sybex Web site) describes each core control property, the type of value the property can hold, and information about setting or reading the value.

Most controls have numerous additional properties; at the extreme, the Combo Box control has more than 80 properties. Table 14.8 (on the Sybex Web site) lists some of the properties for controls that are particularly important when you create programs to automate an application.

The Screen Object

The Screen object refers to the particular form, report, or control that currently has the focus or to the control that previously had the focus. By using the Screen object in a macro or VBA procedure, you can refer to the active object without knowing the object's name. Referring to the Screen object does not, however, make the form, report, or control the active object. Table 14.9 (on the Sybex Web site) lists the properties of the Screen object; all properties are read-only and return a reference to the object.

The selection-centric approach to programming requires that a macro or VBA procedure establish a connection with an object before performing an action on it. You can use the properties of the Screen object to make the connection to the active object.

The VBA-Only Application Objects

The Access Application object model includes several objects that are available only in VBA programming. These objects include the DoCmd object, the Module object and the Modules collection, and the Reference object and the References collection.

THE ACCESS VISUAL BASIC OBJECT MODEL

The Access Visual Basic model provides three objects: the Debug, Err, and Collection objects. Only the Debug object is used in macro programming, and only one of its features, the Immediate Window, is used.

The Debug Object

The Debug object is an extraordinary object available in both macro and VBA programming. You use the Debug object to send output to a special window called the Debug window. You can display the Debug window when any window is active by pressing Ctrl+G. The Debug window consists of three panes: the lower pane is called the Immediate pane, while the upper pane has tabs for the Locals and Watch panes (see Figure 14.8).

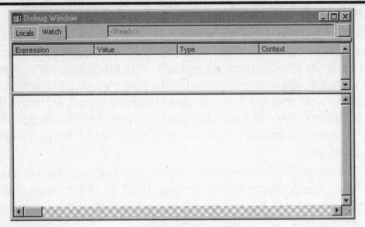

FIGURE 14.8: The panes of the Debug window

You can use the Immediate pane like a scratch pad to evaluate expressions, view and set the values of properties, and run macros and procedures. The Immediate pane is available in both macro and VBA programming. You can use the Locals pane to view the values of variables that may change when a VBA procedure runs. You can use the Watch pane to view the value of an expression or a variable while a VBA procedure is running. The Locals and Watch panes are available only in VBA.

The Debug object has no properties.

THE MACRO PROGRAMMING ENVIRONMENT

When you create macros, you write instructions that manipulate the Access interface directly. You don't manipulate the Jet database engine directly; instead macros make requests for database management services in the Access interface and rely on Access to arrange for Jet database services in response to the requests. In the macro-programming environment, you use a simplified version of the programming objects defined for VBA programming; you use a restricted set of the built-in properties and you don't use the concept of methods at all.

The macro-programming environment uses objects from the following sources:

▶ Three of the collections and objects in the Access object model shown in Figure 14.5: Forms, Reports, and Controls. In macro programming you use the Screen object to refer to the active object and the Immediate pane of the Debug window to evaluate references and expressions and to run macros.

▶ Three of the objects in the data access object model shown in Figure 14.6. In macro programming you work with the Table (called TableDef in DAO), Query (called QueryDef in DAO), and Field objects. You set properties for all other data access objects using the property sheets and dialogs of the Access interface.

▶ The macro Database window objects.

▶ The Customize dialog of the Access interface. You use it to create custom menu bars, shortcut menus, and toolbars.

NOTE

The Access Application object hierarchy shown in Figure 14.5 doesn't include macros. Microsoft could define Macros as a collection of Macro objects and a Macro as the object that refers to a macrosheet. Microsoft could define properties and macro actions or VBA methods that would allow you to create and modify macros directly from other macros or VBA procedures. Microsoft just doesn't do this.

REFERRING TO OBJECTS AND PROPERTIES BY NAME

Before manipulating an object in a macro or a VBA procedure, you must identify the object using the Access rules for referring to objects. (While you may use a naming standard to identify and document the objects you create, Access has its own rules for referring to objects that you must follow when you write programs.) There are four ways you can refer to an object. Only one of these methods, referring to an object explicitly by its name, is available in macro programming, so that is the only method we'll discuss in this chapter.

Referring to an Object by Name

One way to refer to an object is to start with the top object in the hierarchy and traverse along the hierarchical path to the object, recording the names of the specific objects and collection objects you encounter as you move along the path. You use the exclamation point (!), or bang, operator and the dot (.) operator to distinguish between steps and between objects and collections as follows:

▶ Use the bang operator when you are stepping from a collection to one of its members, that is, *collectionname!objectname*

▶ Use the dot operator when you are stepping from an object to one of its collections, that is, *objectname.collectionname*

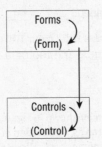

Use ! to step from the Forms
collection to a form:
Forms!formname

Use . to step from a form
to its Control collection:
Forms!formname.Controls

Use ! to step from the Controls
collection to a control:
Forms!formname.Controls!controlname

Referring to a Form or Report

To refer to an open form, say the Switchboard form in the Expenses application, start with the Application object and traverse to the Forms collection and then to the Switchboard form in the collection:

Application.Forms!Switchboard

To refer to an open report, for example, the Expense Report, start with the Application object and traverse to the Reports collection and then to the Expense Report in the collection:

Application.Reports![Expense Report]

When an object's name contains spaces, you must enclose the name in square brackets; otherwise, you can omit the square brackets. (Access may enter the square brackets for you.)

You can decrease the length of a reference by using defaults. For example, Access assumes that you are in Access when you refer to objects; this means you don't have to refer explicitly to the Application object and the references become

Forms!Switchboard

Reports![Expense Report]

These references are still full path references that refer to the specific form or report by name.

Referring to Form and Report Properties

You use the dot operator to separate an object from a property of the object, that is, *objectname.propertyname*. For example, to refer to the RecordSource property of the Expense Categories form see the following:

Forms![Expense Categories].RecordSource

NOTE

When the name of a property contains more than one word the property sheet displays spaces between the words; for example, the property sheet for a form displays the label for the RecordSource property as Record Source. You have to omit the spaces when you create a reference to a property.

Using the Immediate Pane to Evaluate an Object Property

You can use the Immediate pane of the Debug object to determine the setting of an object property. Here's how to use the Immediate pane of the Debug window to determine the value of an object property for a form or a report.

1. Press Ctrl+G to open the Debug window.

2. With the form or report open, type **Print** or **?**, followed by the property reference you want to evaluate, and then press Enter. Access evaluates the property reference immediately and displays the value of the property setting in the next line of the Immediate pane.

The Immediate pane executes a single line each time you press Enter. You can use many of the familiar text editing commands in the Immediate pane including the Cut, Copy, Paste, Delete, and Select All commands in the Edit menu. You can edit a line that you have already executed and then press Enter to execute the edited line (Access inserts a new line below the edited line and displays the result of the execution).

Figure 14.9 shows several examples for the Expenses application. Note that when the value is a Yes/No value, such as the value for the Navigation-Buttons property, Access converts Yes to True and No to False. Also, if no value has been set for the property, Access displays a blank line.

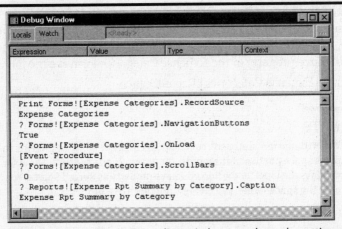

FIGURE 14.9: Using the Immediate window to evaluate the setting of a property

If the property is one that you can set in Design view (design-time property), then the form or report can be open in any view when you evaluate the property. If the property has a value that is determined only when the form or report is in run mode, such as the Dirty property, then the form or report must be in its run mode or else Access displays the error message such as the one shown in Figure 14.10a.

The Immediate pane can display only text values. If you type a reference for an open form such as **?Forms![Expense Reports by Employee]** and then press Enter, Access displays the error message shown in Figure 14.10b. If the form or report is closed when you try to evaluate a property such as ?Forms![Expense Categories].RecordSource, Access displays the same error message.

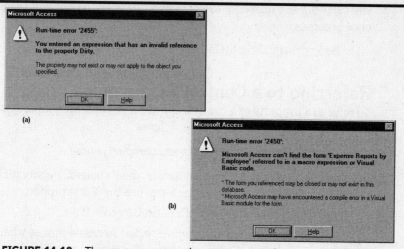

FIGURE 14.10: The error messages when you try to evaluate a run mode property when the form or report is in Design view (a), and when you try to evaluate a reference to an object or a reference to a property of a closed form or report (b)

Referring to a Control

To refer to a control on an open form, you start at the top of the hierarchy with the Application object, traverse to the Forms collection, step to the specific form, traverse to the Controls collection, and finally step to the control:

> Forms!*formname*.Controls!*controlname*

For example, to refer to the command button named Option1 on the Switchboard, step along the path first to the Controls collection and then to the specific control:

> Forms!Switchboard.Controls!Option1

However, you can shorten the reference by using defaults. An object can have a *default collection* that Access assumes when you specify a member of a default collection without specifying the collection. The Form and Report objects have the Controls collection as the default collection, so you can omit the reference to Controls along with the dot and the reference becomes:

Forms!Switchboard!Option1

Referring to a Control's Properties

To refer to a property of a control, append a dot and the property name to the end of the control reference as follows:

Forms!*formname!*controlname.*propertyname*

For example, to refer to the saved data in the ExpenseCategory text box control on the Expense Categories form, use the Value property:

Forms![Expense Categories]!ExpenseCategory.Value

An object may have a *default property* that Access assumes when you don't explicitly specify a property name. The default property for a text box control is the Value property. Using the defaults, the reference to the saved data in the text box is

Forms![Expense Categories]!ExpenseCategory

NOTE

The Text property of a text box also refers to the text contained in a text box control. The difference between the Value and Text properties is that the Value property is the value last saved to the field while the Text property is the current value in the active control. If you edited the text box but haven't saved the change, the Text and Value properties contain different values. When you save the record without leaving the text box, the control is updated and the Text and Value properties contain the same data.

To explore the Value and Text properties:

1. Open the Expense Categories form in Form view and change the Expense Category for the first record to Meal.

2. Without saving the record, type each of the following lines and press Enter to evaluate the expression (see Figure 14.11).

   ?Forms![Expense Categories]!ExpenseCategory

   ?Forms![Expense Categories]!ExpenseCategory.Text

   ?Forms![Expense Categories]!ExpenseCategory.Value

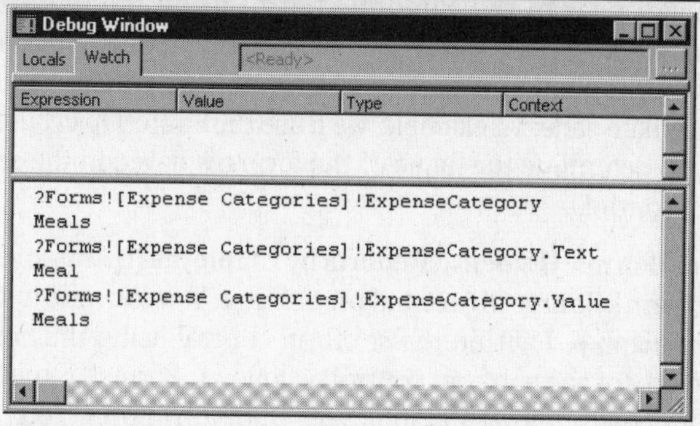

FIGURE 14.11:   Exploring the Text and Value properties for a text box control

Properties That Represent Other Objects

Most properties have a text value as their setting; you can display the value in the Immediate window. Some objects have special properties that you can use to refer to another object. For example, a control's Parent property refers to the control's parent object. A label's Parent property refers to the control the label is linked to and a text box's Parent property refers to the form that contains the text box. Table 14.10 (on the Sybex Web site) lists the objects having properties that refer to other objects. (For completeness, this table includes the Me and RecordsetClone properties that are available only in VBA.) Because these properties refer to an object and not a value, you can't test these references in the Immediate window. For example, you can use the Parent property of a text box to refer to the form itself, but if you type the expression **?Forms![Expense Categories]!ExpenseCategory.Parent** and press Enter, Access displays an error message.

Referring to a Subform

A common way to display data from two tables is to create forms based on each of the tables, place a subform control on one of the forms, and display the second form within the subform control. In this arrangement, the form containing the subform control is called the *main form* and the form displayed within the subform control is called the *subform*.

To explore the references for a subform, do the following:

1. Open the Expense Reports by Employee form in Form view. The Name property of the subform control is Employees Subform, so

you can refer to the subform control using the reference Forms![Expense Report By Employee]![Employees Subform]. You can evaluate properties of the subform control in the Immediate pane; for example, we'll use the SourceObject property to determine the name of the form displayed in the subform control.

2. Type **?Forms![Expense Reports by Employee]![Employees Subform].SourceObject** and press Enter. You can refer to the form displayed within the subform control using the Form property of the subform control as follows: Forms![Expense Report By Employee]![Employees Subform].Form. You can evaluate properties of this form in the Immediate pane; for example, we'll evaluate the DefaultView property.

3. Type **?Forms![Expense Reports by Employee]![Employees Subform].Form.DefaultView** and press Enter. Access displays the integer 2, which represents Datasheet view. You can refer to a control on a form displayed in a subform control by first referring to the form then traversing to the Controls collection and stepping to the specific control. For example, we'll refer to the value in the Total Expenses control on the subform.

4. Type **?Forms![Expense Reports by Employee]![Employees Subform].Form.Controls![Total Expenses]** and press Enter. Fortunately, you can use defaults to simplify the reference to a control on a subform. The default collection for the subform is the Controls collection, so the first simplification is to omit the reference to the Controls collection.

5. Type **?Forms![Expense Reports by Employee]![Employees Subform].Form![Total Expenses]** and press Enter. In addition, Access treats the Form property as the default property for the subform control when you are referring to a control on the subform, so you can omit the reference to the Form property.

6. Type **?Forms![Expense Reports by Employee]![Employees Subform]![Total Expenses]** and press Enter.

The general syntax for referring to a control on a subform is

Forms!*formname*!*subformcontrolname*!*controlname*

Figure 14.12 shows the results of testing these references in the Immediate window.

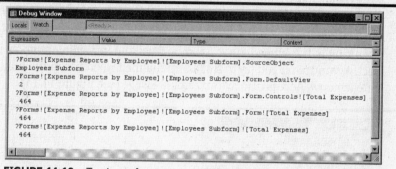

FIGURE 14.12: Testing references to a subform control and to the form displayed in the subform control in the Immediate pane

Referring to Controls on the Active Form or Report

The references, or *identifiers*, we've been exploring are full path references obtained by starting at the top of the object hierarchy and traversing the path to the object. We've shortened the references by referring to the Application object implicitly and using default collections and default properties. You can also shorten the reference when you want to refer to a control on the active form or the active report. Because Access knows which form is the active form, you can reference the active form implicitly; in other words, you can omit the reference to the active form or report. For example, if Expense Reports By Employee is the active form, you can identify the FirstName text box control using simply

FirstName

or, the Total Expenses control displayed in the Employees Subform control using

[Employees Subform]![Total Expenses]

An identifier that refers to the active form or report implicitly is called the *short syntax* or *unqualified reference,* while an identifier that includes the full hierarchical path (and uses defaults and an implicit reference to the Application object) is called the *fully qualified reference.* Normally, you can use the fully qualified reference without problems, but there are exceptions

Part iv

when you must use the short syntax instead. For example, you must use the short syntax when you use the GoToControl macro action to specify the name of the control on the active object that you want to move the focus to.

You can't test identifiers that refer to the active object when you are working in the Immediate window because the Immediate window is the active window. If you try to test an unqualified reference in the Immediate window, Access displays an error message (see Figure 14.13).

FIGURE 14.13:   The error message you get when you enter the short reference in the Immediate window

Using the Screen Object to Refer to the Active Object

Access has a way to uniquely identify the active form, report, or control, or even the control that last had the focus without using the specific names you've given the object. Avoiding specific names is necessary when you create objects that you want to reuse in your application. You can use the properties of the Screen object to identify the active object. For example, to refer to the RecordSource property of the active form, use the reference

Screen.ActiveForm.RecordSource

and to refer to the Locked property of a control named LastName on the active form, use the reference

Screen.ActiveForm!LastName.Locked

Additionally, you can refer to the active control on the active form using the Screen object as follows:

Screen.ActiveControl

For example, to refer to the name of the active control, you use the reference

Screen.ActiveControl.Name

As another example, you can refer to the TabIndex property of the control on the active form that previously had the focus using the reference

Screen.PreviousControl.TabIndex

You can use the Screen object in calculated controls on forms, in macros, and in VBA procedures to refer to an object without naming it explicitly.

You can't test references that use the Screen object when you are working in the Immediate window. When you enter a statement in the Immediate window, the Immediate window itself is the active window. If you try to refer to one of the Screen object's properties, such as **?Screen.ActiveControl.Name**, Access displays an error message (see Figure 14.14).

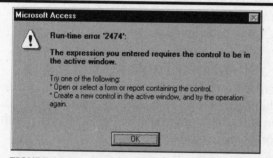

FIGURE 14.14: You can't test references to the Screen object in the Immediate window because the Immediate window is the active window.

Referring to a Field

Often you need to refer to a field in a table or query. The syntax for the reference depends on whether the table or query is in the underlying record source of an open form.

Referring to a Field in the Form's Record Source

You can refer to a field in the table or the query that is the record source for the form whether or not the field is bound to a control on the form, using the reference

Forms!*formname*!*fieldname*

For example,

1. Add a DateHired field to the Employees table and enter sample hire dates for each employee. Do not add a control to the Expense Reports by Employee form.

2. Type **?Forms![Expense Reports by Employee]!DateHired** and press Enter. The Debug window displays the sample hire date for the employee.

NOTE

By default, when you create a form using a form wizard, the Name property of each control created is the same as the name of the field the control is bound to. Or, when you add a control to a form by dragging a field from the field list, the control inherits the field name. However, the control name and the field name need not be the same.

Referring to a Field in a Table or Query

When you are designing a query or an SQL statement, you often need to refer to a field in a table or query. In each case, the Field object belongs to the Fields collection of the table or query. The Fields collection is the default collection for tables and queries so you can use the syntax

tablename.Fields!*fieldname* or *tablename*!*fieldname*

queryname.Fields!*fieldname* or *queryname*!*fieldname*

However, tables and queries are managed by the Jet database engine, which uses either the dot operator or the bang operator when you step from a collection to one of its members. For example, you can use either Employees!LastName or Employees.LastName to refer to the LastName field in the Employees table.

You can't test table and query references in the Immediate window directly. When you work in the Immediate window, you can use the DLookup() function to test a reference to a field in a table or a query. For example, to look up the first value in the LastName field in the Employees table, type **?DLookup("LastName", "Employees")** in the Immediate pane and press Enter. Access displays Davolio.

USING THE EXPRESSION BUILDER TO CREATE REFERENCES

The expressions for referring to properties and controls on forms and subforms can be very complex. Fortunately, Access provides the Expression Builder that helps in creating expressions of any kind, including expressions for query criteria and property settings as well as references for macro and VBA programming. Unfortunately, the Expression Builder is not available in the Immediate pane of the Debug window.

 Start the Expression Builder by right-clicking in the location where you want the expression and choosing the Build command from the shortcut menu, or start it by clicking in the location and then clicking the Build button in the toolbar. When you are creating an expression in a property edit box or an argument edit box of a macro action, you can also summon the Expression Builder by clicking the Build button that appears to the right of the edit box. Figure 14.15a shows the Expression Builder dialog. The Expression Builder is context sensitive; the contents displayed in the edit box in the upper pane and in the list boxes in the lower pane depend on where you are when you start the builder.

The lower pane contains three list boxes. The list box on the left contains folders for all of the tables, queries, forms, and reports in your database. There are also folders for built-in functions, constants, operators, common expressions, and custom Visual Basic functions. The set of folders that appears in the first list box depends on where you started the builder; in Figure 14.15, the builder was started from one of the programming windows (a Macro or Module window). Folders that contain other folders have a plus sign; when you click to expand the folder, the plus sign changes to a minus sign. The Forms and Reports folders contain folders for each of your forms and reports and separate folders for the open forms (in the Loaded Forms folder) and for the open reports (in the Loaded Reports folder). If a form with a subform is open when you start the Expression Builder, Access recognizes the relationship between the form and the subform and shows a folder for the subform within the folder for the form. In Figure 14.15b the Forms folder is fully expanded. The figure shows that the Switchboard and the Expense Reports by Employee forms are the only open forms and that the builder recognizes the Employees Subform as a subform of the Expense Reports by Employee form.

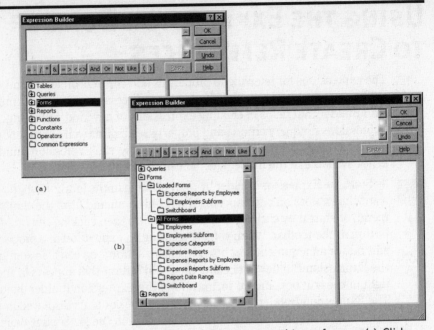

FIGURE 14.15: Use the Expression Builder to create object references (a). Click the plus sign to expand the Forms folder (b).

When you select a specific object in the list box on the left, the list box in the center changes to show the objects contained in the selected object. If you select a form, the first item in the center list is <Form> representing the form itself, the second item is <Field List> representing the field list for the table or query that underlies the form, and the remaining items are the controls and sections on the form. When you select an item in the center list box, the list box on the right changes to display the properties of the item you selected. Figure 14.16 shows the choices for the Total Expenses text box on the Employees Subform form. The duplicate names in the center list box correspond to a label and its linked text box, which have the same name on this form.

After you have made your choices, click the Paste button. The Expression Builder creates the reference based on your choices and also based on the context where you started the builder and pastes the reference in the edit box in the upper pane. Figure 14.16 shows the qualified reference for the Total Expenses text box (note that the Expression Builder includes the default Form reference). You create expressions in the edit box by

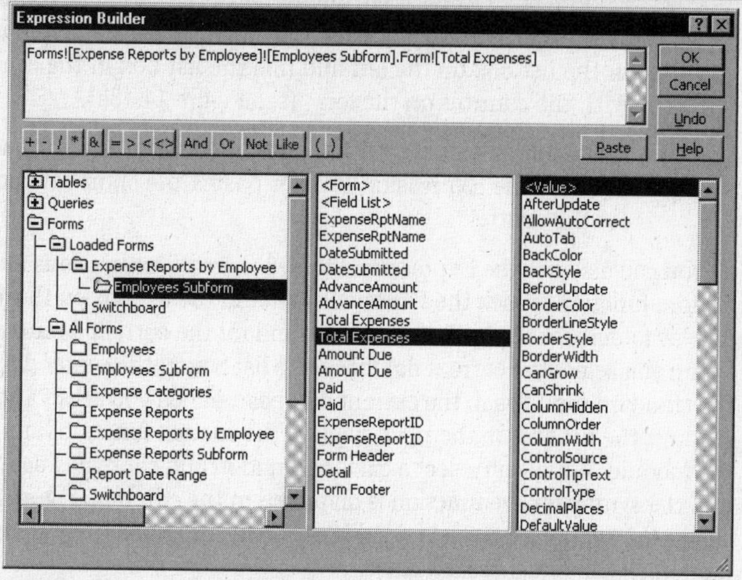

FIGURE 14.16:   The qualified reference for a control on a subform

pasting references and editing them using the keyboard and the operator buttons in the Builder dialog. In this example, you can edit the reference to delete the Form reference, or you can shorten the reference to the unqualified reference.

To show how the starting location affects the Expression Builder, you can start the builder with the Expense Reports by Employee form as the active object.

1. With the Expense Reports by Employee form in Design view, select the form and click the Build button in the toolbar. Access displays the Choose Builder dialog (see Figure 14.17).

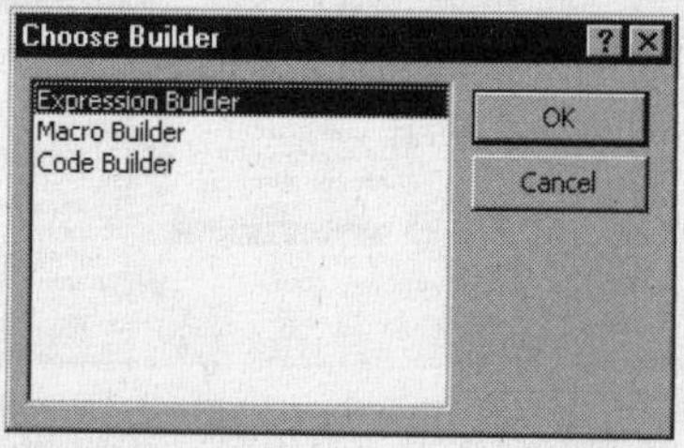

FIGURE 14.17:   The Choose Builder dialog

2.   Choose the Expression Builder and click OK. The Expression Builder displays a folder for the form as the first folder in the list box on the left and fills the list box in the center with the controls on the form (see Figure 14.18a).

3.   Make the choices shown in Figure 14.18b and click the Paste button. The Expression Builder pastes the short reference for the control.

You can also use the Expression Builder to create expressions involving custom functions. Click the Functions folder in the list box on the left to display folders for the built-in functions and for the current database. When you select the current database, the list box in the center displays the standard modules in the current database. When you select a standard module, the list box on the right displays the custom functions stored in the module. When you select a custom function and click the Paste button, the syntax for the function is displayed in the edit box. Figure 14.19 shows the syntax for the IsLoaded function in the GlobalCode standard module in the Expenses database.

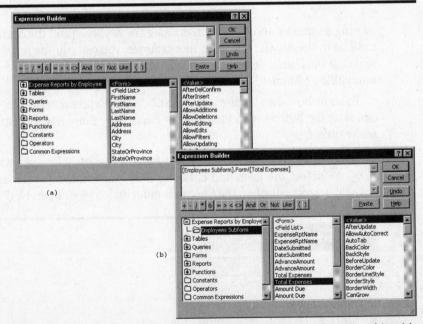

FIGURE 14.18:   Opening the Expression Builder with a form as the active object (a) allows the Expression Builder to create an unqualified reference (b).

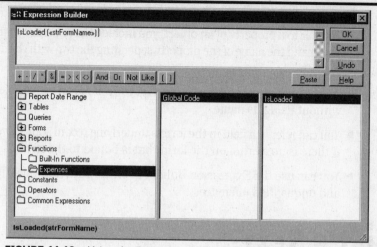

FIGURE 14.19: Using the Expression Builder to display the syntax for a custom function

SUMMARY

This chapter has taken you on an introductory tour of the Access object model that focuses on the objects and properties that are common to both macro and VBA programming. The important points are

- ▶ Objects are related to each other in two ways: they can be similar to other objects or they can contain other objects in a parent-child relationship. The parent-child relationships are used to arrange objects in a hierarchy.

- ▶ The Microsoft Access application has two major components each with its own object hierarchy: the Access Application and the Jet database engine.

- ▶ In general, to refer to an object in a macro or VBA procedure, you must use a fully qualified reference. To obtain the fully qualified reference you start at the top of the object hierarchy and traverse down to the object, recording the names of all of the collections and objects you step through on the way. In the Access object hierarchy, you use the dot operator to indicate stepping from an object to one of its collections and the exclamation point operator to indicate stepping from a collection to one of its members.

Part iv

- ▶ You can use default collections and properties to shorten references.

- ▶ To refer to a property of an object, you include the reference to the object and the name of the property separating the two with the dot operator.

- ▶ The properties of the Screen object let you refer to an active object without using its name.

- ▶ You can refer to a field in the form's underlying record source even if there is no control on the form that is bound to the field.

- ▶ You can use the Expression Builder to create both fully qualified and unqualified references.

WHAT'S NEXT?

In the next and final chapter, you'll learn about some aspects of professional development with VBA. This will include understanding error handling, exploring VBA debugging tools, examining debugging strategies, and adding professional design elements to your applications.

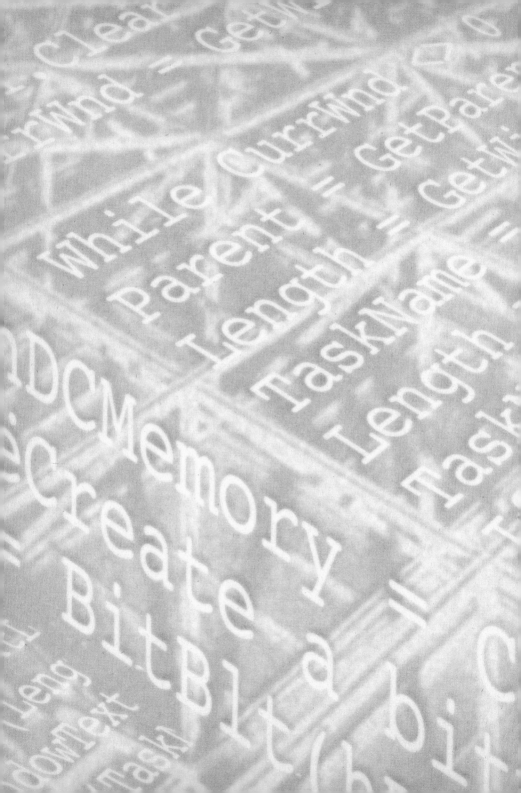

Chapter 15

PROFESSIONAL DEVELOPMENT WITH VBA

This chapter discusses a variety of topics that fall under the category of professional development. Included are things like error handling, debugging, naming standards, and object model design. Our goal is to suggest techniques you can use to create VBA code that is robust, portable, and bug free. (Well, the last is tough, but we give it our best shot.)

Adapted from *VBA Developer's Handbook*
by Ken Getz and Mike Gilbert
ISBN 0-7821-1951-4   976 pages $49.99

Table 15.1 lists the sample files provided for this chapter on the Sybex Web site (www.sybex.com). Once there, go to the Catalog page and enter **2469** (the first four digits of the last five in the book's ISBN) into the search engine. Follow the link for this book that comes up, and then click the Downloads button, which will take you to a list of files organized by chapter.

TABLE 15.1: Sample Files

File Name	Description
ERRORS.XLS	Excel 97 file with sample code
ERROR.MDB	Access 97 databases with sample code
BASERROR.BAS	Generic error-handling functions
BASERREX.BAS	Error-handling examples from this chapter
LOG.CLS	Log class module code
PSTACK.CLS	Stack class module code
PSTACKIT.CLS	StackItem class module code

HANDLING ERRORS THE RIGHT WAY

This chapter starts with error handling because it's a basic feature of a professionally designed application. Inevitably, your program will eventually encounter a situation its code was not designed to handle. How you cope with this situation affects the application and those using it. This section looks at the three types of errors you'll find in your code, shows you how to handle them, and suggests some guidelines for building error handling into every procedure you write.

The Three Types of Errors

As you develop your applications, you'll encounter three types of errors:

- ▶ Compile-time errors
- ▶ Run-time errors
- ▶ Logic errors

Compile-time errors surface while you're writing your code and usually result from syntax errors or an invalid use of a function or property. Under most circumstances, these errors are easy to locate and correct. VBA checks the syntax of each line of code as you enter it and informs you, by means of highlighted text and a warning message, when it contains a syntax error. For errors in syntax that requires multiple lines, like a For...Next loop, and other compile-time errors, VBA warns you of problems when you compile your application. Regardless of the VBA host you're using, there is a way to compile your code while you're working on it.

TIP

As you become more experienced as a VBA programmer, you may find VBA's syntax error dialog annoying. You can prevent it from appearing by unchecking the Auto Syntax Check box in VBA's Options dialog. Despite its name, this option does not turn off syntax checking. (VBA still checks and warns you by highlighting the errant line.) It simply suppresses the message box.

Run-time errors are a bit more insidious than compile-time errors because, as the term implies, they don't surface until you run your application. Run-time errors occur when a syntactically correct line of code can't execute because of the current environmental circumstances. For instance, suppose you tried to use the VBA Kill procedure, which deletes a disk file, and passed the name of a file that did not exist. Even if the statement is free of syntax errors, it cannot execute, because an input parameter is invalid. When this happens, VBA raises an error that your program can intercept and cope with. (This process is called *trapping* the error.) If your program does not trap the error, VBA handles it itself. Depending on the VBA host you're using, this may or may not leave your application in a recoverable state. That's why it's important to ensure that your program traps all run-time errors that occur. This section shows you how to do that. The good news regarding run-time errors is that through thorough testing, you can weed out most of the problems that result from them.

The most insidious errors of them all are *logic errors*. Logic errors (affectionately known to programmers as *bugs*) occur when your code compiles without errors and runs without errors but produces incorrect results. These errors normally result from a mistake or oversight on the programmer's part and can be very difficult to track down. For example, consider the code shown in Listing 15.1.

Listing 15.1: Perfectly Good Code That Doesn't Work Right

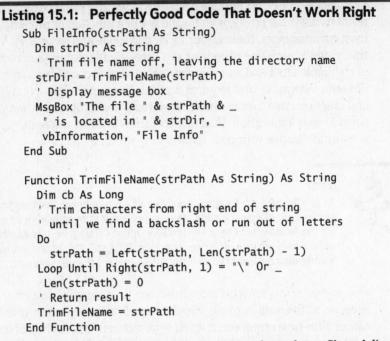

```
Sub FileInfo(strPath As String)
   Dim strDir As String
   ' Trim file name off, leaving the directory name
   strDir = TrimFileName(strPath)
   ' Display message box
   MsgBox "The file " & strPath & _
   " is located in " & strDir, _
   vbInformation, "File Info"
End Sub

Function TrimFileName(strPath As String) As String
   Dim cb As Long
   ' Trim characters from right end of string
   ' until we find a backslash or run out of letters
   Do
      strPath = Left(strPath, Len(strPath) - 1)
   Loop Until Right(strPath, 1) = "\" Or _
   Len(strPath) = 0
   ' Return result
   TrimFileName = strPath
End Function
```

The FileInfo procedure is designed to accept the path to a file and display a message box showing the full path and the directory name. It calls the TrimFileName function to trim the file name from the path, leaving the directory name. When you call TrimFileName from the Immediate window, it works as expected. On the other hand, when you call FileInfo, the Msg-Box statement displays the directory twice rather than the full path. What's wrong? The error is caused by an oversight common to those new to VBA. The strPath argument to TrimFileName is passed *by reference* instead of *by value,* so when TrimFileName operates on the argument, it is also modifying the variable in FileInfo.

In the case of compile- or run-time errors, VBA eventually tells you what the error is and shows you the line of code causing the error. With logic errors, it's up to you to track them down. Fortunately, VBA does provide some tools to assist you, as described in the section "Debugging Like the Pros" later in this chapter.

Trapping Run-Time Errors

Unless you tell it otherwise, VBA handles all run-time errors itself by displaying an error message and halting execution at the offending line of code. While this might be acceptable and is often helpful during the development and testing phases, it is rarely so in a production application. Instead, your code should trap and deal with its own errors, even if the only thing it does is display the same error message VBA would.

The key to this behavior is the error trap, which you set using the On Error statement. In effect, you set a trap in a procedure, and that trap then lies in wait for an error to occur. When the error occurs, your error trap springs into action, executing other statements that cope with the error.

VBA's On Error statement has three forms:

- ▶ On Error GoTo Label
- ▶ On Error Resume Next
- ▶ On Error GoTo 0

The sections that follow explain each of these in turn.

NOTE

You must handle errors in VBA on a procedure-by-procedure basis. There is no way to create a general error handler that is triggered in response to all run-time errors. While you can create a single procedure to handle errors, you still have to add to code to every other procedure to call it in response to an error.

On Error GoTo Label

On Error GoTo Label is the most powerful error trap because it gives you the greatest degree of flexibility in handling a run-time error. Using the On Error GoTo Label statement causes VBA to jump to a specific location in your code if an error occurs. When an error occurs in code after executing an On Error GoTo Label statement, control passes to the assigned label. Listing 15.2 shows a sample procedure that illustrates the most common format for an error handler.

Listing 15.2:   Sample Procedure Containing an Error Trap

```
Sub GenericProcWithErrorTrap()
    ' Stub showing standard way to construct an error handler
    ' Set the error trap
On Error GoTo HandleError
    ' Some code that might generate a run-time error
    ' would go here
```

```
ExitHere:
    ' Important! Exit proc before error handler
    Exit Sub
HandleError:
    ' Error handling goes here!
    Resume ExitHere
End Sub
```

Everything begins with an On Error GoTo Label statement. Normally, this is the first statement to execute, and it appears just before or after local variable declarations. (Whether you place it before or after the variable declarations is a matter of style and personal preference.) In our example, the label used is "HandleError".

NOTE

Prior versions of Basic required that all label names be unique across an entire project. VBA no longer has this restriction. Therefore, you can use the label "HandleError" in every one of your procedures should you so desire.

If an error occurs in the code that follows the On Error GoTo Label statement, VBA begins executing code with the statement immediately following the label. The label must appear in the same procedure as the On Error GoTo Label statement.

It is standard practice to place the error-handling code at the end of the procedure. This is because, in the event that no error occurs, you must exit the procedure before reaching the error handler. Otherwise, VBA executes your error-handling code. Note the Exit Sub statement (and its associated ExitHere label) in the sample procedure.

Once an error has occurred and VBA has begun executing your error-handling code, VBA is in a special state. While in this state, the following is true:

▶ The error handler defined by the On Error GoTo Label statement is no longer in effect. This means any run-time error that occurs within the error handler is treated as an untrapped error.

▶ You can use a Resume statement (described in the section "The Resume Statement" later in this chapter) to return control to the main procedure and resume normal error handling.

▶ You cannot execute an End Sub or End Function statement to "fall out of" an error handler. You must explicitly use an Exit Sub or Exit Function statement to exit the procedure. Commonly accepted software engineering practice says a procedure should have only one entry point and one exit point, so an even better idea is to use Resume Label to return control to the main code, where the procedure can be exited at a common point (as the example does).

On Error Resume Next

Creating an error handler with the On Error GoTo Label statement can require a considerable amount of code. Sometimes you'll want to ignore errors. Other times you'll know exactly which error to expect and want to handle it without having to write a full error handler. The On Error Resume Next statement does just that. It tells VBA to suppress the standard error message and simply execute the next line of code. For example, if you're attempting to delete a file and don't care whether the file actually exists, you might use code like that shown in Listing 15.3. If the file exists, the procedure deletes it. If the file does not exist, a run-time error occurs, VBA suppresses it, and the procedure terminates normally.

Listing 15.3:   Use On Error Resume Next to Ignore a Possible Run-Time Error

```
Sub DeleteFile(ByVal strFileName As String)
    ' Example showing an On Error Resume Next
    ' Deletes a file if it exists
    On Error Resume Next
    Kill strFileName
End Sub
```

The On Error Resume Next statement lets the program ignore the error and continue.

On Error GoTo 0

When you use an On Error GoTo Label or On Error Resume Next statement, it remains in effect until the procedure terminates, another error handler is declared, or the error handler is canceled. The On Error GoTo 0 statement cancels the error handler. VBA (or an error handler in a calling procedure, as described in the section "VBA's Error-Handling Hierarchy" later in this chapter) again traps subsequent errors. This statement also resets the value of the Err object (see the section "Determining Which Error Has Occurred"), so if you need the values it contains, you must store away its properties.

Responding to Trapped Errors

Now that you know how to set an error trap, what do you do when an error occurs? Generally, that depends on the type of error that occurred, what other error handling you have in place, and how you want to cope with the error. This section examines your options.

Determining Which Error Has Occurred

In most cases, the key piece of information you need to know in order to respond intelligently to errors is which error has occurred. VBA provides this information to you in the form of an object, Err. Err has a number of properties (listed in Table 15.2) that give you the information you need. The most important properties are Number, which returns the distinct error code associated with the error, and Description, which provides the informational message that VBA would normally display.

TABLE 15.2: Properties of the VBA Err Object

PROPERTY	DESCRIPTION
Number	Distinct error code associated with the error
Description	Informational message associated with the error
Source	Object or application that caused the error
HelpFile	Windows help file with additional information about the error
HelpContext	Context ID of the help topic with the help file
LastDLLError	Error code returned by the last DLL function executed

Somewhere inside your error handler (the lines of code between the error label and the end of the procedure), you should check the value of Err.Number against one or more anticipated values. Depending on the result, you should take some action to either correct the problem or gracefully terminate your procedure.

Listing 15.4 shows the CopyToFloppy procedure, which attempts to copy a given file to a floppy disk after deleting the existing version. A number of run-time errors could occur in this procedure. The source file or an existing version might not exist, or the user might forget to put a disk in the floppy drive. How the procedure copes with the error depends on which of these errors occurs.

NOTE

The CopyToFloppy procedure contained in the sample code features a complete error handler. We build up to that, step by step, in this section.

Listing 15.4:   Examine the Number Property of the Err Object

```
Sub CopyToFloppy(strFile As String)
  Dim strDest As String
  ' Set the error trap
  On Error GoTo HandleError
  ' Construct destination file path
  strDest = "A:\" & TrimDirectory(strFile)
  ' Delete file from the floppy
  Kill strDest
  ' Attempt to copy the file
  FileCopy strFile, strDest
ExitHere:
  Exit Sub
HandleError:
  Select Case Err.Number
    Case Else
      MsgBox Err.Description, vbExclamation, _
        "Error " & Err.Number & " in CopyToFloppy"
  End Select
End Sub
```

You'll notice that CopyToFloppy uses a Select Case statement in the error handler to examine the error number. In this example, the only thing the error handler does is display a message box with the error information. The following sections explain other ways to cope with the error.

Even an error handler this simple provides the user with useful information. If you examine the MsgBox statement, you'll see that it displays the standard error text (using the Err object's Description property), the error number, and the name of the procedure in which the error occurred. Figure 15.1 illustrates the error message that appears if you attempt to run this procedure without having a disk in the floppy drive.

FIGURE 15.1: Standard error information displayed by an error handler

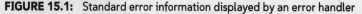

Part iv

While you can take action in response to particular error codes (we'll explain how in a moment), we recommend that you always include a MsgBox statement like the one shown in Listing 15.4 for the Case Else result. At a minimum, it informs the user of the error condition. With this information (the error number, description, and procedure name), you or the user will find it easier to diagnose the source of the problem.

The Resume Statement

In the example, CopyToFloppy terminates immediately after displaying the message box. While informative, this behavior is far from optimal in terms of user friendliness. It would be far better to correct the error if possible. To do that, there must be a way to tell VBA to retry an action rather than just terminate the procedure. The Resume statement takes care of this. In general, Resume redirects execution to a specific point in a procedure after an error has occurred. The Resume statement has three forms:

- ► Resume
- ► Resume Next
- ► Resume Label

Resume   Using Resume by itself returns control to the statement that caused the error. Use Resume when your error handler fixes the problem that caused the error and you want to continue from the place where you encountered the problem. In the example, the user can correct error 71 ("Drive not ready") by placing a disk in the floppy drive. Then VBA can retry the CopyFile statement.

Listing 15.5 shows a modified version of the CopyToFloppy procedure. The error handler now looks specifically for error number 71, using a Case statement.

Listing 15.5:   Use a Case Statement to Check for Error 71

```
Sub CopyToFloppy(strFile As String)
   Dim strDest As String
   ' Set the error trap
   On Error GoTo HandleError
   ' Construct destination file path
   strDest = "A:\" & TrimDirectory(strFile)
   ' Delete file from the floppy
   Kill strDest

   ' Attempt to copy the file
```

```
      FileCopy strFile, strDest
   ExitHere:
      Exit Sub
   HandleError:
      Select Case Err.Number
        Case 71 ' Drive not ready
          If MsgBox("Please place a floppy disk in the " & _
            "drive.", vbExclamation + vbOKCancel, _
            "Load Diskette") = vbOK Then
             Resume
        Case Else
          MsgBox Err.Description, vbExclamation, _
            "Error " & Err.Number & " in CopyToFloppy"
      End Select
      Resume ExitHere
   End Sub
```

If the error handler finds error 71, it displays a message box instructing the user to put a disk in the floppy drive. The dialog, shown in Figure 15.2, has OK and Cancel buttons. If the user clicks OK, the error handler issues a Resume statement, instructing VBA to try the FileCopy statement again. Note, however, that if the problem is still not resolved, an endless loop occurs when the original statement fails again. That's why the dialog has a Cancel button. Clicking that button terminates the procedure.

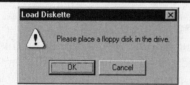

FIGURE 15.2: Customized error message in response to a specific error

Resume Next If you can't correct an error condition but the error is not critical and doesn't affect the outcome of the procedure, you can use the Resume Next statement. Resume Next instructs VBA to execute the line of code *following* the one that caused the error. The CopyToFloppy procedure is very simple and does not contain other statements to execute.

Resume Label Use the Resume Label statement when you want to return to a line other than the one causing the error or the line that follows it. Resume Label is similar to a GoTo statement, but you can use it only from inside an error handler. The example in Listing 15.5 shows this

Part iv

use of the Resume statement to jump to the label ExitHere. This approach to exiting a procedure after a run-time error is preferred because there is only one exit point.

Using a Standard Error Handler

All the variations of CopyToFloppy presented thus far have included a MsgBox statement to alert the user of any run-time error the procedure doesn't specifically handle. You should include this code (or code similar to it) in every substantive procedure in your application. (For exceptions to this rule, see the section "VBA's Error-Handling Hierarchy" later in the chapter.) One way to do this is to create and use a standard error-handling procedure.

Why Use a Standard Procedure?

Using a standard procedure to handle errors has two benefits. First, it provides you with a single routine for doing such things as displaying error messages. As your error-handling needs change, you need only add code to a single procedure. Second, a common procedure makes writing error handlers easier. You can pass information you want the user to see to the error-handling procedure as necessary.

A Sample Error-Handling Procedure

Listing 15.6 shows the error-handling procedure we've written for this book. The procedure, dhError, collects error information and displays it in a dialog box. It accepts three arguments: a pointer to a VBA ErrObject object, the name of the procedure that called the error routine, and a Boolean flag. The flag controls whether the dialog box features both OK and Cancel buttons or simply a single OK button. Note that all the arguments are optional.

Listing 15.6:   dhError, a General-Purpose Error-Handling Procedure

```
Function dhError( _
  Optional strProc As String = "<unknown>", _
  Optional fRespond As Boolean = False, _
  Optional objErr As ErrObject) _
  As Boolean
   Dim strMessage As String
   Dim strTitle As String
```

```
      Dim intStyle As Integer
      ' If the user didn't pass an ErrObject, use Err
      If objErr Is Nothing Then
         Set objErr = Err
      End If
      ' If there is an error, process it
      ' otherwise just return True
      If objErr.Number = 0 Then
         dhError = True
      Else
         ' Build title and message
         strTitle = "Error " & objErr.Number & _
          " in " & strProc
         strMessage = "The following error has occurred:" & _
          vbCrLf & vbCrLf & objErr.Description

         ' Set the icon and buttons for MsgBox
         intStyle = vbExclamation
         If fRespond Then
            intStyle = intStyle Or vbOKCancel
         End If
         ' Display message and return result
         dhError = (MsgBox(strMessage, _
          intStyle, strTitle) = vbOK)
      End If
   End Function
```

We've made all the arguments optional so you can call the procedure using just its name. At a minimum, though, you should pass dhError the name of the procedure where the error occurred. This information appears in the title of the dialog and can help you track down problems.

If you pass True as the value of the second argument, fRespond, dhError displays a dialog with OK and Cancel buttons. If the user clicks the OK button, dhError returns True; otherwise, it returns False. You might use this style of dialog to give users the option of canceling the current operation.

An example of using dhError is shown in Listing 15.7. ForceError creates an error condition by attempting to divide a number by 0. When the error occurs, ForceError's error handler calls dhError inside a conditional statement. Figure 15.3 shows the resulting error dialog. If the user responds by clicking the Cancel button, execution halts on the Stop statement in ForceError. Obviously, in this situation you would want to do something besides halt code execution (exit the procedure, return to your application's main window, and so on), but ForceError does demonstrate how you can use the dhError function.

Part iv

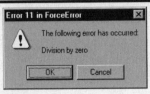

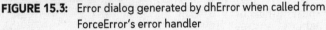

FIGURE 15.3: Error dialog generated by dhError when called from ForceError's error handler

---

Listing 15.7: ForceError Creates a Run-Time Error That Is Handled by dhError

```
Sub ForceError()
  On Error GoTo HandleError
  Debug.Print 1 / 0
ExitHere:
  Exit Sub
HandleError:
  If Not dhError("ForceError", True) Then
    Stop
  End If
  Resume ExitHere
End Sub
```

Keeping the Error Handler Simple

Over the years, we've seen lots of error-handling procedures, many of which are quite complex, allowing for various message permutations, user responses, and related actions, such as logging error information to a file. In our experience, however, simpler generic error handlers are better. Why? Simply put, there are very few situations in which you need to do more than display an informative message to the user. You will probably find some situations that do require complex error handling in the normal course of testing your applications. When necessary, add the required logic in each procedure's code. Trying to account for every possible condition and result in a single procedure is an impractical, if not impossible, task.

VBA's Error-Handling Hierarchy

To cope effectively with run-time errors, it's important to understand how and when VBA chooses to generate them. Error handling adheres to a hierarchical structure such that when an error occurs in a procedure that contains no error handler, VBA searches each procedure in the call chain looking for one.

Consider the example illustrated in Figure 15.4. It depicts four procedures, A, B, C, and D. Procedure A calls procedure B, which calls procedure C, and so on. Procedure A contains an error trap. None of the other procedures do.

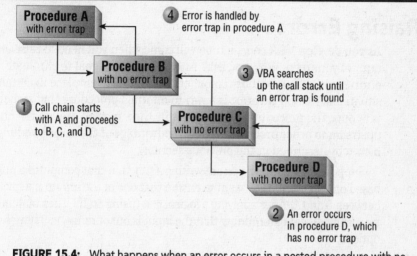

FIGURE 15.4: What happens when an error occurs in a nested procedure with no error trap

When an error occurs in procedure D, VBA searches backward, up the call chain, until it reaches the error trap in procedure A. Procedure A's error trap then handles the error. If no procedure in the call chain contains an error trap, VBA displays its standard error dialog and halts code execution.

You can use this hierarchy to your advantage. It eliminates the need to add error traps to *every* procedure, as long as at least one procedure upstream in the call chain contains one.

There are, however, two drawbacks to relying on the error-handling hierarchy to cope with run-time errors. First, there is no way to tell which lower-level procedure an error occurred in. Second, depending on the error, it might not make sense to handle it in the higher-level procedure. In other words, it might be too late to handle the error effectively. If you can recover from the error by trapping it in the lower-level procedure, add an error trap there.

TIP

Utility functions (those that perform such tasks as string manipulation and mathematical calculations) typically don't require error handling because they are almost always called by other procedures. Error handling does add some overhead. Unless you want to cope with specific errors, avoid putting error traps in utility functions.

Raising Errors

As you develop VBA code, a time will come when you need to raise an error of your own. Why, you ask? After all, isn't the goal to eliminate errors? It is, of course, but custom errors do have their place in certain situations. Raising an error is a way to inform a procedure that something is wrong. The procedure can then handle the situation or pass the error upstream to other procedures (taking advantage of the error-handling hierarchy described in the previous section).

Suppose, for example, you are writing a function that computes a number based on two inputs. You want to ensure that one of the inputs is a fraction between 0 and 1. After applying a logical test (using an If...Then statement, for instance) and determining that the input is out of range, you have several options:

- ▶ Simply abort the function and return a Null or 0.

- ▶ Display an error message and return a Null or 0.

- ▶ Return an error code.

- ▶ Prompt for a valid value.

All these options have their drawbacks, rooted in the fact that the function itself is attempting to cope with the error condition. Another, better option is to raise a run-time error and let the calling procedure cope with it. You do this using the Raise method of VBA's Err object. The procedure in Listing 15.8 illustrates this. Note that it has no error trap of its own.

Listing 15.8: Use the Raise Method to Generate a Run-Time Error

```
Function ComputeValue(dblAmount As Double, _
  sngRate As Single) As Double
  If sngRate < 0 Or sngRate > 1 Then
    Err.Raise 12345, "ComputeValue", _
```

```
         "Argument must be between 0 and 1."
      End If
      ComputeValue = dblAmount * sngRate
   End Function
```

Raise takes three arguments:

▸ An error number that should be unique among all other possible error numbers (those used by VBA as well as by the host application)

▸ A source string, which lets you designate the source of the error (such as the application or procedure name)

▸ An error message, which should be a short description of the problem

The Raise method will generate a run-time error and abort the function. When an upstream error handler is activated, it will be able to retrieve the error information in the Err object's properties.

Since the function may be called from a variety of procedures, it is impractical to decide on a single error-handling strategy for all situations. The advantage of the Raise method is that it lets the upstream procedure handle the error in a way that makes sense.

TIP

In general, utility functions should return custom error information using the Raise method.

DEBUGGING LIKE THE PROS

Handling run-time errors is only part of a programmer's job. You need to decide what to do about an error when it occurs. Should you let your error handler display a message and then return control the user? Should you try to change your program logic so the error doesn't happen? And what about code that generates no errors but does not work as desired? Devising solutions to these problems requires *debugging*.

In a way, debugging an application is like performing exploratory surgery on a sick patient. The goal of each is to identify, and eventually correct, some sort of problem or anomaly. Initially, you have only a limited number of clues as to the source of the problem. You use both the tools at hand and your own intuition and experience to carefully expose the problem and correct it.

In this chapter we discuss the tools VBA provides and share some of our experiences in debugging applications.

VBA Debugging Tools

Any development environment can be measured by the sophistication of its debugging tools. The VBA debugging environment has been evolving for several versions and now provides several tools to aid you in hunting down bugs and logic errors. They include

- ▶ The Immediate window
- ▶ Breakpoints and single step mode
- ▶ The call stack
- ▶ Watch expressions
- ▶ Quick watches
- ▶ Data Tips
- ▶ The Locals window
- ▶ Debugging options in the Options dialog

The Immediate Window

The Immediate window, shown in Figure 15.5, gives you a place to investigate the effects of VBA code directly, without the intervention of macros, forms, or other methods of running the code. Think of the Immediate window as a command line for VBA. You can use it to launch procedures and evaluate expressions. In fact, you can do almost as many things in the Immediate window as you can in VBA procedure code. You open the Immediate window by clicking the Immediate Window button on the toolbar, selecting View ➤ Immediate Window, or pressing Ctrl+G.

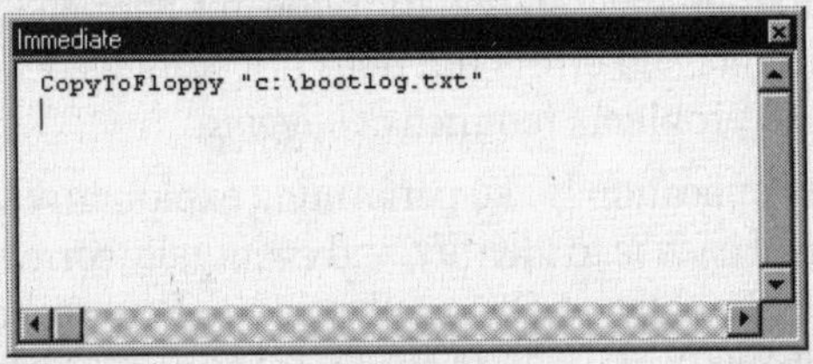

Immediate

```
CopyToFloppy "c:\bootlog.txt"
```

FIGURE 15.5: Immediate window showing how to call the CopyToFloppy procedure

The Immediate window displays the last 200 lines of output at all times. As more output is appended to the end, older lines disappear from the top of the list. With the capability to scroll back the Immediate window, you can position the cursor on an evaluation line and press Enter, and VBA will recalculate the expression and display its value. If you want to remove the lines in the Immediate window above your current location, use Ctrl+Shift+Home to select them all and press Del. To remove lines below your current location, first select them with Ctrl+Shift+End.

Breakpoints

Breakpoints allow you to set locations in your code at which VBA will temporarily halt its execution of the code. The screen in Figure 15.6 shows code halted at a breakpoint. Note the highlighted line of code. This is the line of code about to be executed.

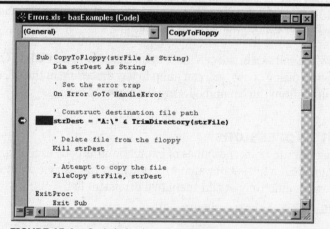

FIGURE 15.6:   Code halted at a breakpoint

The Call Stack

VBA has the ability to display the call stack when a procedure is paused at a breakpoint. The call stack lists each active procedure, with the current procedure at the top of the list, the one that called it next on the list, and so on. If the procedure was originally called from the Immediate window, this is noted at the end of the list. If the procedure is called from elsewhere in the VBA environment (for example, directly from a control's event procedure), there is no way to know where it was called from. The screen in Figure 15.7 shows the call stack as it might appear at a break-point in your code.

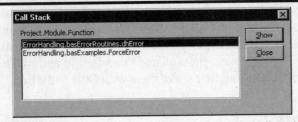

FIGURE 15.7: VBA Call Stack dialog showing the call stack

NOTE

You may occasionally see an entry for "<Non-Basic Code>" in the Call Stack dia-log. This indicates that another process, such as the VBA host application, VBA, or a DLL function, is involved in the call chain.

To view the call stack, select View ➤ Call Stack or press Ctrl+L. Once the Call Stack dialog opens, you can jump to any procedure in the call stack by selecting it from the list and clicking the Show button.

Watch Expressions

You use *watches* to track the values of expressions as code executes. VBA has implemented a full set of watch functionality. You can view watch expressions interactively or add them to a persistent list.

Watches come in three varieties:

▶ Watch expression

▶ Break When Expression Is True

▶ Break When Expression Has Changed

Normal watch expressions are displayed in a separate window (shown in Figure 15.8). Anytime VBA is in break mode, it evaluates and displays all watch expressions. Watch expressions are useful if you are single-stepping through code and want to watch the contents of a variable or an expression. It is also much more convenient than using the Immediate window to print the contents of variables after each line of code executes.

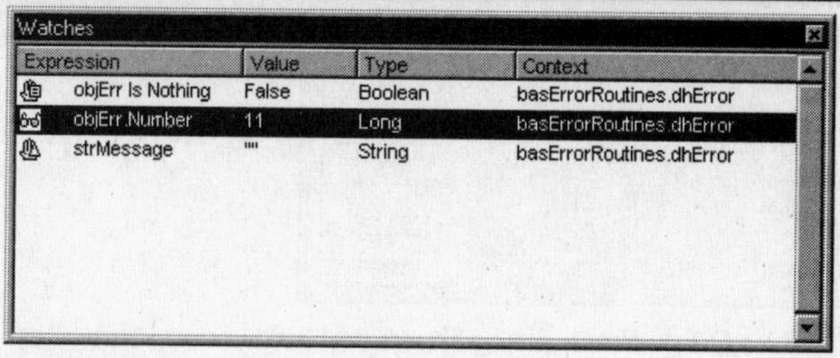

FIGURE 15.8:   The Watches window shows all watch expressions you have defined.

The Break When Expression Is True and Break When Expression Has Changed watch types allow you to specify a logical condition or expression. When that condition is true or changes, VBA immediately halts execution and puts you into break mode. These types of watches are useful for determining when and how a variable's value was changed. For example, say you know that somewhere in your code, a global variable named gintValue is getting set incorrectly to 0. The problem is that you don't know where or how. You can set a Break When Expression Is True watch with the expression "gintValue = 0". Then, as soon as gintValue becomes equal to 0, VBA puts you into break mode.

Quick Watches

The Quick Watch dialog is useful for quickly seeing the value of a variable. To use this dialog, position the cursor anywhere within a variable name and press Shift+F9. This dialog, shown in Figure 15.9, then shows you the present contents of a variable. You can also select an expression, and VBA will evaluate the expression. Clicking the Add button adds the expression as a regular Watch Expression.

Data Tips

Data Tips work like ToolTips in module windows. To use Data Tips, move the mouse over any variable or property while your code is in break mode. VBA displays a small ToolTip-type rectangle with the value of the expression. This is even quicker than using a quick watch!

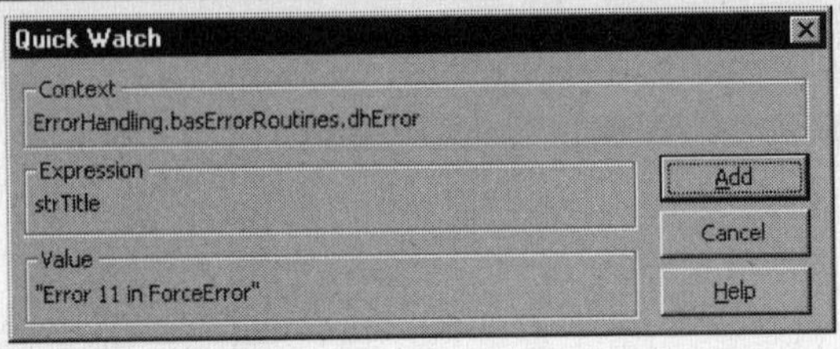

FIGURE 15.9: VBA's Quick Watch dialog shows you the current value of an expression.

The Locals Window

Another very useful feature is the Locals window. This window, shown in Figure 15.10, lists all the variables currently in scope while your code is in break mode. You can expand and collapse objects to view their properties. In effect, this window creates watch expressions for every variable in your code.

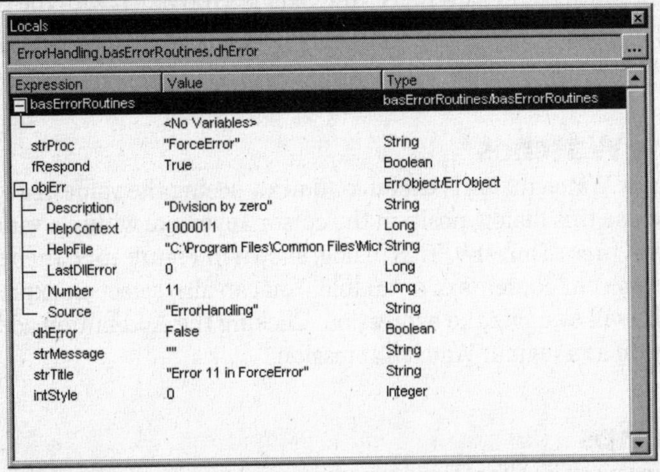

FIGURE 15.10: The Locals window shows all variables in the current scope.

Debugging Options in the Options Dialog

The VBA Options dialog has two sections that let you fine-tune how VBA handles errors and debugging. The first is a text box for conditional compilation constants. You can include the constants that control the behavior of conditional #If...#Then statements in your code or enter them in the Options dialog. If you want to define more than one constant, separate them with colons.

The other option controls error trapping when VBA enters break mode in response to run-time errors. You can choose among three options:

▶ **Break on All Errors:** Causes VBA to enter break mode whenever a run-time error occurs, even if you've defined an error handler. Normally, you'll want to use this option only while debugging an application, not after you distribute it.

▶ **Break in Class Module:** The default setting, this causes VBA to enter break mode on all errors in global or class modules for which there is no error trap defined.

▶ **Break on Unhandled Errors:** Causes VBA to enter break mode, in global modules only, on all errors for which there is no error trap defined. If an error occurs in a class module, VBA enters break mode on the global module statement that called the property or method code of the class.

NOTE

Unfortunately, these options appear at various locations in different VBA host applications. For instance, in Microsoft Access, they appear on the Advanced tab of the Options dialog. In the VBA IDE that ships with Microsoft Excel, PowerPoint, and Word, they are split between the VBA Options dialog and the Options dialog for the current project. You may have to consult your host application's documentation in order to find these options.

USING THE IMMEDIATE WINDOW

You can use the Immediate window to test parts of an application interactively. From this window, you can launch procedures, view and change the values of variables, and evaluate expressions. You can also write VBA code to print information to the Immediate window without your intervention.

Running Code from the Immediate Window

You can easily run any function or subroutine that's in scope from the Immediate window. To run a procedure, simply type its name (along with any parameter values) on a blank line in the Immediate window and press

Enter. VBA runs the procedure and then returns control to the Immediate window. This technique works for both functions and subroutines. If, on the other hand, you want to run a function and have VBA return the *result* to the Immediate window, you have to use the Print statement. For example, if you enter the following expression in the Immediate window, VBA runs the function called MyFunction and prints the return value:

```
Print MyFunction()
```

VBA provides a shortcut for the Print method, as have most previous versions of Basic. In the Immediate window, you can just use the ? symbol to replace the word *Print*. All our examples use this shortcut. Therefore, the preceding statement could be rewritten as follows:

```
?MyFunction()
```

Scoping rules apply as in normal code. That is, variables are available from the Immediate window only if they're currently in scope. If you have the Locals window open, you can tell what the current scope is by looking at the text box at the top of the window. It always reflects what VBA sees as the current scope.

Working with Expressions in the Immediate Window

You can use the Immediate window to evaluate expressions, be they simple variables or complex calculations. For example, you can view the current value of the variable intMyVar by typing the following statement in the Immediate window:

```
?intMyVar
```

Of course, the variable must already be declared elsewhere in your code and must be in scope at the time. You cannot enter a Dim statement (or any of its cousins, including ReDim, Global, and Const) in the Immediate window.

In addition to viewing expression results, you can use the Immediate window to change variable values. To change the contents of intMyVar, you could use an expression like this:

```
intMyVar = 97
```

Any code that executes subsequent to your changing the variable value will see the new value.

Any statement you enter for direct execution in the Immediate window must fit on a single line. You cannot, for example, enter a multiline If... Then...Else statement for evaluation in the Immediate window, although you can execute a single-line If...Then statement. To get around this limitation, you can use the colon (:) to separate multiple VBA statements on the same line.

For example, the following code executes a loop:

```
For intCount = 0 To 10:Debug.Print intCount:Next intCount
```

Printing Information to the Immediate Window

You can use the Immediate window as a way of tracking a running procedure by printing messages or expression values to it while your code is running. You use the Print method of the Debug object to display any expression from within your running code. The prior example used the Print method to print the value of intCount to the Immediate window.

Placing Debug.Print statements at strategic points in your code can greatly aid you in debugging problems. Here are a few suggestions for when to use Debug.Print statements:

- ▶ At the head or foot of a procedure
- ▶ While iterating objects or values in a collection or loop
- ▶ After a complex calculation
- ▶ After accepting user input
- ▶ Before deleting files or other objects

Alas, the Print method is really useful only while you're developing your application. Usually, you won't want your users viewing the Immediate window. To trace your application's behavior after distributing it, consider using the logging class described in the section "Application Logging" later in this chapter.

Handling Remnant Debug.Print Statements

You can safely leave Debug.Print lines in your shipping code if you wish. As long as the user does not have the Immediate window displayed, these lines will have no visible effect and only a slight performance penalty. However, if you are concerned about the performance hit of these lines, you can surround your debug code with conditional compilation statements. For example,

```
' In the declarations section:
#Const fDebug = True
```

```
' In some procedure:
#If fDebug Then
   Debug.Print "Some output"
#End If
```

Using Breakpoints

Using a breakpoint is the equivalent of putting a temporary roadblock in your code. When you set a breakpoint, you tell VBA to stop executing your code at a particular line but to keep the system state in memory. This means that all the variables in the current scope are available for your inspection in the Immediate window. You can also use the Step Into and Step Over functionality (using the menu items, the toolbar buttons, or the F8/Shift+F8 keys) to move through your code statement by statement so you can watch it execute in slow motion.

To set a breakpoint on a particular line of code, place the cursor anywhere on the line and do one of the following: click the Breakpoint button on the toolbar, choose Debug ≻ Toggle Breakpoint, or press the F9 key. You can also create a breakpoint by clicking the mouse in the margin of the module window. VBA highlights the chosen line in the window. (You can control the highlighting colors through the Options dialog.) When VBA encounters a breakpoint while running code, focus switches to the module window with the breakpoint showing and the current statement highlighted. VBA also displays a small arrow in the left margin. VBA suspends execution *before* it executes the statement. This allows you to check or set the values of variables in your code before VBA executes the chosen line of code.

TIP

VBA does not save breakpoints with your code when you close a project. If you need to preserve your breakpoints across sessions, you can use the Stop statement, which acts as a permanent breakpoint. Just as with a breakpoint, VBA halts the execution of your code as soon as it encounters the Stop statement. Of course, you'll need to remove Stop statements from your code (or surround them with conditional compilation statements) before you distribute your application since they will stop the execution of your running code in any environment.

You can reset breakpoints manually with the Debug ≻ Toggle Breakpoint command, the F9 key, or the Breakpoint button on the toolbar. You can also clear all breakpoints you have set with the Debug ≻ Clear All Breakpoints command.

Single Step Mode

When VBA halts your code at a breakpoint, you can choose how to continue. You can proceed at full speed by clicking the Run button on the toolbar, selecting Run ➤ Continue, or pressing F5. You can also use single step mode to execute statements one at a time. To execute the current statement, press F8. After executing the current line of code, VBA brings you back to break mode at the next line.

When VBA encounters one of your own procedures while in single step mode, it continues in one of three ways, depending on which single step command you use:

- ▶ **Step In (F8):** Causes VBA to step into your procedure, executing it one line at a time.

- ▶ **Step Over (Shift+F8):** Also executes code one line at a time, but only within the context of the current procedure. Calls to other procedures are considered atomic by the Step Over action; it executes the entire procedure at once. Step Over is especially useful if you are calling code you've previously debugged. Rather than take the time to walk through working procedures, you can use the Step Over functionality to execute them at full speed while you're debugging.

- ▶ **Step Out (Ctrl+Shift+F8):** Causes VBA to step out of the current procedure. If it was called from another procedure, VBA returns to the line in that procedure following the call to the current one. This is useful if you have inadvertently stepped into a procedure you don't want to debug and want to return to the procedure from which you called it.

Finally, you can use the Run to Cursor functionality to continue to a given line. To do so, highlight any line after the current one and press Ctrl+F8. Run to Cursor is also available from the right-click context menu. Run to Cursor causes VBA to continue execution until the line before the selected one is executed and then reenter break mode.

Other Single Step Options

While in single step mode, you can move the current execution point to another location. Placing the insertion point on any statement in the halted procedure and choosing Debug ➤ Set Next Statement causes execution to begin at that statement when you continue the function. This command is also available from the right-click context menu. You can also change the current execution point by clicking and dragging the arrow in the module margin bar. You cannot skip to another procedure in this fashion, though.

TIP

If you are wading through several open code windows, the Debug ➤ Show Next Statement item brings you back to the currently executing statement.

Occasionally, your code will become so hopelessly bug ridden that during the course of single-stepping through it, you'll want to throw up your hands and surrender. In this case, you can choose the Run ➤ End command or click the End button on the toolbar to stop executing code. While this stops executing code and takes you out of break mode, it retains the contents of any module or global variables. To clear the contents of these variables, choose the Run ➤ Reset command or click the Reset toolbar button.

WARNING

While in break mode, it is possible to launch other procedures. VBA maintains the current execution point for the first procedure while other procedures are executed. This can lead to unpredictable results, especially when you are running procedures that use the same data or variables. If you witness unpredictable behavior, make sure you don't have an outstanding break mode condition by selecting the Show Next Statement command, looking at the call stack, or selecting the Stop or Reset command.

Winning Strategies for Bug-Free Code

It's close to impossible to write a substantial application without any bugs, but certain strategies can help you avoid adding unnecessary ones. You should develop the necessary discipline to use these strategies whenever you write code, even if you think you're writing a function to use only in testing or for your own internal application. Good habits are hard to develop but are also hard to lose once you develop them. The next few sections describe how you can avoid letting bugs slip into your code (and how you can get them out) by following these rules:

▶ Fix bugs as they appear.

▶ Use comments.

- ► Organize your code.

- ► Modularize your code.

- ► Use Option Explicit.

- ► Avoid Variants if at all possible.

- ► Beware the simple Dim statement.

- ► Group your Dim statements.

- ► Use the tightest possible scope.

- ► Use consistent naming conventions.

- ► Use assertions.

Putting these suggestions to use will help you develop a good mind-set for avoiding bugs and for removing the ones that inevitably creep into your code.

As a single rule of thumb, the best bug-avoidance strategy is to take your time and to avoid the urge to make your code "cleverer" than necessary. At times you simply must use the newest, most complex features of any programming language, but in general, the simpler way is the better way. With this strategy in mind, there are some specific tactics that work well in VBA coding to help avoid bugs.

Fix Bugs as They Appear

It's critical that you fix bugs as they reveal themselves rather than wait until you have more features implemented. Hurried cleanup at the end of a project will pressure you to apply bandages instead of real fixes. Fixing bugs as they appear requires steady and systematic testing, which is something programmers tend to avoid. Would you rather write 500 lines of code or try 50 test cases on existing code? Most of us would choose the former since writing code is fun and testing is boring. But if you keep in mind how little fun you'll have if your application doesn't work when it's shipped, you'll buckle down and do the boring testing work, too.

Use Comments

Old code is harder to debug than new code because it is less fresh in your mind. Depending on how busy you are, old code could be two weeks old, two days old, or two hours old! One way to help keep your code from aging rapidly is to insert comments. There's an art to sensible commenting: it depends on adding just enough to tell you what's going on without going overboard and cluttering up your code.

The comment should state the intention of the code rather than tell how the code is implemented. This is an important point. You should highlight the overall structure of the code and note any particularly tricky spots for future programmers, including yourself. Remember that if you've named your variables using a consistent standard, their names will act as mini-comments in the code itself.

A comment that is not maintained is worse than no comment at all. Have you ever read a comment and then stared at the code below it and discovered it didn't seem to do what the comment said it did? Now you have to figure out whether it is the comment or the code that is wrong. If your code change requires a comment change, make sure you do it now, because you probably won't get around to doing it later.

NOTE

One reason for keeping the number of comments to a reasonable level is that comments do take up space in memory while your VBA project is loaded (unless you're using Visual Basic or another tool that lets you create compiled versions of your project). Some programmers encourage comment stripping, the practice of removing all comments from production code. If you choose to do this, make sure you do it only right before shipping and that you don't make changes to the stripped code. Otherwise, you might end up with two different versions of your project.

Organize Your Code

In addition to commenting in your code, you should do whatever you can to keep it organized. This means you should use indentation to organize the flow of code. It also means you should split large procedures into smaller ones.

Indent your code so that statements that should "go together" are at the same indentation level and statements that are subordinate to others are indented one more tab stop. Most VBA programmers use indentation both to match up traditional control structures (For...Next, If...Then... Else, Do...Loop, For Each) and to indicate levels of data access object activity (BeginTrans/CommitTrans, AddNew/Update, and so on).

Modularize Your Code

Modularization is a fancy term for a simple idea: breaking up your code into a series of relatively small procedures rather than a few mammoth ones. There are several key benefits to writing code this way:

▸ You make it easier to understand each procedure. Code that is easier to understand is easier to maintain and to keep bug free.

▸ You can localize errors to a smaller section of the total code. If a variable is used only in one ten-line function, any error messages referring to that variable are most likely generated within that function.

▸ You can lessen the dangers of side effects caused by too-wide scoping of variables. If you use a variable at the top of a 500-line function and again at the bottom for a different loop, you may well forget to reinitialize it.

Use Option Explicit

In the VBA Options dialog, you'll find a check box labeled "Require Variable Declaration." Selecting this check box causes VBA to insert the line "Option Explicit" at the top of any new module it creates. This statement forces you to declare all your variables before referring to them in your code. This will prevent some hard-to-find errors from cropping up in your code. Without Option Explicit, VBA allows you to use any syntactically correct variable in your code, regardless of whether you declare it. This means that any variable you forget to declare will be initialized to a variant and given the value Empty at the point where you first use it. The hours you save in debugging time will make using this option well worth the effort.

Using Option Explicit is an easy way to avoid errors such as the one you'll find in the code in Listing 15.9. Errors like this are almost impossible to catch late in the development cycle, since they're buried in existing code. (Don't feel bad if you don't immediately see the error in the fragment; it's difficult to find.)

Listing 15.9:   Can You Find the Error in This Procedure?

```
Function UpdateLog(intSeverity As Integer, _
  strProcedure As String, strTracking As String) As Integer
  Dim dbCurrent As Database
  Dim rstUsageLog As Recordset
```

```
    Dim intFull As Integer
    Dim qryArchive As QueryDef
    Const dhcMinSeverity = 1
    ' Don't log activities that aren't severe enough to
    ' bother with
    If intSeverity < dhcMinSeverity Then
      Exit Function
    End If
    ' Append a new record to the usage log
    Set dbCurrent = CurrentDb()
    Set rstUsageLog = dbCurrent.OpenRecordset _
     ("zstblUsageLog", dbOpenDynaset)
    rstUsageLog.AddNew
      rstUsageLog![Severity] = intSeverity
      If Err.Number Then
         rstUsageLog![ErrorCode] = Err.Number
         rstUsageLog![ErrorText] = Err.Description
      End If
      rstUsageLog![User] = CurrentUser()
      rstUsageLog![Date] = Now
    rstUsageLog.Update
  End Function
```

In case you missed it, the error occurred on this line of code:

```
    rstUsageLog![Severity] = intSeverty
```

A small spelling error like this would cause only zeros to be stored in the Severity field and could cause you several hours of debugging time. Option Explicit lets you avoid these kinds of errors.

Avoid Variants If Possible

The Variant datatype is convenient, but it's not always the best choice. It's tempting to declare all your variables as Variants so you don't have to worry about what's in them. The VBA design teams did not put in explicit types to make your life difficult; they put them in because they're useful. If you think something will always be an Integer, dimension it as an Integer. If you get an error message later because you've attempted to assign an invalid value to that variable, the error message will point straight to the problem area of your code and give you a good idea of what went wrong. Variants are also slower than explicitly dimensioned variables for the same operations since they have the overhead of tracking which type of data they are holding at any given time. In addition, Variants are larger than almost any other datatype and so take longer to move around in memory. These last two reasons alone should be enough to make you reconsider using variants whenever possible.

NOTE

In some instances, you have no choice about your datatypes. If you're assigning values to variables that might at some point need to contain a null value, you must use the Variant datatype. This is the only datatype that can contain a null value, and attempting to assign a null value to a non-Variant variable triggers a run-time error. The same goes for function return values. If a function might need to return a null value, the return value for that function must be a Variant.

Use ByVal with Care

Be careful about passing information to procedures that have parameters declared using ByVal. While this is a good way to prevent subroutines from modifying variables passed to them (since ByVal creates a copy), you may lose information when calling the procedure. This is because VBA coerces information passed to the procedure to the datatype of the parameter. Therefore, if you pass a variable with the Single datatype to a parameter of type Integer, VBA truncates the fractional component when it creates the Integer. You will have no warning of this, however, so make sure you know which datatype the procedures expect if you've used ByVal in the declaration.

Beware the Simple Dim Statement

Even the simple Dim statement can introduce subtle bugs into your code. Consider this statement:

```
Dim strFirst, strLast As String
```

The intent here is clearly to define two String variables on one line. If you've ever programmed in C or C++, you know that a similar declaration would do just that. However, this is not the way VBA works. The As clause applies only to the variable it immediately follows, not to all variables on the line. The result of the preceding declaration is that strLast is a String variable but strFirst is a Variant variable, with slightly different behavior. For example, strFirst will be initialized to Empty and strLast to a zero-length string. You must explicitly define the datatype of every single variable in VBA. The simplest way to ensure this is to get into the habit of declaring only one variable for each statement.

Group Your Dim Statements

You can declare your variables anywhere in your procedures, as long you declare them before they are actually used, and VBA will understand and accept the declarations. For the sake of easier debugging, though, you should get into the habit of declaring variables at the top of your procedures. This makes it easy to see exactly what a particular procedure is referring to and to find the declarations when you are in the midst of debugging.

Use the Tightest Possible Scope

Always use the tightest possible scope for your variables. Some beginning programmers discover global variables and promptly declare all their variables as global to avoid the issue of scope altogether. This is a sloppy practice that will backfire the first time you have two procedures, both of which change the same global variable's value. If a variable is used solely in a single procedure, declare it there. If it is used only by procedures in a single module, declare it with module scope. Save global scope for only those few variables you truly need to refer to from widely scattered parts of your code.

Use Consistent Naming Conventions

In addition to the conventions discussed here that help structure your code, consider adopting a consistent naming convention for objects and variables in your code. We (along with many other programmers) have standardized our naming conventions based on the RVBA naming conventions.

A consistent naming standard can make it simple for you to find errors lurking in your programs, in addition to making them simpler for multiple programmers to maintain. By using the RVBA naming conventions, you gain two pieces of information about every variable: which datatype it is and what scope it has. This information can be very helpful during the debugging process.

Your Friend, the MsgBox Function

As an alternative to setting breakpoints, you can use the MsgBox function to indicate your program's state. With this strategy, you decide what you would like to monitor and call the MsgBox function to return the information. You can enhance this technique by writing a wrapper for the Msg-Box function so that these messages are posted only when you have a conditional compilation constant set to indicate that you want to see debugging messages. An example is shown in Listing 15.10. Only if the fDebug conditional constant is True does the MsgBox function get called.

Listing 15.10:   Sample Wrapper for the MsgBox Function

```
#Const fDebug = True
Function dhMsgBox(ByVal varMessage As Variant, _
 Optional strCaller As String = "<unknown>") As Integer
   ' Set return value in case fDebug is False
   dhMsgBox = True
   #If fDebug Then
       dhMsgBox = (MsgBox(CStr(varMessage), _
       vbOKCancel Or vbQuestion, "Procedure: " & strCaller) _
       = vbOK)
   #End If
End Function
```

If you click OK, the function returns True. If you click Cancel or press the Esc key, the function returns False. You could take action, such as halting execution with the Stop statement, if this were the case.

Using Assertions

An *assertion* is a statement that enforces a particular logical condition. If the condition is violated, an error message is reported and code execution is halted. Assertions are useful when you want to validate data while running a procedure. For example, Listing 15.11 shows part of a function that computes an invoice total based on a supplied tax rate (sngTax). It uses an assertion (by calling the dhAssert procedure, also shown in Listing 15.11) to ensure that the tax rate supplied is between 0 and 1.

Listing 15.11:   Use Assertions to Validate Data

```
Function InvoiceTotal(lngInvoiceID As Long, _
 sngTax As Single) As Double
   ' Use dhAssert to validate data
   Call dhAssert((sngTax >= 0) And (sngTax <= 1), _
   "Invalid tax rate: " & sngTax)
   ' Other statements
   ' ...
End Function
Sub dhAssert(fCondition As Boolean, Optional _
 strMessage As String = "Assertion failed.")
   ' If condition is False, display error
   ' message and halt execution
```

```
  If Not fCondition Then
    MsgBox strMessage, vbCritical
    Stop
  End If
End Sub
```

Using an assertion in this case is useful because there is no other way to limit the data a Single variable can store. If the condition is satisfied, everything proceeds normally. Otherwise, an error is reported and VBA stops executing code in the dhAssert procedure. When this happens, you can use the Call Stack dialog to see where the error occurred.

While dhAssert does supply default error text, you should pass your own description of the problem. This makes fixing it much easier. Liberal use of assertions in your code will help in finding many logic errors. The trade-off is that they add slightly to the size and reduce the speed of your code.

Systematic Debugging

While the guidelines mentioned thus far will minimize the number of bugs in your programs, some will inevitably creep in. The following paragraphs offer some techniques for getting rid of them.

The first rule of debugging is that you need a reproducible case that causes an error. If you cannot reproduce the error, you will have great difficulty tracking down the bug. You may get lucky and be in a situation in which you can debug the code when the bug appears, but if you can't reproduce it, your chances of fixing it are small. To reproduce the bug, you need as much information about the conditions that produced the bug as possible, but no more than that. If your users give you the hundred steps they performed that morning before the bug occurred, it makes your job difficult. Instead, if users limit the information to the essential three steps that actually cause the bug to occur, you can get somewhere. This isn't always easy. Sometimes you can reproduce a bug only by following numerous steps or, for example, after the user has been using the application for four hours. As you can imagine, these types of bugs are much harder to find and fix.

The second rule of debugging is that you must debug data, not code. This means you should use the debugger to find out what data is producing the error instead of staring at the code and speculating as to what it does. This seems a simple rule, but it is very effective at resolving bugs.

After you have found the bug but before you start fixing code, make sure you understand the nature of the problem. For example, a common error occurs when you declare simple datatype variables (Integer, Long, String, and so on). In your own testing, everything works fine. At the client's site, your application produces "Invalid Use of Null" messages.

There are two solutions to this problem, and each requires some understanding of the particular application. Clearly, you cannot place null values into Integer, Long, or String variables, so you might consider changing them all to Variants. On the other hand, perhaps the solution is to disallow null entries from the user. Your decision on the solution needs to take into account the particular situation. It seems obvious that you should change code only with a reason, but surprisingly, many programmers ignore this principle. "Experience" often masquerades as a reason when it is really a synonym for "wild guess."

Finally, no matter how good you are and how sure you are of your work, make only one change at a time to your code, and then test it again. It's all too easy to fall into the trap of making multiple fixes without keeping records and then having to junk the current version and reload from a backup because you have no idea which things worked and which only made things worse. Take baby steps, and you'll get there faster. As an added measure, document changes to your code using comments in either individual procedures or the declarations section of a module. By logging changes with the date they were made, you can help track down problems introduced by various "fixes."

TIP

Another way to prevent fixes to one procedure from adversely affecting other parts of your program is to use a source code control program that supports versioning. This lets you fall back to a working version of your code so you can try another debugging tactic.

There are two more bits of debugging strategy you might want to consider. Many programmers find "confessional debugging" to be one of the most useful techniques around. Confessional debugging works something like this: you grab your printouts and go into the next cubicle, interrupt the programmer working there, and say, "Hey, sorry to bother you, but I've got this function that keeps crashing. See, I pass in the name of a form here and then declare a form variable and then—oh, wait, that's not the form itself, but the form's name. Never mind; thanks for your help." When you get good at it, you can indulge in this sort of debugging with non-programmers as the audience or even (in times of desperation) by talking things through with your dog or a sympathetic (but bored) loved one.

Of course, there are times when confessing your code isn't enough. If you have the luxury of working with peers, use them. There's a good chance that other programmers can see the bug that you can't.

If all else fails, take a break. It's easy to get stuck in a mental loop in which you try the same things over and over, even though they didn't work the first time. Take a walk. Have lunch. Take a shower. Your mind's background processing can solve many bugs while the foreground processes are thinking about something else altogether. Many programmers have told stories of waking up in the middle of the night, having just dreamed about a bug they weren't even aware existed until then, along with its solution. Having written down the information during the night, they've gone in to work, found the previously unspotted bug, and fixed it on the spot.

OTHER PROFESSIONAL TOUCHES

Providing elegant error handling and relatively bug-free code is only the first step in delivering a professional application. The remainder of this chapter is devoted to several other considerations, such as object model design and providing assistance using online help. You may not choose to follow these guidelines for every project, but they are valuable tools to have at your disposal.

Creating Object Models

Throughout this book, we discuss and present various object models implemented using VBA class modules. As you develop applications using VBA, you'll undoubtedly create object models of your own. Whether they are for your own exclusive use or for use by others, there are some guidelines you can use to create object models that make sense and are easy to understand.

Strive for Simplicity

A good object model is a simple one. When deciding on what classes, properties, and methods you need, choose as few as possible at first. You can always add more later on. Remember that Property statements let you run code when a property value is set or retrieved. This gives you the ability to pack a lot of functionality into a simple property call.

Furthermore, don't feel compelled to include every piece of functionality you think developers will need if they can easily provide it themselves.

For example, if you develop a class that features a Text property, you don't need to include a property like TextLength. Users of your class can easily compute this value from the Text property using the VBA Len function.

Remember that every class member you create should exist for a reason. It should provide essential functionality that cannot be derived from other properties of your class.

Emulate Real-World Processes

The best guide for an object model is a real-world process. Like database design, object model design should reflect an existing set of entities and attributes. Methods should mimic behaviors, either existing or desired. As an example, consider an order entry application. Customers order products and are given an invoice. Each of these (customer, order, and invoice) is a candidate for representation via a class module. Each also has relevant attributes (name, date, amount) that should be modeled using properties. Just as important, each object has characteristics that are irrelevant to the business problem. (For instance, you rarely see a customer's eye color included on an order!)

Model the User Interface

Another guideline when creating an object model is to use your application's user interface, if it has one. If you examine the object models of major Microsoft applications, you'll notice how closely the object models follow the interface. Microsoft Excel's object model, for example, features an Application class at its root. The Application class contains a collection of Workbook objects representing open workbooks (XLS files). Each workbook contains a collection of worksheets. Other elements of the object model, such as the ChartObject and PivotTable classes, adhere to the visual interface.

User interface classes need not be generic. If you are creating a time-reporting application in Excel, for example, you might create a TimeSheet class to refer to the particular style of worksheet you've created for the application. When you subclass a generic object (Worksheet) in this manner, consider creating a property of the derived class to refer to the base object. This lets you access properties of the base object without having to implement your own, duplicate properties. Listing 15.12 illustrates what this might look like.

Listing 15.12:   Implement a Pointer to a Base Class as Part of a Derived Class

```
' Private pointer to the Excel worksheet
Private mobjSheet As Worksheet
Property Set Sheet(objSheet As Worksheet)
  If mobjSheet Is Nothing Then
    Set mobjSheet = objSheet
  End If
End Property
Property Get Sheet() As Worksheet
  Set Sheet = mobjSheet
End Property
```

You could then use a pointer to the TimeSheet class to reference properties of the worksheet:

```
objTimeSheet.Sheet.Visible = False
```

On the other hand, if you don't want other developers to manipulate the base class directly, you can implement some properties in the derived class. When a program accesses these properties, your class simply sets or retrieves properties of the base class. Listing 15.13 shows an alternative version of the TimeSheet class that implements its own Visible property. Changes to this property are passed through to the base class (Worksheet).

Listing 15.13:   Implement a Duplicate Property to "Hide" the Base Class

```
' Private pointer to the Excel worksheet
Private mobjSheet As Worksheet
Property Let Visible(fVisible As Boolean)
  mobjSheet.Visible = fVisible
End Property
Property Get Visible() As Boolean
  Visible = mobjSheet.Visible
End Property
```

Include Standard Properties and Methods

As you use object models developed by companies like Microsoft, you'll come to expect a certain level of consistency among classes, properties, and methods. You should strive to emulate these in your own object models. For example, most classes feature a Name property that indicates the name of the object. Classes that represent user interface elements implement properties such as Visible, Top, Left, and so on.

Collections usually include a Count property as well as Item, Add, and Remove methods. While you can invent your own names, you'll only be making it more difficult for other developers to understand and use your classes.

TO PREFIX OR NOT TO PREFIX

Having said in this chapter that you should strictly adhere to naming standards, we should also point out that you may want to make an exception when it comes to object models. This is especially true if other developers will use your object models. Avoiding the name prefixing that defines most naming standards will make reading and understanding your object models easier when viewed using VBA's Object Browser.

If you look at an object model like VBA's, for instance, you won't see prefixes on method arguments or property names. If you want your object models to look and act like Microsoft's (which, like it or not, are becoming a standard), you should avoid prefixing as well.

As an example, instead of declaring a method like this:

```
Public Sub Display(strFile As String, intMode As _
Integer)
```

declare it like this:

```
Public Sub Display(File As String, Mode As Integer)
```

When viewed with Object Browser, the datatypes will be evident, making the prefixes unnecessary.

The same goes for class names. Many developers prefixed class names with the letter "C" (for class). If you're using Object Browser to view a class, it ought to be clear that it is one!

Creating a Procedure Stack

When you're in the process of debugging an application in the VBA design environment, you can use the Call Stack dialog to see which function caused an error. Unfortunately, VBA doesn't provide any method for retrieving this information from your code. When you get an unexpected error, it's useful to log the code being executed at that point and how it got there. Since VBA provides no way to get at the information it keeps internally (that is, the name of the currently executing procedure), you must maintain the information yourself if you need it.

We've done this by implementing our own procedure stack based on the stack classes. The ProcStack and ProcStackItem classes store information on each procedure in VBA's call stack by implementing a stack of their own. The only catch is that you have to write code in your subroutines and functions to add procedures to the stack—VBA won't do this for you.

NOTE

We've modified the ProcStackItem class in two ways for this example. First, we changed the StackTop property so that instead of returning the value of the top item on the stack, it returns a pointer to the actual item. Second, we added a TimeEntered property. TimeEntered returns the value of a private date/time value that is set during the Initialize event.

To implement a call stack in your own applications, import the two class modules, PSTACK.CLS and PSTACKIT.CLS, from the Sybex Web site and declare a new instance of the ProcStack class in a global module. Call the Push method of the class at the entry point of every routine in your code and the Pop method at the exit point. Listing 15.14 shows an example of how to use these methods. It also shows how to print out the contents of the stack.

Listing 15.14: Example of Using the Procedure Stack Class

```
' Declare global instance of ProcStack class
Global gProcStack As New ProcStack
Sub EnterAndExitExample()
  ' Call Push to place proc name onto the stack
  Call gProcStack.Push("EnterAndExitExample")
  ' Call PrintCallStack, which will print the call stack
  ' to the Immediate window so you can see that it works!
  Call PrintCallStack
  ' Make sure to call Pop!!
  Call gProcStack.Pop
End Sub
Private Sub PrintCallStack()
  Dim objProc As StackItem
  ' Call Push to place proc name onto the stack
  Call gProcStack.Push("PrintCallStack")
  ' Print it out by walking the stack
  Set objProc = gProcStack.StackTop
```

```
Do Until objProc Is Nothing
  Debug.Print "Entered procedure '" & objProc.Value & _
    "' at " & objProc.TimeEntered
  Set objProc = objProc.NextItem
Loop
' Make sure to call Pop!!
Call gProcStack.Pop
End Sub
```

Because you have to call the Pop method at the exit point, you will want to make sure you have only one exit point to your procedures. If you don't, you run the risk of trying to push the wrong procedure off the stack.

The payoff for using this call stack code comes when you are trying to determine the current program state after an error occurs. The information on the stack is the same as that displayed by VBA's Call Stack dialog, but you have programmatic access to it. You can display it on screen, dump it to a log file (using the log class described in the next section), or send it to the printer.

Another advantage of using our modified classes is that the ProcStack-Item class stores the current time when you create a new instance of it. Using this information, you can keep track of how much time is spent in a procedure. This is called *profiling*. You can use the profiling information to help determine which routines need optimization work.

Application Logging

One of the best ways to troubleshoot problems in a deployed application is through log files. Log files contain information about the program's state, variables, and the operating system. A user who is having a problem with your application can enable the log and send you the output to examine. We've developed a log file class you can use in your application. We chose to implement this functionality as a class so you could use multiple log files in the same application. The following sections explain how the class works.

The Log Class

Our log class (called, simply, Log) features a number of properties and methods designed to create or open a log file, delete a log file, and write entries to a log file. Table 15.3 lists each property, along with a short description.

TABLE 15.3: Properties of the Log Class

PROPERTY	DESCRIPTION
Active	A Boolean value indicating whether the log is active. If the log is not active, no output will be written
File	Name of the log file
Options	A bitmask of values that controls whether additional information (such as the date and time) is written to the log file
SeverityLevel	The severity threshold for the log. When writing log entries, you can specify a severity for each. Only those that exceed this value are actually written

In addition to the properties listed in Table 15.3, the class implements two methods, Output and Reset. Output accepts a text string and an optional integer representing the severity of the log entry. Only entries that exceed the SeverityLevel property setting of the class are actually written to the log. This feature lets you distinguish between informational log entries and critical errors. If you don't include a value for the second argument, the Output method assumes a value of 9.

The Reset method deletes the current log file. Normally, log entries are appended to the end of the file. Use the Reset method to purge the file and start over.

Listing 15.15 shows the code behind the Output method. Note that it processes the log information only if the mfActive flag is True. The mfActive variable maps to the Active property of the class and is initially set to False when an instance of the class is created. Note also how the method uses the mlngOptions variable. If it contains certain values (denoted by the conLogDateTime and conLogSeverity constants), the method writes additional information to the log file.

Listing 15.15:   Output Method of the Log Class

```
Public Sub Output(Text As Variant, _
  Optional Severity As Integer = 9)
    Dim hFile As Long
    Dim varText As Variant
    Dim varExisting As Variant
    On Error GoTo HandleError
    ' Only process this if the log is active
```

```
      If mfActive Then
        ' Build up text
        varText = Text
        If mlngOptions And conLogDateTime Then
          varText = Now & vbTab & varText
        End If
        If mlngOptions And conLogSeverity Then
          varText = Severity & vbTab & varText
        End If
        ' Process the log information if Severity
        ' meets or exceeds SeverityLevel
        If Severity >= mintSeverityLevel Then
          ' If SeverityLevel is -1 then put up a message
          ' rather than writing text to the file
          If mintSeverityLevel = -1 Then
            MsgBox varText, vbInformation, "Log"
          Else
            ' Get file handle
            hFile = FreeFile
            ' Open file for append
            Open mstrFile For Append _
             Access Write As hFile
            ' Print the output
            Print #hFile, varText
            ' Close the file
            Close hFile
          End If
        End If
      End If
ExitHere:
    Exit Sub
HandleError:
    mfActive = False
    Err.Raise vbObjectError + 8000, "Log::Output", _
      Err.Description
    Resume ExitHere
End Sub
```

A special SeverityLevel setting of −1 triggers a MsgBox instead of a file entry. You could use this in situations in which you want immediate feedback while your application runs rather than wait to view the log file.

Finally, note that the Output method opens the log file in append mode and closes it in the same procedure. Closing the file is important because if a critical error occurs, resulting in a protection fault, any open files will not be completely written to disk.

Using the Log Class

To use the Log class in your application, you need to import the class module and create at least one instance of the class in your code. (You may also want to copy the constant declarations to a global module.) If you want to experiment with the sample procedures described below, you'll also need to import the BASERROR.BAS file. As an example, you could create a global instance that all procedures could use. Listing 15.16 shows the object declaration as well as a sample procedure that initializes the class and sets various options.

Listing 15.16:   Initialize the Log Class

```
' Declare an instance of the Log class
Global gLog As Log
Sub Main
  ' Initialize the log
  Set gLog = New Log
  ' Set the file name
  gLog.File = "C:\APP.LOG"
  ' Set logging options
  gLog.SeverityLevel = 5
  gLog.Options = conLogDateTime
  ' Other startup code
  '  ...
End Sub
```

Once you have a reference to a class instance, you can begin writing entries to the log file. Listing 15.17 shows a sample procedure that uses logging. Note the different severity level settings.

Listing 15.17:   Sample Procedure That Utilizes Logging

```
Sub ProcessFileName(strFile As String)
  gLog.Output "Entering ProcessFile", 5
  Dim strErrText As String
  gLog.Output "Before: strFile = " & strFile, 6
  ' Do some processing here
  gLog.Output "After: strFile = " & strFile, 6
ExitHere:
  gLog.Output "Exiting ProcessFile", 5
  Exit Sub
HandleError:
  strErrText = "(" & Err.Number & ") " & _
  Err.Description
  Call dhError("ProcessFile")
  gLog.Output "Error in ProcessFile: " & _
```

```
        strErrText, 9
        Resume ExitHere
    End Sub
```

Enabling Log Functionality

After adding support for logging to your application, you should make it easy for users to enable it. For example, you could use a menu command, an option setting, a command-line parameter, or a Registry setting. When a user elects to enable logging, your application should set the Active property of the class to True. Until Active is set to True, no log entries will be made.

Now, many of you astute VBA programmers might be wondering, "Doesn't including all the log code affect performance, even if logging isn't active?" The answer, of course, is yes. Calling the Output method does impart a small amount of overhead each time your application calls it. You have to decide whether the benefits of logging outweigh this cost. This answer is also usually yes, although you'll need to be the final judge.

If performance is a critical issue in your application, you can create what is known as an *instrumented version* that contains the log code. You ship normal users a version without the log code and install the instrumented version only if problems arise. The easiest way to create instrumented and normal versions that share the same code base is to use conditional compilation. Surround all references to logging with #If statements, as the code in Listing 15.18 illustrates. By setting the conditional constant appropriately, you can easily create an instrumented or a normal version of your application.

Listing 15.18:   Use Conditional Compilation to Create an Instrumented Version

```
Sub ProcessFileName(strFile As String)
#If fLog Then
  gLog.Output "Entering ProcessFile", 5
#End If
  ' More statements
  '...
End Sub
```

Providing Online Help

Online help is a valuable resource for today's computer users. In fact, it's often the only form of assistance available. To save money, many large companies do not distribute printed documentation to every user. Furthermore, many users prefer to use online help even when printed manuals are available. Online help can help speed acceptance of your applications as well as cut down on support costs. This section explains how you can tie online help to your applications using VBA. However, it's not a tutorial on creating help files. For that you'll need to consult the documentation that came with your help file creation software.

Help File Basics

Be aware that to reference a help topic, you must know the name of the help file that contains it, as well as the topic's Context ID. A *Context ID* is a unique numeric value that corresponds to a topic in a help file. As you develop help topics, you give each one a unique name. You map these names to numeric Context IDs before compiling the help file.

Help Topics in Code

VBA provides three places where you can reference a help topic in code:

- ▶ The InputBox function
- ▶ The MsgBox function
- ▶ The Err.Raise method

All these procedures have optional arguments for help file and Context ID. When you supply these with the InputBox or MsgBox function, VBA adds a Help button to the proper dialog. For example, Figure 15.11 illustrates the dialog that appears when you execute the following statement:

```
?InputBox(Prompt:="Enter a value below:", _
    Title:="Enter Value", HelpFile:="MYAPP.HLP", _
    Context:=100)
```

If the user presses F1 or clicks the Help button, VBA opens the help file to the given Context ID.

FIGURE 15.11:   Specifying a help file and Context ID causes VBA to display a Help button.

The Err object's Raise method also has optional arguments for help file and Context ID. The standard VBA error dialog features a Help button that normally opens the VBA help file to the "Application defined error" help topic. If you supply your own help file and context information, however, VBA opens your help file in response to the Raise method. If you have an error trap defined, you'll be able to access this information using the HelpFile and HelpContext properties of the Err object. Listing 15.19 shows a test procedure that illustrates this.

Listing 15.19: Use Err.Raise to Supply Help File Information

```
Sub ShowHelpInfo()
  On Error GoTo HandleError
  Err.Raise 12345, "Sub ShowHelpInfo", _
    "This error is by design.", "MAINAPP.HLP", 100
ExitHere:
  Exit Sub
HandleError:
  Debug.Print Err.HelpFile, Err.HelpContext
  Resume ExitHere
End Sub
```

NOTE

While the HelpFile and HelpContext arguments of InputBox, MsgBox, and Raise are optional, if you supply one of them, you must supply the other.

Help for Classes

The final place you can place help information is in a class module. This allows developers to get online assistance for any of the properties or methods of your class. This can be extremely useful if you are distributing your application to developers outside your organization.

You add help information using the Options dialog and Object Browser. First, you specify a help file for your project. To do this, open the project's Properties dialog and enter the name of a help file. You then use Object Browser to specify help Context IDs for each property and method.

To assign a Context ID to a property or method, select it from the Members list in Object Browser. Then select Properties from the right-click context menu. You should see a dialog like the one in Figure 15.12. Note that the help file is filled in for you based on the project settings and cannot be changed. Enter the numeric Context ID in the text box and click OK. VBA saves this information with the member definition.

Member Options	☒
Name: Output	OK
Description:	Cancel
Prints text to the log file	
Help File:	Help Context ID:	Help
CH07.HLP	100|	

FIGURE 15.12:   Specifying a help Context ID for a class member

You should also add a description of the member in the Properties dialog. Object Browser displays the description when a user selects the member.

TIP

You can quickly add descriptions and Context ID numbers to multiple members by editing the source code files directly if your VBA host application supports this ability. (If the host application doesn't use external source files, you can export a module, edit it, and import it.) To add a description, insert a line after the member's declaration and enter the string "Attribute *member*.VB_Description = *text*", replacing *member* with the member name and *text* with the description. To add a Context ID, add the line "Attribute *member*.VB_HelpID = *number*", where *number* is the Context ID. For members with multiple declarations (such as Property Let and Get procedures), you need to add the lines after only one declaration.

SUMMARY

This chapter has covered several topics that figure heavily in the development of professional applications. We discussed error handling and debugging in detail. You should now understand how VBA handles errors in your applications and how you must anticipate and cope with them. We also showed you the various debugging aids VBA provides and offered some guidelines and advice regarding how to eliminate bugs from your programs.

Beyond simple error handling, we also discussed ways to add professional touches to your applications. These included implementing procedure stacks and error logging to aid your users in communicating error conditions to you. We also suggested guidelines for developing object models and online help.

After reading this chapter, you should be familiar with the following concepts:

- ► How VBA handles run-time errors

- ► How to use the On Error and Resume statements

- ► How to use debugging aids such as breakpoints, watches, and the call stack

- ► How to implement professional features such as procedure stacks, application logging, and online help

WHAT'S NEXT?

This chapter concludes your tour of VB and VBA. You now have many of the tools necessary to create an effective VB application and to develop in the VBA environment. The following two reference appendices place even more tools at your fingertips. You'll find a wealth of information about the built-in functions and statements in VB and about the API functions used in Chapter 7. If you'd like more information about any of the topics discussed in this book, please refer to the Sybex books that contributed to this collection.

PART V

VISUAL BASIC REFERENCE

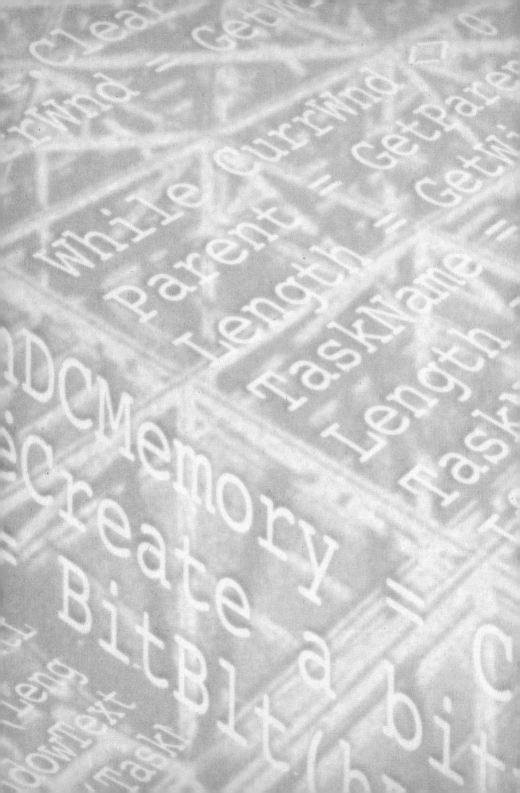

Reference 1

THE COMPLETE VISUAL BASIC 6 LANGUAGE REFERENCE

by Evangelos Petroustos

T his reference describes all Visual Basic built-in functions and statements, grouped by category. Table LR.1 lists the individual functions and statements by type. We chose to group the entries of this reference according to their function because we believe this is how most people read reference material. When you're searching for the statement that opens a file, you probably want to locate all file I/O commands in one place. By grouping all related functions and statements together, we can present examples that combine more than one function or statement.

If you wish to know which ones are functions and which are statements, they're easy to distinguish; functions are followed by a pair of parentheses, which enclose the functions' arguments, while statements are followed by their arguments. As a reminder, function calls take this form:

```
Result = FunctionName(arguments)
```

Statement calls look like this:

```
StatementName arguments
```

The difference between statements and functions is that statements act on their arguments, but they don't return a result. Functions return a result, and that's why they appear on the right side of an equals sign. The following statement deletes a file from the hard disk:

```
Kill "c:\temp\resume.old"
```

This action does not return a result. However, the following function calculates the logarithm of its argument and returns a result:

```
result = Log(4.999)
```

It is possible to call a function as a statement, without storing the result to a variable. The line

```
log(4.999)
```

is perfectly legal, but it doesn't make sense to have Visual Basic perform calculations and then discard the results. This statement causes Visual Basic to calculate the logarithm of 4.999 and then discard the result.

You will also notice that arguments follow the name of the statement without parentheses. Function arguments must appear in parentheses, unless you don't need the result; the line

```
Log 4
```

is a valid statement.

Some statements make use of *keywords*. A keyword is a reserved word, which can appear as part of a statement. The Open statement, for example, has the following syntax:

```
Open "c:\samples\vb\cust.dat" For Input As #1
```

This statement opens the specified file, so your application can write to it and assigns it the value 1. The words *For* and *As* are keywords. All Visual Basic keywords are reserved words, and they can't be used in other contexts (for example, as variable or procedure names); they can only appear in a statement. These two keywords are not unique to the Open statement. The For...Next loop, which repeats a block of statements a number of times, uses the *For* keyword (as well as the *Next* and *To* keywords), as shown in this statement:

```
For counter = 1 To 100
   {statements}
Next
```

The *As* keyword is also used with the Dim statement, which declares a variable:

```
Dim counter1 As Integer, counter2 As Long
```

Everything that's not a statement name, a function name, or an argument (arguments are italicized in the text) is a keyword. For the benefit of readers who are new to Visual Basic, we will list the keywords here. You will be familiar with most of them (and you will see most of these keywords in the entries on the following pages). The Public, Private, and Static keywords are included in this appendix because they are often used as synonyms for the Dim statement.

As	Binary	ByRef	ByVal	Else	Empty	False
For	Friend	Is	Me	New	Next	Nothing
Null	On	Private	Public	Static	Step	Then
To	True	WithEvents				

The functions and statements in Table LR.1 are described in the following sections, along with examples.

TABLE LR.1: Functions and Statements by Type

TYPE	FUNCTION
Input/Output	InputBox()
	MsgBox()
File and Folder Manipulation	ChDir
	ChDrive
	CurDir()
	Dir()
	FileCopy
	FileDateTime()
	GetAttr()
	Kill
	MkDir
	Name
	RmDir
	SetAttr

TABLE LR.1 (continued): Functions and Statements by Type

TYPE	FUNCTION
Variable and Array Declaration	Const
	Declare
	DefType
	Dim
	Enum...End Enum
	Erase
	Private keyword
	Public keyword
	ReDim
	Static keyword
Variable and Array Types	Array()
	IsArray()
	IsDate()
	IsEmpty()
	IsError()
	IsNull()
	IsNumeric()
	IsObject()
	LBound()
	Type ... End Type
	TypeName()
	UBound()
	VarType()
Variable Type Conversion	CBool()
	CByte()
	CCur()
	CDate()
	CDec()
	CDbl()
	CInt()
	CLng()
	CSng()
	CStr()
	CVar()
	CVErr()
String Manipulation Functions	Asc(), AscB(), AscW()
	Chr(), ChrB(), ChrW()
	Filter()
	InStr(), InStrB()
	InStrRev()
	Join()
	LCase()
	Left(), LeftB()
	Len(), LenB()
	LTrim()

TABLE LR.1 (continued): Functions and Statements by Type

TYPE	FUNCTION
String Manipulation Functions	Mid(), MidB() Mid statement Replace() Right(), RightB() RTrim() Space() Split() Str() String() StrComp() StrConv() StrReverse() Trim() UCase()
Data Formatting Functions	Format() FormatCurrency() FormatDateTime() FormatNumber() FormatPercent() LSet statement RSet statement
Math Functions	Abs() Atn() Cos() Exp() Int() Fix() Round() Log() Oct() Hex() Randomize Statement Rnd() Sgn() Sin() Sqr() Tan() Val()
Date and Time	Date() Date Statement DateAdd() DateDiff() DatePart() DateSerial() DateValue()

TABLE LR.1 (continued): Functions and Statements by Type

TYPE	FUNCTION
Date and Time	Day() Hour() Minute() Month() MonthName() Now() Time() Time Statement Second() Timer() TimeSerial() TimeValue() Weekday() WeekdayName() Year()
Financial	IPmt() PPmt() Pmt() FV() PV() NPV() NPer() Rate() IRR() MIRR() DDB() SYD() SLN()
File I/O	Close EOF() FileAttr() FileLen() FreeFile() Get # Input # Line Input # LOF() Loc() Lock Open Print # Put # Reset Seek UnLock

TABLE LR.1 (continued): Functions and Statements by Type

TYPE	FUNCTION
File I/O	Write #
	Width #
Graphics	LoadPicture()
	QBColor()
	RGB()
	SavePicture
Registry	DeleteSetting
	GetAllSettings()
	GetSetting()
	SaveSetting
Resource Files	LoadResData()
	LoadResPicture()
	LoadResString()
Control Flow Statements	Do...Loop
	For...Next
	If...Then
	If...Then...Else
	Select Case
	While...Wend
Application Collaboration	AppActivate
	SendKeys
	Shell()
Objects	CreateObject()
	Event
	For Each...Next
	GetObject()
	Load
	Property Get
	Property Let
	Property Set
	RaiseEvent
	Set
	Unload
	With...End With
Option Statements	Option Base
	Option Compare
	Option Explicit
Error Trapping and Handling	Error
	On Error
	Resume

TABLE LR.1 (continued): Functions and Statements by Type

TYPE	FUNCTION
Miscellaneous	Beep
	CallByName()
	Choose()
	DoEvents
	Environ()
	IIf()
	Rem
	Switch()
Obsolete Functions and Statements	On...GoSub
	On...GoTo
	GoTo
	GoSub, Return

The entries in the following sections are not listed alphabetically within each category but rather start with the simpler ones. This way, we can provide more useful examples by combining more than one function or statement of the same category.

INPUT/OUTPUT FUNCTIONS

Visual Basic provides two basic functions for displaying (or requesting) information to the user: MsgBox() and InputBox(). Windows applications should communicate with the user via nicely designed Forms, but the MsgBox() and InputBox() functions are available and quite useful.

InputBox(prompt[, title][, default][, xpos] [, ypos][, helpfile, context])

The InputBox() function displays a dialog box with a prompt and a TextBox control and waits for the user to enter some text and click the OK or Cancel button. The arguments of the InputBox() function are shown in Table LR.2.

TABLE LR.2: The Arguments of the InputBox() Function

ARGUMENT	DESCRIPTION
prompt	The prompt that appears in the dialog box. If necessary, the prompt is broken into multiple lines automatically. To control line breaks from within your code, use a carriage return character (Chr(13)) or a linefeed character (Chr(10)).
title	The title of the dialog box. If you omit this argument, the application's name is displayed as the title.
default	The default input (if any). If you anticipate the user's response, use this argument to display it when the dialog box is first opened.
xpos, ypos	The coordinates of the upper left corner of the dialog box, expressed in twips.
helpfile	The name of the Help file. Use this argument to provide context-sensitive help for the dialog box.
context	The number of the specific topic within the Help file.

The simplest format of the InputBox() function is as follows:

```
SSN = InputBox("Please enter your social security number")
```

The string that the user enters in the dialog box is assigned to the variable *SSN*. The return value is always a string, even if the user enters numeric information. When prompting for input with the InputBox() function, always check the value returned by the function. At the very least, check for a blank string. Use the IsNumeric() function if you expect the user to enter a number, use the IsDate() function if you expect the user to enter a date, and so on.

```
BDay = InputBox("Please enter your birth date")
If IsDate(Bday) Then
  MsgBox "Preparing your Horoscope"
Else
  MsgBox "Please try again with a valid birth date"
End If
```

MsgBox(prompt[, buttons][, title] [, helpfile, context])

The MsgBox() function displays a dialog box with a message and waits for the user to close it by clicking a button. The message is the first argument (*prompt*). The simplest form of the MsgBox() function is as follows:

```
MsgBox "Your computer is running out of memory!"
```

This function displays a message in a dialog box that has an OK button. The MsgBox() function can display other buttons and/or an icon in the dialog box and return a numeric value, depending on which button was clicked. Table LR.3 summarizes the values for the *buttons* argument.

TABLE LR.3: The Values for the Buttons Argument

CONSTANT	VALUE	DESCRIPTION
BUTTON VALUES		
VbOKOnly	0	Displays OK button only.
VbOKCancel	1	Displays OK and Cancel buttons.
VbAbortRetryIgnore	2	Displays Abort, Retry, and Ignore buttons.
VbYesNoCancel	3	Displays Yes, No, and Cancel buttons.
VbYesNo	4	Displays Yes and No buttons.
VbRetryCancel	5	Displays Retry and Cancel buttons.
ICON VALUES		
VbCritical	16	Displays Critical Message icon.
VbQuestion	32	Displays Warning Query icon.
VbExclamation	48	Displays Warning Message icon.
VbInformation	64	Displays Information Message icon.
DEFAULT BUTTON		
vbDefaultButton1	0	First button is default.
vbDefaultButton2	256	Second button is default.
vbDefaultButton3	512	Third button is default.
vbDefaultButton4	768	Fourth button is default.
MODALITY		
VbApplicationModal	0	Application modal; the user must respond to the message box before switching to any of the Forms of the current application.
VbSystemModal	4096	System modal; all applications are suspended until the user responds to the message box.

Button values determine which buttons appear in the dialog box. Notice that you can't choose which individual buttons to display; you can only choose groups of buttons.

Icon values determine an optional icon you can display in the dialog box. These icons are commonly used throughout the Windows user interface to notify the user about an unusual or exceptional event.

Default Button values determine which button is the default one; pressing Enter activates this button.

The values 0 and 4096 determine whether the message box is modal. To combine these settings into a single value, simply add their values.

Finally, the MsgBox() function returns an integer, which indicates the button pressed, according to Table LR.4.

TABLE LR.4: The Values of the Buttons

CONSTANT	VALUE	DESCRIPTION
vbOK	1	OK
vbCancel	2	Cancel
vbAbort	3	Abort
vbRetry	4	Retry
vbIgnore	5	Ignore
vbYes	6	Yes
vbNo	7	No

To display a dialog box with the OK and Cancel buttons, as well as the Warning Message icon, add the values 1 and 48 as follows:

```
cont = MsgBox("This operation may take several minutes", 48+1)
```

Your program will continue with the operation if the value of *cont* is 1 (OK button), or it will abort the operation if *cont* is 2.

To display a dialog box with the Yes and No buttons and the Critical Message icon, add the values 4 and 16 as follows:

```
cont = MsgBox("Incomplete data. Would you like to retry?", _
4 + 16)
If cont = 6 Then    ' user clicked Yes
    {prompt again}
Else            ' user clicked No
```

```
    {exit procedure}
   End If
```

The *title* argument is the title displayed in the message box's title bar. See the description of the InputBox() function earlier in the reference for an explanation of the *helpfile* and *context* arguments.

FILE AND FOLDER MANIPULATION

The following Visual Basic functions manipulate files and folders (move and rename files, create new folders, delete existing ones, and so on). The statements and functions discussed in this reference do not manipulate the contents of the files. Most of the functions and statements discussed in this section are equivalent to the members of the FileSystemObject object (discussed in Chapter 10, "Scripting Objects"). They are also equivalent to the basic DOS commands for manipulating files and folders.

GetAttr(filename)

This function returns an integer representing the attributes of a file or a directory (folder), according to Table LR.5.

TABLE LR.5: The Values Returned by the GetAttr() Function

CONSTANT	VALUE	DESCRIPTION
vbNormal	0	Normal
vbReadOnly	1	Read-only
vbHidden	2	Hidden
vbSystem	4	System
vbDirectory	16	Directory or folder
vbArchive	32	File has changed since last backup

To determine which attributes are set, use the AND operator to perform a bitwise comparison of the value returned by the GetAttr() function and the value of one or more attributes. If the result is not zero, that attribute is set for the named file. For example, to find out whether a file is read-only, use the following statement:

```
Result = GetAttr(FName) And vbReadOnly
```

If the file *Fname* has its read-only attribute set, *Result* will be 1. If not, Result will be 0, regardless of the values of any other attributes. To find out whether a file has its archive attribute set, use the following statement:

```
Result = GetAttr(FName) And vbArchive
```

This statement will assign the value 32 to the *Result* variable. If the file has both its archive and read-only attributes set, the GetAttr() function will return the value 33. However, you must AND this value with the appropriate constant to find out whether a certain attribute is set or not.

SetAttr file_name, attributes

The SettAttr statement sets the attributes of a file. The argument *file_name* is the path name of an existing file and *attributes* is a numeric value that specifies one or more attributes. To set an attribute without affecting any existing attributes, use a statement like the following one:

```
SetAttr file_name, GetAttr(file_name) Or new_attribute
```

The *new_attribute* argument can have any of the values shown in Table LR.6. To change multiple attributes, combine the corresponding values with the logical OR operator. Notice that the statement

```
SetAttr file_name, new_attribute
```

will turn on a specific attribute, but it will clear all other attributes. If a file is Read-only and Hidden, its Attributes property is 3 (1+2 according to Table LR.6). If you attempt to turn on the Archive attribute by setting its Attributes property to 32, the other two attributes will be cleared. By combining the new attribute (32) and the existing attributes with the OR operator, the file will be Read-only, Hidden, and Archive.

The following code segment shows how you can use the MsgBox() function to prompt the user before changing a file's read-only attribute. You should always examine a file's read-only attribute before deleting it. The Kill statement, which deletes the specified file, is discussed in the following section.

```
If GetAttr(file_name) And 32 Then
    reply = MsgBox("This is a read-only file. _
        Delete it anyway?", vbYesNo)
    If reply = vbYes Then
      SetAttr file_name, GetAttr(file_name) And vbReadOnly
      Kill file_name
    End If
Else
```

```
     Kill file_name
   End If
```

To remove a specific attribute, find out whether this attribute is already set, and then subtract its value from the value returned by the GetAttr() function. To remove the Hidden attribute, use a structure like the following:

```
If GetAttr(file_name) And 2 Then
   SetAttr file_name, GetAttr(file_name) - 2
End If
```

Kill file_name

The Kill statement deletes the specified file permanently from the hard disk. The argument *file_name* specifies one or more filenames to be deleted. Unlike the FileCopy statement (discussed shortly), the Kill statement supports the use of multiple-character (*) and single-character (?) wildcards to specify multiple files. If the specified file does not exist, a run-time error is generated. The Kill statement is frequently used as follows:

```
On Error Resume Next
Kill "C:\RESUME.OLD"
On Error GoTo 0
```

The On Error statement tells Visual Basic to ignore errors and continue execution with the following statement. If the file C:\RESUME.OLD does not exist, then it will not abort with an error message. It simply won't kill it (since it doesn't exist) and will proceed with the next statement, which turns off error trapping.

The Kill statement does not move the specified file to the Recycle Bin; it permanently deletes the file from the disk. If you move the file to the Recycle Bin with the FileCopy statement, the file will appear in the Recycle Bin's window, but you won't be able to restore it.

FileDateTime(filename)

This function returns the date and time when a file was created or last modified. The following statement

```
Print FileDateTime("MYDOCUMENT.TXT")
```

returns a date/time value, such as 21/1/97 14:13:02 PM

FileLen(filename)

The FileLen() function returns a long integer value indicating the file's length. The name of the file whose length you want to find out is passed as an argument to the function. The following statement

```
MsgBox FileLen(".\DOCS\MYDOCUMENT.TXT")
```

displays the length of the specified file in a message box.

The FileLen() function is different from the LOF() function, which returns the length of a file that has already been opened. See the description of the LOF() function in the section "File I/O."

MkDir path

The MkDir statement creates a new folder (directory). The *path* argument can be the full path of the new folder or just a folder name, in which case a new folder is created under the current folder. The statement

```
MkDir "C:\Users\New User"
```

will create the New User folder under C:\Users but only if the parent folder exists already. If the C:\Users folder doesn't already exist, you must call the MkDir statement twice, to create two folders, as shown next:

```
MkDir "C:\Users"
MkDir "C:\Users\New User"
```

Alternatively, you can switch to the parent folder and then create the subfolder:

```
ChDrive "C:\"
ChDir "C:\"
MkDir "C:\Users"
ChDir "Users"
MkDir "New Users"
```

You should also use the appropriate error-trapping code, because if a folder you attempt to create exists already, a runtime error will occur.

RmDir path

The RmDir statement deletes a folder (directory), specified by the *path* argument. The argument can't contain wild-card characters. The folder must be empty; if not, a runtime error will occur. To remove a folder containing files, use the Kill statement to delete the files first. In addition, you must remove all subfolders of a given folder before you can remove the parent folder.

The statement

```
RmDir "C:\Users"
```

will generate an error message. You must first remove the subfolder "New User" and then the parent folder:

```
RmDir "C:\Users\New User"
RmDir "C:\Users"
```

To remove multiple folders or remove folders recursively, use the methods of the FileSystemObject, described in Chapter 10, "Scripting Objects."

ChDir path

The ChDir statement changes the current folder (directory). If your application opens disk files or accesses images in disk files, you can either specify the path name of the desired file or switch to the folder where the file resides and use its name only.

To switch to the folder C:\Windows, use the statement

```
ChDir "C:\Windows"
```

If the argument of the ChDir statement doesn't include a drive name, then ChDir will attempt to switch to the specified folder on the current drive. If no such folder exists, then the current folder won't change, and Visual Basic will generate a "Path not found" error message.

The ChDir statement changes the current folder but not the current drive. For example, if the current drive is C, the following statement changes the current folder to another folder on drive D, but C remains the current drive:

```
ChDir "D:\TMP"
```

To change the current drive, use the ChDrive statement, described next.

You can also use relative folder names. The statement

```
ChDir ".."
```

takes you to the parent folder of the current folder, whereas the statement

```
ChDir "..\MyFiles"
```

takes you to the MyFiles folder of the parent folder (both the current and the MyFiles folders are subfolders of the same folder).

ChDrive drive

The ChDrive statement changes the current drive. The *drive* argument must be the name of an existing drive. If the *drive* argument is a multiple-character string, ChDrive uses only the first letter.

Let's say you distribute an application, which copies a number of auxiliary files to the same folder as the application. You can access your files by their names only if you switch to the application's folder with the following statements:

```
ChDrive App.Path
ChDir App.Path
```

The App.Path property is the path where the application (the VBP of the project, or the EXE file) is stored. Do not use the App.Path property before saving the project to its own folder. Before the project is saved, the application's path is the path to the Visual Basic folder (usually `C:\Program Files\Microsoft Visual Studio\VB6`).

CurDir([drive])

The CurDir() function, when called without an argument, returns the name of the current folder in the current drive. To find out the current folder on another drive, supply the drive's name as an argument. The function

```
CDir = CurDir()
```

returns the current folder on the current drive. To find out the current folder on drive D, call the function CurDir() as follows:

```
DDir = CurDir("D")
```

Dir [path_name[, attributes])]

The Dir() function accepts two optional arguments and returns a string with the name of a file or folder that matches the specified folder or file attribute(s).

If you specify the first argument, which supports wild-card characters, Dir() will return the name of the file or folder that matches the specification. If no file or folder matches the specification, an empty string is returned (""). The second argument is a numeric value, which specifies one or more attributes, as shown in Table LR.6. If the argument is omitted, only normal files (files without attributes) are returned.

TABLE LR.6: The Attributes Recognized by the Dir() Function

CONSTANT	DESCRIPTION
vbNormal	Specifies files with no attributes.
vbReadOnly	Specifies read-only files in addition to files with no attributes.
vbHidden	Specifies hidden files in addition to files with no attributes.
vbSystem	Specifies system files in addition to files with no attributes.
vbVolume	Specifies volume label; if any other attribute is specified, vbVolume is ignored.
vbDirectory	Specifies folders in addition to files with no attributes.

A common use of the Dir() function is to check whether a specific file or folder exists. The statement

```
OCXFile = Dir("C:\WINDOWS\SYSTEM\MSCOMCTL.OCX")
```

will return MSCOMCTL.OCX if the specified file exists, otherwise it will return an empty string.

To find out how many OCX files exist in your Windows\System folder, you must specify a wild-card specification and call the Dir() function repeatedly:

```
OCXFile = Dir("C:\WINDOWS\SYSTEM\*.OCX")
If OCXFile <> "" Then OCXFiles = OCXFiles + 1
While OCXFile <> ""
  OCXFile = Dir()
  OCXFiles = OCXFiles + 1
Wend
```

The Dir() function is called for the first time with an argument. If an OCX file is found, its name is returned. Then, the function is called repeatedly, this time without arguments. Each time, it returns the name of the next OCX file, until all OCX files that match the original specification are exhausted. After the loop, the variable *OCXFiles* contains the number of OCX files in the Windows\System folder. (There should be a few dozen OCX files there, even on a bare-bones system.)

If you want to find out whether there are any hidden OCX files in the Windows\System folder, supply the *attributes* argument to the Dir() function:

```
HiddenFile = Dir("C:\WINDOWS\SYSTEM\*.OCX", vbHidden)
```

You can also combine multiple attributes by adding the corresponding constants or ORing them together. The following statement will return the first hidden system file in the Windows\System folder:

```
HiddenSystemFile = Dir("C:\WINDOWS\SYSTEM\*.*", vbHidden Or _
vbSystem)
```

To list all the subfolders in a given folder, you must specify the vbDirectory attribute, which returns folder names as well as the names of normal files. To check whether an entry is a folder or a file, you must also examine its attributes with the GetAttr() function. The following loop counts the subfolders of the Windows\System folder.

```
Path = "C:\WINDOWS\SYSTEM\"
FFName = Dir(Path, vbDirectory)
While FFName <> ""
  If (GetAttr(Path & FFName) And vbDirectory) = vbDirectory _
Then
    Debug.Print FFName
    TotFolders = TotFolders + 1
  End If
  FFName = Dir()
Wend
```

If you run this code segment, the following list of folders should appear in the Immediate window. You may see more files than the ones listed here but notice the first two entries.

```
.
..
VMM32
IOSUBSYS
COLOR
inetsrv
ShellExt
dcom98
setup
Mts
DTCLog
cache
LogFiles
```

The first two strings returned by the Dir() function represent the current and parent folders. (You see these two symbols every time you run the DIR command from a DOS Prompt window.) You should exclude these two entries either with an If statement or by decreasing the *TotFolders* variable by two.

FileCopy source_file, dest_file

The FileCopy statement copies a file to a new location on the hard disk. The name of the file to be copied is *source_file*. If the file is in the current folder, then you can specify its name only. Otherwise, you must specify the file's path name. The *dest_file* argument specifies the target filename and may include a folder and drive name. Notice that the file can't be copied if an application is using it at the time.

To copy the file C:\VB6 Material\Examples\Files.txt to D:\VB6 Complete\Files.txt, use the following statements:

```
Source = "C:\VB6 Material\Examples\Files.txt"
Destination = "D:\VB6 Complete\Files.txt"
FileCopy Source, Destination
```

The FileCopy statement does not allow wild-card characters. In other words, you can't use this statement to copy multiple files at once. To manipulate files en masse, use the FileSystemObject described in Chapter 10, "Scripting Objects."

Name oldpath As newpath

The Name statement renames a disk file or folder. The existing file or folder's name is specified with the *oldpath* argument, and the new name is specified with the *newpath* argument. The path specified by the *newpath* argument should not exist already. The word *As* in the syntax of the Name command is a keyword and must appear as is. The statement

```
Name "C:\Users" As "C:\All Users"
```

will rename the folder C:\Users to C:\All Users. The folder will be renamed even if it contains subfolders. If you attempt to rename two nested folders at once with a statement like the following one

```
Name "C:\Users\New User" As "C:\All Users\User1"
```

a runtime error will be generated. Rename them one at a time. (It doesn't make any difference which one is renamed first.)

The Name statement can rename a file and move it to a different directory or folder, if necessary. However, it can't move a folder (with or without its subfolders and files). If the D:\New User folder exists, the following statement will move the file UserProfile.cps to the folder New User on the D drive and rename it, as well:

```
Name "C:\AllUsers\User1\Profile1.cps" As "D:\New User\ _
UserProfile.cps"
```

If the folder D:\New User does not exist, it will not be created automatically. You must first create it and then move the file there. The Name statement cannot create a new file, directory, or folder.

Notice that the Name statement can not act on an open file. You must first close it and then rename it. Like most file and folder manipulation statements of Visual Basic, the Name statement's arguments don't recognize wildcard characters. To manipulate files or folders en masse, use the FileSystemObject described in Chapter 10, "Scripting Objects."

VARIABLE AND ARRAY DECLARATION

The following statements are used to declare variables, arrays, and external functions (such as the Windows API functions). They usually appear at the beginning of a module, and the scope of the variables, or functions, they declare is limited to the module in which the declaration appears. To declare variables that can be accessed by all the modules of an application, place the corresponding declarations in a general Module and prefix them with the keyword Public.

Dim

The Dim statement is used to declare variables and arrays. When you declare a variable before using it, Visual Basic allocates the appropriate memory to it, and the variable is ready to be used at runtime. There's a slight overhead in setting up a variable, so it's best to declare variables before using them. If you do not, Visual Basic will set up a new variable every time a new variable is referenced in your code. Even worse, without any additional information about the variable's type, Visual Basic will create a Variant (discussed shortly), which is the least effective variable type.

The syntax of the Dim statement is quite simple, but there are several ways to use it. To declare variables, use the following syntax:

```
Dim var_name As var_type
```

The variable's name is *var_name*, and its type is *var_type*. Visual Basic supports the following data types: Integer, Long, Currency, Single, Double, Byte, String, Boolean, Date, and Variant. In addition, you can specify user-defined types (which have already been defined with the Type...End Type statement) and objects.

You can use the Dim statement to declare single variables, as shown here:

```
Dim counter As Long
Dim length As Double
```

You can also combine multiple declarations in the same line:

```
Dim counter As Long, length As Double
```

If you declare variables without type, Visual Basic creates Variants for you. The statement

```
Dim var1, var2
```

will create two variables of the Variant variety. (They can store all types of information, but some overhead is required before they can be used in a calculation.) Notice that the statement

```
Dim i, j As Integer
```

will not create two integer variables. The first one does not have a type, and it's assumed to be a Variant. The second one is an integer variable.

When variables are initialized, a numeric variable is initialized to 0, a variable-length string is initialized to a zero-length string (""), and a fixed-length string is filled with zero characters (Chr(0)). Variant variables are initialized to Empty. Each element of a user-defined type variable is initialized as if it were a separate variable.

The Dim statement is used to declare arrays, too. When you declare an array, you must supply a pair of parentheses next to its name. In most cases, the array's dimensions appear between the parentheses. To declare an array of 100 integers, use the statement

```
Dim scores(99) As Integer
```

The only difference between declaring variables and arrays is the parentheses that follow the array's name, which enclose the array's size. The number in the parentheses is the subscript of the last element of the array. Array subscripts (or array indexing, as it's sometimes called) start at 0. The first element of the previous array is scores(0), the second one is scores(1), and so on up to the last element, which is scores(99).

This is the default behavior of Visual Basic, and you can change it with the Option Base 1 statement, which tells Visual Basic to start indexing arrays with 1 instead of 0. You can bypass the default subscripting methods of Visual Basic by specifying explicitly the lower and upper bounds of an array with the *To* keyword:

```
Dim Names(1 To 15) As String
Dim Salary(1 To 15) As Currency
```

The array's lower bound can have any other value, provided it's smaller than the upper bound value. The following statements are valid, although most arrays start at 0 or 1:

```
Dim Array1(10 To 20) As Double
Dim Array2(100 to 900) As Long
```

You can even specify negative subscripts, should your application require a really odd indexing scheme:

```
Dim OddArray(-10 to 10) As Double
```

In some situations we want to store sets of multidimensional data. Let's say you want to store city names and city temperatures. One way to do so is to declare two arrays, as the following code shows:

```
Dim Cities(100) As String
Dim Temperatures(100) As Single
```

(From now on, we'll assume that the Option 1 is in effect to avoid the zero array indexing oddity).

You can also declare multidimensional arrays, with a statement like the following:

```
Dim CityTemperatures(2, 100)
```

This array consists of 2 columns and 100 rows. The first column stores city names, and the second row stores temperatures. The two cells on the same row must match. (They should contain a city and the city's temperature.) That's why the array was dimensioned without a type. If all elements hold the same data type, you could have assigned a type to the array. Finally, you can create a custom data type like the following:

```
Type CityTemp
   City As String
   Temperature As Single
End Type
```

Then declare an array of this type with a statement like

```
Dim CityTemperatures(100) As CityTemp
```

(For more information on custom data types, see the entry Type...End Type in this reference).

The benefit of using multidimensional arrays is that they are conceptually easier to manage. Suppose you're writing a game and you want to track the positions of the pieces on the board. Each square on the board is identified by two numbers: its horizontal and vertical coordinates. The obvious structure for tracking the board's squares is a two-dimensional array, in which the first index corresponds to the row number, and the second index corresponds to the column number. The array could be declared as follows:

```
Dim Board(10, 10) As Integer
```

When a piece is moved from the square on the first row and first column to the square on the third row and fifth column, you assign the value 0 to the element that corresponds to the initial position:

```
Board(1, 1) = 0
```

Then, you assign the value 1 to the element that corresponds to the square to which it was moved, indicating the new state of the board:

```
Board(3, 5) = 1
```

This notation can be extended to more than two dimensions. The following statement creates an array with 1,000 elements (10 x 10 x 10):

```
Dim Matrix(10, 10, 10) As Integer
```

You can think of three-dimensional arrays as cubes made up of overlaid two-dimensional arrays.

Sometimes you don't know how large to make an array in advance. Instead of making it large enough to hold the maximum number of data (which means that most of the array may be empty), you can declare a Dynamic array. The size of a Dynamic array can vary during the course of execution of the application. Or you might need an array until the user has entered a bunch of data, and the application has processed it and displayed the results. Why keep the data in memory, when the information is no longer needed? With a Dynamic array, you can discard the data and return the resources occupied by the array to the system.

To create a Dynamic array, declare it as usual with the Dim statement, but don't specify its dimensions:

```
Dim DynArray() As Long
```

Later in the program, when you know how many elements you want to store in the array, use the ReDim statement to redimension the array, this time specifying the actual size of the array:

```
ReDim DynArray(userCount)
```

In this statement, *userCount* is a variable that has been initialized by the application.

For more information on the ReDim statement, see the "ReDim" section later in this reference.

Finally, you can use the Dim statement to declare objects of any type. An object could be an instance of a control on a Form, such as the TextBox control, the Form itself, or any object exposed by a server application. Like variables, objects can be declared as generic or of a specific type. It's recommended that you declare objects using specific types whenever possible.

The following statement declares an object variable that represents a CommandButton control:

```
Dim myButton As CommandButton
```

The *myButton* variable is an object variable because it references an object. At this point, it's capable of referencing a CommandButton, but it doesn't refer to any object. To assign a value to this object variable, use the Set command, where *Command1* is the name of an existing Command Button:

```
Set myBox = Command1
```

Through the *myBox* variable you can manipulate the Command1 control. The statement

```
myBox.Caption = "Click me!"
```

will change the caption of the Command1 button on the Form to the specified string.

Object variables are commonly used to access the objects exposed by other applications. For example, you can create an object variable that references the Document object exposed by Word. To do so, you must first add a reference to the Microsoft Word 8.0 Object Library (Project > References). Then, you can declare object variables that reference the Document object exposed by Word:

```
Dim WordDoc As New Word.Document
```

Through the *WordDoc* object variable you can access a new Word document and manipulate it from within your Visual Basic application (insert text, format it, print it, and so on). The *New* keyword tells Visual Basic to start a new instance of Word in the background and connect the WordDoc variable to a Word document.

The following lines show you how to start Word, use its spell checking capabilities from within your VB application, and shut down the instance of Word when done:

```
Dim WordObject As New Word.Application
Debug.Print WordObject.CheckSpelling("antroid")
Set WordObject = Nothing
```

The correct spelling is *android*, and the above statement will print False in the Immediate window.

With similar statements you can contact Excel, ask it to perform a few calculations, and return a result. When you're done, you must shut down Excel by setting the object variable that represents it to Nothing:

```
Dim ExcelObject As New Excel.Application
Debug.Print _
    ExcelObject.Evaluate("1/sin(0.044)*exp(3.09/log(999.99))")
Set ExcelObject = Nothing
```

This code segment will display the value 63.6812278964161 in the Immediate window.

To be able to reference Excel from within a Visual Basic application, don't forget to add a reference to the Microsoft Excel 8.0 Object Library to your project. For more information on object variables, see the entries CreateObject() and GetObject() in this reference.

Private, Public

These two keywords are equivalent to the Dim statement, in that they can be used to declare variables and arrays. Their syntax is identical to the syntax of the Dim statement. In addition, they modify the default scope of the variables. The Private keyword tells Visual Basic that the variable(s) is local to the module in which it's declared. In other words, variables can't be accessed from within other modules.

Another difference between the Private and Public keywords and the Dim statement is that the Private and Public keywords can also be used with procedures to modify the scope of the procedures (whether they can be called from within other project components or not).

Let's see how the Private and Public keywords are used in a Form. Create a new application, and add a new Form. The project should have two Forms: Form1 and Form2. All variables declared in Form1 (and outside any procedure) with the Dim statement are visible to all procedures in Form1, but you can't access them from within the code of Form2. The same is True if you declare them with the Private keyword. The procedures of Form1 are also local to Form1 and can't be accessed from within the code of Form2. If you want to be able to invoke an event handler in Form1 from within Form2, you must change the Private keyword that precedes the declaration to Public.

If Form1 contains a button named Command1 and you want to be able to invoke its Click event handler from within Form2, change the default declaration of the event handler from

```
Private Command1_Click()
  {your code}
End Sub
```

to

```
Public Command1_Click()
  {your code}
End Sub
```

Then, you can invoke this event handler from within the code of Form2 with the statement

```
Form1.Command1_Click
```

Likewise, if you want to declare some variables in Form1 that can be accessed from within the code of Form2, use the Public statement, as shown here:

```
Public var1, var2
```

These two variables can be accessed from within the code of Form2:

```
Form1.var1
```

and

```
Form1.var2
```

If some variables must be accessed from anywhere in the project's code, you should declare them in a Module with the Public statement. If you insert the following lines in a project's Module, then all the procedures in the project will see them:

```
Public Total As Long, Sum As Double
```

If there are variables that must be shared among the procedures of the Module but not by other project components, use the Private statement to declare them. If the following statement appears in a Module, then the variables *counter1* and *counter2* can be accessed from within any procedure that belongs to the Module but not from within procedures outside the Module.

```
Private counter1 As Integer, counter2 As Integer
```

Static

All variables declared in a procedure are local to the procedure, and every time you call the procedure, its local variables are initialized. If you want some variables to maintain their values between calls, declare them with the Static keyword. Let's say you're writing an application that calculates the average of a user-specified data set. You can store all values to an array and calculate the average after the last value has been entered. Or you can declare two variables at the Form level to keep track of the sum and the count of the data values. Here's a function that calculates the running average (a value that's updated every time a new data value is supplied):

```
Function RunningAverage(newValue As Double) As Double
    CurrentTotal = CurrentTotal + newValue
    TotalItems = TotalItems + 1
    RunningAverage = CurrentTotal / TotalItems
End Function
```

This function will work only if the variables *CurrentTotal* and *TotalItems* are declared outside the function (at the Form level).

You can avoid the introduction of two Form-wide variables by declaring them as Static in the function's body:

```
Function RunningAverage(newValue As Double) As Double
Static CurrentTotal As Double, TotalItems As Long
    CurrentTotal = CurrentTotal + newValue
    TotalItems = TotalItems + 1
    RunningAverage = CurrentTotal / TotalItems
End Function
```

The first time this function is called, the *CurrentTotal* and *TotalItems* variables are zero. After that, they keep increasing because they maintain their value between calls. The advantage of using static variables is that they help you minimize the number of total variables in the application. All you need is the running average, which the RunningAverage() function provides without making its variables' values visible from within other procedures.

You can declare all the variables in a procedure as static by prefixing the procedure definition with the keyword *Static*. The function could have been declared as

```
Static Function RunningAverage(newValue As Double) As Double)
```

and the local variables could be declared with the Dim statement as usual. The keyword *Static* may appear in front of every subroutine or function, including event handlers.

ReDim [Preserve] array_name [As array_type]

The ReDim statement changes the dimensions of a Dynamic array. Dynamic arrays must be declared with a pair of parentheses following their names, without any dimensions:

```
Dim DynArray() As Long
```

Later in your code you can redimension this array with the ReDim statement:

```
ReDim DynArray(100)
```

The ReDim statement doesn't require a data type because you can't change its type. If the original type was Variant, you are allowed to change its type to a different one the first time you redimension it. Let's assume that you have declared a Dynamic array of Variants with the statement

```
Dim Varray()
```

After the following statement has been executed, the array can no longer change its type:

```
ReDim Varray(100) As Long
```

In addition to changing a Dynamic array's type, you can change its dimensions, too. The DynArray() of the first example can be resized with the following statement:

```
ReDim DynArray(9, 9, 9)
```

Once the array has been redimensioned the first time, its number of dimensions can no longer change. It must remain a three-dimensional array. However, you can change its bounds with another ReDim statement:

```
ReDim DynArray(20, 20, 20)
```

Each time you execute the ReDim statement, all the values currently stored in the array are lost. Visual Basic resets the values of the elements as if they were just declared. (Variants are reset to Empty values, numeric types to 0, and string values to zero-length strings, "".) It is possible to change the size of the array without losing its data. The *Preserve* keyword tells Visual Basic to resize the array without discarding the existing data. For example, you can enlarge an array by one element, without losing the values of the existing elements. You can do this by using the UBound() function, as shown in this code:

```
ReDim Preserve DynArray(UBound(DynArray) + 1)
```

There's a catch with redimensioning Dynamic arrays with the *Preserve* keyword: only the last dimension can change. Let's say you've declared a Dynamic array with the statement

```
Dim DynArray() As Long
```

and later you redimension it as

```
ReDim DynArray(10, 10, 10)
```

If you have to redimension it again, yet maintain its data, you can only change the last dimension:

```
ReDim Preserve DynArray(10, 10, 20)
```

If you attempt to change the upper bound of another dimension, a trappable runtime error will be generated.

Erase array_list

The Erase statement "erases" one or more arrays, as specified in the *array_list* argument. When a fixed-size array is erased, its elements are reinitialized, but its dimensions remain the same. This means that the data is lost, but the memory allocated to the array is not returned to the system. Here's how array elements are initialized:

Numeric array	Each element is reset to zero.
Variable-length string array	Each element is reset to a zero-length string ("").
Fixed-length string array	Each element is reset to character Chr(0).
Variant array	Each element is set to Empty.
Array of objects	Each element is set to Nothing.

When the Erase statement is used with a Dynamic array, the memory allocated to the array is also freed. This brings the array to the state it was in after the execution of the statement

```
Dim DynArray()
```

After erasing a Dynamic array, you must redimension it with the ReDim statement. The ReDim statement could also change the dimensions of the array, as if it had never been used before.

DefType

Visual Basic provides a number of statements that set the default type of the variables in a module, based on the first character of their name. The syntax of all these statements is similar. The DefType statement is followed by a range of letters. Variables beginning with a letter in the specified range are automatically declared with the type determined by the DefType statement. The DefType statements are shown next (actually, there's no DefType statement; only the Defxxx statements listed here):

DefBool	Boolean variable	**DefByte**	Byte variable
DefInt	Integer variable	**DefLng**	Long variable
DefCur	Currency variable	**DefSng**	Single variable
DefDbl	Double variable	**DefDate**	Time and Date variable

DefStr	String variable	**DefObj**	Object variable
DefVar	Variant variable		

The DefType statement can be followed by one or more characters separated with commas. The following statement specifies that all variables beginning with *A* or *D* (like *aCounter* or *Age*) are integer variables:

```
DefInt A, D
```

You can specify ranges of letters, using a hyphen, as in the following statement:

```
DefInt A-D, Q-Z
```

This statement specifies that all variables beginning with a letter in the ranges *A* through *D* and *Q* through *Z* are integer variables. You can overwrite the default declaration with the usual variable declaration statements. The following statement declares a Currency variable, even if a previous DefType statement has declared all variables beginning with *A* as integers:

```
Dim Amount As Currency
```

Const

The Const statement is similar to the Dim statement; only instead of declaring variables, it declares constants. A constant is a symbolic name (like a variable) for a value that doesn't change during the course of the application. Math applications, for example, may frequently use the π constant (3.14159...). This value may be used in many calculations, but it doesn't change at run time. Constant values should be declared with the Const statement, so that you can't change them in your code by mistake. Even more important, Visual Basic can handle constants faster than regular variables.

To declare the constant π, use the following statement:

```
Const pi As Double = 3.14159265358979
```

If you don't declare the constant's type with the *As* keyword, Visual Basic uses the type that best describes the value of the constant. Notice that you can't use built-in functions in the declarations of constants. A convenient method for calculating the value of π is the following:

```
Pi = 4 * Atn(1)
```

Unfortunately, you can't use a declaration like the following one:

```
Const Pi As Double = 4 * Atn(1)    ' W R O N G
```

However, you can use other constants that have already been declared and the usual operators, as shown in the following example:

```
Const pi As Double = 3.14159265358979
Const pi2 As Double = 2 * pi
```

Enum...End Enum

A data type that can hold a small number of values is called Enumerated type. The Integer, Double, and other numeric data types are generic and can represent numeric values. If your application uses a variable that can take on only a limited number of integer values, you can use the Enumerated data type. Typical examples of enumerated types are the control properties that have limited values (which are also displayed in a drop-down list in the Properties window). The BackStyle property of many controls, for example, has two possible settings: 0-Opaque and 1-Transparent. You can't specify another value for this property in the Properties window.

To declare an enumerated data type, use the Enum statement, the syntax of which is shown here:

```
Enum name
    membername [= const]
    membername [= const]
    . . .
End Enum
```

The type's name is specified with the *name* argument; you can declare variables of this type with the Dim statement, just as you would declare custom data types with the Type statement. *membername* is an identifier that corresponds to a numeric value. Visual Basic uses numeric values, but in your code you can use more meaningful names.

The *const* argument is a constant that's mapped to the *membername*. If omitted, the first member has the value 0, the next one has the value 1, and so on. Let's say you are building a custom ActiveX control, and you want it to expose the TextAlignment property, which determines how the text is to be aligned on the control. A possible enumerated type for the TextAlignment property is shown here:

```
Enum Align
    [Top Left]
    [Top Middle]
    [Top Right]
    [Center Left]
    [Center Middle]
```

```
    [Center Right]
    [Bottom Left]
    [Bottom Middle]
    [Bottom Right]
End Enum
```

This declaration tells Visual Basic that any variable defined as Align can have the values 0 through 8. (Enumerated types correspond to numeric values, starting with 0.) The strings that appear in the declaration are synonyms of the corresponding numeric values, which will be displayed in the Properties window. The square brackets are necessary only if the corresponding strings have embedded spaces (or, in general, are invalid variable names).

The Property Get and Set procedures for the TextAlignment property must be declared as follows:

```
Public Property Get TextAlignment() As Align
    TextAlignment = m_TextAlignment
End Property

Public Property Let TextAlignment(ByVal New_TextAlignment As Align)
    m_TextAlignment = New_TextAlignment
    PropertyChanged "TextAlignment"
End Property
```

Notice that there's no need for validation code in the Property Let procedure because the user can't select an invalid value for this property in the Properties window. If you attempt to set an enumerated property to an invalid value from within your code, a trappable runtime error will be generated. For more information on Property procedures, see the corresponding entries in the section "Objects," later in this reference.

Declare

The Declare statement is used to declare references to external procedures, which are implemented as functions or subroutines in dynamic-link libraries (DLL). You can develop your own custom functions and package them as DLLs, using a language like Visual C++, but this isn't a common practice among VB programmers. Many VB programmers, however, often use API functions in their applications. API functions, which reside in the DLL files installed with Windows itself, must be declared before they can be used in a VB application.

Depending on whether you declare a function, or subroutine, the Declare statement has two forms:

```
Declare Sub name Lib "libname" [Alias "aliasname"] [arglist]
Declare Function name Lib "libname" [Alias "aliasname"] _
    [arglist] As type
```

The Declare statement can be prefixed by the keywords *Private* or *Public*. Procedures declared in a Form's code must be *Private*. Procedures declared in Modules can be either *Private* or *Public*, depending on the desired scope. If the procedures are going to be called from other procedures in the same Module and not from procedures in other Forms or Modules, they can be *Private*. Usually, DLL procedures are declared in Modules and are *Public*.

The *name* argument is the procedure's name. (DLL entry points are case sensitive.) The *libname* argument is the name of the DLL (library) that contains the procedure being declared. The argument *aliasname* is optional, indicating that the procedure being called has another name in the DLL. Aliases are used when the external procedure name is the same as a keyword. You can also use an alias when a DLL procedure has the same name as a public variable, constant, or any other procedure in the same scope. Aliases are also useful if any characters in the DLL procedure name aren't allowed by the DLL naming convention. If the first character of the alias is a number sign (#), it must be followed by a numeric value that indicates the ordinal number of the procedure's entry point. Finally, *arglist* is a list of arguments that are passed to the procedure when it's called. If the procedure being declared is a function, it must be followed by the type of value it returns.

The arguments are declared just like the arguments of a VB procedure. Because most DLL procedures used in Visual Basic projects belong to the Windows API, their arguments are usually passed by value, not by reference (the default argument-passing mechanism of Visual Basic). When an argument value is passed by value, Visual Basic makes a copy of the original value and passes the copy to the procedure. As a result, the procedure can't alter the original variable in the calling program. Even if the procedure changes the value of the argument, the calling program doesn't see the changes. Arguments are declared as follows:

```
ByVal|ByRef argument_name As argument_type
```

The name of the argument is *argument_name*, and the type of the argument is *argument_type*.

Normally, when you call a DLL procedure, Visual Basic checks the number of arguments and their types against the ones specified in the procedure declaration. If they don't match, Visual Basic raises a trappable runtime error. If not, an error in DLL would occur with unpredictable results. Because DLL procedures are developed in languages such as Visual C++ or Delphi and these languages don't share the same data types as Visual Basic, you may not be able to map the argument's type to a standard Visual Basic data type. In these cases, you can use the Any data type. When an argument is declared with the Any type, Visual Basic doesn't check the type of the actual argument before passing it to the procedure. It's your responsibility to make sure that the actual value you pass to the procedure is of the proper type.

VB programmers use the Declare statement almost exclusively with API function declarations. For more information on declaring Windows API functions, see Chapter 7, "Visual Basic and the Windows API."

Here's the declaration of an API function that's commonly used in VB applications. The sndPlaySound() function plays back a WAV sound file, and it must be declared as follows:

```
Declare Function sndPlaySound Lib "WINMM.DLL" Alias _
    "sndPlaySoundA" (lpszSoundName As Any, _
    ByVal uFlags As Long) As Long
```

The first argument, *lpszSoundName*, is the name of the WAV file to be played back or the name of an array that holds the samples of the sound. The second argument, *uFlags*, can have one of the following values:

```
Global Const SND_ASYNC = &H1
Global Const SND_NODEFAULT = &H2
Global Const SND_MEMORY = &H4
```

To play back the file C:\SOUNDS\WELCOME.WAV call the sndPlaySound() function as follows:

```
success = sndPlaySound("C:\SOUNDS\WELCOME.WAV", _
    SND_ASYNC Or SND_NODEFAULT Or SND_MEMORY)
```

As you can see, after an API function (or any other function stored in a DLL) has been declared in the application's module, it can be called as if it were a built-in function.

VARIABLE TYPES

The following functions examine array and variable types. Some functions let you determine a variable's exact type from within your code, and a series of functions determine the general type of a variable (such as numeric, date, and so on). In addition, three functions let you populate array elements and quickly check array bounds.

VarType(variable)

The VarType() function returns a value indicating the subtype of a variable, according to Table LR.7. The *variable* argument is the actual name of a variable.

TABLE LR.7: The Values Returned by the VarType() Function

CONSTANT	VALUE	DESCRIPTION
vbEmpty	0	Empty (uninitialized)
vbNull	1	Null (no valid data)
vbInteger	2	Integer
vbLong	3	Long integer
vbSingle	4	Single-precision floating-point number
vbDouble	5	Double-precision floating-point number
vbCurrency	6	Currency value
vbDate	7	Date value
vbString	8	String
vbObject	9	Object
vbError	10	Error value
vbBoolean	11	Boolean value
vbVariant	12	Variant (used only with arrays of variants)
vbDataObject	13	A data-access object
vbDecimal	14	Decimal value
vbByte	17	Byte value
vbArray	8192	Array

The VarType() function doesn't return the type of an array's elements directly. Instead, the value of the elements' type is added to 8192. If you pass array of strings to the VarType() function, the return value is 8200 (which is 8192 + 8).

TypeName(variable_name)

This function returns a string that identifies the variable's type. It's similar to the VarType() function, only instead of returning an integer, it returns the name of the variable's type. The variable whose type you're examining with the TypeName function may have been declared implicitly or explicitly. Suppose you declare the following variables:

```
Dim name As String
Dim someVar
```

The following statements produce the results shown. (You can issue the statements in the Debug window and watch the values they return in the same window.)

```
Print TypeName(name)
    String
Print TypeName(someVar)
    Empty
someVar = "I'm a string"
Print TypeName(someVar)
    String
someVar = #5/11/97#
Print TypeName(someVar)
    Date
Print TypeName(anotherVar)
    Empty
```

Notice that the variable *anotherVar,* which wasn't declared, is Empty but not Null.

Array(argument_list)

This function returns a Variant containing an array whose elements are assigned values from the *argument_list.* The *argument_list* variable is a comma-delimited list of values that are assigned to consecutive elements of the array. If you omit the *argument_list* variable, the Array() function will create an array with no elements. To use this array, you must redimension it with the ReDim command. The following statements create an array with the names of the days of the week:

```
Dim WeekDays
WeekDays = Array("Monday", "Tuesday", "Wednesday",
"Thursday", "Friday", Saturday", "Sunday")
FirstDay = WeekDays(0)     ' Monday
SecondDay = WeekDays(1)     ' Tuesday
```

The lower bound of an array created using the Array function is always 0. Notice also that the Array function *does not dimension the array*. It only assigns values to its elements.

By the way, if you need weekday or month names, use the Weekday-Name() and MonthName() functions.

LBound(array_name[, dimension])

This function returns the smallest subscript for the indicated dimension of an array. The *array_name* variable is the name of the array, and *dimension* is an integer indicating the dimension whose lower bound will be returned. If *dimension* is omitted, the first dimension is assumed. The LBound() function returns the smallest subscript of a dimension of a given array. You must use both the Lbound() and Ubound functions to determine the size of the array.

UBound(array_name[, dimension])

This function returns the largest subscript for the indicated dimension of an array. The *array_name* variable is the name of the array, and *dimension* is an integer indicating the dimension whose upper bound will be returned. If *dimension* is omitted, the first dimension is assumed.

To scan all the elements of a one-dimensional array, use both the LBound() and the UBound() functions. The following statements convert the elements of the string array *Strings()* to uppercase:

```
Lower = LBound(Strings)
Upper = UBound(Srtings)
For i = Lower to Upper
    Strings(i) = Ucase(Strings(i))
Next
```

IsArray(variable)

This function returns True if its argument is an array. If the variable *Strings* has been defined as `Dim Strings(100)`, the function `IsArray(Strings)` returns True.

IsDate(expression)

This function returns True if *expression* is a valid date. Use the IsDate() function to validate user data. Dates can be specified in various formats, and validating them without the help of the IsDate() function would be a task on its own.

```
Bdate = InputBox("Please enter your birth date")
If IsDate(BDate) Then
    MsgBox "Date accepted"
End If
```

IsEmpty(variable)

This function returns True if the *variable* is empty. (An empty variable hasn't been initialized or explicitly set to Empty.) After the execution of the following statements, the variables *numVar* and *stringVar* are not empty because they have been initialized:

```
numVar = 0
stringVar = ""
```

If a variable has not been declared with a Dim statement, or otherwise used by your program, it's empty. A variable that has been declared is not empty; when a variable is declared, it is also initialized. The following code segment demonstrates Empty variables:

```
Dim Var1 As Integer

If IsEmpty(Var1) Then
  MsgBox "Variable Var1 is empty"
Else
  MsgBox "Variable Var1 has been initialized"
End If

If IsEmpty(Var2) Then
  MsgBox "Variable Var2 is empty"
Else
  MsgBox "Variable Var2 has been initialized"
End If
```

If you execute these statements (place them in the Click event of a Command Button), you will see two message boxes indicating that *Var1* has been initialized and *Var2* is Empty.

IsNull(expression)

This function returns True if *expression* is Null. A Null value is an invalid value and is different from an Empty value. Regular variables can't be Null; only Object variables can be Null.

Uninitialized variables that refer to database fields are Null, not Empty, and are frequently used in programs that access databases:

```
If Not IsNull(fldName) Then
  {process field fldName}
Else
  {skip field}
End If
```

IsNumeric(expression)

This function returns True if *expression* is a valid number. Use this function to check the validity of strings containing numeric data as follows:

```
age = InputBox("Please enter your age")
If Not IsNumeric(age) Then
  MsgBox("Please try again, this time with a valid number")
End If
```

IsError(expression)

The IsError() function returns True if its argument is a variant of Error type. The Error type allows you to write functions that can return a value (if the calculations were carried out successfully) or an error value (if the calculations failed). The IsError() function and its use in programming is discussed in the CVErr() entry in the section "Variable Type Conversion Functions."

IsObject(expression)

This function returns a Boolean (True/False) value indicating whether *expression* represents an object variable. To find out the type of object, use the TypeName() or VarType() functions, which are described next.

Type...End Type

Most programs don't manipulate isolated variables or even arrays of data of the same type. They manipulate sets of data of different types. A checkbook-balancing application, for instance, must store several pieces of information for each check: the check's number, its amount, the date, and so on. All these pieces of information are necessary to process the checks, and ideally, they should be stored together.

A structure for storing multiple values (of the same or different type) is called a *record*. Each entry in the checkbook-balancing application is stored in a separate record, which contains all the items of a specific check, and each check is stored in a different record, as well. Because the type of information required for each check is the same (only the values change), the records must also have the same structure.

To define a record in Visual Basic, use the Type statement, which has the following syntax:

```
Type varType
    Variable1 As varType1
    Variable2 As VarType2
    ...
    VariableN As VarTypeN
End Type
```

VariableX is a variable name, and *varTypeX* is a data type. With a declaration like this, you have, in essence, created a new (custom) data type that you can use in your applications. You can declare variables of this type and manipulate them as you manipulate all other variables (with a little extra typing). The declaration for the record structure of a checkbook-balancing application could be something like the following:

```
Type CheckRecord
    CheckNumber As Integer
    CheckDate As Date
    CheckAmount As Currency
    CheckPaidTo As String * 50
End Type
```

The *CheckRecord* structure can be used in the same way as regular variables. To define variables of this type, use a statement such as

```
Private check1 As CheckRecord, check2 As CheckRecord
```

To assign values to these variables, you must separately assign a value to each one of its components (they are called *fields*), which can be accessed by combining the name of the variable and the name of a field with a period between them, as follows:

```
Check1.Number = 275
```

You can think of the record as an object and its fields as properties. Here are the assignment statements for a check:

```
check2.CheckNumber = 275
check2.CheckDate = #02/12/98#
check2.CheckAmount = 104.25
check2.CheckPaidTo = "Gas Co."
```

You can also create arrays of records with a statement like

```
Private Checks(100) As CheckRecord
```

Each element in this array is a *CheckRecord* record and holds all the fields of a given check. To access the fields of the third element of the array, use the following notation:

```
checks(2).CheckNumber = 275
checks(2).CheckDate = #02/12/98#
checks(2).CheckAmount = 104.25
checks(2).CheckPaidTo = "Gas Co."
```

Records are frequently used to read from and write to random-access files. For more information using files, see the entries in the File I/O section of this reference.

The Type statement can be used only at module level. Once you have declared a custom data type with the Type statement, you can declare variables of that type anywhere within the scope of the declaration. In standard modules and class modules, user-defined types are public by default. This visibility can be changed using the *Private* keyword. To use the Type statement in a code module, prefix it with the Private keyword.

Finally, you can assign a custom type variable to another one with the same type, as demonstrated by the following example. If you place the following lines in the Click event of a Command button and then execute them, the fields of the *check2* variable will have the same values as the fields of the *check1* variable:

```
Dim check1 As CheckRecord, check2 As CheckRecord
    check1.CheckNumber = 275
    check1.CheckDate = #2/12/1998#
    check1.CheckAmount = 104.25
    check1.CheckPaidTo = "Gas Co."
    check2 = check1
Debug.Print check2.CheckNumber
Debug.Print check2.CheckDate
Debug.Print check2.CheckAmount
Debug.Print check2.CheckPaidTo
```

VARIABLE TYPE CONVERSION

These functions convert their numeric argument to another type (whenever this is possible). With the introduction of the Variant data type, these functions are of little use. You can use them to document your code and show that the result of an operation should be of the particular type. Keep in mind, however, that all operands in an arithmetic operation are first converted to double precision numbers for the greatest possible accuracy. Table LR.8 lists the Variable Type Conversion functions and describes what they do.

TABLE LR.8: The Variable Type Conversion Functions

FUNCTION	WHAT IT DOES
CBool(expression)	Converts its argument to Boolean (True/False) type.
CByte(expression)	Converts its argument to Byte type.
CCur(expression)	Converts its argument to Currency type.
CDate(expression)	Converts its argument to Date type.
CDec(expression)	Converts its argument to Decimal type.
CDbl(expression)	Converts its argument to Double type.
CInt(expression)	Converts its argument to Integer type.
CLng(expression)	Converts its argument to Long type.
CSng(expression)	Converts its argument to Single type.
CStr(expression)	Converts its argument to String type.
CVar(expression)	Converts its argument to Variant type. Numeric expressions are converted to doubles, and alphanumeric expressions are converted to strings.

CVErr()

This function accepts as an argument a numeric value (which is an error number) and returns a variant of Error type containing the specified error number. The CVErr() function does not generate a runtime error. It can be the return value of a function, which may return a result (if no error occurred), or it can be an error object (if something went wrong during its execution).

Let's say you have written the Calculate() function, which performs some complicated operations and returns a result. If everything goes well, the Calculate() function will return its result as usual. If an error occurs during the calculations, the function should return an error object. In the Calculate() function, you could use the following lines:

```
If Err.Number <> 0 Then
   Calculate = CVError()
```

```
      Else
         Calculate = XFinal
      End If
```

The procedure that calls the Calculate() function can examine the function's return value and determine whether an error occurred:

```
      Result = Calculate(arguments)
      If IsError(Result) Then
         {handle error}
      Else
         {continue}
      End If
```

The *Result* variable must be a Variant so that it can store both the actual result (a Double, for math calculations) and the error object returned by the function. Therefore, the Calculate() function's return type must also be Variant.

STRING MANIPULATION

The following functions manipulate strings. Visual Basic provides an impressive array of functions for string manipulation, as the average application spends most of its time operating on strings and not numbers. This group contains a single statement, the Mid statement, which happens to have the same name as the Mid() function.

Asc(string), AscB(string), AscW(string)

The Asc() function returns the character code corresponding to the *string* argument, and it works on all systems, regardless of whether they support Unicode characters. The Asc(), AscB() and AscW() functions will process the first character of the string and ignore the rest of them (if they exist). The following function calls will both return the value 65—the ASCII value of the character *A*:

```
      Debug.Print Asc("A")
      Debug.Print Asc("ABC")
```

The AscB() function is similar, except that instead of returning the character code for the first character, it returns the first byte.

The AscW() function returns the Unicode character code except on platforms that do not support Unicode, in which case, the behavior is identical to that of the Asc() function.

Chr(number), ChrB(number), ChrW(number)

The Chr() function is the inverse of the Asc() function and returns the character associated with the specified character code. Use this function to print characters that don't appear on the keyboard (such as line feeds or special symbols). To insert a tab in a string, use a statement like the following:

```
Debug.Print "Col 1" & Chr(9) & "Col 2"
```

The ChrB() function is used with byte data contained in a string. Instead of returning a character, which may be one or two bytes, ChrB() always returns the ASCII value of a single byte.

The ChrW() function returns a string containing the Unicode character, except on platforms that don't support Unicode, in which case, the behavior is identical to that of the Chr() function.

LCase(string), UCase(string)

The LCase() function accepts a string as an argument and converts it to lowercase; the UCase() function does the opposite: it accepts a string as an argument and converts it to uppercase. After these statements are executed

```
Title = "VB6 Complete"
LTitle = LCase(Title)
UTitle = UCase(Title)
```

the variable *LTitle* contains the string "vb6 complete," and the variable *UTitle* contains the string "VB6 COMPLETE." Notice that the LCase() and UCase() functions know how to handle numbers, punctuation and other special symbols.

To demonstrate these two functions, we'll build a function that converts a string so that it has title capitalization. In other words, the function will convert all the characters in the string to lowercase and then convert the first character of each word to uppercase. (Visual Basic provides a built-in function that does the same thing, the StrConv() function, discussed later in this section.) You can write a LowerCaps() function, which uses the UCase() and LCase() functions, as follows:

```
Function LowerCaps(str As String) As String

position = InStr(str, " ") ' Locate first space
While position ' while there are spaces in the string
   newWord = Left$(str, position) ' extract word
   ' and convert its first character to upper case
   newStr = newStr & UCase$(Left$(newWord, 1)) & Mid$(newWord, 2)
```

```
    str = Right$(str, Len(str) - position) ' remove word from _
    string
      position = InStr(str, " ")
Wend
newWord = str ' convert the last word in the string
newStr = newStr & UCase$(Left$(newWord, 1)) & Mid$(newWord, 2)
LowerCaps = newStr ' return string in Lower Caps

End Function
```

The LowerCaps() function uses the Instr() built-in function to locate successive instances of the space character in the string (the InStr() function is discussed next). It then isolates the words between spaces, changes their first characters to uppercase and the rest of the characters to lowercase, and appends them to the *NewStr* string. When the function exits, its value is the original string formatted in lower caps. If you call the Lower-Caps() function with the following argument

```
CompanyName = "ABC industrial, inc."
UCString = LowerCaps(CompanyName)
```

the *UCString* variable's value will be

```
"ABC Industrial, Inc."
```

InStr([startPos,] string1, string2[, compare]) and InStrB([startPos,] string1, string2[, compare])

The InStr() function returns the position of *string2* within *string1*. The first argument, which is optional, determines where in *string1* the search begins. If the *startPos* argument is omitted, the search begins at the first character of *string1*. If you execute the following statements

```
str1 = "The quick brown fox jumped over the lazy dog"
str2 = "the"
Pos = InStr(str1, str2)
```

the variable *Pos* will have the value 33. If you search for the string "he" by setting

```
str2 = "he"
```

the *Pos* variable's value will be 2. If the search begins at the third character in the string, the first instance of the string "he" after the third character will be located:

```
Pos = InStr(3, str1, str2)
```

This time the *Pos* variable will be 34.

The search is by default case sensitive. To locate "the", "The", or "THE" in the string, specify the last optional argument whose value is 0 (default) for a case-sensitive search and 1 for a case-insensitive search.

The following statement locates the first occurrence of "the" in the string, regardless of case:

```
str1 = "The quick brown fox jumped over the lazy dog"
str2 = "the"
Pos = InStr(1, str1, str2, 1)
```

The value of *Pos* will be 1. If you set the last argument to 0, the *Pos* variable becomes 33. If you want to use the last optional argument of the InStr() function, you must also specify the first argument.

The InStrB() function is used with byte data contained in a string. Instead of returning the character position of the first occurrence of one string within another, InStrB() returns the byte position.

InStrRev(string1, string2[, start][, compare])

This function returns the position of one string within another, as does the InStr() function, but it starts from the end of the string. The *string1* argument is the string being searched, and the *string2* argument is the string being searched for. The other two arguments are optional. The *start* argument is the starting position for the search. If it is omitted, the search begins at the last character. The *compare* argument indicates the kind of comparison to be used in locating the substrings, and its values are explained in the InStr() entry above. If the *compare* argument is *omitted,* a case-sensitive (or binary) comparison is performed.

StrComp(string1, string2 [, compare])

This function compares two strings and returns a value indicating the result, according to Table LR.9.

TABLE LR.9: The Values That the StrComp() Function Returns

VALUE	DESCRIPTION
-1	*string1* is less than *string2*
0	*string2* is equal to *string2*
1	*string1* is greater than *string2*
Null	*string1* and/or *string2* is Null

The last argument of the StrComp() function determines whether the comparison will be case sensitive. If *compare* is 0 (or omitted), the comparison is case sensitive. If it's 1, the comparison is case insensitive.

The following function

```
StrComp("Sybex", "SYBEX")
```

returns 1 ("Sybex" is greater than "SYBEX", because the lowercase *y* character is after the uppercase *Y* in the ASCII sequence). The following function performs a case-insensitive search and returns 0

```
StrComp("Sybex", "SYBEX", 1)
```

Left(string, number), LeftB(string, number)

This function returns a number of characters from the beginning of a string. It accepts two arguments: the string and the number of characters to extract. If the string *date1* starts with the month name, the following Left() function can extract the month's abbreviation from the string, as follows:

```
date1 = "December 25, 1999"
MonthName = Left(date1, 3)
```

The value of the *MonthName* variable is "Dec".

Use the LeftB() function with byte data contained in a string. Instead of specifying the number of characters, the arguments specify numbers of bytes.

Right(string, number), RightB(srting, number)

This function is similar to the Left function, except that it returns a number of characters from the end of a string. The following statement assigns the value "1999" to the *Yr* variable:

```
Yr = Right(date1, 4)
```

Use the RightB() function with byte data contained in a string. Instead of specifying the number of characters, the arguments specify numbers of bytes.

Mid(string, start, [length]), MidB(string, start[, length])

The Mid() function returns a section of a string of *length* characters, starting at position *start*. The following function extracts the name of the month from the specified string:

```
Mid("09 February, 1957", 4, 8)
```

If you omit the *length* argument, the Mid() function returns all the characters from the starting position to the end of the string. If the specified length exceeds the number of characters in the string after the start position, the remaining string from the start location is returned. The following statement returns all the characters of the string variable *strVar*, starting with the fifth character:

```
NewStr = Mid(strVar,5,len(s)-4)
```

A simpler, but equivalent, coding of the same line is the following:

```
NewStr = Mid(strVar, 5)
```

Use the MidB() function with byte data contained in a string. Instead of specifying the number of characters, the arguments specify numbers of bytes.

Mid(string, start, length) = new_string

In addition to the Mid() function, there's a Mid statement, which does the opposite. Instead of extracting a few characters from a string, the Mid statement replaces a specified number of characters in the *string* argument with another string (the argument *new_string*). The location and count of characters to be replaced are specified with the arguments *start* and *length*. These two arguments are optional. If the *start* argument is omitted, Visual Basic assumes it's the first character in the string. If the *length* argument is omitted, all the characters from the starting character to the end of the string will be replaced.

Let's say you're building a long string by appending characters to it, one at a time. Let's also assume that the characters are generated randomly. In a practical situation, the characters would be coming from a text file, a TextStream object, and so on. One way to code this operation would be the following:

```
For i = 1 To 255
  newString = newString & chr(rnd()*26+48)
Next
```

This is how most VB programmers would go about it. It doesn't take more than a few milliseconds to fill up the string, and the code works fine. If you change the length of the string from 255 to 20,000, however, you'll find out that it takes Visual Basic nearly 40 seconds to generate the string. (That's how it long it took on my Pentium 233 system.) Let's see how this time can be improved with the help of the Mid statement. This time, we'll start with a string variable of 20,000 characters:

```
Dim newString As String * 20000
```

Alternatively, you can create a string of 20,000 spaces with the statement

```
newString = Space(20000)
```

Then modify the loop, so that instead of appending characters to the *newString* variable, it replaces the existing ones:

```
For i = 1 To 20000
   Mid(newString, i, 1) = Chr(rnd()*26+48)
Next
```

This loop will fill the 20,000-character string in less than a second. Keep in mind that Mid is also a statement, and it can simplify your code.

Len(string), LenB(string)

The Len() function returns the length of a string. After the following statements, execute

```
Name = InputBox("Enter your first Name")
NameLen = Len(Name)
```

The variable *NameLen* contains the length of the string entered by the user in the Input Box.

The Len() function is frequently used as a first test for invalid input, as in the following lines:

```
If Len(Trim(Name)) = 0 Then
   MsgBox "NAME field can't be empty"
Else
   MsgBox "Thank you for registering with us"
EndIf
```

The Trim() function, discussed next, removes leading and trailing spaces, so that a string made up of spaces will not be accepted.

Use the LenB() function with byte data contained in a string. Instead of returning the number of characters in a string, LenB() returns the number of bytes used to represent that string.

LTrim(string), RTrim(string), Trim(string)

These functions trim the spaces in front of, after, and on either side of a string respectively. They are frequently used in validating user input, as in the following string:

```
If EMail <> "" Then
   MsgBox "Applications without an e-mail address won't be _
processed"
End If
```

The preceding won't, however, catch a string that only has spaces. To detect empty strings, use the Trim() function instead:

```
If Trim(EMail) = "" Then
    MsgBox "Invalid Entry!"
End If
```

Str(number)

The Str() function converts a numeric value to a string. The *number* argument can be any numeric expression that evaluates to a Long value. When numbers are converted to strings, a leading space is always reserved for the sign of the number. This space is filled with the minus sign for negative numbers and remains unchanged for positive numbers.

The functions

```
Str(100 - 0.99)
Str(-99.01)
```

will return the strings " 99.01" and "-99.01" respectively.

The Str() function is included for compatibility reasons and you should use either the CStr() function, or the Format() function to convert numeric values to strings.

Space(number)

This function returns a string consisting of the specified number of spaces. The *number* argument is the number of spaces you want in the string. This function is useful for formatting output and initializing fixed-length strings.

String(number, character)

This function returns a string of *number* characters, all of which are *character*. The following function returns the string "************":

```
String(12, "*")
```

Use the String() function to create long patterns of special symbols.

StrConv(string, conversion)

This function returns a string variable converted as specified by the *conversion* argument, whose values as shown in Table LR.10.

TABLE LR.10: The Values Returned by the StrConv() Function

CONSTANT	VALUE	DESCRIPTION
vbUpperCase	1	Converts the string to uppercase characters (similar to the LCase() function)
vbLowerCase	2	Converts the string to lowercase characters (similar to the UCase() function)
vbProperCase	3	Converts the first letter of every word in the string to uppercase
vbWide*	4*	Converts narrow (single-byte) characters in the string to wide (double-byte) characters
vbNarrow*	8*	Converts wide (double-byte) characters in the string to narrow (single-byte) characters
vbKatakana*	16*	Converts Hiragana characters in the string to Katakana characters
vbHiragana*	32*	Converts Katakana characters in the string to Hiragana characters
vbUnicode	64	Converts the string to Unicode using the default code page of the system
vbFromUnicode	128	Converts the string from Unicode to the default code page of the system

*Applies to Far East locales.

To perform multiple conversions, add the corresponding values. To convert a string to lowercase and to Unicode format, use a statement such as the following:

```
newString = StrConv(txt, vbLowerCase + vbUnicode)
```

StrReverse(string)

This function reverses the character order of its argument. Its syntax is

```
StrReverse(string1)
```

The *string1* argument is the string whose characters will be reversed.

Filter(InputStrings, Value [, Include [, Compare]])

This function returns a zero-based array containing part of a string array, based on specified filter criteria. The *InputStrings* argument is a one-dimensional array of the strings to be searched, and the *Value* argument is the string to search for. The last two arguments are optional, and they indicate whether the function should contain substrings that include or exclude the specified value. If True, the Filter() function returns the subset of the array that contains *Value* as a substring. If False, the Filter() function returns the subset of the array that does not contain *Value* as a substring. The *Compare* argument indicates the kind of string comparison to be used, and it can be any of the values in Table LR.11.

TABLE LR.11: The Values of the *Compare* Argument

VALUE	WHAT IT DOES
vbBinaryCompare	Performs a binary (case-sensitive) comparison
vbTextCompare	Performs a textual (case-insensitive) comparison
vbDatabaseCompare	Performs a comparison based on information contained in the database in which the comparison is to be performed

The array returned by the Filter() function contains only enough elements to contain the number of matched items. To use the Filter() function, you must declare an array without specifying the number of elements. Let's say you have declared the *Names* array as follows:

```
Dim Names
Names = Array("Abe","John", "John", "Ron","Jimmy")
```

You can find out whether the name stored in the variable *myName* is in the *Names* array by calling the Filter function as follows:

```
b = Filter(a, myName)
```

If the name stored in the variable *myName* isn't part of the Names array, b is an array with no elements. The function

```
UBbound(b)
```

will return -1. If the name stored in the variable *myName* is "Abe," the upper bound of the array b will be 0, and the element b(0) will be "Abe." If the value of the *myName* variable is "John," the upper bound of the Names array will be 1 and the elements b(0) and b(1) will have the value "John."

You can also create an array that contains all the elements in the original, except for a specific value. The array b, created with the statement

```
b = Filter(a,"Ron", False)
```

will have four elements, which are all of the elements of the array Names except for "Ron."

Replace(expression, find, replacewith[, start [, count [, compare]]])

This function returns a string in which a specified substring has been replaced with another substring a specified number of times. The *expression* argument is a string containing the string to be replaced, on which the Replace function acts. The *find* argument is the substring to be replaced, and *replacewith* is the replacement string. The remaining arguments are optional. The *start* argument is the character position where the search begins. If it is omitted, the search starts at the first character. The *count* argument is the number of replacements to be performed. If it is omitted, all possible replacements will take place. Finally, the *compare* argument specifies the kind of comparison to be performed. The values of the *compare* argument are described in the Filter entry.

The following statement will replace all instances of the word *the* to the word *a* in the *str1* string variable:

```
str2 = Replace(str1, "the", "a", , , vbTextCompare )
```

If the value of str1 is

```
str1 = "The quick brown fox jumped over the lazy dog"
```

then the following string will be stored in the variable str2 after the Replace() function is executed:

```
"a quick brown fox jumped over a lazy dog"
```

Join(list, delimiter)

This function returns a string created by joining a number of substrings contained in an array. The *list* argument is a one-dimensional array containing substrings to be joined, and the optional *delimiter* argument is a character used to separate the substrings in the returned string. If it is omitted, the space character (" ") is used. If *delimiter* is a zero-length string, all items in the list are concatenated with no delimiters. See the next entry for an example.

Split(expression [, delimiter [, count [, compare]]])

This function is the counterpart of the Join() function. It returns a zero-based, one-dimensional array containing a number of substrings. The *expression* argument is a string that contains the original string that will be broken into substrings, and the optional *delimiter* argument is a character used to delimit the substrings. If *delimiter* is omitted, the space character (" ") is assumed to be the delimiter. If *delimiter* is a zero-length string, a single-element array containing the entire expression string is returned. The *count* argument is also optional, and it determines the number of substrings to be returned. If it's -1, all substrings are returned. The last argument, *compare,* is also optional and indicates the kind of comparison to use when evaluating substrings. Its valid values are described in the Filter entry.

Let's say you have declared a string variable with the following path name:

```
path = "c:\win\desktop\ActiveX\Examples\VBSCRIPT"
```

The Split() function can extract the path's components and assign them to the parts array, with this statement:

```
parts = Split("c:\win\desktop\ActiveX\Examples\VBSCRIPT", "\")
```

To display the parts of the path, set up a loop such as the following:

```
For i = 0 To UBound(parts)
    MsgBox parts(i)
Next
```

The following statement will combine the members of the parts() array into a single string, using the backward slash ("/") as delimiter:

```
Debug.Print Join(parts,"/")
```

The string printed by the previous statement is

```
c:/win/desktop/ActiveX/Examples/VBSCRIPT
```

FORMATTING FUNCTIONS

Up through Visual Basic 5, there was only one function for formatting numbers and dates, the Format() function. Visual Basic 6 features a number of new formatting functions, which are specific to the data type they apply to (numbers, dollar amounts, and dates).

Format(expression[, format[, firstdayofweek[, firstweekofyear]]])

This function returns a string containing an expression formatted according to instructions specified with the *format* argument. The *expression* variable is the number, string, or date to be converted, and *format* is a string that tells Visual Basic how to format the value. The string "hh:mm.ss", for example, displays the expression as a time string. The Format() function is used to prepare numbers, dates, and strings for display. If you attempt to display the following expression

```
Print atn(1) * 4
```

then the number 3.14159265358979 is displayed. If this value must appear in a text control, chances are good that it will overflow the available space.

You can control the number of decimal digits to be displayed with the following call to the Format() function:

```
Print Format(atn(1)*4, "##.####")
```

This statement displays the result 3.1416. If you are doing financial calculations and the result turns out to be 13,454.332345201, it would best to display it as $13,454.33, with a statement such as the following:

```
amount = 13454.332345201
Print Format(amount, "$###,###.##")
```

These statements display the value $13,454.33, which is a proper dollar amount.

The *firstdayofweek* argument, which is used only in formatting dates, determines which is the week's first day and can have one of the values in Table LR.12.

TABLE LR.12: The Values of the *firsdayofweek* Argument

CONSTANT	VALUE	DESCRIPTION
vbUseSystem	0	Uses NLS API setting
vbSunday	1	Sunday (default)
vbMonday	2	Monday
vbTuesday	3	Tuesday
vbWednesday	4	Wednesday
vbThursday	5	Thursday
vbFriday	6	Friday
vbSaturday	7	Saturday

Similarly, the *firstweekofyear* determines which is the first week of the year, and it can have one of the values in Table LR.13.

TABLE LR.13: The Values of the *firstweekofyear* Argument

CONSTANT	VALUE	DESCRIPTION
vbUseSystem	0	Uses NLS API setting
vbFirstJan1	1	Starts with the week of January 1
vbFirstFourDays	2	Starts with the week that has at least four days in the year
vbFirstFullWeek	3	Starts with the first full week of the year

The *firstdayofweek* and *firstweekofyear* arguments are used only in formatting dates.

There are many formatting strings for all three types of variables: numeric, string, and date and time. Table LR.14, Table LR.15, and Table LR.16 show them.

TABLE LR.14: User-Defined Time and Date Formatting

CHARACTER	DESCRIPTION
:	Time separator. In some locales, other characters may be used to represent the time separator. The time separator separates hours, minutes, and seconds when time values are formatted.
/	Date separator. In some locales, other characters may be used to represent the date separator. The date separator separates the day, month, and year when date values are formatted.
c	Displays date as *ddddd* and time as *ttttt*.
d	Displays day as a number (1–31).
dd	Displays day as a number with a leading zero (01–31).
ddd	Displays day as an abbreviation (Sun–Sat).
dddd	Displays day as a full name (Sunday–Saturday).
ddddd	Displays complete date (including day, month, and year), formatted according to the system's short date format setting. The default short date format is *m/d/y*.
dddddd	Displays complete date, formatted according to the long date setting recognized by the system. The default long date format is *mmmm dd, yyyy*.

TABLE LR.14 (continued): User-Defined Time and Date Formatting

CHARACTER	DESCRIPTION
w	Displays day of the week as a number (1 for Sunday through 7 for Saturday).
ww	Displays week of the year as a number (1–54). A year has 52 complete weeks, but usually the first and last weeks are incomplete.
m	Displays month as a number (1–12). If *m* immediately follows *h* or *hh*, the minute rather than the month is displayed.
mm	Displays month as a number with a leading zero (01–12). If *m* immediately follows *h* or *hh*, the minute rather than the month is displayed.
mmm	Displays month as an abbreviation (Jan–Dec).
mmmm	Displays month as a full month name (January–December).
q	Displays quarter of the year as a number (1–4).
y	Displays day of the year as a number (1–366).
yy	Displays year as a 2-digit number (00–99).
yyyy	Displays year as a 4-digit number (100–9999).
h	Displays hours as a number (0–23).
hh	Displays hours with leading zeros (00–23).
n	Displays minutes without leading zeros (0–59).
nn	Displays minutes with leading zeros (00–59).
s	Displays seconds without leading zeros (0–59).
ss	Displays seconds with leading zeros (00–59).
ttttt	Displays complete time (including hour, minute, and second), formatted using the time separator defined by the time format of the system. The default time format is *h:mm:ss*.
AM/PM	Uses the 12-hour format and displays the indication A.M./P.M.
am/pm	Uses the 12-hour format and displays the indication am/pm.
A/P	Uses the 12-hour format and displays the indication A/P
a/p	Uses the 12-hour format and displays the indication a/p.
AMPM	Uses the 12-hour format and displays the A.M./P.M. string literal as defined by the system. Use the Regional Settings program in the Control Panel to set this literal for your system.

TABLE LR.15: User-Defined Number Formatting

CHARACTER	WHAT IT IS OR DOES	DESCRIPTION
None		Displays the number with no formatting.
0	Digit placeholder	Displays a digit or a zero. If the expression has a digit in the position where the 0 appears in the *format* argument, display it; otherwise, display a zero in that position. If the number has fewer digits than there are zeros in the *format* argument, leading or trailing zeros are displayed. If the number has more digits to the right of the decimal separator than there are zeros to the right of the decimal separator in the *format* argument, round the number to as many decimal places as there are zeros. If the number has more digits to the left of the decimal separator than there are zeros to the left of the decimal separator in the *format* argument, display the extra digits without modification.
#	Digit placeholder	Displays a digit or nothing. If the expression has a digit in the position where the # appears in the *format* argument, display it; otherwise, display nothing in that position. This symbol works like the 0 digit placeholder, except that leading and trailing zeros aren't displayed if the number has the same or fewer digits than there are # characters on either side of the decimal separator in the *format* argument.
.	Decimal placeholder	The decimal placeholder determines how many digits are displayed to the left and right of the decimal separator. If the *format* argument contains only number signs to the left of this symbol, numbers smaller than 1 begin with a decimal separator. To display a leading zero displayed with fractional numbers, use 0 as the first digit placeholder to the left of the decimal separator.
%	Percentage placeholder	The expression is multiplied by 100. The percent character (%) is inserted in the position where it appears in the *format* argument.

TABLE LR.15 (continued): User-Defined Number Formatting

CHARACTER	WHAT IT IS OR DOES	DESCRIPTION
,	Thousand separator	Separates thousands from hundreds within a number greater than 1,000. Two adjacent thousand separators or a thousand separator immediately to the left of the decimal separator (whether or not a decimal is specified) means "scale the number by dividing it by 1000, rounding as needed." For example, you can use the format string "##0,," to represent 100 million as 100. Numbers smaller than 1 million are displayed as 0. Two adjacent thousand separators in any position other than immediately to the left of the decimal separator are treated simply as specifying the use of a thousand separator.
:	Time separator	Separates hours, minutes, and seconds when time values are formatted.
/	Date separator	Separates the day, month, and year when date values are formatted.
E+, e-, e+	Scientific format	If the *format* argument contains at least one digit placeholder (0 or #) to the right of *E-*, *E+*, *e-*, or *e+*, the number is displayed in scientific format, and *E* or *e* is inserted between the number and its exponent. The number of digit placeholders to the right determines the number of digits in the exponent. Use *E-* or *e-* to place a minus sign next to negative exponents. Use *E+* or *e+* to place a minus sign next to negative exponents and a plus sign next to positive exponents.
+ $ (space)	Displays a literal character	To display a character other than one of those listed, precede it with a backslash (\) or enclose it in double quotation marks (" ").
\	Displays the next character in the format string	To display a character that has special meaning as a literal character, precede it with a backslash (\). The backslash itself isn't displayed. Using a backslash is the same as enclosing the next character in double quotation marks. To display a backslash, use two backslashes (\\). Examples of characters that can't be displayed as literal characters are the date-formatting and time-formatting characters (*a, c, d, h, m, n, p, q, s, t, w, y, /*, and *:*), the numeric-formatting characters (#, 0, %, *E, e*, comma, and period), and the string-formatting characters (@, &, <, >, and !).

TABLE LR.15 (continued): User-Defined Number Formatting

CHARACTER	WHAT IT IS OR DOES	DESCRIPTION
"ABC"	Displays the string inside the double quotation marks (" ")	To include a string in format from within code, you must use Chr(34) to enclose the text (34 is the character code for a quotation mark (")).

TABLE LR.16: User-Defined String Formatting

CHARACTER	WHAT IT IS OR DOES	DESCRIPTION
@	Character placeholder	Displays a character or a space. If the string has a character in the position where the "at" symbol (@) appears in the *format* argument, it is displayed. Otherwise, a space in that position is displayed. Placeholders are filled from right to left unless there is an exclamation point character (!) in the format string.
&	Character placeholder	If the string has a character in the position where the ampersand (&) appears, it is displayed. Otherwise, nothing is displayed. Placeholders are filled from right to left unless there is an exclamation point character (!) in the format string.
<	Force lowercase	All characters are first converted to lowercase.
>	Force uppercase	All characters are first converted to uppercase.
!	Scans placeholders from left to right	The default order is to use placeholders from right to left. Use this character to reverse the default order.

FormatCurrency(Expression [, NumDigits-AfterDecimal [, IncludeLeadingDigit [, UseParensForNegativeNumbers [, Group-Digits]]]])

This function returns a numeric expression formatted as a currency value (dollar amount) using the currency symbol defined in Control Panel. All arguments are optional, except for the *Expression* argument, which is the number to be formatted as currency. *NumDigitsAfterDecimal* is a value indicating how many digits will appear to the right of the decimal point. The default value is -1, which indicates that the computer's regional settings must be used. *IncludeLeadingDigit* is a tristate constant that indicates whether a leading zero is displayed for fractional values. The *UseParensFor-NegativeNumbers* argument is also a tristate constant that indicates whether to place negative values within parentheses. The last argument, *GroupDigits*, is another tristate constant that indicates whether numbers are grouped using the group delimiter specified in the computer's regional settings.

NOTE

A tristate variable is one that has three possible values: True, False, and Use-Default. The last value uses the computer's regional settings. When one or more optional arguments are omitted, values for omitted arguments are provided by the computer's regional settings.

FormatDateTime(Date [,NamedFormat])

This function formats a date or time value. The *Date* argument is a date value that will be formatted, and the optional argument *NamedFormat* indicates the date/time format to be used. It can have the values shown in Table LR.17.

TABLE LR.17: The Values for the *NamedFormat* Argument

VALUE	WHAT IT DOES
vbGeneralDate	Displays a date and/or time. If a date part is present, it is displayed as a short date. If a time part is present, it is displayed as a long time. If both parts are present, both parts are displayed.
vbLongDate	Displays a date using the long date format, as specified in the client computer's regional settings.
vbShortDate	Displays a date using the short date format, as specified in the client computer's regional settings.
vbLongTime	Displays a time using the time format specified in the client computer's regional settings.
vbShortTime	Displays a time using the 24-hour format.

FormatNumber(Expression [, NumDigits-AfterDecimal [, IncludeLeadingDigit [, UseParensForNegativeNumbers [, GroupDigits]]]])

This function returns a numeric value formatted as a number. The arguments of the FormatNumber() function are identical to the arguments of the FormatCurrency() function.

FormatPercent(Expression [, NumDigits-AfterDecimal [, IncludeLeadingDigit [, UseParensForNegativeNumbers [, GroupDigits]]]])

This function returns an expression formatted as a percentage (multiplied by 100) with a trailing % character. Its syntax and arguments are identical to the FormatCurrency() and FormatNumber() functions.

LSet stringVar = string and RSet stringVar = string

These two statements left or right align a string within a string variable. The string variable (specified with the *stringVar* argument) may be declared as a fixed-length string or initialized as needed. Let's say you have declared two string variables with the statements

```
Private LName As String * 20
Private FName As String * 12
```

If you want to assign a string value to these variables, the characters will be left aligned in the variable. The statements

```
RSet LName = "Hohnecker"
LSet FName = "Richard"
Debug.Print "[" & LName & ", " & FName & "]"
```

will print the following string in the Immediate window:

```
[         Hohnecker, Richard      ]
```

The last name is right aligned in a string of 20 characters, and the first name is left aligned in a string of 12 characters. If you create multiple strings like the previous one and place them one below the other (on a

TextBox or ListBox control, for example), the commas will not align unless a monospaced font, such as Courier, is used.

The LSet and RSet statement can also be used with numeric values. If you want to right align a list of numbers, copy them to a fixed-length string with the RSet statement, and then print them. The first line in the following example initializes the *FString* variable and sets the length of the variable, in which the output values will be aligned. The statements

```
FString = "1234567.00"
RSet FString = 34.56
Debug.Print FString
RSet FString = 4356.99
Debug.Print FString
RSet FString = 4.01
Debug.Print Fstring
```

will produce the following output on the Immediate window:

```
   34.56
 4356.99
    4.01
```

MATH FUNCTIONS

The following functions perform math operations. Their arguments and results are double-precision values. Keep in mind that trigonometric functions assume that angle arguments are expressed in radians. Angles returned by these functions are also expressed in radians. If you'd rather work with degrees, convert angle values to radians, before passing them as arguments to trigonometric functions like Sin() or Cos(). To convert an angle from degrees to radians, multiply it by the value $\pi/180$, where π is 3.14159265358979.... A convenient formula for calculating the value of π is 4 * Atn(1). To calculate the Sine of a 30 degrees angle, use the statements

```
Dim angle As Double, pi As Double
angle = 30
pi = 4 * Atn(1)
RadAngle = angle * (pi / 180)
MsgBox "The Sine of angle is " & Sin(RadAngle)
```

Abs(expression)

This function returns the absolute value of its argument. Both Abs(1.01) and Abs(-1.01) return the value 1.01.

Atn(expression)

This function returns the arctangent of an angle. The value returned is in radians. To convert it to degrees, multiply by $180/\pi$, where π is 3.14159.... To calculate π with double precision, use the following statement:

```
Atn(1)*4
```

Cos(expression)

This function returns the cosine of an angle. The value of the angle must be expressed in radians. To convert it to degrees, multiply by $180/\pi$, where π is 3.14159.... To calculate π with double precision, use the following statement:

```
Atn(1)*4
```

Exp(expression)

This function returns the base of the natural logarithms to a power. The *expression* variable is the power, and its value can be a noninteger, positive or negative. The Exp() function complements the operation of the Log() function and is also called *antilogarithm*.

Int(expression), Fix(expression)

Both these functions accept a numeric argument and return an integer value. If *expression* is positive, both functions behave the same. If it's negative, the Int() function returns the first negative integer less than or equal to *expression,* and Fix() returns the first negative integer greater than or equal to *expression*. For example, Int(-1.1) returns -2, and Fix(-1.1) returns -1.

The functions Int(1.8) and Fix(1.8) both return 1. If you want to get rid of the decimal part of a number and round it as well, use the following expression:

```
Int(value + 0.5)
```

The *value* argument is the number to be rounded. The following function

```
Int(100.1 + 0.5)
```

returns 100, and the function

```
Int(100.8 + 0.5)
```

returns 101. This technique works with negative numbers, as well. The following function returns −100:

```
Int(-100.1 + 0.5)
```

And the following function returns −101:

```
Int(-100.8 + 0.5)
```

Round(expression [,numdecimalplaces])

This function returns a numeric expression rounded to a specified number of decimal places. The *numdecimalplaces* argument is optional and indicates how many places to the right of the decimal are included in the rounding. If it is omitted, an integer value is returned.

The expression Round(3.49) returns 3, and the expression Round(3.51) returns 4. Use this new function to avoid statements such as Int(value + 0.5), which was used with previous versions of Visual Basic to round a floating-point number to an integer.

Log(expression)

The Log() function returns the natural logarithm of a number. The *expression* variable must be a positive number. The expression

```
Log(Exp(N))
```

returns N, as will this expression:

```
Exp(Log(N))
```

If you combine the logarithm with the antilogarithm, you end up with the same number.

The natural logarithm is the logarithm to the base *e*, which is approximately 2.718282. The precise value of *e* is given by the function Exp(1). To calculate logarithms to other bases, divide the natural logarithm of the number by the natural logarithm of the base. The following statement calculates the logarithm of *number* in base 10:

```
Log10 = Log(number) / Log(10)
```

Hex(expression), Oct(expression)

These two functions accept a decimal numeric value as an argument and return the octal and hexadecimal representation of the number in a string. The function Hex(47) returns the value 2F, and the function Oct(47) returns the value 57. To specify a hexadecimal number, prefix it with &H. The equivalent notation for octal numbers is &O. Given the following definitions

```
Dvalue = 199: Ovalue = &O77
```

the function Oct(Dvalue) returns the string 307, and the function Hex(Ovalue) returns 3F. To display the decimal value of 3F, use a statement such as the following:

```
MsgBox ("The number 3F in decimal is " & &H3F)
```

The actual value that will be displayed is 63.

Rnd([expression])

This function returns a pseudo-random number in the range 0 to 1. The optional argument is called *seed* and is used as a starting point in the calculations that generate the random number.

If the *seed* is negative, the Rnd() function always returns the same number. As strange as this behavior may sound, you may need this feature to create repeatable random numbers to test your code. If *seed* is positive (or omitted), the Rnd() function returns the next random number in the sequence. Finally, if *seed* is zero, the Rnd() function returns the most recently generated random number.

In most cases, you don't need a random number between 0 and 1 but between two other integer values. A playing card's value is an integer in the range 1 through 13. To simulate the throw of a dice, you need a number in the range 1 through 6. To generate a random number in the range *lower* to *upper,* in which both bounds are integer numbers, use the following statement:

```
randomNumber = Int((upper - lower + 1)*rnd() + lower);
```

The following statement displays a random number in the range 1 to 49:

```
Debug.Print Int(Rnd * 49 + 1)
```

NOTE

The sequence of random numbers produced by Visual Basic is always the same! Let's say you have an application that displays three random numbers. If you stop and rerun the application, the same three numbers will be displayed. This is not a bug. It's a feature of Visual Basic that allows you to debug applications that use random numbers. (If the sequence were different, you wouldn't be able to re-create the problem.) To change this default behavior, call the Randomize statement at the beginning of your code. This statement will initialize the random number generator based on the value of the computer's Timer, and the sequences of random numbers will be different every time you run the application.

Randomize [seed]

The Randomize statement initializes the random-number generator. The *seed* argument is a numeric value, used to initialize the random-number generator. To create a different set of random numbers every time the application is executed, use the current date as *seed*. However, using the same *seed* will not return the same run of random numbers. If you omit the *seed* argument, Visual Basic will use the value returned by the system timer to initialize the random number generator. If you want to generate the same run of random numbers (to test an application, for instance), call the Rnd() function with a negative argument immediately before calling the Randomize statement.

Sgn(expression)

This function returns an integer indicating the sign of its argument: 1 if the argument is greater than zero, 0 if the argument is zero, and −1 if the argument is less than zero.

Sin(expression)

This function returns the Sine of an angle, specified in radians. See the Cos() entry.

Sqr(expression)

This function returns the square root of a positive number. If the argument number is negative, the Sqr() function causes a runtime error because, by definition, the square root of a negative number is undefined. If your program uses the Sqr() function, you must include an error-trapping code such as the following:

```
If var>=0 Then
    sqVar = Sqr(var)
Else
    MsgBox "The result can't be calculated"
End If
```

Tan(expression)

This function returns the tangent of an angle, which must be expressed in radians.

Val(string)

This function returns the numeric value of a string made up of digits. The Val() function starts reading the string from the left and stops when it reaches a character that isn't part of a number. If the value of the variable *a* is

```
a = "18:6.05"
```

the statement

```
Debug.Print Val(a)
```

returns 18.

DATE AND TIME

A sore point in many programming languages is the lack of appropriate tools for manipulating dates and times. Figuring out the number of hours, days, or weeks between two days could be a project on its own. Not with Visual Basic. There are so many functions and statements for manipulating time and date values, all you have to do is select the one you need for your calculations and look up its arguments.

Timer()

This function returns a single number representing the number of seconds elapsed since midnight. It is frequently used for timing purposes, as long as the desired accuracy is not less than a second. To time an operation that takes a while to complete, use a structure such as the following:

```
T1 = Timer
    {lengthy calculations}
Debug.print Int(Timer - T1)
```

The last statement displays the integer part of the difference, which is the number of seconds elapsed since the calculations started.

Date()

This function returns the current date in month/day/year format, unless you specified the UK date format (day/month/year). The following statement

```
MsgBox "The system date is " & Date()
```

displays a date, such as 9/22/1998, in a message box. To set the system date, use the following statement:

```
date = "01/01/97"
```

Date Statement

The Date statement is the counterpart of the Date() function. Instead of returning the current date, the Date statement sets the system date, and it must be followed by an expression that evaluates to a valid date. Use either of the following statements to set the computer's system date to January 2, 2001:

```
Date = #1/2/2001#
Date = #January 2, 2001#
```

In general, you should avoid setting the date and time from within your application. It is best to let the user set the system date and time through the Control Panel.

Time()

This function returns the system's time in A.M./P.M. format. The following statement

```
MsgBox "The system time is " & Time()
```

displays a time such as 5:13:05 PM in a message box. To set the system time, use the following statement:

```
Time = "13:00.00"
```

Time Statement

The Time statement is the counterpart of the Time() function. Instead of returning the current time, the Time statement sets the system time, and it must be followed by an expression that evaluates to a valid time value. Use the following statement to set the computer's system time to 15 minutes past noon:

```
Time = #12:15.00#
```

In general, you should avoid setting the date and time from within your application. It is best to let the user set the system date and time through the Control Panel.

Now()

This function returns both the system date and time, in the same format as they are reported by the Date() and Time() functions. The following statement

```
Debug.print Now()
```

displays a date/time combination such as 9/13/1998 09:23:10 PM in a message box. There's only one space between the date and the time.

The Now() function is equivalent to the following pair of functions:

```
Date() & " " & Time()
```

Day(date)

This function returns the day number of the date specified by the argument. The *date* argument must be a valid date (such as the value of the Date() or the Now() function). If the following function were called on 12/01/99, it would have returned 1.

```
Day(Date())
```

The Day(Now()) function returns the same result.

Weekday(date [, firstdayofweek])

This function returns an integer in the range 1 through 7, representing the day of the week (1 for Sunday, 2 for Monday, and so on). The first argument, *date,* can be any valid date expression. The second argument, which is optional, specifies the first day of the week. Set it to 1 to start counting from Sunday (the default), or set it to 2 to start counting from Monday. The value 3 corresponds to Tuesday, the value 4 corresponds to Wednesday, and so on.

The following code segment displays the name of the day:

```
DayNames = Array("Sunday", "Monday", "Tuesday", "Wednesday", _
"Thursday", "Friday", "Saturday")
dayname = "Today it is " & DayNames(Weekday(Now)-1)
Debug.Print dayname
```

Notice that the code subtracts 1 from the weekday to account for the array being zero-based. Notice that Visual Basic provides the Weekday-Name() function, which returns the name of the weekday (see next entry).

WeekdayName(weekday[, abbreviate[, firstdayofweek]])

This function returns the name of the weekday specified by the *weekday* argument (a numeric value, which is 1 for the first day, 2 for the second day, and so on). The optional *abbreviate* argument is a Boolean value that indicates if the name is to be abbreviated. By default, day names are not abbreviated. The last argument, *firstdayofweek,* is also optional, and it determines the first day of the week. It can have one of the values shown in Table LR.19 (see the entry DateDiff(), later in this section). By default, the first day of the week is Sunday.

Month(date)

This function returns an integer in the range 1 through 12, representing the number of the month of the specified date. Month(Date) returns the current month number.

MonthName(month[, abbreviate])

This function returns the name of the month specified by the *month* argument (a numeric value, which is 1 for January, 2 for February, and so on). The optional *abbreviate* argument is a Boolean value that indicates if the month name is to be abbreviated. By default, month names are not abbreviated.

Year(date)

This function returns an integer representing the year of the date passed to it as an argument. The following function returns the current year:

```
Year(Now())
```

Hour(time)

This function returns an integer in the range 0 through 24 that represents the hour of the specified time. The following statements

```
Debug.Print Now
Debug.Print Hour(Now)
```

produce the following output:

```
2/27/98 11:32:43 AM
11
```

Minute(time)

This function returns an integer in the range 0 through 60 that represents the minute of the specified time. The following statements

```
Debug.Print Now
Debug.Print Minute(Now)
```

produce the following output:

```
2/27/98 11:57:13 AM
57
```

Second(time)

This function returns an integer in the range 0 through 60 that represents the seconds of the specified time. The following statements

```
Debug.Print Now
Debug.Print Second(Now)
```

produce the following output:

```
2/27/98 11:57:03 AM
 3
```

DateSerial(year, month, day)

This function accepts three numeric arguments that correspond to a year, a month, and a day value, and it returns the corresponding date. The following statement

```
MsgBox DateSerial(1999, 10, 1)
```

displays the string "10/1/99" in a message box.

Although hardly a useful operation, the DateSerial function can handle arithmetic operations with dates. For example, you can find out the date of the 90th day of the year by calling DateSerial() with the following arguments:

```
DateSerial(1996, 1, 90)
```

(This is 30/3/96, if you are curious.) To find out the date 1,000 days from now, call the DateSerial function as follows:

```
DateSerial(Year(Date), Month(Date), Day(Date)+1000)
```

You can also add (or subtract) a number of months to the *month* argument and a number of years to the *year* argument.

DateValue(date)

This function returns a variant of type Date. This function is handy if you are doing financial calculations based on the number of days between two dates. The difference in the following statement

```
MsgBox DateValue("12/25/1996") - DateValue("12/25/1993")
```

is the number of days between the two dates, which happens to be 1,096 days. You can verify this result by adding 1,096 days to the earlier date

```
MsgBox DateValue("12/25/1993") + 1096
```

or subtracting 1,096 days from the later date:

```
MsgBox DateValue("12/25/1996") - 1096
```

TimeSerial(hours, minutes, seconds)

This function returns a time, as specified by the three arguments. The following function

```
TimeSerial(4, 10, 55)
```

returns

```
4:10:55 AM
```

The TimeSerial() function is frequently used to calculate relative times. The following call to TimeSerial() returns the time 2 hours, 15 minutes, and 32 seconds before 4:13:40 P.M.:

```
TimeSerial(16 - 2, 13 - 15, 40 - 32)
```

This is 1:58:08 PM.

TimeValue(time)

This function returns a variant of type Time. Like the DateValue() function, it can be used in operations that involve time. If the variables *Time1* and *Time2* are defined as follows

```
Time1 = "04.10.55"
Time2 = "18.50.00"
```

you can find out the hours, minutes, and seconds between the two times with the following statements:

```
Diff = TimeValue(Time2) - TimeValue(Time1)
HourDiff = Hour(Diff)
MinDiff = Minute(Diff)
SecDiff = Second(Diff)
```

In this example, the values returned will be

```
HourDiff=14
MinDiff=39
SecDiff=05
```

DateAdd(interval, number, date)

This function returns a date that corresponds to a given date plus some specified interval. The *interval* variable is a time unit (days, hours, weeks, and so on), *number* is the number of intervals to be added to the initial date, and *date* is the initial date. If *number* is positive, the date returned by DateAdd is ahead of the *date* argument. If it's negative, the date returned is behind the *date* argument. The *interval* argument can take one of the values in Table LR.18.

TABLE LR.18: The Values for the *Interval* Argument

VALUE	DESCRIPTION
yyyy	Year
q	Quarter
m	Month
y	Day of year
d	Day
w	Weekday
ww	Week
h	Hour
n	Minute
s	Second

To find out the date one month after January 31, 1996, use the following statement:

```
Print DateAdd("m", 1, "31-Jan-96")
```

The result is

```
2/29/96
```

and not an invalid date, such as February 31.

DateAdd() also takes into consideration leap years. The following statement displays the date 2/29/96 in the Immediate window:

```
Print DateAdd("m", 1, "31-Jan-96")
```

The DateAdd() function is similar to the DateSerial() function, but it takes into consideration the actual duration of a month. For DateSerial(), each month has 30 days. The following statements

```
day1=#1/31/1996#
```

```
Print DateSerial(year(day1), month(day1)+1, day(day1))
```

result in

```
3/2/96
```

which is a date in March, not February.

DateDiff(interval, date1, date2[, firstdayofweek[, firstweekofyear]])

This function is the counterpart of the DateAdd() function and returns the number of intervals between two dates. The *interval* argument is the interval of time you use to calculate the difference between the two dates (see Table LR.18 for valid values). The *date1* and *date2* arguments are dates to be used in the calculation, and *firstdayofweek* and *firstweekofyear* are optional arguments that specify the first day of the week and the first week of the year.

Table LR.19 shows the valid values for the *firstdayofweek* argument, and Table LR.20 shows the valid values for the *firstweekofyear* argument.

TABLE LR.19: The Values for the *firstdayofweek* Argument

CONSTANT	VALUE	DESCRIPTION
vbUseSystem	0	Use the NLS API setting.
vbSunday	1	Sunday (default).
vbMonday	2	Monday.
vbTuesday	3	Tuesday.
vbWednesday	4	Wednesday.
vbThursday	5	Thursday.
vbFriday	6	Friday.
vbSaturday	7	Saturday.

TABLE LR.20: The Values for the *firstweekofyear* Argument

CONSTANT	VALUE	DESCRIPTION
vbUseSystem	0	Use the NLS API setting.
vbFirstJan1	1	Start with the week in which January 1 occurs (default).
vbFirstFourDays	2	Start with the first week that has at least four days in the new year.
vbFirstFullWeek	3	Start with the first full week of the year.

You can use the DateDiff() function to find the number of days, weeks, and even seconds between two dates. The following statements display the number of minutes until the turn of the century (or the time elapsed after the turn of century, depending on when you execute it):

```
century=#01/01/2000 00:00.00#
Print DateDiff("n", now(), century)
```

If you place this code in a Timer's Timer event, you can update a text control every second or every minute with the countdown to the end of the century. If you were to use the DateValue() function, as in the following

```
Print minute(DateValue("01/01/2000 00:00.00") - _
DateValue(now()))
```

the result is a number in the range 0 through 60. You would have to take into consideration the difference of years, months, days, hours, and minutes to calculate the correct value.

DatePart(interval, date[,firstdayofweek[, firstweekofyear]])

This function returns the specified part of a given date. The *interval* argument is the desired format in which the part of the date will be returned (see Table LR.18 for its values), and *date* is the part of the date you are seeking. The optional arguments *firstdayofweek* and *firstdayofmonth* are the same as for the DateDiff() function. The following Print statements produce the results shown after each Print statement:

```
day1=#03/23/1996 15:03.30#
Print DatePart("yyyy", day1)
    1996
```

```
Print DatePart("q", day1)
  1
Print DatePart("m", day1)
  3
Print DatePart("d", day1)
  23
Print DatePart("w", day1)
  7
Print DatePart("ww", day1)
  12
Print DatePart("h", day1)
  15
Print DatePart("n", day1)
  3
Print DatePart("s", day1)
  30
```

FINANCIAL FUNCTIONS

The following functions can be used to calculate the parameters of a loan or an investment. This section discusses only the functions that return the basic parameters of a loan (such as the monthly payment or the loan's duration). The more advanced financial functions are described in the Visual Basic online documentation.

IPmt(rate, per, nper, pv[, fv[, type]])

The IPmt() function returns the interest payment for a given period of an annuity based on periodic, fixed payments, and a fixed interest rate. The result is a Double value.

The *rate* argument is a Double value specifying the interest rate for the payment period. For example, if the loan's annual percentage rate (APR) is 10 percent, paid in monthly installments, the rate per period is 0.1/12, or 0.0083.

The *per* argument is a Double value specifying the current payment period; *per* is a number in the range 1 through *nper*.

The *nper* argument is a Double value specifying the total number of payments. For example, if you make monthly payments on a five-year loan, *nper* is 5 * 12 (or 60).

The *Pv* argument is a Double value specifying the principal or present value. The loan amount is the present value to the lender of the monthly payments.

The *fv* argument is a Variant specifying the future value or cash balance after the final payment. The future value of a loan is $0 because that's its value after the final payment. If you want to accumulate $10,000 in your savings account over 5 years, however, the future value is $10,000. If the *fv* argument is omitted, 0 is assumed.

The *type* argument is a Variant specifying when payments are due. Use 0 if payments are due at the end of the payment period; use 1 if payments are due at the beginning of the period. If the *type* argument is omitted, 0 is assumed.

Suppose you borrow $30,000 at an annual percentage rate of 11.5 percent, to be paid off in three years with payments at the end of each month. Here's how you can calculate the total interest, as well as the monthly interest:

```
PVal = 30000&
FVal = 0&
APR = 0.115 / 12
MPayments = 3 * 12
For Period = 1 To Mpayments
    IPayment = IPmt(APR, Period, MPayments, -PVal, FVal, 1)
    Debug.Print IPayment
    TotInt = TotInt + IPayment
Next Period
Debug.Print "Total interest paid: " & TotInt
```

The interest portion of the first payment is $278.11, and the interest portion of the last payment is less than $10. The total interest is $5,276 (approximately).

PPmt(rate, per, nper, pv[, fv[, type]])

This function is similar to the IPmt() function, except that it returns the principal payment for a given period of a loan based on periodic, fixed payments and a fixed interest rate. For a description of the function's arguments, see the IPmt entry.

The code for calculating the principal payment of the previous example is nearly the same as that for calculating the interest:

```
PVal = 30000&
FVal = 0&
APR = 0.115 / 12
MPayments = 3 * 12
For Period = 1 To Mpayments
    PPayment = PPmt(APR, Period, MPayments, -PVal, FVal, 1)
```

```
        Debug.Print PPayment
        TotPrincipal = TotPrincipal + PPayment
    Next Period
    Debug.Print "Total principal paid: " & TotPrincipal
```

In this example, the payments increase with time. (That's how the total payment remains fixed.) The total amount will be equal to the loan's amount, of course, and the fixed payment is the sum of the interest payment (as returned by the IPmt() function) and the principal payment (as returned by the PPmt() function).

Pmt(rate, nper, pv[, fv[, type]])

This function is a combination of the IPmt() and PPmt() functions. It returns the payment (including both principal and interest) for a loan based on periodic, fixed payments and a fixed interest rate. For a description of the function's arguments, see the IPmt() entry. Notice that the Pmt() function doesn't require the *per* argument because all payments are equal.

The code for calculating the monthly payment is similar to the code examples in the IPmt() and PPmt() entries:

```
PVal = 30000&
FVal = 0&
APR = 0.115 / 12
MPayments = 3 * 12
For Period = 1 To Mpayments
    MPayment = Pmt(APR, MPayments, -PVal, FVal, 1)
    Debug.Print MPayment
    TotAmount = TotAmount + MPayment
Next Period
Debug.Print "Total amount paid: " & TotAmount
```

FV(rate, nper, pmt[, pv[, type]])

This function returns the future value of a loan based on periodic, fixed payments and a fixed interest rate. The arguments of the FV() function are explained in the IPmt() entry, and the *pmt* argument is the payment made in each period.

Suppose you want to calculate the future value of an investment with an interest rate of 6.25 percent, 48 monthly payments of $180, and a present value of $12,000. Use the FV() function with the following arguments:

```
Payment = 180
APR = 6.25 / 100
TotPmts = 48
```

```
PVal = 12000
FVal = FV(APR / 12, TotPmts, -Payment, -PVal, PayType)
MsgBox "After " & TotPmts & " your savings will be worth _
$"& FVal
```

The actual result is close to $25,000.

NPer(rate, pmt, pv[, fv[, type]])

This function returns the number of periods for a loan based on periodic, fixed payments, and a fixed interest rate. For a description of the function's arguments, see the IPmt entry.

Suppose you borrow $25,000 at 11.5 percent, and you can afford to pay $450 per month. To figure out what this means to your financial state in the future, you would like to know how many years it will take you to pay off the loan. Here's how you can use the Nper() function to do so:

```
FVal = 0
PVal = 25000
APR = 0.115 / 12
Payment = 450
PayType = 0
TotPmts = NPer(APR, -Payment, PVal, FVal, PayType)
If Int(TotPmts) <> TotPmts Then TotPmts = Int(TotPmts) + 1
Debug.Print "The loan's duration will be: " & TotPmts & " _
months"
```

The actual duration of this loan is 80 months, which corresponds to nearly 6.5 years. If the payment is increased from $450 to $500, the loan's duration will drop to 69 months, and a monthly payment of $550 will bring the loan's duration down to 60 months.

Rate(nper, pmt, pv[, fv[, type[, guess]]])

You use this function to figure out the interest rate per payment period for a loan. Its arguments are the same as with the previous financial functions, except for the *guess* argument, which is the estimated interested rate. If you omit the *guess* argument, the value 0.1 (10 percent) is assumed.

Suppose you want to borrow $10,000 and pay it off in 48 months with a monthly payment of $250 or less. Here's how you can use the Rate() function to calculate the interest rate:

```
FVal = 0
PVal = 10000
Payment = 250
```

```
Payments = 48
PayType = 0
guess = 0.1
IRate = Rate(Payments, -Payment, PVal, FVal, PayType, guess)
Debug.Print "The desired interest rate is: " & Irate * _
12 * 100 & "%"
```

The interest rate is approximately 9.25 percent.

Table LR.21 lists and describes the remaining financial functions.

TABLE LR.21: Additional Financial Functions

FUNCTION	WHAT IT CALCULATES
PV	The present value of an investment
NPV	A Double specifying the net present value of an investment based on a series of periodic cash flows and a discount rate
IRR	The internal rate of return for an investment
MIRR	A Double specifying the modified internal rate of return for a series of periodic cash flows
DDB	A Double specifying the depreciation of an asset for a specific time period using the double-declining balance method or some other method you specify
SYD	A Double specifying the depreciation of an asset in a specific time period using the asset's lifetime in years
SLN	A Double specifying the straight-line depreciation of an asset for a single period

FILE I/O

An important aspect of any programming language is its ability to access and manipulate files. In this section, we'll present all the statements and functions for opening, reading from and writing to, and closing files.

Visual Basic supports three types of files:

- ▶ Sequential
- ▶ Random-access files
- ▶ Binary files

Sequential files are mostly text files (the ones you can open with a text editor, such as NotePad). These files store information as it's entered, one byte per character. Even the numbers in a sequential file are stored as string and not as numeric values (that is, the numeric value 33.4 is not stored as a single or double value, but as the string "33.4"). These files are commonly created by simple text-processing applications and are used for storing mostly text, not numbers. You can also use sequential files to store a column of numeric data, but more complicated data should be stored in binary or random-access files.

Sequential files are read from the beginning to the end. Therefore, you can't read and write at the same time to a sequential file. If you must read from and write to the file simultaneously, you must open two sequential files, one for reading from and another one for writing to. If the size of the file is small, you can read all the data into the memory, process them, and open the same file for output and overwrite the old data.

If your application requires frequent access to the file's data (as opposed to reading all the data into memory and saving them back when it's done), you should use random-access files. Like the sequential files, random-access files store text as characters, one byte per character. Numbers, however, are stored in their native format (as integers, doubles, single, and so on). You can display a random-access file in a DOS window with the Type command and see the text, but you won't be able to read the numbers.

Random-access files are used for storing data that are organized in segments of equal length. These segments are called *records*. Random-access files allow you to move to any record, as long as you know where the desired record is located. Because all records are of the same length, it's easy to locate any record in the file by its index. Moreover, unlike sequential files, random-access files can be opened for reading and writing at the same time. If you decide to change a specific record, you can write the new record's data on top of the old record, without affecting the adjacent records.

Binary files, finally, are similar to sequential files, and they make no assumption as to the type of data stored in them. The bytes of a binary file can be characters or the contents of an executable file. Images, for instance, are stored in binary files.

The manipulation of files is more or less independent of its type and involves three stages:

Opening the file The operating system reserves some memory for storing the file's data. If the file does not exist, it's first created and then opened. To open a file (and create it if necessary), use the Open statement.

Processing the file   A file can be opened for reading from, writing to, or reading and writing. Data are read, processed, and then stored back to the same, or to another, file.

Closing the file   When the file is closed, the operating system releases the memory reserved for the file. To close an open file, use the Close statement or the Reset statement to close all open files.

In the following sections, we'll look at Visual Basic's file-manipulation statements and functions.

FreeFile(file_number)

Each file is identified with a unique number, which is assigned to the file the moment it's opened. During the course of an application, you may open and close many files and you may not always know in advance which file numbers are available. Visual Basic provides the FreeFile() function, which returns the next available file number. The FreeFile() function is used in conjunction with the Open statement to open a file:

```
fNum = FreeFile()
Open "c:\samples\vb\cust.dat" For Random As #fNum Len=Len(Mrec)
```

After these two statements execute, all subsequent commands that operate on the specified file can refer to it as *fNum*. The FreeFile() function returns the next available file number, and unless this number is assigned to a file, FreeFile() returns the same number if called again. The following statements will not work:

```
fNum1 = FreeFile()
fNum2 = FreeFile()
Open "file1" For Input As #fNum1
Open "file2" For Output As #fNum2
```

Each time you call FreeFile() to get a new file number, you must use it. The previous statements should have been coded as follows:

```
fNum1 = FreeFile()
Open "file1" For Input As #fNum1
fNum2 = FreeFile()
Open "file2" For Output As #fNum2
```

Open file_name For file_type [Access access_type] [lock_type] As #file_number [Len=record_length]

To use a file, you must first open it—or create it, if it doesn't already exist. The Open statement, which opens files, accepts a number of arguments, most of which are optional. The *For, Access, As,* and *Len* arguments are Visual Basic keywords and will be discussed shortly. Notice that the order of these keywords can't be changed.

The simplest form of the Open statement is

```
Open fileName As #1
```

This line opens a file and assigns it the number 1. Subsequent statements use the numeric value 1 to identify this file.

The argument *file_name* is the name of the file to be opened (the name of an existing or a new disk file). The argument *file_type* determines the file's type and can be one of the constants listed below.

Input	File is opened for input (reading from) only.
Output	File is opened for output (writing to) only.
Append	File is opened for appending new data to its existing contents.
Random	File is opened for random access (reading or writing one record at a time).
Binary	File is opened in binary mode.

The first three file types refer to sequential files. *Random* is used with random-access files, and *Binary* is used with binary files. When you open a sequential file, you can't change its data. You can either read them (and store them to another file) or overwrite the entire file with the new data. To do so, you must open the file for *Input*, read its data, and then close the file. To overwrite it, open it again (this time for *Output*), and save the new data to it.

If you don't want to overwrite an existing file but want instead to append data to it (without changing any of the existing data), open it for *Append*. If you open a file for *Output*, Visual Basic wipes out its contents, even if you don't write anything to it. Moreover, VB won't warn you that it's about to overwrite a file, as applications do. This is how the Open statement works, and you can't change your mind after opening a sequential file for *Output*.

The *access_type* argument is used with random-access files and determines whether the file can be opened for reading from (Read), writing to (Write), or both (Read Write). If you open a file with Read access, your program can't modify it even by mistake. The access method has nothing to do with file types. Sequential files are open for Input or Output only because they can't be opened in both modes. The access type is specified for reasons of safety. If you need to open a file only to read data from it, open it with Read access. (There's no reason to risk modifying the data.)

The *lock_type* argument allows you to specify the rights of other Windows applications, while your application keeps the file open. Under Windows, many applications can be running at the same time, and one of them may attempt to open a file that is already open. In this case, you can specify how other applications are to access the file. The *lock_type* argument can have one of the values listed below.

The File-Locking Options of Visual Basic

Shared	Other applications can share the file.
Lock Read	The file is locked for reading.
Write Lock	The file is locked for writing.
Lock Read Write	Other applications can't access this file.

File locking is a very important function, especially in a networked environment. Imagine two users attempting to write to the same file at the same time. Using the file-locking features, you can write programs that work properly in networked environments. However, if you are going to build applications that will be run by many users who access the same files, you should probably consider building a database.

A numeric value, which uniquely identifies the file, follows the *As* keyword. Every file you open must have its own unique number. This number is used by subsequent commands to identify the specific file. The Close statement, for example, which closes an open file when it's no longer needed, must know which file to close. The statement

```
Close #1
```

closes the file that was opened as #1. The file number has nothing to do with the actual file on the disk. The same file can be opened later with another number. Without the file number, you'd have to specify the file's name with each command that accesses the file. The file's number is therefore a shorthand notation for identifying files from within our code.

Finally, if the file is a random-access one, you must declare the length of the record with the *Len* keyword. The *record_length* argument is the record's length in bytes. When you create a random-access file, Visual Basic doesn't record any information regarding the record's length, or structure, to the file. You should know, therefore, the structure of each record in a random-access file before you can open it. The record's length is the sum of the bytes taken by all record fields. You can either calculate it, or you can use the function *Len(record)* to let Visual Basic calculate it. The *record* argument is the name of the structure you use with the random-access file.

The following command opens the file `c:\samples\vb\cust.dat` as a sequential file with the number 1:

```
Open "c:\samples\vb\cust.dat" For Input As #1
```

To open a random-access file, you must know its record's length. The record is the basic element of a random-access file, and the record is the smallest piece of information you can write to a random-access file. To find the length of the record, you must first decide how the data will be organized in fields and declare the record's type. Let's say you want to create a random-access file for storing music records. You can use the following structure for the purposes of this application:

```
Type MRecord
    Title As String*60
    Group As String*30
    Style As String *3
    Year As Date
End Type
```

This structure is very simple, but you can extend it by adding any other field you need. The length of this structure can be easily calculated, if you know how many bytes a Date type takes. To avoid mistakes, you should let Visual Basic calculate the record's length with the Len() function—the same function that returns the length of a string. The following statement opens a random-access file for reading from and writing to, using the record structure shown above:

```
Open "c:\samples\vb\cust.dat" For Random As #1 Len=Len(Mrec)
```

MRec is a variable declared as MRecord type.

Close(file_number)

The Close statement closes an open file, whose number is passed as argument. The following statement closes the file opened as #fNum1:

```
Close #fNum1
```

You can also call the Close statement with multiple file numbers, as in

```
Close #fNum1, fNum2, fNum3
```

This statement closes the three files that were opened as #fNum1, #fNum2, and #fNum3.

Reset

The Reset statement closes all files opened with the Open statement. Use this statement to close all the files opened by your application.

EOF(file_number) and LOF(file_number)

These are two more frequently used functions in file manipulation. The EOF() function accepts as an argument the number of an open file and returns True if the end of the file (EOF) has been reached. The LOF() function returns the length of the file, whose number is passed as an argument.

You use the EOF() function to determine whether the end of the file has been reached, with a similar loop as the following:

```
{get first record}
While Not EOF(fNum)
  {process current record}
  {get next record}
Wend
```

With the help of the LOF() function, you can also calculate the number of records in a random-access file:

```
Rec_Length = LOF(file_number) / Len(record)
```

FileAttr(file_number, return_type)

The FileAttr() function returns a long integer value representing the file mode for files already opened with the Open statement. The *file_number* argument is the number of an open file. The second argument should be 1 (it was used in developing 16-bit applications with previous versions of Visual Basic). The FileAttr() function returns one of the values in Table LR.22.

TABLE LR.22: The Values Returned by the FileAttr() Function

RETURN VALUE	DESCRIPTION
1	Input
2	Output
4	Random
8	Append
32	Binary

Print #file_num, variable, variable, ...

The Print statement writes data to a sequential file. The first argument is the number of the file to be written, and the following arguments (you can supply any number of arguments after the first one) are the variables to be written to the file. After all variable values have been written to the file, the Print # statement inserts a line break. The following statements write two lines of text to the file opened as #fNum and insert a line break between them:

```
Print #fNum, "this is the first line of text"
Print #fNum, "and this is the second line of text"
```

The semicolon (;) and the comma (,) characters determine the *screen position,* where the pointer will be moved before printing the next value. The semicolon specifies that the first character of the new value will be placed right after the last character of the last value. The comma specifies that the next character will be printed in the next *print zone.* Each print zone corresponds to 14 columns. In other words, the Print # statement writes data to the file exactly as the Type command (of DOS) displays them on the screen. (That's why the data saved by the Print # statement is called *display-formatted* data.) You must keep in mind that the text will be displayed correctly only when printed with a monospaced typeface, such as Courier. If you place the text on a TextBox with a proportional typeface, the columns will not align.

Data saved with the Print # statement can be read with the Line Input and Input statement. However, isolated fields are not delimited in any way, and you must provide the code to extract the fields from the line read. The Print # statement is used to create text files that can be viewed on a DOS window. To format the fields on each line, you can use the Tab to position the pointer at the next print zone or Tab(n) to position the pointer at an absolute column number. The following statements created a text file, which is shown after the listing:

```
On Error Resume Next
Kill "TEST.TXT"
Open "TEST.TXT" For Output As #1
Print #1, "John"; Tab(12); "Ashley"; Tab(25); "Manager"; _
Tab(45); 35
Print #1, "Michael"; Tab(12); "Staknovitch"; Tab(25); _
"Programmer"; Tab(45); 28
Print #1, "Tess"; Tab(12); "Owen"; Tab(25); "Engineer"; _
Tab(45); 41
Print #1, "Joe"; Tab(12); "Dow"; Tab(25); "Administrator"; _
Tab(45); 25
Print #1, "**************************"
Print #1, "John"; Tab; "Ashley"; Tab; "Manager"; Tab; 3
Print #1, "Michael"; Tab; "Staknovitch"; Tab; "Programmer"; _
Tab; 28
Print #1, "Tess"; Tab; "Owen"; Tab; "Engineer"; Tab; 41
Print #1, "Joe"; Tab; "Dow"; Tab; "Administrator"; Tab; 25
Close #1
```

This is the output produced by the previous example:

```
John      Ashley        Manager        35
Michael   Staknovitch   Programmer     28
Tess      Owen          Engineer       41
Joe       Dow           Administrator  25
**************************
John      Ashley        Manager        3
Michael   Staknovitch   Programmer     28
Tess      Owen          Engineer       41
Joe       Dow           Administrator  25
```

Input #file_num, varlist

The Input# statement reads data from a sequential file and assigns them to the variables listed in the *varlist* argument. *varlist* is a comma-separated list of arguments. The following line reads two values from the open file, a numeric value and a date:

```
Dim numVal As Long, DateVal As Date
Input #1, numVal, DateVal
```

This statement is used to read data written to the file with the Write # statement (see the entry Write # for more information).

Line Input #file_number, strVar

To read from sequential files, use the Line Input # statement. The *file_number* argument is the file's number, and *strVar* is the name of a variable where the data read from the file will be stored. The Line Input statement reads a single line of text from the file and assigns it to a string variable. This statement reads all the characters from the beginning of the file to the first newline character. When you call it again, it returns the following characters, up to the next newline character. The newline characters are not part of the information stored to or read from the file, and they are used only as delimiters. If we close the file of the last example and open it again, the following lines will read the first two text lines and assign them to the string variables *line1* and *line2:*

```
Line Input #fNum, line1
Line Input #fNum, line2
```

If you want to store plain text to a disk file, create a sequential file and store the text there, one line at a time. To read it back, open the file and read one line at a time with the Line Input statement, or use the Get statement to read the entire text.

Put #file_number, [record_number], record and Get #file_number, [record_number], record

These statements are used for writing records to and reading records from a random-access file and binary files. Both statements need to know the record number you want to access (write or read). We'll start by examining the use of the Put and Get statements with random access files.

The *record_number* argument is the number of the record we are interested in, and *record* is a record variable that is written to the file. The *record_number* argument is optional; if you omit it, the record will be written to the current record position. After a record is written to or read from the file, the next record becomes the current one. If you've read the second record, the Put statement will store the field values in the third record in the file. If you call the Put statement ten times sequentially without specifying a record number, it will create (or overwrite) the first ten records of the random-access file.

The arguments of the Get statement have the same meaning. The Get statement must be used to read data saved to a file with the Put statement (as you will see shortly, there are more statements for writing to and reading from files).

At this point, we'll outline the basics of random-access file manipulation because this is the most flexible file type. Let's say you want to create a random-access file for storing a product list. Each product's information is stored in a *ProductRecord* variable, whose declaration is shown next:

```
Type ProductRecord
    ProductID As String*10
    Description As String*100
    Price As Currency
End Type
```

The Type *ProductRecord* will be used for storing each product's information before moving it to the file. Let's start by defining a variable of type *ProductRecord*:

```
Dim PRec As ProductRecord
```

You can then assign values to the fields of the *PRec* variable with statements such as the following:

```
PRec.ProductID = "TV00180-A"
PRec.Description = "SONY Trinitron TV"
PRec.Price = 799.99
```

The *PRec* record variable can be stored to a random-access file with the Put statement. Of course, you must first create the file with the following statements:

```
FNum = FreeFile()
Open "PRODUCTS.DAT" For Random Len=Len(ProductRecord) As #FNum
```

You can then write the *Prec* variable to the file with the statement

```
Put #FNum, , PRec
```

Notice that you can omit the number of the record where the data will be stored. If you omit the record number, Visual Basic will store the data at the current record's position. If a record exists at the specified location, it will be overwritten. You can change the values of the fields and keep storing additional records with the same Put statement (as long as *PRec* is populated with a different value). New records will be stored after each other in the file. After all the values are stored to the file, you can close the file with this statement:

```
Close #FNum
```

To read the records, open the file with the same Open statement you used to open it for saving the records:

```
FNum = FreeFile()
Open "PRODUCTS.DAT" For Random Len=Len(ProductRecord) As #FNum
```

You can then set up a loop to read the records in an array of *PRec* structures. Assuming that the array Products has been declared with the statement

```
Dim Products(100) As PRec
```

you can scan the records of the file with the following loop:

```
TotRecords = LOF(fNum) / Len(ProductRecord)
For i = 1 to TotRecords
  Get #FNum, , Products(i)
Next
```

The function LOF() returns the length of the file (in bytes). By dividing this number by the length of each record (also in bytes), we get the number of records in the file. This value is used by the For...Next loop to scan all records in the file.

The Put and Get statements can also be used with binary files. To store information to a binary file, specify a variable's name as the last argument to the Put statement. Assuming that the variables IntVar and DoubleVar hold an integer and double precision number respectively, the following statements store their values to a binary file with the Put statement:

```
Open "TEST.DAT" For Binary As 1
Put #1, , IntVar
Put #1, , DoubleVar
Close #1
```

To read the values back, you must use variables of the same type and in the same order as the ones you have stored in the file. In other words, you must know the type of data you have stored in the file in order to read it back. The following statements will open the same file and read two numeric values, an integer and a double one:

```
Open "TYPES.DAT" For Binary As #1
Get #1, , IntVar
Get #1, , DoubleVar
Close #1
```

Have you ever wondered how Visual Basic stores the various data types to a file (or how it stores them into variables, for that matter)? To find out, you can write a small program that stores variables of several types to a binary file, then opens the same file and reads its bytes. Here's the code that creates a binary file and stores four variables in it (an integer, double, date, and string variable):

```
Dim fNum As Long
Dim IntVar As Integer
Dim StrVar As String * 20
Dim DoubleVar As Double
```

```
Dim DateVar As Date

  fNum = FreeFile
  Open "TYPES.DAT" For Binary As #fNum
  IntVar = 104
  StrVar = "VISUAL BASIC"
  DoubleVar = 34.599088
  DateVar = Now
  Put #fNum, , IntVar
  Put #fNum, , StrVar
  Put #fNum, , DoubleVar
  Put #fNum, , DateVar
  DateVar = DateVar + 1 / 24
  Put #fNum, , DateVar
  Close #1
```

Notice that the DateVar is stored twice. The two values differ by one hour. You can add the constant $1/(24 * 60)$ to add a minute and so on.

The following statements open the TYPES.DAT file and read its contents, one byte at a time. As each byte is read, it's printed in the Immediate window as a decimal and a character value.

```
Dim fNum As Long
Dim ByteVar As Byte

  fNum = FreeFile
  Open "TYPES.DAT" For Binary As #fNum
  While Not EOF(fNum)
    Get #fNum, , ByteVar
    Debug.Print ByteVar, Chr(ByteVar)
  Wend
  Close #1
```

The integer variable corresponds to the first two bytes in the file, which are 104 and 0. The eight bytes making up the double value 34.599088 are 137, 182, 99, 234, 174, 76, 65, and 64. Date variables are stored in eight bytes, and here are the bytes making up the two date and time values (which differ by one hour). They are printed in two rows, so that you can compare which bytes differ (the actual values will be quite different when you execute the same lines):

19	229	12	233	57	165	225	64
74	159	244	148	58	165	225	64

As you can see, the four most significant bytes hold the date and the four least significant bytes hold the time. You can use this simple trick to locate date and time values in a binary file.

The Get and Put statements can also be used to store an entire array with a single line of code. Assuming that the array *Scores()* has been declared as

```
Dim Scores(1 To 100) As Integer
```

you can store the entire array to a binary file with the following statements:

```
Open "ARRAY.DAT" For Binary As #fNum
Put #1, , Scores()
Close #1
```

To read the data stored in the *Scores()* array, declare an array of the same type, open the file as binary again, and use the Get statement, as shown here:

```
Dim Scores(1 To 100) As Integer
Open "ARRAY.DAT" For Binary As #fNum
Get #1, , Scores()
Close #1
```

If you run into a random access file and you don't know the record structure (or you can't decipher it by looking at the data), you can open the file as Binary and read its contents one byte at a time. If you open the same file with a binary editor, you should be aware of how Visual Basic stores information into random-access files.

If the length of the record variable you're using to read from a random-access file is less than the length specified in the Open statement with the Len keyword, Get uses the record variable to read data. It reads as many bytes as required to fill its fields. Subsequent record locations are calculated according to the length of the record variable you use to read data from the file. In general, the record length specified in the Open statement must match the length of the record you're using with the Get statement.

When you store variable-length strings with the Put statement, Visual Basic inserts an integer value (two bytes) containing the actual length of the string. The Get statement will read these two bytes to find out the length of the string, then read the actual characters. If you're reading the data of a random-access file one byte at a time, you should take into consideration these two bytes.

When you store variants with the Put statement, Visual Basic inserts an integer (two bytes) containing the actual type of the variant. This integer has the same value as the one reported by the VarType() function, when applied to the variant being saved. For example, if the variant holds a date value, Visual Basic stores the integer value 7 (which corresponds to the Date type) and then the eight bytes of the variant that holds the date value (a total of 10 bytes). If the variant happens to hold a string, Visual Basic will first store two bytes with the value 8 (which corresponds to the String type), then two more bytes with the length of the string and then the actual characters of the string.

Seek #file_number, record_number

An important concept in processing random-access files is that of the *current record*. Visual Basic maintains a pointer to the current record for each open random-access file. Each time you read a record or save one in the file, the pointer is increased by one to point to the next record. The numbers of the records are not stored on disk. Since all records have the same length, the operating system can calculate where each record begins and move to the corresponding byte instantly.

Visual Basic provides the Seek statement, which lets you move to any record in the random-access file, and the Loc() function, which returns the number of the current record. In other words, the Seek statement manipulates the record pointer, and the Loc() function simply reads its value.

The argument *record_number* is the number of the record to which you want to move. The Seek statement can't locate a record based on its contents. It's like accessing an array element with its index.

Loc(file_number)

The Loc() function returns the number of the current record in a random-access file. To move to the next record in a random-access file, use the following statements:

```
fPointer = Loc(fNum) + 1
Seek(fNum, fPointer)
```

The value returned by the Loc() function is a Long Integer, which means a random-access file can hold more records than can physically fit on an average disk.

The Seek statement and Loc() function can be used with random-access files, as well as binary files, only in this case there are no record numbers. We usually set the length of the record to 1 byte, and we seek for a specific byte number in the file. If you want to read a number of bytes starting at a specified location in the file, use the Seek method to move to the first byte you're interested in, and then read as many bytes as you need.

Lock #file_number [,record_range] and Unlock #file_number [,record_range]

The Lock statement allows you to lock a file or some of the records in a file. The locked records or bytes are not available to other applications that are currently running. Your application, however, has access to all records (or bytes). If another application attempts to open a locked file or to access one of the locked records, Visual Basic will generate a trappable runtime error.

With the Lock command you can lock an entire file. The following statement locks the entire file opened as #fNum:

```
Lock #fNum
```

If the file was opened as a sequential file, the entire file must be locked. If the file was opened as a random-access file, you can lock one or more records. The following statement locks records 99 through 110 of the file opened as #fNum:

```
Lock #fNum 99,100
```

If the file was opened as binary, bytes 99 through 100 will become unavailable to other applications.

The Unlock statement has the same syntax but the opposite effect. If the file is locked, it unlocks it. The Lock and Unlock statements are essential in building applications that access files in an operating system, such as Windows, in which multiple applications can access the same file and act on it. You should always take into consideration the possibility of another application accessing the same files as yours. However, if the situation gets too complicated, you should probably switch to a database.

Write #file_num[, output_list]

The Write # statement writes data to a sequential file. The data to be written is supplied in the *output_list*, which is a comma-separated list of variables and literals. Data written with the Write # statement are usually read with the Input # statement. The following line will write a numeric and a date value to a sequential file:

```
NumVal = 3300.004
DateVal = #04/09/1999#
Write #1, NumVal, DateVal
```

The following lines write the same data as the example of the Print # statement, explained earlier in this reference:

```
Open "c:\test.txt" For Output As #1
Write #1, "John Ashley", 33, "Manager"
Write #1, "Michael Staknovitch", 24, "Programmer"
Write #1, "Tess Owen", 37, "Engineer"
Write #1, "Joe Dow", 28, "Administrator"
Close #1
```

The structure of the text file, however, is quite different. Here's the output of the Write # statements:

```
"John Ashley",33,"Manager"
"Michael Staknovitch",24,"Programmer"
"Tess Owen",37,"Engineer"
"Joe Dow",28,"Administrator"
```

Width #fNum, length

This is another useful statement that applies to sequential files only. The Width statement sets the maximum line length that can be written to a file. The maximum line length is specified by the second argument, *length*. A line with fewer characters than *length* is stored to the file as is. Longer lines are broken; Visual Basic automatically inserts new line characters to enforce the specified maximum line length.

FileAttr(file_number, return_type)

The FileAttr() function returns a long integer representing the file mode for files opened using the Open statement. The *file_number* argument is the number of the file, and *return_type* must be 1. The value returned is one of those in Table LR.23.

TABLE LR.23: The Values Returned by the FileAttr() Function

VALUE	MODE
1	Input
2	Output
4	Random
8	Append
32	Binary

GRAPHICS

This section discusses the two Visual Basic functions for color definition, as well as the statements and functions for loading (and saving) pictures to any control that exposes a Picture property (Forms, PictureBox, and ImageBox controls).

QBColor(color)

This function returns a Long Integer representing the RGB color code corresponding to the specified color number. The *color* argument is a number in the range 0 through 15. Each value returns a different color, as shown in Table LR.24.

TABLE LR.24: The Values for the *Color* Argument

NUMBER	COLOR
0	Black
1	Blue
2	Green
3	Cyan
4	Red
5	Magenta
6	Yellow
7	White
8	Gray
9	Light Blue
10	Light Green
11	Light Cyan
12	Light Red
13	Light Magenta
14	Light Yellow
15	Bright White

Use the QBColor() function to specify colors if you want to address the needs of users with the least-capable graphics adapter (one that can't display more than the basic 16 colors). Also use it for business applications that don't require many colors.

RGB(red, green, blue)

This function returns a Long Integer representing a color value. The *red*, *green*, and *blue* arguments are integer values in the range 0 through 255, representing the values of the three basic colors. Table LR.25 lists some of the most common colors and their corresponding red, green, and blue components. The colors correspond to the eight corners of the RGB color cube, shown in Figure LR.1.

TABLE LR.25:

Common Colors and Their Corresponding RGB Components

COLOR	RED	GREEN	BLUE
Black	0	0	0
Blue	0	0	255
Green	0	255	0
Cyan	0	255	255
Red	255	0	0
Magenta	255	0	255
Yellow	255	255	0
White	255	255	255

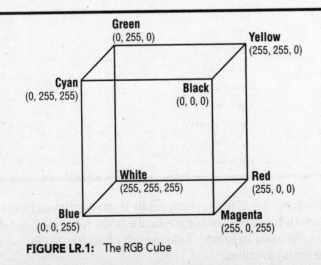

FIGURE LR.1: The RGB Cube

The following statement assigns a pure red color to the background of the Text1 control:

```
Text1.BackColor = RGB(255, 0, 0)
```

The following code segment will fill up a PictureBox control with a gradient between the colors *StartColor* and *EndColor*. The two end colors in this example are red and yellow respectively, but you can modify the values of the variables *StartColor* and *EndColor* to draw a linear gradient between any two colors.

```
' Extract the basic color components of the starting and _
ending colors
StartRed = StartColor Mod 256
EndRed = EndColor Mod 256
StartGreen = (StartColor And &HFF00FF00) / 256&
EndGreen = (EndColor And &HFF00FF00) / 256&)
StartBlue = (StartColor And &HFF0000) / (256& * 256&)
EndBlue = (EndColor And &HFF0000) / (256& * 256&)
' Calculate each basic color's increment along the gradient
Pwidth = Picture1.ScaleWidth
RedInc = (EndRed-StartRed) / Pwidth
GreenInc = (EndGreen-StartGreen) / Pwidth
BlueInc = (EndBlue-StartBlue) / Pwidth
' and draw the gradient
For ipixel = 0 To Pwidth-1
  NewColor = RGB(StartRed + redInc * ipixel, _
          StartGreen + greenInc * ipixel _
          StartBlue + blueInc * ipixel)
  Picture1.Line (ipixel, 0) -(ipixel, Picture1.Height-1), _
        NewColor
Next
```

To achieve a gradient, we must draw successive lines of similar color, starting with *StartColor* and ending with *EndColor*. Along the way, each color component must be increased (or decreased) by an amount that's equal to the difference between the two end colors, divided by the number of lines drawn. This is what the first half of the code does: it calculates the basic color components at the two ends of the gradient and the increments for each color component along the way. The second half of the code generates the gradient by drawing vertical colors that differ from the previous line by a small amount (redInc, greenInc and blueInc). Insert this code segment in a Command Button's Click event handler, place a PictureBox control on the same Form, and click the button to draw the gradient. You should also set the PictureBox control's ScaleMode to 3-pixel so that the vertical lines are drawn for every pixel across the PictureBox control.

LoadPicture([file_name,] size[, colordepth] [,x,y])

Use this function to load a graphic from a disk file on a Form object or a PictureBox or an ImageBox control. The LoadPicture() function returns a Picture object, which must be assigned to the Picture property of a Form object or control.

Notice that all arguments of the LoadPicture() function are optional. The *file_name* argument is the name of the file that contains the image. Visual Basic recognizes the following graphics formats: bitmap files (.bmp) files, icons (.ico), cursors (.cur), run-length encoded files (.rle), metafiles (.wmf), enhanced metafiles (.emf), GIF (.gif) files, and JPEG (.jpg) files. If you omit the *file_name* argument, the LoadPicture() function clears the current image on the Form or the control. To clear the graphic on the Picture1 control, call the LoadPicture() function without arguments:

```
Picture1.Picture = LoadPicture()
```

If the image is a cursor or an icon, the *size* argument specifies the desired cursor or icon size. Likewise, if the image is a cursor or an icon, the *colordepth* argument specifies the desired color depth. Both arguments are variants and must be assigned one of the constants listed in Tables LR.26 and LR.27.

The arguments *x* and *y* specify the width and height of a cursor or icon graphic. If the specified file contains multiple images, the image that matches the specified dimensions will be used. If no exact match can be found, then the best possible match will be used. For icon files, the maximum value for these two arguments is 255. Notice that you can't use the *x* and *y* arguments to resize an image as you load it with the LoadPicture() function.

TABLE LR.26: The Settings of the *Size* Argument

CONSTANT	VALUE	DESCRIPTION
vbLPSmall	0	Small system icon
vbLPLarge	1	Large system icon size, as determined by the video driver
vbLPSmallShell	2	Small shell icon size, as determined by the Caption Buttons size setting on the Appearance tab in the Display dialog box in the Control Panel
vbLPLargeShell	3	Large shell icon size, as determined by the Icon size setting on the Appearance tab in the Display dialog box in the Control Panel
vbLPCustom	4	Custom size, values provided by *x* and *y* arguments

TABLE LR.27: The Settings of the *Colordepth* Argument

CONSTANT	VALUE	DESCRIPTION
vbLPDefault	0	Best available match in the specified file
vbLPMonochrome	1	2 colors
vbLPVGAColor	2	16 colors
vbLPColor	3	256 colors

To load a graphic as a background on a Form, assign the return value of the LoadPicture() function to the Form's Picture property:

```
Form1.Picture = LoadPicture('BGROUND.BMP')
```

Icons are usually assigned to the Icon and DragIcon properties of various controls:

```
Text1.DragIcon = LoadPicture('MOVINGTEXT.ICO')
```

SavePicture picture, file_name

This statement saves the graphic on a control, or Form, to a disk file. The *picture* argument is the Picture or Image property of a control that can display images. This statement is commonly used with the PictureBox control and Forms. The second argument, *file_name*, is the name of a disk file where the bitmap will be stored.

The SavePicture method creates an uncompressed BMP file, and the disk file's extension should be BMP. This is true even if the control's bitmap is a GIF image, loaded at design time (by means of the control's Picture property) or loaded at runtime with the LoadPicture() function. Notice that only the items drawn while the control's AutoRedraw property is set to True are stored in the bitmap. Any shapes placed on the control while AutoRedraw = False will not be saved.

Let's assume you have a Form with a PictureBox control on it. You can load an image to the control and/or draw shapes on it with the control's drawing methods. You can save the bitmap on the control with the SavePicture method, with the following line:

```
SavePicture Picture1.Image, "c:\counter.bmp"
```

The following lines create a counter (a small image that displays the number of visitors to your Web site). The program creates the bitmap of the counter and stores it to a disk file. Then, you can display it on a Web page. (We won't show you here how this is done.)

```
Private Sub Command1_Click()
    SetBackground  Picture1.CurrentX = 60
    Picture1.CurrentY = 0
    Picture1.ForeColor = RGB(255, 0, 0)
    Picture1.Font.Name = "Comic Sans MS"
    Picture1.Font.Size = 24
    Picture1.Print "ACME Inc."
    Picture1.Font.Size = 16
    Picture1.CurrentX = 70
    Picture1.Print "Vistor # 3999"
    SavePicture Picture1.Image, "c:\counter.bmp"
End Sub
```

You can change the hard-coded value 3,999 to any other value. The Set-Background() subroutine (which is not shown in this appendix) draws a gradient on the control's background (see the RGB() entry for more information on drawing gradients). You should also make sure that the Picture-Box control's AutoRedraw property is True. You can insert the following line before the line that prints the visitor number:

```
Picture1.AutoRedraw = False
```

If you execute these lines again and then open the Counter.bmp file, you will see that it has the proper background and text, except for the last line, which was placed on the control while the AutoRedraw property was set to False. In other words, the bitmap will display a gradient background and the name of the company only.

REGISTRY FUNCTIONS

Visual Basic provides a few special functions for storing values in the Registry. These functions are safer than the Registry API functions, and they access only a single branch of the Registry. (In other words, you can't ruin the branch of another application by mistake.)

SaveSetting appname, section, key, setting

This is a statement that stores a new setting in the Registry or updates an existing one. The *appname* argument is the name of the application (or project) that stores the information in the Registry. It doesn't have to be the actual name of the application; it can be any string you supply, as long as it's unique for your application and you use the same value when you read the setting from the Registry with the GetSetting() function. The *section* argument is the name of the section under the application's branch in which the key setting will be saved. The *key* argument is the name of the key setting that will be saved. The last argument, *setting*, is the value of the key to be saved. If *setting* can't be saved for any reason, a runtime trappable error is generated.

The following statements store the keys "Left" and "Top" in the Startup section of the application's branch in the Registry:

```
SaveSetting "MyApp", "Startup", "Top", Me.Top
SaveSetting "MyApp", "Startup", "Left", Me.Left
```

These values should be saved to the Registry when the application ends, and they should be read when it starts, to place the Form on the desktop (they are the coordinates of the Form's upper left corner on the desktop).

DeleteSetting appname, section[, key]

This statement deletes a section or key setting from an application's entry in the Windows registry. Its arguments are the same as the arguments by the same name of the SaveSettings statement, and only the last one is optional. If the last argument is omitted, then all the keys in the specified section are deleted. The following statements delete the "Top" and "Left" keys stored in the Registry with the sample statements of the previous entry:

```
DeleteSetting "MyApp", "Startup", "Top"
DeleteSetting "MyApp", "Startup", "Left"
```

To delete both keys, along with any other keys that may have been saved to the Startup section, use this statement:

```
DeleteSetting "MyApp", "Startup"
```

GetSetting(appname, section, key[, default])

This function returns a key setting from an application's branch in the Registry. The arguments *appname*, *section*, and *key* are the same as in the previous entry. The last argument, *default*, is optional and contains the value to return if no value for the specified key exists in the Registry.

To read the key values stored in the Registry by the statements of the example in the SaveSettings() entry, use the following statements:

```
Me.Top = GetSetting("MyApp", "Startup", "Top", 100)
Me.Left = GetSetting("MyApp", "Startup", "Left", 150)
```

Don't omit the default values here because the Form may be sized oddly if these keys are missing.

GetAllSettings(appname, section)

This function returns a list of keys and their respective values from an application's branch in the Registry. The *appname* argument is the name of the application (or project) whose key settings are requested. The *section* argument is the name of the section whose key settings are requested. The GetAllSettings() function returns all the keys and settings in the specified section of the Registry in a two-dimensional array. The element (0, 0) of the array contains the name of the first key, and the element (0, 1) contains the setting of this key. The next two elements (1, 0) and (1, 1) contain the key and setting of the second element and so on. To find out how many keys are stored in the specific section of the Registry, use the LBound() and UBound() functions on the array returned by the GetAllSettings() function.

The following statement retrieves all the keys in the Startup section for the MyApp application and stores them in the array AllSettings:

```
AllSettings = GetAllSettings("MyApp", "Startup")
```

You can then set up a loop that scans the array and displays the key and setting pairs:

```
For i = LBound(AllSettings, 1) To UBound(AllSettings, 1)
    Debug.Print AllSettings(i, 0) & " = " & AllSettings(i, 1)
Next
```

RESOURCE FILES

To survive in a global market, you should develop applications that can be easily adapted for foreign languages. The ad hoc method of doing so is to allow other developers to edit your source code and translate all the strings used on the application's interface, replace your images and sound files with different ones, and so on.

A better way to build applications that can be easily localized is to use Resource files. Resource files contain information used for the appearance of the user interface and no code at all. When a developer in another country wants to localize your application, all they have to do is edit the Resource file and translate the strings, sounds, and other resources to the target language. The code of the application remains the same, and you don't have to worry about copyright issues.

Visual Basic 6 comes with a Resource Editor that simplifies the compilation of the Resource file. Using these resources in your application, however, requires that you call certain functions, which are described in this section.

Using Resource files has an added benefit: they are loaded faster. (You load one resource at a time as needed, as opposed to opening multiple files and reading more information than required.) Moreover, you don't have to install numerous files (images, sounds, text files) on the user's hard disk. All the resources are included in a single resource file.

LoadResData(index, format)

This loads data from a resource (RES) file and returns a Byte array. Each data item in the resource file (string, bitmap, sound, and so on) is identified by an index. The index of the desired item is specified with the *index* argument. The second argument, *format*, specifies the format of the data being returned and can have one of the values shown in Table LR.28. It can also be the name of a user-defined resource.

TABLE LR.28:

The Values of the *format* Argument

SETTING	DESCRIPTION
1	Cursor resource
2	Bitmap resource
3	Icon resource
4	Menu resource
5	Dialog box
6	String resource
7	Font directory resource
8	Font resource
9	Accelerator table
10	User-defined resource
12	Group cursor
14	Group icon

The data loaded from a resource file with the LoadResData function cannot exceed 64 Kbytes. If you attempt to load a bitmap, icon, or cursor resource with the LoadResData() function, the function will return a string with the actual bits in the resource. These resources should be loaded with the LoadResPicture() function, which returns a bitmap object.

Let's assume you have created a Resource file (with the Resource Editor add-in), and it contains a number of WAV sound files, each one with a message in a different language. First, you must assign the proper value to a variable for each of the languages the application was designed. This variable will identify the locale. Let's say you have programmed the application for three different languages. All the strings, sounds, and so on used by the application must be translated into three different languages and stored in a Resource file. The variable, which we'll call ResID, should be set when the application starts with statements like the following:

```
Select Case Language
   Case "English": ResID = 16
   Case "French": ResID = 48
   Case "German": ResID = 80
End Select
```

Later in the code, you can retrieve a resource for a specific language by specifying its Resource ID. The IDs will be generated while you create the Resource file. To play back a sound, you must first retrieve the bytes of the WAV file, store them to a local buffer, and then play back the sound with the sndPlaySound() API function. The buffer must be declared as an array of bytes with a statement like the following:

```
Dim SoundBuffer() As Byte
```

There's no need to specify the array's size; the array will be resized while the data is being loaded. The following two statements retrieve the sound's bytes and play them back:

```
SoundBuffer = LoadResData(ResID, "Sounds")
sndPlaySound SoundBuffer(0), SND_ASYNC Or SND_NODEFAULT Or _
SND_MEMORY
```

To complete the example, here are the declarations of the API function and the related constants:

```
Declare Function sndPlaySound Lib "WINMM.DLL" Alias _
"sndPlaySoundA" _
    (lpszSoundName As Any, ByVal uFlags As Long) As Long

Global Const SND_ASYNC = &H1
Global Const SND_NODEFAULT = &H2
Global Const SND_MEMORY = &H4
```

For more information on API functions, see Chapter 7, "Visual Basic and the Windows API."

LoadResPicture(index, format)

This function loads bitmap, icon, and cursor data from a Resource file. The LoadResPicture() function returns an Image object, which you assign to the Picture or Icon property of a control. Each data item in the Resource file (string, bitmap, sound, and so on) is identified by an index. The index of the desired item is specified with the *index* argument. The second argument, *format*, specifies the format of the data being returned and can have one of the values shown in Table LR.29. It can also be the name of a user-defined resource.

TABLE LR.29: The Value of the Format Argument for Picture Resources

CONSTANT	VALUE	DESCRIPTION
vbResBitmap	0	Bitmap resource
vbResIcon	1	Icon resource
vbResCursor	2	Cursor resource

Let's assume you have stored a few bitmaps for each language in the Resource file. To retrieve the first bitmap of the current language, use the index *ResID*. For the second bitmap, use the index *ResID + 1*, and so on. In addition to the index of the desired resource, you must also specify the type of bitmap. The following function will retrieve the second bitmap for the current language:

```
LoadResPicture(ResID+1, vbResBitmap)
```

To display the bitmap on a PictureBox control, use the statement

```
Picture1.Picture = LoadResPicture(ResID+1, vbResBitmap)
```

LoadResString(index)

The LoadResString() function loads a string from a Resource file. The *index* argument specifies the ID of the string in the Resource file.

Loading strings from a Resource file is quite trivial, but in addition to the resource's ID, you must also specify an index that corresponds to the desired string. Let's say that the first string is a welcome message and the following three strings are the captions of three Command buttons. You must specify four strings for each language.

To retrieve the captions of the three buttons in the current language, use the following statements:

```
Command1.Caption = LoadResString(ResID+1)
Command2.Caption = LoadResString(ResID+2)
Command3.Caption = LoadResString(ResID+3)
```

The first string in the Resource file has a zero index.

CONTROL FLOW STATEMENTS

The capability to examine external conditions and act accordingly makes programming languages flexible and capable of handling every situation and programming challenge. Programs are not monolithic sets of commands that carry out the same calculations every time they are executed. Instead, they adjust their behavior depending on the data supplied; on external conditions, such as a mouse click or the existence of a peripheral; or even on abnormal conditions generated by the program itself. In addition, they can repeat the same calculations a fixed number of times or while a condition is True. This section of the reference discusses the conditional and looping statements of Visual Basic.

CONDITIONAL STATEMENTS

An application needs a built-in capability to test conditions and take a different course of action depending on the outcome of the test. Visual Basic provides three decision structures:

- ▶ If...Then
- ▶ If...Then...Else
- ▶ Select Case

If...Then and If...Then...Else

The If structure tests the condition specified and, if it's True, executes the statement(s) that follow. The If structure can have a single-line or a multiple-line syntax. To execute one statement conditionally, use the single-line syntax as follows:

```
If condition Then statement
```

Visual Basic evaluates the condition and, if it's True, executes the statement that follows. If the condition is not True, it continues with the statement following the If structure.

You can execute multiple statements by separating them with a colon:

```
If condition Then statement: statement: statement
```

Here's an example of a single-line If statement:

```
If Month(date) = 1 Then Year = Year + 1
```

You can break this statement into multiple lines, as shown here:

```
If Month(date) = 1 Then
  Year = Year + 1
End If
```

Some programmers prefer the multiple-line syntax of the If...Then statement, even if it contains a single statement, because the code is easier to read.

A variation of the If...Then statement is the If...Then...Else statement, which executes one block of statements if the condition is True and another if the condition is False. The syntax of the If...Then...Else statement is as follows:

```
If condition Then
   statementblock-1
Else
   statementblock-2
End If
```

Visual Basic evaluates the condition. If it's True, it executes the first block of statements and then jumps to the statement following the End If statement. If the condition is False, Visual Basic ignores the first block of statements and executes the block following the *Else* keyword.

Another variation of the If...Then...Else statement uses several conditions, with the *ElseIf* keyword:

```
If condition1 Then
   statementblock-1
ElseIf condition2 Then
   statementblock-2
ElseIf condition3 Then
   statementblock-3
Else
   statementblock-4
End If
```

You can have any number of ElseIf clauses. The conditions are evaluated from the top, and if one of them is True, the corresponding block of statements is executed. The Else clause will be executed if none of the previous expressions were True. Here's an example of an If statement with ElseIf clauses:

```
score = InputBox("Enter score")
If score < 50 Then
  Result = "Failed"
ElseIf score < 75 Then
  Result = "Pass"
ElseIf score < 90 Then
  Result = "Very Good"
Else
  Result = "Excellent"
End If
MsgBox Result
```

Notice that once a True condition is found, Visual Basic executes the associated statements and skips the remaining clauses. It continues executing the program with the statement immediately after End If. That's why you should prefer the complicated structure with ElseIf statements to the equivalent series of simple If statements:

```
If score < 50 Then
 Result = "Failed"
End If
If score < 75 And score >= 50 Then
 Result = "Pass"
End If
If score < 90 And score > =75 Then
 Result = "Very Good"
End If
If score >= 90 Then
 Result = "Excellent"
End If
```

You may have also noticed that the order of the comparisons is vital in a nested If...Then structure that uses ElseIf statements. Had you written the previous code segment as follows (we switched the first two conditions), then the results would be quite unexpected.

```
If score < 75 Then
 Result = "Pass"
ElseIf score < 50 Then
 Result = "Failes"
ElseIf score < 90 Then
 Result = "Very Good"
```

```
Else
 Result = "Excellent"
End If
```

A student who made 49 would have passed the test! The code would compare the score variable (49) to the value 75. Because 49 is less than 75, it would assign the value "Pass" to the variable Result, and then it would skip the remaining clauses. Be extremely careful and thoroughly test your code if it uses multiple ElseIf clauses.

Because the multiple ElseIf structure can create efficient but difficult-to-read code, an alternative is available: the Select Case statement.

Select Case

The Select Case structure compares the same expression to a different value. The advantage of the Select Case statement over multiple If...Then...Else statements is that it makes the code easier to read and maintain.

The Select Case structure tests a single expression, which is evaluated once at the top of the structure. The result of the test is then compared with several values, and if it matches one of them, the corresponding block of statements is executed. Here's the syntax of the Select Case statement:

```
Select Case expression
Case value1
   statementblock-1
Case value2
   statementblock-2
      .

      .

      .
Case Else
   statementblock
End Select
```

Here's a practical example based on the Select Case statement:

```
Select Case WeekDay(Date)
Case 1
 DayName = "Monday"
 Message = "Have a nice week"
Case 6
 DayName = "Saturday"
 Message = "Have a nice weekend"
Case 7
```

```
    DayName = "Sunday"
    Message = "Did you have a nice weekend?"
  Case Else
    Message = "Welcome back!"
  End Select
```

The term *expression,* which is evaluated at the beginning of the statement, is the number of the weekday, as reported by the WeekDay() function (a value in the range 1 to 7). The value of *expression* is then compared with the values that follow each *Case* keyword. If they match, the block of the following statements up to the next *Case* keyword is executed, and the program skips to the statement following the End Select statement. The block of the Case Else statement is optional and is executed if none of the previous Case values match the expression.

Some Case statements can be followed by multiple values, which are separated by commas. Here's a revised version of the previous example:

```
  Select Case WeekDay(Date)
  Case 1
    Message = "Have a nice week"
    DayType = "Workday"
  Case 2, 3, 4, 5
    Message = "Welcome back!"
    DayType = "Workday"
  Case 6, 7
    Message = "Have a nice weekend"
    DayType = "Holiday"
  End Select
```

The five workdays and the two weekend days are handled by two Case statements with multiple values. This structure doesn't contain a Case Else statement because all values are examined in the Case statements. The WeekDay() function can't return another value.

If more than one Case value matches the expression, only the statement block associated with the first matching Case will execute.

Here is the equivalent If...Then...Else statement that would implement the previous example:

```
  today = WeekDay(Date)
  If today > 0 And today < 6 Then
    Message = "Welcome back!"
    DayType = "Workday"
  Else
    Message = "Have a nice weekend"
    DayType = "Holiday"
  End If
```

A glance at this coding shows it is overdone. If you attempt to implement a more elaborate Select Case statement with If...Then...Else statements, the code becomes even more difficult to read. Here is the first example, implemented with If...Then...Else statements:

```
today = WeekDay(date)
If today = 1 Then
  DayName = "Monday"
  Message = "Have a nice week"
Elseif today = 6 Then
  DayName = "Saturday"
  Message = "Have a nice weekend"
Elseif today = 7 Then
  DayName = "Sunday"
  Message = "Did you have a nice weekend?"
End If
```

Of course, the Select Case statement can't substitute for any If...Then structure. The Select Case structure evaluates the expression at the beginning only. In contrast, the If...Then...Else structure can evaluate a different expression for each ElseIf statement.

LOOP STATEMENTS

Loop statements allow you to execute one or more lines of code repetitively. Many tasks consist of trivial operations that must be repeated, so looping structures are an important part of any programming language. Visual Basic supports the following loop statements:

- ▶ Do...Loop
- ▶ For...Next
- ▶ While...Wend

Do...Loop

The Do...Loop executes a block of statements for as long as a condition is True. There are two variations of the Do...Loop statement, but both use the same basic model. Visual Basic evaluates an expression, and if it's True, the statements are executed. If the expression is not True, the program continues, and the statement following the loop is executed.

The loop can be executed either while the condition is True or until the condition becomes True. The two variations of the Do...Loop use the keywords *While* and *Until* to specify how long the statements are executed. To execute a block of statements while a condition is True, use the following syntax:

```
Do While condition
  statement-block
Loop
```

To execute a block of statements until the condition becomes True, use the following syntax:

```
Do Until condition
  statement-block
Loop
```

When Visual Basic executes the previous loops, it first evaluates *condition*. If *condition* is False, the Do While or Do Until loop is skipped (the statements aren't even executed once). When the Loop statement is reached, Visual Basic evaluates the *condition* again. It will repeat the statement block of the Do While loop if the *condition* is True, or it will repeat the statements of the Do Until loop if the *condition* is False.

The Do...Loop can execute any number of times as long as the *condition* is True (or nonzero if the condition evaluates to a number). Moreover, the number of iterations need not be known before the loop starts. If the *condition* is initially False, the statements may never execute.

Here's a typical example of using Do...Loops. Suppose the string MyText holds a piece of text (perhaps the Text property of a TextBox control) and you want to count the words in the text. We will assume that there are no multiple spaces in the text and that the space character separates successive words. To locate an instance of a character in a string, use the InStr() function, which accepts three arguments:

▶ The starting location of the search

▶ The text to be searched

▶ The character being searched

The following loop repeats for as long as there are spaces in the text. Each time the InStr() function finds another space in the text, it returns the location (a positive number) of the space. When there are no more spaces in the text, the InStr() function returns zero, which signals the end of the loop.

```
position = 1
Do While position > 0
  position = InStr(position + 1, MyText, " ")
```

```
        words = words + 1
        Loop
        Debug.Print words
```

The Do...Loop is executed while the InStr() function returns a positive number, which happens for as long as there are more words in the text. The variable *position* holds the location of each successive space character in the text. The search for the next space starts at the location of the current space plus 1 (so that the program won't keep finding the same space). For each space found, the program increments the value of the *words* variable, which holds the total number of words when the loop ends.

You may notice a problem with the previous code segment. It assumes that the text contains at least one word and starts by setting the *position* variable to 1. If the *MyText* variable contains an empty string, the program reports that it contains one word. To fix this problem, you must specify the condition as follows:

```
        Do While InStr(position + 1, MyText, " ")
        position = InStr(position + 1, MyText, " ")
        words = words + 1
        Loop
        Debug.Print words
```

This code segment counts the number of words correctly, even if the *MyText* variable contains an empty string. If the *MyText* string variable doesn't contain any spaces, the function InStr(position + 1, MyText, " ") returns 0, which corresponds to False, and the Do...Loop isn't executed.

You can code the same routine with the *Until* keyword. In this case, you must continue to search for spaces until the position becomes zero. Here's the same code with a different loop (the InStr() function returns 0 if the string it searches for doesn't exist in the longer string):

```
        position = 1
        Do Until position = 0
        position = InStr(position + 1, MyText, " ")
        words = words + 1
        Loop
        Debug.Print words
```

Another variation of the Do...Loop executes the statements first and evaluates the condition after each execution. This Do...Loop has the following syntax:

```
        Do
            {statements}
        Loop While condition
```

or

```
Do
   {statements}
Loop Until condition
```

The statements in this type of loop execute at least once because the condition is examined at the end of the loop. Could we have implemented the previous example with one of the last two types of loops? The fact that we had to do something special about zero-length strings suggests that this problem shouldn't be coded with a loop that tests the condition at the end. Because the loop's body will be executed once, the *words* variable is never going to be zero.

As you can see, you can code loops in a number of ways with the Do...Loop statement, and which one you use depends on the problem at hand and your programming style. Of course, text is not made up of words separated by single spaces. You may have multiple spaces between words, tabs, and multiple lines of text. The following code counts the words in a TextBox control, taking into consideration multiple spaces and carriage return and line feed characters:

```
Dim position As Long
Dim words As Long
Dim myText As String

    position = 1
    myText = Text1.Text
' replace line feeds with spaces
    myText = Replace(myText, Chr(13) & Chr(10), " ")
' replace tabs with single spaces
    myText = Replace(myText, Chr(9), " ")
    myText = Trim(myText)
' Count the first word
' Because the last word isn't delimited by
' a space, if the string isn't blank, then it
' contains at least one word.
' By setting words=1, we won't have to increase the
' number of words by 1 when we are done counting.
    If Len(myText) > 0 Then words = 1
' while the string contains spaces...
    Do While position > 0
       position = InStr(position, myText, " ")
       ' ... increase word count
       If position > 0 Then
          words = words + 1
          ' and skip additional spaces
          While Mid(myText, position, 1) = " "
```

```
            position = position + 1
         Wend
      End If
   Loop
   MsgBox "The TextBox contains " & words & " words"
```

For...Next

The For...Next Loop is one of the oldest loop structures in programming languages. Unlike the Do...Loop, the For...Next Loop requires that you know how many times the statements in the loop will be executed. The For...Next Loop uses a variable (it's called the loop's counter) that increases or decreases in value during each repetition of the loop. The For...Next Loop has the following syntax. (The keywords in square brackets are optional.)

```
For counter = start To end [Step increment]
statements
Next [counter]
```

The arguments *counter*, *start*, *end*, and *increment* are all numeric. The loop is executed as many times as required for the counter to reach (or exceed) the end value.

In executing a For...Next Loop, Visual Basic does the following:

1. Sets *counter* equal to *start*.

2. Tests to see if *counter* is greater than *end*. If so, it exits the loop. If *increment* is negative, Visual Basic tests to see if *counter* is less than *end*, in which case it exits the loop.

3. Executes the statements in the block.

4. Increments *counter* by the amount specified with the *increment* argument. If the *increment* argument isn't specified, *counter* is incremented by 1.

5. Repeats the statements.

The following For...Next Loop scans all the elements of the numeric array data() and calculates their average:

```
For i = 0 To UBound(data)
 total = total + data(i)
Next i
Debug.Print total / UBound(a)
```

The single most important thing to keep in mind when working with For...Next loops is that the loop's counter is set at the beginning of the loop. Changing the value of the end variable in the loop's body won't have any effect. The following loop will be executed 10 times, not 100 times:

```
endValue = 10
For i = 0 To endValue
 endValue = 100
 {more statements}
Next i
```

You can, however, adjust the value of the counter from within the loop. The following is an endless, or infinite, loop:

```
For i = 0 To 10
 Debug.Print i
 i = i - 1
Next i
```

This loop never ends because the loop's counter, in effect, is never increased. (If you try this, press Control+Break to interrupt the endless loop.)

Manipulating the counter of a For...Next Loop is strongly discouraged. This practice will most likely lead to bugs, such as infinite loops, overflows, and so on. If the number of repetitions of a loop isn't known in advance, use a Do...Loop or a While...Wend structure (discussed in the following section).

The *increment* argument can be either positive or negative. If *start* is greater than *end,* the value of *increment* must be negative. If not, the loop's body will not be executed, not even once.

Finally, the counter variable need not be listed after the Next statement, but it makes the code easier to read, especially when For...Next loops are nested within each other (nested loops are discussed in the section "Nested Control Structures" later in this reference).

While...Wend Loop

The While...Wend Loop executes a block of statements while a *condition* is True and its syntax is

```
While condition
 statement-block
Wend
```

If *condition* is True, all statements are executed, and when the Wend statement is reached, control is returned to the While statement, which evaluates condition again. If *condition* is still True, the process is repeated. If *condition* is False, the program resumes with the statement following the Wend statement.

The following While...Wend loop prompts the user for numeric data. The user can type a negative value to indicate that all values are entered:

```
number = 0
While number => 0
  total = total + number
  number = InputBox("Please enter another value")
Wend
```

You assign the value 0 to the number variable before the loop starts because this value can't affect the total. Another technique is to precede the While statement with an InputBox function to get the first number from the user.

Application Collaboration

In this section we present the Shell() function, which allows you to start another application from within your VB application. Once the application has been started successfully, you can activate its window remotely and send keystrokes to it as if they were typed in the remote application's window. This is a rude way of automating another application, but if the application you want to automate doesn't support VBA, the Shell() function and related statements are the only options.

Shell(path_name [,windowstyle])

This function starts another application and returns a value representing the program's task ID if successful; otherwise, it returns zero. The task ID is a unique number that identifies the application and is used by other statements to contact the application. The *path_name* argument is the full path name of the application to be started and any arguments it may expect. The optional argument *windowstyle* determines the style of the window in which the application will be executed, and it can have one of the values shown in Table LR.30.

TABLE LR.30: The Values of the *windowstyle* Argument

Value	Description
vbHide (0)	The window is hidden, and the focus is passed to it.
vbNormalFocus (1)	The window has the focus and is restored to its original size and position.

TABLE LR.30 (continued): The Values of the *windowstyle* Argument

Value	Description
vbMinimizedFocus (2)	The window is displayed as an icon that has the focus.
vbMaximizedFocus (3)	The window is maximized and has the focus.
vbNormalNoFocus (4)	The window is restored to its most recent size and position. The currently active window remains active.
vbMinimizedNoFocus (6)	The window is displayed as an icon. The currently active window remains active.

The Shell function runs other programs asynchronously. This means that a program started with Shell might not finish executing before the statements following the Shell function are executed.

To start Notepad from within your VB application, use the following statement:

```
NPAD = Shell("notepad.exe")
```

Notice that you need not specify the path name of the executable file, if it's on the path (the `Notepad.exe` file resides in the Windows folder). The NPAD value identifies the specific instance of the Notepad application and you can use it from within your code to manipulate the external application. As you have guessed, starting an application would be a nearly useless feature if you couldn't manipulate it from within your VB code. There are two statements, the AppActivate and SendKeys statement, which allow you to manipulate the application you started with the Shell() function. The statements are discussed next.

AppActivate title [, wait]

This statement lets you activate an application that you started previously from within your VB code with the Shell() function. The first argument, *title*, specifies the title of the application (as it appears in the title bar of the application's window). You can also use the ID of the application returned by the Shell() function. The *wait* argument is optional, and it's a Boolean value that determines whether the calling application has the focus before activating another. If it's False (the default value), the specified application is immediately activated, even if the calling application does not have the focus. If it's True, your application must wait until it gets the focus before it can activate the external application. The

AppActivate statement changes the focus to the named application or window but does not affect whether it is maximized or minimized.

If you're using the application's title to activate it, make sure you provide enough information to make it unique. Word's title is "Microsoft Word" followed by the name of the active document. If you specify the string "Microsoft Word" only and there are multiple instances of Word running, you don't know which one will be activated by the AppActivate statement. It is best to use the ID of the application you started with the Shell() function.

SendKeys string[, wait]

Use the SendKeys statement to send keystrokes to the active window, as if typed at the keyboard. Every task that can be carried out in the active application with the keyboard (without using the mouse) can also be automated from within your VB application with the SendKeys statement.

The *string* argument is a string that specifies the keystrokes to be sent to the active application. The *wait* optional argument specifies whether control is relinquished to your application immediately after the keys are sent (the default) or whether keystrokes must first be processed before control is returned to the VB application.

To start Calculator and calculate the logarithm of 77.999, use the following statements:

```
CALC = Shell("Calc.exe")
AppActivate CALC
SendKeys "77.999L", True
```

At this point, the result will appear on the calculator's display (1.892089034777). The digits sent to the Calculator application will appear on its display. When the L key is sent, it will simulate the press of the Log button, which calculates the logarithm of the value displayed and replaces the original value on the display with the result of the calculation. You will soon see how you can retrieve the result and use it in your application.

To specify single keyboard characters, use the characters themselves. To display the string "Visual Basic" in a word processor's window, use the statement

```
SendKeys "Visual Basic"
```

A few characters have special meaning with SendKeys. These special characters are the plus sign (+), caret (^), percent sign (%), tilde (~), and parentheses ( ). To specify one of these characters, enclose it within braces ({ }). For example, to specify the plus sign, use

```
SendKeys "{+}"
```

Brackets ([ ]) have no special meaning to SendKeys, but you must enclose them in braces. Finally, to specify braces, use the strings {{} and {}} for the opening and closing braces respectively.

Some keys don't produce visible characters on the screen, but they usually cause the application to perform some action. To specify these keys, use the codes in the second column of Table LR.31.

TABLE LR.31: The Special Key Codes Used by SendKeys

KEY	CODE
Backspace	{BACKSPACE}, {BS}, or {BKSP}
Break	{BREAK}
Caps Lock	{CAPSLOCK}
Del or Delete	{DELETE} or {DEL}
Down Arrow	{DOWN}
End	{END}
Enter	{ENTER} or ~
Esc	{ESC}
Help	{HELP}
Home	{HOME}
Ins or Insert	{INSERT} or {INS}
Left Arrow	{LEFT}
Num Lock	{NUMLOCK}
Page Down	{PGDN}
Page Up	{PGUP}
Print Screen	{PRTSC}
Right Arrow	{RIGHT}
Scroll Lock	{SCROLLLOCK}
Tab	{TAB}
Up Arrow	{UP}
F1	{F1}

TABLE LR.31 (continued): The Special Key Codes Used by SendKeys

KEY	CODE
F2	{F2}
F3	{F3}
F4	{F4}
F5	{F5}
F6	{F6}
F7	{F7}
F8	{F8}
F9	{F9}
F10	{F10}
F11	{F11}
F12	{F12}
F13	{F13}
F14	{F14}
F15	{F15}
F16	{F16}

To specify keys combined with any combination of the Shift, Ctrl, and Alt keys, precede the key code with one or more of the following codes:

Key	Code
Shift	+
Ctrl	^
Alt	%

To specify that any combination of Shift, Ctrl, and Alt should be held down while several other keys are pressed, enclose the code for those keys in parentheses. For example, if you want to hold down Shift while V and B are pressed, use "+(VB)". The expression "+VB" would produce the keystrokes Shift+V, then B. To specify that Shift and Control must be down while 1 is pressed, use "+^1" (or "^+1").

You can also specify repeating keys, using the form {key number}. To move the cursor 10 places to the right, use the string "{RIGHT 10}".

The following code segment performs the following. First, it starts the WordPad and Calculator accessories. The IDs of the two windows are stored in the variables WPAD and CALC respectively. Then, it sends the appropriate keystrokes to the Calculator accessory to calculate the sine of 0.399. Start the Calculator, and type the following: **Alt V**, **S**, **0.399**, **S**, **=**, **Ctrl C** and **Alt F4**. Then, open the Clipboard accessory and you'll see the result pasted there. If you send the same keystrokes to Calculator, the result will be copied to the Clipboard, and you'll be able to use it in any other application. The keystrokes Alt+V and S invoke the Scientific command of the View menu. Then the value 0.399 is entered and the S keystroke simulates the click of the Sin button, which calculates the sine of the value on the display. Finally, the Ctrl+C keystroke invokes the Copy command, which copies the result to the Clipboard. The last keystroke closes the Calculator application.

The program then activates WordPad and sends it the following keystrokes:

Alt F   Starts a new document

Enter   Closes the New Document dialog box

Then it sends some text, which is entered as is. Notice that new lines are entered with the code "{ENTER}".

Alt EL   Invokes the Select All command of the Edit menu

Alt OF   Invokes the Font command of the Format menu

Then, the program enters the name of the new font, tabs to the next box, and selects Bold. It sends another Enter to close the Font dialog box. The result of these operations is to format the entire text.

Finally, it moves to the end of the text with the Ctrl+End keystrokes and inserts the result of the previous calculations (which is on the Clipboard) with the Shift Insert keystroke.

```
Private Sub Command1_Click()
    WPAD = Shell("C:\Program Files\ACCESS~1\WORDPAD.EXE", _
        vbMinimizedFocus)
    CALC = Shell("Calc.exe")
    AppActivate CALC
    SendKeys "%V", True
    SendKeys "S", True
    SendKeys "0.399", True
    SendKeys "s", True
    SendKeys "=", True
    SendKeys "^C", True
```

```
    SendKeys "%{F4}", True
    AppActivate WPAD
    SendKeys "%FN", True
    SendKeys "{ENTER}"
    SendKeys "This is some text", True
    SendKeys "{ENTER}", True
    SendKeys "and these are some special symbols", True
    SendKeys "{ENTER}", True
    SendKeys "{&}{^}{+}", True
    SendKeys "%EL", True
    SendKeys "%OF", True
    SendKeys "Comic Sans MS{TAB}Bold", True
    SendKeys "{ENTER}", True
    SendKeys "^{END}", True
    SendKeys "{ENTER}", True
    SendKeys "The sine of 0.399 is: ", True
    SendKeys "+{INSERT}", True
End Sub
```

OBJECTS

The following functions and statements create and manipulate object variables, custom component properties and events, and so on. If you are developing custom ActiveX controls, Classes, or even simple applications to automate other applications through VBA, you will run into these entries quite frequently. The presentation of the entries in this section is rather brief, and you should be familiar with object programming in order to use this reference material.

CreateObject(class[, server_name])

The CreateObject() function starts an OLE compliant application and returns a reference to the application or one of the objects it exposes. The application's Class name is *class*, and *server_name* is the name of the server on which the object will be created (the name of the machine on the network where the application executes). The Class name of Microsoft Word is "Word.Application," and the Class name of Excel is "Excel.Application." To start Word on your own computer, use the following statements:

```
    Dim WordApp As Word.Application
    Set WordApp = CreateObject("Word.Application")
```

You must also add a reference to the Microsoft Word 8.0 Object Library to the project (through the Project ➤ References dialog box). If Word is installed on the machine Toolkit on the network, use this statement to start a new instance of Word remotely:

```
Set WordApp = CreateObject("Word.Application", "Toolkit")
```

Through the object variable returned by the CreateObject() function, you can control (automate) the other application from within your VB application. If you type **WordApp.** in the editor, you will see the names of the members exposed by the referenced application. The property WordApp.Name returns the string "Microsoft Word." To access a document, use the Documents collection. To start a new document, use the statement

```
WordApp.Documents.Add
```

In general, use the *WordApp* variable to access the members exposed by Word and manipulate it from within your VB application. By default, the new instance of Word is invisible. To make it visible, set its Word-App.Visible property to True.

When you are done, you must close this instance of Word by calling its Quit method:

```
WordApp.Quit
```

Finally, you must reset the object variable *WordApp*, when you no longer need it, by setting it to *Nothing:*

```
Set WordApp = Nothing
```

Make sure that you terminate all the instances of applications you start with the CreateObject() function and release the corresponding object variable by setting them to Nothing. Because the instances of applications started with the CreateObject() function remain invisible, you can easily start a dozen instances of an application and have them all open. While you're testing your application, press Ctrl+Alt+Delete to see the Close Program window, which displays all running applications. If you see too many instances of Winword or any other application you have started with the CreateObject() function, shut it down manually.

In addition to contacting applications like Word, or Excel, the Create-Object() function is used to contact custom Classes (ActiveX EXE or ActiveX DLL code components). Let's say you have created a Class called Crypto-Class, which encrypts text. To use it in your applications, you must create an object variable and set it to this Class with the following statements:

```
Dim cryptoObject As CryptoClass
Set cryptoObject = CreateObject("Crypto.CryptoClass")
```

Here *Crypto.CryptoClass* is the Class's ID. You can also use the New keyword in the declaration of the object variable and skip the CreateObject() function altogether:

```
Dim cryptoObject As New CryptoClass
```

GetObject([path_name] [, class])

The CreateObject() function starts a new instance of the specified application, even if one is already running. If you don't need a new instance (and in most situations you don't), you can contact the existing instance of an application with the GetObject() function. In addition to contacting an existing instance of the application, the GetObject() function can also open an existing document with its application (a DOC file with Word, for example).

Both arguments of the GetObject() function are optional, but one of them must be specified. The *class* argument has the same meaning as the CreateObject() function. The *path_name* argument is the name of the document you want to open. The following statement will contact a running instance of Word and open the specified document:

```
Set WordDoc = GetObject("C:\PERSONAL\STATEMENTS.DOC")
```

The WordDoc object variable does not represent the application this time. It represents the document opened with the GetObject() function. For example, you can find out the number of words in the document with the statement

```
totalWords = WordDoc.Words.Count
```

You can use any property or methods exposed by the Document application to manipulate the `Statements.doc` document. After you are done, close the document with the statement

```
WordDoc.Close
```

and release the WordDoc object variable by setting it to Nothing. You should not shut down the application because it may be processing another document at the time.

If you want to contact an existing application but not open a document, you can use the GetObject() function but specify its second argument only. Let's contact the running instance of Excel to carry out some calculations:

```
Dim EXLApp As Excel.Application
Set EXLApp = GetObject(, "Excel.Application")
Result = EXLApp.Evaluate("2/log(9.5/0.56)")
```

After you are done, you can set the *EXLApp* object variable to Nothing but don't close Excel. If you have added any new worksheets, you should also close them.

You're probably wondering how your application knows whether an instance of the application it needs to contact is already running? Well, it doesn't, but there are several ways to find out. One way is to attempt to contact a running instance of the application. If an error occurs, start a new instance of the application. The following code segment attempts to contact Excel; if it's not running, start a new instance of Excel:

```
On Error Resume Next
Set EXLApp = GetObject(, "Excel.Application")
If EXLApp Is Nothing Then
  Set EXLApp = CreateObject("Excel.Application")
  If EXLApp Is Nothing Then
    MsgBox "Could not start Excel, will abort"
    End
  End If
End If
```

The statement On Error Resume Next tells VB to continue execution, even if an error occurs. If the GetObject() function doesn't return a valid reference to Excel (because it's not running), then we attempt to start a new instance of the application with the CreateObject() function. If this function fails too, then Excel probably isn't installed on the host system and the program terminates. The *EXLApp* variable must be declared as Object or Excel.Application (the latter is recommended).

Set variable_name = [New] objectreference

The Set statement is used to assign an object reference to another object or object variable. The name of the object variable is *object_variable*, and *objectreference* is an object or a reference to an object (that is, another object variable that has already been set). The *New* keyword is optional and tells Visual Basic to create a new instance of the object being referenced. Here's an example. A TextBox control on a Form is an object, which is referenced by its name (Text1). You can assign this control to an object variable, with a statement like the following:

```
Set myText = Text1
```

(You can't use the *New* keyword with controls. If you need information on how to create new controls at runtime, see the section "Load" in this reference.) After the previous statement is executed, Visual Basic will create an object variable and assign it a reference to the Text1 control. In other words, you'll be able to refer to the properties of the Text1 control on the Form either with its name, as in

```
Text1.Text = "This is Text1"
```

or with the *myText* variable, as in

```
MyText.Text = "This is also Text1"
```

Object variables can be Variants (i.e., they can store references to any object) or have a specific type (and store objects of this type only). To make an object variable that can store references to TextBox controls, use a declaration like

```
Dim myText As TextBox
```

If you insert the last declaration in a module, you can type **myText.** (notice the period following the name of the variable) to see the list of members (provided the AutoList Members feature of the editor is turned on). Visual Basic knows the type of object you are referring to and can check the syntax of the statements as you enter them. This is called *early binding* (the variable is bound to the object at design time). If you don't declare your object variables, Visual Basic doesn't know whether the member you specified exists or not. A property like *myText.Text* is as good as *MyText.Caption*. Because Visual Basic can't check your code at design time, it must at runtime contact the object, find out whether it exposes a specific member, and only then use it. In the case of *MyText.Caption*, it will find out that the TextBox control doesn't support a Caption property, and it will generate a runtime error. This is called *late binding* (the variable is bound to the object at runtime) and can lead to runtime errors. I recommend that you declare your object variables before using them. You can also create dynamic object variables, which reference different objects in the course of the application. In this case, you must declare your variables as

```
Dim dynVar1 As Object, dynVar2 As Object
```

Let's look at an example of the *New* keyword. One of the most common objects of Visual Basic is the stdFont object, which represents a Font. You can create a new Font object in your application by declaring it as

```
Dim newFont As New StdFont
```

The *New* keyword tells Visual Basic to create a reference to a new Font (and not an existing one). Later in your code, you can manipulate the properties of the new Font with statements like the following:

```
newFont.Name = "Comic Sans MS"
newFont.Size = 24
newFont.Bold = True
```

The new font isn't used anywhere. To see the font you have created, assign it to the Font property of a control on the Form, using the Set statement, as shown here:

```
Set Text1.Font = newFont
```

The text on the Text1 control will be rendered in the new font, as if you had changed the property *Text1.Font.*

Property Get

This statement declares a procedure that retrieves the value of a property of a custom control or an object exposed by a Form. The procedures that manipulate properties are called Property procedures, and they are declared as follows:

```
Property Get property_name [(arglist)] [As type]
  {statements}
  property_name = expression
  Exit Property
  {more statements}
  property_name = expression
End Property
```

The *Property* keyword can be prefixed by one of the following modifiers:

Public   The procedure can be called from other applications.

Private   The procedure can be called only from other components of the same module.

Friend   The procedure can be called from other components in the same project but not from other applications. The Friend modifier can be used only in a Class Module.

If no scope modifier is specified explicitly, the procedure is Public (and so is the corresponding property).

The procedure is called *property_name.* Normally, the same name will be used with a Property Let procedure, which sets the value of the same property (unless the property is read only). *arglist* is a list of arguments that must be passed to the procedure by the calling module. Each argument must be declared as

```
argument_name As argument_type
```

Multiple arguments are separated by commas. The name and data type of each argument in a Property Get procedure must be the same as the corresponding argument in a Property Let procedure (if one exists). The return type of a Property Get procedure must be of the same data type as the actual property. A property that can be assigned integer values, for example, should be declared As Integer. Each argument must be prefixed with the keyword ByVal, if it's going to be passed by value. The *ByRef* keyword is not needed because this is the default argument-passing mechanism of Visual Basic.

The Exit Property statement is equivalent to the Exit Sub or Exit Function statement, and it may appear many times in the body of the procedure. Property Get procedures are implemented as functions because they return a value, which is the value of the property. The value of the property is usually stored in a local variable, and this variable is assigned to the name of the Property Get procedure.

Let's say you have implemented a custom ActiveX control that exposes the *TextAlignment* property. The value of this property is stored in the *m_TextAlignment* local variable. When the application that hosts the custom control requests the value of this property, the Property Get Text-Alignment() procedure is called. This is a simple property, and no arguments need be passed by the calling program. Here's the implementation of the procedure:

```
Private m_TextAlignment As Integer

Public Property Get TextAlignment () As Integer
   TextAlignment = m_TextAlignment
End Property
```

The Declaration statement is included to show that the *TextAlignment* property is mapped to a private variable in the control's code (the *m_TextAlignment* variable). This variable changes value through the Property Let procedure, which is invoked when the host application sets the value of the property. The Property Let procedure is discussed next.

Many of the properties of a custom ActiveX control are mapped directly to properties of the UserControl object. If your custom control has a Back-Style property, it's very likely that this property is mapped to the BackStyle property of the UserControl object. The Property Get procedure of a property that's mapped to a UserControl object is shown next:

```
Public Property Get BackStyle() As Integer
   BackStyle = UserControl.BackStyle
End Public
```

Properties that are mapped to properties of the UserControl object are not stored in local variables.

As you probably know, the BackStyle property is not an integer but an enumerated type (its possible values are Opaque and Transparent). To declare properties with custom enumerated types, use the Enum statement, which is discussed in the section "Variable and Array Declarations" of this reference.

Property Let

This is the counterpart of the Property Get procedure, and it assigns a value to a property. Property Let procedures are usually more complicated than Property Get procedures because the value assigned to the property must also be validated. The syntax of the Property Let procedure is

```
Property Let property_name ([arglist,] value)
    {statements}
    Exit Property
    {more statements}
End Property
```

The *Property* keyword must be prefixed by one of the keywords listed in the Property Get section. The name of the Property Let procedure is *property_name*, and it should be the same as the name of the matching Property Get procedure. The value to be assigned to the property is *value*, and your code must first validate it and then assign it to the local variable that maintains the property's value.

To set the *TextAlignment* property of a custom ActiveX control, declare a private variable where the value of the property will be stored and then write a Property Let procedure like the following:

```
Private m_TextAlignment As Integer
Property Let TextAlignment(NewAlignment As Integer)
    If NewAlignment < 0 Or NewAlignment > 8 Then
        MsgBox "Invalid property value"
    Else
        m_TextAlignment = NewAlignment
        Propertychanged "TextAlignment"
    End If
End Property
```

The procedure accepts a single argument, which is the new value of the property. The code validates the property value. (In this specific example, the property value must be an integer in the range 1 through 8 inclusive.) If the argument has a valid value, it is assigned to the *m_Text-Alignment* private variable. If not, a message is displayed, and the property doesn't change value.

To set a custom property that's mapped to a property of the UserControl object, use a Property Let procedure like the following:

```
Public Property Let BackStyle(NewStyle As Integer)
   If NewStyle = 0 Or NewStyle = 1 Then
      UserControl.BackStyle = NewStyle
      PropertyChanged "BackStyle"
   Else
      MsgBox "Invalid property value"
   End If
End Property
```

Notice the statement

```
PropertyChanged "BackStyle"
```

which tells Visual Basic that a specific property has changed. This line is required for the changes to be saved in the PropertyBag object.

This method of handling errors (namely, popping a message box) will work with custom ActiveX controls but not with Classes (code components). A Class may be registered on another computer on the network, in which case the message box will appear on the remote computer's screen. To handle errors in Classes, you must raise an error with the Raise method of the Err object. To raise a trappable error from within your code, you can call the Err.Raise method with the following syntax:

```
Err.Raise error_number, source, description, heplfil, _
   helpcontext
```

To raise an error from within your Class's code, use a statement like the following:

```
Err.Raise 1000 + vbObjectError, "MyClass.MyProperty", _
   "Invalid Property Value"
```

Property Set

Some properties of your custom ActiveX controls or Classes will be objects. The Font property is a trivial example. Nearly every custom control with a visible interface provides a Font property that lets the host application set the attributes of the text displayed on the control. The Font property can't be set with a Property Let procedure because it's not a simple data type. The property is an object that provides its own properties (Name, Size, Bold, Italic, and so on). To set an object property, you must implement a Property Set procedure, which has the same structure as a Property Let procedure, but the assignment of the property is done with the Set statement. Here's the Property Set procedure for the Font property:

```
Public Property Set Font(ByVal NewFont As Font)
    Set UserControl.Font = New_Font
    PropertyChanged "Font"
End Property
```

Likewise, the equivalent Property Get procedure must use the Set statement to assign the current value of the Font property to the name of the property procedure:

```
Public Property Get Font() As Font
    Set Font = UserControl.Font
End Property
```

The Font Property Set procedure is invoked every time the host application invokes a property of the Font object. When the host application sets the font's size or typeface with the following statements, the Property Set procedure of the Font property is invoked:

```
MyControl1.Font.Name = "MS Comic Sans MS"
MyControl1.Font.Size = 24
```

The same procedure will be invoked if the host application assigns an instance of an existing Font object to the Font property, as in the following statement:

```
Set MyControl1.Font = Text1.Font
```

Event event_name [(arglist)]

The Event statement is used in a Class Module, custom ActiveX control, or Form to declare a user-defined event. Your component can raise any event, under any conditions you choose, with the RaiseEvent method (described next). However, you can't raise an event you have not already declared at the beginning of the module.

The name of the event is *event_name*, and *arglist* is a comma-separated list of the arguments that Visual Basic must report to the event's handler. If you raise a Click event, for example, you need not supply any arguments. Let's say you've built a custom ListBox control, which raises the Selected event. The Selected event is fired when the user clicks (or double-clicks) an item in the list, and it must pass two values to its event handler: the selected item and its index in the list. The declaration of the Selected event should be

```
Public Event Selected(ByVal SelItem As String, ByVal _
SelIndex As Long)
```

The ByVal keyword is used because most event handlers don't allow the developer to alter the arguments. If your event must return a value to your component, you must supply an argument by reference (such as the *Cancel* argument, which cancels the operation or action that triggered the event). Events can't have named or optional arguments and do not have return values.

If the host application contains an instance of this control, named *DeluxeList*, it must provide the following event handler to react to this event:

```
Private Sub DeluxeList_Selected(SelItem As String, _
SelIndex As Long)
    {statements to handle the event}
End Sub
```

The name of the Selected event will appear automatically in the VB editor's Events drop-down list whenever you select the DeluxeList Object in the Object drop-down list.

Once the event has been declared, use the RaiseEvent statement to fire the event.

RaiseEvent event_name [(arglist)]

The RaiseEvent statement fires a custom event from within a Class module, ActiveX control, or Form. The argument *event_name* is the name of the event, and the event handler for this event in the host application must be named after the component's name, followed by an underscore character, followed by the name of the event. The name of the event must match one of the Event declarations inserted at the beginning of the module.

If you're building a custom ActiveX control and you want it to fire a Selected event, the host application must provide the Control1_Selected event handler (assuming that the name of the control on the Form is Control1). The name of the Selected event will appear automatically in the Events drop-down list of the editor, when Control1 is selected in the Objects drop-down list.

In a pair of parentheses following the event's name, you must provide the list of arguments (which Visual Basic should pass to the event handler) when the specific event is fired. If the Selected event must report a string and an index value (say, the name of the selected item and its index), you should raise the event with the following statement:

```
RaiseEvent Selected (Names(i), i)
```

Here *Names()* is a string array that holds the values that can be selected on the custom control. The values you pass to the event's handler in the host application must match the arguments in the definition of the event. If the event doesn't report any values to its handler, you must omit the parentheses.

The RaiseEvent statement can be used anywhere in the component's code to raise an event. For example, you can call it from within the Click event of the UserControl object or the DblClick event of a constituent control. You can even raise an event when a special key is pressed while a specific constituent control has the focus. Any actions that can be detected by Visual Basic can be used as triggers for raising custom events, as long as the event's name has been declared with an Event statement.

Here's the code you must include in your custom component's code to raise an event:

```
Public Event Selected(ByVal SelItem As String, ByVal _
SelIndex As Long)


Private Sub UserControl_DblClick()
  {statements}
  RaiseEvent Selected (Names(i), i)
  {more statements}
End Sub
```

The host application should provide a handler for the Selected event. Assuming that the control's name on the Form is *DeluxeList,* here's a sample handler for the control's Selected event:

```
Private Sub DeluxeList_Selected(ByVal SelItem As String, _
                ByVal SelIndex As Long)
  MsgBox "You have selected the " & SelIndex & _
    "th item in the list" & _
      vbCrLf & "The selected item's text is " & SelItem
  End Sub
```

The same techniques apply to Class components. However, when you declare an object variable to represent the Class in the host application, you must use the WithEvents keywords, as shown here:

```
Private WithEvents MyCalc As Calculator.Matrix
```

Calculator.Matrix is the ID of the Class, which your code can contact through the *MyCalc* object variable. Had you omitted the WithEvents keyword, the host application wouldn't have received the events raised by the Class.

Load object_name

The Load statement loads a form into memory or adds a new element of a control array on a Form. The *object_name* argument is the name of a Form object or a control array element to be loaded. Of course, the form must already contain a control array in order to create new elements in the array (see the example at the end of this entry).

When you start an application, the startup Form is loaded and displayed automatically (unless you have specified that the startup object is the Main subroutine). To load another Form, you can call its Show method, which loads the Form into memory and displays it. Sometimes we want to load a Form but not display it. To load a Form, but keep it hidden, use the Load statement. After the Form has been loaded, you can display it with the Show method. The advantage of this approach is that the Form is displayed instantly because it has already been loaded. Keep in mind, however, that even though they are invisible, loaded Forms consume system resources.

To load the Statistics Form, use the statement

```
Load Statistics
```

Once the Form has been loaded, you can access its properties and controls, even though the Form remains invisible. By the way, Forms are also loaded automatically when you access their properties or controls.

The same statement can be used to load new control instances on a Form. Let's say you have a Form with a TextBox control on it (the Text1 control). If you want to be able to add TextBox controls on the Form at run time, set the Text1 control's Index property to 0. The new name of the TextBox control is now Text1(0). In effect, you have created an array of controls. The array contains a single member, the Text1(0) control, but you can add as many instances of this control as needed with the Load statement. The following lines will place two more instances of the TextBox control on the Form:

```
Load Text1(1)
Text1(1).Visible = True
Text1(1).Top = Text1(0).Top + Text1(0).Height
Text1(1).Text = "I'm the second member of the array"
Load Text1(2)
Text1(2).Visible = True
Text1(2).Top = Text1(1).Top + Text1(1).Height
Text1(2).Text = "I'm the third member of the array"
```

Each new control placed on the Form with the Load statement is initially invisible and is placed exactly on top of the first member of the array and has the same dimensions. (It's an exact copy of the existing control.) The additional statements in the previous example make the control visible and move it below the previous member of the control array.

To unload a Form from memory or a control from a Form, use the Unload statement.

Unload object_name

This statement unloads a Form from memory or a control from a Form. The *object_name* argument is the name of a Form object or a control array element to be unloaded. Instead of unloading a Form, you can make it invisible by calling its Hide method, so that the next time you need it, Visual Basic won't have to load it into memory again. You should always unload Forms and controls that are no longer needed to claim the allocated memory.

To unload the Statistics Form use the statement

```
Unload Statistics
```

To unload the second and third elements of the Text1 control array of the last example of the Load entry, use the following statements:

```
Unload Text1(1)
Unload Text1(2)
```

With Object...End With

The With statement executes several statements on the same object or a user-defined type. To change a number of properties on an object or invoke several of its methods, you should use repeat statements of the form

```
object.property
object.property
...
object.property
```

or

```
object.method
...
object.method
```

Using the With statement, you can list the name of the object outside the body of statements that access the properties (or methods) of the object and skip the name of the object when calling its properties and methods. Here's how you'd access the same properties and methods using the With statement:

```
With object
   .property = value
   .property = value
   .method arguments
   .method arguments
End With
```

Sometimes, objects have fairly lengthy expressions. To manipulate the font of a cell in an Excel Worksheet, you'd use an expression like the following:

```
Worksheet.Cells(2,4).Font
```

To set the size of the font and a few attributes, you'd have to repeat the same object name several times:

```
Worksheet.Cells(2,4).Font.Name = "Comic Sans MS"
Worksheet.Cells(2,4).Font.Size = 14
Worksheet.Cells(2,4).Font.Bold = True
Worksheet.Cells(2,4).Font.Italic = True
```

Use the With statement to manipulate all the font properties as shown here:

```
With Worksheet.Cells(2,4).Font
   .Name = "Comic Sans MS"
   .Size = 14
   .Bold = True
   .Italic = True
End With
```

For Each...Next Statement

This statement is similar to the For...Next statement, and it iterates through the members of an array or collection. The difference between the two loop structures is that you don't have to specify the number of iterations explicitly. The For Each ... Next structure will loop automatically through all the members of the collection or array. The syntax of the For Each...Next statement is

```
For Each element In Collection
   {statements}
   [Exit For]
   {statements}
Next
```

The *element* variable is of the same type as the members of the collection or array. At each iteration, the *element* variable assumes the value of the next member of the collection or array. Of course, it can be a Variant or a generic object variable if the collection contains objects. *Collection* is the name of the collection or array you want to scan.

Once the loop has been entered, all the statements in the loop are executed for the first element. The statements are repeated as many times as there are elements in the collection.

Let's say you have declared and initialized an array with the following statements:

```
Dim Scores(100) As Double
For i = 1 To 100
   Scores(i) = Rnd * 10000
Next
```

You can use a similar loop to scan the elements of the array, but you can also use a For Each...Next loop to process its elements:

```
For Each element In Scores()
   Debug.Print element
Next
```

At each iteration of the loop, the element variable takes on a new array element's value. You can use the *element* variable's value in your calculations, but you can't change its value. Notice that you can assign a new value to the *element* variable (it's a Variant), but this value isn't going to be assigned to the current array element. This action will not generate a message error either. You may think you have changed the array's elements, but in reality, you have only changed the value of a variable temporarily. At the next iteration, the *element* variable will be assigned the value of the next array element.

The For Each...Next statement is commonly used with built-in or custom collections. The following lines scan the Contacts folder of Outlook 98 and print the names of the contacts:

```
Dim allContacts As Object
Dim mContact As ContactItem

Set allContacts = _
      mNameSpace.GetDefaultFolder(olFolderContacts).Items
For Each mContact In allContacts
   List1.AddItem mContact.FullName
Next
```

If you want to test this code segment with your installation of Outlook, you must add a reference to the component Outlook 98 Type Library to your project and then execute the following lines in the Form's Load event:

```
On Error GoTo OutlookNotStarted
  Set OLApp = CreateObject("Outlook.Application")
On Error GoTo NoMAPINameSpace
  Set mNameSpace = OLApp.GetNamespace("MAPI")
  List1.Clear
  Exit Sub
OutlookNotStarted:
  MsgBox "Could not start Outlook"
  Exit Sub
NoMAPINameSpace:
  MsgBox "Could not get MAPI NameSpace"
  Exit Sub
```

These lines will start Outlook and create the *mNameSpace* object variable. The GetDefaultFolder(olFolderContacts).Items property of the *mNameSpace* variable returns the items of the Contacts folder, which form a collection. You can then scan them with the For Each...Next statement.

Option Statements

The Option statements let you specify options (such as the subscripting of arrays and sorting order) in a module. The Option statements appear at the beginning of a module, and they affect the code in the specific module.

Option Base

This statement declares the default lower bound for array subscripts. By default, array subscripts start at zero. To specify that array subscripts should start at one, use the statement

```
Option Base 1
```

The Option Base 0 statement is never really required (unless you want to overwrite the Option Base 1 setting for a specific module). The Option Base statement can appear only once in a module and before any procedure. Moreover, it affects the lower bound of arrays in the module where the statement appears.

The Option Base statement affects only the arrays declared without explicit lower bounds, which are declared with statements like the following:

```
Dim Scores(100) As Integer
```

Arrays declared with the *To* keyword, as in the following declaration, are not affected by the Option Base 0 statement:

```
Dim Scores(10 To 99) As Integer
```

Option Compare

This statement, which takes effect in the module in which it appears, determines how Visual Basic will perform string comparisons. Although comparing numeric values is straightforward and there's no question as to the order of numeric values, things aren't as trivial with strings. Does the string "alias" come before "Branch" or after all the words that begin with an uppercase character? And how about foreign symbols? Should words beginning with $\grave{E}$, ..., or $\hat{E}$ appear after the words beginning with E, or should they appear after the English characters? The way you compare strings depends on the application, and there are several options for sorting strings. The Option Compare statement has three variations:

Option Compare Binary   Sorts strings based on the internal binary representation of the characters. With the Binary sort option, all uppercase characters come before the lowercase characters, and foreign symbols are at the end, again with uppercase characters ahead of lowercase characters:

$A < B < C ... < Z < a < b < c ... < z < \grave{A} < \acute{A} < \hat{A} < ...<\grave{a} < \acute{a} <\hat{a} ...$

Option Compare Text   Sorts strings using case-sensitive order (that is, $A = a < \grave{A} = \grave{a} < ... B = b < ...$ so on). This is the natural sort order for names.

Option Compare Database   Affects operations on Microsoft Access databases. The sorting order is determined by the locale ID of the database.

Option Explicit

This statement tells the compiler to check each variable in the module before using it and to issue an error message if you attempt to use a variable without having previously declared it. If you decide to declare all variables in your projects (to avoid excessive use of variants), you can ask Visual Basic to insert the Option Explicit statement automatically in every module by checking the Require Variable Declaration checkbox in the Options dialog box (choose Tools ➤Options).

When Option Explicit appears in a module, you must explicitly declare all variables using the Dim, Private, Public, ReDim, or Static statements. If you don't use the Option Explicit statement, all undeclared variables are of Variant type unless the default type is otherwise specified with a Deftype statement.

Let's examine the side effects of implicit variable declaration in your application. You could use the following statements to convert German marks to U.S. dollars:

```
DM2USD = 1.6588
USDollars = amount * DM2USD
```

The first time your code refers to the *DM2USD* variable name, Visual Basic creates a new variable and then uses it as it was declared.

Suppose the variable *DM2USD* appears in many places in your code. If in one of these places you type *DM2UDS* instead of *DM2USD* and the application doesn't enforce variable declarations, the compiler will create a new variable, assign it the value zero, and then use it. Any amount converted with the mistyped variable (*DM2UDS*) will be zero! If the application enforces variable declarations, the compiler will complain (the *DM2UDS* variable hasn't been declared and therefore can't be used), and you'll catch the error.

ERROR TRAPPING AND HANDLING

The applications you develop must not only carry out their calculations but also communicate with users in a robust, bulletproof manner. Users are going to make mistakes, enter the wrong type of data, and even abuse your application. Yet your application should be able to handle everything users can throw at it.

Developing well-behaved, robust applications means that you must foresee every possible mistake, validate every piece of information entered by the user, and guide users when they don't know what to do. And even if you develop a user interface that can't be fooled, you have to deal with unexpected events, such as a full disk, an attempt to write to a CD-ROM, printing to a disconnected printer, and so on. To help you develop more robust applications, Visual Basic provides a few statements for trapping and handling errors, which are discussed next.

On Error

This statement is at the heart of your application's error-trapping logic. As you know, when an error occurs, Visual Basic aborts execution with an error message that indicates what caused the application to fail. The error message has a unique number and a short description (which, in most cases, is a cryptic one). This default behavior is clearly unacceptable. To change it, you can include the On Error statement, which tells Visual Basic what to do when an error occurs. The On Error statement has the following variations:

On Error GoTo Label   Program control is transferred to the line specified with the *label* argument. The code segment starting at this label is called an *error handler*, and it should handle the error. After the error has been handled, you must tell Visual Basic how to proceed. You do so with the Resume statement. There are several variations of the Resume statement, which allow you to repeat the same statement that caused the error, resume execution with the following line, or transfer program control to another line in the procedure.

On Error Resume Next   Program execution continues with the line following the line that contains the error. In other words, the line that caused the error is ignored and execution continues. This is like hiding the dust under the rug, so don't use it frequently in your applications. Use the On Error Resume Next statement if you plan to insert inline error handlers. Here's an example of the correct use of the On Error Resume Next statement:

```
On Error Resume Next
{statement}
If Err.Number <> 0 Then
    {an error occurred, handle it here!}
End If
```

If you expect an error to happen on a specific statement, use an inline error handler. The inline error handler examines the value of the Err.Number property, and if it's not zero, then an error occurred, which is handled on the spot.

The On Error Resume Next statement can be used in simple error situations as well. Let's say you want to delete the file C:\TEMP.DOC. If the file does not exist or if for any other reason the Kill command can't delete the file, a runtime error will be generated. To avoid the runtime error, use the following statements:

```
On Error Resume Next
Kill "D:\TEMP.DOC"
On Error GoTo 0
```

If the file can't be deleted, then the program continues with the next statement. Use this statement if the file might not exist. Of course, if it's imperative that the file be killed, you should examine why the Kill statement failed and act accordingly. The last line turns off the error trapping. You don't want your program to go on ignoring any other error and pretend everything is fine. If you forget to turn off the On Error Resume Next statement, your application will not be interrupted by other errors (Visual Basic will keep ignoring them) and you will not get a chance to fix them.

On Error GoTo 0   This statement turns off any error-trapping method set up with the other two statements earlier in the code. Use this statement to return to Visual Basic's default behavior (no trapping).

When dealing with errors, the most important object is the Err object, which supports two properties: Number and Description. They return the number and description of the most recent error. The description is useful if you want to display a message to the users, but your code must figure out what happened and how to handle the error based on the error's number.

The error handler is a code segment that examines the source of the error and attempts to handle it. Each procedure has its own error handler and the error handler can't be a separate procedure. In other words, you can't tell Visual Basic to call another procedure when an error occurs.

Let's say you have a code segment that attempts to save data to a disk file. Any number of things can go wrong: the user may select a file that's already open, the selected file may be read-only, and so on. You may actually start saving the data when a "disk full" error is encountered or there is a disk malfunction. It's neither the user's fault nor your application's fault, but it's something that must be dealt with. Let's see how you can trap similar errors and handle them with the On Error statement. The following code segment opens the Save File common dialog control and saves the data. If an error occurs, then the program will jump to the File-Error line. The error handler consists of the statements following the line FileError.

```
On Error GoTo FileError
CommonDialog1.ShowSave
{statements to save file}
Exit Sub
FileError:
MsgBox "The following message occurred" & vbCrLf & _
    Err.Description & vbCrLf & "File not saved!"
Exit Sub
```

The error handler for this example is quite trivial. It displays the error message that Visual Basic would have displayed, warns the user that the save operation did not complete successfully, and exits the subroutine. It's up to the user to figure out the source of the problem (based on the description) and try to save the file again. That's not a very helpful handler, but it's still better than the default behavior of Visual Basic—which would abort execution, causing the user to lose all the information.

To write better event handlers, you should use one of the several variations of the Resume statement, which is discussed next.

The On Error statement traps errors that occurred in the same module in which the statement appears. If no error trap is in effect in a specific routine, then the error propagates up, through the Call Stack, and is caught by the first error trap it encounters. Let's say the subroutine SubA has an error handler, and it calls SubB. If SubB has its own error handler, then all errors are trapped and handled by the subroutine in which they occurred. If SubB doesn't have an error handler of its own, then any errors that occur in this subroutine will be caught and handled by the error handler of SubA.

Let's examine the following listing:

```
Function FunctionA() As Integer

On Error GoTo ErrHandler
    Debug.Print "FUNCTIONA: Ready to call FunctionB"
    FunctionB
    Debug.Print "FUNCTIONA: Just called FunctionB"
    Exit Function
```

```
ErrHandler:
    Debug.Print "FUNCTIONA: Handling Error # " & Err.Number
    Resume Next

End Function

Function FunctionB() As Integer

    Debug.Print "FUNCTIONB will raise an 'Object Required' _
    error "
    s2 = Text1.Text
    Debug.Print "This line will never be reached, because _
         FunctionB raised an error that's handled _
         outside the procedure"

End Function
```

FunctionA() has its own error handler, which simply displays the error description. FunctionA() calls FunctionB(), which doesn't have an error handler. FunctionB() should raise an "Object Required" error when it attempts to read the Text property of the Text1 control because the Form doesn't contain a Text1 control. If you call FunctionA(), you will see the following messages in the Immediate Window:

```
FUNCTIONA: Ready to call FunctionB
FUNCTIONB will raise an 'Object Required' error
FUNCTIONA: Handling Error # 424
FUNCTIONA: Just called FunctionB
```

If you call FunctionB() directly, its execution will be interrupted with a run-time error because it contains no error message. Visual Basic will raise error # 424 ("Object required") when it attempts to access the Text1 object.

Resume

The Resume statement resumes execution after the error handler has completed. The Resume statement has several variations, which are

> **Resume**   If the error occurred in the same procedure as the error handler, execution resumes with the statement that caused the error. Presumably, the error handler has done something to fix it. If the error was caused by a line that attempts to open a file that's already open, you should give the user a chance to close the file (which is probably open in another application) and then try to execute the same statement again.

If the error occurred in another subroutine, then execution will resume with the statement that called the procedure in which the error occurred. In effect, when you allow errors to be handled outside the procedures that caused them, you must resume execution by starting the offending procedure from the beginning. Things can get messy if SubA calls SubB and SubB calls SubC and only SubA has an error handler. Should an error occur in SubC, it will be handled by SubA. If you use the Resume statement, then program execution will resume with the line of SubA that called SubB.

Resume Next   If the error occurred in the same procedure as the error handler, execution resumes with the statement that follows the statement that caused the error. If the error occurred in another procedure, execution resumes with the statement following the statement that called the procedure in which the error occurred. In effect, the Resume Next statement ignores the line that caused the error and continues with the next one. Unlike the Resume Next statement, however, it executes an error handler before resuming execution. If the error was caused in a procedure without an error handler and was caught in the calling procedure, then the statement that called the procedure with the error is skipped and program execution continues (the entire subroutine that caused the error will be skipped).

Resume *label*   Program execution resumes at the specified line in the same procedure that trapped the error. Let's say your code prompts the user for a bunch of numeric values and then proceeds to perform some calculations. If the calculations lead to errors (such as the square root of a negative number), your only option is to warn the user and prompt them for new data. Here's the structure of an error handler that uses the Resume label statement:

```
GetData:
  {get data, most likely through a form or dialog box}
On Error Goto MathError
  {perform calculations}
  {display result and exit}
MathError:
  Msg = "There is no solution for the data you supplied." & _
     VbCrLf & "Do you want to enter another data set?"
  reply = InputBox(Msg, vbYesNo)
  If reply = vbYes Then
```

```
    Resume GetData
Else
   {exit procedure or terminate application}
End If
```

The Resume *label* statement is used when you can't remedy the situation from within your code and you must restart the operation that caused the error.

Before you write an event handler, you must decide on which errors it should react and how. The Visual Basic errors and their numbers are listed in Table LR.32.

TABLE LR.32: Visual Basic Error Codes and Descriptions

ERROR NUMBER	ERROR DESCRIPTION
3	Return without GoSub.
5	Invalid procedure call or argument.
6	Overflow.
7	Out of memory.
8	Application-defined or object-defined error.
9	Subscript out of range.
10	This array is fixed or temporarily locked.
11	Division by zero.
13	Type mismatch.
14	Out of string space.
16	Expression too complex.
17	Can't perform requested operation.
18	User interrupt occurred.
20	Resume without error.
28	Out of stack space.
35	Sub or Function not defined.
47	Too many DLL application clients.
48	Error in loading DLL.
49	Bad DLL calling convention.
51	Internal error.
52	Bad filename or number.

TABLE LR.32 (continued): Visual Basic Error Codes and Descriptions

ERROR NUMBER	ERROR DESCRIPTION
53	File not found.
54	Bad file mode.
55	File already open.
57	Device I/O error.
58	File already exists.
59	Bad record length.
61	Disk full.
62	Input past end of file.
63	Bad record number.
67	Too many files.
68	Device unavailable.
70	Permission denied.
71	Disk not ready.
74	Can't rename with different drive.
75	Path/File access error.
76	Path not found.
91	Object variable or With block variable not set.
92	For loop not initialized.
93	Invalid pattern string.
94	Invalid use of Null.
96	Unable to sink events of object because the object is already firing events to the maximum number of event receivers that it supports.
97	Cannot call friend function on object, which is not an instance of defining class.
98	A property or method call cannot include a reference to a private object, either as an argument or as a return value.
321	Invalid file format.
322	Can't create necessary temporary file.
325	Invalid format in resource file.
380	Invalid property value.

TABLE LR.32 (continued): Visual Basic Error Codes and Descriptions

ERROR NUMBER	ERROR DESCRIPTION
381	Invalid property array index.
382	Set not supported at runtime.
383	Set not supported (read-only property).
385	Need property array index.
387	Set not permitted.
393	Get not supported at runtime.
394	Get not supported (write-only property).

Let's say you want to provide an error handler for the SaveFile subroutine, which saves data to a disk file. The data to be saved could be the text on a TextBox control, the cells of a MSFlexGrid control, and so on. When you write code that accesses disk files, you must be ready to cope with a number of different errors. Most of these errors will be beyond your program's or the user's control, like a disk malfunction, or a disk full error.

The first step is to go trough the errors of Table LR.31 and figure out which ones may occur in your code. In the following example we will handle the following errors:

55	File already open	We will give the user a chance to close the file (by switching to another application) and then attempt to repeat the statement that caused the error.
61	Disk full	We'll prompt the user as to whether they want to delete the files in the Temp folder and then attempt to repeat the statement that caused the error.
68	Device unavailable	We'll give the user a chance to select another drive or a write-capable drive (should the error be caused because a CD-ROM drive was initially selected by the user).

| 71 | Disk not ready | We'll give the user a chance to select another drive or fix the error (perhaps insert a floppy in the drive) and then resume by executing the line that opens the File Save dialog box. |
| 76 | Path not found | We'll give the user a chance to select another filename and then resume by executing the line that opens the File Save dialog box. |

The outline of the SaveFile subroutine is shown next:

```
Private Sub SaveFile()
On Error GoTo FileError
GetFileName:
  CommonDialog1.DefaultExt = "*.TXT"
  CommonDialog1.Filter = "Text Files|*.TXT"
  CommonDialog1.ShowSave
  If CommonDialog1.FileName = "" Then Exit Sub
  {code to save data to file}
EndRoutine:
  Exit Sub

FileError:
  Select Case Err.Number
    Case 55:
      Msg = "The file is already open by another _
          application"
      Msg = Msg & vbCrLf
      Msg = Msg & "Do you want to close it and try again?"
      reply = MsgBox(Msg, vbYesNo)
      If reply = vbYes Then
        Resume
      Else
        {close any open file(s)}
        Resume GetFileName
      End If
    Case 68, 71, 76:
      Msg = "Disk I/O Error"
      Msg = Msg & vbCrLf & "Try again with a _
          different drive"
      MsgBox Msg
      {close any open file(s)}
      Resume GetFileName
```

```
    Case 61:
      Msg = "Disk is full"
      Msg = Msg & vbCrLf & "Delete files in Temp folder?"
      reply = MsgBox(Msg, vbYesNo)
      If reply = vbYes Then
                ClaimDiskSpace
        Resume
      Else
        {close any open file(s)}
        Resume GetFileName
      End If
    Case Else
      Msg = "Error in saving file"
      Msg = Msg & vbCrLf & "Click OK to return to the _
        editor"
      MsgBox Msg
      {close any open file(s)}
      Resume EndRoutine
    End Select
  End Sub
```

As you can see, the error handler has more lines than the actual sub-routine (which shouldn't surprise you). The subroutine displays the File Save dialog box, where the user can select a filename or specify a new one. If an error occurs while the program attempts to save the data, the program will jump to the *FileError* error handler. All statements following the *FileError* label form the error handler. Some errors that can be handled by the user are dealt with the Resume statement. For instance, if the program can't save the data because the file is already open, it prompts the user to close the file and attempts to execute the statement that caused the error again. If the error persists, the user can specify a different file name or a different drive/path name.

If the save operation failed because the disk was full, the program presents two choices. Claim some disk space by deleting the files in the Temp folder (the ClaimDiskSpace subroutine is supposed to delete the files), or try to save the file on a different drive. If the user agrees to claim the necessary disk space, the program calls the ClaimDiskSpace subroutine and then executes the line that caused the error again. If the user wants to try a different drive, the program resumes with the GetFileName line. The File Save dialog box will be displayed again, and this time the user must select a different drive.

Notice that in the first case (where the program will attempt to claim some disk space), we don't close the file(s) already open because we'll attempt to execute the offending line again. If the user decides to fix the problem himself, we close the open file(s) so that we can open another one.

This error handler is by no means complete, but it demonstrates the complexity of error trapping and handling. Other error handlers are simpler, but it's quite common for an error handler to be lengthier (and frequently more complicated than the code that processes the data). Your task is to make sure that the application doesn't quit on the user no matter what. The more help and guidance you can offer the user, the better.

Error error_number

The Error statement simulates the occurrence of the error specified by its argument, *error_number*. While you can reproduce many error conditions, you'll find it hard to generate errors such as Disk Full or Device Unavailable. Use the Error statement anywhere in your code to simulate any error condition. The Err object's properties will take the same values as if the actual error had occurred, and you'll be able to test and debug your error-handling routines.

To see how the error handler we discussed in the previous handler will handle error 61, insert the following statement somewhere in the statements that save the data:

```
Error 61
```

Be warned, however, that you can't test the Resume statement with this technique. If the error is simulated, the Resume statement will attempt to execute the Error statement again, causing the same error to surface. In this case, you must break the program by pressing Ctrl+Break. Use the Error statement to test your error-trapping code in combination with the Resume Next statement.

MISCELLANEOUS FUNCTIONS

This section describes the functions and statements that don't fit in any other category.

Choose(index, choice1[, choice2, ...])

The Choice() function selects and returns a value from a list of arguments. The *index* argument is a numeric value between 1 and the number of available choices. The following arguments, *choice1*, *choice2*, and so on are the available options. The function will return the first choice if *index* is 1, the second option if *index* is 2, and so on.

One of the uses of the Choose() function is to translate single digits to strings. The function IntToString() returns the name of the digit passed as an argument:

```
Function IntToString(int As Integer) As String
    IntToString = Choose (i+1, "zero", "one", "two", "three", _
        "four", "five", "six", "seven", "eight", "nine")
End Sub
```

If *index* is less than one or larger than the number of options, the Choose function returns a Null value.

IIf(expression, truepart, falsepart)

This function returns one of two parts, depending on the evaluation of *expression*. If the *expression* argument is True, the *truepart* argument is returned. If *expression* is not True, the *falsepart* argument is returned. The IIf() function is equivalent to the following If clause:

```
If expression Then
    result = truepart
Else
    result = falsepart
End If
```

In many situations, this logic significantly reduces the amount of code. The Min() and Max() functions, for instance, can be easily implemented with the IIf() function:

```
Min = IIf(a<b, a, b)
Max = IIf(a>b, a, b)
```

Switch(expression1, value1[, expression2, value2,....])

This function evaluates a list of expressions and returns a value associated with the first expression in the list that happens to be True. If none of the expressions are True, the function returns Null. The following statement selects the proper quadrant depending on the signs of the variables X and Y:

```
Quadrant = Switch(X>0 and Y>0, 1, X<0 and Y>0, 2, _
        X<0 and Y<0, 3, X>0 and Y<0, 4)
```

If both *X* and *Y* are positive, the *Quadrant* variable is assigned the value 1. If *X* is negative and *Y* is positive, *Quadrant* becomes 2, and so on. If either *X* or *Y* is zero, none of the expressions are True, and *Quadrant* becomes Null.

DoEvents()

The DoEvents() function yields execution of your VB application and returns the control to the operating system so it can process other events. After the operating system has finished processing all pending events, control is returned to your application. The DoEvents() function accepts no arguments, but it returns an Integer representing the number of open forms in Visual Basic. For all other applications, it returns zero.

The DoEvents() function should be called from within tight segments of code (such as loops) that take a long time to complete. Let's say you have written a subroutine that scans the entire hard disk for a specific file or iterates some complicated math operations. Both operations may take seconds to minutes to complete. Without the DoEvents() function, the program would appear frozen. The user would be able to switch to other applications but would not be able to interrupt the VB application.

Let's say you have coded a subroutine that takes a long time to complete, and you want the user to be able to interrupt it. To do so, you can include a Command button with its Cancel property set to True. Every time the user clicks this button or presses the Esc key, the button's event handler is executed. Obviously, you must insert a statement in the button's Click handler, such as the following one, where *InterruptNow* is a global variable:

```
InterruptNow = True
```

The same variable's value is examined in the subroutine to interrupt the lengthy calculations. Somewhere in your subroutine, you must include the lines

```
DoEvents()
If InterruptNow = True Then
   InterruptNow = False
   Exit Sub
End If
```

If the subroutine doesn't yield control to the operating system, the button's event handler will never get a chance to be executed, and the user will not be able to interrupt the calculations.

Environ()

This function returns the *environment variables* (operating system variables set with the SET command). To access an environment variable, use a numeric index or the variable's name. If you access the environment variables by index, as in

```
Print Environ(2)
```

you'll get a string that contains both the name of the environment variable and its value:

```
TMP=C:\WINDOWS\TEMP
```

(The actual folder name may be different on your system.) To retrieve only the value of the TMP environment variable, use the expression

```
Print Environ("TMP")
```

and the function will return the value

```
C:\WINDOWS\TEMP
```

If you specify a nonexistent environment variable name, a zero-length string ("") is returned.

Beep Statement

This statement sounds a tone of short duration through the computer's speaker. The pitch and duration of the beep depend on the target computer and can't be adjusted. This is the simplest form of audio warning you can add to your application because it doesn't require a sound board.

Rem

This statement appears usually at the beginning of a code line followed by remarks. Everything to the left of the Rem statement is ignored by the compiler. (It's for the programmer's eyes only.) The Rem statement has been replaced by the character ' (apostrophe). The following lines are typical examples of code with remarks:

```
' Now set up array
Score(1) = 45: Score(2) = 41: Score(3) = 54
' and calculate averages
For i = 1 To 30 ' This loop scans all the elements of the _
array
  Total = total + Score(i)
Next
```

If the Rem keyword (or apostrophe) follows other statements on a line (such as the case of the For statement in the previous example), it must be separated from the statements by a colon (:). To use the Rem statement to insert a comment after the For statement, use the following syntax:

```
For i = 1 To 30: REM This loop scans all the elements of _
the array
```

CallByName(object, procedurename, calltype,[arguments()])

This function executes a method of an object or sets/returns an object property. The *object* argument is the name of the object whose method will be called or whose property will be set or read. *procedurename* is the name of a property or method of the object on which the function will act. The *calltype* argument specifies the type of procedure being called, and it can have one of the values shown in Table LR.33.

TABLE LR.33: The Values of the *Calltype* Argument

CONSTANT	MEANING
vbGet	Reads a property value
vbLet	Sets a property value
vbSet	Sets a property value
vbMethod	Calls a method of the object

The last argument is an array, which contains the arguments required by the method or the value of the property to be set.

To set the Text property of the Text1 control, you'd write a statement like

```
Text1.Text = "Welcome to VB6"
```

You can call the CallByName() function to set the same property to the same value as follows:

```
CallByName Text1, "Text", vbLet, "Welcome to VB6"
```

Notice that the first argument is the actual object, not a string variable with the name of the object. The following statements will generate a runtime error:

```
ObjectName = "Text1"
CallByName ObjectName, "Text", vbLet, "Welcome to VB6"
```

If you want to use a variable, you must first set it to an existing object, as shown here:

```
Set MyObject = Text1
CallByName MyObject, "Text", vbLet, "Welcome to VB6"
```

To retrieve the value of the Text property of the same control, use the following statement:

```
MyText = CallByName(Text1, "Text", vbGet)
```

The CallByName() function can be used to invoke a method of an object. The following statement invokes the AddItem method of the List1 control:

```
CallByName List1, "AddItem", VbMethod, "Joe Doe"
```

It's simpler to invoke methods and set or read property values with the notation object.property or object.method. There may be situations where you must call one of several methods at runtime, and this is when the CallByName() function will come in handy.

OBSOLETE STATEMENTS

Visual Basic provides a few more statements, which are leftovers from older versions of BASIC. They are seldom used in modern VB programming, but they are included for compatibility reasons. Of the statements listed in this section, the GoTo statement is not obsolete, but you should only use it in extreme situations.

GoTo label

The GoTo statement is the most commonly used branching statement. It transfers program control to the line specified by the *label* argument. This statement was used routinely with previous versions of BASIC and has attracted serious criticism because it was responsible for enormous amounts of so-called *spaghetti code* (programs with too many GoTo statements are impossible to read).

The label is nothing more than a name followed by a colon (:). Here's a short code segment that (ab)uses the GoTo statement:

```
StartCalculations:
Total = Total + i
i = i + 1
If Total < 30 Then GoTo StartCalculations
MsgBox "The sum is " & Total
```

The following loop is a far more elegant way of coding the same calculations:

```
While Total < 30
  Total = Total + i
  i = i + 1
Wend
MsgBox "The sum is " & Total
```

Don't confuse the unconditional GoTo statement with the On Error GoTo statement. The latter is neither obsolete (quite the opposite) nor does it produce spaghetti-code. It transfers program control to a specific line when an error occurs and you should use it to trap run-time errors.

GoSub and Return

This statement branches to another line, just like the GoTo statement, but it remembers where it branched from. As soon as the Return statement is reached, program control is transferred automatically to the line following the GoSub statement. The GoSub statement was the only way to implement procedures with early versions of BASIC and is included in Visual Basic for compatibility reasons. Here's a small code segment that uses the GoSub statement:

```
FName = "Joe": LName = "Doe"
Gosub FormatName
MsgBox FormattedName
End

FormatName:
FormattedName = LName & ", " & FName
Return
```

When the GoSub statement is reached, the program control is transferred to the line labeled FormatName. The following line formats the name and stores it into the variable *FormattedName*. Then the Return statement is reached, and program control returns to the line following the GoSub statement, which displays the formatted name.

Notice that all the variables are common to the calling section and the "subroutine" section. Obviously, the same operation could have been implemented with a function, which accepts the two strings (first and last names) and returns the formatted name. The advantage of using a function is that the variables of the calling program and the function are separate.

On expression GoTo destination_list and On expression GoSub destination_list

These two statements are similar to the GoTo and GoSub statements, but they transfer program control to another line depending on the value of the specified *expression*. The *expression* argument is evaluated when the statement is reached at runtime, and its value should be an integer in the range 0 to 255.

▶ If *expression* is zero, the program continues with the statement following the On...Goto or On...GoSub statement.

▶ If *expression* is a positive number, but less than 255, its value determines the line in the *destination_list* to which the program will branch. If it's 1, then program control is transferred to the first line in the *destination_list*; if it's 2, then program control is transferred to the second line in the destination list; and so on.

▶ If *expression* evaluates to a negative value or a positive value larger than 255, a runtime error occurs.

▶ If *expression* evaluates to a number that does not correspond to an option in the *destination_list* (if, for example, *expression* evaluates to 10 and there are only 9 labels in the *destination_list*), then the program will not branch. Instead, it will drop to the line following the On...GoTo statement.

The following statements calculate the discount of a ticket, based on a child's age. Notice that ages 1, 2, and 3 cause the program to branch to the same line (for a 70 percent discount), ages 4 and 5 also branch to the same line (for a 50 percent discount), and ages 6 and 7 branch to Level3 (for a 30 percent discount). There is no discount for children of age 8 or higher.

```
age = Int(Rnd() * 12 + 1)
cost = 275
Discount = 0#
On age GoSub Level1, Level1, Level1, Level2, Level2, Level3, Level3
cost = cost * (1 - Discount)
MsgBox "The ticket for a " & age & " year old child will cost " & cost
Exit Sub
Level1:
  Discount = 0.7
```

```
    Return
Level2:
  Discount = 0.5
  Return
Level3:
  Discount = 0.3
  Return
```

Insert this code segment in the Click event handler of a command button and check it out. The child's age is generated randomly, in the range from 1 to 12.

The Select Case statement is a more flexible and elegant way to perform multiple branching. Here's the same example implemented with a Select Case statement:

```
age = Int(Rnd() * 12 + 1)
cost = 275
discount = 0#
Select Case age
  Case 1, 2, 3:
    discount = 0.7
  Case 4, 5:
    discount = 0.5
  Case 6, 7:
    discount = 0.3
  Case Else
    discount = 0
  End Select
cost = cost * (1 - discount)
MsgBox "The ticket for a " & age & _
    " years old child will cost " & cost
```

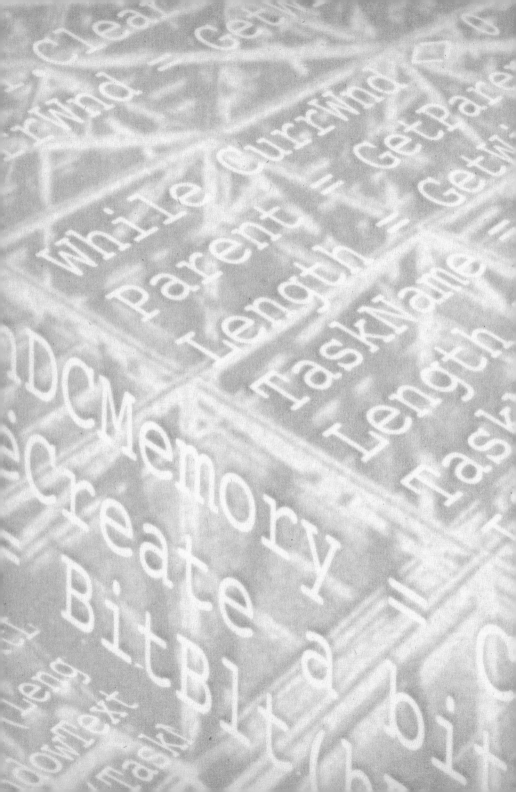

Reference 2

VISUAL BASIC 6 FUNCTION REFERENCE

This appendix includes the declarations, parameters, and return values for Win32API functions used in Chapter 7. A Remarks section is included about some functions to provide additional information.

API FUNCTIONS FOR THE FINDWINDOW PROJECT

The API functions in this section deal with Windows handles and windows.

ClientToScreen

Converts the client coordinates of a given point or rectangle on the display to screen coordinates.

Declaration

```
Declare Sub ClientToScreen Lib "user32" (ByVal hwnd _
    As Long, lpPoint As POINT)
```

Parameters

hWnd   Long. Handle of the window whose client area is used for the conversion.

lpPoint   POINT. Points to a POINT structure that contains the client coordinates to be converted.

Return Values

If the function succeeds, the return value is TRUE. If the function fails, the return value is FALSE.

Remarks

The ClientToScreen function replaces the client coordinates in the POINT structure with the screen coordinates. The screen coordinates are relative to the upper-left corner of the screen.

GetWindowText

Copies the text of the specified window's title bar (if it has one) into a buffer. If the specified window is a control, the text of the control is copied.

Declaration

```
Declare Function GetWindowText Lib "user32" Alias _
"GetWindowTextA" (ByVal hwnd As Long, ByVal lpString As _
String, ByVal cch As Long) As Long
```

Parameters

hWnd   Long. Identifies the window or control containing the text.

lpString   String. Points to the buffer that will receive the text.

cch   Long. Specifies the maximum length of the buffer. If the text exceeds this limit, it is truncated.

Return Values

If the function succeeds, the return value is the length, in characters, of the copied string, not including the terminating null character. If the window has no title bar or text, if the title bar is empty, or if the window or control handle is invalid, the return value is zero. Sets GetLastError.

Remarks

This function causes a WM_GETTEXT message to be sent to the specified window or control. This function cannot be used to retrieve the text of an edit control in another application.

GetWindowRect

Retrieves the dimensions of the rectangle of the specified window. The dimensions are given in screen coordinates that are relative to the upper-left corner of the screen.

Declaration

```
Declare Function GetWindowRect Lib "user32" (ByVal _
hwnd As Long, lpRect As RECT) As Boolean
```

Parameters

hWnd   Long. Identifies the window.

lpRect   Rect. Points to a RECT structure that receives the screen coordinates of the window.

Return Values

If the function succeeds, the return value is TRUE. If the function fails, the return value is FALSE. Sets GetLastError.

WindowFromPoint

Retrieves the handle of the window that contains the specified point.

Declaration

```
Declare Function WindowFromPoint Lib "user32" (ByVal _
    ptY As Long, ByVal ptX As Long) As Long
```

Parameter

Point   Specifies a POINT structure (X,Y) that defines the point to be checked.

Return Values

If the function succeeds, the return value is the handle of the window that contains the point. If no window exists at the given point, the return value is NULL.

Remarks

The WindowFromPoint function does not retrieve the handle of a hidden or disabled window. An application should use the ChildWindowFromPoint function for a nonrestrictive search.

LoadCursor

Loads the specified cursor.

Declaration

```
Declare Function LoadCursor Lib "user32" Alias "LoadCursorA" _
    (ByVal hInstance&, ByVal lpCursor&) As Long
```

Parameters

hInstance   Long. Identifies an instance of the module whose executable file contains the cursor to be loaded.

lpCursor   String. Points to a null-terminated string that contains the name of the cursor resource to be loaded.

To use one of the Win32 predefined cursors, the application must set the hInstance parameter to NULL and the lpCursor parameter to one of the values shown in Table FR.1.

TABLE FR.1: Predefined Cursor Values

Value	Description
IDC_APPSTARTING	Standard arrow and small hourglass.
IDC_ARROW	Standard arrow.
IDC_CROSS	Crosshair.
IDC_IBEAM	Text I-beam.
IDC_ICON	Obsolete for applications marked version 4 or later.
IDC_NO	Slashed circle.
IDC_SIZE	Obsolete for applications marked version 4 or later. Use IDC_SIZEALL.
IDC_SIZEALL	Four-pointed arrow.
IDC_SIZENESW	Double-pointed arrow pointing northeast and southwest.
IDC_SIZENS	Double-pointed arrow pointing north and south.
IDC_SIZENWSE	Double-pointed arrow pointing northwest and southeast.
IDC_SIZEWE	Double-pointed arrow pointing west and east.
IDC_UPARROW	Vertical arrow.
IDC_WAIT	Hourglass.

Return Values

If the function succeeds, the return value is the handle of the newly loaded cursor. If the function fails, the return value is NULL. Sets GetLastError.

Remarks

LoadCursor loads the cursor resource only if it has not already been loaded; otherwise, it retrieves the handle of the existing resource. If lpCursor points to any type of resource other than a cursor, the return value is not NULL, even though it is not a valid cursor handle.

The LoadCursor function searches the cursor resource most appropriate for the cursor for the current display device. The cursor resource can be a color or a monochrome bitmap.

DrawIcon

Draws an icon in the client area of the window of the specified device context.

Declaration

```
Declare Function DrawIcon Lib "user32" (ByVal hdc As Long, _
    ByVal x As Long, ByVal y As Long, ByVal hIcon As _
    Long) As Long
```

Parameters

hDC   Long. Identifies the device context for a window.

X   Long. Specifies the logical x-coordinate of the upper-left corner of the icon.

Y   Long. Specifies the logical y-coordinate of the upper-left corner of the icon.

hIcon   Long. Identifies the icon to be drawn.

Return Values

If the function succeeds, the return value is nonzero. If the function fails, the return value is zero. To get extended error information, call GetLastError.

Remarks

DrawIcon draws the icon's upper-left corner at the location specified by the X and Y parameters. In Windows NT, the icon resource must have been previously loaded by using the LoadIcon function. In Windows 95/98, the icon resource must have been previously loaded by using the Load-Icon or LoadImage functions.

ShowWindow

Sets the specified window's visibility.

Declaration

```
Declare Function ShowWindow Lib "user32" (ByVal hwnd As _
    Long, ByVal nCmdShow As Long)
```

Parameters

hWnd   Long. Identifies the window.

nCmdShow   Long. Specifies how the window is to be shown. Use one of the constants in Table FR.2 for this parameter.

TABLE FR.2: The ShowWindow Visibility Values

VALUE	DESCRIPTION
SW_HIDE	Hides the window and activates another window.
SW_MAXIMIZE	Maximizes the specified window.
SW_MINIMIZE	Minimizes the specified window and activates the next top-level window in the Z order.
SW_RESTORE	Activates and displays the window. If the window is minimized or maximized, Windows restores it to its original size and position. An application should specify this flag when restoring a minimized window.
SW_SHOW	Activates the window and displays it in its current size and position.
SW_SHOWDEFAULT	Sets the show state based on the SW_ flag specified in the STARTUPINFO structure passed to the CreateProcess function by the program that started the application.
SW_SHOWMAXIMIZED	Activates the window and displays it as a maximized window.

TABLE FR.2 (continued): The ShowWindow Visibility Values

VALUE	DESCRIPTION
SW_SHOWMINIMIZED	Activates the window and displays it as a minimized window.
SW_SHOWMINNOACTIVE	Displays the window as a minimized window. The active window remains active.
SW_SHOWNA	Displays the window in its current state. The active window remains active.
SW_SHOWNOACTIVATE	Displays a window in its most recent size and position. The active window remains active.
SW_SHOWNORMAL	Activates and displays a window. If the window is minimized or maximized, Windows restores it to its original size and position. An application should specify this flag when displaying the window for the first time.

Return Values

If the window was previously visible, the return value is nonzero. If the window was previously hidden, the return value is zero.

Remarks

ShowWindow must be called only once per application for the main window. Subsequent calls must use one of the values listed in Table FR.2.

IsWindowVisible

Retrieves the visibility state of the specified window.

Declaration

```
Declare Function IsWindowVisible Lib "user32" (ByVal hwnd _
   As Long) As Long
```

Parameter

hWnd   Long. Identifies the window.

Return Values

If the specified window and its parent window have the WS_VISIBLE style, the return value is nonzero.

Remarks

Any drawing to a window with the WS_VISIBLE style will not be displayed if the window is obscured by other windows or is clipped by its parent window.

IsWindowEnabled

Determines whether the specified window is enabled.

Declaration

```
Declare Function IsWindowEnabled Lib "user32" (ByVal hwnd _
    As Long) As Long
```

Parameter

hWnd   Long. Identifies the window to test.

Return Values

If the window is enabled, the return value is TRUE; otherwise, it is FALSE.

Remarks

A child window receives input only if it is both enabled and visible.

IsZoomed

Determines whether a window is maximized.

Declaration

```
Declare Function IsZoomed Lib "user32" (ByVal hwnd As _
    Long) As Long
```

Parameter

hWnd   Long. Identifies the window.

Return Values

If the window is zoomed, the return value is nonzero; otherwise, it is zero.

IsIconic

Determines whether the specified window is minimized (iconic).

Declaration

```
Declare Function IsIconic Lib "user32" (ByVal hwnd _
    As Long) As Long
```

Parameter

hWnd   Long. Identifies the window.

Return Values

If the window is iconic, the return value is nonzero; otherwise, it is zero.

SetWindowPos

Changes the size, position, and Z order of a child, pop-up, or top-level window. Child, pop-up, and top-level windows are ordered according to their appearance on the screen. The topmost window receives the highest rank and is the first window in the Z order.

Declaration

```
Declare Function SetWindowPos Lib "user32" (ByVal hwnd _
    As Long, ByVal hWndInsertAfter As Long, ByVal x As Long, _
    ByVal y As Long, ByVal cx As Long, ByVal cy As Long, _
    ByVal wFlags As Long) As Long
```

Parameters

hWnd   Long. Identifies the window.

hWndInsertAfter   Long. Identifies the window to precede the positioned window in the Z order. This parameter must be a window handle or one of the values in Table FR.3.

TABLE FR.3: SetWindowsPos Values

VALUE	DESCRIPTION
HWND_BOTTOM	Places the window at the bottom of the Z order. If the hWnd parameter identifies a topmost window, the window loses its topmost status and is placed at the bottom of all other windows.
HWND_NOTOPMOST	Places the window above all nontopmost windows (that is, behind all topmost windows). This flag has no effect if the window is already a nontopmost window.
HWND_TOP	Places the window at the top of the Z order.
HWND_TOPMOST	Places the window above all nontopmost windows. The window maintains its topmost position even when it is deactivated.

X   Long. Specifies the new position of the left side of the window.

Y   Long. Specifies the new position of the top of the window.

cx   Long. Specifies the new width of the window, in pixels.

cy   Long. Specifies the new height of the window, in pixels.

uFlags   Long. Specifies the window sizing and positioning flags. This parameter can be a combination of the values in Table FR.4.

TABLE FR.4: SetWindowsPos Sizing and Position Values

VALUE	DESCRIPTION
SWP_DRAWFRAME	Draws a frame (defined in the window's class description) around the window.
SWP_FRAMECHANGED	Sends a WM_NCCALCSIZE message to the window, even if the window's size is not being changed. If this flag is not specified, WM_NCCALCSIZE is sent only when the window's size is being changed.

TABLE FR.4 (continued): SetWindowsPos Sizing and Position Values

VALUE	DESCRIPTION
SWP_HIDEWINDOW	Hides the window.
SWP_NOACTIVATE	Does not activate the window. If this flag is not set, the window is activated and moved to the top of either the topmost or nontopmost group (depending on the setting of the hWndInsertAfter parameter).
SWP_NOCOPYBITS	Discards the entire contents of the client area. If this flag is not specified, the valid contents of the client area are saved and copied back into the client area after the window is sized or repositioned.
SWP_NOMOVE	Retains the current position (ignores the X and Y parameters).
SWP_NOOWNERZORDER	Does not change the owner window's position in the Z order.
SWP_NOREDRAW	Does not redraw changes. If this flag is set, no repainting of any kind occurs. This applies to the client area, the nonclient area (including the title bar and scroll bars), and any part of the parent window uncovered as a result of the window being moved. When this flag is set, the application must explicitly invalidate or redraw any parts of the window and parent window that need redrawing.
SWP_NOREPOSITION	Same as the SWP_NOOWNERZORDER flag.
SWP_NOSENDCHANGING	Prevents the window from receiving the WM_WINDOWPOSCHANGING message.
SWP_NOSIZE	Retains the current size (ignores the cx and cy parameters).
SWP_NOZORDER	Retains the current Z order (ignores the hWndInsertAfter parameter).
SWP_SHOWWINDOW	Displays the window.

Return Values
If the function succeeds, the return value is nonzero; otherwise, it is zero. Sets GetLastError.

Remarks
A window cannot be moved or sized if the SWP_SHOWWINDOW or SWP_HIDEWINDOW flag is set.

You can make a window topmost either by setting the hWndInsertAfter parameter to HWND_TOPMOST and ensuring that the SWP_NOZORDER flag is not set or by setting a window's position in the Z order so that it is above any existing topmost windows. When a nontopmost window is made topmost, all of its owned windows are also made topmost. Its owners, however, are not changed.

If an application makes an inactive window active, it will also bring it to the top of the Z order. An application can change an activated window's position in the Z order without restrictions, or it can activate a window and then move it to the top of the topmost or nontopmost windows.

FlashWindow

Flashes the specified window once.

Declaration

```
Declare Function FlashWindow Lib "user32" (ByVal hwnd _
    As Long, ByVal bInvert As Long) As Long
```

Parameters

hWnd   Long. Identifies the window to be flashed. The window can be either open or minimized (iconic).

bInvert   Long. Specifies whether the window is to be flashed or returned to its original state. The window is flashed from one state to the other if this parameter is TRUE. If it is FALSE, the window is returned to its original state (either active or inactive).

Return Values

The return value specifies the window's state before the call to the Flash-Window function. If the window was active before the call, the return value is nonzero. If the window was not active before the call, the return value is zero.

Remarks

Flashing a window means changing the appearance of its caption bar as if the window were changing from inactive to active status or vice versa.

(An inactive caption bar changes to an active caption bar; an active caption bar changes to an inactive caption bar.)

Typically, a window is flashed to inform the user that the window requires attention but that it does not currently have the keyboard focus.

You can create a system timer to cause repeated flashing.

If the window is minimized, FlashWindow simply flashes the window's icon; bInvert is ignored for minimized windows.

APPLICATION MANIPULATION API FUNCTIONS

This section details the API functions used in the AppShell project in Chapter 7. These API functions make it possible for you to verify and control applications running concurrently with your Visual Basic application.

CloseHandle

Closes an open object handle.

Declaration

```
Declare Function CloseHandle Lib "kernel32" Alias
"CloseHandle" (ByVal hObject As Long) As Long
```

Parameter

hObject   Long. Identifies an open object handle.

Return Values

If the function succeeds, the return value is nonzero; otherwise, it is zero. Sets GetLastError.

Remarks

CloseHandle invalidates the specified object handle, decrements the object's handle count, and performs object retention checks. Once the last handle to an object is closed, the object is removed from the operating system.

This function does not close module objects.

CreateProcess

Creates a new process and its primary thread. The new process executes the specified executable file.

Declaration

```
Declare Function CreateProcess Lib "kernel32" Alias _
"CreateProcessA" (ByVal lpApplicationName As String, ByVal _
lpCommandLine As String, lpProcessAttributes As _
SECURITY_ATTRIBUTES, lpThreadAttributes As _
SECURITY_ATTRIBUTES, ByVal bInheritHandles As Long, ByVal _
dwCreationFlags As Long, lpEnvironment As Any, ByVal _
lpCurrentDirectory As String, lpStartupInfo As STARTUPINFO, _
lpProcessInformation As PROCESS_INFORMATION) As Long
```

Parameters

lpApplicationName   String. Pointer to a null-terminated string that specifies the module to execute. The string can specify the full path and filename of the module to execute. The string can also specify a partial name. In that case, the function uses the current drive and current directory to complete the specification.

The lpApplicationName parameter can be NULL. In that case, the module name must be the first white-space-delimited token in the lpCommandLine string.

The specified module can be a Win32-based application. It can be some other type of module (for example, MS-DOS or OS/2) if the appropriate subsystem is available on the local computer.

In Windows NT, if the executable module is a 16-bit application, lpApplicationName should be NULL, and the string pointed to by lpCommandLine should specify the executable module. A 16-bit application is one that executes as a VDM (Virtual DOS Machine) or WOW (Window on Windows) process.

lpCommandLine   String. Pointer to a null-terminated string that specifies the command line to execute. The lpCommandLine parameter can be NULL. In that case, the function uses the string pointed to by lpApplication-Name as the command line.

If both lpApplicationName and lpCommandLine are non-NULL, *lpApplicationName specifies the module to execute, and *lpCommand-Line specifies the command line. The new process can use GetCommand-Line to retrieve the entire command line. C run-time processes can use the argc and argv arguments.

If lpApplicationName is NULL, the first white-space-delimited token of the command line specifies the module name. If the file name does not contain an extension, EXE is assumed. If the file name ends in a period (.) with no extension or if the file name contains a path, EXE is not appended. If the file name does not contain a directory path, Windows searches for the executable file in the following sequence:

1. The directory from which the application loaded.

2. The current directory for the parent process.

3. The Windows 95/98 system directory. Use the GetSystem-Directory function to get the path of this directory.

4. In Windows NT, the 32-bit Windows system directory. Use the GetSystemDirectory function to get the path of this directory. The name of this directory is SYSTEM32.

5. The Windows directory. Use the GetWindowsDirectory function to get the path of this directory.

6. The directories that are listed in the PATH environment variable.

If the process to be created is an MS-DOS-based or Windows-based application, lpCommandLine should be a full command line in which the first element is the application name. Because this also works well for Win32 applications, it is the most robust way to set lpCommandLine.

lpProcessAttributes   SECURITY_ATTRIBUTES. Pointer to a SECURITY_ATTRIBUTES structure that determines whether the returned handle can be inherited by child processes. If lpProcess-Attributes is NULL, the handle cannot be inherited.

In Windows NT, the lpSecurityDescriptor member of the structure specifies a security descriptor for the new process. If lpProcessAttributes is NULL, the process gets a default security descriptor.

In Windows 95/98, the lpSecurityDescriptor member of the structure is ignored.

lpThreadAttributes SECURITY_ATTRIBUTES. Pointer to a SECURITY_ATTRIBUTES structure that determines whether the returned handle can be inherited by child processes. If lpThread-Attributes is NULL, the handle cannot be inherited.

In Windows NT, the lpSecurityDescriptor member of the structure specifies a security descriptor for the main thread. If lpThreadAttributes is NULL, the thread gets a default security descriptor.

In Windows 95/98, the lpSecurityDescriptor member of the structure is ignored.

bInheritHandles Long. Indicates whether the new process inherits handles from the calling process. If TRUE, each inheritable open handle in the calling process is inherited by the new process. Inherited handles have the same value and access privileges as the original handles.

dwCreationFlags Long. Specifies additional flags that control the priority class and the creation of the process. The creation flags in Table FR.5 can be specified in any combination, except as noted.

TABLE FR.5: Creation Flags

FLAG	DESCRIPTION
CREATE_SEPARATE_WOW_VDM	Windows NT only. This flag is valid only when starting a 16-bit Windows-based application. If set, the new process is run in a private Virtual DOS Machine (VDM). By default, all 16-bit Windows-based applications are run as threads in a single, shared VDM. The advantage of running separately is that a crash kills only the single VDM; any other programs running in distinct VDMs continue to function normally. Also, 16-bit Windows-based applications that are run in separate VDMs have separate input queues. If one application hangs momentarily, applications in separate VDMs continue to receive input.
CREATE_SHARED_WOW_VDM	Windows NT only. The flag is valid only when starting a 16-bit Windows-based application. If the Default-SeparateVDM switch in the Windows section of WIN.INI is TRUE, this flag causes the CreateProcess function to override the switch and run the new process in the shared Virtual DOS Machine.
CREATE_SUSPENDED	The primary thread of the new process is created in a suspended state and does not run until the ResumeThread function is called.

Table FR.6 lists the priority constants that can be used with the Create-Process function.

TABLE FR.6: CreateProcess Priorities

PRIORITY	DESCRIPTION
HIGH_PRIORITY_CLASS	Indicates a process that performs time-critical tasks that must be executed immediately for it to run correctly. The threads of a high-priority class process preempt the threads of normal-priority and idle-priority class processes. For example, Windows Task List must respond quickly when called by the user, regardless of the load on the operating system. Use extreme care when using the high-priority class, because a high-priority class CPU-bound application can use nearly all available cycles.
IDLE_PRIORITY_CLASS	Indicates a process whose threads run only when the system is idle and are preempted by the threads of any process running in a higher priority class. An example is a screen saver. The idle-priority class is inherited by child processes.
NORMAL_PRIORITY_CLASS	Indicates a normal process with no special scheduling needs.
REALTIME_PRIORITY_CLASS	Do not use with Visual Basic.

lpEnvironment   Any. Points to an environment block for the new process. If this parameter is NULL, the new process uses the environment of the calling process.

An environment block consists of a null-terminated block of null-terminated strings. If an application provides an environment block rather than passing NULL for this parameter, the current directory information of the system drives is not automatically propagated to the new process.

lpCurrentDirectory   String. Points to a null-terminated string that specifies the current drive and directory for the child process. The string must be a full path and file name that includes a drive letter. If this parameter is NULL, the new process is created with the same current drive and directory as the calling process. This option is provided primarily for shells that need to start an application and specify its initial drive and working directory.

lpStartupInfo   STARTUPINFO. Points to a STARTUPINFO structure that specifies how the main window for the new process should appear.

lpProcessInformation   PROCESS_INFORMATION. Points to a PROCESS_INFORMATION structure that receives identification information about the new process.

Return Values

If the function succeeds, the return value is nonzero; otherwise, it is zero. Sets GetLastError.

Remarks

In addition to creating a process, CreateProcess also creates a thread object. The thread is created with an initial stack whose size is described in the image header of the specified program's executable file. The thread begins execution at the image's entry point.

GetExitCodeProcess

Retrieves the termination status of the specified process.

Declaration

```
Declare Function GetExitCodeProcess Lib "kernel32" Alias _
"GetExitCodeProcess" (ByVal hProcess As Long, lpExitCode As _
Long) As Long
```

Parameters

hProcess   Long. Identifies the process. A handle of the process whose exit code you want to obtain.

lpExitCode   Long. Points to a 32-bit variable to receive the process termination status.

Return Values

If the function succeeds, the return value is nonzero; otherwise, it is zero. Sets GetLastError.

Remarks

If the specified process has not terminated, the termination status returned is STILL_ACTIVE.

GetParent

Retrieves the handle of the specified child window's parent window.

Declaration

```
Declare Function GetParent Lib "user32" Alias "GetParent" _
(ByVal hwnd As Long) As Long
```

Parameter

hWnd   Long. Identifies the window whose parent window handle is to be retrieved.

Return Values

If the function succeeds, the return value is the handle of the parent window. If the window has no parent window, the return value is NULL. Sets GetLastError.

GetWindow

Retrieves the handle of a window that has the specified relationship (Z order or owner) to the specified window.

Declaration

```
Declare Function GetWindow Lib "user32" Alias "GetWindow" _
(ByVal hwnd As Long, ByVal wCmd As Long) As Long
```

Parameters

hWnd   Long. Identifies a window. The window handle retrieved is relative to this window, based on the value of the uCmd parameter.

uCmd   Long. Specifies the relationship between the specified window and the window whose handle is to be retrieved. This parameter can be one of the values in Table FR.7.

TABLE FR.7: Window Types for GetWindow

VALUE	DESCRIPTION
GW_CHILD	The retrieved handle identifies the child window at the top of the Z order.
GW_HWNDFIRST	The retrieved handle identifies the window of the same type that is highest in the Z order.
GW_HWNDLAST	The retrieved handle identifies the window of the same type that is lowest in the Z order.
GW_HWNDNEXT	The retrieved handle identifies the window below the specified window in the Z order.
GW_HWNDPREV	The retrieved handle identifies the window above the specified window in the Z order.
GW_OWNER	The retrieved handle identifies the specified window's owner window, if any.

Return Values

If the function succeeds, the return value is a window handle. If no window exists with the specified relationship to the specified window, the return value is NULL. Sets GetLastError.

GetWindowLong

Retrieves information about the specified window. The function also retrieves the 32-bit (long) value at the specified offset into the extra window memory of a window.

Declaration

```
Declare Function GetWindowLong Lib "user32" Alias _
    "GetWindowLongA" (ByVal hwnd As Long, ByVal nIndex As Long) _
    As Long
```

Parameters

hWnd   Long. Identifies the window and, indirectly, the class to which the window belongs.

nIndex Long. Specifies the zero-based offset to the value to be retrieved. Valid values are in the range zero through the number of bytes of extra window memory, minus 4; for example, if you specified 12 or more bytes of extra memory, a value of 8 would be an index to the third 32-bit integer. To retrieve any other value, specify one of the values in Table FR.8.

TABLE FR.8: Window Values

VALUE	ACTION
GWL_EXSTYLE	Retrieves the extended window styles.
GWL_STYLE	Retrieves the window styles.
GWL_WNDPROC	Retrieves the address of the window procedure or a handle representing the address of the window procedure. You must use the CallWindowProc function to call the window procedure.
GWL_HINSTANCE	Retrieves the handle of the application instance.
GWL_HWNDPARENT	Retrieves the handle of the parent window, if any.
GWL_ID	Retrieves the identifier of the window.
GWL_USERDATA	Retrieves the 32-bit value associated with the window. Each window has a corresponding 32-bit value intended for use by the application that created the window.

The values in Table FR. 9 are also available when the hWnd parameter identifies a dialog box.

TABLE FR.9: Dialog Box Values

VALUE	ACTION
DWL_DLGPROC	Retrieves the address of the dialog box procedure or a handle representing the address of the dialog box procedure. You must use the CallWindowProc function to call the dialog box procedure.
DWL_MSGRESULT	Retrieves the return value of a message processed in the dialog box procedure.
DWL_USER	Retrieves extra information private to the application, such as handles or pointers.

Return Values

If the function succeeds, the return value is the requested 32-bit value; otherwise, it is zero. Sets GetLastError.

Remarks

Reserve extra window memory by specifying a nonzero value in the cbWndExtra member of the WNDCLASS structure used with the RegisterClass function.

GetWindowText

Copies the text of the specified window's title bar (if it has one) into a buffer. If the specified window is a control, the text of the control is copied.

Declaration

```
Declare Function GetWindowText Lib "user32" Alias _
"GetWindowTextA" (ByVal hwnd As Long, ByVal lpString As _
String, ByVal cch As Long) As Long
```

Parameters

hWnd   Long. Identifies the window or control containing the text.

lpString   String. Points to the buffer that will receive the text.

nMaxCount   Long. Specifies the maximum number of characters to copy to the buffer, including the NULL character. If the text exceeds this limit, it is truncated.

Return Values

The length, in characters, of the copied string, not including the terminating null character. If the window has no title bar or text, if the title bar is empty, or if the window or control handle is invalid, the return value is zero. Sets GetLastError.

Remarks

This function causes a WM_GETTEXT message to be sent to the specified window or control. This function cannot retrieve the text of an edit control in another application.

GetWindowTextLength

Retrieves the length, in characters, of the specified window's title bar text (if the window has a title bar). If the specified window is a control, the function retrieves the length of the text within the control.

Declaration

```
Declare Function GetWindowTextLength Lib "user32" Alias _
"GetWindowTextLengthA" (ByVal hwnd As Long) As Long
```

Parameter

hWnd   Long. Identifies the window or control.

Return Values

If the function succeeds, the return value is the length, in characters, of the text; otherwise it is zero. Sets GetLastError.

Remarks

This function causes a WM_GETTEXTLENGTH message to be sent to the specified window or control.

IsWindow

Determines whether the specified window handle identifies an existing window.

Declaration

```
Declare Function IsWindow Lib "user32" Alias "IsWindow" _
(ByVal hwnd As Long) As Long
```

Parameter

hWnd   Long. Specifies the window handle.

Return Values

If the window handle identifies an existing window, the return value is nonzero; otherwise, it is zero.

OpenProcess

Returns a handle of an existing process object.

Declaration

```
Declare Function OpenProcess Lib "kernel32" Alias _
"OpenProcess" (ByVal dwDesiredAccess As Long, ByVal _
bInheritHandle As Long, ByVal dwProcessId As Long) As Long
```

Parameters

dwDesiredAccess   Long. Specifies the access to the process object. For operating systems that support security checking, this access is checked against any security descriptor for the target process. Any combination of the access flags in Table FR.10 can be specified in addition to the STANDARD_RIGHTS_REQUIRED access flags:

TABLE FR.10: OpenProcess Access Flags

ACCESS	DESCRIPTION
PROCESS_ALL_ACCESS	Specifies all possible access flags for the process object.
PROCESS_CREATE_PROCESS	Used internally.
PROCESS_CREATE_THREAD	Enables using the process handle in the CreateRemoteThread function to create a thread in the process.
PROCESS_DUP_HANDLE	Enables using the process handle as either the source or target process in the DuplicateHandle function to duplicate a handle.
PROCESS_QUERY_INFORMATION	Enables using the process handle in the GetExitCodeProcess and GetPriorityClass functions to read information from the process object.
PROCESS_SET_INFORMATION	Enables using the process handle in the SetPriorityClass function to set the priority class of the process.
PROCESS_TERMINATE	Enables using the process handle in the TerminateProcess function to terminate the process.
PROCESS_VM_OPERATION	Enables using the process handle in the VirtualProtectEx and WriteProcessMemory functions to modify the virtual memory of the process.

TABLE FR.10 (continued): OpenProcess Access Flags

ACCESS	DESCRIPTION
PROCESS_VM_READ	Enables using the process handle in the ReadProcess-Memory function to read from the virtual memory of the process.
PROCESS_VM_WRITE	Enables using the process handle in the Write-ProcessMemory function to write to the virtual memory of the process.
SYNCHRONIZE	Windows NT only. Enables using the process handle in any of the wait functions to wait for the process to terminate.

bInheritHandle   Long. Specifies whether the returned handle can be inherited by a new process created by the current process. If TRUE, the handle is inheritable.

dwProcessId   Long. Specifies the process identifier of the process to open.

Return Values
If the function succeeds, the return value is an open handle of the specified process. If the function fails, it is NULL. Sets GetLastError.

Remarks
The handle returned by the OpenProcess function can be used in any function that requires a handle to a process.

PostMessage
Posts a message in the message queue associated with the thread that created the specified window and then returns without waiting for the thread to process the message. Messages in a message queue are retrieved by calls to the GetMessage or PeekMessage function.

Declaration
```
Declare Function PostMessage Lib "user32" Alias _
"PostMessageA" (ByVal hwnd As Long, ByVal wMsg As Long, ByVal
wParam As Long, ByVal lParam As Long) As Long
```

Parameters

hWnd   Long. Identifies the window whose window procedure is to receive the message.

HWND_BROADCAST is posted to all top-level windows in the system, including disabled or invisible unowned windows, overlapped windows, and pop-up windows. The message is not posted to child windows. Use NULL to post a thread message.

Msg   Specifies the message to be posted.

wParam   Long. Specifies additional message-specific information.

lParam   Long. Specifies additional message-specific information.

Return Values

If the function succeeds, the return value is nonzero; otherwise, it is zero. Sets GetLastError.

Remarks

Good for sending messages that do not have to be processed immediately.

WaitForSingleObject

Returns when the specified object is in the signaled state or when the time-out interval elapses.

Declaration

```
Declare Function WaitForSingleObject Lib "kernel32" Alias _
"WaitForSingleObject" (ByVal hHandle As Long, ByVal _
dwMilliseconds As Long) As Long
```

Parameters

hHandle   Long. Identifies the object. For a list of the object types whose handles can be specified, see the following "Remarks" section. In Windows NT, the handle must have SYNCHRONIZE access.

dwMilliseconds   Long. Specifies the time-out interval in milliseconds. The function returns if the interval elapses, even if the object's state is nonsignaled. If dwMilliseconds is zero, the function tests the object's state and returns immediately. If dwMilliseconds is INFINITE, the function's time-out interval never elapses.

Return Values

If the function succeeds, the return value indicates the event that caused the function to return. If the function fails, the return value is WAIT_FAILED. Sets GetLastError. The return value on success is one of the values in Table FR.11.

TABLE FR.11: Successful WaitForSingleObject Return Values

VALUE	DESCRIPTION
WAIT_ABANDONED	The specified object is a mutex object that was not released by the thread that owned the mutex object before the owning thread terminated. Ownership of the mutex object is granted to the calling thread, and the mutex is set to nonsignaled.
WAIT_OBJECT_0	The state of the specified object is signaled.
WAIT_TIMEOUT	The time-out interval elapsed, and the object's state is nonsignaled.

Remarks

The WaitForSingleObject function checks the current state of the specified object. If the object's state is nonsignaled, the calling thread enters an efficient wait state. The thread consumes little processor time while waiting for the object state to become signaled or for the time-out interval to elapse.

ANALYZEMENUS PROJECT API FUNCTIONS

The API functions in this section allow you to analyze, verify, and access the menus of other applications from your Visual Basic application.

FindWindow

Retrieves the handle to the top-level window whose class name and window name match the specified strings. This function does not search child windows.

Declaration

```
Declare Function FindWindow Lib "user32" Alias _
    "FindWindowA" (ByVal lpClassName As String, ByVal _
    lpWindowName As String) As Long
```

Parameters

lpClassName   String. Points to a null-terminated string that specifies the name of the class of the window. If this parameter is zero, all window names match.

lpWindowName   String. Points to a null-terminated string that specifies the window name (the window's title). If this parameter is NULL, all window names match.

Return Values

If the function succeeds, the return value is the handle to the window that has the specified class name and window name. If the function fails, the return value is NULL. Sets GetLastError.

GetMenu

Retrieves the handle of the menu assigned to the given window.

Declaration

```
Declare Function GetMenu Lib "user32" (ByVal hwnd _
    As Long) As Long
```

Parameter

hWnd   Long. Identifies the window whose menu handle is retrieved.

Return Values

If the function succeeds, the return value is the handle of the menu. If the given window has no menu, the return value is NULL. If the window is a child window, the return value is undefined.

GetMenuItemCount

Determines the number of items in the specified menu.

Declaration

```
Declare Function GetMenuItemCount Lib "user32" (ByVal _
    hMenu As Long) As Long
```

Parameter

hMenu   Long. Identifies the handle of the menu to be examined.

Return Values

If the function succeeds, the return value specifies the number of items in the menu. If the function fails, the return value is -1. Sets GetLastError.

GetMenuItemID

Retrieves the menu item identifier of a menu item located at the specified position in a menu.

Declaration

```
Declare Function GetMenuItemID Lib "user32" (ByVal _
    hMenu As Long, ByVal nPos As Long) As Long
```

Parameters

hMenu   Long. Identifies the menu that contains the item whose identifier is to be retrieved.

nPos   Long. Specifies the zero-based relative position of the menu item whose identifier is to be retrieved.

Return Values

The menu ID for the specified entry is 0 if the entry is a separator; it is −1 if the entry is a pop-up menu

GetMenuState

Retrieves the menu flags associated with the specified menu item. If the menu item opens a submenu, this function also returns the number of items in the submenu.

Declaration

```
Declare Function GetMenuState Lib "user32" (ByVal hMenu _
    As Long, ByVal wID As Long, ByVal wFlags As Long) As Long
```

Parameters

hMenu   Identifies the menu that contains the menu item whose flags are to be retrieved.

wID   Long. Specifies the menu item for which the menu flags are to be retrieved, as determined by the uFlags parameter.

wFlags   Long. MF_BYCOMMAND indicates that the uId parameter gives the identifier of the menu item. The MF_BYCOMMAND flag is the default if neither the MF_BYCOMMAND nor the MF_BYPOSITION flag is specified. MF_BYPOSITION indicates that the uId parameter gives the zero-based relative position of the menu item.

Return Values

If the specified item does not exist, the return value is 0xFFFFFFFF.

If the menu item opens a submenu, the low-order byte of the return value contains the menu flags associated with the item, and the high-order byte contains the number of items in the submenu opened by the item. Otherwise, the return value is a mask (Boolean OR) of the menu flags. Table FR.12 lists and describes the menu flags associated with the menu item.

TABLE FR.12: The GetMenuState Return Values

VALUE	DESCRIPTION
MF_CHECKED	Places a checkmark next to the item (for drop-down menus, sub-menus, and shortcut menus only)
MF_DISABLED	Disables the item
MF_GRAYED	Disables and grays the item
MF_HILITE	Highlights the item
MF_MENUBARBREAK	Functions the same as the MF_MENUBREAK flag, except for drop-down menus, submenus, and shortcut menus, for which the new column is separated from the old column by a vertical line
MF_MENUBREAK	Places the item on a new line (for menu bars) or in a new column (for drop-down menus, submenus, and shortcut menus) without separating columns
MF_SEPARATOR	Creates a horizontal dividing line (for drop-down menus, sub-menus, and shortcut menus only)

GetMenuString

Copies the text string of the specified menu item into the specified buffer.

Declaration

```
Declare Function GetMenuString Lib "user32" Alias _
  "GetMenuStringA" (ByVal hMenu As Long, ByVal wIDItem _
  As Long, ByVal lpString As String, ByVal nMaxCount _
  As Long, ByVal wFlag As Long) As Long
```

Parameters

hMenu   Long. Identifies the menu.

wIDItem   Long. Specifies the menu item to be changed, as determined by the uFlag parameter.

lpString   String. Points to the buffer that is to receive the null-terminated string.

nMaxCount   Long. Specifies the maximum length, in characters, of the string to be copied + 1.

wFlag   Long. Specifies how the uIDItem parameter is interpreted. MF_BYCOMMAND indicates that uIDItem gives the identifier of the menu item. If neither the MF_BYCOMMAND nor the MF_BYPOSITION flag is specified, the MF_BYCOMMAND flag is the default flag. MF_BYPOSITION indicates that uIDItem gives the zero-based relative position of the menu item.

Return Values

If the function succeeds, the return value specifies the number of characters copied to the buffer, not including the terminating null character; otherwise, it is zero.

Remarks

The nMaxCount parameter must be one larger than the number of characters in the text string to accommodate the terminating null character.

GetSubMenu

Retrieves the handle of the drop-down menu or submenu activated by the specified menu item.

Declaration

```
Declare Function GetSubMenu Lib "user32" (ByVal hMenu _
    As Long, ByVal nPos As Long) As Long
```

Parameters

hMenu   Long. Identifies the menu.

nPos   Long. Specifies the zero-based relative position in the given menu of an item that activates a drop-down menu or submenu.

Return Values

If the function succeeds, the return value is the handle of the drop-down menu or submenu activated by the menu item; otherwise, it returns NULL.

SendMessage

Sends the specified message to a window or windows. The function calls the window procedure for the specified window and does not return until the window procedure has processed the message.

Declaration

```
Declare Function SendMessage Lib "user32" Alias _
  "SendMessageA" (ByVal hwnd As Long, ByVal wMsg As _
  Long, ByVal wParam As Long, lParam As Any) As Long
```

Parameters

hWnd   Long. Handle of the window to receive the message. If this parameter is HWND_BROADCAST, the message is sent to all top-level windows in the system, but not to child windows.

Msg   Long. Specifies the message to be sent.

wParam   Long. Specifies additional message-specific information.

lParam   Long. Specifies additional message-specific information.

Return Values

Depend on the message sent.

Remarks

If the specified window was created by the calling thread, the window procedure is called immediately as a subroutine. If the specified window was created by a different thread, Windows switches to that thread and calls the appropriate window procedure.

BITMAPS AND GRAPHICS

Bitmaps and graphics have become a staple in most of the applications created today. Table FR.13 lists the members of a bitmap's structure.

TABLE FR.13: Bitmap Structure

MEMBERS	DESCRIPTION
bmType	Specifies the bitmap type. This member must be zero.
BmWidth	Specifies the width, in pixels, of the bitmap. The width must be greater than zero.
BmHeight	Specifies the height, in pixels, of the bitmap. The height must be greater than zero.
BmWidthBytes	Specifies the number of bytes in each scan line. This value must be divisible by 2, because Windows assumes that the bit values of a bitmap form an array that is word-aligned.
BmPlanes	Specifies the count of color planes.
BmBitsPixel	Specifies the number of bits required to indicate the color of a pixel.
BmBits	Points to the location of the bit values for the bitmap. The bmBits member must be a long pointer to an array of character (1-byte) values.

Device-Dependent Bitmaps

You can copy and display a device-dependent bitmap (DDB) much faster than you can copy and display a device-independent bitmap (DIB). All Windows needs to do to move a DDB is copy memory. You can use the function BitBlt to do this. The key to using DDBs is compatibility. The easiest way to determine if a bitmap is compatible with a device is to use the CreateCompatibleBitmap function. On the other hand, you can use DIBS to copy or display bitmaps across devices.

Device-Independent Bitmaps

A device-independent bitmap is a color bitmap in a format that eliminates the problems that occur in transferring DDBs to devices having a different bitmap format. DIBs provide bitmap information that any display or printer driver can translate. The main purpose of DIBs is to allow bitmaps to be moved from one device to another.

Transferring bitmaps from one device to another was not possible in Microsoft Windows before version 3. Now, with DIBs, every device can display a bitmap to the extent of its color resolution. An application can store and display a bitmap regardless of the output device.

A bitmap file consists of a BITMAPFILEHEADER structure and the DIB itself. Table FR.14 lists and describes the fields in this structure.

TABLE FR.14: The BITMAPFILEHEADER Structure

FIELD	DESCRIPTION
bfType	WORD that defines the type of file. It must be BM.
BfSize	A DWORD that specifies the size of the file in bytes. The Microsoft Windows Software Development Kit (SDK) documentation claims otherwise. To be on the safe side, many applications calculate their own sizes for reading in a file.
bfReserved1, bfReserved2	WORDs that must be set to zero.
BfOffBits	A DWORD that specifies the offset from the beginning of the BITMAPFILEHEADER structure to the start of the actual bits. The DIB header immediately follows the file header, but the actual image bits need not be placed next to the headers in the file.

The DIB header immediately follows the BITMAPFILEHEADER, and Table FR.15 lists and describes its fields. The header is made up of two parts—the header and the color table. They are combined in the BITMAPINFO structure, which is what all DIB APIs expect.

TABLE FR.15: The BITMAPINFOHEADER Structure

FIELD	DESCRIPTION
BiSize	Should be set to sizeof(BITMAPINFOHEADER). This field defines the size of the header (minus the color table). If a new DIB definition is added, it is identified by a new value for the size. This field is also convenient for calculating a pointer to the color table, which immediately follows the BITMAPINFOHEADER.
biWidth, biHeight	Defines the width and the height of the bitmap in pixels. They are DWORD values for future expansion, and the code in Windows versions 3 and 3.1 ignores the high word (which should be set to zero).

TABLE FR.15 (continued): The BITMAPINFOHEADER Structure

FIELD	DESCRIPTION
BiPlanes	Should always be 1. All DIB definitions rely on biBitCount for color resolution definition.
BiBitCount	Defines the color resolution (in bits per pixel) of the DIB. Only four values are valid for this field: 1, 4, 8, and 24. New resolutions (16-bit, for example) may be added in the future, but for now, only these four define a valid DIB. Choosing the appropriate value when doing a GetDIBits is discussed below. When performing a Set operation, the value should already be defined for the bits.
BiCompression	Specifies the type of compression. Can be one of three values: BI_RGB, BI_RLE4, or BI_RLE8. The most common and useful choice, BI_RGB, defines a DIB in which all is as it seems. Each block of biBitCount bits defines an index (or RGB value for 24-bit versions) into the color table. The other two options specify that the DIB is stored (or will be stored) using either the 4-bit or the 8-bit run-length encoding (RLE) scheme that Windows supports. The RLE formats are especially useful for animation applications and also usually compress the bitmap. BI_RGB format is recommended for almost all purposes. RLE versions, although possibly smaller, are slower to decode, not as widely supported, and extremely painful to band properly.
BiSizeImage	Should contain the size of the bitmap proper in bytes.
biXPelsPerMeter, biYPelsPerMeter	Define application-specified values for the desirable dimensions of the bitmap. This information can be used to maintain the physical dimensions of an image across devices of different resolutions. GDI never touches these fields. When not filled in, they should both be set to zero.
BiClrUsed	Provides a way for getting smaller color tables. When this field is set to zero, the number of colors on the biBitCount field (1 indicates 2 colors, 4 indicates 16, 8 indicates 256, and 24 indicates no color table) is used. A nonzero value specifies the exact number of colors in the table. So, for example, if an 8-bit DIB uses only 17 colors, only those 17 colors need be defined in the table, and biClrUsed is set to 17. Of course, no pixel can have an index pointing past the end of the table.

TABLE FR.15 (continued): The BITMAPINFOHEADER Structure

FIELD	DESCRIPTION
BiClrImportant	Specifies that the first *x* colors of the color table are important to the DIB. If the rest of the colors are not available, the image still retains its meaning in an acceptable manner. BiClrImportant is purely for application use; GDI does not touch this value. When this field is set to zero, all the colors are important, or rather, their relative importance has not been computed.

The color table follows the header information. The number of entries in the color table matches the number of colors supported by the DIB, except for a 24-bit color bitmap, which does not have a color table. Table FR.16 lists and describes the fields for the structure of a color table for a 16-color DIB.

TABLE FR.16: The Color Table

FIELD	DESCRIPTION
bmiHeader	BITMAPINFOHEADER information
BmiColors(15)	Colors

API FUNCTIONS FOR THE SCREENCAPTURE PROJECT

Capturing a screen is beyond the scope of Visual Basic alone. This section includes the API functions used in Chapter 7 to capture and display screen shots from within a Visual Basic application.

BitBlt

Performs a bit-block transfer of the color data corresponding to a rectangle of pixels from the specified source device context into a destination device context.

Declaration

```
Private Declare Function BitBlt Lib "GDI32" ( _
    ByVal hDCDest As Long, ByVal XDest As Long, _
    ByVal YDest As Long, ByVal nWidth As Long, _
    ByVal nHeight As Long, ByVal hDCSrc As Long, _
    ByVal XSrc As Long, ByVal YSrc As Long, ByVal dwRop As _
    Long) As Long
```

Parameters

hdcDest   Long. Identifies the destination device context.

nXDest   Long. Specifies the logical x-coordinate of the upper-left corner of the destination rectangle.

nYDest   Long. Specifies the logical y-coordinate of the upper-left corner of the destination rectangle.

nWidth   Long. Specifies the logical width of the source and destination rectangles.

nHeight   Long. Specifies the logical height of the source and the destination rectangles.

hdcSrc   Long. Identifies the source device context.

nXSrc   Long. Specifies the logical x-coordinate of the upper-left corner of the source rectangle.

nYSrc   Long. Specifies the logical y-coordinate of the upper-left corner of the source rectangle.

dwRop   Long. Specifies a raster-operation code. These codes define how the color data for the source rectangle is to be combined with the color data for the destination rectangle to achieve the final color. Table FR.17 shows some common raster-operation codes.

TABLE FR.17: Common Raster-Operation Codes

VALUE	DESCRIPTION
BLACKNESS	Fills the destination rectangle using the color associated with index zero in the physical palette. (This color is black for the default physical palette.)

TABLE FR.17: Common Raster-Operation Codes

VALUE	DESCRIPTION
DSTINVERT	Inverts the destination rectangle.
MERGECOPY	Merges the colors of the source rectangle with the specified pattern by using the Boolean AND operator.
MERGEPAINT	Merges the colors of the inverted source rectangle with the colors of the destination rectangle by using the Boolean OR operator.
NOTSRCCOPY	Copies the inverted source rectangle to the destination.
NOTSRCERASE	Combines the colors of the source and destination rectangles by using the Boolean OR operator and then inverts the resultant color.
PATCOPY	Copies the specified pattern into the destination bitmap.
PATINVERT	Combines the colors of the specified pattern with the colors of the destination rectangle by using the Boolean XOR operator.
PATPAINT	Combines the colors of the pattern with the colors of the inverted source rectangle by using the Boolean OR operator. The result of this operation is combined with the colors of the destination rectangle by using the Boolean OR operator.
SRCAND	Combines the colors of the source and destination rectangles by using the Boolean AND operator.
SRCCOPY	Copies the source rectangle directly to the destination rectangle.
SRCERASE	Combines the inverted colors of the destination rectangle with the colors of the source rectangle by using the Boolean AND operator.
SRCINVERT	Combines the colors of the source and destination rectangles by using the Boolean XOR operator.
SRCPAINT	Combines the colors of the source and destination rectangles by using the Boolean OR operator.
WHITENESS	Fills the destination rectangle using the color associated with index 1 in the physical palette. (This color is white for the default physical palette.)

Return Values

If the function succeeds, the return value is nonzero; otherwise, it is zero. Sets GetLastError.

Remarks

If the color formats of the source and destination device contexts do not match, the BitBlt function converts the source color format to match the destination format.

When an enhanced metafile is being recorded, an error occurs if the source device context identifies an enhanced-metafile device context.

BitBlt returns an error if the source and destination device contexts represent different devices.

CreateCompatibleBitmap

Creates a bitmap compatible with the device that is associated with the specified device context.

Declaration

```
Private Declare Function CreateCompatibleBitmap Lib _
    "GDI32" (ByVal hDC As Long, ByVal nWidth As Long, _
    ByVal nHeight As Long) As Long
```

Parameters

hdc   Long. Identifies a device context.

nWidth   Long. Specifies the bitmap width, in pixels.

nHeight   Long. Specifies the bitmap height, in pixels.

Return Values

If the function succeeds, the return value is a handle to the bitmap; otherwise, it is NULL.

Remarks

The color format of the bitmap created by the CreateCompatibleBitmap function matches the color format of the device identified by the hdc parameter.

Because memory device contexts allow both color and monochrome bitmaps, the format of the bitmap returned by the CreateCompatibleBitmap function differs when the specified device context is a memory device context. However, a compatible bitmap that was created for a nonmemory device context always possesses the same color format and uses the same color palette as the specified device context.

When you no longer need the bitmap, call the DeleteObject function to delete it.

CreateCompatibleDC

Creates a memory device context compatible with the specified device.

Declaration

```
Private Declare Function CreateCompatibleDC Lib "GDI32" ( _
ByVal hDC As Long) As Long
```

Parameter

hdc   Long. Identifies the device context. If this handle is NULL, the function creates a memory device context compatible with the application's current screen.

Return Values

If the function succeeds, the return value is the handle to a memory device context; otherwise, it is NULL.

Remarks

Before an application can use a memory device context for drawing operations, it must select a bitmap of the correct width and height into the device context. Once a bitmap has been selected, the device context can be used to prepare images that will be copied to the screen or printed.

The CreateCompatibleDC function can only be used with devices that support raster operations.

When you no longer need the memory device context, call the DeleteDC function to delete it.

CreatePalette

Creates a logical color palette.

Declaration

```
Private Declare Function CreatePalette Lib "GDI32" ( _
lpLogPalette As LOGPALETTE) As Long
```

Parameter

lplgpl   LOGPALETTE. Points to a LOGPALETTE structure that contains information about the colors in the logical palette.

Return Values

If the function succeeds, the return value is a handle that identifies a logical palette; otherwise, it returns NULL. Sets GetLastError.

Remarks

An application can determine whether a device supports palette operations by calling the GetDeviceCaps function and specifying the RASTER-CAPS constant.

When you no longer need the palette, call the DeleteObject function to delete it.

GetDesktopWindow

Returns the handle of the Windows Desktop window. The Desktop window covers the entire screen. The Desktop window is the area on top of which all icons and other windows are painted.

Declaration

```
Private Declare Function GetDesktopWindow Lib "USER32" () _
As Long
```

Parameters

This function has no parameters.

Return Values

The return value is the handle of the Desktop window.

GetDeviceCaps

Retrieves device-specific information about a specified device.

Declaration

```
Private Declare Function GetDeviceCaps Lib "GDI32" ( _
ByVal hDC As Long, ByVal iCapability As Long) As Long
```

Parameters

hdc   Long. Identifies the device context.

iCapability   Long. Specifies the item to return. This parameter can be one of the values in Table FR.18.

TABLE FR.18: The GetDeviceCaps Values

INDEX	MEANING
DRIVERVERSION	The device driver version
TECHNOLOGY	Device technology

The TECHNOLOGY index can be any of the values in Table FR.19.

TABLE FR.19: The TECHNOLOGY Index Values

VALUE	MEANING
DT_PLOTTER	Vector plotter.
DT_RASDISPLAY	Raster display.
DT_RASPRINTER	Raster printer.
DT_RASCAMERA	Raster camera.
DT_CHARSTREAM	Character stream.
DT_METAFILE	Metafile.
DT_DISPFILE	Display file.
HORZSIZE	Width, in millimeters, of the physical screen.
VERTSIZE	Height, in millimeters, of the physical screen.
HORZRES	Width, in pixels, of the screen.
VERTRES	Height, in raster lines, of the screen.
LOGPIXELSX	Number of pixels per logical inch along the screen width.
LOGPIXELSY	Number of pixels per logical inch along the screen height.

TABLE FR.19 (continued): The TECHNOLOGY Index Values

VALUE	MEANING
BITSPIXEL	Number of adjacent color bits for each pixel.
PLANES	Number of color planes.
NUMBRUSHES	Number of device-specific brushes.
NUMPENS	Number of device-specific pens.
NUMFONTS	Number of device-specific fonts.
NUMCOLORS	Number of entries in the device's color table if the device has a color depth of no more than 8 bits per pixel. For devices with greater color depths, –1 is returned.
ASPECTX	Relative width of a device pixel used for line drawing.
ASPECTY	Relative height of a device pixel used for line drawing.
ASPECTXY	Diagonal width of the device pixel used for line drawing.
PDEVICESIZE	Reserved.
CLIPCAPS	Flag that indicates the clipping capabilities of the device. If the device can clip to a rectangle, it is 1. Otherwise, it is zero.
SIZEPALETTE	Number of entries in the system palette.
NUMRESERVED	Number of reserved entries in the system palette.
COLORRES	Actual color resolution of the device, in bits per pixel.
PHYSICALWIDTH	For printing devices: the width of the physical page, in device units.
PHYSICALHEIGHT	For printing devices: the height of the physical page, in device units.
PHYSICALOFFSETX	For printing devices: the distance from the left edge of the physical page to the left edge of the printable area, in device units.
PHYSICALOFFSETY	For printing devices: the distance from the top edge of the physical page to the top edge of the printable area, in device units.
VREFRESH	Windows NT only. For display devices: the current vertical refresh rate of the device, in cycles per second (Hz).
DESKTOPHORZRES	Windows NT only. Width, in pixels, of the virtual desktop.
DESKTOPVERTRES	Windows NT only. Height, in pixels, of the virtual desktop.
BLTALIGNMENT	Windows NT only. Preferred horizontal drawing alignment, expressed as a multiple of pixels.
RASTERCAPS	Value that indicates the raster capabilities of the device, as shown in the following table.

Table FR.20 shows the raster capabilities of the RASTERCAPS value.

TABLE FR.20: The Raster Capabilities of the RASTERCAPS Value

Capability	Meaning
RC_BANDING	Requires banding support
RC_BITBLT	Capable of transferring bitmaps
RC_BITMAP64	Capable of supporting bitmaps larger than 64K
RC_DI_BITMAP	Capable of supporting the SetDIBits and GetDIBits functions
RC_DIBTODEV	Capable of supporting the SetDIBitsToDevice function
RC_FLOODFILL	Capable of performing flood fills
RC_GDI20_OUTPUT	Capable of supporting features of Windows 2
RC_PALETTE	Specifies a palette-based device
RC_SCALING	Capable of scaling
RC_STRETCHBLT	Capable of performing the StretchBlt function
RC_STRETCHDIB	Capable of performing the StretchDIBits function
CURVECAPS	Value that indicates the curve capabilities of the device, as shown in the following table

Table FR.21 shows the curve capabilities of CURVECAPS.

TABLE FR.21: The Curve Capabilities of CURVECAPS

Value	Meaning
CC_NONE	Device does not support curves
CC_CIRCLES	Device can draw circles
CC_PIE	Device can draw pie wedges
CC_CHORD	Device can draw chord arcs
CC_ELLIPSES	Device can draw ellipses
CC_WIDE	Device can draw wide borders
CC_STYLED	Device can draw styled borders
CC_WIDESTYLED	Device can draw borders that are wide and styled
CC_INTERIORS	Device can draw interiors
CC_ROUNDRECT	Device can draw rounded rectangles
LINECAPS	Value that indicates the line capabilities of the device, as shown in the following table

Table FR.22 shows the line capabilities of LINECAPS.

TABLE FR.22: The LINECAPS Values

VALUE	MEANING
LC_NONE	Device does not support lines
LC_POLYLINE	Device can draw a polyline
LC_MARKER	Device can draw a marker
LC_POLYMARKER	Device can draw multiple markers
LC_WIDE	Device can draw wide lines
LC_STYLED	Device can draw styled lines
LC_WIDESTYLED	Device can draw lines that are wide and styled
LC_INTERIORS	Device can draw interiors
POLYGONALCAPS	Value that indicates the polygon capabilities of the device, as shown in the following table

Table FR.23 lists and explains the values of POLYGONALCAPS.

TABLE FR.23: The Values of POLYGONALCAPS

VALUE	MEANING
PC_NONE	Device does not support polygons
PC_POLYGON	Device can draw alternate-fill polygons
PC_RECTANGLE	Device can draw rectangles
PC_WINDPOLYGON	Device can draw winding-fill polygons
PC_SCANLINE	Device can draw a single scanline
PC_WIDE	Device can draw wide borders
PC_STYLED	Device can draw styled borders
PC_WIDESTYLED	Device can draw borders that are wide and styled
PC_INTERIORS	Device can draw interiors
TEXTCAPS	Value that indicates the text capabilities of the device, as shown in the following table

Table FR.24 lists and explains the values of TEXTCAPS.

TABLE FR.24: The Values of TEXTCAPS

BIT	MEANING
TC_OP_CHARACTER	Device is capable of character output precision.
TC_OP_STROKE	Device is capable of stroke output precision.
TC_CP_STROKE	Device is capable of stroke clip precision.
TC_CR_90	Device is capable of 90-degree character rotation.
TC_CR_ANY	Device is capable of any character rotation.
TC_SF_X_YINDEP	Device can scale independently in the x- and y-directions.
TC_SA_DOUBLE	Device is capable of doubled character for scaling.
TC_SA_INTEGER	Device uses integer multiples only for character scaling.
TC_SA_CONTIN	Device uses any multiples for exact character scaling.
TC_EA_DOUBLE	Device can draw double-weight characters.
TC_IA_ABLE	Device can italicize.
TC_UA_ABLE	Device can underline.
TC_SO_ABLE	Device can draw strikeouts.
TC_RA_ABLE	Device can draw raster fonts.
TC_VA_ABLE	Device can draw vector fonts.
TC_RESERVED	Reserved; must be zero.
TC_SCROLLBLT	Device cannot scroll using a bit-block transfer. This meaning may be the opposite of what you expect.

Return Values

The return value specifies the value of the desired item.

GetForegroundWindow

Returns the handle of the foreground window (the current window). The system assigns a slightly higher priority to the thread that creates the foreground window than it does to other threads.

Declaration

```
Private Declare Function GetForegroundWindow Lib "USER32" () _
    As Long
```

Parameters

This function has no parameters.

Return Values

The return value is the handle of the foreground window.

GetSystemPaletteEntries

Retrieves a range of palette entries from the system palette that is associated with the specified device context.

Declaration

```
Private Declare Function GetSystemPaletteEntries Lib _
    "GDI32" (ByVal hDC As Long, ByVal wStartIndex As Long, _
    ByVal wNumEntries As Long, lpPaletteEntries _
    As PALETTEENTRY) As Long
```

Parameters

hdc   Long. Identifies the device context.

iStartIndex   Long. Specifies the first entry to be retrieved from the system palette.

nEntries   Long. Specifies the number of entries to be retrieved from the system palette.

lppe   PALETTEENTRY. Points to an array of PALETTEENTRY structures to receive the palette entries. The array must contain at least as many structures as specified by the nEntries parameter. If this parameter is NULL, the function returns the total number of entries in the palette.

Return Values

If the function succeeds, the return value is the number of entries retrieved from the palette; otherwise, it returns zero. Sets GetLastError.

Remarks

An application can determine whether a device supports palette operations by calling the GetDeviceCaps function and specifying the RASTERCAPS constant.

GetDC

Retrieves a handle of a display device context (DC) for the client area of the specified window. The display device context can be used in subsequent GDI functions to draw in the client area of the window.

Declaration

```
Private Declare Function GetDC Lib "USER32" ( _
    ByVal hWnd As Long) As Long
```

Parameter

hWnd   Long. Identifies the window whose device context is to be retrieved.

Return Values

If the function succeeds, the return value identifies the device context for the given window's client area; otherwise, it returns NULL.

Remarks

After painting with a common device context, the ReleaseDC function must be called to release the device context.

GetWindowRect

Retrieves the dimensions of the rectangle of the specified window. The dimensions are given in screen coordinates that are relative to the upperleft corner of the screen.

Declaration

```
Declare Function GetWindowRect Lib "user32" (ByVal _
    hwnd As Long, lpRect As RECT) As Boolean
```

Parameters

hWnd   Long. Identifies the window.

lpRect   Rect. Points to a RECT structure that receives the screen coordinates of the window.

Return Values

If the function succeeds, the return value is TRUE. If the function fails, the return value is FALSE. Sets GetLastError.

GetWindowDC

Retrieves the device context (DC) for the entire window, including title bar, menus, and scroll bars. A window device context permits painting anywhere in a window, because the origin of the device context is the upper-left corner of the window instead of the client area. This function assigns default attributes to the window device context each time it retrieves the device context. Previous attributes are lost.

Declaration

```
Private Declare Function GetWindowDC Lib "USER32" ( _
    ByVal hWnd As Long) As Long
```

Parameter

hWnd   Long. Identifies the window with a device context that is to be retrieved.

Return Values

If the function succeeds, the return value is the handle of a device context for the specified window; otherwise, it is NULL.

Remarks

GetWindowDC is intended for special painting effects within a window's nonclient area. Painting in nonclient areas of any window is not recommended.

After painting is complete, the ReleaseDC function must be called to release the device context.

OleCreatePictureIndirect

Creates a new picture object initialized according to a PICTDESC structure.

Declaration

```
Private Declare Function OleCreatePictureIndirect _
    Lib "olepro32.dll" (PicDesc As PicBmp, RefIID As GUID, _
    ByVal fPictureOwnsHandle As Long, IPic As IPicture) As Long
```

Parameters

pPictDesc   PicBmp. Pointer to a caller-allocated structure containing the initial state of the picture.

riid   GUID. Reference to the identifier of the interface describing the type of interface pointer to return in ppvObj.

fOwn   Boolean. If TRUE, the picture object is to destroy its picture when the object is destroyed. If FALSE, the caller is responsible for destroying the picture.

ppvObj   Long. Indirect pointer to the initial interface pointer on the new object. If the call is successful, the caller is responsible for calling Release through this interface pointer when the new object is no longer needed. If the call fails, the value of ppvObj is set to NULL.

Return Values

This function supports the standard return values E_INVALIDARG, E_OUTOFMEMORY, and E_UNEXPECTED, as well as the values shown in Table FR.25.

TABLE FR.25: OleCreatePictureIndirect Return Values

VALUE	MEANING
S_OK	The new picture object was created successfully.
E_NOINTERFACE	The object does not support the interface specified in riid.
E_POINTER	The address in pPictDesc or ppvObj is not valid. For example, it may be NULL.

RealizePalette

Maps palette entries from the current logical palette to the system palette.

Declaration

```
Private Declare Function RealizePalette Lib "GDI32" ( _
    ByVal hDC As Long) As Long
```

Parameter

hdc   Long. Identifies the device context (DC) into which a logical palette has been selected.

Return Values

If the function succeeds, the return value is the number of entries in the logical palette mapped to the system palette. If the function fails, the return value is GDI_ERROR. Sets GetLastError.

Remarks

An application can determine whether a device supports palette operations by calling the GetDeviceCaps function and specifying the RASTER-CAPS constant.

The RealizePalette function modifies the palette for the device associated with the specified device context.

A logical color palette is a buffer between color-intensive applications and the system, allowing these applications to use as many colors as needed without interfering with colors displayed by other windows.

ReleaseDC

Releases a device context (DC), freeing it for use by other applications. It frees only common and window device contexts. It has no effect on class or private device contexts.

Declaration

```
Private Declare Function ReleaseDC Lib "USER32" ( _
    ByVal hWnd As Long, ByVal hDC As Long) As Long
```

Parameters

hWnd   Identifies the window whose device context is to be released.

hDC   Identifies the device context to be released.

Return Values

The return value specifies whether the device context is released. If the device context is released, the return value is 1. If the device context is not released, the return value is zero.

Remarks

The application must call the ReleaseDC function for each call to the GetWindowDC function and for each call to the GetDC function that retrieves a common device context.

SelectObject

Selects an object into the specified device context. The new object replaces the previous object of the same type.

Declaration

```
Private Declare Function SelectObject Lib "GDI32" ( _
    ByVal hDC As Long, ByVal hObject As Long) As Long
```

Parameters

hdc   Long. Identifies the device context.

hObject   Long. Identifies the object to be selected. The specified object must have been created by using one of the functions shown in Table FR.26.

TABLE FR.26: SelectObject Functions

OBJECT	FUNCTIONS
Bitmap	CreateBitmap, CreateBitmapIndirect, CreateCompatible-Bitmap, CreateDIBitmap, CreateDIBSection. (Bitmaps can be selected for memory device contexts only, and for only one device context at a time.)

TABLE FR.26 (continued): SelectObject Functions

OBJECT	FUNCTIONS
Brush	CreateBrushIndirect, CreateDIBPatternBrush, CreateDIB-PatternBrushPt, CreateHatchBrush, CreatePatternBrush, CreateSolidBrush.
Font	CreateFont, CreateFontIndirect.
Pen	CreatePen, CreatePenIndirect.
Region	CombineRgn, CreateEllipticRgn, CreateEllipticRgnIndirect, CreatePolygonRgn, CreateRectRgn, CreateRectRgnIndirect.

Return Values

If the selected object is not a region and the function succeeds, the return value is the handle of the object being replaced. If the selected object is a region and the function succeeds, the return value is one of the values in Table FR.27. If an error occurs and the selected object is not a region, the return value is NULL. Otherwise, it is GDI_ERROR.

TABLE FR.27: SelectObject Region Return Values

VALUE	MEANING
SIMPLEREGION	Region consists of a single rectangle.
COMPLEXREGION	Region consists of more than one rectangle.
NULLREGION	Region is empty.

Remarks

This function returns the previously selected object of the specified type.

An application cannot select a bitmap into more than one device context at a time.

SelectPalette

Selects the specified logical palette into a device context.

Declaration

```
Private Declare Function SelectPalette Lib "GDI32" ( _
    ByVal hDC As Long, ByVal hPalette As Long, _
    ByVal bForceBackground As Long) As Long
```

Parameters

hdc   Long. Identifies the device context.

hPalette   Long. Identifies the logical palette to be selected.

bForceBackground   Long. Specifies whether the logical palette is forced to be a background palette. If this value is TRUE, the Realize-Palette function causes the logical palette to be mapped to the colors already in the physical palette in the best possible way. If this value is FALSE, RealizePalette causes the logical palette to be copied into the device palette when the application is in the foreground.

Return Values

If the function succeeds, the return value identifies the device context's previous logical palette; otherwise, it is NULL. Sets GetLastError.

Remarks

An application can determine whether a device supports palette operations by calling the GetDeviceCaps function and specifying the RASTER-CAPS constant.

STATISTICS PROJECT API FUNCTIONS

In this section, we will look at the API functions that give your Visual Basic applications access to the system statistics for the current user.

GetDeviceCaps

Retrieves device-specific information about a specified device.

Declaration

```
Declare Function GetDeviceCaps Lib "gdi32" (ByVal _
    hdc As Long, ByVal nIndex As Long) As Long
```

Parameters

hdc   Long. Identifies the device context.

nIndex   Long. Specifies the item to return. This parameter can be one of the values in Table FR.28.

TABLE FR.28: GetDeviceCaps Values

INDEX	MEANING
DRIVERVERSION	The device driver version.
TECHNOLOGY	Device technology. The values are shown in the following table.

The TECHNOLOGY index can be any of the values in Table FR.29.

TABLE FR.29: The TECHNOLOGY Index Values

VALUE	MEANING
DT_PLOTTER	Vector plotter.
DT_RASDISPLAY	Raster display.
DT_RASPRINTER	Raster printer.
DT_RASCAMERA	Raster camera.
DT_CHARSTREAM	Character stream.
DT_METAFILE	Metafile.
DT_DISPFILE	Display file.
HORZSIZE	Width, in millimeters, of the physical screen.
VERTSIZE	Height, in millimeters, of the physical screen.
HORZRES	Width, in pixels, of the screen.
VERTRES	Height, in raster lines, of the screen.
LOGPIXELSX	Number of pixels per logical inch along the screen width.
LOGPIXELSY	Number of pixels per logical inch along the screen height.
BITSPIXEL	Number of adjacent color bits for each pixel.
PLANES	Number of color planes.
NUMBRUSHES	Number of device-specific brushes.

TABLE FR.29 (continued): The TECHNOLOGY Index Values

VALUE	MEANING
NUMPENS	Number of device-specific pens.
NUMFONTS	Number of device-specific fonts.
NUMCOLORS	Number of entries in the device's color table if the device has a color depth of no more than 8 bits per pixel. For devices with greater color depths, −1 is returned.
ASPECTX	Relative width of a device pixel used for line drawing.
ASPECTY	Relative height of a device pixel used for line drawing.
ASPECTXY	Diagonal width of the device pixel used for line drawing.
PDEVICESIZE	Reserved.
CLIPCAPS	Flag that indicates the clipping capabilities of the device. If the device can clip to a rectangle, it is 1. Otherwise, it is zero.
SIZEPALETTE	Number of entries in the system palette.
NUMRESERVED	Number of reserved entries in the system palette.
COLORRES	Actual color resolution of the device, in bits per pixel.
PHYSICALWIDTH	For printing devices: the width of the physical page, in device units.
PHYSICALHEIGHT	For printing devices: the height of the physical page, in device units.
PHYSICALOFFSETX	For printing devices: the distance from the left edge of the physical page to the left edge of the printable area, in device units.
PHYSICALOFFSETY	For printing devices: the distance from the top edge of the physical page to the top edge of the printable area, in device units.
VREFRESH	Windows NT only. For display devices: the current vertical refresh rate of the device, in cycles per second (Hz).
DESKTOPHORZRES	Windows NT only. Width, in pixels, of the virtual desktop.
DESKTOPVERTRES	Windows NT only. Height, in pixels, of the virtual desktop.
BLTALIGNMENT	Windows NT only. Preferred horizontal drawing alignment, expressed as a multiple of pixels.
RASTERCAPS	Value that indicates the raster capabilities of the device, as shown in the following table.

Table FR.30 shows the capabilities of the RASTERCAPS value.

TABLE FR.30: The Capabilities of the RASTERCAPS Value

CAPABILITY	MEANING
RC_BANDING	Requires banding support
RC_BITBLT	Capable of transferring bitmaps
RC_BITMAP64	Capable of supporting bitmaps larger than 64K
RC_DI_BITMAP	Capable of supporting the SetDIBits and GetDIBits functions
RC_DIBTODEV	Capable of supporting the SetDIBitsToDevice function
RC_FLOODFILL	Capable of performing flood fills
RC_GDI20_OUTPUT	Capable of supporting features of Windows 2
RC_PALETTE	Specifies a palette-based device
RC_SCALING	Capable of scaling
RC_STRETCHBLT	Capable of performing the StretchBlt function
RC_STRETCHDIB	Capable of performing the StretchDIBits function
CURVECAPS	Value that indicates the curve capabilities of the device, as shown in the following table

Table FR.31 shows the values of the CURVECAPS capability.

TABLE FR.31: The Values of CURVECAPS

VALUE	MEANING
CC_NONE	Device does not support curves.
CC_CIRCLES	Device can draw circles.
CC_PIE	Device can draw pie wedges.
CC_CHORD	Device can draw chord arcs.
CC_ELLIPSES	Device can draw ellipses.
CC_WIDE	Device can draw wide borders.
CC_STYLED	Device can draw styled borders.
CC_WIDESTYLED	Device can draw borders that are wide and styled.
CC_INTERIORS	Device can draw interiors.
CC_ROUNDRECT	Device can draw rounded rectangles.
LINECAPS	Value that indicates the line capabilities of the device, as shown in the following table.

Table FR.32 shows the values of LINECAPS.

TABLE FR.32: The Values of LINECAPS

VALUE	MEANING
LC_NONE	Device does not support lines.
LC_POLYLINE	Device can draw a polyline.
LC_MARKER	Device can draw a marker.
LC_POLYMARKER	Device can draw multiple markers.
LC_WIDE	Device can draw wide lines.
LC_STYLED	Device can draw styled lines.
LC_WIDESTYLED	Device can draw lines that are wide and styled.
LC_INTERIORS	Device can draw interiors.
POLYGONALCAPS	Value that indicates the polygon capabilities of the device, as shown in the following table.

Table FR.33 shows the values of the POLYGONALCAPS value.

TABLE FR.33: The Values of POLYGONALCAPS

VALUE	MEANING
PC_NONE	Device does not support polygons.
PC_POLYGON	Device can draw alternate-fill polygons.
PC_RECTANGLE	Device can draw rectangles.
PC_WINDPOLYGON	Device can draw winding-fill polygons.
PC_SCANLINE	Device can draw a single scanline.
PC_WIDE	Device can draw wide borders.
PC_STYLED	Device can draw styled borders.
PC_WIDESTYLED	Device can draw borders that are wide and styled.
PC_INTERIORS	Device can draw interiors.
TEXTCAPS	Value that indicates the text capabilities of the device, as shown in the following table.

Table FR.34 shows the values of TEXTCAPS.

TABLE FR.34: The Values of TEXTCAPS

BIT	MEANING
TC_OP_CHARACTER	Device is capable of character output precision.
TC_OP_STROKE	Device is capable of stroke output precision.
TC_CP_STROKE	Device is capable of stroke clip precision.
TC_CR_90	Device is capable of 90-degree character rotation.
TC_CR_ANY	Device is capable of any character rotation.
TC_SF_X_YINDEP	Device can scale independently in the x- and y-directions.
TC_SA_DOUBLE	Device is capable of doubled character for scaling.
TC_SA_INTEGER	Device uses integer multiples only for character scaling.
TC_SA_CONTIN	Device uses any multiples for exact character scaling.
TC_EA_DOUBLE	Device can draw double-weight characters.
TC_IA_ABLE	Device can italicize.
TC_UA_ABLE	Device can underline.
TC_SO_ABLE	Device can draw strikeouts.
TC_RA_ABLE	Device can draw raster fonts.
TC_VA_ABLE	Device can draw vector fonts.
TC_RESERVED	Reserved; must be zero.
TC_SCROLLBLT	Device cannot scroll using a bit-block transfer. This meaning may be the opposite of what you expect.

Return Values

The return value specifies the value of the desired item.

GetDiskFreeSpace

Retrieves information about the specified disk, including the amount of free space on the disk.

Declaration

```
Declare Function GetDiskFreeSpace Lib "kernel32" Alias _
   "GetDiskFreeSpaceA" (ByVal lpRootPathName As String, _
   lpSectorsPerCluster As Long, lpBytesPerSector As Long, _
   lpNumberOfFreeClusters As Long, lpTotalNumberOfClusters _
   As Long) As Long
```

Parameters

lpRootPathName   String. Points to a null-terminated string that specifies the root directory of the disk to return information about. If lpRootPathName is NULL, the function uses the root of the current directory.

lpSectorsPerCluster   Long. Points to a variable for the number of sectors per cluster.

lpBytesPerSector   Long. Points to a variable for the number of bytes per sector.

lpNumberOfFreeClusters   Long. Points to a variable for the total number of free clusters on the disk.

lpTotalNumberOfClusters   Long. Points to a variable for the total number of clusters on the disk.

Return Values

If the function succeeds, the return value is nonzero; otherwise, it is zero. Sets GetLastError.

Remarks

Windows 95/98 OSR 2: The GetDiskFreeSpaceEx function is available on Windows 95/98 systems beginning with OEM Service Release 2 (OSR 2). The GetDiskFreeSpaceEx function returns correct values for all volumes, including those that are greater than 2 gigabytes.

GlobalMemoryStatus

Retrieves information about current available memory. The function returns information about both physical and virtual memory. This function supersedes the GetFreeSpace function.

Declaration

```
Declare Sub GlobalMemoryStatus Lib "kernel32" _
    (lpBuffer As MEMORYSTATUS)
```

Parameter

lpBuffer MEMORYSTATUS. Loads a MEMORYSTATUS structure in which information about current memory availability is returned.

Return Values
This function does not return a value.

Remarks
This function replaces the GetFreeSpace function.

GetUserName

Retrieves the username of the current thread. This is the name of the user currently logged on to the system.

Declaration
```
Declare Function GetUserName Lib "advapi32.dll" Alias _
    "GetUserNameA" (ByVal lpBuffer _
    As String, nSize As Long) As Long
```

Parameters

lpBuffer String. Points to the buffer to receive the null-terminated string containing the user's logon name. The function fails if this buffer is not large enough to contain the entire username.

nSize Long. A variable initialized to the length of lpBuffer.

Return Values
If the function succeeds, the return value is nonzero; otherwise, it is zero. Sets GetLastError.

Remarks
If the current thread is impersonating another client, the GetUserName function returns the user name of the client that the thread is impersonating.

GetVersionEx

Obtains extended information about the version of the operating system that is currently running.

Declaration

```
Declare Function GetVersionEx Lib "kernel32" Alias _
    "GetVersionExA" (lpVersionInformation As OSVersionInfo) _
    As Long
```

Parameter

lpVersionInformation OSVERSIONINFO. Pointer to an OSVER-SIONINFO data structure that the function fills with operating system version information. You must set the OSVersionInfoSize field of this structure to the size of the structure (148) before calling this function.

Return Values

If the function succeeds, the return value is nonzero; otherwise, it returns zero. Sets GetLastError.

Remarks

The GetVersionEx function supersedes the GetVersion function and is the preferred method for obtaining operating system version number information.

GetSystemInfo

Returns information about the current system.

Declaration

```
Declare Sub GetSystemInfo Lib "kernel32" _
    (lpSystemInfo As SYSTEM_INFO)
```

Parameter

lpSystemInfo SYSTEM_INFO. Loads a SYSTEM_INFO structure with information about the underlying hardware platform.

Return Values

This function does not return a value.

INDEX

Page numbers in *italics* refer to figures; page numbers in **bold** refer to primary discussions of the topic.

B

D

P

S

About the Contributors

Some of the best—and best-selling—Sybex authors have contributed chapters to *Visual Basic 6 Complete*.

Steve Brown   contributed chapters from *Visual Basic 6 In Record Time*.

In his 15 years of experience developing custom network and multimedia software, Mr. Brown has mastered writing innovative code and teaching programmers to do the same. He is president and owner of MYLE Software and Consulting, www.myle.com, and also the author of *Visual Basic 5: No Experience Required*.

Wayne S. Freeze   contributed chapters from *Expert Guide to Visual Basic 6*.

Mr. Freeze is a full-time computer book author and computer-technology consultant. He has more than 20 years of experience in technical support, previously working as the tech support manager for the University of Maryland. Previous books include *Visual Basic 5 Programmer's Reference*, *Programming ISAPI with Visual Basic 5*, and *Leveraging Visual Basic with ActiveX Controls*.

Ken Getz   contributed a chapter from *VBA Developer's Handbook* (coauthored with Mike Gilbert).

Mr. Getz splits his time between programming, training, and writing. He is Senior Consultant with MCW Technologies, a frequent speaker at developer conferences throughout the world, and contributing editor for Informant Publishing's *MS Office & VBA Developer* magazine and Advisor Publication's *Access-Office-VBA Advisor* magazine. He has coauthored all editions of the *Access Developer's Handbook* from Sybex.

Mike Gilbert   contributed a chapter from *VBA Developer's Handbook* (coauthored with Ken Getz).

Mr. Gilbert is Product Manager with Microsoft's Developer Tools division. His mission is to spread the word about VB technology to developers everywhere. He is a regular columnist for *MS Office & VBA Developer* magazine and a regular speaker at Microsoft TechEd and other developer conferences. He coauthored *Access 97 Developer's Handbook*.

Guy Hart-Davis   contributed a chapter from *Word 97 Macro & VBA Handbook*.

Mr. Hart-Davis is the author of *The ABCs of Word 97* and *The ABCs of Microsoft Office 97 Professional Edition* and coauthor of *Mastering Lotus 1-2-3 Release 5*, all from Sybex. He also writes macros for Sybex and other companies.

Kevin Hough   contributed chapters from *Visual Basic 6 Developer's Handbook* (coauthored with Evangelos Petroutsos).

Mr. Hough is an author and consultant specializing in high-level client-server applications written using Visual Basic and SQL Server. His advanced custom controls have been used in large-scale commercial projects and custom software applications. He is the author of *MCSD: SQL Server 6.5 Database Design Study Guide* from Sybex.

Susann Novalis   contributed a chapter from *Access 97 Macro & VBA Handbook*.

Dr. Novalis is a Professor of Mathematics and Associate Dean of the College of Science and Engineering at San Francisco State University. She is the author of *Automating Microsoft Access with Macros* and *Mastering Microsoft FrontPage 97*. Her work has appeared in *Access Visual Basic Advisor* and *Internet Advisor* magazines.

Evangelos Petroutsos   contributed chapters from *Visual Basic 6 Developer's Handbook* (coauthored with Kevin Hough) and *Mastering Visual Basic 6*, and he wrote "The Complete Visual Basic 6 Language Reference" especially for this book.

Mr. Petroutsos is a computer engineer who has worked for several corporations and organizations, including the California Institute of Technology and MCI. Currently, he writes computer books and articles, teaches networking and programming courses, and works as a computer communications consultant. He has authored and coauthored many programming books.

WORD 97 MACRO & VBA HANDBOOK
GUY HART-DAVIS
848 pages; 7 1/2" x 9"
ISBN 0-7821-1962-X
$44.99 US

Not for programmers only! This unintimidating guide show
experienced Word users how to create their own timesaving
productivity-enhancing macros based on Visual Basic fo
Applications (VBA) and begin writing their own code in VBA
Tips and tricks lead to more advanced skills, including
solid foundation in VBA. The companion CD includes all o
the book's code, presented in an easy-access format, an
video walkthroughs of key procedures.

ACCESS 97 MACRO & VBA HANDBOOK
SUSANN NOVALIS
1,104 pages; 7 1/2" x 9"
ISBN 0-7821-1977-8
$54.99 US

Improve your database productivity with this task-oriente
guide to creating timesaving Access macros. See ho
Visual Basic for Applications (VBA) makes it easier tha
ever to write and record macros, create Wizards, and desig
VBA links to other Office Suite products — even with n
prior programming experience. The companion CD contair
all code from the book, as well as shareware and evalua
tion copies of Access add-ins.